ADULT DEVELOPMENT AND AGING

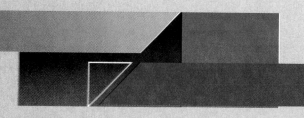

DIANE E. PAPALIA

CAMERON J. CAMP
Myers Research Institute

RUTH DUSKIN FELDMAN

The McGraw-Hill Companies, Inc.
New York ▪ St. Louis ▪ San Francisco ▪ Auckland ▪ Bogotá ▪ Caracas ▪ Lisbon ▪ London
Madrid ▪ Mexico City ▪ Milan ▪ Montreal ▪ New Delhi ▪ San Juan ▪ Singapore
Sydney ▪ Tokyo ▪ Toronto

McGraw-Hill

A Division of The McGraw-Hill Companies

ADULT DEVELOPMENT AND AGING

This book is printed on acid-free paper.

234567890 AGM AGM 909876

ISBN 0-07-048756-1

This book was set in Palatino by The Clarinda Company.
The editors were Leslye Jackson, Jeannine Ciliotta, and Susan Gamer;
the designer was Wanda Lubelska;
the design manager was Joan E. O'Connor;
the production supervisor was Elizabeth J. Strange.
The photo editor was Inge King.
Quebecor Printing was printer and binder.

Library of Congress Cataloging-in-Publication Data

Papalia, Diane E.
    Adult development and aging / Diane E. Papalia, Cameron J. Camp,
Ruth Duskin Feldman.
      p.   cm.
    Includes bibliographical references and indexes.
    ISBN 0-07-048756-1
    1. Adulthood—Psychological aspects.   2. Aging—Psychological
aspects.   3. Adulthood.   4. Aging.   5. Developmental psychology.
I. Camp, Cameron J.   II. Feldman, Ruth Duskin.   III. Title.
BF724.5P37   1996
155.6—dc20   95-39802

ABOUT THE AUTHORS

As a professor, **Diane E. Papalia** taught thousands of undergraduates at the University of Wisconsin-Madison. She received her bachelor's degree, majoring in psychology, from Vassar College, and both her master's degree in child development and family relations and her Ph.D. in lifespan developmental psychology from West Virginia University. She has published numerous articles in such professional journals as *Human Development, International Journal of Aging and Human Development, Sex Roles, Journal of Experimental Child Psychology,* and *Journal of Gerontology.* Most of these papers have dealt with her major research focus, cognitive development from childhood through old age. She is especially interested in intelligence in old age and in factors that contribute to the maintenance of intellectual functioning in late adulthood. She is a Fellow in the Gerontological Society of America. She is coauthor, with Sally Wendkos Olds, of *Human Development, A Child's World,* and *Psychology,* college textbooks published by McGraw-Hill.

Cameron J. Camp is a noted psychologist specializing in applied research in gerontology. He received a bachelor's degree in psychology from the University of Houston, where he graduated summa cum laude, and master's and doctoral degrees in experimental psychology from the same institution. For 16 years, he taught undergraduate courses in adult development and aging, as well as in memory, general psychology, child development, and experimental design, first at Fort Hays State University in Kansas, and then at the University of New Orleans. He is the author of numerous articles in professional journals such as *Psychology and Aging, Journal of Gerontology, The Gerontologist, Experimental Aging Research, Human Development,* and *Clinical Gerontologist.* He has contributed chapters to books on memory and aging, problem solving, and lifespan development and is coauthor of a college textbook, *Human Sexuality Today.* Currently he is Research Scientist at the Myers Research Institute of Menorah Park Center for the Aging in Cleveland, Ohio. Much of his research involves the development of behavioral and cognitive interventions to help persons with dementia live more independent and fulfilling lives and to reduce burdens on caregivers. He is a member of the Gerontological Society of America and is on the executive committee of the American Psychological Association's division on adult development and aging.

Ruth Duskin Feldman is an award-winning professional writer. She is the author or coauthor of four books addressed to general readers, including *Whatever Happened to the Quiz Kids? Perils and Profits of Growing Up Gifted,* and was coauthor of the Fourth Edition of Diane E. Papalia and Sally Wendkos Olds's widely used textbook *Human Development.* A former teacher, she has developed educational materials for all levels from elementary school through college. She has written hundreds of articles for newspapers and national magazines on education and other topics and has lectured extensively throughout the United States. She prepared the test banks to accompany the Fifth Edition of *Human Development* and the Sixth Edition of another Papalia/Olds text, *A Child's World,* as well as the *Study Guide with Readings* to accompany the Fifth, Sixth, and Seventh Editions of *A Child's World.* She received her bachelor's degree from Northwestern University, where she graduated with highest distinction and was elected to Phi Beta Kappa. She is a member of several professional associations, including the Authors' Guild and the American Society of Journalists and Authors.

To our parents,
Edward and Madeline Papalia;
Cameron, Frieda, and Paula Camp;
and Boris and Rita Duskin,
who lighted the way
and encouraged us on our chosen paths.

And to our life partners
Jonathan L. Finlay,
Linda Camp,
and Gilbert Feldman,
who helped us over the rough spots
and exulted with us at the peaks.

And to our children,
Anna Victoria Finlay;
Kathy, Karen, and Jenson Camp;
and Steven, Laurie, and Heidi Feldman,
who will continue the journey
in directions we can barely imagine.

CONTENTS

LIST OF BOXES   xi

PREFACE   xiii

TO THE STUDENT   xvii

PART ONE
EXPLORING THE WORLD
OF ADULTHOOD   1

CHAPTER 1
ADULT DEVELOPMENT
AND AGING IN A CHANGING
WORLD   2

FOCUS: *Betty Friedan*   3

**Approaching the Study of Adult
Development and Aging:
An Overview**   5
What is Adult Development? ▪ How the
Study of Adult Development and Aging
Evolved ▪ A Lifespan Developmental
Approach

Basic Concepts   9
Aspects of Development ▪ Periods of
Adulthood ▪ Meanings of Age
▪ Influences on the Course of Adult
Development and Aging

**Changing Images and Realities
of Aging**   18
Cultural Views of Aging ▪ The Shifting
Demographics of Aging ▪ The Aging
Population: A Profile of Diversity
▪ Challenges and Dilemmas of a Graying
World ▪ New Roles for Older Adults

Summary   33

Key Terms   34

CHAPTER 2
METATHEORETICAL PERSPECTIVES
AND RESEARCH METHODS   36

FOCUS: *Erik H. Erikson*   37

Metatheories   39
Three Metatheories: Mechanistic,
Organismic, and Contextual ▪ Applying
Metatheories

Basic Research Methods   46
Sampling ▪ Data Collection

Basic Research Designs   54
Case Studies ▪ Correlational Studies
▪ Experiments

**Quasi-Experimental Designs:
The Problem of Internal Validity**   61
Cross-Sectional Studies ▪ Longitudinal
Studies ▪ Time-Lag Studies ▪ Sequential
Designs

Ethics of Research   68

Summary   71

Key Terms   73

PART TWO
THE WORLDS
OF BODY AND MIND   75

CHAPTER 3
LONGEVITY AND
PHYSIOLOGICAL AGING   76

FOCUS: *Martha Graham*   77

Lifespan and the Aging Process   79
Trends in Life Expectancy ▪ How Far Can
the Human Lifespan Be Extended? ▪ Quality
versus Quantity of Life ▪ Theories of Biological
Aging ▪ Predicting Individual Longevity

Physical Appearance   90

Sensorimotor Functioning   92
Vision • Hearing • Taste and Smell
• Touch, Pain, and Temperature
• Motor Functions

**Sexual and Reproductive
Functioning**   104
The Female Reproductive System
• The Male Reproductive System
• Sexuality and Aging

Summary   112

Key Terms   113

CHAPTER **4**
HEALTH AND
BODY SYSTEMS   114

FOCUS: *Stephen Hawking*   115

**Health and Aging: A Lifespan
Developmental Approach**   119

Changes in Body Systems   123
Skeletal System • Cardiovascular System
• Respiratory System • Immune System
• Neurological System

"Dread Diseases" of Aging   136
Alzheimer's Disease • Cancer: A Disorder
of Many Systems

Indirect Influences on Health   143
Age and Gender • Socioeconomic Status,
Race, and Ethnicity • Relationships

**Factors in Maintaining
and Improving Health**   147
Harmful Substances • Stress • Diet
• Dental Care • Exercise

Summary   154

Key Terms   157

CHAPTER **5**
MEMORY   158

FOCUS: *Laurence Olivier*   159

Studying Memory Systems   161

**Information-Processing Approach:
Software of Memory**   162
Processes: Encoding, Storage, and Retrieval
• "Storehouses": Sensory, Short-Term,
and Long-Term • Aging and Long-Term
Memory: Stability or Decline?
• Summing Up: Memory and Age

**Biological Approach:
Hardware of Memory**   176
Structures Controlling Conscious Memory
• Structures Controlling Unconscious
Memory

New Directions for Research   182

**Aspects of Memory and
Forgetting in Adulthood**   183
Intrusion Errors: Remembering What Did
Not Happen • Prospective Memory:
Remembering to Do Something
• Production Deficiencies in Strategies for
Remembering • Metamemory: The View
from Within • Mnemonics: Making the
Most of Changing Memory • Forgetting
and Its Surprising Benefits

Summary   194

Key Terms   196

CHAPTER **6**
INTELLIGENCE
AND CREATIVITY   198

FOCUS: *Akira Kurosawa*   199

**Intelligence and Its Measurement:
The Psychometric Approach**   201
What Is Intelligence? • Intelligence Tests
and Scores • Tests and Cultural Bias
• Influences on Older Adults' Test
Performance • Psychometric Testing:
A Preliminary Evaluation

**Intellectual Development
in Adulthood: Basic Issues**   210
Is Intelligence One Ability or Many? •
Does Intelligence Grow or Decline during
Adulthood? • Do Changes in Intelligence
Vary? • Does Intelligence Show Plasticity?
• Summing Up: Intelligence and Age

Creativity 227
What Is Creativity? ▪ Studying and
Measuring Creativity ▪ Creativity
and Age

Summary 237

Key Terms 239

CHAPTER **7**
MATURE THOUGHT,
WISDOM, AND
MORAL INTELLIGENCE 240

FOCUS: Nelson Mandela 241

The Role of Experience 243
Applying Expertise ▪ Solving Everyday
Problems ▪ Thinking Integratively

Postformal Thought:
Beyond Piaget's Stages 248
How Postformal Thought Develops
▪ Social Reasoning and Postformal
Thought ▪ Cultural Change and
Postformal Thought ▪ Criteria for
Postformal Thought

A Lifespan Model
of Cognitive Development 254

Wisdom 255
Wisdom in Folklore, Myth, and Philosophy
▪ Psychological Concepts and
Assessments ▪ Summing Up: Wisdom
and Age

Moral Development 265
Kohlberg's Theory: Moral Reasoning
▪ Gilligan's Theory: Gender and
Postformal Morality ▪ Evaluating
Kohlberg's and Gilligan's Theories

Intelligence, Creativity,
Wisdom, and
Moral Development: A Last Word 274

Summary 276

Key Terms 278

PART THREE
THE SOCIAL WORLD 279

CHAPTER **8**
EDUCATION, WORK,
LEISURE, AND RETIREMENT 280

FOCUS: Jimmy Carter 281

Education 284
College ▪ Lifelong Learning
▪ Adult Illiteracy

Work and Leisure 289
Vocational Choice and Career Development
▪ Changing Occupational Patterns
▪ Age and Job Performance
▪ Occupational Stress ▪ Unemployment
▪ Work, Leisure, and Intellectual Growth

Retirement and
Other Late-Life Options 304
To Retire or Not to Retire ▪ Financing
Retirement ▪ Preparing for Retirement
▪ How Do Retired People Use Their Time?
▪ How Does Retirement Affect Well-Being?
▪ How Does Retirement Affect Society?

Summary 318

Key Terms 319

CHAPTER **9**
INTIMATE RELATIONSHIPS
AND LIFESTYLES 320

FOCUS: Louise Erdrich
and Michael Dorris 321

Foundations of Intimate Relationships 323
Friendship ▪ Love ▪ Sexuality

Nonmarital Lifestyles 329
Single Life ▪ Homosexual Relationships
▪ Cohabitation

Marital and Postmarital Lifestyles 332
Marriage ▪ Divorce and Remarriage
▪ What Makes Marriages Succeed?

Family Life   343
Changing Family Structures ▪ Parenthood
Today ▪ Parenthood as a Developmental
Experience ▪ When Children Leave:
The "Empty Nest" ▪ Parenthood, Role
Changes, and Marital Satisfaction
▪ Remaining Childless

Summary   356

Key Terms   358

CHAPTER **10**
MATURE KINSHIP TIES AND
LIVING ARRANGEMENTS   360

FOCUS: Marian Anderson   361

The Adult Family:
Changing Roles and Relationships   363
Young Adult Children and Middle-Aged
Parents ▪ Middle-Aged Children
and Elderly Parents ▪ Siblings
▪ Multigenerational Late-Life Families

Grandparenthood and
Great-Grandparenthood   372
The Grandparent's Role ▪ The Great-
Grandparent's Role ▪ Raising
Grandchildren and Great-Grandchildren

Living Arrangements, Caregiving,
and Community Support   380
Adult Children at Home: The Not-So-Empty
Nest ▪ Living Arrangements for Older
Adults ▪ Family Caregiving ▪ Care of the
Old-Old: An International Perspective

Summary   397

Key Terms   399

PART FOUR
THE WORLD WITHIN   401

CHAPTER **11**
PERSONALITY DEVELOPMENT   402

FOCUS: Eva Perón   403

Defining and Studying
Personality   405
What Is Personality? ▪ Measuring
Personality ▪ Origins of Personality:
Inheritance and Experience

Models of Adult Personality:
Stability or Change   410
Trait Models ▪ Self-Concept Models
▪ Stage Models ▪ The Timing-of-Events
Model

Gender and Personality   429
Gender Stereotypes, Gender Roles, and
Gender Identity ▪ Women's Personality
Development: The Mills Studies

Synthesizing Approaches to
Adult Personality Development   440

Summary   441

Key Terms   443

CHAPTER **12**
MENTAL HEALTH, COPING,
AND ADJUSTMENT TO AGING   444

FOCUS: Arthur Ashe   445

Models of Coping   448
Environmental Models ▪ Behavioral
Models ▪ Coping-Style Models
▪ Cognitive-Appraisal Model

"Successful Aging"   455
Normative Models ▪ Balance Models
▪ Laypeople's Views about Successful
Aging

Destructive Behavior Patterns   463
Substance Use Disorders ▪ Partner Abuse
▪ Child Abuse and Neglect
▪ Abuse of the Elderly

Mental Health in Late Life:
A Lifespan Developmental Approach 472
Mental Health and Life Satisfaction
▪ Mental Disorders ▪ Assessing Strengths

Summary   483

Key Terms   485

CHAPTER **13**
DEALING WITH DEATH
AND BEREAVEMENT 486

FOCUS: Louisa May Alcott 487

**Changing Perspectives
on Death and Dying** 489
Biological, Social, and Psychological
Aspects of Death • The Study of Death:
Thanatology and Death Education
• Hospice Care

Facing Death 492
Attitudes toward Death and Dying
• Approaching Death

Facing Bereavement 503
Forms and Patterns of Grief • Surviving
a Spouse • Losing a Parent • Losing
a Child

Controversial Issues 514
Suicide • Euthanasia

**Finding Meaning and Purpose
in Life and Death** 521
Reviewing a Life • Overcoming Fear
of Death • Development: A Lifelong
Process

Summary 524

Key Terms 525

GLOSSARY 527

BIBLIOGRAPHY 537

ACKNOWLEDGMENTS 583

NAME INDEX 587

SUBJECT INDEX 599

LIST OF BOXES

1-1 The Multicultural Context: Meanings of Age and Family in the Kalahari Desert 14

1-2 The Art of Aging: New Environments for an Aging Population 22

1-3 The Cutting Edge: The Oldest Old 26

2-1 The Cutting Edge: Early Studies of Sexuality 47

2-2 The Multicultural Context: Avoiding Cultural Bias in Research 50

2-3 The Art of Aging: What Longitudinal Studies Can Tell Us 64

3-1 The Cutting Edge: Can We Push Out the Boundaries of Life? 82

3-2 The Art of Aging: New Ways to Better Vision and Hearing 94

3-3 The Multicultural Context: Japanese Women's Experience of Menopause 108

4-1 The Cutting Edge: Genetic Testing 117

4-2 The Multicultural Context: How Traditional Beliefs Influence the Course of Disease 122

4-3 The Art of Aging: The Estrogen Decision 125

5-1 The Cutting Edge: Everyday Memory—A Case of Conflict among Researchers 163

5-2 The Art of Aging: The Best Memory Aid—A Healthy Lifestyle 177

5-3 The Multicultural Context: Memory and Culture 186

6-1 The Multicultural Context: Is Intelligent Behavior the Same in All Cultures? 202

6-2 The Cutting Edge: Are Intelligence Tests the Best Predictor of Job Performance? 212

6-3 The Art of Aging: Creativity Takes Hard Work at Any Age 232

7-1 The Multicultural Context: Postformal Thinking and Cultural Change 251

7-2 The Cutting Edge: Comparing Wisdom with Intelligence and Creativity 256

7-3 The Art of Aging: Moral Leadership in Middle and Late Adulthood 274

8-1 The Art of Aging: Computer Training—Teaching Older Adults New Tricks 286

8-2 The Cutting Edge: Age Discrimination and Public Safety 299

8-3 The Multicultural Context: Work and Retirement in China 309

9-1 The Art of Aging: How Dual-Earner Couples Cope 334

9-2 The Multicultural Context: Divorce in France—A Two-Track System 336

9-3 The Cutting Edge: Motherhood After Menopause 348

10-1 The Multicultural Context: The Extended-Family Household in Hispanic Cultures 364

10-2 The Cutting Edge: Establishing
Mature Relationships with Parents   366

10-3 The Art of Aging:
Choosing Living Arrangements   382

11-1 The Cutting Edge: Can Personality
Patterns Cause Disease?   407

11-2 The Art of Aging:
Navigating the Midlife Crossing   422

11-3 The Multicultural Context:
Druze Men—New Roles
in Late Middle Age   434

12-1 The Cutting Edge: Both Job
and Family Roles Affect Men's
Psychological Well-Being   447

12-2 The Multicultural Context:
Coping with Economic
Change in Rural Malaysia   454

12-3 The Art of Aging: Religion
and Emotional Well-Being
in Late Life   456

13-1 The Cutting Edge:
Near-Death Experiences   498

13-2 The Multicultural Context:
Postponing Death   502

13-3 The Art of Aging:
Evoking Memories for
a Life Review   523

PREFACE

To write a textbook about adult development and aging is an exciting challenge. This rapidly growing field of study about a vital, diverse, and expanding population draws on the findings of many academic disciplines. This book takes a topical rather than a chronological approach. We discuss each aspect of development—physical, cognitive, social, and personality development—in relation to all periods of the adult lifespan, with special emphasis on late adulthood.

By combining the talents and experience of the author of a leading textbook on lifespan development, a noted researcher in adult development and aging who has extensive teaching experience in the field, and a professional writer who has written textbook material and peripherals in developmental psychology, we believe we have achieved not only a high degree of accuracy and thoroughness, but also a tone and a writing style that are fresh, lively, clear, engaging, thought-provoking, and accessible.

What sets this book apart from others in the field? What were our aims in writing it?

- We depict adult development as a very human story. Each chapter begins with a biographical vignette about a real person. The subjects are well-known men and women (such as Betty Friedan and Nelson Mandela) of varying racial, national, and ethnic origins, whose lives dramatize important themes in the chapter. Students will enjoy and identify with these stories, which lead directly and smoothly into the body of each chapter.

- We take a consistently cross-cultural perspective. Extensive multicultural and multiethnic material is woven into topical discussions throughout the book. In addition, a series of boxes called "The Multicultural Context" focuses on specific topics such as how traditional beliefs influence the course of disease, whether intelligent behavior is the same in all cultures, and how rural Malaysians cope with economic change. Photographs reinforce the themes of diversity and demographic balance.

- We discuss contemporary trends and lifestyles in a complex, changing world. The introductory chapter, which includes a section on the "graying of the planet," sets the tone for current, issue-oriented coverage. As an integral part of our discussions of relationships and family life, we deal with such topics as single parenting, dual-earner families, homosexuality, and caregiving grandparents. We include a number of topics not covered (or mentioned only in passing) in most adult development texts, such as domestic violence, the effects of no-fault divorce, and the surprising benefits of forgetting.

- We take a positive yet realistic view of aging. We believe that all periods of adulthood are equally important and provide opportunities for growth. Throughout the book, we point out insights to be gained from a lifespan developmental perspective and a multidisciplinary approach.

- We balance theoretical, empirical, and practical concerns. To emphasize the evolving nature of scientific knowledge, a series of boxes called "The Cutting Edge" describes groundbreaking and controversial research, past and present. Another series of boxes, "The Art of Aging," features specific research applications such as environmental adaptations to meet the needs of an aging population, pros and cons of estrogen replacement therapy, and computer training for older adults. Where controversy exists, we explore it. We present the field of adult development as it is: a developing field whose practitioners still have much to discover.

xiii

AUDIENCE

This book is designed primarily for undergraduates—sophomores or juniors—taking courses in adult development and aging. Such courses are typically offered by departments of psychology, sociology, or gerontology and by programs in social work, health education, human services, or nursing. Because of its comprehensive, up-to-date content, *Adult Development and Aging* may also be used for advanced and graduate-level courses. It is also appropriate for lifespan developmental courses, in conjunction with a text on child and adolescent development. No prior knowledge of psychology is necessary, because basic concepts and methods are explained as needed.

ORGANIZATION AND COVERAGE

The thirteen chapters are grouped into four parts. Part One, "Exploring the World of Adulthood," includes an introductory overview of the field and a chapter on metatheories and research methods. Part Two, "The Worlds of Body and Mind," covers physical, cognitive, and moral development. Part Three, "The Social World," explores education, work, retirement, and leisure; relationships and lifestyles; and living arrangements, caregiving, and community support. Part Four, "The World Within," turns to personality development, mental health and coping, and death and bereavement. We believe that this organization provides a clear, logical treatment of the most salient topics in the study of adult development and aging.

LEARNING AIDS

This book contains a number of pedagogical aids for the student:

- *Part overviews.* Each part begins with an overview that explains the rationale and sets the tone for the chapters that follow.
- *Chapter openings.* Each chapter opening includes a chapter outline that previews the major topics, and a short biographical vignette that brings those topics into focus.

- *Examples.* In addition to the opening vignette, each chapter has many examples and anecdotes—real events that happened to real people in real life. These are drawn from news reports, from research, or from our own experience and observations.
- *Chapter summaries.* Brief statements, organized around the main topics in the chapter, review the important concepts.
- *Boxes.* Each chapter has three boxes—one from each of three series: The Multicultural Context, The Cutting Edge (research), and The Art of Aging (application).
- *Illustrations, figures, and tables.* Drawings, graphs, charts, and photographs are carefully chosen to underscore important points in the text.
- *Key terms.* As each important new term is introduced, it is highlighted and defined in the text. Key terms, and the pages on which they first appear, are listed at the end of each chapter.
- *Glossary.* Key terms and their definitions appear in alphabetical order in an end-of-book glossary.
- *Bibliography.* A complete listing of references appears alphabetically by author at the end of the book.

SUPPLEMENTARY MATERIALS

Adult Development and Aging is accompanied by a complete learning and teaching package consisting of a combined Instructor's Manual and Test Bank prepared by Cheryl Rickabaugh, University of Redlands, California. Computerized versions of the Test Bank will be available for Macintosh and IBM systems.

ACKNOWLEDGMENTS

We would like to express our appreciation to the following friends and colleagues, who reviewed drafts of *Adult Development and Aging* and whose valuable suggestions helped us clarify our thinking and improve the final product: James A. Blackburn, University of Wisconsin –Milwaukee (who helped in the initial planning);

Fredda Blanchard-Fields, Georgia Institute of Technology; Victor Cicirelli, Purdue University; Joan Erber, Florida International University; Susan Hillier, Sonoma State University; William Hoyer, Syracuse University; Paul Klaczynski, Western Carolina University; Dale Lund, University of Utah; Richard Metzger, University of Tennessee; Catherine Murray, St. Joseph's University; Eileen Nelson, James Madison University; Sarah O'Dowd, Community College of Rhode Island; Stuart Offenbach, Purdue University; Karen Rook, University of California, Irvine; and Steven Zarit, Penn State University.

We deeply appreciate the strong support of our publisher. We wish to express special thanks to Jane Vaicunas, our original editorial sponsor, who conceived the idea for the book and assembled the team of authors; to Leslye Jackson, who came on board in midstream and helped keep the project on course; to Jeannine Ciliotta, whose superb editorial skills and attentiveness to detail helped shape the book's organization and content, and who sharpened its focus and shepherded it through all phases of preparation and production; to Susan Gamer, our thorough and precise editing supervisor; and to Beth Kaufman, who supervised the review process and the supplements. Inge King, our photo editor, found excellent photographs that visually reinforce important concepts. Wanda Lubelska produced an innovative, attractive cover and book design.

We are grateful to Sally Wendkos Olds for her considerable contribution to the writing of parts of the book. We also wish to thank Linda Camp and the many students at the University of New Orleans who contributed their time and talents to assisting with research. Space does not permit mention of all, but a short list includes Alan Stevens, Leslie McKitrick, Ann O'Hanlon, Jean Foss, Cecile Brookover, Sandra Bologna, Dave Vance, Patricia Ford, Amy Mandella, Cricket Gaumer, Shawn Arrillaga, Mary Ursin, Michelle Bertoniere, Kelly Robinson, Robin Beniger, Shirley Turco, Christine Altobello, Toni Ronquille, Wendy Barlow, Rhoda Noto, Opal Hornig, Lynn Chauvin, Leah Steele, Laurie Weisberg, and Wendy Watrous.

Diane E. Papalia
Cameron J. Camp
Ruth Duskin Feldman

TO THE STUDENT

When you look through your family photo album, do you wonder about the people whose images are frozen at moments in time? When you see that portrait of your grandparents on their wedding day, do you wonder whether they were nervous about the new life they were starting together? Did their lives turn out as they hoped? There is your grandmother, holding your father as a baby. How did that young bride turn into the woman with an infant in her arms, and then into the older woman you may have known or still know?

Snapshots tell us little about the processes of inward and outward change that make up an adult life. Even a series of home movies or videotapes, which can follow people from moment to moment as they grow older, will not capture changes so subtle that we often cannot detect them until after they have occurred. The processes that produce those changes—the processes by which adults develop across time—are the subject of this book.

The study of adult development and aging is endlessly fascinating because it is the study of real lives. Even though scientists may someday find a way to clone a human embryo, there is no way to duplicate an adult human being with the peculiar blend of characteristics and experiences that makes that individual unique. How does this special mix come about? How did you become the person you are? How will you become the person you will be tomorrow? Because human personality is complex, developmentalists do not have definitive answers. But they have learned much about adult human beings: what their needs are, how they respond to the many influences on and within them, and how they can best fulfill their potential as individuals and as a species.

Of course, development does not begin with adulthood. The processes that govern it are extensions of those that began at or before birth. But distinct features and themes, such as practical intelligence and wisdom, appear—or become more important—in adulthood. Studying adult development and aging can help professionals and laypeople deal with life's transitions. For example, the more we know about the nature of aging, the better we can distinguish between things we can easily control (such as fitness) and those we can't control so easily (loss of nerve cells). Even up to the end of life, people can grow and change. By examining the course of adult development, you will come to know more about yourself and other human beings. And you may be able to help yourself and others to live happier, more fulfilled lives.

HOW THIS BOOK IS ORGANIZED

Writing a textbook about adult development and aging is a challenge because the subject covers almost every aspect of the lives of adult human beings and the societies they live in. Students of adult development and aging need information about how adults respond to their biological heritage and their environment, and how they affect the world they live in. Theory and research on adult development draw on many disciplines, including psychology, sociology, anthropology, biology, education, and medicine.

In Part One of this book, you begin an exploration of the ever-changing world of adult development and aging with a "guidebook" to basic concepts, current population trends, and the explorer's tools: the theoretical perspectives that developmentalists bring to their work and the kinds of research methods they use. Part Two describes the worlds of body and mind: physical and intellectual development throughout adulthood. Part Three expands your horizons to the wider social world: relationships with family members and friends, social institutions, and the choices adults make regarding work, retirement, and leisure. Part Four explores the inner world of personality development, mental and emotional health, and how adults cope with the challenges of aging and the prospect of the end of life.

HOW THIS BOOK RELATES TO YOUR LIFE

Much of what you will read in this book is directly relevant to your life today—such topics as sexual orientation, establishing a mature relationship with parents, career development, and what makes for marital success. Some of the information is as pertinent to you as your next paycheck. Did you know, for example, that a substantial portion of your tax money finances federal programs related to aging? Did you know that as of 1995 there were 28 federally funded Alzheimer's Disease Research Centers across the United States? How will the need to fund social security benefits for a growing elderly population affect your earnings?

The way society looks at aging will affect the way people think about you in the future, and perhaps the way you think about yourself. What do you think older people are like? How is today's aging population different from older generations in the past? What will you be like when you grow old?

Reading this book may affect the person you will become in later life. For example, establishing good health habits can prevent problems that sometimes afflict middle-aged and older adults. And new findings may help you maximize your intellectual potential throughout your life.

THE AUTHORS' PERSPECTIVE

Every book is written by real people, whose selection of subject matter, examples, and interpretations is inevitably colored by their own experiences and attitudes. We three authors make up a diversified team. Our ages range from the early forties to just past 60; our combined life experience encompasses the periods from the Great Depression of the 1930s to the present. Our ethnic origins are Italian, eastern European Jewish, Irish, Norwegian, and Native American. Between us, we have lived in 11 states of the union. All of us are married, all are parents, and one is a grandparent.

Despite our varied backgrounds and interests, the three of us share some basic beliefs about adult human beings. To help you assess what we say, we want to outline the perspectives from which we wrote this book.

- We believe that people have the potential to develop as long as they live. Each part of adulthood has its own special nature and its own developmental tasks.

- Although we look separately at physical, intellectual, social, and personality development, we recognize that each of these aspects of development is entwined with the others.

- Adults live in a wide array of cultures that exhibit the richness and complexity of human aspirations and experience. Since what happens around and to adults affects them in many ways, we look at development in the context in which it occurs.

- We believe that adults help shape their own development. They actively affect their own environment and then respond to the environment they have helped create.

- We look at aging realistically, as a natural process of development that includes both losses and gains. Older people are not all the same "age" in abilities, energy, activity, or interests; and a person who has declined physically may still be growing mentally and emotionally.

Real adults are not abstractions. They are human beings who live, work, love, laugh, weep, ask questions, and make decisions. To personalize the information from hundreds of scientific studies, we open each chapter with a vignette about a real person—someone you may well have heard of—whose life brings into focus concepts discussed in the chapter. The subjects of these vignettes—such as the feminist author Betty Friedan, the British actor Laurence Olivier, the African American tennis champion Arthur Ashe, and the Native American writers Louise Erdrich and Michael Dorris—reflect the diversity as well as the underlying unity of adult life. Although these are famous people, they are (or were) people first and foremost, with needs, hopes, fears, motivations, and resources.

Ultimately, it is you who must apply what you learn from this book. Observe the adults around you—your parents, your sisters and brothers, your friends, your spouse or lover. Observe the strangers you see in supermarkets and fast-food restaurants, in department stores and offices, on construction projects and on farms, on buses and airplanes, in movie theaters and sports centers. Pay attention to them as they confront and experience the challenges of everyday life. See how they get along with others, how they go about solving problems, how they spend their leisure time. Think about your own experiences and how they relate to the concepts and issues discussed in this book. With the insights you gain as you proceed on your journey through the world of adult development and aging, you will be able to look at yourself and at every adult you see with new eyes.

As you begin your exploration of the world of adulthood, you enter a terrain both familiar and unfamiliar. Like an explorer of the physical world, you will find much that you may not yet know. Just as the study of a geographic area can make your journey through it more meaningful, the study of the world of adulthood—the changing world you will live in for the rest of your life—can help you see it more clearly. In Part One, we prepare the way.

Chapter 1 gives you an "itinerary": a description of how this "guidebook" is organized and of what kinds of "sights" you will see. We briefly describe the aging population of today's adult world, and we introduce some of the questions you will need to ask as you go along.

Just as an explorer of the physical world needs tools (such as a compass and a telescope) for guidance, so do scientists whose life work is to explore the world of adulthood. In Chapter 2, we discuss theoretical perspectives and research methods that help scientists search out new directions for study and test the soundness of a path.

Learning about the journey through adulthood can show you what to expect. It can suggest things you can do to make your trip as pleasant as possible. And it can prepare you to illuminate the way for those who come after you.

PART ONE

EXPLORING THE WORLD OF ADULTHOOD

CHAPTER 1

ADULT DEVELOPMENT AND AGING IN A CHANGING WORLD

APPROACHING THE STUDY OF
ADULT DEVELOPMENT AND
AGING: AN OVERVIEW
What Is Adult Development?
How the Study of Adult Development
   and Aging Evolved
A Lifespan Developmental Approach

BASIC CONCEPTS
Aspects of Development
Periods of Adulthood
Meanings of Age
Influences on the Course
   of Adult Development and Aging

CHANGING IMAGES AND
REALITIES OF AGING
Cultural Views of Aging
The Shifting Demographics of Aging
The Aging Population:
   A Profile of Diversity
Challenges and Dilemmas
   of a Graying World
New Roles for Older Adults

BOXES
1-1 The Multicultural Context:
   Meanings of Age and Family
   in the Kalahari Desert
1-2 The Art of Aging:
   New Environments
   for an Aging Population
1-3 The Cutting Edge: The Oldest Old

There is nothing permanent except change.

Heraclitus, fragment (sixth century B.C.)

(Joyce Ravid)

Betty Friedan* stands a feisty 5 feet 2 inches tall and does not shrink from a fight. At age 42, she wrote *The Feminine Mystique* (1963), a call to arms for the women's movement in the United States. Three decades later, Friedan has become a standard-bearer for another crusade with *The Fountain of Age* (1993), aimed at freeing older adults from a restrictive image of aging.

Both books and both causes are deeply rooted in Friedan's own experience. Her odyssey from her beginnings in Peoria, Illinois, a small town in the American heartland, tells much, not only about her personal development as an adult but about the changing social context of adult development and aging. Not wanting to be like her mother, who always regretted having given up her career for marriage, the bright, energetic young woman went east to Smith College, a prestigious women's school. She majored in psychology, graduated summa cum laude, and later did postgraduate work with such leaders in the field as Kurt Lewin and Erik Erikson. She also worked as a reporter for a labor news service but was bumped by a returning World War II veteran—a common experience for working women who had been recruited to fill in for fighting men, only to be told, after the war, to go home where they "belonged."

In 1947, Friedan was married. Two years later, fired from a newspaper job for being pregnant, she (like most other young women of her time and place) became a self-described housewife, seeking the feminine fulfillment her mother had failed to achieve. But somehow she wanted more. During the 1950s, while raising her three

*Sources for biographical information about Betty Friedan are Carlson and Crowley (1992), Friedan (1963, 1976, 1981, 1993, 1994), Klagsbrun (1993), and *Who's Who in America* (1994).

children in a New York suburb, she wrote articles for national women's magazines and secretly began work on her myth-shattering book, *The Feminine Mystique*.

"I did not set out consciously to start a revolution when I wrote *The Feminine Mystique*," Friedan (1976, pp. xiii, xv) later recalled, "but it changed my life, as a woman and as a writer, and other women tell me it changed theirs."

The book, which has so far sold 3 million copies, expressed Friedan's growing frustration with her role in a male-dominated society in which a woman's "place" was in the home and her sole identity was "wife and mother." It articulated the unacknowledged rage, emptiness, and desperation of millions of women who chafed under the bonds of domesticity yet succumbed to societal pressures against having lives and careers of their own. The message was threatening to many women but liberating to many others.

Friedan became an organizer of the women's movement, the founder and first president of the National Organization for Women (NOW), and the convener of the National Women's Political Caucus. On August 26, 1970, a year after she divorced her husband, she called a "Women's Strike for Equality" and led an estimated 50,000 marchers down Manhattan's Fifth Avenue. Friedan (1976, 1981) gradually broadened her sights, pressing for new approaches to divorce, abortion reform, housing, employment, and education; for equality within marriage as well as in the workplace; and for societal supports for women who wanted to balance a career and children.

Now in her early seventies, the woman who raised the consciousness of a generation of young and middle-aged women is determined to do the same for older adults. Before starting 10 years of research for *The Fountain of Age*, she had to break through her psychological denial of her own aging. Ultimately, Friedan (who has six grandchildren and two step-granddaughters and is a visiting professor at New York University) set out "to debunk the 'age mystique' that defines older people as passive objects of care and . . . denies them their 'personhood,' just as the feminine mystique denied women theirs" (Carlson & Crowley, 1992, pp. 20, 15).

The Fountain of Age has been hailed by some critics, but dismissed by others as too upbeat. It seeks to change the prevalent view of aging as a process of inevitable deterioration, helplessness, and disease, and of older adults as a burden and a drain on society—an image that does not match the real lives of vast numbers of older adults. Instead of defining old age merely as a loss of youth, Friedan sees it as another stage of development with its own, as yet largely untested, possibilities and strengths—"an adventure, not a problem" (Carlson & Crowley, 1992). In fact, she suggests, freeing themselves from "clinging blindly to the mask of youth" can help adults "sustain a good, vital life at any age" (Friedan, 1994, pp. 4, 5).

Betty Friedan's adult life and work demonstrate what she learned from her teachers of psychology: that human beings develop in a context. Her story dramatizes how an individual adult can affect and be affected by changing social conditions. Friedan's dissatisfaction with her role as a suburban wife and mother in the 1950s sparked a movement that changed the lives of many American women—and her own as well. Now, with the "baby boom" generation—fully one-third of the nation's population—approaching later life, a major shift is occurring in how adults think about and deal with their own development.

This shift is reflected in a growing interest in the study of adult development and aging. In introducing you to that study, we start with basic questions and concepts: What does it mean for an adult to develop? Is aging more than a process of decline? How has adult development been studied? Does age have more than one meaning? Why do some people seem to age differently from others? What kinds of influences can alter the course of adult development? We go on to discuss changing views and realities of aging. We briefly describe the diverse composition of a graying population in the United States and worldwide, and the challenges and dilemmas it presents.

APPROACHING THE STUDY OF ADULT DEVELOPMENT AND AGING: AN OVERVIEW

Before beginning a study of adult development and aging, we need to raise a basic question: Do adults actually *develop*, or do human beings reach maturity in their early twenties and then decline? Until the middle of the twentieth century, most psychologists would have given the second answer. Sigmund Freud, the father of psychoanalysis, saw puberty as the end point of development. Researchers limited their attention to children; even adolescence was not considered a separate stage of life until the turn of the twentieth century. Only during the past few decades has there been serious, scientific study of adult development. That study is still in an early phase, and many of its discoveries are still quite tentative; but developmentalists are asking and exploring important questions.

WHAT IS ADULT DEVELOPMENT?

We've been speaking about *development;* but what, precisely, does this term mean? In ordinary speech, forms of the word are used in many contexts. For example:

- Horace is developing a cold.
- Flowers develop from buds.
- Many developing nations are rapidly becoming industrialized.
- Lindsay took a roll of film to be developed.
- Detectives reported a new development in the murder case.

Obviously, development involves change. But not all change is developmental. If a person changes clothes, or changes the bedsheets, we hardly would call that *development*.

Change is simply a difference in something or someone from one time to another. Change is continual and inevitable. Changes in a human being over the course of adult life are too numerous, too diverse, and often too random to study usefully. *Development* is a systematic process of adaptive change in behavior in one or more directions. Development is *systematic* in that it is coherent and organized. It is *adaptive* in that it is aimed at dealing with the ever-changing internal and external conditions of existence. Development tends to progress from simple to complex forms (as when a nation's economy evolves from family farming to large-scale industry). It may take more than one route and may or may not have a definite goal; but there is some connection between the often-imperceptible changes of which it is composed. The child you were shaped the adult you have become, and the adult you are today will shape the adult you become tomorrow. Developmentalists study how people change—and also how they do *not* change—throughout the lifespan.

Development may involve *learning:* long-lasting changes in behavior as a result of experience. Or it may be the result of *maturation* of body and brain: the unfolding of a biologically determined sequence of behavior patterns, including readiness to master new abilities. More often, development involves a complex interaction between the two, as when a young child says the first word or the first sentence. While children pass such milestones at pretty much the same ages, individual differences widen as people grow older and experience becomes more of a factor. Adult development may not be as rapid or as obvious as childhood development and may involve losses as well as gains; but even older adults can continue to develop new skills, such as learning to use computers.

HOW THE STUDY OF ADULT DEVELOPMENT AND AGING EVOLVED

The first serious interest in the study of adulthood appeared in the early decades of the twentieth century. In 1922, at age 78, G. Stanley Hall, who had been a pioneer in the study of childhood and adolescence, published *Senescence: The Last Half of Life*. Six years later, Stanford University opened the first major scientific research unit devoted to aging. But not until a generation later did this area of study blossom. By 1946, the National Institutes of Health (NIH) had established a large-scale research unit, and specialized organizations and journals were reporting the latest findings.

Since the late 1930s, a number of long-term studies have focused on adults. The Grant Study of Adult Development followed Harvard University students through adulthood. In the mid-1950s Bernice Neugarten and her associates at the University of Chicago began studies of middle-aged people, and K. Warner Schaie launched the still-ongoing Seattle Longitudinal Study of adult intelligence. Paul Costa and Robert McCrae have conducted a study of personality traits based on data collected beginning in the late 1950s to mid-1960s on thousands of adults of all ages in Boston and Baltimore.

Full lifespan studies in the United States grew out of programs designed to follow children through adulthood. The Stanford Studies of Gifted Children

The psychologist G. Stanley Hall (1846–1924) was a pioneer in the study of aging, as well as of childhood and adolescence. He was a founder and the first president of the American Psychological Association, and he established the nation's first professional psychology journal and its first psychology laboratory.

(begun in 1921 under the direction of Lewis Terman) continue to trace the development of people who were identified as unusually intelligent in childhood. Other major studies that began around 1930—the Berkeley Growth Study, the Oakland Growth Study, and the Fels Research Institute Study—have yielded information on long-term development.

These and other studies we discuss in this book have drawn on a variety of research tools and have added much to our understanding of adulthood. However, we still know much more about children and older adults than we do about those in between. A growing emphasis on studies about young and middle-aged adults should yield fruit in years to come.

A LIFESPAN DEVELOPMENTAL APPROACH

Today, most psychologists accept the idea that human development goes on throughout life. This concept of development as a lifelong process of adaptation is known as *lifespan development.* Scientific study of lifespan development is the primary task of *lifespan developmental psychology.*

One of the newest, most influential, and most fully elaborated perspectives on lifespan development is that of Paul B. Baltes, a leader in shaping the concept and study of lifespan development, particularly in the intellectual sphere. Baltes (1987) has identified key features of a lifespan developmental approach (summarized in Table 1-1), to which we will refer throughout this book:

1. *Multidirectionality.* According to Baltes, development throughout life is *multidirectional:* it involves both growth and decline. As people gain in one area, they may lose in another, and at varying rates. Children grow mostly in one

TABLE 1-1 KEY FEATURES OF A LIFESPAN DEVELOPMENTAL APPROACH

Feature	Explanation
Multidirectionality	Development can result in both increases and decreases, at varying rates, within the same person, age period, or category of behavior.
Plasticity	It is possible to improve functioning throughout the lifespan, though there are limits on how much a person can improve at any age.
History and context	People develop within a physical and social context, which differs at different points in history. Individuals not only respond to their context but interact with and actively influence it.
Multiple causality	Development has multiple causes. Because no single perspective can adequately describe or explain the complexities of development, the study of lifespan development requires cooperative, multidisciplinary efforts of scholars from many fields.

SOURCE: Adapted from Baltes, 1987.

direction—up—both in size and in abilities. In adulthood the balance gradually shifts toward the negative side. Some capacities, such as vocabulary, continue to increase; others, such as the ability to solve unfamiliar problems, normally diminish; and some new attributes, such as wisdom, may emerge.

2. *Plasticity.* Adaptive capacities are not set in concrete. **Plasticity** means that many skills can be significantly modified with training and practice, even in late life. But the potential for change is not unbounded. Researchers are now testing the limits of improvement, for example, in memory training.

3. *History and context.* Each person develops within a specific set of circumstances or conditions defined by time and place. During the course of development, human beings influence, and are influenced by, their historical and social context. Like Betty Friedan, they not only respond to their environment but interact with and change it.

4. *Multiple causation.* Because development has a variety of causes, to view behavior from the standpoint of psychology alone would be short-sighted. The study of adult development requires a multidisciplinary partnership of scholars from many fields, looking at adult development and aging from different perspectives. How, for example, can we fully understand the psychological impact of menopause without knowing about the biological changes occurring in a woman's body or how different cultures treat this transition?

The idea that development goes on throughout the lifespan has several important implications. It suggests that each phase of a person's life is influenced by what has already occurred and will affect what is to come. Thus each part of the lifespan has its own unique characteristics and value. No part of life is more or less important than any other.

BASIC CONCEPTS

An extremely useful way to visualize adult development is as a product of *multiple concurrent forces acting on a complex system.* This concept allows us to look at several aspects of the same person, who may be—for example—growing intellectually while experiencing some physical decline. We can view a person as having not one but several different ages: not only chronological but also functional, biological, psychological, and social. And we can measure the effects of many kinds of factors that influence development.

ASPECTS OF DEVELOPMENT

One reason adult development is complex is that changes occur in several aspects of the self. In this book, we speak of physical, intellectual, personality, and social development. Changes in the body and the brain—including sensory capacities, organic and nervous systems, health and fitness, and motor skills—are all parts of *physical* development. To some extent, physical development may be genetically programmed; but research now suggests that people can control their own physical development to a much greater extent than once was thought possible. Changes in mental functioning—such as memory, intelligence, practical problem solving, moral reasoning, and wisdom—are aspects of *intellectual*, or *cognitive*, development. *Personality* development involves the unique way each

Adult development is about all adults and each adult. Adults vary widely in physical characteristics, intellectual abilities, personality, lifestyle, and cultural background; and differences often increase with age.

(Joel Gordon)

person deals with the world and expresses thoughts and emotions. *Social development* refers to changes in an individual's social world—the world of relationships, living arrangements, work, and leisure.

Both rates and results of development vary widely. Individuals differ in height, weight, and body build, in such constitutional factors as health and energy level, and in how their bodies adapt to aging. They differ in intellectual abilities and in emotional reactions; in the work they do, how well they do it, and how much they like it; in the homes and communities they live in, the people they see, and the relationships they have; and in how they use their leisure.

Although we talk separately about physical, intellectual, social, and personality development, these domains are interrelated, and each aspect of development affects the others. Physical and intellectual capacities, for example, contribute greatly to self-esteem and can affect choice of occupation—important elements of personality and social development. Decisions about work and retirement can affect physical and intellectual functioning. Anxiety about taking a test can impair physical or intellectual performance. And grief can literally make a bereaved person ill.

PERIODS OF ADULTHOOD

When does a person become an adult? When does an adult reach middle or old age? These questions are not as simple as they may seem. The demarcation of periods of the lifespan varies in different times and in different societies. Still, most research divides adulthood into three periods: young adulthood (approximately ages 20 to 40), middle age (ages 40 to 65), and late, or older, adulthood (age 65 or more). At least in most western societies today, each of these periods has characteristic events and concerns (see Table 1-2).

Young adults are generally at the height of their physical powers and many aspects of their intellectual powers. During these years, they make career choices and form intimate relationships that may be lifelong.

Middle-aged adults typically see some decline in health and physical abilities but develop more mature patterns of thinking based on practical experience. Some middle-aged people are at the height of their careers; others have reached dead ends. Some dust off mothballed dreams or pursue new goals. Many have children who are leaving the nest. A growing consciousness of the inevitability of death may bring on personality changes and exploration of new opportunities for growth.

Most *older adults* are physically active and mentally alert. Free from the pressures of childrearing and, often, of full-time employment, they have more time for personal relationships. But they must deal with the decline of some faculties, the loss of friends and loved ones, and the prospect of death.

MEANINGS OF AGE

A number of common sayings suggest that there can be discrepancies between chronological age and how old a person feels and acts:

TABLE 1-2 MAJOR DEVELOPMENTS OF THE THREE PERIODS OF ADULTHOOD

Age Period	*Major Developments*
Young adulthood (20 to 40 years)	Physical health peaks, then declines slightly. Intellectual abilities assume more complexity. Decisions are made about intimate relationships. Most people marry; most become parents. Career choices are made. Sense of identity continues to develop.
Middle age (40 to 65 years)	Some deterioration of physical health, stamina, and prowess takes place. Women experience menopause. Wisdom and practical problem-solving skills are high; ability to solve novel problems declines. Double responsibilities of caring for children and elderly parents may cause stress. Launching of children typically leaves empty nest. For some, career success and earning powers peak; for others, "burnout" occurs. Typically, women become more assertive, men more nurturant and expressive. Search for meaning in life assumes central importance. Time orientation changes to "time left to live." For some, there may be a midlife "crisis."
Late adulthood (65 years and over)	Most people are healthy and active, although health and physical abilities decline somewhat. Slowing of reaction time affects many aspects of functioning. Most people are mentally alert. Although intelligence and memory deteriorate somewhat, most people find ways to compensate. Retirement from work force creates more leisure time but may reduce economic circumstances. Need arises to cope with losses in many areas (loss of one's own faculties, loss of loved ones). Need arises to find purpose in life to face impending death.

"Act your age!"

"You're only as old as you feel."

"He is wise beyond his years."

"She's old before her time."

Just as most Americans identify themselves as "middle-class," many adults think of themselves as "thirtysomething." Young adults generally feel just about their own age, but middle-aged and older adults tend to feel younger than they are (Montepare & Lachman, 1989). One anthropologist, on the basis of interviews with older adults in a California metropolitan area, coined the term *ageless self* to capture this perception that the self remains the same despite chronological aging and physical change (Kaufman, 1986). Some very old people feel like young people inhabiting an old body. One man, at age 84, was still working as an engineer and talking about putting money aside for his "twilight years." A 94-year-old man does not like to go to the senior center because "too many old people show up."

All this suggests that a person can age in a number of ways, which are not necessarily "in sync."* *Chronological age* is simply a count of how many times an inhabitant of this planet has orbited the sun. Minimum age limits for drinking, driving, voting, and the like assume that chronological age is a barometer of the ability to perform certain functions. However, that assumption is not necessarily accurate. The mere passage of time does not cause development. Not only can the pace of development differ among individuals; the same person may also develop more quickly or more slowly in certain areas. For example, a college student who is physically and sexually mature may be immature when it comes to knowing how to act in a social situation.

Functional age is a measure of how well a person can function in a physical and social environment as compared with other people of the same chronological age. A 70-year-old who is "young at heart" may be functionally younger than a 50-year-old who finds life's challenges overwhelming. *Gerontologists,* social scientists who study aged people and the aging process, sometimes divide today's older people into two categories. The *young-old*, the majority, are those who—regardless of chronological age—are vital, vigorous, and active. The *old-old* are the frail, infirm minority (Neugarten & Neugarten, 1987). So, while this book—for convenience and consistency with much of the research literature—refers to adults as falling into conventional categories based on chronological age, in actuality these divisions are approximate and arbitrary.

Three components of functional age are biological age, psychological age, and social age, and these may differ greatly. *Biological age* is a measure of how far a person has progressed along a potential lifespan; it is predicted by the person's physical condition. We can measure biological age by examining how well vital organ systems, such as the respiratory and circulatory systems, are functioning. A 50-year-old who has exercised regularly is likely to be biologically younger than a 40-year-old whose most strenuous exercise is clicking a remote control. To some extent, it's possible to reverse the march of biological age by making healthful changes in lifestyle, such as quitting smoking. Giving up cigarettes can add years to life expectancy; taking up smoking (a disturbing trend among teenagers and young adults today) increases a person's biological age.

The ability to deal with an unexpected pregnancy, an accident, a move, or a change in job depends on *psychological age:* how well, in comparison with same-aged peers, a person can cope with environmental challenges. A 50-year-old who lives with his or her parents, has no job, and cannot form a meaningful personal relationship may be psychologically younger than a 20-year-old who is independent and exerts control over life choices.

*This discussion is indebted to Birren and Cunningham (1985) and Birren and Renner (1977).

Social age depends on how closely behavior conforms to the roles a person of a certain chronological age is expected to play in society. A woman having her first child in her mid-forties is adopting the role of parent later than most of her peers; she thus has a younger social age. Likewise, older adults who sign up for a college course in archaeology are socially younger than most of their peers. A 23-year-old widow is relatively advanced in social age.

The concept of social age assumes that social development follows a typical pattern based on a particular society's set of expectations. (Box 1-1 describes the meaning of social age in two African tribes.) As the lifespan developmental approach points out, history too is a factor in development. Social roles differ markedly at different periods of time. For example, in the not-too-distant past, Americans typically married at an earlier age than they do today. Such a historical role shift exemplifies one of the major kinds of influences on the course of adult development, which we look at now.

INFLUENCES ON THE COURSE OF ADULT DEVELOPMENT AND AGING

Development is subject to many influences. Some originate with *heredity*—the inborn genetic endowment that human beings receive from their biological parents. Others come from the external *environment*—the world outside the self. But this distinction soon blurs: people change their world even as their world changes them.

In discussing how adults develop, we look at influences that affect many or most people and also at those that affect people differently: gender, race, ethnicity, culture, socioeconomic status (social class, education, occupation, and income), lifestyles, family constellations, and the presence or absence of physical or mental disabilities. Some influences are purely individual, while others are common to certain groups—age groups, generations, or people who live in or were raised in particular societies.

Normative and Nonnormative Influences

Some researchers distinguish between normative and nonnormative influences on development (Baltes, Reese, & Lipsitt, 1980).

An event is *normative* when it occurs in a similar way for most people in a given group. *Normative age-graded influences* are very similar for people in a particular age group. They include biological events (such as menopause and diminution of sexual potency) and cultural events (such as retirement). *Normative history-graded influences* are common to a particular *cohort:* a group of people who share a similar experience, in this case growing up at the same time in the same place. Some examples are the worldwide economic depression of the 1930s, the Vietnamese war, the massive famines in Africa during the 1980s, and the Persian Gulf war of the early 1990s. Also in this category are such cultural developments as the changing roles of women and the impact of television and computers.

BOX 1-1

Meanings of Age and Family in the Kalahari Desert

In the Kalahari Desert of Botswana in southwest Africa live two very different neighboring tribes: the !Kung San Bushmen and the Herero.

Since the 1960s, the !Kung have given up their traditional nomadic ways and settled down in encampments beside government-dug wells, storing the food they hunt and gather. Each family has a low hut of branches and grass, not so much to live in as to mark its territory and to keep its food, skins, and tools dry.

The Herero, by contrast, are literate and relatively prosperous; they keep cattle, goats, and sheep. The women dress in bright colors with ruffles and flounces, and they build thatched mud houses, with smooth white walls decorated with painted flowers. The village patriarch owns all the houses and cattle and children and has several wives.

In 1987, a husband-and-wife team—Patricia Draper and Henry Harpending of Pennsylvania State University—moved their family to Botswana to live with these tribes and find out what each of the two peoples thought about the meaning of age (Brown, 1990). Both Draper and Harpending had lived among the !Kung before. This time they went as part of a team of anthropologists working on four continents. Each researcher was to interview 200 people, including 50 older adults.

It soon became apparent that a question such as "How old are you?" does not make sense to the !Kung. In this culture, people do not count the number of years they have been alive. They do not even count their children or how many times they have moved. A mother would recount having had a child at a certain place and time; she could recall each birth perfectly, and what had happened to each child. But she left it to the researcher to figure out how many children this recital added up to.

In fact, the !Kung do not regard age as useful information. They know only who is older or younger than someone else, not how old specific people are. When asked what they call people of different ages, the !Kung name individuals. Although they do have words for *teenaged* and *middle-aged*, they rarely respond by using them.

Furthermore, social roles of adults are not determined by age. Women in their twenties and their sixties do the same things: tending gardens, drawing water from wells, and taking care of children (their own or other women's).

The Herero, on the other hand, are quite age-conscious. They fear old age, which they equate with inability to work—inability to replace a rotten gatepost, say, or to water cattle. Like many people in western countries, they prepare for retirement by arranging for a place to move to and for children to help them.

But while the Herero concept of age is more

Nonnormative life events are unusual events that have a major impact on individual lives. They are either (1) typical events that occur at an atypical time of life, such as becoming a father at age 60, or (2) atypical events, such as being in an airplane crash or winning a lottery. Whether such an event is positive or nega-

(Marjorie Shostak / Anthro-Photo)

Age can have different meanings in different cultures. The !Kung San of Botswana in southwest Africa do not keep track of their age and do not consider it important. Social roles such as hunting, gathering, and preparing food are performed by adults of all ages.

like that in western countries than that of the !Kung, their concept of family is quite foreign to ours. In their culture, the care of older adults is valued the way Americans value the care and nurture of children; high praise for a woman would be not "Look how well she takes care of her children" but "Look how well she takes care of her mother!" Young children are expected to take care of adults, rather than the other way around—doing errands, fetching wood and water, cooking, and helping with other everyday chores.

Most Herero men and women do not marry for love, and many women return to their own families after some years of marriage. A wife who has had no children may arrange for someone else's daughter to take her place. When unmarried women become pregnant, older people who have no children of their own place "orders" for them. Many Americans would consider this buying and selling of children shocking, but the system seems to work for the Herero.

Clearly, the meanings of age and family, and the way a society deals with older adults, are strongly influenced by culture. Looking at cultures different from our own allows us to see the values and customs of our own culture from a fresh perspective. That is one of the benefits of cross-cultural research.

tive, it is likely to cause stress when a person does not expect it, is not prepared for it, and needs special help in adapting to it. People often create their own non-normative life events—by, say, applying for a challenging job or taking up a risky hobby like skydiving—and thus participate actively in their own development.

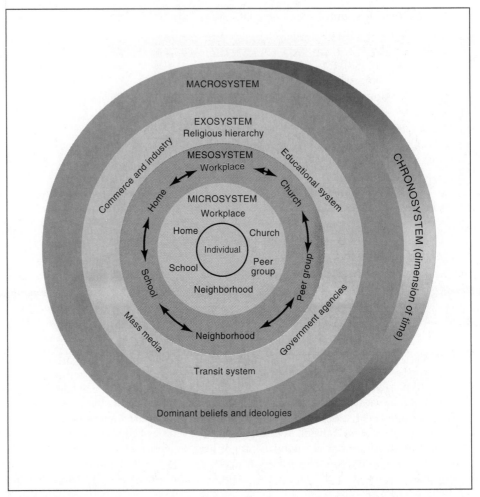

FIGURE 1-1

Ecological view of influences on development. Concentric circles indicate the most intimate environment (innermost area) to the broadest, all within the dimension of time.
(SOURCE: Adapted from Cole & Cole, 1989.)

Contexts of Influences: An Ecological Approach

Another way of classifying influences is by immediacy of impact. Urie Bronfen-brenner's (1979, 1994) *ecological approach* to development identifies five levels of environmental influence, ranging from very intimate to very broad: microsystem, mesosystem, exosystem, macrosystem, and chronosystem (see Figure 1-1). To understand the complexity of influences on development, we must see a person within the context of these multiple environments.

A *microsystem* is the everyday environment of home, school, work, or neighborhood, including face-to-face relationships with spouse, children, friends, classmates, teachers, employers, or colleagues. How does a new baby affect the parents' lives? How do male professors' attitudes affect a young woman's performance in college?

The *mesosystem* is the interlocking of various microsystems—linkages between home and school, work and neighborhood. How does a bitterly contested divorce affect a person's performance at work? How does unhappiness on the job affect a parent-child relationship?

The *exosystem* consists of linkages between a microsystem and outside systems or institutions that affect a person indirectly. How does a community's transit system affect job opportunities? Does television programming that may encourage criminal behavior make people less secure in their homes?

The *macrosystem* consists of overarching cultural patterns, such as dominant beliefs, ideologies, and economic and political systems. How is an individual affected by living in a capitalist or socialist society?

Finally, the *chronosystem* adds the dimension of time: change or constancy in the person and the environment. This can include changes in family structure, place of residence, or employment, as well as larger cultural changes such as wars and economic cycles.

By looking at systems that affect individuals in and beyond the family, this ecological approach helps us to see the variety of influences on adult development. The relative importance of each system may vary from one society to another and from one cultural group to another within the same society. This is one reason for doing cross-cultural research.

The Role of Culture

When adults in the Kpelle tribe in central Liberia were asked to sort 20 objects, they consistently sorted on the basis of functional categories (that is, they matched a knife with an orange, or a potato with a hoe). Western psychologists associate functional sorting with a low level of thought; but since the participants kept saying that this was how a "wise man" would do it, the experimenter finally asked, "How would a fool do it?" He then received the "higher-order" categories he had originally expected—four neat piles with food in one, tools in another, and so on (J. Glick, 1975, p. 636).

By conducting research among various cultural groups, developmentalists can recognize biases that often go unquestioned—"as with the fish who reputedly is unaware of water until removed from it" (Rogoff & Morelli, 1989, p. 343). Cross-cultural research can tell us which aspects of development are universal (and thus seem to be intrinsic to the human condition) and which are cultural. This book discusses several influential theories developed from research on western subjects that do not hold up when tested in other cultures—theories about gender roles, abstract thinking, moral reasoning, and a number of other concepts. In each chapter, we look at adults in cultures other than the dominant one in the United States, to show how closely adult development is tied to society and culture and to understand normal development in a variety of settings.

CHANGING IMAGES AND REALITIES OF AGING

▼

Imagine that you are listening to the radio in the year 2030 and you hear the following commercial message:

> Are you tired of looking younger than you feel? Do you want to get the respect that you deserve? Are other people being promoted ahead of you, even when you know they are no older than you? What do they have that you don't? They may be using GRAY DAYS. Yes, GRAY DAYS is a natural product, used by millions, which gradually puts that look of wisdom into your hair. Used once a day, this colorless, odorless formula will make you look like the experienced, level-headed person you know you are. Of course you could wait until the gray came naturally to your hair, but remember this: some people don't start to show the color of prestige until their fifties or even later! Don't take that chance. Start now. Make the changes in your life that will put you at the head of the line. Don't be embarrassed by the doorman at the seniors' bar who keeps asking you to prove you're old enough to get in. Let GRAY DAYS give you a start toward great days—TODAY!
>
> And, for that "I've been alive a long time" look, try our new WRINK-AID. Just rub it in at bedtime. In the morning your skin will show the lines and wrinkles of maturity. WRINK-AID's "natural look of aging" lasts all day. Use WRINK-AID every day, and you'll never again be called a "baby face." Show the world you've been around and have what it takes. Why wait? Get WRINK-AID and wrink it up, NOW!

It may seem implausible that any such switch in attitudes could take place in the United States. Yet a look at portraits of George Washington and our other founding fathers tells us that there was a time when men in this country wore powdered wigs as a mark of distinction (in fact, barristers and judges in Great Britain still wear wigs today). The men who wrote our Constitution also set minimum age limits for candidates for public office. For example, a person under 35 years of age cannot serve as president of the United States.

In the year 2030, more than half of the population of the United States will be over age 40 (Quinn, 1993), and one-fifth will be 65 or older (American Association of Retired Persons, AARP, 1994). Is it unreasonable to predict that age may again be valued more highly than youth?

CULTURAL VIEWS OF AGING

In most western countries, it is considered rude to ask a person's age. But in Japan, where old age has high status, it is traditional for travelers checking into hotels to be asked their age to ensure that they receive proper deference. A man celebrating his sixtieth birthday wears a red vest, symbolizing rebirth into an advanced phase of life (Kimmel, 1988).

In American culture today, aging is seen as undesirable—unless one considers the alternative. Try browsing through a rack of greeting cards. Do most cards express positive or negative sentiments about arriving at a fortieth, fiftieth, or sixtieth birthday? Although everybody wants to live long, hardly anybody wants to

(Robin Laurance/Photo Researchers)

In England, white-wigged barristers (lawyers) and judges command respect. In the United States today, a youthful appearance is highly prized.

be *old*, a word that connotes physical frailty, narrow-mindedness, incompetence, and loss of attractiveness. People of advanced years are called "senior citizens," "golden-agers," "the elderly," "older Americans," or even "chronologically gifted." Such language is an effort to counteract *ageism:* prejudice or discrimination, usually against older persons, based on age. Ageism has been said to arise from a "deep and profound dread of growing old" (R. N. Butler, 1987a, p. 22)—a need to distance oneself from older people and from one's own future self.

The media are full of stereotypes about aging. An article in *Time* magazine on detective programs built around older stars such as Angela Lansbury was titled "Murder, They Wheezed." The central characters of "these arthritic whodunits" were described as "old codgers" or as "easygoing dilettantes" who "would rather be napping." The illustration accompanying the article depicted these crime fighters as doddering and decrepit (Zoglin, 1994).

Such stereotypes reflect widespread misconceptions about aging: that older people are usually tired, poorly coordinated, and prone to infections; that they have many accidents and spend most of their time in bed; that they live in institutions; that they can neither remember nor learn; that they have no interest in sexual relationships; that they are isolated from others and depend on television or radio; that they do not use their time productively; and that they are grouchy, self-pitying, touchy, and cranky. These negative stereotypes do real harm. A physician who does not bring up sexual issues with a 75-year-old heart patient may deny the patient an important source of fulfillment. An overprotective adult child may encourage an aging parent to become infantile. A social worker who considers depression "to be expected" in old age may in effect abandon an elderly client.

Evidence of ageism showed up in an analysis of forty-three studies. Older people were judged more negatively than younger people on all characteristics studied, especially on competence and attractiveness (Kite & Johnson, 1988). Such judgments can have practical effects, as pervasive as unwillingness of younger adults to listen to an older person's opinions and as serious as loss of a job. Positive stereotypes, which picture old age as a "golden age" of peace and relaxation when people harvest the fruits of their lifelong labors, or as a carefree second childhood spent idly on the golf course or at the card table, are no more accurate or helpful.

Ageism affects middle-aged adults, too. It is during this period that anxiety over slipping faculties and loss of attractiveness often sets in, especially among women. One of the most prized compliments for a woman is to be told that she looks younger than her age. In men, gray hair, coarsened skin, and "crow's feet" are indicators of experience and mastery; in women, they are signs of being "over the hill." Such physical changes are more likely to affect a husband's sexual responsiveness to his wife than vice versa (Margolin & White, 1987). Once the appearance of youth is gone, so (in many men's eyes) is a woman's value as a sexual and romantic partner.

According to evolutionary psychology, this traditional double standard of aging goes back to the universal drive to perpetuate the species. Since women lose their reproductive capacity earlier than men, loss of youthful appearance may have warned a man that a woman was no longer desirable as a mate (Katchadourian, 1987). Today, when the value of relationships is not measured only by the biological mandate to reproduce, a societal standard "that regards beauty as the exclusive preserve of the young . . . makes women especially vulnerable to the fear of aging. . . . The relentless social pressures to retain a slim 'girlish' figure make women self-conscious about their bodies . . . [and] can be detrimental to the midlife woman's personal growth and sense of self-worth" (Lenz, 1993, pp. 26, 28).

Efforts to combat ageism are making headway, in part thanks to writers such as Betty Friedan and in part because of the visibility of a growing cadre of active, healthy middle-aged and older Americans. Articles with such titles as "The Flaming Fifties" (Sheehy, 1993), "Achievers After the Age of 90" (adapted from Wallechinsky & Wallace, 1993), and "100 Years Old—and Counting" (K. Read, 1993) appear more and more frequently in newspapers and magazines.

On television, older people are less frequently portrayed as "comical, stubborn, eccentric, and foolish" and more often as "powerful, affluent, healthy, active, admired, and sexy" (Bell, 1992, p. 305). But negative stereotypes persist; and even positive stereotypes fail to acknowledge diversity among older adults. Furthermore, older women still are rarely shown, and when they are shown, they are generally subordinate to men. Meanwhile, "the media continue to bombard us with advertising for cosmetic surgery, hair coloring, anti-wrinkle creams, pills, potions, tonics and diet programs that, they assure us, will make it possible to maintain our youthful attractiveness forever" (Lenz, 1993, p. 26).

We need to look beyond distorted images of age to its true, multifaceted reality, gazing neither with rose-colored glasses nor with dark ones. Aging adults are an extremely diverse lot, with individual strengths and weaknesses. And they are becoming more so as they grow increasingly numerous.

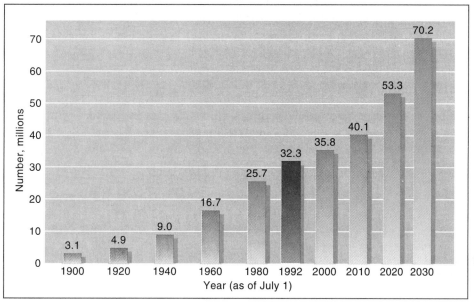

FIGURE 1-2

There are about 10 times as many older Americans today as there were in 1900; in 2030, there will be more than twice as many as today. The percentage of the population age 65 and older is growing, too—from 4 percent at the turn of the twentieth century to about 13 percent at the turn of the twenty-first—and may reach 20 percent by 2030.

(SOURCE: Adapted from AARP, 1994, including data from U.S. Bureau of the Census, 1995.)

THE SHIFTING DEMOGRAPHICS OF AGING

There are no 45-year-olds being born today—nor 28-year-olds, nor 67-year-olds. Thus we can count a definite number of people of a given age group who are now alive and, on the basis of that figure, project how many will be alive in 2010, 2020, 2030, and so on. Using census data, international population studies, and other sources, we can obtain fairly accurate descriptions of the current population and can predict (barring famines or other disasters) how many people will be of a certain age at a certain date. It is much harder, of course, to predict how it will feel to be alive at that time, or what quality of life people of different ages will experience. One thing, however, is clear: both as a nation and as a global population, we are growing older.

The population of the United States in the first half of the twenty-first century will look quite different from today's. By 2030, the median age will rise from 34 to 42, and fully one-third of the people will be 55 or older (Quinn, 1993; U.S. Bureau of the Census, 1995). By 2050, 1 in 5 Americans—more than 80 million in all, and more than twice the present number—will be age 65 and above (U.S. Bureau of the Census, 1995; see Figure 1-2). Meanwhile, the under-55 population will grow hardly at all (U.S. Bureau of the Census, 1989; U.S. Senate, 1991).

Startling as these predictions may seem, our population has been aging for quite some time. In 1994 there were 33 million older adults—11 times as many as

BOX 1-2

THE ART OF AGING

New Environments for an Aging Population

Have you ever watched a left-handed person try to turn a doorknob designed for right-handers, or have you experienced this challenge yourself? It's not easy—and it gives an idea of how difficult many everyday tasks can be for older adults. To a middle-aged or older person trying to live and work in an environment geared toward young adults, simple daily activities such as reading product labels, reaching high shelves, getting dressed, cleaning house, driving a car, and taking a bath can be annoying or even hazardous. The Gallup Organization confirmed this when it polled 1,500 adults age 55 and over about obstacles to independent living (Gallup, 1984).

As the population ages, we can expect many changes in our physical environment and in the products we use. Already, pain relievers, previously packaged in childproof bottles that stymied arthritic adults, are being repackaged in easier-to-open containers.

The gerontologist Ken Dychtwald, in *Age Wave* (Dychtwald & Flower, 1990), predicts ways in which the environment of the twenty-first century will be redesigned to accommodate physical changes that often accompany aging (discussed in Chapters 3 and 4). Here are some examples; a few of them are already becoming available:

Aids to Vision

Signals now given visually will be spoken as well. There will be talking exit signs, talking clocks, talking appliances that tell you when they get hot, talking cameras that warn you when the light is too low, and talking automobiles that caution you when you're about to collide with something. Windshields will adjust their tint automatically to varying weather and light conditions and will be equipped with large, liquid-crystal displays of speed and other information (so that older drivers need not take their eyes off the road and readjust their focus). Reading lights will be brighter, and books will have larger print. Floors will be carpeted or textured, not waxed to a smooth, glaring gloss.

Aids to Hearing

Public address systems and recordings will be engineered to an older adult's auditory range. Telephones will have adjustable volume and tone controls and extra-loud ringers. Park benches and couches will be replaced by angled or clustered seating so that older adults can communicate face to face.

Aids to Manual Dexterity

To compensate for stiff, aging fingers and other joints, it will become increasingly common to find such items as comb and brush extenders, stretchable shoelaces, Velcro tabs instead of buttons, lightweight motorized pot-and-pan scrubbers and garden tools, tap turners on faucets and stove handles, foot mops that eliminate bending, voice-activated telephone dials or dials with large buttons, long-handled easy-grip zippers, and contoured eating utensils.

Aids to Mobility and Safety

Ramps will become more common, knobs will replace levers, street lights will change more slowly, and traffic islands will let slow walkers pause and rest. Closet shelves and bus platforms will be lower—as will windows, for people who sit a lot. Bathtubs and showers will have built-in seats and grab bars; regulators will keep tap water from scalding; and "soft tubs" will prevent slips, add comfort, and keep bath water from cooling too fast. Automobiles will be programmed to operate windows, radio, heater, lights, wipers, and even the ignition by verbal commands.

Temperature Adjustments

Because older bodies take longer to adjust to temperature changes and have more trouble keeping warm, homes and hotels will have heated furniture and thermostats in each room. Some people will wear heated clothing and eat heat-producing foods.

Such innovations will make life easier and more convenient for everyone. An environment designed for older rather than younger adults can be more user-friendly for all age groups.

in 1900—and they had grown from 4 percent to more than 12½ percent of the population (U.S. Bureau of the Census, 1995).

The graying of the population has several causes: the high birthrates of the late 1800s and the early to mid-1900s, the high immigration rates of the twentieth century, and longer life due to medical progress (see Chapter 3). A child born in 1900 could expect to live only about 47 years. A child born in 1993 could expect to live 75.4 years—a gain of more than 28 years in one century (Wegman, 1992; "Wellness Facts," 1995). However, because relatively few babies were born during the Great Depression of the 1930s, the growth of the older population has begun to slow. As many of the 76 million "baby boomers" born between 1946 and 1964 reach old age, the proportion of older Americans will peak about a third of the way into the twenty-first century, and then will drop again (C. Farrell, Palmer, Atchison, & Andelman, 1994; U.S. Bureau of the Census, 1995).

Not only is the population aging; the population of older adults is itself getting older. The fastest-growing group of adults in the United States is those over 85. In 1990, an estimated 36,000 people were over age 100 (U.S. Bureau of the Census, 1992a).

Today's young adults, then, can expect to spend a much larger portion of their adult lives in old age than their grandparents did. The "aging avalanche" may bring significant changes in the physical and social environment in which all of us live (see Box 1-2). It is raising serious questions about our ability to support a graying population. Similar trends worry policymakers in other parts of the world. For these reasons, and because more data are available on people age 65 and over than on any other adult age group, let's take a closer look at our own older adult population and then at the global picture.

THE AGING POPULATION: A PROFILE OF DIVERSITY

> It is useful, maybe even necessary, to imagine that there is a definable group called "the elderly." But all such conceptions inevitably fail. It is accurate only to say that a certain part of the population has lived longer than other parts of the population, and that they differ widely. (Kidder, 1993, p. 53)

Are there more older men or more older women? Do men or women have a better quality of life in old age? What percentage of older Americans are members of minority groups, and does their experience of aging differ from that of white people? How likely are older adults to live in nursing homes? To be employed? To be poor? To have finished high school? To be in ill health? We discuss such questions in more depth later in this book. For now, let's take a snapshot of our aging population.

Gender

Because women typically live longer than men, older women outnumber older men nearly 3 to 2, and the ratio increases with advancing age (U.S. Bureau of the Census, 1995; see Figure 1-3). In 1993, there were 122 women for every 100 men age 65 to 69; among people age 85 and older, there were 256 women for every 100 men (AARP, 1994).

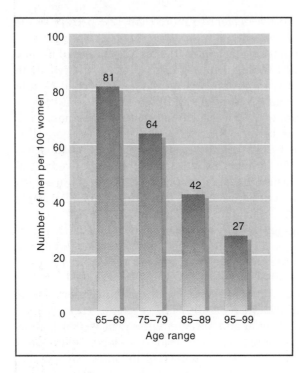

FIGURE 1-3
As the population ages, the proportion of men for every 100 women declines. One result is that older women are more likely than older men to live alone and to need help from their families and from society.
(SOURCE: U.S. Bureau of the Census, 1992b.)

Older women are more likely than older men to be widowed, to remain unmarried afterward, and to have more years of poor health and fewer years of active life and independence (Katz et al., 1983; Longino, 1987; U.S. Bureau of the Census, 1992b, 1995). Older women are much more likely than older men to be poor, to live alone, and to need help with such necessities of daily living as eating, dressing, bathing, preparing meals, managing money, and getting outside (AARP, 1994; U.S. Bureau of the Census, 1995).

Race and Ethnicity

The United States began as a nation of immigrants. Since 1980, because of tight immigration laws, the flow has slowed to a trickle. But as a result of shifting *patterns* of immigration, high minority birthrates, and declining births among the white majority, the American population is becoming far more racially and ethnically diverse. Between 1980 and 1990, minorities grew by 31 percent, almost 8 times as much as non-Hispanic whites (Outtz, 1993). If current immigration policies and levels continue, by 2050 white people may be only 53 percent of the population, Hispanics 21 percent, African Americans 15 percent, and Asians 10 percent (Day, 1992). Today, only 10 percent of older Americans are nonwhite, but this proportion is expected to double by 2050. Older Hispanics will quadruple from 4 percent to 16 percent (U.S. Bureau of the Census, 1995).

Many aging members of minority groups are at great risk because of poverty, spotty histories of work and education, and inadequate health care. Older African

Americans and Hispanics tend to be less educated and to have lower incomes than white people (AARP, 1994). They are also likely to die younger (see Chapter 3). Although their need for social and medical services is greater, they often live in areas where services are least available. Older people in various ethnic groups, especially those born in other countries, often fail to take advantage of community and government services because they lack information about these services, because they are too proud to accept help, or because they feel uncomfortable dealing with agency staff members who do not understand their way of life (Gelfand, 1982). Instead, adults in minority groups often turn to family members. African American and Hispanic American families have large kinship networks, with high levels of interaction and strong emotional bonds (R. J. Taylor & Chatters, 1991). The generations commonly help each other with money, child care, advice, and other forms of support (Gibson, 1986; Mindel, 1983).

Living Arrangements

Negative images of aging suggest that most older adults live alone or in nursing homes. Actually, only 5 percent of all older Americans—but 24 percent of those 85 and above—live in institutions (AARP, 1994). Since women live longer than men, women are more likely to end up in nursing homes. About 3 out of 10 older adults outside of institutions* live alone: 41 percent of older women, but only 16 percent of older men (AARP, 1994).

Socioeconomic Status

Stereotypes depict older adults either as too infirm to work or as mindlessly enjoying a life of idleness. In reality, about 11 percent of older Americans are in the work force; more than half of these (mostly women) work part time. Nearly 1 in 4 of the working elderly (mostly men) are self-employed (AARP, 1994). Although most older adults are defined as retired, many of them have active, productive lifestyles. Retired older adults also make valuable contributions to other generations, such as taking care of grandchildren.

Other images of older adults suggest that most are poor and live solely on social security. Actually, social security accounts for only 40 percent of older adults' income (AARP, 1994). And although median family income peaks when the chief breadwinner is in middle age and declines thereafter (Schick & Schick, 1994), most older adults are relatively secure financially and have more assets than younger adults. Older adults living with their families have higher incomes than those living alone or with nonrelatives; men are better off than women; and white people have more income than blacks or Hispanics (AARP, 1994; U.S. Bureau of the Census, 1995). The discrepancy in income between white and minority adults exists throughout adulthood (Schick & Schick, 1994).

About 1 in 5 older adults was classified as poor or near poor in 1993 (AARP, 1994); but the poverty rate for this age group is only one-third of what it was in

*Unless otherwise noted, data on living arrangements, socioeconomic status, education, and health refer to noninstitutionalized older adults.

BOX 1-3

THE CUTTING EDGE

The Oldest Old

Since the number of healthy, vigorous people over age 65 is growing rapidly, we may soon begin to talk of old age as starting at 85. This age group, the fastest-growing segment of the United States population, numbered 3 million in 1994. This figure represented a whopping increase of 274 percent since 1960, a period in which the total population grew by only 45 percent. By the middle of the twenty-first century, these "oldest old" could be nearly one-fourth of the elderly population (U.S. Bureau of the Census, 1995).

Who are the oldest old? Where and how do they live? How healthy are they? What do they like to do? Some of the answers, according to 1990 census data, are predictable, but others are unexpected.

Because of men's lower life expectancy, there are fewer than 39 men for every 100 women age 85 and over (U.S. Bureau of the Census, 1992b; refer back to Figure 1-3). Women are three times as likely as men to be poor, mainly because their husbands have died. When wives die, widowers tend to remarry quickly, an option rarely available to women because there are fewer men.

Most people over 85 live in their own homes, and 30 percent live alone. One-fourth are in nursing homes, hospitals, or other institutions, and 1 in 6 is poor. Many never went beyond eighth grade. Future generations, though, will be both better educated and more affluent (Longino, 1988; U.S. Bureau of the Census, 1995).

A surprisingly large number of these oldest citizens need little medical care, but many do have health problems. Almost 10 percent of those outside institutions are disabled and isolated—unable to use public transportation (Longino, 1987, 1988)—and 50 percent need assistance with everyday activities (U.S. Bureau of the Census, 1995). Costs of health care for the "oldest old" are expected to soar; by 2040 Medicare costs may increase sixfold (Schneider & Guralnik, 1990). Cost containment will depend on the ability to prevent or cure disorders of old age that entail the greatest need for long-term care.

Most of these people spend time with other people. More than half of an Iowa sample belong to professional, social, recreational, or religious groups and go to religious services at least once a week. More than 3 out of 4 see their children or other close relatives once a month (Meer, 1987).

Even at the last stage of life, then, it is misleading to generalize about people. What emerges is a picture not of "the elderly" but of individual human beings—some needy and frail, but most independent, healthy, and involved.

(AP/Wide World Photos)

Paul Clark, who keeps up with the stock market by computer in his apartment in Atlanta, Georgia, is one of an estimated 36,000 Americans past their hundredth birthday. The oldest old—those over age 85—form the fastest-growing segment of the United States population. Most are independent, healthy, and active.

1959 (Littman, 1991). The poverty rate for older adults is slightly higher than the rate for young adults but much higher than the poverty rate for the middle-aged; and it continues to rise in late adulthood (U.S. Bureau of the Census, 1991a, b; 1995). Most likely to be impoverished are women (especially widows), blacks, Hispanics, single people, people living alone or with nonrelatives, people who did not finish high school, former unskilled laborers, and the ill or disabled (AARP, 1994; Hurd, 1989; U.S. Bureau of the Census, 1992b, 1995).

Individuals who have multiple risk factors are most likely to be poor. For example, 44 percent of older black women who live alone are poor (AARP, 1994). Thus, while most older adults do not live in poverty, some elements of the older population are at extreme risk.

Education

Older Americans are better educated today than in the past; their median educational level has risen steadily (Schick & Schick, 1994). In 1970, only 28 percent of older Americans had completed high school; by 1993, 60 percent had (compared with 85 percent of people age 25 to 64), and about 12 percent of the elderly had finished college. However, only 33 percent of older African Americans and 26 percent of older Hispanics were high school graduates. And, on average, older adults did worse than any other age group on the 1992 Adult Literacy Survey (AARP, 1994; U.S. Bureau of the Census, 1995). With adults of all ages increasingly continuing their education, we can expect that future generations will be better-educated than previous ones (U.S. Bureau of the Census, 1995).

Health

Three out of 4 noninstitutionalized Americans 65 to 74 years old, and 2 out of 3 of those 75 and older, consider themselves in good to excellent health (Schick & Schick, 1994; U.S. Bureau of the Census, 1995). Fewer than 3 out of 10 call their health "fair" or "poor" (compared with 8 percent of persons under 65). This less healthy group includes many more elderly African Americans (44 percent) than white people (27 percent). Most older people have one or more chronic conditions, such as arthritis, hypertension, heart disease, cataracts, sinusitis, diabetes, tinnitus, and visual, hearing, or orthopedic impairments. About 3 out of 4 older adults can manage without help; the proportion falls steeply with age (AARP, 1994; see Figure 4-1 in Chapter 4).

Since many adults remain vigorous and active into their seventies, eighties, and beyond, it is becoming harder to tell where middle age leaves off and old age begins. In fact, one author has called the years between 50 and 75 a "second middle age" (Bronte, 1993). As we discuss in Chapter 4, many problems of the "old-old" are due to lifestyle factors or health problems that may or may not accompany aging. Research in gerontology and *geriatrics*, the branch of medicine concerned with treating and managing diseases related to aging, has underlined the need for support services for the frail elderly, many of whom have outlived their savings and cannot pay for their own care. (We take a look at the "oldest old" in Box 1-3.)

Clearly, older adults are a heterogeneous group. Like people of all ages, they are individuals with varying needs, desires, abilities, lifestyles, and cultural backgrounds. As we move into the twenty-first century and our society becomes increasingly older and more diverse, dealing with this aging population will require a great deal of knowledge, sophistication, and flexibility.

CHALLENGES AND DILEMMAS OF A GRAYING WORLD

The graying of the population is far from unique to the United States. Worldwide, the older adult population is growing faster than any other age group and nearly twice as fast as the population as a whole (Chawla, 1993). The number of adults age 65 and over—about 332 million in 1991—is expected to more than double by the year 2020, to 722 million. Even more dramatic, the number of people age 80 and over will jump from 57 million in 1991 to 139 million in 2020 (U.S. Bureau of the Census, 1992c; 1993). The most striking growth will be in what is today the economically developing world, where fertility is still high and mortality has decreased—Africa, Latin America, and most of Asia and the Pacific Islands (Cassel, 1992; see Figure 1-4). By 2025, more than 7 out of 10 adults age 60 and over (and 84 percent of the entire global population) are likely to be living in those regions (Chawla, 1993).

In absolute numbers, the older adult populations of today's economically developed regions (North America, Japan, Europe, Australia, New Zealand, and the former Soviet Union) will not be as large. Still, by 2025 the 60-plus age group will amount to fully one-quarter of the people in those parts of the world, as compared with 12 percent in the developing regions (Chawla, 1993).

(AP/Wide World Photos)

Most older Americans consider themselves in good to excellent health. At age 111, Rutherford B. Hayes Elmore, shown getting a birthday kiss from his 6-year-old great-great-great-granddaughter, said he had never been sick a day in his life.

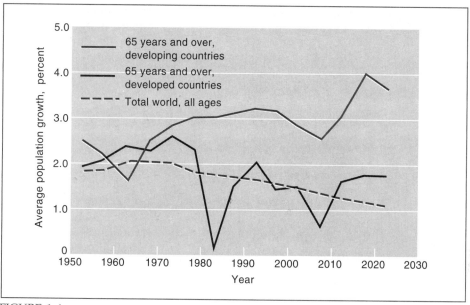

FIGURE 1-4

Rate of growth in the world's elderly population has shifted dramatically: developing countries are now experiencing the greatest percentage increase. The pace of growth in both developing and developed regions is projected to slow during the first decade of the twenty-first century, but it will rise again during the second decade, particularly in developing areas.
(Source: Schick & Schick, 1994.)

This demographic explosion poses serious challenges to both developed and developing countries. As an example, let's look at the changing situation in Asia; we'll then consider some economic issues.

Aging in Asia

It is hard to generalize about Asian countries. In Japan, a highly developed nation, people live longer than anywhere else in the world: on average, approximately 81 years for women and 76 for men (Nishio, 1994). In Nepal, a very poor nation, the average woman lives to only 52 and the average man to 55 (Central Bureau of Statistics, 1992). There is at least one link among the diverse Asian nations: a great respect for elders and an expectation that when old people can no longer care for themselves, their families will care for them. But today, while both patterns remain more prevalent than in the west, they are disintegrating under the pressure of a rising older population.*

Since the 1940s, Asia has been the most successful region of the world in reducing fertility. In China, for example, government policy limits families to one

*Unless otherwise indicated, this discussion is based on Martin (1988).

(Du Jie/Sovfoto/Eastfoto)

Respect for elders is traditional in Asian cultures. The famous Chinese writer Bing Xin (on right, shown here with a well-known colleague, Wang Meng) was still writing newspaper columns at 94.

child (MacAdam, 1993). Meanwhile, higher standards of living, better sanitation, and immunization programs have extended the adult lifespan. As a result, it is projected that by 2025, the elderly in China, Hong Kong, Singapore, and Sri Lanka will constitute more than 10 percent of the population; in Japan, they will make up more than 20 percent.

Although about three-quarters of elderly Asians live with their children, they are less likely to do so than older people were in the past. Along with the shifting balance between old and young, such trends as urbanization, migration, and an increase in the proportion of women in the work force make home care of elderly relatives less feasible. While most Asians want to help care for aging family members, doing this is becoming a difficult challenge. In Korea, a survey taken in 1981 found that only 7 percent of adults thought their children would care for them in old age; 64 percent expected to care for themselves.

To halt this erosion in care of the aged, China, Japan, and Singapore have passed laws obliging people to care for elderly relatives, and Japan and Singapore provide tax relief to those who give older relatives financial help. In Japan, lotteries for tenancy in public housing give households with a member age 60 or older a 10 times greater chance of winning. Institutionalization is still seen as a last resort, only for those who are destitute or without families—in part because few such homes exist. The proportion of older adults living in homes for the aged ranges from 0.33 percent in China to 2.5 percent in Singapore.

Such limited access to institutional care places severe strains on the traditional family. In Japan, where suicide among older women is more prevalent than anywhere else in the world (MacAdam, 1993), older adults living in three-generation households are more likely to take their lives than those living alone.

A major controversy in Asia, as in the west, is whether housing, health care, and other social services should be offered on the basis of age. Young adults with small children worry that, in order to fund services for the old, governments may have to cut back what little social welfare exists for the young. In Japan, Korea, Indonesia, the Philippines, Singapore, and Thailand, older adults are joining senior citizens' clubs, which may strengthen their political clout. The establishment of Respect for the Aged Day (September 15) in Japan and National Aging Day (April 13) in Thailand reflects this growing "gray power." But the need for such symbolism underlines a decline in the tradition of reverence for age.

In some ways, however, this tradition continues to set Japan apart from other advanced industrial nations. A survey of approximately 900 older adults in Japan, Germany, Canada, the United Kingdom, and the United States found that only 10 percent of older adults in Japan live alone, as compared with 31 to 46 percent in the four western countries. Older adults in the United States and Canada are least likely to get help from their families when they are ill or need money. Still, about 6 out of 10 older adults in those two countries are very satisfied with their lives, as compared with only 28 percent in Japan (Commonwealth Fund, 1992).

Economic Development and Aging

The issues presented by a graying population are somewhat different in developed and developing nations. Planners and politicians in almost all industrialized nations fear that the cost of supporting a growing contingent of retirees will place an insupportable burden on a shrinking group of working adults (Crown, 1993). In the United States, some analysts fear that the cost of medical care for older adults will bankrupt the health care system and reduce the quality of care available to younger adults and their families (Binstock, 1993). A drastic solution, suggested in some quarters, would be a "renegotiation" of the implied "social contract" that has called for younger, able-bodied adults to support retired and disabled workers (Adamchak, 1993, p. 6).

The key to supporting an aging population may be an economy capable of meeting the demographic challenge. If incomes go up faster than the taxes needed to fund social programs for the elderly, the actual burden on workers may not increase: "The affordability of an aging population will be dictated largely by future economic growth" (Crown, 1993).

That is likely to be true in the developing world as well. In such countries as the Dominican Republic, Sri Lanka, and Thailand, where large numbers of older adults must continue to work for a bare subsistence (Kaiser, 1993), worries about retirement benefits and government-funded health care, though still down the road, are likely to arise in the not-too-distant future (MacAdam, 1993). Certain observers predict that as labor loses its ties to the land and becomes dependent on a market economy, some form of western-style welfare state will be necessary (J. H. Schulz, 1993a). Others call for developing countries to find solutions rooted in their traditional, family-centered cultures.

In developing countries, issues of economic development and aging are closely linked. The graying of the population is a direct result of economic improvement and the amelioration of widespread deprivation, hunger, and disease. But this "success story" is often seen as a burden rather than a boon: will older adults drain scarce resources, impeding further development (Chawla, 1993; Kaiser, 1993)?

The International Plan of Action on Ageing, adopted by the United Nations in 1982, takes a radically different approach. It recognizes that older adults can "contribute to, as well as share in, the benefits of development" (Chawla, 1993, p. 21). As international planners begin to stress the human dimension of economic development (United Nations Committee for Development Planning, 1988), developing societies need to find ways to diminish dependency by expanding the productive abilities of older adults. This concept of *productive aging* "views older persons as potentially unlimited human resources contributing to the goods, services, and products available for themselves and society" (Kaiser, 1993, p. 66). In Zambia, destitute older adults learn basic farming skills and then are given small farms on which they can raise grain and poultry to feed their families (Kerschner, 1992). In Bogotá, Colombia, a group of older adults opened a bakery and used the proceeds to provide medical and other services to the poor and institutionalized elderly (Checkoway, 1992). Such examples suggest ways in which a growing older population can present "an opportunity rather than a crisis, a solution rather than a problem, an asset rather than a burden, a resource rather than a drain on resources" (Kerschner, 1992, p. 4).

NEW ROLES FOR OLDER ADULTS

An emphasis on productive aging, whether in developed or developing countries, may help solve the economic dilemmas posed by an aging global population. It also fits in with current thinking on adult development and aging.

Social roles for younger and middle-aged adults, though more flexible now than they were in the past, generally remain fairly clear: spouse, worker, parent, grandparent. But as the lifespan increases and more years stretch out after retirement, what new expectations will society have for older adults? Will there be greater freedom for them to play a variety of social roles and to maximize control of their own lives?

Ken Dychtwald, the gerontologist who wrote *Age Wave*, has divided the human lifespan, and human history, into three "ages" (Dychtwald & Flower, 1990). The first age, from birth to about age 25, represents nearly the full average lifespan in premodern times, when the primary tasks of life were physical development, basic learning, and survival. The second age, from about 26 to 60, represents the normal lifespan before the mid-twentieth century, when adult concerns were centered on work, family, and parenting. The third age, only now coming into its own, is the period from the sixties on, a period when many of the tasks of the second age are already done. This can be a time of less external pressure and more internal development—a time "for giving back to society the lessons, resources, and experiences accumulated and articulated over a lifetime" (p. 347).

SUMMARY

APPROACHING THE STUDY OF ADULT DEVELOPMENT AND AGING: AN OVERVIEW

- The idea that adults develop is relatively recent. Today most psychologists believe that human development goes on throughout life.
- The lifespan developmental approach of Paul Baltes emphasizes multidirectionality, plasticity, historical and cultural influences, and multidisciplinary research.

BASIC CONCEPTS

- A useful way to visualize adult development is as a product of multiple concurrent forces acting on a complex system. Each aspect of development encompasses a wide range of individual differences.
- The periods of adulthood—young adulthood, middle age, and late adulthood or old age—are somewhat arbitrarily demarcated, but most people go through a fairly typical sequence of development.
- Chronological age is not necessarily an indicator of functional age. Functional age has three dimensions—biological, psychological, and social. They are not necessarily synchronized.
- Both heredity and environment influence development. Some investigators distinguish among normative age-graded influences, normative history-graded influences, and nonnormative life events. Bronfenbrenner's ecological approach identifies levels of environmental influence.
- Cross-cultural research can indicate whether certain aspects of development are universal or cultural.

CHANGING IMAGES AND REALITIES OF AGING

- Cultural attitudes toward aging contrast markedly across both time and space.
- Both the United States and the world are experiencing a "graying of the population."
- In the United States, women live longer than men and tend to have more difficulties in old age. The adult population is becoming more racially and ethnically diverse.
- Only 5 percent of older adults are in institutions. Many older adults work, and most are relatively secure financially. Still, about 1 in 5 older adults is poor or near poor.
- Older Americans today are increasingly well-educated, and most (the "young-old") have good to excellent health. The "old-old" are the frail, infirm minority who need support services.
- Worldwide, the most dramatic growth in the older adult population is in developing regions. This growth, which can place great strains on societal institutions such as the family, and on the economy, has led to an emphasis on productive aging. In developed nations, concerns center on retirement and health benefits for an aging population.

KEY TERMS

▼

change (page 6)
development (6)
learning (6)
maturation (6)
lifespan development (7)
lifespan developmental
    psychology (7)
multidirectional (7)
plasticity (8)
ageless self (11)
chronological age (12)
functional age (12)
gerontologists (12)
biological age (12)

psychological age (12)
social age (13)
heredity (13)
environment (13)
normative age-graded influences (13)
normative history-graded
    influences (13)
cohort (13)
nonnormative life events (14)
ecological approach (16)
ageism (19)
geriatrics (27)
productive aging (32)

META-THEORETICAL PERSPECTIVES AND RESEARCH METHODS

CHAPTER 2

META-THEORETICAL PERSPECTIVES AND RESEARCH METHODS

METATHEORIES
Three Metatheories: Mechanistic,
  Organismic, and Contextual
Applying Metatheories

BASIC RESEARCH METHODS
Sampling
Data Collection

BASIC RESEARCH DESIGNS
Case Studies
Correlational Studies
Experiments

QUASI-EXPERIMENTAL DESIGNS: THE PROBLEM OF INTERNAL VALIDITY
Cross-Sectional Studies
Longitudinal Studies
Time-Lag Studies
Sequential Designs

ETHICS OF RESEARCH

BOXES
2-1 The Cutting Edge: Early Studies
     of Sexuality
2-2 The Multicultural Context:
     Avoiding Cultural Bias in Research
2-3 The Art of Aging: What
     Longitudinal Studies Can Tell Us

FOCUS: ERIK H. ERIKSON

(UPI/Bettmann)

Erik H. Erikson,* one of the first investigators to extend the systematic study of personality development into adulthood, wrote: "I have . . . learned from life histories that everything that is new and worth saying . . . has a highly personal aspect" (Erikson, personal communication, in Coles, 1970, p. 181). Erikson's own life and work demonstrate his point.

One of the key concepts Erikson introduced was the *identity crisis*—an unsettling period, usually in adolescence or young adulthood, in which people search for a sense of self and of meaning in their lives. In his research, Erikson repeatedly found echoes of his own prolonged identity crisis, which included coping with his father's absence, growing up among peers who regarded him as a stranger, stumbling onto his career path in his mid-twenties and then, in his mid-thirties, resettling in a new land and learning a new language.

Themes of "identity confusion" and alienation run through Erikson's life story, beginning with the dubious circumstances of his birth. He was born in 1902 near Frankfurt, Germany, to a Danish-Jewish woman; he never knew his father. His mother's Danish husband apparently left her before the child's birth, after discovering that the father was another man. Her second husband, a Jewish doctor named Theodor Homburger, gave the child his name and raised him as a Jew.

An outsider among both his anti-Semitic German schoolmates and his non-Nordic Jewish peers, the youth left school at the age of 18, dabbled in art, and wandered around Europe for seven years, "trying to come to grips with himself" (Coles, 1970,

*Sources of biographical material on Erikson are Coles (1970), Hall & Lindzey (1978), P. Miller (1983), Roazen (1976), Stevens (1983), and Erikson's obituary in *The New York Times*, May 13, 1994, p. C16.

p. 15). At 25, he was hired as a children's tutor in Vienna and helped found a small progressive school for children whose parents were involved in Sigmund Freud's growing psychoanalytic movement. (*Psychoanalysis* is a therapeutic method designed to free patients from emotional disturbances traced to long-buried memories of early, traumatic experiences.) "Herr Erik" eventually took psychoanalytic training (though he lacked the usual medical background, having only a high school diploma) and became a member of Freud's circle.

In 1933, when Hitler came to power, the young psychoanalyst, his Canadian-born wife, and their two sons moved to the United States. In 1939, when he became an American citizen, he took the name Erikson (son of Erik), perhaps identifying with the Norwegian discoverer of his adopted country, but also suggesting that he was the child of himself—that his identity was his own creation.

Although Erikson was a child psychiatrist by training and profession, his greatest contributions may well have been in illuminating the inner world of adulthood. His own experiences of rootlessness and immigration as a young adult convinced him that Freud was wrong in believing that personality development stops at puberty. Erikson's wide-ranging research among American combat veterans, normal and disturbed adolescents, Native Americans, and Hindus in India, as well as his studies of the lives of Martin Luther and Mahatma Gandhi, led him to place more importance on the influences of society and culture than Freud, whose psychoanalytic theory grew out of clinical work with a limited Viennese clientele. In his later years Erikson, in the belief that development continues throughout life, sought a deeper understanding of middle and old age—unlike Freud, who saw no point in working with older adults at all. Erikson's last works, written in his eighties with his wife, Joan, elaborated on his view that people in late life achieve wisdom based on the positive resolution of earlier emotional crises.

Erikson died in 1994 at age 91. He had, as *The New York Times* reported, "profoundly reshaped" our view of human—and particularly of adult—development.

The story of Erik H. Erikson underlines several important points about the study of adult development and aging. First, research on human beings is not dry, abstract, or esoteric. It deals with the substance of real life.

Second, theory and research are interwoven strands in the seamless fabric of scientific study. A *theory* is a coherent set of related concepts, which seeks to organize and explain *data,* the information gathered from research. As painstaking research adds, bit by bit, to the body of knowledge, theoretical concepts, such as Erikson's "identity crisis," help us make sense of, and see connections between, these isolated pieces of data. Theories, in turn, inspire further research and predict its results. Research can indicate whether a theory is accurate in its predictions but cannot conclusively prove a theory. Scientists must always be ready to change their theories to account for new and unexpected data.

Finally, developmental science cannot be completely objective. Theories and research about human behavior are products of very human individuals, whose inquiries and interpretations are inevitably influenced by their own values and experience. As Erikson observed, this personal dimension can yield enriching insights; but it can also produce blind spots. In striving for greater objectivity, researchers must scrutinize how they and their colleagues conduct their work, the assumptions on which it is based, and how they arrive at their conclusions.

Throughout this book, we examine many, often conflicting, theories. In assessing them, it is important to keep in mind that they reflect the outlooks of the human beings who originated them. In the first part of this chapter, we present three basic perspectives that underlie much of the theoretical and research work in adult development and aging, as well as in other fields of science. In the remainder of the chapter, we look at how researchers gather information, so that you will be better able to judge whether or not it is on solid ground.

METATHEORIES

▼

Imagine that a shaman (spiritual healer) from India wanders into a convention where an American university professor is presenting a paper on how age affects recall of stories. The professor reports that older and younger adults are equally able to remember the main points of a story, but younger adults recollect many more details than older adults do. She suggests that perhaps memory aids can ameliorate this problem. On hearing this, the shaman says: "I understand your concern, but your own numbers give you cause for hope. Some day the young will simply outgrow their affliction."

Why do the professor and the shaman give opposite interpretations of the same data, and which interpretation is correct? The fact is that the shaman and the professor view adult development from different perspectives, both of which may be equally valid because they start from different assumptions and focus on different problems.

The professor emphasizes *quantitative development*—changes in number or amount. The problem she sees is a decrease in the number of details that older adults can extract from a story and remember. She views aging as a time of decline; an older adult cannot remember as much as a younger adult. She assumes that older people need help to compensate for this quantitative deficiency.

The shaman, on the other hand, emphasizes *qualitative development*—changes in the *kinds* of things older and younger adults can do, or how they do them. He sees the problem in terms of ability to *retell* a story. Concentration on recalling details can get in the way; fresh details drawn from personal experience lend vividness and immediacy. The shaman views aging as one of a series of progressive developments throughout life. He assumes that experience will eventually make a young adult a more effective storyteller.

In the shaman's eyes, the professor is inexplicably trying to make older adults act like younger adults. To the professor, the shaman has an overly rosy view of aging.

The perspectives from which people, including scientists, view phenomena such as aging are called *metatheories*. A **metatheory** is a broad hypothesis, or tentative explanation, about how the world works (Pepper, 1942, 1961). It is like a lens through which a person looks at the universe: a set of assumptions and values that filter perceptions and focus one's view of reality. A metatheory is a "supertheory." Operating in various branches of science, it embraces a family of theories that take a similar approach (though some theories seem to fall into more than one metatheoretical camp). Metatheory can critically influence a research design. It can shape the questions researchers ask, the topics they think it important to study, the methods they use, the kinds of evidence they look for, and the way they interpret their results.

At the heart of differences among theories of adult development and aging are fundamental issues concerning how human beings change as they go through life and interact with their environment. Is development primarily quantitative or qualitative? Is it continuous, or does it start and stop? Does it progress in a series of universal stages, or is it idiosyncratic? Does it move in one direction or more than one? The positions investigators take on these issues reflect their metatheoretical orientation. Different thinkers, looking through different lenses, come up with different explanations for how people behave. And these scientists may have as much trouble communicating with one another as the shaman and the professor.

THREE METATHEORIES: MECHANISTIC, ORGANISMIC, AND CONTEXTUAL

Let's look at three metatheories and some developmental theories and models that flow from them. (A **model** is a concrete image or structural representation of theoretical relationships.) None of these metatheories is necessarily better or truer than any of the others. Each offers a singular perspective that can shed light on adult development and aging, as well as on other natural phenomena. Each has a basic metaphor—a central image or analogy that captures its essential character. Table 2-1 summarizes major features of the three metatheories: mechanistic, organismic, and contextual.

The Mechanistic Perspective

The **mechanistic perspective** views all things in nature, including adult human beings, as if they were machines (Pepper, 1942, 1961). A machine is the sum of its parts. To understand it, we can break it down into its smallest components and then reassemble it.

Machines do not operate of their own volition; they react automatically and passively to physical forces or inputs. Fill a car with gas, turn the ignition key, press the accelerator, and the vehicle will move. In the mechanistic view, human behavior is much the same: it results from the operation of biological parts in response to external or internal stimuli. In principle, if we know enough about how the human "machine" is put together and about the forces impinging upon it, behavior is perfectly predictable. Of course, just as a car may not start in sub-

TABLE 2-1 COMPARISON OF THREE METATHEORIES

	Mechanistic	*Organismic*	*Contextual*
Basic metaphor	Machine	Developing organism (e.g., embryo)	Ongoing act in context
View of development	Continuous (no stages)	Discontinuous (stages)	Continuous and discontinuous (shifting goals and contexts)
Type of change emphasized	Quantitative	Qualitative	Quantitative and qualitative
View of causality	Internal and external environment	Internal; directed to optimal endpoint	Individual goals within contextual opportunities and constraints
Predictability	Very high	Moderate to high	Low to moderate
Direction of change	Unidirectional; decline or decline with compensation	Unidirectional; ever more integrated and adaptive	Multidirectional; gains and losses at each point of life
Value of old age	Low	Neutral to high	Neutral

zero temperatures or a part may break down under excessive stress, special external or internal conditions can affect human responses.

Mechanistic theorists (like the professor in our story) deal with quantitative development—for example, how much or how quickly a person can remember, rather than what memory is or how it operates. They see development as continuous and as moving in one direction at a time. One unidirectional view of development is the traditional view of adulthood and aging as unbroken physical and intellectual decline—the idea that people, like flowers, develop in a steadily positive direction until maturity and then undergo unremitting decay.

Information-processing theory explains how the human mind works by breaking the complex processes of thinking and remembering into their component parts. Information-processing researchers study the processes people go through in manipulating information and solving problems. In this model, human beings, like computers, register incoming information, code and store it, and then retrieve it when the right "keys" are pushed. Much as the parts of a machine wear down, information processing seems to become slower with age. The human "machine" reaches peak efficiency in young adulthood and then declines. Thus information-processing researchers design *interventions*—techniques to boost older adults' functioning. However, information-processing theories are not necessarily purely mechanistic. Many psychologists who study information processing believe that nonmechanical characteristics such as emotions and motivations play a part in thought and memory.

While the mechanist analyzes phenomena by breaking them down into simpler elements, the other two perspectives synthesize data. For them, a phenomenon is more than the sum of its parts. The meaning of a family relationship, for example, goes beyond what can be learned from studying its individual members and their day-to-day interactions. Also, in the other two metatheories people play a more active role in their own development.

The Organismic Perspective

The *organismic perspective* sees people as developing organisms (Pepper, 1942, 1961). Like embryos, they are growing, maturing beings with internally generated patterns of development. They initiate events; they do not just react. Environmental influences do not cause or significantly alter development, though they can speed it up or slow it down.

For organicists, development has an underlying, orderly structure, though it may not be obvious from moment to moment. As a fertilized egg cell develops into an embryo and then into a fetus, it goes through a series of qualitative changes not overtly predictable from what came before. Swellings on the head become eyes, ears, mouth, and nose. The brain begins to coordinate breathing, digestion, and elimination. Sex organs form. Similarly, organicists describe development after birth as a progressive sequence of stages, moving in one direction: toward full maturation.

A *stage* is a pattern of behavior typical of a certain period of development, which leads to a different, usually more advanced pattern. (As with a teenager's sulky moods, what may appear to be a reversion to less mature behavior prepares the way for a resumption of forward movement.) At each stage, people cope with different kinds of problems and develop different kinds of abilities. Transitions between stages tend to be abrupt, but there is continuity, too; each stage builds on the previous one and lays the foundation for the next. Organicists see this unfolding structure of development as universal: everyone goes through the same stages in the same order, though the precise timing varies.

It might seem logical that organicists would view old age as the climax of development rather than a time of decline (as in mechanistic models). However, classic stage theories, such as those of Freud and the Swiss cognitive theoretician Jean Piaget, placed the normal endpoint of maturation around puberty. Erikson was the first influential thinker to view adulthood and old age as unique stages of life with their own issues to be resolved. (Table 2-2 lists the stages in each of these theories.) Today, many theorists believe that new stages of development occur across the adult lifespan, especially in cognition and personality.

Erikson's theory of personality development illustrates an important feature of organismic development: integration driven by conflict. At each stage, resolution of a "crisis" or turning point depends on achieving a healthy balance between opposing traits (such as intimacy versus isolation); this resolution results in development of a "virtue" (such as love). Without satisfactory resolution of a crisis, a person will continue to struggle with it, impeding healthy development.

TABLE 2-2 STAGES OF HUMAN DEVELOPMENT: THREE MAJOR THEORIES

Psychosexual Stages (Freud)	Psychosocial Stages (Erikson)	Cognitive Stages (Piaget)
Oral (birth to 12–18 months). Baby's chief source of pleasure is mouth-oriented activities like sucking and eating.	Basic trust versus mistrust (birth to 12–18 months). Baby develops sense of whether world can be trusted. Virtue: hope.	Sensorimotor (birth to 2 years). Infant changes from a being who responds primarily through reflexes to one who can organize activities in relation to the environment. Uses sensory and motor abilities to comprehend world.
Anal (12–18 months to 3 years). Child derives sensual gratification from withholding and expelling feces.	Autonomy versus shame and doubt (12–18 months to 3 years). Child develops a balance of independence over doubt and shame. Virtue: will.	Preoperational (2 to 7 years). Child develops a representational system and uses symbols such as words to represent people, places, and events.
Phallic (3 to 6 years). Child becomes attached to parent of other sex; later identifies with same-sex parent.	Initiative versus guilt (3 to 6 years). Child develops initiative when trying out new things and is not overwhelmed by failure. Virtue: purpose.	
Latency (6 years to puberty). Time of relative calm between more turbulent stages.	Industry versus inferiority (6 years to puberty). Child must learn skills of the culture or face feelings of inferiority. Virtue: skill.	Concrete operations (7 to 12 years). Child can solve problems logically if they are focused on the here and now.
Genital (puberty through adulthood). Time of mature adult sexuality.	Identity versus identity confusion (puberty to young adulthood). Adolescent must determine own sense of self. Virtue: fidelity.	Formal operations (12 years through adulthood). Person can think in abstract terms, deal with hypothetical situations, and think about possibilities.
	Intimacy versus isolation (young adulthood). Person seeks to make commitments to others; if unsuccessful, may suffer from sense of isolation and self-absorption. Virtue: love.	
	Generativity versus stagnation (middle adulthood). Mature adult is concerned with establishing and guiding the next generation or else feels personal impoverishment. Virtue: care.	
	Integrity versus despair (old age). Elderly person achieves a sense of acceptance of own life, allowing the acceptance of death, or else falls into despair. Virtue: wisdom.	

NOTE: All ages are approximate.

The Contextual Perspective

The central image of the *contextual perspective* is the ongoing act in its context—a dynamic event in a setting that is always in flux. An act is never isolated. Its immediate context grows out of the past and affects the future. For purposes of study, we can look at an event at a given moment in time, but this is an artificial separation that distorts reality.

In contextualism, as in organicism, people actively shape their own development. But contextualists place more emphasis on interaction with the environment. Every act is produced by, and irrevocably changes, both the actor and the context, creating new conditions for development—much as, in a price war, each round of price reductions alters the circumstances within which the next round occurs. The changing person acts on and changes the environment, and the changing environment acts on and changes the person.

Individuals set goals within a particular context as they perceive it, and then select new goals within the new context that they seek out or that then presents itself. Thus, although development is continuous from one moment to the next, it is also discontinuous, as goals and contexts shift. Furthermore, the context is not just "out there." It includes a person's own aspirations, beliefs, and interpretations. Individuals influence and are influenced by the context of which they are a part.

Charlotte Bühler (1933, 1968a, 1968b) was one of the first theorists to talk about development as focused on setting and attaining personal goals. On the basis of more than 200 biographical studies and years of intensive interviews, she concluded that self-fulfillment is the key to healthy development and depends on the achievement of self-defined goals—though people may not always be conscious of them at the time.

Contextualists view development as both quantitative and qualitative; they look at changes in what people do as well as in how much they can do. Unlike organicists, contextualists do not see development as directed toward any particular endpoint. Instead, they emphasize individual differences. People develop in many directions, and no path is intrinsically superior. Success hinges on how appropriate behavior is to its context. For example, making fishing boats may be highly adaptive on an island until the coming of a factory whose polluted discharge kills the fish.

In the "activated lifespace" model (Sansone & Berg, 1993), a current example of the contextualist perspective, each person has a unique set of experiences and abilities; and each activity occurs within a unique context, which may include physical setting, social pressures, rewards, feedback, and other features. In trying to solve a problem, a person "activates" (uses) only those personal resources and contextual features within his or her "lifespace" that seem relevant at the moment. At different times of life, a person may bring different experiences and abilities to bear on a task in different contexts. An older adult who can't solve a math problem on a timed test may be able to solve a similar problem while shopping.

Although the lifespan developmental approach (Baltes, 1987), discussed in Chapter 1, blends aspects of all three metatheories, many of its key features—history and context, multiple avenues of research, and multidirectional development—fit within contextualism. The lifespan approach is coming to the fore at a time when older adults are becoming more numerous and diverse, and when technological innovations allow researchers in different fields to communicate rapidly and effectively.

Indeed, from a contextual perspective, metatheories themselves are grounded in particular social, political, and economic conditions (Riegel, 1977). The mechanistic perspective was developed chiefly in the United States and Great Britain, highly competitive societies in which "the main criterion for intellectual and personal excellence was the amount of information accumulated, just as the criterion for social respectability was the amount of wealth and property acquired" (p. 71). The organismic perspective emerged in stratified continental European societies in which different age groups had their own special roles. Contextualism seems to reflect a contemporary world in which notions of orderly progress have broken down, the universe (science tells us) is in flux, the planet Earth is becoming an interdependent global village, and people's life choices are dynamic, ever-changing, and highly individual.

APPLYING METATHEORIES

How would representatives of the three metatheoretical perspectives approach the same research problem? Think back to the professor and the shaman. The professor represents a mechanistic perspective. She focuses on quantitative differences in the amount of detail that older and younger adults can recall. Since an older adult's "machinery" appears to be functioning less efficiently, she proposes interventions to bring it up to speed. The shaman represents an organismic perspective. He sees the professor's findings as reflecting a natural course of qualitative development requiring no intervention. Each age group is acting as it should and must.

A contextual researcher in the audience might comment that the study was incomplete. He might suggest further research to compare older and younger adults in a variety of situations: working alone, working with another person, or working with a group of people. Since remembering often takes place in a social context, he might predict that some older individuals would be more motivated and better able to recall details in cooperation with others.

As you read this book, keep asking yourself: Which metatheoretical perspective does this theory, research finding, or interpretation represent? What is *my* metatheoretical perspective on this issue? Everyone uses metatheories. Your attitude toward your own development, the way you deal with the inevitable process of growing older, will depend on the metatheory under which you operate. Remember that no metatheory has an exclusive claim to truth. You may choose one metatheoretical approach toward one type of problem and a different approach toward another. Indeed, some developmentalists maintain that the ability to select the most appropriate metatheoretical perspective on a particular situation is a sign of mature thought.

BASIC RESEARCH METHODS

▼

The purpose of research is to draw valid, reliable conclusions about the world and the human beings who inhabit it—*valid* in that the conclusions appropriately apply to the phenomena and populations being studied, and *reliable* in that the results are reasonably consistent across time. For example, an intelligence test is valid if it actually measures the abilities it claims to measure. It is reliable if a person's scores do not vary greatly from one testing to another.

While researchers in various branches of the physical and social sciences use varying methods, the term *scientific method* refers to principles and processes that characterize scientific inquiry in any field. These are: careful observation and recording of data; testing of hypotheses; and widespread public dissemination of findings and conclusions so that other observers can check, learn from, analyze, repeat, and build on them.

Let's look now at the basic methods researchers use; then, in the next section, at some basic research plans, or designs. In the final section of this chapter, we'll turn to special problems in doing research on adult development and aging.

Two key issues at the outset of any investigation are how the participants will be chosen and how the data will be collected. These decisions often depend on what questions the research is intended to answer. All these issues play a part in a research plan or design.

SAMPLING

How similar are you to the other members of your family? To your neighbors? To people you go to school with, or work with? To people who have more money than you do? To people who have less money than you do? To people from the same ethnic background? To people from different ethnic backgrounds? To people of your gender? To people of the other gender? How comfortable would you feel if the results of a study about you were applied to each of these groups? How comfortable would you be if their results were applied to you?

Your answers may depend in part on the kinds of questions being studied. But a way to make *sure* that the results of a study have *external validity*—that they can be generalized to people other than those in the study—is to control who gets into the study. Of course, if an entire population (all members of the group being studied) could take part, any findings would be valid for them; but studying an entire population is usually too costly and time-consuming. Therefore, investigators select a *sample,* a smaller group within the population. Only if the sample is truly representative can the results properly be generalized to the population as a whole.

Researchers ensure representativeness by *random selection,* which gives every person in a population an equal chance of being chosen. The result of random selection is a *random sample.* One way to select a random sample of the students in an adult development class, for example, would be to put all their names into a hat, shake it, and then draw out a certain number of names. A random sample, especially a large one, is likely to represent the population well—that is, to show relevant characteristics and behavior in the same proportion in which they are found in the entire population.

To make sure that a sample includes representative percentages of certain subgroups, such as women, minorities, and older adults, polling organizations often randomly select within each of these subgroups. This type of sample is sometimes called a *stratified random sample.*

Although precise stratification is not always necessary, it is important that a sample does not leave out or greatly underrepresent major segments of the population. For example, in Box 2-1 we discuss sampling problems in Alfred Kinsey's pioneering studies of sexuality.

BOX 2-1

THE CUTTING EDGE

Early Studies of Sexuality

What percentages of American men and women have had homosexual experiences? What percentages have engaged in sex outside of marriage? What percentages are impotent or infertile?

Answers to such questions are widely available today. But scientific data about human sexual behavior were virtually nonexistent in 1938, when Alfred C. Kinsey, a zoology professor at Indiana University, began to survey students about what kinds of sexual activities they had engaged in, when, and how often. Kinsey soon switched from questionnaires to in-person interviews, which allowed more flexibility and detail. Ultimately, he and his colleagues interviewed 5,300 men and nearly 6,000 women nationwide and produced two eye-opening reports: *Sexual Behavior in the Human Male* (1948) and *Sexual Behavior in the Human Female* (1953). The latter, which found, among other things, that 62 percent of women masturbate, was especially controversial. At a time when women's sexual needs were neither widely recognized nor openly discussed, the report was attacked as "offensive . . . amoral, antifamily, and even tainted with communism" (Masters, Johnson, & Kolodny, 1988, p. 20).

Critics were quick to point out methodological flaws. The most serious problem was that Kinsey's *sample,* the group of participants chosen

Alfred C. Kinsey and his wife arrive in Paris in October 1955, carrying a French translation of his groundbreaking book, Sexual Behavior in the Human Female. *Despite some methodological flaws, Kinsey's work became the foundation for scientific study of human sexuality.*

(UPI/Bettmann)

to represent the population, was in fact unrepresentative. For example, the original sample contained very few black people; the elderly, too,

(CONTINUED)

BOX 2-1

CONTINUED

were underrepresented. And the fact that the participants were volunteers could have distorted the findings.

Still, a committee of the American Statistical Association gave the Kinsey reports a favorable overall rating (Cochran, Mosteller, & Tukey, 1953). In retrospect, William H. Masters and Virginia E. Johnson attribute the methodological "quibbles" about Kinsey's work largely to "an attempt to discredit the credibility of Kinsey's 'shocking' findings" (Masters et al., 1988, p. 31).

Although Masters and Johnson's own study of the physical processes of human sexual arousal, *Human Sexual Response* (1966), appeared at a time when societal attitudes toward sexuality were becoming more liberal, it, too, aroused furious controversy. If concerns about Kinsey's methodology may have masked outrage at the subject matter of his research, objections to Masters and Johnson's work centered on the methods themselves. In a marked departure from Kinsey's relatively tame interviews, Masters and Johnson for 11 years directly observed and recorded the physical responses of 382 women and 312 men engaging in various types of sexual activity in their laboratory at Washington University Medical School in St. Louis. In addition to machinery to measure heart rate and rhythm and muscular tension and contractions, their equipment included an artificial penis that could film vaginal changes during simulated intercourse.

One criticism was that people who would agree to be in such studies would not be typical of the population. However, Masters and Johnson did interview prospective participants to assess emotional stability and motivations. Besides, they argued, a true cross-section of the population is not generally required in research on normaal

bodily functions, "as long as the sample is both diverse and healthy" (Masters et al., 1988, p. 40). The sample included a modest number of older people, and some of the findings addressed sexual capacity in older men and women.

Another criticism was that the participants' responses might have been affected by the artificiality of the setting. But to help the couples feel at ease, the researchers first had them engage in an unobserved "practice session," without the equipment. In addition, the investigators soundproofed the laboratory and shifted sessions to the evening, when fewer curiosity seekers would be hanging around.

Ultimately, Masters and Johnson rest their case for the value of their work on its successful application to contraceptive design, infertility counseling, sex education, and particularly to sex therapy, a profession that grew out of their clinical studies reported in *Human Sexual Inadequacy* (1970).

These groundbreaking forays into the field of human sexuality demonstrate the importance of methodology in scientific research. The progression of methods used by Kinsey and then by Masters and Johnson, from questionnaires to interviews to laboratory observation to clinical treatment, shows how research can evolve to meet changing goals or unforeseen problems and outcomes. And the controversy over these reports demonstrates how methodological weaknesses can endanger the acceptance of research that delves into culturally "taboo" subjects or uses unorthodox methods.

NOTE: Unless otherwise indicated, this discussion of early investigations of human sexuality is based on Masters et al. (1988).

To take another example, after 1977 the U.S. Food and Drug Administration excluded women who might bear children from early clinical trials of new drugs, testing instead mainly with men; but can results of research on men be generalized to women? In fact, the exclusionary policy has now been reversed; and the National Institutes of Health has launched a large-scale study specifically of women's health.

Similarly, we must be careful about generalizing the results of studies done in one culture to other cultures that may have different characteristics (see Box 2-2 and Figure 2-1 on the following page). Also, if a significant proportion of a randomly chosen sample refuse to participate, the sample's representativeness may be compromised.

DATA COLLECTION

Common ways of gathering data include self-reports (verbal reports of a person's own thoughts, feelings, or actions); tests and other behavioral measures; and observation. Researchers may use one or more of these data-collection techniques in any research design.

Self-Reports: Diaries, Interviews, and Questionnaires

The simplest form of self-report is a diary or log. People may be asked, for example, to record their daily diet, times when they feel depressed, or times when they forget something. Other types of self-reports are interviews and questionnaires.

In an *interview,* a researcher asks questions about a person's attitudes, opinions, or behavior. The questioning may be face to face or by telephone; telephone interviews can reach a greater number of people more efficiently. In a *structured interview,* every participant gets the same fixed set of questions or tasks. In an *open-ended interview,* the interviewer has more flexibility with regard to determining topics and order of questions and asking follow-up questions based on the responses. Some interviews combine the two approaches. For example, an interviewer may ask a group of adults to complete a series of sentences such as: "The thing I dislike most about my job is . . . ." Then the interviewer may probe further: "You said you don't like your boss. What is it about him or her that you don't like?"

Questionnaires are written instruments, given either in person or by mail. Because questionnaires are easier than interviews to tabulate and summarize, they are often used in large-scale surveys.

Any kind of self-report can be prone to inaccuracy. Participants' memory may be faulty, or a respondent may consciously or unconsciously edit replies to make them more acceptable. The wording of a question can affect the answer. One example was a Roper survey published by the American Jewish Committee in 1993. The original results were startling: 22 percent of the adult respondents said it seemed "possible" rather than "impossible" that the Holocaust (the Nazis'

BOX 2-2

Avoiding Cultural Bias in Research

Many studies have found that as people get older, their hearing—especially for high-pitched sounds—gradually deteriorates, necessitating the use of hearing aids. Is hearing loss entirely a physiological phenomenon of aging, or do environmental and cultural factors make a difference?

To find out, one group of researchers (Baltes, Reese, & Nesselroade, 1977) compared samples of older adults in rural and urban American areas and also among the Mabaans, a tribe in the African nation of Sudan who live in an especially noise-free environment (see Figure 2-1). Older Mabaans showed less hearing loss than *any* of the American samples, male or female. Men in the United States showed more hearing loss than women; and, among men, the degree of hearing impairment was related to how much noise they heard in their everyday environments. Rural men, who heard less noise throughout their lives than urban factory workers, experienced less hearing loss in late adulthood than the factory workers did.

Findings like these illustrate how cross-cultural research can provide *external validity*. A study using only an American sample (especially a sample using only American males, or American urban males), could overestimate the amount of hearing loss associated with normal physiological aging. Clearly, such a study could not be generalized to American women or to Mabaans in Sudan—or perhaps to other cultures as well. By looking at people from various cultural and ethnic groups, researchers can learn which aspects of development seem to be universal (and thus a part of the aging process everywhere), and which are cultural.

Just as travelers returning from abroad may see familiar aspects of their own world in a new light, learning about the ideas and practices of other cultures can give us a new perspective on our own. Throughout this book, we present many examples of cross-cultural research. These studies demonstrate how closely adult development is tied to society and culture and how greatly "normal" development can vary in different cultural settings.

FIGURE 2-1

Cross-cultural differences in hearing loss showed up in a study that compared American men and women, exposed to varying noise levels in their everyday environment, with older people in a Sudanese tribe exposed to unusually low noise levels. These findings suggest that hearing loss is not purely physiological but is environmentally influenced.
(SOURCE: Baltes, Reese, & Nesselroade, 1977.)

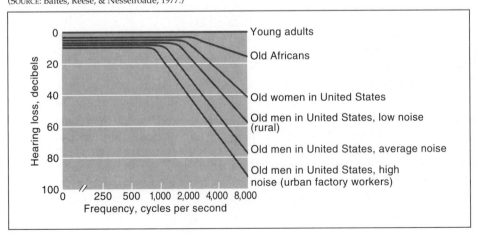

Questionnaires and interviews are common techniques for gathering data about adults' attitudes and behavior, but their usefulness may be limited by their subjectivity.

annihilation of Jews during World War II) had never happened (Siano, 1993; T. W. Smith, 1995; "Testing Awareness," 1993). However, when the survey was repeated twice using a more clearly worded question, only 1 to 3 percent said it seemed possible that the Holocaust had not occurred (T. W. Smith, 1995). Sometimes the identity of the questioner makes a difference. In a Northwestern University survey, men were twice as likely to admit to having engaged in sexual harassment in the workplace when questioned by a man as by a woman (Secter, 1995).

Self-reports have an important place in psychological investigation but are limited by their subjectivity. They depend on awareness of processes that may be less than fully conscious; and they are inevitably filtered through each participant's interpretive screen. For many kinds of research, investigators seek greater objectivity through measures that do not depend on verbal reports.

Behavioral Methods: Tests and Other Measures

A behavioral measure such as an intelligence test *shows* something about a person rather than asking the person to *tell* about it. Tests and other behavioral measures, including mechanical and electronic devices, may be used to assess abilities, skills, knowledge, or physical responses.

Observation

A scientist must . . . be absolutely like a child. If he sees a thing, he must say that he sees it, whether it was what he thought he was going to see or not. See first, think later, then test. But always see first. Otherwise you will only see what you were expecting. (D. Adams, 1985, pp. 164-165).

Seeing is a common word for what scientists call *observation*. Observation can take two forms: naturalistic observation and laboratory observation.

Naturalistic observation takes place in real-life settings. Researchers do not manipulate the environment or the participants' activities. They simply record what they observe.

Systematic, sustained observation can reveal information missed by casual observation. In one study of nursing home residents who had been reported by staff members to wander, the residents wore electronic ankle tags that automatically activated video recorders. Staff members viewed the videotapes and identified patterns of movement. About 81 percent of the movement of residents reported to be "wanderers" (compared with 94 percent for "nonwanderers") turned out to be direct travel from one place to another. Apparently, much of what staff members ordinarily saw as aimless wandering was actually efficient movement (Martino-Saltzman, Morris, & McNeal, 1991).

(Joel Gordon)

Many caregivers have observed the "mirror phenomenon," in which a person with Alzheimer's disease reacts to his or her own reflection as if it were another person. Such naturalistic observations can suggest questions for further study.

Sometimes naturalistic observation raises questions that it cannot conclusively answer. A 68-year-old woman with Alzheimer's disease became agitated and refused to enter the bathroom, claiming there was a stranger inside. Her daughter gently led her into the bathroom and said, "Show me the stranger." The mother hesitantly went to the mirror and pointed to her own reflection. A number of caregivers have reported this "mirror phenomenon," in which demented patients react to their own reflection as if it were another person. Might particular features of the situation, or degree of dementia, have something to do with this phenomenon? Answers can come from *laboratory observation*—which may or may not take place in an actual laboratory—in which researchers observe a group of people under identical, controlled conditions. By manipulating the environment, the investigators can observe any differences in behavior.

In one study in a French geriatric center (Biringer, Anderson, & Strubel, 1988), eighteen women at three discrete, progressively advanced stages of Alzheimer's disease (stages 5, 6, and 7) sat, by turns, before a mirror. The researchers observed each woman from the next room for 5 minutes to see whether she would act as if she knew that she was facing her own reflection. Next, an investigator entered the room and, while rearranging the woman's hair (a common procedure at the center), smudged her forehead with soot from a burnt cork. The investigator again left the room and observed the woman for 5 minutes. Finally, the investigator again returned and put a mark on the woman's hand, where she could see it without looking in the mirror, and then observed her for 5 more minutes.

Most of the women at a less advanced stage of the disease (stage 5) recognized themselves in the mirror during the first observation period, and every one of them showed an understanding that the mark on the forehead of the reflection in the mirror was actually on her own forehead. Some of the women at stage 6 could recognize themselves and respond appropriately to the marks on their foreheads, and some could not. However, all these women responded appropriately to the marks on their hands, suggesting that lack of response to a mark on the forehead was not due simply to lack of interest in strange marks on the body. At stage 7, all the women failed to respond to marks on their reflections, and all but one failed to respond to marks on their hands.

Observation can yield much useful descriptive information. But even under controlled laboratory conditions, observation by itself cannot explain behavior. The studies described above do not tell us why patients with advanced Alzheimer's disease seem to lose the ability to recognize themselves before they lose the ability to notice a mark on their hands. Two additional cautions: First, an observer's presence may affect behavior. If adults know they are being observed, they may act differently. Researchers may be able to obtain a clear, accurate picture only through long-term observation in which they gradually fade into the background, or when the observation is made so unobtrusively that the person being observed is unaware of it. Second, the value of observation may be limited by *observer bias:* a tendency to misinterpret or distort observed data to fit the observer's expectations, perhaps by emphasizing some aspects and minimizing others.

TABLE 2-3   THREE BASIC RESEARCH DESIGNS

	Major Characteristics	Advantages	Disadvantages
Case Study	Study of single individual in depth	Provides detailed picture of one person's behavior	May not generalize to others; may reflect observer bias
Correlational Study	Study that measures direction and magnitude of a relationship between variables	Allows predictions from one variable about another	Does not determine cause-effect relationships
Experiment	Controlled procedure in which independent variable is manipulated to determine its effects on dependent variable	Establishes cause-effect relationship; may be repeated by other researchers	Findings may not generalize, especially when research is done in a lab setting

BASIC RESEARCH DESIGNS

▼

A research design is a plan for conducting a scientific investigation: what questions are to be answered, how participants are to be selected, how data are to be collected and interpreted, and how valid conclusions can be drawn. Three basic designs used in developmental research are case studies, correlational studies, and experiments. Each design has advantages and drawbacks, and each is appropriate for certain kinds of research problems (see Table 2-3).

CASE STUDIES

A *case study* is a study of a single case or individual. A number of theories, such as those of Freud and Erikson, have grown out of clinical case studies—some later modified or fleshed out by other types of research. Both Freud and Erikson also did historical case studies, using biographical, autobiographical, and documentary materials. Case studies can achieve great depth and breadth in exploring sources of behavior and developing and testing treatments for problems.

One advantage of a case study is flexibility. The researcher is free to explore avenues of inquiry that arise during the course of the study. One of the authors of this textbook (R. D. Feldman, 1982) conducted open-ended interviews with several middle-aged men and women who, like her, had been frequent panelists on *Quiz Kids*, a popular radio and television quiz show featuring precocious youngsters. One, Claude Brenner, was a 52-year-old engineer with a varied career ranging from space technology to energy conservation. After reflecting at length on the effects of *Quiz Kids* on his personal and professional life, Brenner concluded:

> So the question comes back to the extent to which we were influenced, controlled, governed and shaped by the Quiz Kids experience. I would say strongly, but not exclusively. Perhaps I was laying all my emotional difficulties on that experience, and that is unfair. There were other factors going on in our lives. Our families—but our families themselves were inevitably shaped by our Quiz Kid experience. There's an interweaving of cause and effect that becomes a seamless web. . . . We will never know whether we were Quiz Kids because of the kind of people we were or whether we're the kind of people we are because we were Quiz Kids. (p. 135)

In the 1940s, Claude Brenner (far right) was a panelist on Quiz Kids, *a popular radio quiz show featuring bright children. At age 52, Brenner was one of several former Quiz Kids who participated in case studies by their fellow panelist Ruth Duskin Feldman (center), one of the authors of this textbook. Another former Quiz Kid, James Dewey Watson (second from left), won a Nobel prize in 1962 for the discovery of the structure of DNA, the substance that determines hereditary characteristics.*

(Courtesy of Quiz Kids, Inc.)

Brenner's comment illuminates an important limitation of case studies: they do not yield unequivocal information about causal relationships, because there is no way to test the validity of an explanation. Also, case studies are particularly prone to observer bias. In one notorious case, Freud rebuked an 18-year-old girl, who complained of a family friend's sexual advances, for her "hysterical" refusal to follow what Freud maintained was her true desire to have sex with the man (Lakoff & Coyne, 1993). Finally, while a case study may offer a rich description of a single individual, it is questionable how the information applies to people in general.

Despite their limitations, however, case studies can provide valuable information about individual personality and behavior and can suggest hypotheses to be tested by other research. In one famous case study, an epileptic known as H. M. lost his memory of recent events but not his ability to learn new skills—such as solving puzzles—after his hippocampus and neighboring brain structures were removed in an attempt to stop his seizures (Kalat, 1992). Case studies such as this one have stimulated research about distinctions between memory for facts and for skills, and the brain structures that seem to be involved in each.

CORRELATIONAL STUDIES

Suppose we want to see whether blood pressure has something to do with the risk of heart attack. By carefully measuring both phenomena, we might find that people with high blood pressure are more likely to have heart attacks than people with low blood pressure. If so, we have found a *correlation*, or relationship, between blood pressure and heart attacks.

Researchers are often interested in identifying relationships among *variables*—phenomena that change or vary among people. (*Constants* are things that do not change or vary.) Researchers are particularly interested in finding variables (such as blood pressure and risk of heart attack) that change together, that is, are related to one another.

A *correlational study* is designed to find out whether a statistical correlation can be calculated showing the direction and strength of a relationship between variables. It can show whether two variables are related *positively* (that is, both increase or decrease together, like blood pressure and heart attacks) or *negatively* (as one increases, the other decreases), and to what degree. A negative correlation does *not* mean "no correlation." It means that the two factors change in opposite directions. For example, studies in a number of countries show a negative correlation between educational level and the risk of dementia due to Alzheimer's disease. In Shanghai, people over age 75 with little or no education are twice as likely to become demented as those who have had some schooling. In other words, *less* schooling is associated with *more* dementia (Katzman, 1993).

Numerical correlations range from +1.0 (a perfect positive, or direct, relationship) to −1.0 (a perfect negative, or inverse, relationship). Of course, perfect correlations are rare. The closer a correlation comes to +1 or −1, the stronger the relationship, either positive or negative. A correlation of zero means that the variables have no relationship (see Figure 2-2).

Correlations allow researchers to make predictions but not to draw conclusions about cause and effect. A rooster's crow heralds, but does not bring, the

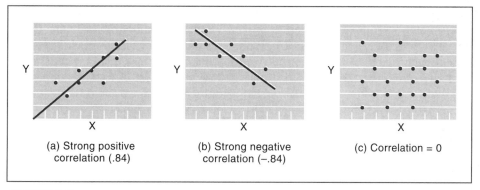

FIGURE 2-2
Correlational studies may find positive or negative correlations or no correlation. (a) In a positive correlation, data plotted on a graph cluster around a line showing that one variable (X) increases as the other variable (Y) increases. (b) In a negative correlation, one variable (X) increases as the other variable (Y) decreases. (c) No correlation—zero correlation—exists when increases and decreases in two variables show no consistent relationship (that is, data plotted on a graph show no pattern).

dawn. A strong positive correlation suggests, but cannot tell us with certainty, that high blood pressure causes heart attacks. Heart disease (and, perhaps, high blood pressure as well) might result from an unknown third factor. Similarly, the negative correlation between education and dementia might be due to another variable, such as socioeconomic status, which might explain *both* lower levels of schooling *and* higher levels of dementia. Compared with people who can afford advanced schooling, people who cannot afford it may have poorer diets, more exposure to environmental toxins, less adequate health care, or other deprivations that may contribute to a greater likelihood of mental deterioration. If a study found a correlation between education and brain development, it would be a strong indication that intellectual activity can protect against dementia; but it still could not definitively establish a causal connection. Only an experiment could do that. (In this case, however, for both practical and ethical reasons that will become clear later, such an experiment could not be conducted.)

EXPERIMENTS

An *experiment* is a rigorously controlled procedure in which the experimenter systematically manipulates one or more variables to see whether this manipulation causes change in other, uncontrolled variables. This manipulation is what permits experimenters to establish cause and effect. Experiments must be conducted and reported in such a way that other investigators can replicate (repeat) them to verify the results and conclusions.

Designing an Experiment

Let's imagine that we see an advertisement for a pill that is supposed to improve eyesight. How might we design an experiment to test that claim?

VARIABLES AND GROUPS The first step is to identify the variables. An *independent variable* is something over which the experimenter has direct control—in this case, ingestion of vision pills. A *dependent variable*—in this case, visual acuity—is something that may or may not change as a result of changes in the independent variable; that is, it may or may not depend on the independent variable. The experimenter manipulates the independent variable (the pills) to see whether and how it affects the dependent variable (eyesight). This manipulation of the independent variable—the thing the experimenter wants to study—is called the *treatment.*

After identifying the variables, the experimenter must divide the participants into two groups: an *experimental group,* which will be given the treatment, and a *control group,* which will not. A control group is an essential element; it consists of people similar to the experimental group who are exposed to everything that group experiences except the treatment. A control group shows what the people who got the treatment would have been like without it.

In our experiment, the experimental group would take the vision pills, while the control group would take a placebo, which looked exactly like the vision pill but had no active ingredients. None of the participants would know which type of pill they were getting. This is called a *single-blind test.* Ideally, the person who gave out the pills also would be unaware of the purpose of the study and would not know which participants got the vision pills and which got the placebo. Such a procedure is commonly called a *double-blind test.*

Before giving the experimental group the treatment, we could test both groups to make sure that their visual acuity was approximately equal. After both groups had taken equal numbers of pills, we would test them again, once or more, to

(Steve Goldberg/Monkmeyer)

In a double-blind study, neither the participants nor the persons administering a treatment know who is getting the treatment and who is getting a placebo.

measure the effect of the treatment. (Again, ideally the person administering the test would not know who had taken which pill, or even why the test was being given.) We would compare any changes in average performance of the groups and determine whether they were statistically significant; that is, whether the difference was greater than that attributable to chance.

RANDOM ASSIGNMENT   In our vision pill experiment, if a significant difference emerged in the performance of the experimental and control groups, could we validly conclude that the pills were the cause? Not necessarily. We would have to be sure that initially the two groups were similar in all relevant ways, not just in visual acuity.

We have already discussed how random sampling can ensure external validity: generalizability of results beyond the study sample. The question here is one of *internal validity* for the sample itself—assurance that the outcome was due to the treatment and only to the treatment. How can we be sure that the vision pills and not some other factor (such as physical changes that might coincidentally have occurred during the course of the study) caused the difference in performance of the two groups?

The answer hinges on control of who gets the treatment. Experimenters achieve this control through *random assignment* of participants to experimental and control groups. This means that all members of a sample have an equal chance of being in the group that receives the treatment. If the sample is large enough, random assignment ensures that differences in such factors as age, sex, race, and socioeconomic status will be evenly distributed by chance, so that the experimental and control groups are as alike as possible in every way but one: receipt of the treatment. Random assignment controls for all other variables; it prevents these other variables from affecting the results, so that the outcome of the experiment will reflect only the impact of the independent variable (the treatment).

In our vision pill study, we could achieve internal validity if, after selecting the sample, we alternately drew names for the experimental and control groups. Of course, we could instead attempt to deliberately match the experimental and control groups for any and all factors that might have an effect. But no matter how carefully we matched groups for certain characteristics, we would probably miss others that might turn out to be just as important. The best way to control for such unforeseen factors is to assign participants randomly to experimental and control groups. Together, random sampling and random assignment can give an experiment both external and internal validity.

What makes scientific research so fascinating is that investigators can never be sure of the outcome of a study in advance. Although scientists often have hunches or hypotheses about what might occur in an experiment, nature seems ever ready to hand out surprises. For example, the experiment outlined above, if actually conducted, might show that the vision pills *decreased* visual acuity. Then we would have to look for, and test, a new hypothesis to explain that unexpected result.

Laboratory, Field, and Natural Experiments

Methods such as random assignment are most easily used in *laboratory experiments*, in which researchers have full control and can isolate groups and variables for study. Not all studies can be neatly confined within a laboratory, but it's possible to achieve internal validity in experiments outside the laboratory—if researchers control who gets the treatment. A *field experiment* is a controlled study conducted in a setting (such as a supermarket, singles bar, or nursing home) that is part of everyday life.

Sometimes, for practical or ethical reasons, it is impossible to conduct a true experiment (though, as we discuss at the end of this chapter, scientists have at times done experiments that today would be considered unethical). For example, an experiment testing whether education has a protective effect against dementia would have to deprive the control group of education.

However, nature may cooperate by providing the raw materials for a *natural experiment*. Here the investigator compares people who were divided into different groups by circumstances of life—one group who were exposed to, say, famine, venereal disease, a birth defect, or advanced education; and another group who were not. Natural experiments, because they do not permit manipulation of variables or control of assignment to groups, are actually correlational studies.

Issues of Construct Validity and Factorial Invariance

A boy received a voice-activated toy car for his fifth birthday. The car would careen across the floor when the boy said "Go!" After awhile, the boy decided to pull the wheels off the car and see what would happen. When he said "Go!" the car stood still. "Look," said the boy to his mother, "If you pull off all of a car's wheels, it goes deaf."

What is wrong with the boy's statement? Clearly, the treatment (removing the wheels) produced the effect he identified (failure to move when commanded). If he were to check his conclusion experimentally by removing the wheels of a randomly selected and assigned experimental group of voice-activated toy cars and not those of a control group, the cars in the control group would move on command, and those in the experimental group would not. Thus the experiment would have internal and external validity. Furthermore, the results should be easy to replicate.

The problem is that the boy was not studying the thing he thought he was studying. He thought he was studying hearing loss when he was actually studying physical mobility. His experiment lacked **construct validity**, because the manipulations and measures he used were not pertinent to the *construct*, the phenomenon under study.

Researchers ensure construct validity in two ways: first, by precisely defining the construct; second, by finding more than one way to produce or measure it. The boy used only one criterion: the car's failure to move when commanded. Another measure (such as observing whether the axles still turned when the boy said "Go!") might suggest a different conclusion.

A related problem in research on adult development and aging is *factorial invariance.* It may not be appropriate to use the same instrument to measure a construct (phenomenon) in different age groups. For example, affirmative responses to such statements as "I feel a lot of aches and pains" and "I don't have as much energy as I used to" may be a valid index of depression in young adults. But those statements may be true for many older adults who are *not* depressed. One way to check for factorial invariance is to find out whether two or more items in a questionnaire show similar correlations in all age groups. For example, items about pains and energy may be positively related to items about feeling sad in almost all young adults, but not in almost all older adults.

QUASI-EXPERIMENTAL DESIGNS: THE PROBLEM OF INTERNAL VALIDITY

If we want to know how age affects some aspect of development, we are asking a question about a causal relationship; thus the appropriate research design would seem to be an experiment. Unfortunately, a true experiment on the effects of aging can't be done because the "treatment" under study is chronological age, and age is not subject to control.

Actually, the passage of time in itself does not change anything. When researchers set out to study effects of age, they are really studying the effects of processes associated with aging, such as long-term exposure to sunlight, which may cause wrinkles. But these processes vary among individuals, and investigators cannot randomly assign people to age groups so as to control for the variations; an experimenter cannot tell a participant, "Today you will be 45 years old." Without random assignment, we cannot be sure that age is the *only* relevant difference between groups. Therefore, most studies of age effects (as well as studies of other unalterable conditions, such as gender) use a special type of correlational design called a *quasi experiment.*

A *quasi experiment* looks something like an experiment. It may measure differences between groups, or changes following a treatment. But (like a natural experiment) it lacks a critical feature of all true experiments: control based on random assignment. Without the ability to randomly assign who gets a treatment, the researcher cannot confidently rule out alternative explanations for the outcome. Quasi experiments, then, have problems of internal validity. Let's look at several types of quasi-experimental design used in research on adult development and aging.

CROSS-SECTIONAL STUDIES

Investigators who want to study effects of aging on, say, memory or physical strength typically compare the ability of groups of younger and older adults to recall a string of numbers or lift a certain weight. This research design, in which people of different ages are assessed on one occasion, is a *cross-sectional study—* the design most commonly used in research on adult development and aging.

Effects of cohort can be difficult to disentangle from effects of age. Middle-aged adults who grew up in the youth counterculture of the 1960s are likely to have been influenced by that formative phenomenon.

A cross-sectional study can measure differences between groups of younger and older adults; but, lacking random assignment of ages, a researcher cannot conclude that aging *causes* those differences. Thus cross-sectional studies are actually correlational studies; they show a relationship between age and some other phenomenon.

Advantages of cross-sectional research include speed and economy; data can be gathered fairly quickly from large numbers of people. But a serious drawback is that participants of different ages belong to different *cohorts*. A **cohort** is a group of people who have shared a common experience; in this case, the experience of growing up at approximately the same time. People in different cohorts are affected by different formative cultural events (such as a war, a stock market crash, the assassination of a president, or the advent of computers). For example, the war in Vietnam was a formative influence for the cohort growing up in the mid-1960s to the mid-1970s, just as the Great Depression was for the cohort growing up in the 1930s.

When we try to compare younger and older groups, then, how do we know whether to attribute our observations to age differences or to cohort (generational) differences? The effects of age and cohort are *confounded* (mixed together). This confounding, or confusion, of age and cohort effects is an intrinsic flaw of cross-sectional research. Cross-sectional studies are sometimes misinterpreted as yielding information about developmental changes—information that may be misleading, as the gerontologist Robert Kastenbaum suggests in this tongue-in-cheek observation:

> Occasionally I have the opportunity to chat with elderly people who live in the communities near Cushing Hospital. I cannot help but observe that many of these people speak with an Italian accent. I also chat with young adults who live in these same communities. They do *not* speak with an Italian accent. As a student of human behavior and development . . . I indulge in some deep thinking and come up with the following conclusion: as people grow older they develop Italian accents. (Quoted in Botwinick, 1984, p. 381)

What if, instead of observing a difference in accents, Kastenbaum had noted more rigid personality traits among elderly people than among younger adults? Could he validly attribute that difference to aging? Such an inference may seem more reasonable, and sometimes is made; but it still may be false. Older adults who are more rigid than younger adults may also have been more rigid in their youth. We cannot know unless they were studied then—and that would have required a longitudinal design.

LONGITUDINAL STUDIES

While cross-sectional research provides information about *differences* among age groups, a **longitudinal study** shows *changes* in the same person or persons (see Figure 2-3 and Box 2-3). In longitudinal research, the participants are studied more than once over a period of time, sometimes years apart. Researchers may measure one characteristic—such as IQ, height, aggressiveness, or size of vocabulary—or several characteristics. Longitudinal studies, then, can track long-term individual development. However, they are more time-consuming and expensive than cross-sectional studies and are subject to *attrition:* participants may die or drop out. Another likely shortcoming is *sampling bias:* people who volunteer for such studies (and especially those who stay with them) tend to be above average in intelligence and socioeconomic status. Still another problem is *testing effects:* people who are tested repeatedly tend to do better because of practice with the questions or familiarity with the procedures.

Much as cohort effects threaten the internal validity of cross-sectional studies, longitudinal studies have problems of external validity. Conclusions from a study of a particular cohort (say, people born in 1930) may not apply to other cohorts (say, people born in 1980).

Furthermore, just as cross-sectional studies confound age effects and cohort effects, longitudinal studies confound age effects and time-of-measurement effects: cultural changes that occur between the times when measurements are taken. For example, intelligence test scores in the United States increased between World War I and World War II. Was this because people became smarter as they grew older, or because of a widening of educational opportunity? Lacking a control group that does not age, a longitudinal study cannot establish with certainty that the changes it reveals are effects of aging.

BOX 2-3

THE ART OF AGING

What Longitudinal Studies Can Tell Us

In 1932, Stuart Campbell, age 11, became one of more than 500 children recruited for three studies known collectively as the Berkeley Longitudinal Studies. Stuart had been effectively orphaned at age 6 (his mother died and his alcoholic father abandoned him) and was being raised in near-poverty by a stern but loving grandmother. The study in which Stuart was enrolled was the (Oakland) Adolescent Growth Study, which was designed to assess social and emotional development through the senior high school years. Twenty years later, a full-scale follow-up study began. A succession of interviews and tests enabled investigators to track Stuart's life through age 63.

Measures

All participants had medical examinations, and their family histories and current living situations were recorded. They took periodic intelligence and psychological tests, including personality inventories (instruments that yield psychometric, or quantitative, ratings of certain traits or groupings of traits). On the basis of recorded data and interviews, the researchers developed detailed life histories (case studies) of 60 participants.

Eventually the research began to focus on a theoretical construct (phenomenon) which the personality inventories called *planful competence*, a combination of self-confidence, intellectual commitment, and dependable effectiveness. Of the 60 participants for whom case studies were developed, Stuart Campbell had the highest score for planful competence.

Findings

The sociologist John A. Clausen (1993), analyzing the results of this longitudinal study, concluded that planful competence helps people mobilize resources and cope with difficulties. Planful com-

petence did not *guarantee* success, nor did its absence ensure failure. But it did turn out to be the most powerful influence on the course of a person's life. Competent people made good choices in adolescence and early adulthood, which often led to promising opportunities (scholarships, good jobs, and competent spouses); less competent teenagers made poorer early decisions and then tended to lead crisis-ridden lives.

Stuart Campbell, for example, knew by age 17 that he wanted to be a doctor. He became a pediatrician, married early in life, went through an amicable divorce, married again (this time happily), had five children, and established a home and a solid professional and civic reputation in an upper-middle-class community. He was a strong family man, a man who could be counted on. At age 61, he was self-confident, intellectually involved, and dependable, as well as outgoing, warm, agreeable, and modestly assertive—all qualities he had shown since early adolescence.

Methodological Issues

"Longitudinal studies do not approach the neat precision of a well-conceived research design," said Clausen. "In some ways, they are messy and have loose ends. . . . Human lives are that way too" (p. 35).

For example, planful competence initially was a dependent variable. Researchers wanted to see whether and to what extent it was influenced by such independent variables as parenting practices, intelligence test scores, and social class. Later, during the adult phase of the study, planful competence became an independent variable; researchers measured its influence on success in life.

The report of these studies is entitled *American Lives*, but it is actually a report of only *some* American lives. The participants were a cohort born in the 1920s in one part of the country (the San Francisco Bay area). The sample (reflecting the population living there at the time) was almost entirely white, mostly native-born, Chris-

BOX 2-3

CONTINUED

tian, and middle-class. Thus, the findings may lack external validity. Also, of the approximately 200 participants who dropped out, a disproportionate number were from families with financial or interpersonal problems, skewing the ultimate sample toward those with fewer problems.

Still, with these caveats, the findings can be useful as an indication of the persistence of personality traits throughout adulthood and of how human beings can help shape their own lives.

FIGURE 2-3

Three designs for studying adult development. In a cross-sectional study, *adults of different ages are measured at the same time to obtain data about age-related* differences *in performance. Here, groups of 20-, 40-, and 60-year-olds were tested in 1975. In a* longitudinal study, *a group of adults is measured more than once to show age-related* changes *in individual performance. Here, young adults were first measured in 1975, when they were 20 years old. They were retested in 1995 at age 40 and are to be tested again in 2005 at age 60. In a* time-lag comparison, *which shows historical influences, different groups of people are measured at different times when they are the same age. Here, a group of 20-year-olds was tested in 1975; another group of 20-year-olds was tested in 1995; and a third group will be tested in 2005.*

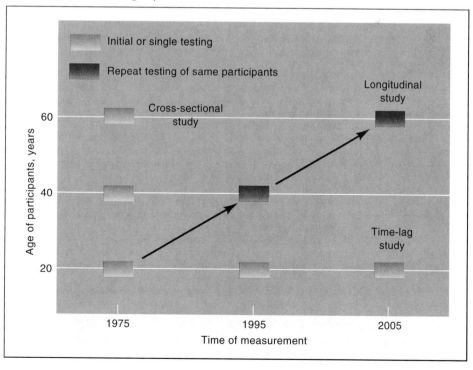

TABLE 2-4   THREE SIMPLE QUASI-EXPERIMENTAL DESIGNS

Design	Measures	Holds Constant	Confounds
Cross-sectional	Differences among age groups	Time of measurement	Age and cohort
Longitudinal	Changes with aging	Cohort	Age and time
Time-lag	Historical influences	Age	Cohort and time

TIME-LAG STUDIES

Erland Nelson (1954), in a longitudinal study of college students, attempted to untangle age from time-of-measurement effects. First, he tested students' attitudes toward a wide variety of issues. When he retested the participants 14 years later, he found their attitudes more liberal. Did this mean that liberalism increases during young adulthood? Such a conclusion might have seemed likely—except that, at the same time he retested his original sample, Nelson tested a *new* sample of college students the same age as the original sample had been when first tested. This new sample was just as liberal as the retested sample and more liberal than the original group had been 14 years earlier—not surprisingly, since the years from 1940 to 1954 had been a period of growing liberalism in American society. Nelson concluded that this historical change was probably the major influence on the change in the original participants' attitudes.

A *time-lag study*—what Nelson did in comparing the two groups of students—measures different cohorts at different times, when they are the same age (refer back to Figure 2-3). Parents often make informal time-lag comparisons ("When I was your age . . . "). While time-lag comparisons avoid confounding age with other effects, they do confound cohort and time of measurement. Both effects result from important cultural influences at particular times in history; but cohort effects, unlike time of measurement effects, may have occurred before the period under study. (Table 2-4 compares time-lag with cross-sectional and longitudinal designs.)

SEQUENTIAL DESIGNS

None of the research designs described above completely avoids the problem of internal validity; all involve some confounding of variables. Is there any way to overcome this problem? Some researchers might wish for a time machine, which would allow them to regress a representative sample of older adults to their younger selves and test them on, say, cognitive functioning.

Then the machine would transport them back to the present. If a second test showed improvement or decline, it would be clear that age was the cause, since nothing else would have changed. In reality, of course, it is impossible to test the same group of people on the same day at different ages; and "experiments we perform in real life are efforts to approximate, as closely as possible, this nearly ideal state of affairs" (Lachman, Lachman, & Taylor, 1982, p. 282).

The most ambitious attempts to overcome the drawbacks of cross-sectional, longitudinal, and time-lag designs involve combining them into more complex *sequential designs.* *Cross-sequential designs* combine longitudinal and cross-sectional data; researchers test a cross-sectional sample more than once to determine differences in each age cohort over a period of time. Similarly, *cohort-sequential designs* combine time-lag comparisons with longitudinal studies; and *time-sequential designs* combine time-lag comparisons with cross-sectional studies.

Perhaps the ultimate combination is what K. Warner Schaie (1965, 1977), who devised it, calls the "most efficient" sequential design, which combines all three sequential designs. Suppose we start with a cross-sectional comparison in 1975, when five cohorts (age groups) ranging from ages 15 to 55 take an intelligence test (see Figure 2-4 on the following page). We then test these people every 10 years through 2015, providing longitudinal data for each cohort. In addition, we make time-lag comparisons between cohorts; for example, we can compare 25-year-olds born in 1950 and tested in 1975 with 25-year-olds born in 1960 and tested in 1985. At each retesting, we add new participants from each cohort to detect improvements due to testing (practice) effects. For example, we can compare the scores of people tested for the second (or third or fourth or fifth) time in, say, 1995 with scores of people from the same cohort who are tested for the first time that same year.

Such a design permits many other kinds of comparisons that help sort out effects which are confounded in simpler designs. For example, we can compare changes in one cohort's scores between, say, ages 55 and 65 with changes in another cohort's scores between these same ages. If changes during this 10-year period are similar for the two cohorts, then such changes are more likely due to age differences than to cohort or time-of-testing differences. But if cross-sectional differences (differences between scores of cohorts tested at the same time) are larger than longitudinal changes (differences in successive scores for the same cohort), then age-related effects may be less significant than the cross-sectional data alone would suggest.

Most sequential research has focused on intelligence and seems to provide a more accurate assessment of intellectual functioning across the lifespan than cross-sectional or longitudinal studies. Sequential studies have also provided clear evidence of cohort effects on intellectual performance (Schaie, 1990a; see Chapter 6). Their major drawbacks—and these can be daunting—involve time, effort, and complexity. Sequential designs require large numbers of participants and the collection and analysis of huge amounts of data over a period of many years. Interpreting their findings and conclusions can demand a high degree of sophistication.

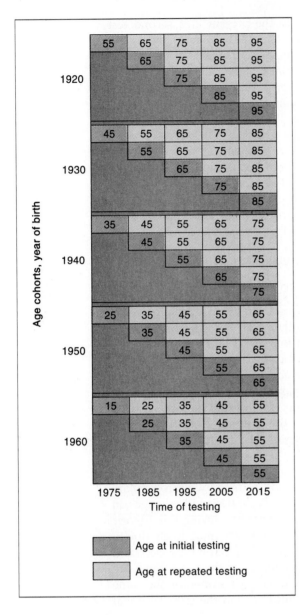

FIGURE 2-4

Schaie's "most efficient" sequential study design combines cross-sectional, longitudinal, and time-lag designs. Participants in five age cohorts are measured five successive times, 10 years apart. Each time, new participants in each cohort are added, to control for testing effects (improvements in performance with repeated testing). Comparisons among cohorts at the same time of testing show cross-sectional differences. Each cohort is also followed longitudinally, showing change through time. Time-lag comparisons are made possible by comparing, for example, 55-year-olds tested in 1975 with 55-year-olds (in other cohorts) tested in 1985, 1995, 2005, and 2015.

ETHICS OF RESEARCH

Should research that might harm its participants ever be undertaken? How can we balance the possible benefits to humanity against the risk of intellectual, emotional, or physical injury to individuals?

Between the late 1940s and the 1970s, the United States government sponsored experiments in which unsuspecting adults and children were fed or injected with radioactive substances to test the effects of radiation in the event of a nuclear attack. The government's shocking disclosure of these studies in late 1993 elicited comparisons with the "medical" experiments the Nazis had perpetrated on Jews during World War II. The radiation research was also chillingly reminiscent of another infamous American government-supported study during approximately the same period: a 40-year study of the effects of untreated syphilis in black males (Jones, 1981).

In 1932, when that study began, syphilis—a progressive, sexually transmitted disease that eventually can produce paralysis, blindness, insanity, and major heart damage, leading to death—was spreading rapidly among the poor, mostly black population in rural Macon County, Alabama. Methods of treatment in existence at that time were of dubious safety and effectiveness. Officials of the U.S. Public Health Service, in cooperation with the respected Tuskegee Institute (which was located in the area) and state and county health agencies, took the opportunity to study the natural evolution of the disease in 399 black men who had never been treated. Free blood tests and medical examinations, hot lunches, and promises of free burial benefits induced the participants to submit to periodic painful spinal taps intended to determine how the disease was progressing.

The sponsors concealed the nature and purpose of the study from the mostly illiterate participants, who were falsely told that the spinal taps were treatments. Nor were they informed that they would be excluded from any future treatment that became available. The goal was "bringing them to autopsy" (Jones, 1981, p. 132). After the discovery of penicillin in the 1940s, information about the drug was withheld from them, and those who found out about it were actively discouraged from taking it. In the view of the sponsors, the growing use of this "wonder drug" made the Tuskegee study a final opportunity to study an untreated group of syphilitics. In reality, methodological defects, such as lack of any control group of treated syphilitics—and the fact that many of the participants did manage to get treatment on their own—made the study's findings worthless.

Although reports of the Tuskegee study were published from time to time in medical journals, no objection was raised until the mid-1960s. After the press broke the story in 1972, there was a congressional investigation that led to the termination of the study. Survivors sued the federal government and won an out-of-court settlement.

Today it is almost inconceivable that such a study would be conducted. Since the 1970s, federally mandated committees have been set up at colleges, universities, and other institutions to review proposed research from an ethical standpoint. The American Psychological Association's guidelines cover such points as protection of research participants from harm and loss of dignity, guarantees of privacy and confidentiality, informed consent, avoidance of deception, the right to decline or withdraw from an experiment at any time, and the responsibility of investigators to correct any undesirable effects. Still, researchers may face troubling ethical questions.

(National Archives—Southeast Region)

Home visits by a nurse, Eunice Rivers, were part of the Tuskegee study of the course of untreated syphilis, a classic illustration of the need for informed consent in research. The participants were mostly poor, illiterate black men in rural Macon County, Alabama, like this cotton farmworker. When safe, effective treatment became available, it was withheld from them. The study, which began in 1932, was ended 40 years later, after a congressional investigation. Ethical standards in effect today would prohibit such research on human beings.

One of the most disturbing aspects of both the radiation studies and the Tuskegee study is lack of informed consent. Informed consent exists when participants voluntarily agree to participate and are fully aware of risks as well as potential benefits. Ethical standards require that participants are competent to give consent and are not being exploited. But studies that seek causes and treatments for Alzheimer's disease, for example, need participants whose mental status may preclude their being fully or even partially aware of what is involved. When, if ever, is it appropriate for a demented person to be part of a study that may be beneficial to people with that condition? (An example would be the study cited earlier involving women with Alzheimer's disease who were tested to see if they could recognize smudges on their foreheads.) What if a person gives consent and later forgets having done so? If caregivers give consent, how can we be sure that they are acting in the patient's best interest? Current practice, to be on the safe side, is to ask *both* participants and caregivers for consent.

Obviously, informed consent cannot exist when participants are deceived about the nature of a study. In a controversial experiment at Yale University, Stanley Milgram (1963) probed how far ordinary Americans would go in obeying orders to hurt an innocent person. Participants who were recruited for a "learning experiment" were actually tested on their willingness to follow instructions to inflict apparently painful, increasingly strong "electric shocks" on an unsuccessful "learner" hidden behind a screen. In retrospect, the moral theorist Lawrence Kohlberg (1974b), who observed the study, called it "a morally dubious experiment" (p. 42) because of its effect on the participants' moral sensibilities. Research like this, which is intrinsically deceptive, may add to knowledge, but at the cost of participants' right to know what they are getting involved in.

It may be that precautions regarding informed consent have gone so far as to work *against* a patient's welfare in some instances. In recent tests, a new plunger-like pump was proving more effective than traditional methods in restoring blood circulation immediately after cardiac arrest. But since the unconscious patients were in no position to give informed consent, the U.S. Food and Drug Administration discontinued the study, even though the technique appeared to boost survival and recovery rates significantly (Hurley, 1994).

Should adults be subjected to research that may harm their self-esteem? Studies on limits of memory, for example, have a built-in "failure factor": the researcher keeps asking questions until the participant cannot answer. Might this inevitable failure affect a participant's self-confidence? Might the publication of studies in which younger adults score higher than older adults create self-fulfilling prophecies, affecting societal expectations and older adults' performance?

What about the right to privacy? Is it ethical to use one-way mirrors and hidden cameras to observe people without their knowledge? How can we protect the confidentiality of personal information that participants may reveal in interviews or questionnaires (for example, about income or family relationships or even about illegal activities, such as smoking marijuana or shoplifting)?

Despite the stringent rules and vastly improved ethical climate that prevail today, specific situations often call for hard judgments. Everyone in the field of adult development and aging must accept the responsibility to try to do good and, at the very least, to do no harm.

SUMMARY

METATHEORIES

- A metatheory embraces theories and models with similar features in various branches of science. Scientists with different metatheoretical perspectives may study different problems, use different methods, and interpret data differently.

- Three important metatheories are the mechanistic, organismic, and contextual perspectives.

- The mechanistic perspective views behavior as machinelike and analyzes phenomena by breaking them down into simpler parts. Mechanists view development as quantitative and see aging as a time of decline. An example is information-processing theory.

- The organismic perspective views adults as organisms developing in a systematic, internally controlled order. Development occurs in a universal series of qualitative stages. An example is Erikson's theory of personality development.

- The contextual perspective views behavior as an ongoing act in a fluid context. Contextualists emphasize individual differences and see development as adaptive, as produced by interaction between the individual and the environment. Bühler's theory of setting goals and Sansone and Berg's "activated lifespace" model are examples.

- The lifespan developmental approach draws upon all three metatheories, particularly the contextual.

BASIC RESEARCH METHODS

- Research based on scientific method can draw valid, reliable conclusions about the world and its inhabitants.

- Random selection of a research sample can ensure external validity. Stratification of a random sample can ensure representation of subgroups within the population.

- Cross-cultural research can check for generalizability of experimental results from one culture to another.

- Forms of data collection include self-reports (diaries, structured or open-ended interviews, and questionnaires), tests and other behavioral measures, and naturalistic or laboratory observation. The value of self-reports is limited by subjectivity; the value of observation is limited by observer bias.

BASIC RESEARCH DESIGNS

- Three basic designs used in developmental research are case studies, correlational studies, and experiments.

- Only experiments can establish causal relationships. Case studies and correlational studies can provide hypotheses or predictions to be tested by experimental research.

- Experiments must be rigorously controlled so as to be valid and reliable. Random assignment of participants to experimental or control groups ensures internal validity.

- In laboratory experiments, researchers have full control and can isolate variables for study. However, controlled field experiments also can achieve internal validity.

- Natural experiments, which are actually correlational studies, may be useful in situations where true experiments would be impractical or unethical.

- To ensure construct validity, a researcher must precisely define the phenomenon being studied and should use more than one way to measure it.

QUASI-EXPERIMENTAL DESIGNS: THE PROBLEM OF INTERNAL VALIDITY

- Because age is beyond the researcher's control, most studies of age effects are quasi experiments, which present problems of internal validity.

- Cross-sectional designs confound age with cohort effects. Longitudinal studies confound age with time-of-measurement effects. Time-lag comparisons confound cohort with time of measurement. Sequential designs combine the simple quasi-experimental designs.

ETHICS OF RESEARCH

- Ethical issues in research on development include informed consent, deception, self-esteem, and privacy of participants.

KEY TERMS

▼

theory (page 38)
data (38)
quantitative development (39)
qualitative development (39)
metatheory (40)
model (40)
mechanistic perspective (40)
information-processing theory (41)
organismic perspective (42)
stage (42)
contextual perspective (44)
valid (46)
reliable (46)
scientific method (46)
external validity (46)
sample (46)
random selection (46)
random sample (46)
naturalistic observation (52)
laboratory observation (53)

observer bias (53)
case study (54)
correlational study (56)
experiment (57)
variables (57)
independent variable (58)
dependent variable (58)
treatment (58)
experimental group (58)
control group (58)
internal validity (59)
random assignment (59)
construct validity (60)
factorial invariance (61)
quasi experiment (61)
cross-sectional study (61)
cohort (62)
longitudinal study (63)
time-lag study (66)
sequential designs (67)

A sound mind in a sound body—these are prerequisites for a good life. If we want to understand adult development and aging, we need to look first at physical and intellectual changes that occur as people grow older.

Chapters 3 and 4 deal with the biology of aging. In Chapter 3, we start with basic questions about how long people live and why their bodies show signs of aging. We describe common changes in appearance, sensorimotor abilities, sexuality, and reproductive capacity. In Chapter 4, we focus on health. We describe typical changes in body systems that regulate breathing, blood circulation, bone growth, and immunity from disease, as well as in brain and nervous system. We suggest how adults of all ages can improve health and ward off life-threatening illnesses.

In Chapters 5 to 7, we turn our attention to the mind. In Chapter 5, we explain how memory works and how its functioning may change with age. In Chapter 6, we look at various ways of studying and measuring intelligence and creativity in adults. In Chapter 7, we discuss the emergence of mature thought patterns, and we examine moral development across the adult lifespan.

"A sound mind in a sound body" is a worthy goal. Reading these chapters may make it easier for you to achieve that goal as you age, and to help others achieve it.

PART TWO

THE WORLDS OF BODY AND MIND

CHAPTER 3

LONGEVITY AND PHYSIOLOGICAL AGING

**LIFESPAN AND
THE AGING PROCESS**
Trends in Life Expectancy
How Far Can the Human Lifespan
  Be Extended?
Quality versus Quantity of Life
Theories of Biological Aging
Predicting Individual Longevity

PHYSICAL APPEARANCE

SENSORIMOTOR FUNCTIONING
Vision
Hearing
Taste and Smell
Touch, Pain, and Temperature
Motor Functions

**SEXUAL AND REPRODUCTIVE
FUNCTIONING**
The Female Reproductive System
The Male Reproductive System
Sexuality and Aging

BOXES
3-1 The Cutting Edge: Can We Push Out
    the Boundaries of Life?
3-2 The Art of Aging: New Ways to
    Better Vision and Hearing
3-3 The Multicultural Context: Japanese
    Women's Experience of Menopause

Don't try to live forever. You will not succeed.

George Bernard Shaw, preface to *The Doctor's Dilemma*

FOCUS: MARTHA GRAHAM

("The Swirl" © Barbara Morgan,
Martha Graham "Letter to the World")

Martha Graham,[*] who is considered the mother of contemporary dance, was a legend in her time. She lived through most of the twentieth century and almost singlehandedly "gave dance a new vocabulary" by daring to express "the starkest . . . truth of the body" (Shapiro, 1991, p. 77). Her motto was "Movement never lies."

Physically, she did not fit the usual image of a dancer. No more than 5 feet 3 inches tall, she was no beauty and was slightly overweight when she became a student of the famous dancer Ruth St. Denis and her husband, Ted Shawn, in Los Angeles. Unlike most serious dancers, who begin studying at an early age, Graham was then in her early twenties and had little or no previous training. "My people were strict religionists who felt that dancing was a sin," she once explained (McDonagh, 1973, p. 13). Ferociously determined, within 3 years she was dancing solos. For the next 4 years she was a leading dancer with the Denishawn company and then on Broadway.

Beginning with her first independent recital in New York City at age 31, Graham gradually unveiled her own revolutionary style. Baring her feet and her feelings, she broke all the graceful rules and illusions of ballet and "pulled the art of dance right down to the floor" (Shapiro, 1991, p. 77). Her body communicated raw emotion. Taking natural biological rhythms as inspiration, she translated the breathing process into sharp, wrenching movements of contraction and release.

[*]Sources for biographical information about Martha Graham are Armitage (1966), De Mille (1991), Duffy (1991), Friedan (1994), Graham (1954, 1991), Leabo (1962), McDonagh (1973), Seibert (1991), Shapiro (1991), Stodelle (1984), and "Tribute" (1991).

Many critics condemned Graham's work. Like abstract art, it was jolting and often misunderstood. As John Martin, a critic for *The New York Times* said, "She does the unforgivable thing for a dancer to do—she makes you think" (Martin, 1937, cited in Armitage, 1966, p. 8). But young dancers flocked to study with her. By the 1930s she had assembled her own troupe and was creating such masterpieces as "Primitive Mysteries," for which she took 23 curtain calls. Her influence extended beyond dance. Bette Davis, Richard Boone, Eli Wallach, Gregory Peck, Joanne Woodward, Woody Allen, Tony Randall, and Madonna were among the actors who studied body movement with her.

Among her severest detractors, early on, were her former mentors at the Denishawn studio. One woman (reportedly either St. Denis or one of her friends) said, "Martha, this is simply dreadful. How long do you expect to keep this up?"

"As long as I have an audience," Graham replied.

Sure enough, when she passed 60 she was still going strong, touring Europe and Asia. Despite advancing arthritis and the advice of friends and critics, she did not stop performing until after her seventy-fourth birthday.

For this woman, ever determined to make her body do her bidding, giving up dancing was like giving up life itself. But after a physical and emotional collapse, she returned to work as a choreographer and teacher, passing on her living legacy to a new generation. At age 91, she said, "The body is your instrument in dance, but your art is outside that creature, the body. I don't leap or jump anymore. I look at young dancers, and I am envious, more aware of what glories the body contains. But sensitivity is not made dull by age" (Friedan, 1994, p. 609). At 96, she premiered her 180th work, "Maple Leaf Gala"—a jazzlike piece unlike anything she had done before.

Six months later, Martha Graham lost a bout with pneumonia. At the time, she was working on a new piece, which she predicted would be her swan song. "I . . . believe in the . . . continuity of life and of energy," she wrote shortly before her death (1991, p. 276). "I am sure it [the new work] will be a terror and a joy . . . and I will feel that I have failed a hundred times and try to dodge those inevitable footsteps behind me. But what is there for me but to go on? That is life for me. My life."

Martha Graham, who as a young adult overrode her physical limitations and lack of early training and defied convention in the world of dance, also defied conventional expectations for physical performance in late life. But even Graham ultimately had to come to terms with the truth of her aging body. When she stopped dancing but continued to choreograph, she learned to model her creations after other people's bodies rather than her own—an adjustment consistent with the lifespan developmental approach, which holds that gains occur along with losses throughout life. Today, with medical advances allowing many people to live longer and better than at any previous time in human history, more and more ordinary adults are defying age by running marathons, lifting weights, climbing mountains, playing competitive sports, and living active and productive lives through their eighties and beyond.

In this chapter and Chapter 4, we look at physical development throughout adulthood. We start with influences on length of life and theories of why bodies age. We describe physiological changes often associated with aging: gradual changes in appearance, sensory and motor abilities, and sexual and reproductive capacities. In Chapter 4, we discuss changes in internal body systems and factors that contribute to health and disease.

LIFESPAN AND THE AGING PROCESS

▼

How long will I live? Why do I have to grow old? Would I want to live forever? Human beings have been wondering about these questions for thousands of years.

The first question involves two different but related concepts: *life expectancy,* the age to which a person born at a certain time and place is statistically likely to live; and *longevity,* how long a particular person actually does live. Life expectancy is based on the average longevity, or lifespan, of members of a population. The second question expresses an age-old theme: a yearning for a fountain or potion of youth. Behind this yearning is a fear, not so much of chronological age, as of biological aging: loss of health and physical powers. Similarly, the third question expresses a concern not just with how long but with how well we live.

TRENDS IN LIFE EXPECTANCY

Today, most people can expect to grow old, often very old. In 1993, life expectancy for a baby born in the United States was nearly 75.4 years, a 60 percent increase since 1900 (Wegman, 1992; "Wellness Facts," 1995). Such longevity is unprecedented in the history of humankind (see Figure 3-1). By the year 2040, life expectancy at birth is predicted to be 83 for women and 75 for men, as compared with 79 for women and 72 for men in 1991 (Schneider & Guralnik, 1990; U.S. Bureau of the Census, 1995). And the longer people live, the longer they are likely to live. Americans who make it to age 65 today can expect to reach 82— about 6½ years more than the life expectancy of people born today (U.S. Bureau of the Census, 1995).

The gain in life expectancy during the twentieth century was due largely to a dramatic reduction in deaths during infancy and from childhood disease. In 1900, 1 in 5 white children and 1 in 3 children of other races died before age 5, and only 41 percent of newborns could be expected to survive to age 65. In 1990, 80 percent could be expected to live that long (U.S. Bureau of the Census, 1992c). Also contributing to increased life expectancy are reduced deaths in young adulthood, particularly during childbirth, and new treatments for many once-fatal illnesses. Worldwide, life expectancy has risen 41 percent since 1950—from 46 years to 65—with the largest increases in developing countries, where a 54 percent rise is credited to dramatic increases in health care, including childhood immunizations, as well as improvements in food production and sanitation (Worldwatch Institute, 1994).

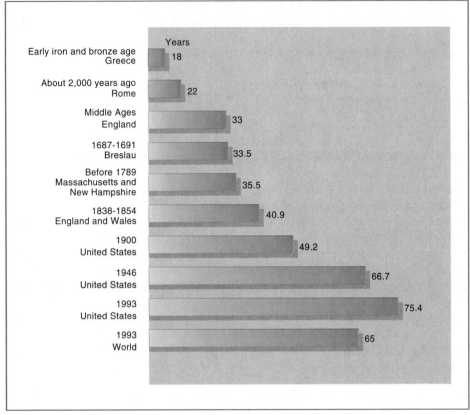

FIGURE 3-1

Changes in life expectancy from ancient to modern times.

(Source: Adapted from Katchadourian, 1987; 1993 data from "Wellness Facts," 1995, and Worldwatch Institute, 1994.)

Race and gender are factors in life expectancy. On average, white Americans live about 4 years longer than nonwhite Americans, and women (including non-white women) live about 7 years longer than men (U.S. Bureau of the Census, 1992b; Wegman, 1992). Because of this gender gap in life expectancy, women are more likely to face problems that may accompany old age.

Along with the increase in life expectancy have come a decrease in deaths from childbirth and infectious disease and a rise in deaths from conditions related to age. Despite progress in staving off the terminal effects of cancer and heart disease, these remain the most common causes of death in later years (Cassel, 1992). If cancer were eliminated as a cause of death, the average lifespan would be increased by somewhat less than 2 years. If we could eliminate deaths due to heart disease, we would add 5 years to life expectancy at age 65 and would greatly increase the proportion of the population age 65 and older (USDHHS, 1991).

HOW FAR CAN THE HUMAN LIFESPAN BE EXTENDED?

In 1986, a Japanese man named Shirechiyo Izumi died of pneumonia at age 120; in March 1995, Jeanne Calment of Arles, in France, had just reached 120. As far as we know, theirs are the longest authentically documented human lives. Many gerontologists long maintained that 110 to 120 years was the upper limit of human longevity—just as the upper limit for dogs is about 20 and for tortoises, 150 (NIA, 1993). Today, however, scientists are reconsidering the idea of a fixed limit of life. Is it possible for a human being to live to 130, 150, or even 200? With continued medical progress, is there any limit to how long people could live?

At least part of the key to the maximum lifespan for each species appears to be in the *genes*, bits of deoxyribonucleic acid (DNA), strung on chromosomes, which govern the inherited characteristics of every living thing. DNA carries the "program"—unique to each individual—that tells each cell what functions to perform and how.

Leonard Hayflick (1974) studied cells of various animals and found a limit on the number of times a cell would divide—about 50 times for human cells; this is called the *Hayflick limit.* Since then, researchers have demonstrated that regulation of cell division is a genetically *dominant* trait (one that is expressed even if an opposing trait is present). It is controlled by a small number of genes, one of which has been found on a specific human chromosome (Schneider, 1992). Thus, there seems to be a biological clock that limits the lifespan of human cells and therefore of human life. According to Hayflick, if all diseases and causes of death were eliminated, humans would remain healthy until about 110 years of age.

(N'Guyen Tien/Gamma Liaison)

Jeanne Calment of Arles, France, is one of the only two human beings known to have lived to age 120, widely believed to be the limit of the human lifespan. (The other was Shigechiyo Izumi of Japan, who died in 1986.) Calment, now the oldest living human being, reached 120 in March 1995. Scientists are investigating whether human beings could live significantly longer.

BOX 3-1

THE CUTTING EDGE

Can We Push Out the Boundaries of Life?

A 100-year-old man was asked, "What can people do to help them live as long as you have?" The centenarian thought for a moment and then responded, "Well, first make sure that you don't die."

Are there ways to slow down the aging process and delay death? The novelist Tom Robbins, in *Jitterbug Perfume* (1984), gives some fanciful but research-based answers to that question. The novel revolves around two characters who find a way to live hundreds of years without aging. Their secret is based on principles related to the four ancient "elements": *air* (breathing deeply and steadily), *fire* (frequent sex), *water* (hot baths, followed by cooling off), and *earth* (eating small portions and fasting periodically). To what extent does research support Robbins's four points?

The first life-extending technique, deep and rhythmic breathing, is supposed to lessen the ravages of stress and of free radicals produced during the metabolism of oxygen, which damage cell tissue. The characters in *Jitterbug Perfume* believe that proper breathing will reduce the level of free radicals in the body. Research to support that idea is scanty or inconclusive. However, deep, rhythmic breathing *is* widely used in yoga and other meditation or relaxation techniques to ward off stress. And stress (as we discuss in Chapter 4) is a special threat to older adults.

As for the second life-extending technique, frequent sexual intercourse, most research has found a direct relationship between sexual activity and health; and people who are sexually active in middle age are more likely to remain sexually active in old age (Katchadourian, 1987). But can sexual activity actually lengthen the normal lifespan? Such an effect is not well-documented—though perhaps the emotional aspects of a healthy sex life with a willing and understanding partner create psychological

(Laima Druskis/Stock, Boston)

Deep, rhythmic breathing—used in yoga and other relaxation exercises—is one of four possible life-extending techniques explored in Tom Robbins's novel Jitterbug Perfume *(1984).*

benefits, such as reduced stress, which might influence longevity.

In an aging body, the autoimmune system tends to attack the body's own cells because it confuses them with invading organisms (see Chapter 4). The third life-extension technique is based on the belief that a sudden contrast between hot and cold will check this tendency by cooling the blood and decreasing body tempera-

BOX 3-1

CONTINUED

ture. Accordingly, the technique consists of a series of hot baths, each followed by getting out and cooling off. However, no research as yet supports this idea.

That leaves Robbins's fourth technique: eating less. Here he may be on somewhat firmer ground. As reported in this chapter, drastically reducing the caloric intake of rodents, fish, worms, and other species, while giving them necessary vitamins and other nutrients, dramatically increases their lifespan while they retain youthful appearance and health. However, there is no evidence—so far—that dietary restriction will extend life in humans or other longer-lived animals.

Roy Walford, one of the researchers responsible for caloric-restriction research on rats, is conducting a similar experiment on himself. Starting in the early 1980s, Walford (1983, 1986) has cut his average daily food intake to 1,500 to 2,000

calories (largely vegetables and grains), as compared with 2,500 for the average man, and has reduced his weight by 25 percent. He eats no more than 15 percent fat and 25 percent protein and takes a long list of vitamin and mineral supplements, including antioxidants to combat free radicals. He runs, swims, and lifts weights to keep in good physical shape.

"There is no doubt at all that the life span of animals can be extended by more than 50 percent by dietary means, corresponding to humans living to be 150 or 160 years old," Walford has written (1986, p. 18). He has predicted that people who adopt a lifestyle like his might double their remaining life expectancy (Angier, 1990) while retaining more youthful appearance and vigor (Weindruch & Walford, 1988). Born in 1925, Walford hopes to continue his experiement until 2065, when, if his hypothesis is borne out, he will have lived to be 140.

Then the cellular clock would run out and they would die, much as the biological clock that controls the female menstrual cycle turns off, typically between ages 45 and 55.

Recent research calls that idea into question. Researchers are currently isolating genes that affect longevity in yeast, worms, and fruit flies. A mutant gene has been identified that extends the lifespan of roundworms by 60 percent—from 26 days to 60—while they remain biologically young (T. E. Johnson, 1990). Fruit flies have been selectively bred to nearly double their normal lifespan (Rose, cited in NIA, 1993).

Perhaps the most promising line of research is on dietary restriction (see Box 3-1). Rats fed 35 to 40 percent fewer calories than usual (along with all necessary vitamins and other nutrients) live as much as 50 percent longer than other laboratory rodents (about 1,500 days as compared with 1,000 days). The reduction in caloric intake seems to delay age-related decline in the ability to fight disease (Weindruch & Walford, 1988). It has been suggested that dietary restriction merely simulates natural feeding patterns, and that these rats live no longer than they would in the wild (Schneider, 1992). But a reduced diet has also been found to extend life in worms and fish—in fact, in virtually all species on which it has been tried (Weindruch & Walford, 1988).

What, if anything, might such research tell us about the human lifespan? Studies of caloric restriction in monkeys and other nonhuman primates are not yet complete; and, so far, there has been no similar, systematic research on humans—though one investigator is trying such a diet on himself (Box 3-1). Nor does there appear to be a simple relationship between diet and longevity in human beings; people who are underweight, as well as those who are overweight, tend to die early (Schneider, 1992).

Some gerontologists point to other evidence for potential lengthening of the human lifespan. Computer studies of death patterns among Danish twins and among genetically identical strains of fruit flies suggest that most deaths result from accidents or disease rather than from old age. Death rates for people over 85 in Sweden have dropped dramatically in the past 50 years (Barinaga, 1991, 1992). Death rates among the "oldest old" have also decreased in the United States and probably will continue to do so as better-educated cohorts, who tend to stay healthier, grow old (U.S. Bureau of the Census, 1992a).

FIGURE 3-2

Survival curves show the percentage of persons born in the United States in selected years who survived, or are expected to survive, to each age. Survival curves have become increasingly "rectangularized" as life expectancy has increased owing to medical advances. But while a larger percentage of the population is surviving to more advanced ages, the curves still drop to zero by about age 100, suggesting that there may be a genetically determined limit to human life. (SOURCE: Katchadourian, 1987.)

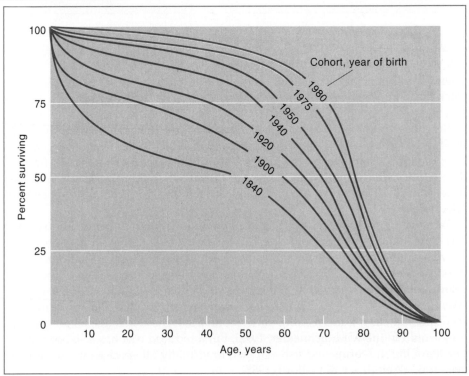

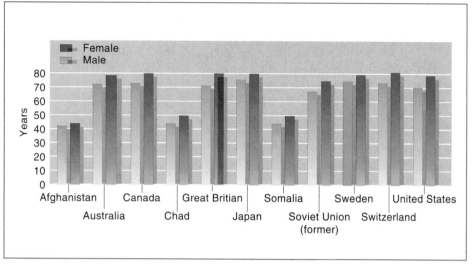

FIGURE 3-3

People in wealthy, industrialized countries, such as Switzerland and Japan, live longer than people in developing countries, such as Afghanistan and Somalia, where more people die prematurely of infectious diseases, starvation, and other ailments. But there is little variance in life expectancy among industrialized countries. For example, the Japanese (who have a low-fat diet) and the Swiss (who eat a good deal of fat) have virtually the same life expectancy—suggesting that there may be a limit to the life-extending potential of diet, health care, and other lifestyle factors.

Still, historical changes in **survival curves**—percentages of people who live to various ages—suggest that there may be a definite limit to human life regardless of health and fitness. Although more and more Americans are living longer, the curves still end around the century mark, suggesting that no matter how healthy people remain throughout adulthood, the lifespan will not go much above 100 (see Figure 3-2). Internationally, average life expectancies in industrialized countries hover between 75 and 79, despite differences in diet and lifestyle (see Figure 3-3).

It seems unlikely, then, that people will someday live forever, or even high into the hundreds. Still, the new life-extension research does suggest that many deaths even in the oldest old are preventable and that life expectancy may well continue to rise, possibly to about 90 or 100.

QUALITY VERSUS QUANTITY OF LIFE

Eos, a mythological goddess, asked Zeus to allow Tithonus, the mortal she loved, to live forever. Zeus granted Tithonus immortality, and the lovers lived happily—for a while. Then Tithonus grew older and older until he became so infirm that he could not move. Yet he was denied the gift of death. Eos had made a grievous error; she had forgotten to ask Zeus to grant Tithonus eternal youth along with eternal life.

If we could find ways to extend human life, should we? The myth of Eos and Tithonus dramatizes the importance of quality of life. In recognition of the tragedy of life too long extended, the motto of the Gerontological Society of America is: "To add life to years, not just years to life." The goal of research is not just to lengthen life but also to lengthen the vigorous and productive years. Eradication of cancer and heart disease might increase the number of people living with such infirmities as arthritis and dementia (Cassel, 1992).

Even if science conquers all diseases and all older adults stay healthy until they reach their genetically predetermined end, will society have a place for all of them? For this to happen, social changes on a massive scale would have to occur. To encourage older people to keep on working, so as not to put an impossible burden on younger generations, we might need to reduce pensions, create flexible work times, and change societal attitudes toward older people in the workplace. Only a thriving economy could support such an expansion of the work force. Such social changes might be "a greater challenge than unlocking the biological mysteries" of longevity and aging (Cassel, 1992, p. 63).

THEORIES OF BIOLOGICAL AGING

Questions of longevity and quality of life are intimately connected with what happens to our bodies as we age. A typical young adult is a fine physical specimen. Strength, energy, agility, endurance, and health are at their peak. The senses are sharpest, and body systems work at top efficiency. From young adulthood through midlife, physical losses are typically so small and so gradual as to be barely noticed. But as people age, their physical differences increase. The onset of *senescence*—the period of the lifespan marked by obvious declines in body functioning generally associated with aging—varies greatly. One 80-year-old man can hear every word of a whispered conversation; another cannot hear the doorbell. One 70-year-old woman runs marathons; another cannot walk around the block.

Why does senescence come earlier for some people than for others? For that matter, why do people age biologically at all? Most theories about biological aging fall into two general categories: *genetic-programming theories* and *variable-rate theories* (see Table 3-1).

Genetic-Programming Theories

Genetic-programming theories hold that bodies age according to a normal developmental timetable built into the genes. Since each species has its own life expectancy and pattern of aging, this pattern must be predetermined and inborn, subject to only minor modifications.

Genetic-programming theory is consistent with the idea of a genetically decreed maximum lifespan. Hayflick's (1981) suggestion that human cells in a laboratory culture go through the same aging process as within the body implies that environmental influences play little or no role in aging (Gerhard & Cristofalo, 1992) and that the human body, like a machine, is biologically programmed to fail at a certain point, even if kept in tiptop condition. Failure may come through *programmed senescence*, in which specific genes "switch off" at times

TABLE 3-1 THEORIES OF BIOLOGICAL AGING	
Genetic-Programming Theories	*Variable-Rate Theories*
Programmed senescence. Aging is the result of the sequential switching on and off of certain genes, with senescence being defined as the time when age-associated deficits are manifested.	*Wear and tear.* Cells and tissues have vital parts that wear out.
	Free radicals. Accumulated damage caused by oxygen radicals causes cells and eventually organs to stop functioning.
Endocrine theory. Biological clocks act through hormones to control the pace of aging.	*Rate of living.* The greater an organism's rate of oxygen basal metabolism, the shorter its lifespan.
Immunological theory. A programmed decline in immune system functions leads to an increased vulnerability to infectious disease and thus to aging and death.	*Error catastrophe.* Damage to mechanisms that synthesize proteins results in faulty proteins, which accumulate to a level that causes catastrophic damage to cells, tissues, and organs.
	Somatic mutation. Genetic mutations occur and accumulate with increasing age, causing cells to deteriorate and malfunction.
	Crosslinking. An accumulation of crosslinked proteins damages cells and tissues, slowing down bodily processes.

Source: Adapted from NIH/NIA, 1993, p. 2.

when age-related losses (for example, in vision, hearing, and motor control) become evident. Or the biological clock may act through genes which control *hormonal changes,* or which cause problems in the *immune system,* leaving the body vulnerable to infectious disease.

A variant of genetic-programming theory is that genes are programmed to enable humans to live long enough to reproduce. Like a booster stage, which has no further function after putting a satellite into orbit and eventually burns out, adults may continue to live past the childbearing years, but the genetic program no longer can help them and may even hurt.

If genes control aging, could tinkering with the genetic program overcome programmed biological declines and extend life? We need to remember that genetic control of a biological process can be extremely complex. Approximately 200 genes seem to be involved in regulating human aging (Schneider, 1992), with specific genes controlling different processes, such as those in the endocrine and immune systems. *Gene therapy* (replacement or insertion of genes to correct a defect, improve functioning, or delay senescence) has been used successfully to treat a disease caused by the genetically induced lack of a particular enzyme produced by cells of the immune system (Freeman, Whartenby, & Abraham, 1992). Such therapy, while unlikely to change the *maximum* lifespan, could increase the *average* lifespan (Gerhard & Cristofalo, 1992).

Variable-Rate Theories

Variable-rate theories, sometimes called *error theories,* view aging as a result of processes that vary from person to person and are influenced by both the internal and the external environments. In most variable-rate theories, aging involves damage due to chance errors in, or environmental assaults on, people's biological systems. Other variable-rate theories focus on internal processes such as metabolism (the process by which the body turns food and oxygen into energy), which may more directly and continuously influence the rate of aging (NIA, 1993; Schneider, 1992).

Wear-and-tear theory holds that the body ages as a result of accumulated damage to the system, like a car that develops one problem after another as its parts wear out. This wearing-out process occurs more swiftly under stress. Today, most theorists do not believe that normal wear and tear is an adequate explanation for aging. For one thing, a human being (unlike a car) is capable of self-repair and can compensate for damage to the system.

Free-radical theory focuses on the harmful effects of *free radicals*—highly unstable molecules formed during metabolism, which react with and can damage cell membranes, cell proteins, fats, carbohydrates, and even DNA. Damage from free radicals accumulates with age and has been associated with such diverse diseases as arthritis, muscular dystrophy, cataracts, and cancer (Stadtman, 1992). It has been suggested that defective molecules (possibly the result of injury induced by free radicals) may cause late-onset diabetes and neurological disorders such as Parkinson's disease (Wallace, 1992). "Antioxidant" supplements of vitamins C and E and beta-carotene are popularly believed to stop free-radical activity, but research on their effects is inconclusive. Also, it is not clear whether accumulation of free radicals (or other "errors") is a *cause* or an *effect* of aging.

Rate-of-living theory suggests that the body can do just so much work, and that's all; the faster it works, the faster it wears out. According to this theory, speed of metabolism determines length of life. For example, fish whose metabolism is lowered by putting them in cooler water live longer than they would in warm water (Schneider, 1992). The research on dietary restriction in rodents also appears to support this theory. A low-calorie diet seems to temper the long-term harmful effects of glucose, or blood sugar (including free-radical formation), and lower the rate of metabolism (Masoro, 1985).

Error-catastrophe theory and *somatic-mutation theory* are based on the fact that as body cells divide, errors (destruction or changes in cellular structure) occur. External and internal stressors, such as exposure to toxic substances and ultraviolet light, may alter the composition of cells and tissues in the brain, liver, and other organs; and as they grow older, they are less able to repair themselves. Eventually, according to this theory, an accumulation of these erroneous occurrences causes deterioration of body parts, malfunctioning, and death.

Cross-linking theory attributes errors to bonds, or links, that form between cellular proteins. For example, cross-linking of the protein collagen makes the skin less flexible. There is some recent evidence that high levels of blood sugar, as in diabetes, cross-link proteins in the lens of the eye and in the kidneys and blood vessels, causing disease (Schneider, 1992).

Comparing Genetic-Programming and Variable-Rate Theories

If human beings are programmed to age at a certain rate, they can do little to retard the process except, perhaps, look for controlling genes and attempt to alter them. But if aging is variable, then lifestyle and health practices may influence it.

Variable-rate theories seem better able to explain the wide variations in physiological aging. It may be, though, that each of these perspectives offers part of the truth. Genetic programming may limit the maximum length of life, but environmental and lifestyle factors may affect how closely a person approaches the maximum and in what condition. For example, people who limit their exposure to the sun may be able to minimize wrinkling and avoid skin cancer.

Some gerontologists make a distinction between *primary* and *secondary* aging. **Primary aging** is a gradual, inevitable process of bodily deterioration that begins early in life and continues through the years. **Secondary aging** consists of results of disease, abuse, and disuse—factors that are often avoidable and within people's control (Busse, 1987; Horn & Meer, 1987). By eating sensibly and keeping physically fit, many older adults can and do stave off secondary effects of aging.

PREDICTING INDIVIDUAL LONGEVITY

Is it possible to predict how long a particular person—you, for example—will live? Life insurance companies make such predictions when they set premium rates on the basis of variables that appear to be correlated with longevity. For example, before the practice was outlawed as discriminatory, men generally paid higher rates than women because women tend to live longer.

Good health is positively correlated with long life. So are exercise, nutrition, education, intelligence, socioeconomic status, satisfaction with work, long-lived parents and grandparents, a positive attitude toward life, and the ability to cope with adversity. Variables that are negatively correlated with long life include being overweight, poor, illiterate, chronically ill, or unmarried; smoking; bearing children after age 35; and having high blood pressure, many children, psychiatric disturbances such as schizophrenia or depression, or a family history of diseases such as cancer or diabetes (Botwinick, 1984).

But while these variables predict life expectancy for certain classes of people, they cannot predict an individual's lifespan. Furthermore, correlational analyses cannot tell us what *causes* long life. The fact that it tends to run in families, for example, doesn't indicate whether the cause is hereditary, environmental, or both. Some predictors of longevity tend to cluster together. People with high-paying jobs are also likely to have higher education and income and better access to medical care than people with low-paying jobs. But do any of these factors actually cause people to live longer? Again, we don't know.

Some scientists, in an attempt to identify biological processes that actually determine an individual lifespan, are searching for **biomarkers** of aging: specific, universally valid measures of biological age. No single biomarker is likely to predict a person's lifespan. Investigators look for a *set* of physical attributes, such as lung capacity, size of heart, strength of grip, and reaction time, which together may be reasonably accurate in predicting how long a person has left to live (Sprott & Roth, 1992; Walford, 1986). Most of the data collected so far have been cross-sectional and therefore cannot measure changes in the same individual. Longitudinal studies of various physiological changes in nonhuman primates are now in progress.

Although it would be premature to draw any conclusions, at least two possible biomarkers seem to be good candidates: declines in immune system functioning and in blood levels of the hormone dehydroepiandrosterone (DHEA), which is produced by the adrenal glands (Sprott & Roth, 1992). Most 70-year-olds have only one-tenth as much DHEA as they did at 25 (August, 1995). Researchers are experimenting with giving DHEA in pill form; this will probably not lengthen life but may help people avoid some unpleasant effects of aging, such as discomfort in the joints and sleeping less soundly (Jaroff, 1995).

Keep in mind that biomarkers of aging and biomarkers of longevity are not necessarily the same. For example, a widely observed drop in cognitive functioning before death (see Chapters 6 and 13) may indicate that a person will soon die but not how rapidly the body is aging (Sprott & Roth, 1992). And increasing the length of life is not identical with increasing the length of time the body remains biologically young. Still, in research on caloric restriction, the long-lived rodents do appear to maintain their vitality and to develop age-related diseases later than normal.

We are a long way from being able to point to biological markers that can accurately predict an individual human lifespan. Even if scientists succeed in finding these markers, to what use should such information be put? Would it affect the cost and availability of health insurance and pension benefits? Would you want to know how long you are likely to live? Would that knowledge change the way you live?

PHYSICAL APPEARANCE

▼

There is no "typical adult." At any age, adults come in many sizes and shapes. They differ in strength, stamina, and other physical abilities. They have different lifestyles. Their body systems age at different rates, and their health varies. Outward appearance also varies; a 30-year-old may look more like 40, and some older adults look middle-aged. Still, we can sketch changes in physical appearance that typically take place with age—changes that can affect how adults are treated and how they feel about themselves.

Young adults normally have smooth, taut skin, and their hair has color, fullness, and sheen. Today's 20-year-olds tend to be taller than their parents because of a *secular trend* in growth that has taken place during the past century in developed countries. Young people in the United States, western Europe, and Japan reach adult height and sexual maturity earlier than in past generations, apparently because of better nourishment and health care (Chumlea, 1982; Eveleth & Tanner, 1976).

Most young adults are quite appearance-conscious. The ideal of a slim, lean physique fuels the diet industry and fosters such eating disorders as anorexia (self-starvation) and bulimia (binging and purging). Still, many young adults are too fat; the risk of being overweight, which threatens not only appearance but health, is highest from ages 25 to 34 (Williamson, Kahn, Remington, & Anda, 1990). (We discuss diet, obesity, and exercise in Chapter 4.)

"Middle age," said the comedian Bob Hope, "is when your age starts to show around your middle." Especially in men who lead sedentary lives, middle-age spread increases markedly until about age 55 to 60, as fat replaces muscle. Habitual facial expressions set into "character" lines (Katchadourian, 1987).

By late adulthood, physical changes become more obvious. The skin tends to become paler and splotchier; it takes on a parchmentlike texture, loses elasticity, and hangs in folds and wrinkles. Varicose veins of the legs are more common. In both men and women, the hair on the head turns white and becomes thinner, and sometimes it sprouts in new places—on a woman's chin, or out of a man's ears. People may become shorter as the disks between their spinal vertebrae atrophy, and they may look even smaller because of stooped posture. In some women a thinning of the bone (see Chapter 4) may cause a "widow's hump" at the back of the neck.

Because our society places a premium on youth, middle-aged and older adults spend a great deal of time, effort, and money trying to maintain a youthful appearance. Although many "anti-aging" treatments are useless, emollient creams and lotions offer temporary improvement in skin tone and moisture. Alpha hydroxy acid products may soften skin and fade "age spots" and freckles. Sunscreens can protect against harmful ultraviolet rays (Brumberg, 1993).

(Susan Lapides/Design Conceptions)

Facial lines and wrinkles, coarser skin texture, and thinning hair are typical in middle age. Because of our society's premium on youth, some adults expend much time, money, and energy on anti-aging treatments. Others manage to accept changes in appearance without loss of self-esteem.

The popularity of such treatments is an indication of the widespread desire to hide the appearance of aging. If your "ideal self" has the body of a 20-year-old, then with each passing year it takes more and more effort—whether by cosmetics, by plastic surgery, or by taking a young lover—to deny what is occurring. Self-esteem suffers when people devalue their physical being. But even in the face of powerful social forces that reinforce a worship of youth, many adults can and do learn to accept the changes taking place in themselves.

SENSORIMOTOR FUNCTIONING

From the mid-twenties until about age 50, changes in sensory and motor capacities are gradual and generally almost imperceptible—until one day a 45-year-old man realizes that he cannot read the telephone directory without eyeglasses, or a 55-year-old woman has to admit that she is not as quick on her feet as she was. Still, most middle-aged people compensate well. And although sensorimotor abilities typically decline in late adulthood, there is much individual variation.

Most aging adults do worry about sensory losses. And no wonder! From the ring of the alarm clock and the aroma of freshly brewed coffee to the softness of the pillow as we shut our eyes at night, our senses are the primary means by which we know our world. Many people also regret declines in muscular strength, endurance, coordination, and reaction time.

Because sensorimotor abilities are the outcome of a complex series of processes involving the nervous system, they may be affected by developmental changes in that system (discussed in Chapter 4). It may take longer for the brain to assess a situation and decide what to do. Slowed reflex responses can result in accidental injuries. Slowed information processing can result in requests to repeat information that has been presented too quickly or not clearly enough. Remember, though, as we describe changes typical with advancing age,[*] that each person has a unique level of ability in each area of sensory and motor activity.

VISION

Ted Williams, a baseball player who is in the Hall of Fame, gave a batting exhibition when he was middle-aged. At that time, it is said, he could still see with the naked eye exactly where his bat met a spinning fast ball when he hit it.

As with all aspects of aging, there are great individual differences in visual ability. Some people in their eighties or older do not need glasses, while some young adults do. Most age-related visual problems occur in five areas: dynamic vision (reading moving signs), near vision, sensitivity to light, visual search (for example, locating a sign), and speed of processing visual information (Kline et al., 1992; Kosnick, Winslow, Kline, Rasinski, & Sekuler, 1988). Corrective lenses or medical or surgical treatment—including some new technologies (see Box 3-2 and Figure 3-4)—can often help people with moderate visual problems.

---

[*]The discussion of sensory changes in the following sections is based largely on Spence (1989).

(Susan Lapides/Design Conceptions)

Sensorimotor abilities, such as riding a bicycle, are the outcome of complex processes involving the nervous system. Each person has a unique level of ability in each area of sensory and motor activity, and even a person with a disability may develop ways to compensate so as to pursue a favorite activity.

Changes in Eye Structure and Function

Aging usually brings a loss of *visual acuity,* ability to distinguish detail. Visual acuity, which is measured when you look at an eye chart in the doctor's office or when you apply for a driver's license, is keenest at about age 20 and begins to decline by about age 50. By age 85, some adults have lost as much as 80 percent of the visual acuity they had in young adulthood.

Dynamic visual acuity is the ability to see moving objects clearly. This ability—even more than acuity for stationary objects—declines with age. Thus information presented in motion, such as credits scrolled down or across a movie or television screen, is much harder for older adults to follow than for younger adults (Kline & Schieber, 1985).

Probably the most common visual problem after about age 40 is a form of far-sightedness called *presbyopia,* which makes many people put on reading glasses. Presbyopia stems from structural changes in the lens of the eye. The lens, unlike most body structures, keeps growing throughout life. As new cells accumulate on the outer part of the lens, the older lens fibers (cells) are squeezed together and pushed toward the center. By age 70, the lens may be at least 3 times thicker than it was originally. Meanwhile, it hardens, flattens, and becomes less elastic—less

BOX 3-2

THE ART OF AGING

New Ways to Better Vision and Hearing

Recent advances in technology have made possible new surgical treatments for nearsightedness, astigmatism, and cataracts and new methods to aid hearing.

Vision

Radial keratotomy (RK) is a surgical technique designed to correct *myopia,* or nearsightedness. The best candidates for RK are 30- to 50-year-olds with mild or moderate overcurvature of the cornea, the outer surface of the eye, which works together with the lens to focus images on the retina (see Figure 3-4). Surgeons make three to sixteen precise microscopic incisions in the cornea to flatten it, allowing images to be projected directly onto the retina rather than in front of it. The surgery takes only 5 to 10 minutes per eye, and only topical anesthesia (eye drops) or local anesthesia is needed. Many patients experience only mild pain, if any, afterward. Although the goal is 20/20 vision, the outcome may fall short of that. About 75 to 95 percent of patients end up with 20/40 eyesight, good enough for a driver's license. There is some controversy about long-term effects, as longitudinal data are sparse so far. The surgery does weaken the eye and make it more injury-prone; and cataracts may be harder to treat (Brint, Nordan, & Herman, 1991; "Surgery," 1994).

An even newer technique still in the investigational stage is the use of lasers to "sculpture" the cornea to correct nearsightedness, farsightedness, or *astigmatism* (blurry vision due to uneven curvature of the cornea). Laser treatment is less harmful to eye tissue but may cause more postoperative pain, and improvement in eyesight may not show up as quickly ("Surgery," 1994).

Corrective surgery for cataracts is now commonplace. Various surgical techniques are used to remove the clouded lens and replace it with an artificial one. Because the stitches required to close the incision made in the bag holding the cornea may cause astigmatism, a one-stitch (or no-stitch) method is gaining popularity. A tiny probe emits an ultrasound wave, which shatters the lens into fine particles. These are vacuumed out through the incision, which is only 3 to 4 millimeters long. The old lens is replaced with a flexible lens that is rolled up and propelled into the eye. Once in place, the new lens unfolds to its proper shape. Only one stitch is needed to close the incision; in some cases the eye seals itself, requiring no stitches at all. This technique lessens the chances of resulting astigmatism, and patients apparently see better sooner. The outpatient procedure usually lasts about 30 minutes and produces very little discomfort. Generally, normal activities may be resumed within 1 to 7 days (Brint, 1989).

Hearing

When older adults complain that people around them are mumbling, it's generally because they have lost their hearing for high-frequency consonants, though they can still hear vowels, which are lower in frequency. New microchip technology for hearing aids can raise the volume of high-frequency sounds without affecting lower frequencies. These **microprocessor-enhanced hearing aids** can filter out distortion and automatically adjust volume. They can be fine-tuned to suit the individual and reprogrammed as needed. The cost is about twice as much as for conventional hearing aids.

For people with profound hearing loss, **cochlear implants** can make a dramatic difference. These electronic devices transform sound into electrical signals and deliver them to the receptor nerve cells of the *cochlea* in the inner ear,

BOX 3-2

CONTINUED

which then channels the impulses to the *auditory cortex* of the brain. The electrodes must be surgically implanted in the cochlea. The patient wears a speech processor, which analyzes and encodes sounds before transmitting them to the implant. People who undergo cochlear implantation should participate in aural rehabilitation programs, which include fitting and adjusting the speech processor, training in speech production, and informational or personal counseling (Gagné, Parnes, LaRocque, Hassan, & Vidas, 1991).

Most implant recipients improve in the ability to read lips, and two-thirds to three-fourths can understand speech without visual clues. With daily activities easier to perform and conversation less stressful, many experience improvements in psychological, social, and emotional health as well (Gagné, 1992). As with any surgery, there are possible complications, including temporary injury to the facial nerve, but surgeons experienced in cochlear implantation generally do not encounter such problems (Cohen et al., 1993).

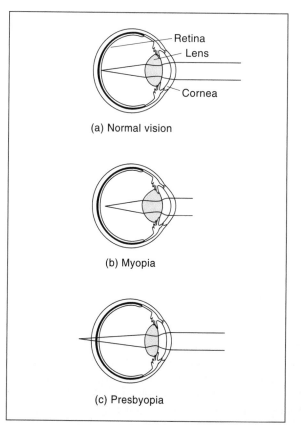

(a) Normal vision

(b) Myopia

(c) Presbyopia

FIGURE 3-4

Normal vision, myopia, and presbyopia. (a) In normal vision, light rays focus on the retina at the rear of the eye. (b) In myopia (nearsightedness), the eyeball is too long, or the curvature of the lens or cornea is too great, so the light rays focus in front of the retina. (c) In presbyopia, a form of farsightedness that often develops with aging, the lens becomes thickened and loses elasticity, so that it cannot curve enough to focus light from nearby objects on the retina; instead, the image focuses behind the retina.

(SOURCE: Adapted from Donn, 1985, p. 649.)

able to change shape to focus on nearby objects (refer back to Figure 3-4). This continuous lifelong process usually becomes noticeable for the first time in middle age, when the eye's ability to accommodate, or adjust its focus, also slows (Whitbourne, 1985). Women usually develop presbyopia about 3 to 5 years earlier than men do (Kline & Schieber, 1985).

Initially, most people try to compensate for presbyopia by holding books, newspapers, or whatever they are reading farther and farther away from the face—until it is so far away that the letters are too small to make out. Some people at this age need nothing more than magnifying lenses. Others need bifocals, which have one focal length for reading and another for distant vision. Presbyopia usually stabilizes at about age 60; and, with corrective lenses, most older people can see fairly well.

The lens also may begin to turn yellow and filter out green, blue, and violet light. Thus these colors should not be used for objects, such as medicines, that older adults need to be able to distinguish. An older person might easily mix up two pills of the same shape if the only apparent difference was that one was violet and the other blue.

Another change is in the size of the *pupil,* the dark opening in the center of the *iris,* the colored portion of the eye. If you look at the eyes of a 5- or 6-year-old child, you will notice that the pupils are larger than in a young adult. If you look at a 75-year-old's pupils, they are likely to be smaller than a young adult's. That is because the muscles in the iris that dilate the pupil in dark places (such as movie theaters) to let in more light become weaker in middle age, and the pupil no longer dilates as much. As a result, middle-aged adults need about one-third more brightness than young adults to compensate for the loss of light reaching the retina (Belbin, 1967; Troll, 1985). This tendency may increase in old age, so older adults need even more light to read or make out objects. Partly for the same reason, the eyes of older adults are slower and less able to adapt to darkness.

Depth perception may diminish with advancing age, which is why older people tend to run into or trip over things, or to miss their footing on steps or curbs. Older adults also become more sensitive to glare. And because they lose visual contrast sensitivity, they have trouble reading either very small or very large characters (Akutsu, Legge, Ross, & Schuebel, 1991).

Visual Disorders and Diseases

Some of the visual impairments discussed above, such as sensitivity to glare and contrast, are aggravated by *cataracts.* More than half of older adults develop these cloudy or opaque areas in the lens, which prevent light from passing through, causing blurred vision (USDHHS, 1993a). Surgery to remove cataracts (refer back to Box 3-2) is the most common operation among Americans over 65 (Steinberg et al., 1993); more than 1.3 million cataract operations were performed in 1993 (Research to Prevent Blindness, 1994). Eating foods high in vitamin A (broccoli, carrots, and spinach) at least five times a week can greatly lower the risk of cataracts, according to a large-scale 8-year study. Taking vitamin A supplements did not necessarily have the same effect (Hankinson et al., 1992).

Cataracts are the most frequent cause of preventable blindness in the world as a whole; but *senile macular degeneration* (or *age-related macular degeneration*), in which the *macula,* the central part of the retina, gradually loses the ability to distinguish fine details, is the leading cause of functional blindness in Americans over 65 years old (Research to Prevent Blindness, 1994). It affects 1 in 5 of those over 75, especially white women and smokers ("The Aging Eye," 1994). Though not limited entirely to older adults, this disorder is more common with advancing age; a diet high in carotenoids such as spinach, collard greens, and carrots apparently reduces the risk (Hankinson et al., 1992). There is no effective medical or surgical treatment so far, but powerful magnifying lenses (worn or held in the hand) can improve acuity. Genes for some forms of the disease have been identified, giving hope for eventual gene therapy (Research to Prevent Blindness, 1994). Also, animal research is exploring possible avenues of treatment, including replacement of damaged retinal cells by transplants. Thalidomide (which causes birth defects when taken by pregnant women) may prevent abnormal growth of tiny blood vessels, a possible cause of retinal degeneration (D'Amato, Loughnon, Flynn, & Folkman, 1994).

Glaucoma occurs when fluid pressure builds up within the eye because of inadequate drainage, damaging the nerve cells. Glaucoma, which affects about 5 percent of Americans over age 65 and 14 percent of those over 80 ("The Aging Eye," 1994), can develop slowly or swiftly. Symptoms include blurred vision, seeing rings of color around light sources (such as a halo of red around a light bulb), severe headache, or pain and watering of the eye. An early symptom of the most common form of the disease is gradual loss of peripheral vision; this can often be detected through routine checkups. When diagnosed early, glaucoma can be treated and controlled with eye drops, medicine, laser treatments, or surgery.

Corneal disease occurs when the cornea, the front surface of the eye, becomes clouded, scarred, or distorted by injury, disease, or hereditary defects. Artificial corneal implants have been developed recently, which can restore vision when conventional treatments fail, and gene mapping holds promise for eventual prevention or cure (Research to Prevent Blindness, 1994).

Dealing with Visual Losses

When the French painter Edgar Degas began to lose his vision in his late sixties, he switched to making wax sculptures, taking advantage of the sense of touch (McMullen, 1984). But even those older adults who do not have serious disorders often have trouble doing things that depend on vision and need to find ways to compensate. Reduced ability to adapt to dim light, tolerate glare, and locate and read signs can make driving (especially at night) particularly difficult and even dangerous. It may also be hard for older adults to read or do close work and even to do such everyday tasks as shopping and cooking. After 65, serious visual problems not only may curtail everyday activities but sometimes cause accidents both inside and outside the home (Branch, Horowitz, & Carr, 1989). Loss of visual abilities can have serious psychological consequences when it deprives older people of activities, social life, and independence.

TABLE 3-2 SAFETY CHECKLIST FOR PREVENTING FALLS IN THE HOME	
Stairways, hallways, and pathways	Free of clutter
	Good lighting, especially at top of stairs
	Light switches at top and bottom of stairs
	Tightly fastened handrails on both sides and full length of stairs
	Carpets firmly attached and not frayed; rough-textured or abrasive strips to secure footing
Bathrooms	Grab bars conveniently located inside and outside of tubs and showers and near toilets
	Nonskid mats, abrasive strips, or carpet on all surfaces that may get wet
	Night lights
Bedrooms	Telephones and night lights or light switches within easy reach of beds
All living areas	Electrical cords and telephone wires out of walking paths
	Rugs well secured to floor
	Inspect for hazards, such as exposed nails and loose threshold trim
	Furniture and other objects in familiar places and not in the way; rounded or padded table edges
	Couches and chairs proper height to get into and out of easily

SOURCE: Adapted from NIA, 1993.

There are simple ways to help people remain safely active and self-reliant. Make sure lighting in work and reading areas is bright enough and directed efficiently. A good fluorescent lamp (yellowish, not blue) can provide a high level of illumination with low glare. Get rid of unnecessary items in cupboards and bookshelves, and highlight often-used items with bright-colored markers. Helpful accessories include sunglasses, so that less adjustment is necessary when coming indoors; a pocket flashlight for reading menus and theater programs; a magnifying glass to put in a pocket or hang on a chain; and large-type reading matter. Since older eyes need sharper contrasts, make stair treads a different color from risers, and edges of counters and tables a different color from the tops; paint bathroom grab bars to contrast with the walls. Carpeting and other textured materials can prevent distracting glare. (Table 3-2 lists additional suggestions for preventing falls.)

HEARING

Hearing, like vision, is at its best at about age 20. A gradual hearing loss typically begins before age 25 and becomes more apparent after that age. This is an age-related impairment, which at first is limited to high-pitched sounds; it is known as *presbycusis.* After about age 55, hearing loss is greater for men than for women, perhaps because men hear more noise at work (Katchadourian, 1987; Troll, 1985). Presbycusis is very common late in life, though usually not severe; about 3 out of 10 people between ages 65 and 74 and about half of those between

75 and 79 have it to some degree. Whereas a young child can hear frequencies as high as 20,000 cycles per second, an older adult is unlikely to hear anything above 8,000 cycles per second.

Most people do not notice their hearing loss during young adulthood and middle age, because it does not affect frequencies used in normal speech. Eventually, these lower frequencies, too, become harder to hear; but it isn't until the seventies that most adults begin to miss words in conversation (Katchadourian, 1987). Women and children, whose voices are higher-pitched than men's, are particularly hard for older people to understand, especially when there is competing noise from radio or television, or a buzz of several people talking at once.

Some high-frequency sounds can be critically important. An older adult might be unable to hear a high-pitched smoke alarm, no matter how loud it is—just as blowing hard on a dog whistle whose sound is above the frequency range of the human ear will not make it easier for a person to hear it. Adults should have their hearing checked if they find it hard to understand words; complain that other people are "mumbling"; cannot hear a dripping faucet or high notes in music; have a hissing or ringing noise in the ears; or do not enjoy parties, television, or concerts because they miss much of what goes on (NIA, 1993).

Causes of Hearing Loss

Most age-related hearing impairment is due to degeneration of structures in the inner ear. There are several patterns of loss, depending on which parts of the inner ear are affected. Hearing also can be damaged by constant exposure to loud noise. Hearing loss occurs at much later ages or to a lesser degree among some

(UPI/Bettmann)

People whose occupations constantly expose them to high noise levels, such as ground personnel on an airfield, must wear protective ear pads to avoid hearing loss.

African peoples than it does in European and American cities, where exposure to blaring auto horns, loud radios, jet airplanes, and other harsh noises is common (Baltes et al., 1977; Timiras, 1972; see Box 2-2 and Figure 2-1). Excessive earwax may interfere with hearing, especially for low frequencies. Sometimes the cause is genetic. Tumors, infections, and drug reactions are other possible causes (Eastman, 1992).

About 10 percent of older adults have *tinnitus*, a persistent ringing or buzzing in the ears. Tinnitus can occur at any point in adulthood, but the number of cases increases with increasing age. It seems to occur more frequently in women. A person who takes large doses of aspirin may have this symptom temporarily, along with a temporary hearing loss. Chronic tinnitus can be extremely stressful.

Dealing with Hearing Loss

Hearing aids, which amplify sound, can compensate for mild hearing loss to some degree. However, they can be hard to adjust to, since they magnify background noises as well as sounds the wearer wants to hear. Furthermore, many people feel that wearing a hearing aid is like wearing a sign saying "I'm getting old." Newer hearing aids using microchip technology provide improved sound quality (refer back to Box 3-2). Medical treatment, special training, and surgery are other ways to deal with hearing impairment.

People who talk to hearing-impaired older adults can take some simple steps to improve communication (Hull, 1980). When speaking to someone with a hearing problem, make sure you are in good light, where the other person can see you, so that your lip movements and gestures can be used as clues to your words. Speak from a distance of 3 to 6 feet, never right into the person's ear. Don't chew, eat, or cover your mouth while speaking, and turn off the radio and television. Speak somewhat more loudly than usual, but don't shout. Speak clearly and not too quickly. Don't exaggerate articulation—exaggeration can distort both sounds and visual cues. If the listener doesn't understand what you say, don't just repeat it; rephrase it in short, simple sentences.

TASTE AND SMELL

Taste and smell generally begin to decline in midlife (Cain, Reid, & Stevens, 1990; Stevens, Cain, Demarque & Ruthruff, 1991), sometimes because of illness or injury, smoking, medications, or environmental pollution (American Academy of Otolaryngology, 1986). Since the taste buds become less sensitive, foods that may be quite flavorful to a younger person may seem bland to a middle-aged person (Troll, 1985). Taste very often depends on smell. When older people complain that their food does not taste good anymore, it may be both because they have fewer taste buds in the tongue and because the *olfactory bulb*—the organ in the brain that is responsible for the sense of smell—has withered. Many older people compensate for these losses by eating more highly seasoned foods. Some oversalt their food, possibly contributing to high blood pressure. Others eat less and may become undernourished.

Gender appears to affect losses of taste and smell. One study of people between ages 19 and 95 found that women retained these senses better than men; but men and women who were taking medicine or were undergoing medical treatment experienced more loss (Ship & Weiffenbach, 1993).

TOUCH, PAIN, AND TEMPERATURE

The skin at the fingertips becomes less sensitive with age (Stevens, 1992). For most people, this lessening of tactile acuity has little impact, but for the visually disabled it can interfere with the ability to read braille.

Along with a decline in sensitivity to touch after age 45, adults at about age 50 begin to lose sensitivity to pain. But at the same time that they feel pain less, they become less able to tolerate it. As a result, many older people find pain more distressing than before (Katchadourian, 1987).

An older person's body adjusts more slowly to cold and becomes chilled more easily than that of a younger person. Exposure to outdoor cold and to poorly heated interiors may lower body temperature—a serious risk for the very old. Older adults cannot cope as well with heat, either. The body's normal cooling mechanisms—sweating and pumping blood to the skin—don't perform as well as in younger persons. During hot weather, or after exercise, older people need to drink plenty of water to replace lost body fluids (M. J. Holland, 1990).

MOTOR FUNCTIONS

Even Martha Graham eventually had to retire. So do professional athletes, usually by age 40; though some, like the pitcher Nolan Ryan, stay on top of their game well past that age. What happens in adulthood that causes motor functioning to decline, and why is this decline faster in some people than in others?

For one thing, the tissue that connects muscles to joints thickens, making the joints less flexible. Manual dexterity generally becomes less efficient after the mid-thirties (Troll, 1985)—though some pianists, such as Vladimir Horowitz, have continued to perform brilliantly in their eighties. Arthritis (degeneration of the joints) can take its toll (see Chapter 4).

Muscle fibers become fewer and contain less protein, diminishing muscular power, speed, and (to a lesser extent) endurance. But individual differences are great and become greater with each passing decade (Spirduso & MacRae, 1990). "Use it or lose it" is the motto of many middle-aged adults, who engage in jogging, raquetball, tennis, aerobic dancing, and other forms of exercise. Even some adults in their seventies still compete in marathons and triathlons. People who lead sedentary lives or have poor health tend to lose muscle tone and energy, while those who are active retain more strength, stamina, and resilience.

Eventually, though, if a person lives long enough, physiological changes do limit motor activity (Spirduso & MacRae, 1990). Generally, older adults can do most things that younger people can, but more slowly (Birren, Woods, & Williams, 1980; Salthouse, 1985). They are not as strong as they used to be and cannot carry as heavy loads. Age also brings changes in coordination and reaction time, which affect such abilities as driving. Let's look at some of these changes.

(Margaret Miller/Photo Reseachers)

(Elaine Rebman/Photo Reseachers)

(Jaye R. Phillips/The Picture Cube)

Although motor functioning declines somewhat after young adulthood, middle-aged and older people who remain active can retain more manual dexterity, strength, and stamina than those who do not.

Muscular Strength and Endurance

Most adults are strongest during their twenties or thirties (Spirduso & MacRae, 1990). They gradually lose about 10 to 20 percent of their strength up to age 70; after that, the loss becomes greater. Some older adults have only half the strength they had at 30 (Spence, 1989). Muscles of the upper body keep their strength better than muscles of the lower body (Spirduso & MacRae, 1990). Most people notice a weakening first in the back muscles, by the early fifties, and then in the arm and shoulder—but not until well into the sixties (Katchadourian, 1987).

The reason for this loss of strength is a loss of muscle mass. Between ages 30 and 80, as much as 30 percent of muscle fiber can atrophy, depending on such factors as heredity, nutrition, and especially how much use a muscle gets. Lost fibers cannot replace themselves; instead, they are replaced by fat (Spence, 1989). By age 65, a man's body is typically 30 percent fat—the same as a woman's, but nearly three times the percentage he had at age 20, even if his weight does not change (Katchadourian, 1987).

Together with good nutrition, an exercise program can increase muscular bulk and density until middle age (Katchadourian, 1987). Even older adults can grow stronger with exercise (Spirduso & MacRae, 1990). One weight training program produced significant gains in muscular strength, size, and functional mobility in ten aged nursing home residents (Fiatarone et al., 1990). After only 8 weeks of weight-lifting, these 90-year-olds increased their muscle strength by an average of 174 percent. Preliminary findings from an expanded study show unprecedented evidence of "actual growth of new muscle fibers" (Fiatarone et al., 1994).

This finding of plasticity even among the oldest old—consistent with the life-span developmental approach—is important because people whose muscles have atrophied are more likely to suffer falls and fractures and to need help with tasks of day-to-day living. Preliminary studies suggest that hormone therapy may increase muscle mass and prevent hip fractures in elderly men (Drinka, Jaschob, Schultz, & Rudman, 1992; Rudman et al., 1991).

Endurance—how long a person can continue to exert maximum force before fatigue sets in—often holds up much better than strength. Probably, that is why many competitive runners, swimmers, and cyclists switch from short to longer races as they get older. Older athletes can do better in an endurance event, such as running a marathon, than in an event that depends on strength, such as the shot put (Spirduso & MacRae, 1990).

Reaction Time and Coordination

Older adults perform more slowly than younger adults on almost all kinds of tasks; in general, the more complex the task, the greater the age difference. Simple reaction time, which involves a single response to a single stimulus (such as pressing a button when a light flashes) slows by about 20 percent, on the average, between ages 20 and 60 (Birren et al., 1980), depending on the amount and kind of information to be processed and the kind of response required. When a vocal rather than a manual response is called for, age differences in simple reaction time are substantially reduced (S. J. Johnson & Rybash, 1993).

Tasks that involve a choice of responses (such as hitting one button when a light flashes and another button when a tone is heard) and complex motor skills involving many stimuli, responses, and decisions (as in playing a video game or driving a car) decline more; but the decline does not necessarily result in poorer performance. Typically, middle-aged adults are better drivers than younger ones (McFarland, Tune, & Welford, 1964), and 60-year-old typists are as efficient as 20-year-olds (Spirduso & MacRae, 1990). In these and other activities, the improvement that comes with experience more than makes up for the decrements that come with age.

Driving becomes riskier for older adults, because of slower information processing, slower reaction time, and less efficient coordination. Drivers over age 65 have a high proportion of accidents, usually because of improper turns, failure to yield the right of way, and failure to obey traffic signs (Sterns, Barrett, & Alexander, 1985). In 1991, nearly 16 percent of people who died in traffic accidents were 75 or older—the most rapidly increasing group of drivers in the United States ("Elderly Driving," 1994).

Training can help reaction time. In one study, for instance, older people who had never before played video games used "joy sticks" and "trigger buttons" for 11 weeks to play such games as Breakout, Kaboom, and Ms. Pacman. At the end of the study period, they showed quicker reaction times than a control group (Dustman, Emmerson, Steinhaus, Shearer, & Dustman, 1992).

For an older adult, driving can make the difference between active participation in society and enforced isolation. Older drivers' vision, coordination, and reaction time need to be retested regularly. They can compensate for any loss of ability by driving more slowly and for shorter distances, choosing easier routes, and driving only in daylight (Sterns et al., 1985). In many communities, courses in defensive driving help to keep older drivers behind the wheel as long as possible. Meanwhile, highway engineers explore ways to make signs easier to read and intersections safer (Schmidt, 1988).

SEXUAL AND REPRODUCTIVE FUNCTIONING

Many adults view sexuality as a hallmark of youth. Actually, despite changes in the male and female reproductive systems (summarized in Table 3-3), sexual activity and pleasure can continue throughout adult life.

THE FEMALE REPRODUCTIVE SYSTEM

The menstrual cycle is a powerful regulator of hormones that fluctuate in a woman's body for some 40 years of her life, from about age 12 until about age 50. To varying degrees, these hormones affect women's physiological, intellectual, and emotional states and even their sensory responses. For example, sight is keenest at the time of ovulation, hearing peaks at the beginning of a menstrual period and again at ovulation, smell is most sensitive at midcycle and is reduced during menstruation, and sensitivity to pain is lowest just before a period (Parlee, 1983). The cessation of menstruation in middle age is an important event with both physical and psychological effects.

Premenstrual Syndrome

Premenstrual syndrome (PMS) is a disorder involving physical discomfort and emotional tension during the 2 weeks before a menstrual period. Symptoms may

TABLE 3-3 AGE-RELATED CHANGES IN HUMAN REPRODUCTIVE SYSTEMS		
	Female	*Male*
Climacteric (approximate age)	45–50	55–60
Hormonal change	Drop in estrogen and progesterone	Drop in testosterone
Symptoms	Hot flashes, vaginal dryness, urinary dysfunction	Undetermined
Sexual changes	Less intense arousal, less frequent and quicker orgasms	Loss of psychological arousal, less frequent erections, slower orgasms, longer recovery between ejaculations, increased risk of impotence
Reproductive capacity	Ends	Continues; some decrease in fertility may occur

include fatigue, food cravings, headaches, swelling and tenderness of the breasts, swollen hands or feet, abdominal bloating, nausea, constipation, weight gain, anxiety, depression, irritability, mood swings, tearfulness, and difficulty concentrating or remembering (American Council on Science and Health, 1985; Harrison, 1982; "PMS: It's Real," 1994; Reid & Yen, 1981). These symptoms are not distinctive in themselves; it is their timing that identifies PMS. Up to 70 percent of menstruating women may have some symptoms; about 3 to 5 percent have symptoms severe enough to interfere with normal functioning and to be considered a mental disorder (American Psychiatric Association, 1994; "PMS: It's Real," 1994; Wurtman & Wurtman, 1989).

The cause of PMS is not known. It may in part be related to biochemical changes of the menstrual cycle: the depletion of neurotransmitters in the brain that affect well-being or relaxation or stimulate the central nervous system. The most effective medications, such as Prozac and certain anti-anxiety medications, build up the levels of these chemicals or mimic their effects. Hormone treatments can be quite effective but can have undesirable side effects. For milder symptoms, some doctors recommend exercise and dietary changes, such as avoiding fat, sodium, caffeine, and alcohol ("PMS: It's Real," 1994). Treatment may target specific symptoms: for example, antidepressants for a woman who feels "blue" or diuretics for a woman who retains fluids. Since some women report relief after binge eating of carbohydrates, one research team suggests a high-carbohydrate diet (Wurtman & Wurtman, 1989).

PMS sometimes is confused with *dysmenorrhea,* menstrual cramps. Cramps tend to afflict adolescents and young women; PMS is more typical in women in their thirties or older. Dysmenorrhea is caused by contractions of the uterus, which are set in motion by prostaglandin, a hormone-like substance; it can be treated with prostaglandin inhibitors.

Menopause

Menopause takes place when a woman stops ovulating and menstruating and can no longer bear children; it is generally considered to have occurred 1 year after the last menstrual period. For American women, this biological event typically happens between ages 45 and 55, at an average age of 51. Some women, however, begin to experience menstrual changes in their thirties, and others not until their sixties.

The period of 2 to 5 years during which a woman undergoes physiological changes that bring on menopause is the **climacteric,** popularly known as the "change of life." During the climacteric, the ovaries and adrenal glands begin to produce less of the female hormone estrogen. As a result, menstruation usually becomes irregular, with less flow than before and a longer time between menstrual periods.

PHYSICAL EFFECTS   Three out of four women experience little or no physical discomfort due to menopause (NIA, 1993). Some, however, have "hot flashes" (sudden sensations of heat that flash through the body) due to expansion and contraction of blood vessels (Spence, 1989).

Other possible symptoms include vaginal dryness, burning, and itching; urinary problems; and vaginal infections. During menopause, the vagina becomes narrower and shorter, its walls become thinner and less elastic, and lubrication diminishes, sometimes causing pain during intercourse or irritation of the bladder. Use of water-soluble gels can prevent or relieve such discomfort. Vaginal secretions also become less acidic, offering less protection against bacterial and yeast infections. The more sexually active a woman is, either with a partner or by masturbation, the less likely she is to experience such changes (Katchadourian, 1987; Spence, 1989).

The hormones most directly linked to sexual desire in both men and women are the androgens (such as testosterone). Therefore, the drop at menopause in estrogen and other female hormones called *progestins* does not affect the sex drive in women as much as reduced testosterone generally does in men at midlife (Katchadourian, 1987). Still, women do go through sexual adjustments. Some do not become aroused as readily as before, and the sexual flush that accompanies arousal diminishes. Breast engorgement, nipple erection, and clitoral and labial engorgement may also diminish. Women can still reach orgasm, especially if they have sex regularly (Masters & Johnson, 1966, 1981), but their contractions are less intense and less frequent and climax more quickly.

Many of the troublesome physical effects of menopause—including higher risks of certain diseases (discussed in Chapter 4)—seems to be related to lower levels of estrogen and may be preventable. Often doctors prescribe **estrogen replacement therapy (ERT),** also called *hormone replacement therapy* (HRT): artificial estrogen, sometimes in combination with progesterone, in the form of a pill, a slow-release skin patch, or a vaginal cream. But hormone therapy may not be advisable for some women, depending on their medical history. (We discuss pros and cons of ERT in Box 4-3 in Chapter 4.)

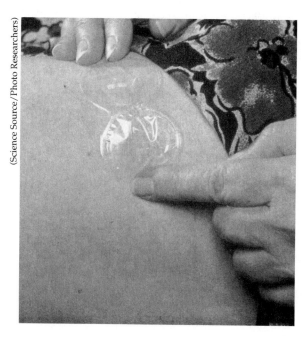

(Science Source/Photo Researchers)

Some postmenopausal women take estrogen in the form of a slow-release skin patch (worn on the thigh), a pill, or a vaginal cream to counteract hot flashes and vaginal dryness and to help prevent osteoporosis and heart disease. The advisability of estrogen therapy for an individual woman may depend on her medical history.

PSYCHOLOGICAL EFFECTS   In rural Ireland, not long ago, women who no longer menstruated would retire to their beds and stay there, often for years, until they died (U.S. Office of Technology Assessment, 1992). This traditional custom may seem extreme, but the attitude it expressed—that a woman's usefulness ends with her ability to reproduce—was typical in western societies until fairly recently (Crowley, 1994a).

For most women in the United States today, menopause is a psychological *non*event. At one time, such problems as irritability, depression, and even insanity were blamed on menopause, but research shows no reason to attribute psychiatric illness to this normal change.

In a classic study, researchers asked several hundred women from ages 21 to 65 about menopause. The responses of women who had already experienced it were much more positive than those of women who had not. In fact, some found the cessation of the aches and pains of menstruation a relief (Neugarten, Wood, Kraines, & Loomis, 1963). In newer research, of 541 healthy women age 42 to 50 who were premenopausal at the beginning of the study, many reported some uncomfortable physical symptoms as they entered the climacteric but tended to report *lower* levels of stress in their daily lives after menopause than they had experienced before it. Although about 10 percent of the women experienced slight depression as menopausal symptoms first appeared, the vast majority did not become depressed either at this time or after menopause (Matthews, 1992).

Psychological problems in midlife are more likely to be caused by attitude than by anatomy—especially by negative societal views of aging. In some cultures, especially those that value older women, few problems are associated with menopause (Dan & Bernhard, 1989; see Box 3-3).

BOX 3-3

THE MULTICULTURAL CONTEXT

Japanese Women's Experience of Menopause

The value of cross-cultural research in making social scientists question long-held and widely accepted beliefs has shown up in the results of a cross-sectional survey of Japanese women between ages 45 and 55 (Lock, 1991). A total of 1,316 factory workers, farm workers, and home-makers answered questionnaires, and 105 were interviewed in their homes. In addition, the researchers interviewed physicians and counselors.

Japanese women's experience of menopause turned out to be quite different from the experience of many western women. For example, fewer than 13 percent of Japanese women whose menstruation was becoming irregular reported having had hot flashes in the previous 2 weeks, compared with more than 47 percent of Canadian women. Fewer than 20 percent of Japanese women had *ever* experienced a hot flash, compared with almost 65 percent of Canadian women.

In fact, there is no specific Japanese term for *hot flash*, although the Japanese language makes many subtle distinctions about all kinds of body states. This linguistic evidence supports the research finding that what most western women report as the most bothersome symptom of menopause has a low incidence in Japan and is rarely perceived as troublesome. Japanese women in this age group are more likely to report headaches, stiffness in the shoulders, ringing in the ears, dizziness, and other complaints that do not appear directly related to the hormonal changes of menopause.

These findings emphasize the importance of doing cross-cultural research and of developing research tools appropriate to a particular culture. It would not be useful, for example, to assess women in Japan by means of a list of menopausal symptoms drawn up in Canada, or vice versa. This research may point to biological variations among populations in such physical symptoms as hot flashes. On the other hand, researchers need to consider that different cultures view events differently. In Japan the end of menstruation may have far less significance than it does for western women.

"Menopause is not a disease, but a life-cycle transition to which powerful symbolic meanings, individual and social, are attached" (Lock, 1991, p. 1272). In Japan, "menopausal syndrome" is seen as an affliction of modernity, which affects women with too much time on their hands. If, says the Japanese government, these women would busy themselves taking care of their elderly parents, they would not have physical complaints. This point of view may well arise from the fact that the greatest health problem in Japan is the aging of the population, and one of the greatest social problems is an erosion of the traditional pattern of the extended family.

It is possible that this official attitude may dissuade Japanese women from reporting uncomfortable symptoms of menopause, or that cultural attitudes may affect how women interpret their physical sensations. Further research may be needed to clarify how biology and culture interact.

THE MALE REPRODUCTIVE SYSTEM

Men, unlike women, do not undergo a sudden reduction in hormone production at midlife; instead, men's testosterone levels gradually decline and then stabilize at about age 60 (King, Camp, & Downey, 1991). Some middle-aged men seem to have cyclic fluctuations in hormone production (Kimmel, 1980). Although men can continue to father children until quite late in life, there is some reduction in sperm count, and some middle-aged men experience a decrease in fertility (Beard, 1975; Spence, 1989).

The *male climacteric* (sometimes inaccurately called the *male menopause*) is a period of physiological, emotional, and psychological change involving a man's reproductive system and other body systems. It generally begins about 10 years later than a woman's climacteric, and its physical effects vary (Weg, 1989). About 5 percent of middle-aged men experience depression, fatigue, lower sexual drive, occasional erectile failure, and vaguely defined physical complaints (Henker, 1981; Weg, 1989), but it is not clear that these conditions are related to the climacteric. The prostate gland (the organ surrounding the neck of the bladder) may enlarge, causing urinary and sexual problems.

Many men, as they grow older, greatly fear loss of sexual potency. Actually, the idea that this is a natural accompaniment of aging is a fallacy (Masters & Johnson, 1970). Although a man's sexual excitation may be slower and shorter-lived than in his youth, sexual activity remains a normal, vital part of life. However, most middle-aged men do not experience sexual tension as often as they did when they were younger: those who wanted intercourse every other day may now be content to go 3 to 5 days between orgasms. Erections arrive less often of their own accord or in response to psychological or visual stimuli such as the sight of a lover, and more often only with direct physical stimulation. Orgasms come more slowly and sometimes not at all. And men need a longer recovery time before they can ejaculate again (Bremner, Vitiello, & Prinz, 1983; Katchadourian, 1987; Masters & Johnson, 1966).

Very often, lessening of sexual activity is due to nonphysiological causes: monotony in a relationship, preoccupation with business or financial worries, mental or physical fatigue, depression, failure to make sex a high priority, and fear of inability to perform. Physical causes include chronic disease (such as diabetes), surgery, some medications, and too much food or alcohol (Weg, 1989).

A minority of middle-aged and especially older men do experience *impotence,* or *erectile dysfunction:* inability to achieve or maintain an erect penis "sufficient for satisfactory sexual performance" (NIH, 1992, p. 6). It is estimated that about 30 million men, most of them over age 65, suffer chronically from this condition to some degree. Its incidence increases with age: it affects about 5 percent of 40-year-old men as compared with 15 to 25 percent of men age 65 or more. Late-onset diabetes, hypertension, high cholesterol, endocrine problems, depression, neurological disorders, and many chronic diseases, especially kidney failure, can lead to erectile dysfunction. Alcohol, drugs, smoking, poor sexual techniques, lack of sexual knowledge, unsatisfying or deteriorating relationships, anxiety, and stress can be contributing factors. About 35 percent of cases can be helped by treating the underlying causes or adjusting medications ("Effective Solutions for Impotence," 1994; NIH, 1992).

The least expensive and safest direct treatment for erectile dysfunction is a wraparound vacuum constrictive device, which draws blood into the penis. Some men find it uncomfortable; it sometimes prevents ejaculation, and some couples find the lack of spontaneity disturbing. Injections of prostaglandin E1 (a drug found in semen, which widens the arteries) can be effective, but the dosage must be carefully adjusted or the erection may persist for hours or days, creating a medical emergency. A third (and most expensive) option is penile implant surgery, using either semirigid rods or an inflatable tube filled with a saline solution. All these devices, especially the inflatable ones, involve a risk of further surgery. Researchers are currently testing two promising treatments: a topical cream and a suppository, both using prostaglandin E1 ("Effective Solutions for Impotence," 1994; NIH, 1992).

If there is no apparent physical problem, psychotherapy, behavioral therapy, or some other type of sex therapy may help. As with any other treatment, the support and involvement of the partner are important (NIH, 1992). Therapeutic exercises are often more successful with homosexuals than with heterosexuals, perhaps because partners of the same sex may better understand each other's needs (King et al., 1991).

SEXUALITY AND AGING

Awareness of changes in the male and female reproductive systems can help couples enjoy more satisfying sexual relations throughout the adult lifespan.

In most young adults, sexual drive and capacity are high. People form relationships, whether heterosexual or homosexual. Today sexual lifestyles are more diverse than in the past. However, the fear of AIDS and other sexually transmitted diseases may be putting a damper on the widespread sexual freedom that has existed in the United States since the 1960s (see Chapter 9).

Most middle-aged adults take changes in reproductive and sexual capacities in stride, and some even experience a kind of sexual renaissance. Freed from worries about pregnancy, and having more time to spend with their partners, many people find their sexual relationship better than it has been in years. Because of men's slowed response, middle-aged lovers may enjoy longer, more leisurely periods of sexual activity. Women may find their partner's longer period of arousal helpful in reaching their own orgasm—often by means other than intercourse. In one study of 160 middle-aged women, most reported having a better sex life than before. They knew their own sexual needs and desires better, felt freer to take the initiative, and had more interest in sex (Rubin, 1982). Homosexual as well as heterosexual couples who hold and caress each other, both in and out of bed, without confining such touching to foreplay for genital sex, can experience heightened sexuality as part of a caring, close relationship (Weg, 1989).

The physical aspect of sex was not scientifically recognized as a normal element of the lives of older people until the 1960s, with the pioneering research of

(CLEO Photo/The Picture Cube)

Older adults often express their sexuality by touching, holding, and hugging, with or without genital intercourse.

Masters and Johnson (see Box 2-1 in Chapter 2) and the findings of the Duke University Longitudinal Study that healthy older adults are both capable and desirous of sexual activity. More recent reports indicate a rich diversity of sexual experience well into late adulthood (Brecher & Editors of Consumer Reports Books, 1984; Starr & Weiner, 1981).

After interviewing men and women over age 60, Masters and Johnson (1966, 1981) concluded that people who have had active sexual lives during their younger years are likely to remain sexually active in later life. A healthy man who has been sexually active can usually continue some form of sexual expression into his seventies or eighties, and women are physiologically able to be sexually active as long as they live. The major barrier to a fulfilling sexual life for older women is lack of a partner.

Sex is, of course, different in late adulthood from what it was earlier. Older people feel less sexual tension, usually have less frequent sexual relations, and experience less intensity. They may express their sexuality by touching, holding, and other intimacies, with or without genital intercourse.

Sexual expression can be more pleasurable for older people if both young and old recognize it as normal and healthy—if older people accept their own sexuality without shame or embarrassment, and younger ones avoid ridiculing or patronizing older persons who show signs of healthy sexuality. Housing arrangements should give older men and women opportunities to socialize with ample privacy. Medical and social workers should consider the sexual needs of the elderly and of people with physical or mental disabilities. When possible, they should avoid prescribing drugs that interfere with sexual functioning; and when such a drug must be taken, the patient should be alerted about its effects. Professionals should discuss sexual activity matter-of-factly—for example, with a heart patient who may be embarrassed to ask about it.

Human beings are sexual beings from birth until death. Sexual expression is part of a healthy lifestyle—a subject we explore in Chapter 4. But even when illness or frailty prevents older people from acting on sexual feelings, the feelings persist. People can express sexuality in many ways other than genital contact—in touching, in closeness, in affection, in intimacy (Kay & Neelley, 1982). An active sexual relationship assures each partner of the other's love and affection and assures both of their continuing vitality.

SUMMARY

LIFESPAN AND THE AGING PROCESS

- Life expectancy has increased greatly as a result of medical advances and is expected to continue to rise. Race and gender are factors in life expectancy.

- Research on extension of the lifespan in several species, especially through caloric restriction, has yielded promising results. However, survival curves suggest that there may be a genetically determined limit to human life.

- Theories of biological aging fall into two categories: genetic-programming theories, which hold that the body is programmed to fail at a certain point; and variable-rate theories, which suggest that environment and lifestyle play an important role.

PHYSICAL APPEARANCE

- Despite individual variations, certain changes in appearance commonly occur during the course of adulthood.

- Because physical attributes of young adults (such as smooth skin and a lean physique) are highly prized in American society, many middle-aged and older adults attempt to maintain a youthful appearance.

SENSORIMOTOR FUNCTIONING

- As age advances, sensory and motor functioning vary widely among individuals. There often is a slowdown in various functions of the central nervous system.

- Aging generally brings a decline in visual acuity (especially for moving objects) and the development of presbyopia (loss of near vision). Corrective lenses and environmental modifications can compensate for most moderate visual problems.

- Visual disorders associated with aging, which may cause varying degrees of blindness, include cataracts, senile macular degeneration, glaucoma, and corneal disease.

- Presbycusis, a gradual hearing loss (at first for high-pitched sounds) begins before age 25 and increases thereafter. It is more pronounced in people frequently exposed to loud noise. Treatments include hearing aids and cochlear implants.

- Losses in taste and smell make food less flavorful to older adults. Older people also have less sensitivity to touch, but less tolerance for pain and temperature changes.

- Muscular strength diminishes gradually until age 70 and more significantly after that. Endurance holds up better. Muscle performance even in the very old can be improved by training and exercise.

■ Reaction time slows with age, more so for complex tasks. But experience more than compensates in middle age. Driving becomes riskier for older adults, but training can improve reaction time.

SEXUAL AND REPRODUCTIVE FUNCTIONING

■ The menstrual cycle regulates hormones in women's bodies until menopause.

■ Premenstrual syndrome (PMS) is most common among women in their thirties or older.

■ Menopause, which usually occurs around age 50, brings a sharp decline in estrogen and progesterone levels; this can produce a number of physical symptoms. Psychologically, most women take menopause in stride.

■ In males, testosterone levels decline gradually until age 60. Most men remain fertile until late in life. The male climacteric begins about 10 years later than the female climacteric.

■ With advancing age, men experience more changes in sexual functioning than women do. Men's responses become slower and their need for sexual activity is less frequent. Impotence, or erectile dysfunction, becomes more common with age.

■ Although forms of sexual expression may change with aging, people can have satisfying sexual relationships throughout adult life.

KEY TERMS

▼

life expectancy (page 79)
longevity (79)
genes (81)
Hayflick limit (81)
survival curves (85)
senescence (86)
genetic–programming theories (86)
gene therapy (87)
variable–rate theories (88)
free radicals (88)
primary aging (89)
secondary aging (89)
biomarkers (89)
visual acuity (93)
dynamic visual acuity (93)
presbyopia (93)
radial keratotomy (RK) (94)

microprocessor-enhanced hearing
   aids (94)
cochlear implants (94)
cataracts (96)
senile (or age-related) macular
   degeneration (97)
glaucoma (97)
corneal disease (97)
presbycusis (98)
tinnitus (100)
premenstrual syndrome (PMS) (105)
dysmenorrhea (105)
menopause (106)
climacteric (106)
estrogen replacement therapy (ERT)
   (106)
male climacteric (109)
impotence (erectile dysfunction) (109)

CHAPTER 4

HEALTH AND BODY SYSTEMS

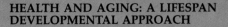

HEALTH AND AGING: A LIFESPAN DEVELOPMENTAL APPROACH

CHANGES IN BODY SYSTEMS
Skeletal System
Cardiovascular System
Respiratory System
Immune System
Neurological System

"DREAD DISEASES" OF AGING
Alzheimer's Disease
Cancer: A Disorder of Many Systems

INDIRECT INFLUENCES ON HEALTH
Age and Gender
Socioeconomic Status, Race, and Ethnicity
Relationships

FACTORS IN MAINTAINING AND IMPROVING HEALTH
Harmful Substances
Stress
Diet
Dental Care
Exercise

BOXES
4-1 The Cutting Edge: Genetic Testing
4-2 The Multicultural Context: How Traditional Beliefs Influence the Course of Disease
4-3 The Art of Aging: The Estrogen Decision

FOCUS: STEPHEN HAWKING

(AP Photo by Dave Weaver/Wide World)

In 1988, in his best-selling book *A Brief History of Time*, the British astrophysicist Stephen Hawking—then in his mid-forties—offered answers to such fundamental questions as: "Where did the universe come from? How and why did it begin? Will it come to an end, and if so, how?" (Hawking, 1988, p. vi). But even more fascinating than his explanations of the origins of black holes or the contradictions between quantum mechanics and Einstein's theory of relativity (which he and other theoretical physicists are trying to combine into a single, unified theory of the universe) is Hawking's own life story.

Hawking is the most famous living person with amyotrophic lateral sclerosis (ALS), commonly called *Lou Gehrig's disease* after a New York Yankees baseball star who died of it in 1941 at age 38. ALS has also claimed the lives of the former United States Senator Jacob K. Javits of New York, the actor David Niven, General Maxwell Taylor, and the jazz bass player Charles Mingus, among others.

ALS is a degenerative disease of the neurological system; it afflicts some 30,000 Americans, with 5,000 new cases diagnosed yearly. In ALS, nerve cells in the brain and spinal cord that control motor activity die, and the unused muscles waste away. So far, there is no known cure. The disease progresses rapidly to paralysis; inability to swallow, speak, or (eventually) breathe; and finally death—usually within 2 to 5 years.

In this, as in his awesome mental abilities (which, fortunately, ALS does not affect), Stephen Hawking is an exception: he has survived for about a quarter of a century. He first showed symptoms of the disease as a graduate student at Cambridge University (Angier, 1993), where he now holds the professorship once graced by Isaac Newton, the discoverer of the force of gravity (Sagan, 1988). Hawking was unusually young when diagnosed with ALS, which usually appears between ages 40 and 70 (ALS Association, undated).

Almost completely paralyzed and confined to a motorized wheelchair, Hawking lacks the physical ability to write or even to speak. He requires 24-hour nursing care. Able to move only the muscles of his face and two fingers of his left hand, he communicates by typing on a computer keyboard connected to a voice synthesizer. His terse remarks "are often laced with humor. . . . But he can be stubborn, abrasive and quick to anger, terminating a conversation by spinning around and rolling off, sometimes running one of his wheels over the toes of an offender" (Jaroff, 1992, p. 88).

Hawking and his former wife have three children. He socializes with students and colleagues. He goes to rock concerts and discos, where he wheels around the dance floor. In July 1995 he announced plans to marry his nurse in September.

"Apart from being unlucky enough to get ALS . . . I have been fortunate in almost every other respect," Hawking (1988, p. vii) wrote in *A Brief History of Time*. "I was . . . fortunate in that I chose theoretical physics, because that is all in the mind. So my disability has not been a serious handicap."

At first glance, it might appear that Stephen Hawking's situation is highly unusual. His intelligence is extraordinary, his disease is relatively rare, and his incapacitation is extreme. And yet, this man and his circumstances reflect themes that run through this chapter.

First, ALS points up the delicate balance involved in the functioning of body systems essential to health. Health is an important aspect of adult development and aging because many of the physical processes that underlie changes in health are developmental. ALS is one of a number of diseases that are more likely to strike in middle or old age. As people age, their body systems tend to undergo structural and functional changes. In order to age successfully and healthfully, they must adapt to those changes. Furthermore, physical health can affect other aspects of development, such as work, retirement, intimate relationships, and mental health. Indeed, although we discuss physical health in this chapter and mental health in Chapter 12, we need to keep in mind that the two are inter-related.

Second, the effort to conquer ALS exemplifies the continual, painstaking quest for control over threats to physical well-being. Until very recently, scientists knew little about the cause of ALS, except that about 1 in 10 patients inherit it. Then, in 1993, researchers discovered a genetic defect that appears to be linked to those familial cases, though it is not clear how. More recent studies have turned up other possible causative factors (Angier, 1993; "Research Update," 1995; Rosen et al., 1993). Eventually, perhaps, one or more of these lines of research will lead to an effective treatment or a cure.

Since a number of other diseases, such as Alzheimer's disease, cancer, and heart disease, seem to have genetic forms, it is likely that genetic screening and therapy for a broad range of conditions will become increasingly common (see Box 4-1). But even when dealing with a hereditary disease, we need to recognize the importance of environmental and lifestyle factors that affect health. Every moment of every day, people make choices about how they live, what they eat, and how they handle stress. Stephen Hawking, for example, evidently spends his time thinking about black holes rather than about what his disease makes him unable to do.

In this chapter, you will learn about how body systems age across the adult lifespan and about direct and indirect influences on health. As you read, ask yourself: What am I doing now that will help me live to a healthy and happy old age? What should I change? Do I understand risk factors for diseases such as cancer, and do I know how to monitor my own health? How do I handle crises and the stresses of daily living? If I were told that I had ALS (or some other fatal disease), how would I react? What would I do with the rest of my life?

BOX 4-1

THE CUTTING EDGE

Genetic Testing

The Human Genome Project, a 15-year, $3 billion research effort under the joint leadership of the National Institutes of Health and the U.S. Department of Energy, is designed to map all the estimated 100,000 human genes and identify those that cause particular disorders. The genetic information gained from such research could save many lives and improve the quality of many others by increasing our ability to control, treat, and cure diseases. Tests for genetic predispositions to some cancers are already becoming available.

But the rush to test individuals to find out whether they carry harmful genes is controversial. What are the implications of such testing? What benefits and concerns are there?

Benefits of Genetic Testing

1. Knowing one's genetic profile may lead to early detection and prevention or more effective treatment of hereditary disorders. For example, a person who learns of a genetic

The sisters of Jan Modeland, who died of breast cancer, are at high risk of the disease. The discovery of genes that may be involved in some breast cancers may lead to genetic testing of women whose family history puts them at risk.

(AP Photo by Dean Wariner/Wide World)

(CONTINUED)

BOX 4-1

CONTINUED

predisposition to lung cancer may be motivated to stop smoking. A woman who learns that she has a genetic tendency to breast cancer might be advised to under-go earlier and more frequent examinations than would otherwise be recommended. But although early detection dramatically reduces the death rate for breast cancer, it is not known whether that is true for women carrying the faulty gene, since the cancer may manifest itself in other forms or locations (Kolata, 1995).

2. Genetic information may be helpful in making decisions such as whether to have children, what occupation to pursue, and what climate to live in; it will also allow more time to plan for illness or death (Post, 1994).

Concerns about Genetic Testing

1. Genetic information may be disseminated in a way that violates privacy. Although medical data are supposed to be confidential, it is almost impossible to keep such information private. A study at the University of Minnesota found that at least 50 people had access to each patient's medical charts (Gruson, 1992). Also, what claim, if any, do parents, children, or siblings have to information that may affect them?

2. A genetic profile may be used to deny a job, insurance, or other benefits. In fact, discrimination on the basis of genetic information has already occurred, even though tests in current use are often imprecise and unreliable, and people deemed at risk of a disease may never develop it. An informal survey found 50 cases in which people had been denied jobs, insurance claims, and other benefits because of their genes (Gruson, 1992). Several states have passed laws prohibiting job discrimination based on genetic information. In April 1995, the federal Equal Employment Opportunity Commission (EEOC) banned such discrimination under the Americans with Disabilities Act (ADA).

3. It might be extremely anxiety-producing for a person to learn that she or he has the gene for an incurable disease. What is the point of knowing you have a potentially debilitating condition when you cannot do anything about it, especially if the financial costs of testing are very high (Post, 1994)? On the other hand, people who have family histories of a disease may be under *less* stress once they know the worst that is likely to happen (Wiggins et al., 1992).

4. Given limited economic resources, the need for genetic testing, which can cost as much as $1,500 for a single disorder, must be weighed against other medical priorities (Post, 1994).

5. Some genetic tests are based on discoveries that are still in the research stage, and it may be unclear how to interpret the results (Kalata, 1995).

Are we, then, premature in using genetic testing? Or do the benefits outweigh the risks?

HEALTH AND AGING:
A LIFESPAN DEVELOPMENTAL APPROACH

▼

The peak of health for most people is in young adulthood, though most middle-aged and older adults continue to be healthy and able-bodied. Almost 95 percent of Americans age 15 to 44 consider their health excellent, very good, or good, as compared with 84 percent of middle-aged people, three-fourths of noninstitutionalized older adults age 65 to 74, and about two-thirds of those 75 and over (Schick & Schick, 1994; U.S. Bureau of the Census, 1992c, 1995; USDHHS, 1992).

Many young adults are never seriously ill or incapacitated; and fewer than 1 percent, as compared with close to 9 percent of middle-aged people, have chronic conditions or impairments that affect their mobility or activities (USDHHS, 1992). Although chronic ailments tend to increase with age, most older adults do not have to limit any major activities for health reasons before age 85, nor do they need help with eating, dressing, bathing, using the toilet, cooking, shopping, or housework (AARP, 1994; see Figure 4-1). Older people do need more medical care than younger ones. They go to the doctor more often, are hospitalized more frequently, stay longer, and spend more than 4 times as much on health care (AARP, 1994; U.S. Bureau of the Census, 1992c).

Why does health often decline with age? A widely accepted explanation is that body systems and organs deteriorate, becoming more susceptible to problems. It is true that tissues and structures throughout the body tend to become less elastic and less efficient, and some normal changes may herald more serious dysfunctions or disorders. But such changes are not inevitable or universal. Individual differences—some of them related to socioeconomic, racial, and ethnic factors—cast doubt on the popular belief in a link between aging and disease.

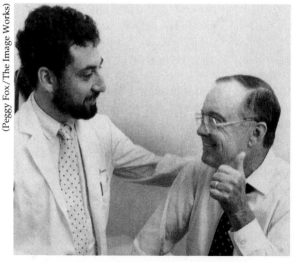

(Peggy Fox/The Image Works)

A survivor of leukemia gives "thumbs-up" to his doctor. Middle-aged and older adults tend to have more chronic ailments than younger ones and to need more medical care. But disease is not an inevitable accompaniment of aging. A healthy lifestyle can help individuals maintain a high level of physical functioning.

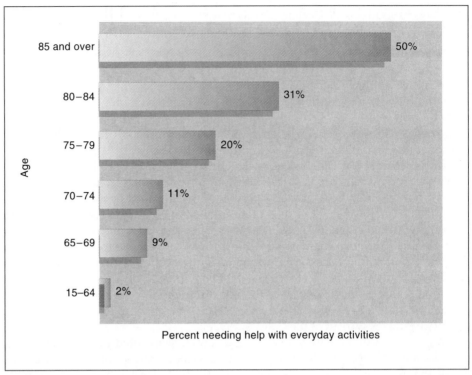

FIGURE 4-1

Percentage (as of 1990–1991) of older adults (noninstitutionalized civilians) of varying ages who needed help with daily activities. Most older adults do not need help with such everyday activities as eating, dressing, bathing, using the toilet, cooking, shopping, or housework. Limitations on what people can do increase with age.

(SOURCE: U.S. Bureau of the Census, 1995.)

Many of the declines commonly associated with aging may actually be effects of disease rather than causes (T. F. Williams, 1992). As the "young old" become more numerous, it is becoming increasingly apparent that health is a matter not so much of age as of genes, lifestyle, and (to some extent) luck. The classic descriptions of age-related physical losses come mainly from cross-sectional studies. For example, cross-sectional observations of apparently healthy adults age 20 to 80 found a general drop in kidney functioning with age (Rowe et al., 1976). But such findings may be due to cohort differences. By contrast, the Baltimore Longitudinal Study of Aging, a long-term study of more than 1,000 adults of all ages, begun in 1958, measured kidney functioning repeatedly in the *same* subjects. Many showed only a slight decline with advancing age, and 35 percent showed no decline (Lindeman, Tobin, & Shock, 1985).

The lifespan developmental approach (Baltes, 1987) sheds new light on why adults age so differently. Why is one man's heart "fit as a fiddle" at age 70, while another needs a bypass operation? Why do some body systems generally decline more rapidly than others (see Figure 4-2), so that a woman may have a "young" heart but "old" eyes and "middle-aged" lungs? The concept of multidirectionality—change occurring in more than one direction or at more than one rate throughout the lifespan—may offer a clue to such differences among and within individuals.

As the lifespan approach suggests, gains in some areas can compensate for losses in others. For example, in adults free of heart disease, the Baltimore Longitudinal Study found that while the heart's ability to pump more rapidly during exercise tends to lessen with age, blood flow diminishes very little because the heart pumps more blood with each stroke (NIH/NIA, 1993; Rodehoffer et al., 1984). In Chapter 3, we cite examples of plasticity, another key concept of the lifespan developmental approach. In this chapter we note the brain's ability to rejuvenate itself by compensating for losses of threadlike *dendrites* that carry messages between nerve cells (NIH/NIA, 1993; Selkoe, 1992).

Finally, the lifespan perspective emphasizes history and context, reminding us that cultural factors such as diet and nutrition, sanitation, environmental pollutants, scientific knowledge, economic development, and even religious beliefs help determine patterns of health and disease, life and death (see Box 4-2). The newer longitudinal findings on organ functioning suggest that today's healthier lifestyles will allow more and more people to maintain a high level of physical functioning well into old age.

FIGURE 4-2

Declines in organ functioning. Differences in functional efficiency of various internal body systems are typically very slight in young adulthood but widen by old age.

(SOURCE: Katchadourian, 1987.)

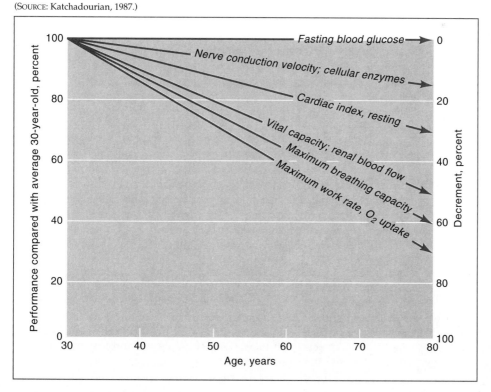

BOX 4-2

THE MULTICULTURAL CONTEXT

How Traditional Beliefs Influence the Course of Disease

In traditional Chinese culture, medicine and astrology are intimately connected. Chinese healers teach that people born in years ending with certain numbers are ill-fated if they contract certain diseases. For example, heart disease is more likely to prove fatal to people born in a "fire year" (a year ending in 6 or 7, such as 1946 or 1967). People born in an "earth year" (ending in 8 or 9) are less likely than others to survive diabetes, peptic ulcers, or cancer. And those born in "metal years" (ending in 0 or 1) do worse than average if they develop such respiratory diseases as bronchitis, emphysema, and asthma.

David P. Phillips (Phillips, Ruth, & Wagner, 1993), a sociologist at the University of California, San Diego, decided to test the effects of these traditional Chinese beliefs. Phillips and his colleagues looked at death certificates of 28,169 Chinese American adults, all of whom had died between 1969 and 1990. The investigators matched each deceased Chinese American with a randomly selected control group of 20 deceased white Americans of the same sex, born in the same year, who had also died in the same year and of the same cause. The researchers also tracked each person's health history to see when the fatal disease had begun.

As a group, Chinese Americans who had an "ill-fated" combination of birth year and disease died of the ailment more quickly than white controls, and about 1 to 5 years sooner than Chinese who had the same disease but were not born in an ill-fated year. Women with ill-fated combinations of disease and birth year died earlier than men. Chinese Americans with unlucky pairings who were presumed to be strongly committed to traditional beliefs—those who had been born in China, lived in large cities, and had not been autopsied (a traditionally disapproved procedure) also tended to have died sooner. For exam-

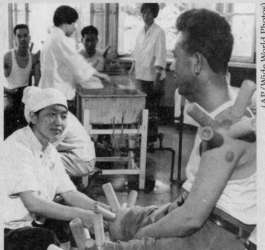

(AP/Wide World Photos)

Traditional healers at a sanatorium in northeast China use methods such as cautery (burning off diseased tissue), along with western techniques. Studies suggest that cultural attitudes can influence the course of disease.

ple, strongly traditional Chinese women born in metal years who had bronchitis, emphysema, or asthma died 8.3 years earlier than other Chinese who died of the same diseases.

The researchers interpreted their findings as showing a psychosomatic influence on the course of illness. People who expected to die early from a certain disease were more likely to do so. However, the study did not consider the possibility that some people with "ill-fated" diseases may have died of other causes. Also, it is possible that people who believe they are destined to die of a certain disease, such as lung cancer, may be less likely to take precautions against it (for example, avoiding smoking).

Still, this research—together with another study by the same group (described in Box 13-2 in Chapter 13), which found that Chinese and Jewish people are less likely to die during ethnic holidays—does suggest that culturally influenced attitudes can play an important role in the course of disease.

CHANGES IN BODY SYSTEMS

▼

One important change that may affect health is a decline in *reserve capacity* (or *organ reserve*), a backup capacity that helps body systems function in times of stress. Reserve capacity is like money in the bank for a rainy day. Normally, people do not use their organs and body systems to the limit. Extra capacity is available for extraordinary circumstances, allowing each organ to put forth 4 to 10 times as much effort as usual. Reserve capacity helps to preserve *homeostasis,* the maintenance of vital functions within their optimum range (Fries & Crapo, 1981).

With age, reserve levels tend to drop. Although the decline is not usually noticeable in everyday life, older people generally cannot respond to the physical demands of stressful situations as quickly or efficiently as before. Someone who used to be able to shovel snow and then go skiing afterward may now exhaust the heart's capacity just by shoveling. Young people can almost always survive pneumonia; older people often succumb to it, as Rose Kennedy, mother of President John F. Kennedy and Senators Robert and Edward Kennedy, did at age 104. Older pedestrians who cannot call on fast reflexes, vigorous heart action, and rapidly responding muscles to get out of harm's way are more likely to be victims of traffic accidents.

However, most normal, healthy middle-aged adults—and even many older ones—barely notice changes in systemic functioning. Although no longer able to reach the peak performance levels of their youth, they retain enough reserve capacity to function well. By pacing themselves, they can do just about anything they need and want to do (Katchadourian, 1987).

Let's "tour" five major body systems—skeletal, cardiovascular, respiratory, immunological, and neurological—and see what changes may occur with age.

SKELETAL SYSTEM

With aging, changes in bones and joints* can lead to two of the most common physical disorders in older adults: osteoporosis and arthritis.

Structural and Functional Changes

Aging often brings problems with the joints. The smooth, protective cushion of cartilage covering the ends of bones tends to deteriorate, perhaps because of repeated stress or internal changes.

The bones themselves, especially in women, become less dense. Throughout life, the body constantly absorbs and replaces calcium in the bones. As people age, there is typically some net loss of bone as more calcium is absorbed than replaced. In women, bone loss usually begins at about age 30, speeds up at

*Unless otherwise noted, this discussion is based on Spence (1989) and Jaffe (1985).

menopause, and then levels off. Men, whose bones contain more calcium to begin with, typically do not have bone loss until after 60 (Exton-Smith, 1985; Spence, 1989).

Excessive loss of calcium can cause bones to become thin and brittle, and, together with visual impairments, can lead to falls. A woman over age 65 has a 1-in-5 chance of breaking a hip (Brody, 1992b). Fractures can be more damaging to older adults than to younger people—harder and slower to heal, and more likely to result in extended loss of mobility and independence.

Older people can minimize the risk of falling by having regular vision and hearing checkups; asking about side effects of medicines that may affect coordination and balance; avoiding alcohol, which can interfere with balance and reflexes; getting up slowly after eating or resting; keeping nighttime temperatures no lower than 65 degrees, since a drop in body temperature can cause dizziness; using a cane, walking stick, or walker on uneven or unfamiliar ground; walking cautiously on wet or icy pavements; wearing rubber-soled or low-heeled shoes (not socks only, or smooth-soled slippers); and exercising regularly. (See Table 3-2 in Chapter 3, a safety checklist for the home.)

Osteoporosis

Osteoporosis ("porous bones"), a disorder in which the bones become extremely thin and brittle as a result of rapid calcium depletion, is present in 1 in 4 women over age 60 and is a major cause of broken bones in old age. Frequent signs of osteoporosis are loss in height and a "hunchbacked" posture due to compression and collapse of weakened bones in the spine. Osteoporosis is most prevalent in white women, those with fair skin or a small frame, those with a family history of the condition, and those whose ovaries were removed at an early age (NIA, 1993). Although most common after menopause, osteoporosis may begin to develop before age 30 in young women who avoid milk products in order to lower their intake of fat, as many American women do. Affected women may lose up to 50 percent of their bone mass between ages 40 and 60 or 70 (Spence, 1989).

Proper nutrition and exercise begun in youth and maintained throughout life, along with avoidance of smoking, can slow the rate of bone loss and prevent osteoporosis (Dawson-Hughes et al., 1990; NIA, 1993; NIH, 1984). Women over age 40 should get 1,000 to 1,500 milligrams of calcium a day from low-fat milk, cheese, and yogurt or other foods, along with recommended daily amounts of vitamin D, which enables the body to absorb calcium (NIA, 1993). Although findings on calcium supplements are mixed, some studies have found value in extra calcium intake by women over age 50 to 55 (Dawson-Hughes et al., 1990; "Should You Take," 1994). The best exercises for increasing bone density are weight-bearing activities, such as walking, jogging, aerobic dancing, and bicycling (NIA, 1993). Men, who have 1 out of 5 cases of osteoporosis, also need to get enough calcium and exercise ("Should You Take," 1994).

Estrogen supplements are sometimes prescribed for women at high risk of developing osteoporosis. This step, while effective in preventing bone loss, is controversial, and 3 out of 4 postmenopausal women decide against it ("Should You Take," 1994; see Box 4-3). Alternative therapies include calcitonin (a hormone) and etridronate (a phosphate additive), but their effectiveness may diminish with long-term use ("Should You Take," 1994).

BOX 4-3

THE ART OF AGING

The Estrogen Decision

The sharp drop in estrogen production after menopause is the leading cause of bone loss in older women, which can lead to osteoporosis. Artificial estrogen, which can make up for the loss of natural estrogen, is the most widely prescribed drug in the United States (Crowley, 1994b), alone or in combination with progestin, a form of the female hormone progesterone. There is strong evidence that hormone-replacement therapy (HRT) can help prevent cardiovascular disease, and there are mixed findings on its role in Alzheimer's disease (Barrett-Connor & Kritz-Silverstein, 1993; Paganini-Hill & Henderson, 1994). Estrogen appears to improve skin tone and memory, help maintain the vitality of the sex organs, help prevent vaginal and urinary infection, and relieve "hot flashes" and other symptoms of menopause. But estrogen therapy is costly (up to $30 a month) and has been linked to higher rates of cancer of the lining of the uterus (endometrial cancer) and possibly to breast cancer. The safety of long-term hormone treatment is still under study, and alternative treatments are being tested. Meanwhile, women need to weigh potential risks and benefits.

Let's look at four possible benefits, and at two warnings.

Reasons to Consider HRT

1. Currently, HRT is the best way of combating bone loss during the first 5 to 7 postmenopausal years. It has proven effective against osteoporosis, especially when started before symptoms appear. However, bones may weaken if the treatment is discontinued ("Should You Take," 1994). The National Institute on Aging (1993) recommends that women at menopause consult their doctors about tests for bone mass and about the advisability of HRT. Recent studies found that estrogen therapy can promote bone formation even in women over 70 (Felson et al., 1993; Prestwood et al., 1994).

2. Some physicians maintain that estrogen's protective effect against heart disease, which kills more women each year than all cancers combined, outweighs any small increase in deaths from cancer (Cobleigh et al., 1994; Goldman & Tosteson, 1991). In a 10-year nonrandomized study of 48,470 postmenopausal nurses, estrogen therapy cut the risk of heart disease almost in half (Stampfer et al., 1991). Estrogen appears to improve the balance between HDL ("good") and LDL ("bad") cholesterol, which we discuss later in this chapter (The Writing Group, 1995), and may stave off atherosclerosis ("Estrogen and the Heart," 1994).

(CONTINUED)

BOX 4-3

CONTINUED

3. Although estrogen taken alone increases the risk of uterine cancer, when it is taken with progesterone this risk falls below that of women who take no hormone at all (Bush et al., 1983; Hammond, Jelovsek, Lee, Creasman, & Parker, 1979). Of course, this issue does not affect women whose uterus has been removed by hysterectomy.

4. Low doses of estrogen may soothe headaches that sometimes develop after menopause. But estrogen can also trigger headaches ("Headache," 1994; see below).

Reasons to Be Wary of HRT

1. Concerns about the possible role of estrogen in breast cancer have yet to be resolved. A meta-analysis of English-language studies found that women who used estrogen after menopause had no special risk of breast cancer (Henrich, 1992). But data from a long-term nonrandomized study of more than 120,000 female nurses suggest that women who use estrogen for more than 5 years do have a significantly increased risk, depending on age (Colditz et al., 1995). Some studies show that estrogen produces very dense breast tissue (the type found in young

women), which has been associated with more aggressive breast cancer and with difficulty in detecting potentially cancerous lumps. It may be possible to reduce the density of breast tissue, and thus the risk of breast cancer, by taking hormones that suppress ovulation, together with small doses of estrogen and progesterone (Spicer et al., 1994).

2. About 10 percent of women taking HRT experience such side effects as weight gain, headaches, nausea, fluid retention, swollen breasts, and vaginal discharge. There also is increased risk of abnormal vaginal bleeding. Women who experience such bleeding should be especially cautious about taking estrogen. So should those who are obese; those who have high blood pressure, migraine headaches, seizures, large uterine fibroids, diabetes, or endometriosis; those with kidney, pancreatic, or gallbladder disease; those with a history of breast or uterine cancer, heart attack, stroke, liver disease, thrombophlebitis, or thromboembolism; and those whose mothers took DES (diethylstilbestrol) during pregnancy. Women who choose HRT should have yearly medical checkups ("Alternatives," 1994; NIA, 1993).

Arthritis

Arthritis is a general term for more than 100 disorders that cause pain and loss of movement, most often involving inflammation of the joints. Arthritis occurs more frequently with advancing age and is the most common chronic health problem of older adults, affecting nearly half of those age 65 and older. But it can strike young people, too; if so, they may have to live with the condition for the rest of their lives (AARP, 1994; Arthritis Foundation, 1993; NIA, 1993).

The most common form is *osteoarthritis,* or degenerative joint disease. Osteoarthritis occurs when a joint becomes chronically inflamed, perhaps because of wear and tear or repeated stress, and cartilage begins to break down.

(Ruth Cincotta/Black Star)

Range-of-movement exercises, done in a swimming pool, can help people who have arthritis.

The rough, exposed ends of the bones rub together, causing the joint to swell and stiffen. Weight-bearing joints in the spinal column, hips, and legs, as well as the fingers and toes, are most commonly affected. Tennis players often develop osteoarthritis in the elbow and knees, and pianists and typists in the fingers.

Rheumatoid arthritis is a crippling disease that progressively destroys joint tissue. It is more common and more severe in women than in men. It can begin at any age; often, symptoms appear before age 50 and become more debilitating over time. Rheumatoid arthritis is most likely to affect the small joints in the hands, wrists, elbows, feet, and ankles. It starts with inflammation of the synovial membrane, which lubricates the joint and nourishes the cartilage. Without treatment, the cartilage may be damaged and the joint may become deformed. In severe cases, the bones may eventually fuse, immobilizing the joint.

The cause of either type of arthritis is unknown. One possibility is that rheumatoid arthritis may be a malfunction of the autoimmune system, which (as we'll discuss later) begins to attack the body's own cells.

Treatment usually involves a combination of medication, rest, physical therapy, application of heat or cold, and some method of protecting the joints from stress, such as canes or splints or just using a joint itself more carefully. Aspirin or other nonsteroidal anti-inflammatory drugs can relieve pain and control inflammation. Range-of-movement exercises can help, especially when done in a heated spa or pool. A radical treatment is replacing a joint, especially the hip. Withdrawal of fluid that may form in the joint cavity can relieve osteoarthritis. So can cortisone injections (especially in the knee). However, since cortisone itself can damage cartilage, this treatment cannot be repeated too often.

CARDIOVASCULAR SYSTEM

Changes in the *cardiovascular system*—the heart and blood vessels, which circulate the blood that carries oxygen and other nutrients to the cells—may lead to life-threatening disease.[*]

Structural and Functional Changes

The heart is a muscle, and, like other muscles, may become less flexible when healthy muscle tissue is replaced with fat or more rigid connective tissue. *Cardiac reserve*—the heart's ability to pump faster under stress—may decline substantially, and the remaining muscle tissue must work harder to compensate. In some older adults, the heart's output may be only half what it was at age 20. Both fat deposits and pumping capacity can be greatly influenced by diet and exercise.

Two interrelated changes in the blood vessels may be forerunners of disease. A gradual increase in **blood pressure** (the force of blood flow against the arterial walls) may begin as early as the twenties. Although a slight elevation of blood pressure is normal with aging, a significant rise may lead to severe health problems in middle or old age. High blood pressure tends to promote thickening and loss of elasticity of the arteries—*arteriosclerosis* ("hardening of the arteries"), which occurs as flexible tissue is gradually replaced by collagen fibers. Like a garden hose that becomes stiff, rigid arteries, in turn, offer greater resistance to blood flow, making the heart work harder and raising blood pressure.

Cardiovascular Diseases

Cardiovascular disease is the leading cause of death in the United States and other developed nations. It has been estimated that nearly 1 in 10 Americans will die of diseases of the heart or blood vessels (Spence, 1989). Although the death rate from cardiovascular disease dropped 48 percent between 1965 and 1989 in the United States, these diseases still kill nearly 1 million men and women each year (American Heart Association, 1990, 1992, 1993, 1994).

Hypertension (high blood pressure) is usually the first cardiovascular disease to develop, typically in midlife, and it often presages a heart attack or stroke. Hypertension is particularly prevalent among African Americans and people living in poverty (NIA, 1993; USDHHS, 1992). Thirty-six percent of noninstitutionalized older adults have it (AARP, 1994). People who experience a great deal of stress, are obese, consume a large amount of alcohol or salt, or have a family history of hypertension are believed to be more at risk (NIA, 1993). *Atherosclerosis,* or *coronary artery disease,* is a buildup of *plaque,* fatty deposits on the inner walls of arteries. As the heart strains to force blood through the narrowed passages, pressure builds, increasing the risk of a swelling (*aneurism*) or rupture. A *myocardial infarction* (heart attack) happens when a blood clot or plaque buildup stops the flow of blood through a coronary artery that feeds the heart. Without oxygen, the affected heart muscle dies. *Congestive heart failure* can occur when a diseased heart can no longer pump an adequate supply of blood. Blood backs up into the lungs and other tissues, and fluid accumulates in the body.

[*]Unless otherwise noted, the discussion in this section is based on Bigger (1985) and Spence (1989).

In *cerebrovascular disease,* clogged blood vessels so restrict the flow of blood to the brain that nerve cells begin to die. If a blood vessel supplying the brain becomes completely choked off, or if a blood vessel in the brain bursts, a cerebrovascular accident—a *stroke*—will occur, causing brain damage, paralysis, or death. Blood pressure screening, low-salt diet, and education have prevented many deaths from heart disease and stroke (NIA, 1984).

Personality, Gender, and Cardiovascular Disease

Is a particular type of personality prone to heart attack? Early studies found that people (mostly men) with a behavior pattern called *type A*—impatient, competitive, aggressive, and hostile—were more likely to suffer heart attacks in their thirties or forties. By contrast, *type B* people—relaxed, easygoing, and unhurried—rarely had heart attacks before age 70, even if they smoked, ate fatty foods, and did not exercise (Friedman & Rosenman, 1974). However, more recent research has cast doubt on the relationship between type A behavior and heart disease. One line of study suggests that only one aspect of type A behavior—hostility—seems to be related to heart disease (Barefoot, Dahlstrom, & Williams, 1983; R. B. Williams, Barefoot, & Shekelle, 1984). A meta-analysis of 101 studies done over a period of four decades seems to suggest the existence of a generally disease-prone personality, rather than a personality specifically prone to heart attack (Friedman & Booth-Kewley, 1987).

In the past, most studies of heart disease—as with many other health conditions—were done on men (Healy, 1991). Today, major new research is seeking information on cardiovascular disease in women. One recent finding is that, while men's blood pressure tends to rise when they are angry, women's blood pressure rises when they are anxious. However, there is no evidence that anxiety—or hostility, or job pressure—increases women's risk of heart disease ("We're Not Like Men," 1994).

Heart disease is the leading cause of death in both sexes. Nearly half of the 500,000 Americans who die of heart attacks each year are women; and cardiovascular diseases kill more than twice as many women as all forms of cancer. The risk is especially great for black women age 35 to 84, whose death rate from heart attacks is 1.4 times that of white women (American Heart Association, 1992). Heart disease is generally thought of as a men's disease because more men have heart attacks and have them earlier in life. But women are less likely to survive a heart attack and, if they do, are more likely to have another.

As in men, women's risk increases with age. Before menopause, atherosclerosis progresses less rapidly in women; but after menopause, arterial clogging and consequent risk of coronary heart disease begin to "catch up" (Katchadourian, 1987). Between ages 45 and 64, 1 in 6 men but only 1 in 9 women has some form of cardiovascular disease; in women over 65, the ratio climbs to 1 in 3. A little more than one-fourth of women age 18 to 54, but more than half of those over 55, have high blood pressure. And an astonishing 83 percent of black women and 66 percent of white women over 65 have high blood pressure (American Heart Association, 1992, 1993). There is evidence that estrogen therapy dramatically lowers these risks (Stampfer et al., 1991; refer back to Box 4-3).

RESPIRATORY SYSTEM

Since breathing is essential, physiological changes that restrict expansion of the lungs and other parts of the respiratory system can be life-threatening.[*]

Structural and Functional Changes

Beginning in the twenties, respiratory structures gradually tend to become more rigid. Cartilage in the walls of the *trachea* (the windpipe), and in the *bronchial tubes* that branch off from its lower end, begins to calcify, as does cartilage in the rib cage. The lungs lose elasticity because of changes in the chemical composition and structure of their fibers; and the bubble-like *alveoli*, the microscopic air sacs in the lungs, shrink. These changes, together with deterioration of the muscular and skeletal systems—which may cause the spine to curve forward, constricting the chest—can make breathing less efficient.

Vital capacity—the amount of air that can be drawn in with a deep breath and then expelled—diminishes beginning at about age 40 and may drop as much as 40 percent by age 70. In an ongoing longitudinal study of most of the population of the town of Framingham, Massachusetts, vital capacity has turned out to be the best single predictor of how much longer a person will live, regardless of level of activity (Walford, 1986), and thus this may be an excellent biomarker of aging.

Respiratory Disorders

It is normal for people to sleep less in their later years. Older people sleep more lightly, dream less, and have fewer periods of deep sleep (Webb, 1987; Woodruff, 1985).

Some "light sleepers" have a disturbance called *sleep apnea,* a halt in breathing for 10 seconds or more, which causes a person (especially an older male) to awaken frequently and then fall back to sleep, resuming normal breathing. An estimated 30 to 50 percent of otherwise-normal older men experience 25 or more such episodes nightly, and some have hundreds. Sufferers may be aware only that they are sleepy in the daytime. Sleep apnea appears to be related to snoring, which also becomes more common, particularly among men, with advancing age (Prinz, 1987; Woodruff-Pak, 1987). People who use sleeping pills, drink alcohol, take daytime naps, sleep on their backs, or are overweight are more prone to sleep apnea. Because the condition is associated with a pronounced rise in blood pressure, adults who have it may be at increased risk of heart disease and strokes (Prinz, 1987; Roff & Atherton, 1989; "Sleep," 1995; Woodruff-Pak, 1987).

Emphysema is an irreversible disease in which chronic irritation from smoking, polluted air, or respiratory infections causes destruction of lung tissue and progressive difficulty in breathing. The lungs become inflexible, making exhaling difficult. Stale air gets trapped in the alveoli, so that they cannot take in fresh air. The walls of the alveoli are damaged, permitting less oxygen to enter the blood-

---

[*]Unless otherwise noted, the discussion in this section is based on Spence (1989).

stream. Symptoms include confusion, disorientation, and sometimes periods of unconsciousness as the brain literally suffocates. People suffering from emphysema often have to breathe pure oxygen on a regular basis. There is no cure. Death often results from heart failure: the disease places an extra load on the heart, whose pumping must become faster and harder to circulate more blood in a futile effort to get more oxygen from the lungs. Emphysema is usually avoidable through better health habits, such as quitting smoking.

IMMUNE SYSTEM

The *immune system* is the body's primary defense against invading foreign substances (*antigens*). The immune system attacks invaders by means of (1) *antibodies*, specialized proteins that counteract specific antigens; and (2) *T cells*, special white blood cells that attach themselves to antigens and destroy them. T cells originate in the bone marrow and mature in the thymus gland before entering the bloodstream (Braveman, 1987; Spence, 1989).

Structural and Functional Changes

With advancing age, the thymus shrinks—by age 50, to perhaps 10 percent of its original size—and the number of mature T cells in the bloodstream decreases (Braveman, 1987; Spence, 1989). As a result, people tend to become more susceptible to infection and less able to recover from it. Because of the decline in the body's defensive capabilities, it is advisable for older adults to get flu shots.

Many scientists believe that heightened *autoimmunity*—a tendency for the body to mistake its own tissues for antigens—is responsible for aging (Spence, 1989). According to this *autoimmune theory* of aging (a variation on the error theories discussed in Chapter 3), the immune system begins to release antibodies that destroy its own cells.

Mature-Onset Diabetes

Autoimmune reactions may play a part in a number of diseases, including *mature-onset diabetes,* which typically develops after age 30 and becomes more prevalent with age (American Diabetes Association, 1992). Unlike *juvenile-onset,* or *insulin-dependent,* diabetes, in which the level of blood sugar rises because the body does not produce enough insulin to metabolize glucose, in mature-onset diabetes glucose levels rise because the cells lose their ability to *use* the insulin the body produces. As a result, the body may try to compensate by producing *too much* insulin (Spence, 1989). At least 90 percent of the 14 million Americans with diabetes have mature-onset, or *non-insulin-dependent,* diabetes. People with mature-onset diabetes often do not realize it until they develop such serious complications as heart disease, stroke, blindness, kidney disease, or loss of limbs (American Diabetes Association, 1992). Diabetes caused nearly 49,000 deaths in 1991 (National Center for Health Statistics, 1994), but the toll is probably much higher, as death certificates often list one of the other chronic conditions associated with the disease.

The definitive symptom of either type of diabetes is sugar in the urine. (Physicians also test the urine for *ketones*, poisons that may form in the blood if the body attempts to burn fats instead of sugar as a source of energy.) Other symptoms include abnormal thirst, frequent urination, rapid weight loss, tiredness, and wounds that will not heal, especially in the feet and hands. Mature-onset diabetes may be controlled by appropriate diet and exercise or may be treated with oral medications.

AIDS

The movie actor Rock Hudson died from it. The beloved basketball star Earvin "Magic" Johnson quit playing because he was infected with the virus that causes it. Millions of people who don't yet know they have it will come down with it in the next few years.

Acquired immune deficiency syndrome (AIDS), a failure of the immune system that leaves affected persons vulnerable to a variety of fatal ailments, has been spreading rapidly since the early 1980s. In the United States, it is now the leading cause of death among 25- to 44-year-olds (Centers for Disease Control and Prevention, 1995; see Figure 4-3). AIDS results from a contagious disease, human immunodeficiency virus (HIV), which destroys the T cells that enable the

FIGURE 4-3

Death rates from leading causes of death among 25- to 44-year-olds in the United States, 1982–1993. Deaths from HIV infection, the virus that causes AIDS, have increased dramatically in comparison with all other leading causes of death in this age group.

(SOURCE: Centers for Disease Control and Prevention, 1995.)

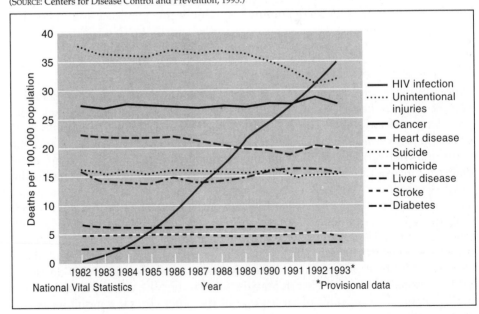

(Terry Bochatey/Reuters/Bettmann)

Elizabeth Glaser caught the HIV virus from a blood transfusion and unknowingly passed it on to her infant daughter in her breast milk. At the 1992 Democratic National Convention, Glaser gave an emotional speech to raise consciousness about the need for AIDS research. Although most AIDS cases in the United States so far are among men, the incidence among women is increasing dramatically, as it is worldwide.

immune system to fight off invasions. HIV is transmitted through bodily fluids (mainly blood and semen) and is believed to stay in the body for life. Symptoms of AIDS—which include extreme fatigue, fever, swollen lymph nodes, weight loss, diarrhea, and night sweats—may not appear until 6 months to 10 or more years after the initial HIV infection. As of now, AIDS is incurable. However, the drug azidothymidine (AZT) and other, more recently developed drugs may prolong life. The average time from HIV infection to death has been 10 years. But about 5 percent of HIV-infected people remain healthy and do not show the same declining blood counts as HIV-infected people whose disease progresses. The eventual fate of "nonprogressors" (as they are called) is not known, but many seem to be staying healthy 10 or more years after being infected with the virus (Baltimore, 1995).

The World Health Organization (WHO) estimates that 15 million adults and 1 million children had been infected with HIV by 1995, up from 12 million in 1992, and that 40 million people will be infected by the year 2000. By 2020, according to the U.S. Census Bureau's World Population Profile, the number of cases will soar to 121 million; in some countries, this will result in life expectancies 9 to 25 years lower than before the AIDS epidemic. At the beginning of 1995, more than 50 percent of the world's cases of HIV were in sub-Saharan Africa, where the virus is believed to have first entered the human population. In some African countries, 1 out of 4 adults has been infected. Currently, HIV is spreading most rapidly in southeast Asia—especially in the cities of Thailand and India—and in South America (King, 1996).

Worldwide, most HIV-infected adults are heterosexual, and the infection rate for women is rising dramatically, particularly in developing countries (A. Larson, 1989; N. Miller & Rockwell, 1988). WHO predicts that by the year 2000 most new HIV infections will be in females (Altman, 1992). According to the U.S. Census Bureau, if people in developing countries increased their use of condoms by 20 percent, they could cut the HIV infection rate in half by the year 2015. In Zaire, a campaign to distribute condoms in drugstores, movie theaters, bars, grocery stores, and clinics resulted in more than a tenfold increase in sales (Altman, 1992).

In the United States, more than 441,500 cases of AIDS were reported among adults and adolescents from 1981 through June 1994 (Centers for Disease Control and Prevention, 1994),* and 1 million people are believed to have HIV. However, many AIDS cases and AIDS-related deaths are probably not reported. Here, unlike most other parts of the world, affected adults so far are predominantly male. Most are drug abusers who have shared contaminated hypodermic needles, homosexual and bisexual men, people who have received transfusions of infected blood or blood products, and people who have had sexual contact with someone in one of these high-risk groups. Prevention efforts focus on education in safer sex practices (such as use of condoms and avoidance of promiscuity) and screening of blood used in transfusions; more controversial are proposals to reduce sharing of hypodermic needles by distributing clean ones to drug users.

Heterosexual transmission was responsible for 9 percent of new AIDS cases in the United States in 1993—up from about 2 percent in 1985—and for more than half of all new cases among American women (King, 1996). Unprotected heterosexual activity with multiple partners—for example, among users of crack cocaine selling sex to support their drug habit—is an increasingly high risk factor for contracting HIV (Edlin et al., 1994).

AIDS does not attack only the young; people over age 50 now account for 11 percent of recorded cases in the United States (Ayya, 1994). About 17 percent of patients in this age group contracted it through contaminated blood transfusions before routine screening began in 1985. The disease seems to be more severe and to progress more rapidly in older adults, perhaps because the immune system is weakened (Brozan, 1990; USDHHS, 1992). Because health professionals and caregivers are often unaware of the risk of AIDS in older persons, and because AIDS-related dementia may be mistaken for dementia due to other causes, AIDS in older people is often misdiagnosed or is diagnosed only when the patient is on the brink of death (Ayya, 1994).

NEUROLOGICAL SYSTEM

The *neurological,* or *nervous, system* is a communication link among the cells and organs of the body and a key to the functioning of many other body systems, including sensory perception and muscular control.

---

*In 1993, Centers for Disease Control (CDC) revised its criteria for AIDS; as a result, there was a dramatic increase in the number of reported cases.

The nervous system has two parts: the *central nervous system* and the *peripheral nervous system*. The central nervous system—brain and spinal cord—is responsible for higher-level functions such as memory, language, and intelligent behavior, as well as reflexes. The peripheral nervous system connects the central nervous system to the rest of the body.

Structural and Functional Changes

Although the brain does change with age, these changes vary considerably from one person to another. In normal, healthy older people, changes are generally modest and make little difference in functioning (Kemper, 1994). The brain increases in weight until about age 30; there is then a slight weight loss and later an increasingly rapid loss. By age 90, the brain may lose up to 10 percent of its weight, probably because of a loss of nerve cells, or *neurons*. Nerve cells, like muscle cells, cannot replace themselves. Because some neurons die every day, the total number of cells in the nervous system declines throughout adulthood. Different parts of the brain lose varying numbers of neurons. The *cerebellum* may lose 25 percent of its cells, noticeably affecting balance and fine motor coordination, while other parts of the brain lose few cells and retain their functioning virtually intact (Spence, 1989).

A functional change that commonly accompanies loss of brain matter is a gradual slowing of responses, beginning in middle age. After age 70, many adults no longer show the knee jerk; by age 90 all such reflexes are typically gone (Spence, 1989). A slowdown of the central nervous system can affect not only physical coordination but also intellectual performance. It can worsen the performance of older adults on intelligence tests, especially timed tests, and can interfere with their ability to learn and to remember (Birren et al., 1980; Salthouse, 1985; Spence, 1989).

Not all brain changes are negative. Between middle age and early old age, nerve cells may sprout additional branches, or dendrites. This may compensate for the loss of neurons by increasing the number of *synapses*, or connections among remaining cells (NIH/NIA, 1993; Sapolsky, 1992; D. J. Selkoe, 1992).

The *autonomic nervous system*, a part of the peripheral nervous system, often declines in old age, making it more difficult to withstand extreme temperatures and lessening control over the anal and urethral sphincter muscles.

Dementia

The confusion, forgetfulness, and personality changes sometimes associated with old age may or may not have physiological causes. The general term for physiologically based intellectual and behavioral deterioration is **dementia;** we discuss this further in Chapter 12. Contrary to stereotype, dementia is not an inevitable part of aging. Nor is moderate memory loss necessarily a sign of dementia. Although most dementias are irreversible, some can be reversed with proper diagnosis and treatment (American Psychiatric Association, 1994; NIA, 1993). Many dementias formerly thought to be due to other causes are now being attributed to Alzheimer's disease (discussed in the next section).

"DREAD DISEASES" OF AGING

Although heart disease kills more people than any other, perhaps the most deeply feared diseases that strike adults are Alzheimer's disease and cancer. Both are progressively debilitating, involve prolonged intense suffering, and are more prevalent with age. In their later stages, they disrupt not only the patient's life but the lives of families, friends, and caregivers. Both have captured immense public and professional attention, and the search for causes, prevention, and treatment continues to have a massive economic and social impact.

ALZHEIMER'S DISEASE

A respected poet cannot remember her own name, much less her poetry. A former industrial tycoon, swathed in a diaper, spends hours polishing his shoes. These are among the victims of *Alzheimer's disease (AD)*, a progressive, irreversible, degenerative brain disorder that gradually robs people of memory, intelligence, awareness, and even the ability to control their bodily functions—and finally kills them.

Alzheimer's disease seems to be the "disease of the 1990s." Even before former president Ronald Reagan revealed that he had it, in 1994, it had been a target of vast research resources and media coverage. Today, it is the fourth leading

(Richard Falco/Black Star)

Alzheimer's disease, a degenerative brain disorder with no known cure, is one of the most dreaded diseases associated with aging.

cause of death in the United States. Yet only 20 years ago most people had not even heard of it. What has happened? Why do so many people today—an estimated 3 to 4 million Americans (Baker, 1994; Edwards, 1994)—seem to have it? Why are so many people worried about getting it?

In 1907 Alois Alzheimer, a German psychiatrist, reported a "strange disease of the cerebral cortex." After the patient, a 56-year-old woman, died, Alzheimer examined her brain and found extensive loss of nerve cells and shrinkage of the cortex, as well as unusually large masses of two structures that tend to form in aging brains: amyloid plaques and neurofibrillary tangles (Banner, 1992; Bogerts, 1993). *Amyloid plaques* are formed outside nerve cells by the protein beta-amyloid and contain decaying dendrites and axons, the cells' message-bearing links. *Neurofibrillary tangles* are masses of twisted, hairlike protein filaments that develop inside nerve cells. Both structures exist in the brains of normal older adults, though not in the same concentrations or locations as in Alzheimer's patients. Excessive formation of plaques and tangles, which interferes with communication between nerve cells, is characteristic of Alzheimer's disease.

The disease is rarely seen in anyone younger than 50, and the risk increases dramatically with age. Estimates of prevalence vary from 2 to 10 percent of adults over age 65 and from 13 to 50 percent of those age 85 and over. Women, who are longer-lived than men, are more at risk (Evans et al., 1989; Folstein, Bassett, Anthony, Romanoski, & Nestadt, 1991; Skoog, Nilsson, Palmertz, Andreasson, & Svanborg, 1993; "Testing for Alzheimer's Disease," 1995). The main reason so many more cases are diagnosed now than in the past, then, aside from increased knowledge about the disease, is that far more people now reach an age when they are likely to show signs of it. The number of Alzheimer's patients is expected to rise to at least 14 million by the year 2040, as the baby boomers grow old (Friend, 1994). The graying of the population also explains why there is so much interest in finding a cure or treatment, or at least a way to postpone onset. A 10-year delay in the average age of onset could mean a 75 percent reduction in the number of cases (Banner, 1992).

The first signs of Alzheimer's disease are often overlooked. An older person may occasionally garble telephone messages, have some trouble playing cards, or go on sudden spending binges. The most noticeable early symptom is loss of memory, especially for recent events. More symptoms follow: confusion, irritability, restlessness, and agitation, accompanied by impaired judgment, concentration, orientation, and speech. (Table 4-1 compares early warning signs of Alzheimer's disease with normal mental lapses.) As the disease progresses, symptoms become more disabling. By the end, a person cannot eat without help, cannot understand or use language, and does not recognize family members.

So far the only definitive way to diagnose Alzheimer's disease is Alois Alzheimer's procedure: analysis of brain tissue after death. Doctors usually diagnose Alzheimer's disease in a living person through neurological, psychiatric, and memory tests and by ruling out other conditions. Diagnoses made in this way are 80 to 90 percent accurate, as confirmed by autopsy (Banner, 1992).

Suggested causes of Alzheimer's disease include biochemical deficiency, viral infection, defect of the immune system, and even aluminum poisoning; but none of these possibilities has generated enough reliable and convincing data to be

TABLE 4-1   ALZHEIMER'S DISEASE VERSUS NORMAL BEHAVIOR: WARNING SIGNS

Normal Behavior	Symptoms of Disease
Temporarily forgetting things	Permanently forgetting recent events; asking the same questions repeatedly
Inability to do some challenging tasks	Inability to do routine tasks, such as making and serving a meal
Forgetting unusual or complex words	Forgetting simple words
Getting lost in a strange city	Getting lost on one's own block
Becoming momentarily distracted and failing to watch a child	Forgetting that a child is in one's care and leaving the house
Inability to balance a checkbook	Forgetting what the numbers in a checkbook mean and what to do with them
Misplacing everyday items	Putting things in inappropriate places where one cannot usefully retrieve them; e.g, a wristwatch in a fishbowl
Occasional mood changes	Rapid, dramatic mood swings and personality changes; loss of initiative

SOURCE: Adapted from Alzheimer's Association (undated).

widely accepted (Farrer et al., 1990; Henderson & Finch, 1989; Manuelidis, deFigueiredo, Kim, Fritch, & Manuelidis, 1988). Recent evidence suggests that at least some cases (perhaps including Reagan, whose mother also had the disease) are genetically based. In one study, relatives of patients with Alzheimer's disease were found to have an almost 50 percent risk of getting it by age 90—about 4 times as high as that of a control group (Mohs, Breitner, Silverman, & Davis, 1987). Mutant genes on chromosomes 21 and 14 seem to be related to an early-appearing form of the disease (Karlinsky, Lennox, & Rossor, 1994; St. George-Hyslop et al., 1987; Schellenberg et al., 1992). The late-onset type may be inherited in much the same way, through a gene pair on chromosome 19 (Roses, 1994).

Such findings raise hopes that researchers may soon be able to develop genetic tests to identify people at high risk of Alzheimer's disease, though at this point forecasting remains very imprecise. Some cases appear to be inherited; many others do not. It may be that Alzheimer's disease is actually a set of related diseases, each with different causes but all resulting in a similar pattern of brain destruction.

There is dispute over which of the two characteristic features of Alzheimer's disease—plaques or tangles—is the main cause of death of nerve cells (Banner, 1992; Roses, 1994). If plaques are the principal cause, then treatment may require finding a way to keep them from proliferating (Banner, 1992). However, researchers at Duke University, such as Allen Roses (1994), suggest that neuro-fibrillary tangles are the primary cause of the disease and plaques are only a secondary symptom. These researchers have been investigating a gene called APOE that can take several different forms, or *alleles*. One of these alleles, APOE4, may permit tangles to develop by inhibiting production of a protein that helps maintain the structure of nerve cells. APOE4 exists in about 30 percent of the population and appears to be a significant risk factor for developing late-onset Alzheimer's disease (Lennox et al., 1994). If Roses is right, the disease might be treated by supplements of the inhibited protein.

Regardless of which of these lines of research eventually proves most accurate, an effective treatment may be many years away. Memory training and memory aids may help in the early stages (Camp et al., 1993; Camp & McKitrick, 1992). Promising new drugs to improve memory and behavior are being tested (K. L. Davis et al., 1992; Farlow et al., 1992). Tacrine (sold under the name *Cognex*), the only medication for Alzheimer's approved so far by the U.S. Food and Drug Administration, is generally prescribed at early stages to maintain or raise brain levels of the neurotransmitter acetylcholine, a chemical involved in communication between nerve cells. Possible side effects of Tacrine include nausea, stomach problems, and—a more serious concern—liver damage from prolonged large doses. Regular monitoring through blood tests to adjust the dosage to safe levels can raise the cost to more than $250 a month. Although some patients respond well to Tacrine, others show little effect; and any gains are lost when its use is discontinued.

Family members often suffer greatly from Alzheimer's disease. In the early stages, there is the stress of uncertainty and the gradual realization that something is very wrong. Normal roles and expectations become confused and eventually reversed. In its later stages the disease destroys intimacy and at the same time imposes an enormous burden of caregiving (see Chapter 10). Strains can affect not only the caregiver (often the spouse or an adult daughter) but other family members, including an adult child's spouse, children, and in-laws. Probably the biggest source of help for both patient and family is social and emotional support from professional counseling and support groups (Blieszner & Shifflett, 1990; Fisher & Lieberman, 1994; Garwick et al., 1994).

CANCER: A DISORDER OF MANY SYSTEMS

Cancer is a term for more than 100 different diseases involving uncontrolled growth of abnormal cells, which, if untreated, eventually invade healthy tissue. Unlike the other diseases discussed so far, cancer can arise in and spread to many body organs and systems.

Cancer is the second leading cause of death in older adults, after cardiovascular disease (USDHHS, 1991). At least 50 percent of the more than 1 million cancers diagnosed annually in the United States—and more than 60 percent of the roughly 500,000 annual cancer deaths—are in people over age 65 (American Cancer Society, 1994; Ershler, 1992; Freeman, Whartenby, & Abraham, 1992; Porterfield & St. Pierre, 1992). One explanation is a weakened immune system. Another is that older people have had more time to develop cancers, which are often slow-growing. Overall, the death rate from cancer rose 7 percent between 1970 and 1990. Actually, it fell 20 percent among young adults; but it increased 15 percent among older people, perhaps as a result of better detection, a decline in deaths from heart disease, and greater longevity ("Are We 'in the Middle,'" 1994).

Some cancers (such as basal cell carcinoma, a skin cancer) are far more curable than others. Although death rates have dropped dramatically for stomach, colorectal, ovarian, and cervical cancer, they have risen even more dramatically for lung cancer, the biggest killer—up 104 percent in men and 452 percent in women since 1960, largely because of smoking (American Cancer Society, 1994).

The discovery of two mutant genes responsible for many cases of cancer of the colon and rectum may someday enable doctors to identify and monitor people at risk of these types of cancer and possibly other types as well. The mutations apparently cause a failure to correct errors in DNA that arise during cell division, permitting cells to multiply uncontrolled (Fackelmann, 1993b; G. Weiss, 1994). *Gene therapy*—insertion of genetic material into the body to alter cellular composition or replace defective genes—is now an experimental treatment but is expected to become important in the next decade (Freeman et al., 1992; "The New Genetic Screens," 1995).

Not all cancers appear to be genetic, however. Suspected or known environmental *carcinogens* (cancer-causing agents) include pollution, pesticides, plastics, and much else. Exposure to the sun can cause skin cancer. The best ways to prevent cancer or to stall its growth are to avoid smoking, drink alcohol only in moderation, exercise, and eat a healthy diet.

In the 1930s, 4 out of 5 cancer patients died within 5 years. Today—thanks to chemotherapy (anticancer drugs), radiation treatments, and surgery—the 5-year survival rate is near 50 percent. But the improvement in long-term survival is considerably less ("Are We 'in the Middle,'" 1994; Taub, 1985). Many more people could be saved through periodic screening (especially of adults over 50 and those with a personal or family history of cancer), which would permit earlier diagnosis and treatment. The recent discovery of telomerase, an enzyme which is present in virtually all cancers and allows tumor cells to grow and proliferate indefinitely, has led to the testing of medications that could block its action. Such treatment might be less dangerous to healthy cells and more effective than present methods (Kim et al., 1994).

Recently there has been an upsurge of concern about two gender-related cancers: breast cancer and prostate cancer.

Breast Cancer

Breast cancer strikes about 182,000 American women a year and kills as many as 46,000. As with other cancers, the chance of developing breast cancer increases with age. More than 90 percent of affected women are 40 or older, and about 80 percent are past 50 (American Cancer Society, 1994). Nine out of 10 women with breast cancer can survive at least 5 years if the cancer is caught before it spreads (Spence, 1989; Taub, 1985). But younger women who develop breast cancer are

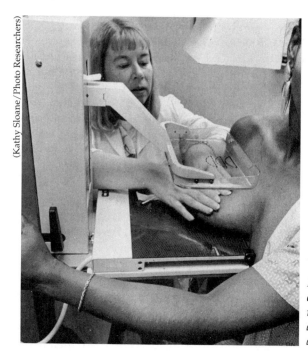

(Kathy Sloane/Photo Researchers)

Routine mammography (x-ray examination of the breasts) is recommended for all women age 50 and over to aid in early detection and treatment of breast cancer.

more likely to have a recurrence within 5 years and less likely to survive (de la Rochefordiere et al., 1993).

There is disagreement about how early and how often women should have *mammography,* diagnostic x-ray examination of the breasts. Findings pointing to radiation itself as a carcinogen and questioning its effectiveness in detecting cancer in younger women led the National Cancer Institute in 1993 to stop recommending routine mammography for women under 50. However, given the far greater chance of cure after early detection, the American Medical Association and American Cancer Society continue to recommend routine mammograms for women in their forties. Experts also continue to urge monthly self-examinations, since mammography misses 10 to 15 percent of breast cancers detected manually ("Breast Imaging," 1995). Women between 40 and 49 should consult with their doctors about the advisability of mammography (Fackelmann, 1993a).

Scientists have recently identified one gene, and located another, which may be involved in some cases of breast cancer and ovarian cancer. These discoveries may lead to genetic screening of women with strong family histories of either. Because women with the flawed genes have an estimated 85 percent chance of developing breast cancer someday, they may wish to have more frequent examinations and possibly even preventive surgery ("The Breast Cancer Genes," 1994). A controversial study is testing the preventive possibilities of *tamoxifen,* a drug which can cut by 40 percent the risk of a relapse in a woman who has had a malignancy surgically removed, but which also is believed to increase the risk of uterine cancer (Raloff, 1994b; Schwartz, 1994).

Since the newly identified genes do not appear to be implicated in the vast majority of breast cancers, lifestyle factors may be important. Even moderate use of alcohol brings a 40 to 100 percent greater risk of breast cancer. Studies differ on whether taking estrogen after menopause increases the risk (refer back to Box 4-3).

Another dispute is over the relative efficacy of *lumpectomy,* in which the tumor and a small amount of surrounding tissue are removed; and *mastectomy,* in which all or part of the breast is removed. Findings from an extensive randomized study suggest that lumpectomy followed by radiation is as effective as mastectomy in treating small breast cancers (B. Fisher et al., 1986, 1989; Fowble et al., 1991; Posner & Wolmark, 1994; Veronesi et al., 1990, 1993).

Prostate Cancer

Cancer of the prostate gland (at the base of a man's bladder) has received extensive news coverage since 1993, when it claimed the lives of the rock musician Frank Zappa and the actors Don Ameche and Bill Bixby. Prostate cancer affects about as many men as breast cancer does women. About one-third of men over age 50 have latent prostate tumors, but many are unaware of the condition because these tumors grow so slowly. Although prostate cancer killed some 38,000 American men in 1994—second only to lung cancer—most men with prostate cancer die of something else ("Keeping Cancer," 1994; "The PSA Debate," 1995; Raloff, 1993). Still, while the death rate from breast cancer has begun to fall (at least among white women under age 50), the death rate from prostate cancer is rising, perhaps because men are now living longer ("Are We 'in the Middle,'" 1994; "Breast Cancer: Up or Down," 1995; Eastman & Crowley, 1995).

Men all over the world are equally likely to develop prostate cancer, but they are not equally likely to die of it. The fatality rate in the United States is almost 4.5 times as high as in Japan, for example (Pienta & Esper, 1993a, 1993b). A diet high in certain types of fat, particularly red meat, butter, and chicken with the skin left on, seems to help the disease advance to a lethal stage (Giovannucci et al., 1993).

Prostate cancer can be cured only when it has not spread beyond the prostate gland. The American Cancer Society recommends annual digital rectal examinations after age 40 and annual blood tests after age 50 (age 40 for African-American men, who are at higher risk, and men who have a family history of prostate cancer). The blood test has improved early detection by 25 percent since 1986 ("The PSA Debate," 1995). The most common treatments are radiation and surgical removal of the prostate. Newer treatments to remove or shrink the prostate include cryosurgery (freezing), laser surgery, thermal therapy, chemotherapy, and implantation of radioactive pellets (Blasko, Ragde, & Grimm, 1991; Bonfield, 1995; Soltes, 1994; Wolinsky, 1994). However, treatment can have side effects, such as impotence and incontinence. Because prostate cancer takes so long to become terminal, some physicians contend that men with small tumors—especially those in their late sixties and older—may be safe in simply keeping a tumor under observation ("Better Prostate," 1994; "The PSA Debate," 1995).

An enlarged prostate is not always a sign of cancer, since this gland continues to grow throughout adulthood. However, even a benign enlargement can eventually cause difficulties with urination and may require surgery, usually after age 50 (B. M. King, Camp, & Downey, 1991).

INDIRECT INFLUENCES ON HEALTH

How people take care of their bodies and how they respond to life's changes and challenges affect their health directly. But there are also indirect influences: age, gender, socioeconomic status, race or ethnicity, and relationships.

AGE AND GENDER

How likely are young, middle-aged, and older men and women to develop specific diseases or disorders, and what are the chief causes of death at each period of adulthood? As we summarize health problems and risks by age and gender, keep in mind that not only do wide individual variations exist, but—as we'll show next—certain groups experience greater problems and risks at any age.

When young adults get sick, it is usually from a cold or other respiratory illness, which is easily shaken off. The most frequent chronic conditions, especially among those with low incomes, are back and spine problems, hearing impairment, arthritis, and hypertension (high blood pressure). Since most young adults are healthy, it is not surprising that accidents are the second leading cause of death (after AIDS) for Americans age 25 to 44. Next comes cancer, followed by heart disease and suicide (refer back to Figure 4-3). At age 35, for the first time since infancy, physical illness becomes the chief cause of death, and the death rate at least doubles for each of the next two decades. Between 35 and 44, cancer and heart disease are the major killers. Men age 25 to 44 are twice as likely to die as women. Aside from AIDS, men at this age are mostly likely to die in automobile crashes; women are most likely to die of cancer (Centers for Disease Control and Prevention, 1995; USDHHS, 1992).

The most common chronic ailments of middle age are asthma, bronchitis, diabetes, nervous and mental disorders, arthritis and rheumatism, impaired sight and hearing, and malfunctions of the circulatory, digestive, and genitourinary systems. These conditions may appear before middle age; while three-fifths of 45- to 64-year-olds have one or more of them, so do two-fifths of people between ages 15 and 44 (Metropolitan Life Insurance Company, in Hunt & Hunt, 1974; USDHHS, 1992). The leading causes of death between ages 45 and 64 are cancer, heart disease, stroke, accidental injuries, and conditions related to chronic obstructions of the lungs (USDHHS, 1992, 1995). Men of this age are almost twice as likely to die as women—3 times more likely to die from heart disease and 25 to 30 percent more likely to die from cancer or stroke. The leading cause of death for women age 45 to 64 is cancer, mainly of the breast, reproductive organs, or lungs (USDHHS, 1982, 1986, 1990, 1992).

Most older adults have at least one chronic medical condition—most commonly, arthritis, hypertension, hearing impairment, heart disease, orthopedic impairments, cataracts, sinusitis, diabetes, tinnitus, or visual impairments, in that order (AARP, 1994). Chronic conditions become more frequent with age and may become disabling. Although people over 65 have fewer colds, flu infections, and acute digestive problems than younger adults, chronic conditions combined with loss of reserve capacity may cause a minor illness or injury to have serious repercussions. While deaths from heart disease have declined since the 1960s, it remains by far the leading killer of people over 65, accounting for 40 percent of deaths. The next most common causes of death in this age group are cancer (21 percent) and stroke (8 percent) (U.S. Bureau of the Census, 1995).

Which are healthier—women or men? Women report being ill more often than men, and they use health services more often. Yet—now that improvements in medical care have dramatically reduced deaths during pregnancy and childbirth—women, on average, live 7 years longer than men (Chapter 3). Women's greater longevity has been attributed to the genetic protection given by the presence of two X chromosomes and, before menopause, to the beneficial effects of female hormones (USDHHS, 1992).

The fact that women report being sick more often than men does not necessarily mean that women are in worse health than men, nor that they are imagining ailments or are preoccupied with illness. Instead, it may well be that women today are simply more health-conscious and take better care of themselves. Menstruation and pregnancy tend to make women aware of the body and its functioning, and cultural standards encourage medical management of those processes. Many women see doctors, not only during pregnancy, but for routine tests such as the Pap smear, which detects cervical cancer; and they are more likely to be hospitalized than men, most often for surgery in connection with the reproductive system.

Women generally know more than men about health, think and do more about preventing illness, are more aware of symptoms and susceptibility, and are more likely to talk about their medical fears and worries. Men may feel that illness is not "masculine" and thus may be less likely to admit that they do not feel well. Employment may be a factor in men's lower rates of reported illness. Likewise, employed women report less illness than homemakers, possibly because workers need to protect their jobs and their image as healthy producers (Nathanson & Lorenz, 1982).

SOCIOECONOMIC STATUS, RACE, AND ETHNICITY

In the United States as a whole, adults are healthier and can look forward to longer lives than ever before. But one segment of the population—African Americans who live in inner-city slums—is in as deplorable a state of health as people in some of the poorest and most underdeveloped nations in the world. Black men under age 65 in New York's Harlem, for example, have a lower life expectancy than men in Bangladesh (see Figure 4-4). African Americans are more than twice as likely as white people to die in young adulthood and about 1.8 times as likely to die in middle age; their death rate in middle age is also higher than that of Hispanics, Asian Americans, and Native Americans (USDHHS, 1992). Death

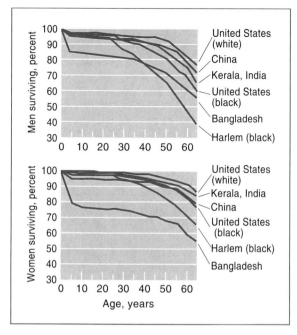

FIGURE 4-4
Variations in survival rates by sex, race, and region.
(SOURCE: Sen, 1993, p. 45.)

rates of African Americans are approximately 35 percent higher than those of white people from cancer and 40 percent higher from heart disease ("Are We 'in the Middle,'" 1994; USDHHS, 1992).

What accounts for this catastrophe in a prosperous, highly developed country? The largest single factor is poverty, which results in poor nutrition, substandard housing, inadequate prenatal care, and limited access to health care (Otten, Teutsch, Williamson, & Marks, 1990). Black women are more than 3 times as likely as white women to die during pregnancy, in part because they are less likely to get early prenatal care ("Differences in Maternal Mortality," 1995). And they are more than twice as likely to die of breast cancer within 5 years of diagnosis, probably because they are less likely to get mammograms and their cancers tend to be diagnosed later (Eley et al., 1994).

Almost one-third (31 percent) of the excessive mortality of black people age 35 to 54 can be attributed to six risk factors: high blood pressure, high cholesterol, overweight, diabetes, smoking, and alcohol (Otten et al., 1990). The first four may be partly attributable to heredity, which also predisposes black people to sickle cell disease. But lifestyle plays a part in these four factors, and of course in the last two—smoking and drinking. By practically every measure, lifestyle factors that contribute to ill health are epidemic in poor African American communities. Poor black people have a high incidence of cancer (especially lung cancer), heart disease, and cirrhosis of the liver (Chissell, 1989; McCord & Freeman, 1990). Because more black people suffer from high blood pressure, they are nearly twice as likely as whites or Hispanics to have strokes, and to die of strokes (Sacco, Hauser, & Mohr, 1991; USDHHS, 1992). One in 10 African Americans has diabetes, and African Americans have higher rates of blindness, kidney failure, and amputation of limbs as a result (American Diabetes Association, 1992).

(Eric Breitenbach/The Picture Cube)

Hispanic Americans are especially prone to high blood pressure.

This gap persists in old age. Affluent and white older people are likely to be healthier than poor and black ones; elderly Hispanic Americans seem to fall in between (Markides, Coreil, & Rogers, 1989).

Poverty is not the only factor. Education is important, too. The less schooling people have had, the greater the chance that they will develop and die from such chronic ailments as hypertension and heart disease (Pincus, Callahan, & Burkhauser, 1987). The disparity between the high death rates of poor and poorly educated people and the lower death rates of more affluent, better-educated people increased from 1960 to 1986 (Pappas, Queen, Hadden, & Fisher, 1993). This does not mean, of course, that formal education *causes* good health. However, education is related to other factors that may be causative. Better health care, together with the benefits of health habits set early in life, may explain why college-educated people, wealthier people, and white people rate their health better than less educated, lower-income, and minority-group people (USDHHS, 1982, 1985, 1990, 1992, 1995).

Severe health problems among Hispanic Americans are related to poverty, low levels of education, and cultural and language barriers. Hispanic Americans suffer disproportionately from high blood pressure, kidney disease, certain cancers, AIDS, lead poisoning, and diabetes (Council on Scientific Affairs of the American Medical Association, 1991). More than one-third of Hispanics age 65 to 74 have diabetes, as compared with one-fourth of African Americans and fewer than 17 percent of white Americans in that age group (American Diabetes Association, 1992). Because Hispanic Americans are less likely than any other ethnic group in the United States to have health insurance, their ailments tend to be diagnosed at a more advanced stage, when they are less likely to benefit from treatment (Council on Scientific Affairs of the American Medical Association, 1991).

RELATIONSHIPS

Relationships have important effects on physical well-being. People who are isolated from friends and family are twice as likely to fall ill and to die as people who maintain social ties (House, Landis, & Umberson, 1988).

Although there is some evidence to the contrary (J. M. White, 1992), marriage seems to be associated with good health. Married people—especially married men—tend to be healthier physically and psychologically than people who are separated, divorced, widowed, or never-married (C. E. Ross, Mirowsky, & Goldsteen, 1990). Married people have fewer disabilities or chronic conditions that limit their activities; and when they go to the hospital, their stays are generally short. Married people live longer, too, according to a study going back to 1940 in 16 industrial countries (Hu & Goldman, 1990). Those who have never married are the next-healthiest group, followed by widowed people and then by people who are divorced or separated.

Why should this be? Healthy people may attract mates more easily, may be more interested in getting married, and may be better marriage partners. Or married people may lead healthier, safer lives than single people. Because spouses can take care of each other, they may be less likely to need care in hospitals or institutions. Married people tend to be better off financially, a factor that seems to enhance physical and mental health (C. E. Ross et al., 1990). Then, even in less-than-ideal marriages, partners usually provide companionship, offer emotional support, and do many things that ease day-to-day life. The loss of these supports through death or separation may make widowed and divorced people more vulnerable to mental and physical disorders (Doherty & Jacobson, 1982). The quality of a marital relationship may make a difference.

The key to the correlation between marriage and health may be simply having another person to live with. A study of more than 25,000 women age 18 to 55 found that those who lived with another adult—whether married or not—were healthier than those who lived alone (Anson, 1989).

FACTORS IN
MAINTAINING AND IMPROVING HEALTH

▼

Health is often directly linked to how adults live from day to day—whether and how much they drink, whether they smoke or abuse drugs, how they react to stress, what and how much they eat, how they take care of their teeth, and whether they get proper exercise. Healthful habits can modify a number of aspects of biological aging, such as cardiac and pulmonary (lung) reserve, glucose tolerance, bone loss, cholesterol levels, and blood pressure (Porterfield & St. Pierre, 1992). Since 1977, mortality has declined 30 percent for Americans age 25 to 64, largely because of changes in personal lifestyle (USDHHS, 1992). Although good health habits can't guarantee protection against disease, they can greatly reduce the risks, especially if started early in life (Porterfield & St. Pierre, 1992; see Table 4-2).

TABLE 4-2   **TACTICS FOR REDUCING RISKS OF SELECTED DISEASES**

√√√ *Highly effective*   √√ *Moderately effective*   √ *Somewhat effective*

	No tobacco	Low-fat diet	High-fiber diet	Avoid alcohol	Avoid salted, pickled foods	Diet high in vegetables and fruits	Exercise, weight control
Cancer							
Lung	√√√	√				√	
Breast		√√√	√			√√	√
Colon		√√√	√√√			√√√	√
Liver				√√√	√	√√	
Heart attack	√√√	√√√				√√	√√
Stroke	√				√√√	√√	√√
Adult diabetes		√√√	√			√√	√√

SOURCES: Porterfield & St. Pierre, 1992, p. 114 (based on data from American Health Foundation).

HARMFUL SUBSTANCES

Two of the most beneficial decisions a person can make are to stop smoking (or, better still, not to start) and to drink alcohol only in moderation.

Tobacco

Smoking is the leading preventable cause of death in the United States, killing 390,000 people yearly and disabling millions (NIA, 1993). *Passive smoking*—inhaling other people's smoke—is third, after alcohol (Correa, Pickle, Fontham, Lin, & Haenszel, 1983; Fielding & Phenow, 1988; Trichopoulos et al., 1992). Non-smokers who live with people who smoke more than two packs of cigarettes a day inhale as much smoke as if they themselves smoked one or two cigarettes a day (Matsukura et al., 1984). Worldwide, 3 million people die each year as a result of smoking, and that number may be rising because of cigarette exports from the United States, which grew by 275 percent between 1985 and 1993, especially to Japan, the former Soviet Union, and South Korea (American Cancer Society, 1994).

The link between smoking and lung cancer is well established. Since 1977, deaths from lung cancer for 25- to 64-year-olds have risen 250 percent. Smoking is estimated to be responsible for more than 80 percent of these deaths and for at least one-third of all cancer deaths in the United States ("Are We 'in the Middle,'" 1994; USDHHS, 1990). A nonsmoking woman who lives with a moderate smoker has a 30 percent higher risk of lung cancer than otherwise; if she lives with a heavy smoker, her risk is 80 percent higher. People exposed to secondhand smoke in the workplace increase their risk by 39 percent ("Environmental Tobacco Smoke," 1994).

Smoking is also linked to cancer of the larynx, mouth, esophagus, bladder, kidney, pancreas, and cervix, to gastrointestinal problems such as ulcers, to respiratory illnesses such as bronchitis and emphysema, and to heart disease (NIA, 1993; USDHHS, 1987). A 45-year-old man who smokes cigarettes has a 70 percent greater chance of a heart attack than a nonsmoker, and a woman who smokes runs more than twice the risk. A woman smoker's risk rises dramatically if she uses oral contraceptives; according to some research, such women have 39 times the chance of a heart attack as women who neither smoke nor use birth control pills. However, some studies suggest that this risk may be lessened with newer, low-dose pills (American Heart Association, 1992; Katchadourian, 1987). Secondhand smoke also may damage the heart (Glantz & Parmley, 1995).

A smoker who has a heart attack is more likely than a nonsmoker to die from it (American Heart Association, 1992). Cigar and pipe smokers are in less danger of heart attack than cigarette smokers, but still at higher risk than nonsmokers; and they are more likely to get cancer of the lips, tongue, and mouth (Katchadourian, 1987).

As these risks have become widely known, smoking has declined—40 percent since 1965, though only 32 percent among women (American Heart Association, 1992). Still, according to a national survey, 30 percent of American adults now smoke, up 5 percent since 1991 (Prevention Research Center, 1993). At least 90 percent of the people who stop smoking do so on their own (Fiore et al., 1990). Others turn to special programs, such as support groups. Nicotine chewing gum and nicotine patches, along with information on the drawbacks of smoking, have been quite successful (NIA, 1993; USDHHS, 1987).

However and whenever people stop smoking, their health is likely to improve immediately. Giving up smoking reduces the risks of heart disease and stroke, even after an initial heart attack (Katchadourian, 1987; Kawachi et al., 1993; NIA, 1993). In one study, women who had given up smoking for at least 3 years had a risk of heart attack no higher than that of women who had never smoked (Rosenberg, Palmer, & Shapiro, 1990). The risk of cancer takes longer to decline but within 10 years is no greater than for a nonsmoker (NIA, 1993).

Alcohol

The United States is a drinking society. Advertising equates liquor, beer, and wine with the good life. According to a national survey, 59 percent of adults say that they sometimes drink. Of those who drink, 46 percent—a modest decline since 1983—say they have one to three drinks a day. However, the proportion who are heavy drinkers, consuming four or more drinks a day, has remained at 12 percent since the early 1980s (Prevention Research Center, 1993).

Although moderate consumption of alcohol seems to reduce the risk of fatal heart disease, the definition of *moderate* is becoming more restricted. A recent large-scale study found that men who take more than one drink a day have much higher death rates. Apparently, increased risk of cancer of the throat, gastric system, urinary tract, and brain outweighs any benefits to the heart (Camargo, Gaziano, Hennekens, Manson, & Stampfer, 1994). And other studies suggest that women can safely drink only about half as much as men.

Long-term heavy use of alcohol may lead to cirrhosis of the liver, other gastrointestinal disorders (including ulcers), certain cancers, heart failure, damage to the nervous system, psychoses, and other medical problems. Alcohol is also a major cause of deaths from automobile accidents; it is implicated in deaths from drowning, suicide, fire, and falls; and it is often a factor in family violence (National Institute on Alcohol Abuse and Alcoholism, 1981). We discuss alcohol abuse and alcoholism further in Chapter 12.

STRESS

You've taken on a heavy course load and feel overwhelmed by deadlines. You're facing a major competitive challenge at work. You've just had an argument with your boyfriend or girlfriend. You can be under stress for an almost infinite number of reasons. *Stress* is an organism's physiological and psychological reaction to difficult demands made on it.

The more stressful the changes that take place in a person's life, the more likely the person is to become ill within the next year or two. That was the finding of a classic study in which two psychiatrists, on the basis of interviews with 5,000 hospital patients, ranked the stressfulness of life events that had preceded illness (Holmes & Rahe, 1976; see Table 4-3). Some of the events seemed positive—for example, marriage, a new home, or an outstanding personal achievement. Even happy events, though, call for adjustments. Change can be stressful, and some people react to stress by getting sick.

Stress—or rather, how people cope with stress—is coming under increasing scrutiny as a factor in causing or aggravating such diseases as hypertension, heart ailments, stroke, and ulcers. The most commonly reported physical symptoms of stress are headaches, stomachaches, muscle aches or muscle tension, and fatigue. The most common psychological symptoms are nervousness, anxiety, tenseness, anger, irritability, and depression. In one study of 227 middle-aged men, the 26 who had had heart attacks were more likely than the others to have worried and to have felt sad, anxious, tired, and lacking in sexual energy in the year before the attack (Crisp, Queenan, & D'Souza, 1984). Another study of 2,320 men who had had heart attacks found that men who were socially isolated and under stress were more likely to die within 3 years after an attack than more sociable men who were under less stress (Ruberman, Weinblatt, Goldberg, & Chaudhary, 1984). We discuss the psychology of coping with stress in Chapter 12. Here, our focus is on its physiological effects.

TABLE 4-3 SOME TYPICAL LIFE EVENTS AND WEIGHTED VALUES

Life Event	Value
Death of spouse	100
Divorce	73
Marital separation	65
Jail term	63
Death of close family member	63
Injury or illness	53
Marriage	50
Being fired at work	47
Marital reconciliation	45
Retirement	45
Change in health of family member	44
Pregnancy	40
Sex difficulties	39
Gain of new family member	39
Change in financial state	38

SOURCE: Adapted from Holmes & Rahe, 1976.

The body's ability to respond to stress tends to become impaired with age. Although body systems may function well under normal circumstances, when challenged by stressful events they do not respond as efficiently as in youth. An older person's body may both underreact and overreact to stress—not stepping up heart output enough during physical exertion, but releasing excessive amounts of adrenalin and other stress hormones well after the stress-provoking event is over (Lakatta, 1990).

Some theories (see Chapter 3) attribute biological aging itself to effects of a lifetime's accumulation of stress. Even adaptive responses can cause stress if repeated often enough. For example, a rise in blood pressure enables a person to flee an attacker; but a person whose blood pressure is consistently elevated for years—perhaps owing to stress on the job—is a prime candidate for a heart attack, ulcers, or colitis (Sapolsky, 1992). Long-term oversecretion of stress hormones may play a part in a number of age-related disorders, from mature-onset diabetes to osteoporosis (Krieger, 1982; Munck, Guyre, & Holbrook, 1984).

There do seem to be limits to such degeneration, and some individuals seem to escape it entirely. By studying individual differences in reactions to stress—particularly to psychological stress, which has less uniform effects than physical stress—we may begin to find a key to prevention or treatment of stress-related disorders.

One reason the same event leads to illness in one person and not in another may have to do with a sense of mastery or control. When people feel that they can control stressful events, they are less likely to get sick. Research on human beings and animals has found links between stressful events perceived as uncontrollable and various illnesses, including cancer (Laudenslager, Ryan, Drugan, Hyson, & Maier, 1983; Matheny & Cupp, 1983; Sklar & Anisman, 1981). One team of researchers suggested that belief in external, rather than personal, control suppresses the functioning of the immune system and creates health problems, including depression (Rodin, Timko, & Harris, 1985). Stress management workshops teach people to control their reactions and to turn stress into an opportunity for constructive change. These workshops frequently incorporate such techniques as relaxation, meditation, and biofeedback.

DIET

"You are what you eat" is not just a cliché. The cumulative effects of diet and nutrition become more apparent with age.

Obesity—an overweight condition technically defined as a skinfold measurement in the 85th percentile—is a serious health hazard. It affects the circulatory system, the kidneys, and sugar metabolism; it contributes to degenerative disorders and tends to shorten life. The National Institutes of Health (NIH, 1985) urges that the 34 million Americans who have medically significant obesity receive the same kind of attention given to patients with life-threatening disorders. Even being modestly overweight can impair health, especially in combination with such conditions as diabetes and hypertension. The risk of being overweight is highest from ages 25 to 34, making young adults a prime target group for prevention (Williamson et al., 1990). The healthiest way to lose weight is to eat less, exercise more, and change eating patterns so as to maintain the loss.

Reducing cholesterol levels in the bloodstream through diet and drugs can lower the risk of heart disease and death (Lipid Research Clinics Program, 1984a, 1984b; Scandinavian Simvastatin Survival Study Group, 1994). There are two kinds of cholesterol: low-density lipoprotein (LDL) cholesterol and high-density lipoprotein (HDL) cholesterol. HDL seems to have a protective function. A favorable ratio between these two, with HDL ("good") cholesterol relatively high and LDL ("bad") cholesterol relatively low, is even more important than total cholesterol level. Although a recent study suggests that the effects of cholesterol may not persist in men and women older than 70, these findings are controversial, and more study is needed ("Aging and Cholesterol," 1995; "Cholesterol," 1995).

Nine major voluntary and government health agencies have proposed a "healthy American diet" for everyone from age 2 up (American Heart Association, 1990). It emphasizes a variety of nutritionally sound foods, with less fat, salt, and cholesterol and more fiber and complex carbohydrates, found in fruits, vegetables, cereals, and grains. The "healthy American diet" takes the risk of cancer into account. Extensive worldwide research points strongly to a link between diet and certain cancers—particularly between a high-fat diet and colon cancer (Willett, Stampfer, Colditz, Rosner, & Speizer, 1990).

DENTAL CARE

Few people keep all their teeth until very late in life. Loss of teeth, usually due to tooth decay or *periodontitis* (gum disease), can have serious implications for nutrition. Because people with poor or missing teeth find many foods hard to chew, they tend to eat less and to shift to softer, sometimes less nutritious foods (Wayler, Kapur, Feldman, & Chauncey, 1982). People with dentures tend to be less sensitive to dangerously hot foods and liquids and less able to detect bones and other harmful objects (NIA, 1993).

Dental health is related to inborn tooth structure and to lifelong eating and dental habits. Extensive loss of teeth—especially among the poor—may reflect inadequate dental care more than effects of aging. In one interview study, more than half of those 65 and over had not seen a dentist for 2 years or more (USDHHS, 1990).

Because the risk of tooth decay continues as long as a person has natural teeth, so does the need for regular checkups. In addition, gum disease becomes an increasingly common cause of tooth loss after age 35. Drinking fluoridated water, brushing daily with fluoride toothpastes, flossing, and using antibacterial or antiplaque mouth rinses can help prevent these conditions (NIA, 1993).

EXERCISE

Today's exercise boom is showing results. According to a recent survey, 78 percent of American adults regularly engage in physical activity, and 37 percent exercise strenuously at least three times a week (Prevention Research Center, 1993). Those who do reap many benefits. Physical activity helps to maintain desirable body weight; build muscles; strengthen heart and lungs; lower blood pressure; protect against heart attacks, cancer, and osteoporosis; relieve anxiety and depression; and possibly lengthen life (Lee, Franks, Thomas, & Paffenbarger, 1981; Lee & Paffenbarger, 1992; McCann & Holmes, 1984; Notelovitz & Ware, 1983).

The benefits of exercise are not confined to marathon runners and aerobics fanatics. In one study, when more than 13,000 healthy men and women were tested on a treadmill, they fell into five categories of heart and respiratory fitness. The least fit led the most sedentary lives; the fittest exercised strenuously. Eight years later, the death rates of the least fit were more than three times the death rates of the most fit. But those who merely walked for ½ hour to 1 hour every day at a fast but comfortable pace also cut their health risks by half or more (Blair et al., 1989). Similarly, a 3-year study of 500 women between ages 42 and 50 found that moderate daily exercise—or even as little as three brisk 20-minute walks each week—can lower the risk of heart disease (Owens, Matthews, Wing, & Kuller, 1992).

Healthful aging is not merely a matter of chance. The message of the new research on biological aging, and the message of the lifespan developmental

(Doug Plummer / Photo Researchers)

Adults who exercise regularly—as more than 3 out of 4 American adults do—can cut their health risks dramatically.

approach, is that individuals have some control over their physical destiny. The choices young and middle-aged adults make, day by day, may well help determine how they look and feel when they reach old age. We may or may not be able to extend the human lifespan, but we can make more of the lifespan vital and healthy. Good health habits can prevent, delay, or even reverse what used to be considered the inevitable ravages of aging. As we discuss in Chapters 5, 6, and 7, adults can also do much to maintain or improve their cognitive functioning, even into old age.

SUMMARY

HEALTH AND AGING: A LIFESPAN DEVELOPMENTAL APPROACH

■ Although most adults remain fairly healthy into old age, the peak of health is generally in young adulthood.

■ Many declines associated with aging may be effects of disease. Large variations between individuals and within the same person can be understood through a lifespan developmental approach.

■ Healthier lifestyles can promote a high level of physical functioning well into old age.

CHANGES IN BODY SYSTEMS

- Despite a decline in reserve capacity, most aging adults can do necessary tasks and desired activities.

- A common change, especially in postmenopausal women, is thinning of the bones due to calcium depletion; excessive depletion can produce osteoporosis.

- Arthritis is the most common chronic health problem of older adults.

- The heart tends to lose elasticity as fat replaces muscular tissue, and the output of blood may diminish. Other age-related changes are a rise in blood pressure and arteriosclerosis.

- Cardiovascular disease is the leading cause of death in the United States and other developed nations, among both women and men. Women's risk rises after menopause.

- Respiratory structures tend to become less elastic with aging, and vital capacity diminishes, making breathing less efficient.

- Changes in the immune system can make older people more susceptible to infections and less able to recover. Heightened autoimmunity may cause or contribute to biological aging.

- Several diseases, including mature-onset diabetes, may result from autoimmune reactions. One is HIV infection, which causes AIDS, an eventually fatal failure of the immune system. AIDS is spreading rapidly throughout the world.

- Changes in the brain are usually minor, and new connections can compensate for loss of nerve cells. A slowing of the central nervous system can affect physical and intellectual functions, but dementia is not an inevitable part of aging.

"DREAD DISEASES" OF AGING

- Both Alzheimer's disease and cancer are prolonged, progressively debilitating, and more prevalent with age.

- The causes of Alzheimer's disease have not been definitively established; but research points to genetic causes in some cases.

- Cancer is the second leading cause of death in older people. Genetic and environmental causes of certain cancers have been identified. Many cancers can be cured if treated early. Death rates have dropped for many cancers but have risen for lung cancer.

INDIRECT INFLUENCES ON HEALTH

- Indirect influences on health include age, gender, socioeconomic status, race or ethnicity, and relationships.

- The prevalence of various chronic conditions and causes of death varies across the lifespan and between men and women.

- Although women report more frequent illness than men, they live longer and may be healthier because of their greater focus on health.

- In the United States, minority groups such as African Americans and Hispanic Americans are in significantly poorer health than white people, largely because of poverty, limited education, lack of access to treatment, and lifestyle factors.

- Supportive relationships, particularly marriage, are related to enhanced physical health.

FACTORS IN MAINTAINING AND IMPROVING HEALTH

- Smoking is the leading preventable cause of death in the United States, and passive smoking is third. Smokers who quit can dramatically improve their health.
- Although alcohol consumption has declined, heavy drinking still causes a number of medical problems, as well as accidental deaths.
- Stress seems to be a factor in illness. The body's ability to respond to stress tends to decline with age. There are also individual differences in ability to handle stress.
- Obesity is a life-threatening condition. The risk of being overweight is greatest in young adulthood.
- A high-fiber, low-fat, low-cholesterol diet can lessen the risk of heart disease and cancer.
- Dental health is related to inborn tooth structure and to lifelong eating and dental habits.
- Exercise improves health and protects against a number of major diseases.

KEY TERMS

reserve capacity (page 123)
homeostasis (123)
osteoporosis (124)
arthritis (126)
cardiac reserve (128)
blood pressure (128)
arteriosclerosis (128)
hypertension (128)
atherosclerosis (128)
myocardial infarction (128)
congestive heart failure (128)
stroke (129)
vital capacity (130)
sleep apnea (130)
emphysema (130)

autoimmunity (131)
mature-onset diabetes (131)
acquired immune deficiency
    syndrome (AIDS) (132)
dementia (135)
Alzheimer's disease (AD) (136)
cancer (139)
carcinogens (140)
mammography (141)
lumpectomy (142)
mastectomy (142)
passive smoking (148)
stress (150)
obesity (152)
periodontitis (153)

CHAPTER 5

MEMORY

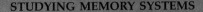

STUDYING MEMORY SYSTEMS

INFORMATION-PROCESSING
APPROACH:
SOFTWARE OF MEMORY
Processes: Encoding, Storage,
  and Retrieval
"Storehouses": Sensory, Short-Term,
  and Long-Term
Aging and Long-Term Memory:
  Stability or Decline?
Summing Up: Memory and Age

BIOLOGICAL APPROACH:
HARDWARE OF MEMORY
Structures Controlling Conscious
  Memory
Structures Controlling Unconscious
  Memory

NEW DIRECTIONS FOR RESEARCH

ASPECTS OF MEMORY AND
FORGETTING IN ADULTHOOD
Intrusion Errors: Remembering
  What Did Not Happen
Prospective Memory: Remembering
  to Do Something
Production Deficiencies in Strategies
  for Remembering
Metamemory: The View from Within
Mnemonics: Making the Most
  of Changing Memory
Forgetting and Its Surprising Benefits

BOXES
5-1 The Cutting Edge: Everyday
    Memory—A Case of Conflict
    among Researchers
5-2 The Art of Aging: The Best Memory
    Aid—A Healthy Lifestyle
5-3 The Multicultural Context:
    Memory and Culture

*"The memory . . . likes to paint pictures.
Experience is not laid away in it like a snapshot
. . . but is returned to us as a portrait painted
in our own psychic colors, its form and pattern
structured on that of our life."*

Lillian Smith, *The Journey*

FOCUS: LAURENCE OLIVIER

(The Bettmann Archive)

In his youth, the great British actor Laurence Olivier* had an exceptional memory. At age 20, while playing one part, he learned the leading role for another play in less than a week, letter-perfect. A noted colleague, Ralph Richardson, said of him, "In this respect [the ability to memorize rapidly] Larry was a genius—better than any of the rest of us" (Kiernan, 1981, p. 50).

At age 57, at the height of his career, Olivier began to experience attacks of paralyzing stage fright. He would become breathless; his throat would tighten; the hall seemed to spin; his mind went blank; his face makeup beaded with perspiration; he had momentary blackouts. These anxiety attacks, which continued for almost 10 years, may have been related to fear of aging, of losing his memory. Indeed, he was having more and more trouble remembering lines (Bragg, 1984; J. Miller, 1987; Spoto, 1992). "I'm such a slow study these days," he complained at age 62. "A single scene takes me three weeks. . . . When I was young I learned [the role of] Romeo in two days." A fellow actor once found him in the wings, desperately going over his lines, when he was supposed to be making his entrance. Olivier looked up from the script and remarked, "This is no profession for an adult person" (Spoto, 1992, p. 351).

Throughout the rest of his long and distinguished career, Olivier was increasingly afflicted with memory lapses. In his late years, he limited himself to film and television work, in which short "takes" permit an actor to keep fewer lines in mind. At 73, in conversations with the theater critic Mark Amory (1987), he rattled off casts of plays in

*Sources of biographical information about Laurence Olivier are Amory (1987), Bragg (1984), Granger (1987), Holden (1988), Kiernan (1981), Miller (1987), and Spoto (1992).

which he had appeared 50 or 60 years before and quoted passages from *Hamlet*, one of the roles that had made him famous on stage and screen. When retelling an incident, he made the scene come alive. Yet he couldn't seem to remember Amory's name. By 76, Olivier "could no longer commit one line of dialogue accurately to memory"; but, on hearing of Richardson's death, he told "in vivid and colorful detail [a] cascade of anecdotes" about their six-decades-long association (Spoto, 1992, p. 403).

A few of Olivier's late-life characterizations—notably, King Lear, Lord Marchmain in *Brideshead Revisited*, and the blind Clifford Mortimer in *A Voyage Round My Father*—showed greater depth than ever (though it was generally agreed, when he retired on his eightieth birthday, that he had held on about 3 years too long). As he told a reporter, "Your mind expands as your body shrinks, and you adjust to it, giving in age what you couldn't give in youth" (Spoto, 1992, p. 398).

Memory is the residue of experience. Without the ability to remember, the oldest adult would be like a newborn baby, greeting the world with ever-naive eyes. Reality would be like a picture that must continually be recreated—a series of fleeting images, no sooner perceived than lost.

Calling on stored experience is a key to thinking and to solving problems. Throughout the lifespan, memory enables human beings to learn from encounters with their environment and to put that knowledge to use. An apparent decline in this essential capacity troubles many middle-aged and older adults, even if their work is not so dependent on memorization as Laurence Olivier's. Small lapses in memory may arouse a fear—usually unfounded—that dementia is setting in.

Actually, as the lifespan developmental approach suggests—and as Olivier's example shows—problems with memory need not signal a general decline in mental abilities. Age may bring gains as well as losses. In fact, forgetting may have a positive side. Could there be a relationship between a tendency to forget detailed information (such as an actor's lines) and the growing depth of thought that often comes with maturity? Perhaps forgetting is not necessarily an enemy in old age but an ally, clearing away clutter so the mind can more readily recall important information and find meaningful connections.

In this chapter (which covers memory) and Chapters 6 and 7 (which deal with other aspects of cognition), we look at such changes—both positive and negative—and at how people of advancing age can maintain or enhance their intellectual powers. The information in this chapter may help you better understand your own memory. Do you remember certain kinds of things better than others? Does your memory fail you at times? Under what circumstances does it function best? Do you think your memory will get worse as you grow older? What strategies might help you make the most of your memory?

STUDYING MEMORY SYSTEMS

▼

Changes in memory are a typical sign of aging. A man who always kept his schedule in his head now has to write it in a calendar. A woman who takes several medicines measures out each day's dosages and puts them where she is sure to see them. Yet in memory as in other respects, individuals vary greatly. Jorge, age 58, can rattle off the batting average of every major league baseball player, but his mind is so occupied with his thoughts that he will come into a room and forget what he came for. Jorge's son Julio, age 35, also has trouble remembering what he was about to do, and he can't remember batting averages as well as his father does. And Jorge's mother Juanita, at 75, shows no obvious changes in memory at all.

What explains memory change during adulthood and its variability? Why, as in Laurence Olivier's case, do certain aspects of memory often seem to be more affected than others? A revolutionary new view of memory has developed since the 1960s, thanks to studies in a variety of disciplines, including psychology, biology, and medicine. Scientists now see memory, not as a single capacity, but as a complex, dynamic system of processes and "storehouses." Some, but not all, of these components may operate differently as people age.

Since computers can be programmed to "learn" and "remember," we may be able to understand how human memory works by comparing it with how a computer processes information. Human memory systems can be studied from two perspectives, each of which has produced an independent line of research. *Information-processing research* explores the mental operations involved in remembering: the software of memory. Using concepts from computer science, such as *encoding, storage, search,* and *retrieval,* information-processing researchers have produced elaborate theoretical models of the path a bit of information takes from the moment we perceive it to the moment—perhaps months or years later—when we call it up from memory. *Biological research* maps the physical structures and "wiring" of the brain and nervous system: the hardware of memory. Through animal studies, through observations of people who have suffered brain damage, and by recording brain activity, neuroscientists have begun to pinpoint the actual physical locations where various memory functions and connections take place.

In the following three sections, we look at changes in the "software" and "hardware" of memory and at new directions for research. In the last section of the chapter, we examine how adults cope with changes in memory and how they use tools of memory and forgetting across the lifespan.

INFORMATION-PROCESSING APPROACH: SOFTWARE OF MEMORY

▼

The goal of the information-processing approach is to discover what people do with information from the time they perceive it until they use it. Because this approach focuses on individual differences in intelligent behavior, it is particularly suited to describing changes that take place over the lifespan. It can distinguish between functions that change a great deal and those that change very little, either in the same person or in one person as compared with another (Lovelace, 1990). Most of the early information-processing research took the form of highly controlled laboratory studies in which people of various ages identified pictures, learned word lists, and repeated strings of numbers. During the 1980s and 1990s, some researchers have attempted direct study of how memory works in everyday life (see Box 5-1).

The information-processing approach assumes that:

- Human beings actively seek useful information about their world.
- Human beings can handle only a limited amount of information at a given time; information not currently being used must be stored in memory.
- Information that comes in through the senses is transformed by a series of mental processes into a form suitable for storage and later recall (Lovelace, 1990).

Let's look more closely at these processes and how they may be affected by aging. As we do, however, keep in mind that most information-processing studies are cross-sectional, and their findings may reflect cohort differences rather than age-related changes.

PROCESSES: ENCODING, STORAGE, AND RETRIEVAL

It is helpful to think of memory as a three-step filing system: *encoding, storage,* and *retrieval.* In order to file something in our memory, we first must decide what "folder" to put it in—for example, "people I know" or "places I've been." *Encoding* attaches a "code" or "label" to the information to prepare it for storage, so that it will be easier to find when needed. Next, we *store* the material (put the folder away in the filing cabinet). The last step is to *retrieve* the information when we need it (search for the file and take it out). The precise mechanisms involved in encoding, storage, and retrieval may vary with the situation, the type of information, and how the information is to be used (Lovelace, 1990); difficulties in any of these steps may impair memory.

How information is encoded and stored can affect access (Lovelace, 1990; Wingfield & Stine, 1989). An item that is misfiled (inappropriately encoded or stored in the wrong place) will be hard to retrieve. For example, you would be unlikely to find information on Alaska if it had been filed under "tropical

BOX 5-1

Everyday Memory: A Case of Conflict among Researchers

Should changes in memory functioning be studied in the laboratory or in the real world? Should these changes be studied by measuring performance on contrived tasks, or by observing how and what younger and older adults remember in everyday life?

In 1978, Ulric Neisser, a psychologist at Emory University, in an address some colleagues regarded as "inflammatory" (Roediger, 1991, p. 37), dismissed the mostly laboratory-based memory research of the previous century as wasted effort—trivial and irrelevant to how memory actually works. If an aspect of memory was interesting and significant, Neisser claimed, it had rarely been investigated. Rather than continuing to focus on such "isolated" tasks as recall of items from word lists, he argued, researchers should study memory the way ethologists study animal behavior: by observing it in real-world settings. Only then would their findings be *ecologically valid*—that is, applicable to naturally occurring behavior.

Memory research—traditional as well as ecologically oriented—has changed radically since Neisser spoke out. Today laboratory researchers are studying such topics as implicit (unconscious) memory, metamemory (awareness of how memory works), motor skills, and cognitive maps. Real-world research, using such tools as questionnaires, diaries, autobiographies, and simulations of experience, has delved into such areas as oral tradition, prospective memory ("things to do"), personal recollections, and eyewitness reports.

Still, it is not surprising that there was an eventual backlash. After all, Neisser had, in effect, suggested that "all of the other psychologists who had ever studied memory, had been and probably still were (a) not very bright, (b) socially irresponsible, (c) lacking in imagination, (d) some of the above, or (e) all of the above" (Tulving, 1991, p. 41). Turning the tables, two psychologists at Yale University, Banaji and

Crowder, in an article in *American Psychologist* entitled "The Bankruptcy of Everyday Memory," charged that the everyday memory movement had yet to produce a single important new principle, theory, or method and had sacrificed rigor for "superficial glitter" (1989, p. 1192). They argued that the main criterion of the value of research is its scientific soundness, not its ecological validity; and results of naturalistic studies, because of the "multiplicity of uncontrolled factors," cannot be generalized to other situations (p. 1189). Indeed, they argued, "the more complex a phenomenon, the greater the need to study it under controlled conditions" (p. 1192).

Of course, Banaji and Crowder's article in turn aroused a storm of protest, the emotional flavor of which is apparent from the titles of rebuttal articles that appeared in the same journal: "The Bankruptcy of Everyday Thinking" (Morton, 1991), "In Defense of Everyday Memory" (Conway, 1991), and "A Case of Misplaced Nostalgia" (Neisser, 1991). Some writers offered examples of everyday memory research that were said to represent, not "glitter," but "gold": significant effects found in natural settings, which could not have been discovered in a laboratory (Loftus, 1991; Neisser, 1991). But another writer argued that the rebuttals had missed the point: the paramount importance of experimental control and generalizability, both inside and outside the laboratory (Roediger, 1991.)

Eventually, cooler heads prevailed. One (Klatzky, 1991), in an article entitled "Let's Be Friends," foresaw fruitful interplay between conventional laboratory studies and everyday research. Observation of everyday phenomena may suggest topics for controlled laboratory study; phenomena that surface only in real-world settings can receive laboratory follow-up. "So let us stop squabbling and go back to more creative work," another writer (Tulving, 1991) urged. "Let us identify genuinely important problems, and let us not worry about whether someone labels them artificial or real. Let us work on these problems in whatever setting is most natural, using whatever methods are most appropriate" (p. 42).

Recognizing a familiar face may be easier for older adults than recalling the name of someone they have just met.

islands." Problems also can arise when an item fits in more than one category. For example, if you had filed the word *base* only under "terms used in baseball" and you wanted a synonym for *foundation,* you might not be able to retrieve it. Also, similar items, such as *principal* and *principle,* can cause confusion unless their encoding is distinctive.

How do these memory processes change with age? One finding is that the ability to retrieve newly encountered information seems to drop off. After several hours, days, or weeks, younger adults can remember word pairs or paragraphs, or recognize pictures, better than older people can (Craik, 1977; Park, Pugiisi, & Smith, 1986; Park, Royal, Dudley, & Morrel, 1988; Poon, 1985). But when older people have trouble remembering, is this due to faulty retrieval or to actual loss of material from memory storage—or does it have more to do with the way they encoded the information in the first place? The answer may be any of the above.

- *Encoding problems.* In general, older adults seem to be less efficient than younger ones at encoding new information to make it easier to remember. For example, older people are less likely to spontaneously arrange material in alphabetical order or create mental associations. Older adults can improve their encoding skills through training or instruction, but how much they benefit in comparison with younger adults depends on the task (Craik & Jennings, 1992). In addition, older people's encoding seems to be less precise (Craik & Byrd, 1982).

- *Storage problems.* One plausible explanation for forgetting is that stored material may deteriorate to the point where retrieval becomes difficult or impossible. Although most studies do not support the idea that older people forget more quickly than younger ones (Poon, 1985), recent research suggests that a small increase in "storage failure" may occur with age (Camp & McKitrick, 1989; Giambra & Arenberg, 1993). But if memories do decay, traces are likely to remain, and it may be possible to reconstruct them—or at least to relearn the material speedily (Camp & McKitrick, 1989; Chafetz, 1992).

- *Retrieval problems.* In retrieving learned information from memory, older adults may be able to answer a multiple-choice question but not an open-ended one. While they have more trouble *recalling* items than younger adults, they do about as well in *recognizing* items they know (Hultsch, 1971; Lovelace, 1990). Even then, it takes older people longer than younger ones to search their memories (Anders, Fozard, & Lillyquist, 1972; Lovelace, 1990). Age differences are minimized when older adults are familiar with the material, have an opportunity to practice, and can work at their own pace (Lovelace, 1990; Poon, 1985).

Why do certain memory processes seem to work less efficiently as people age? Where are breakdowns most likely to occur? To answer these questions, we need to look at the structure of memory—where information is kept and how it is handled during each stage of processing.

"STOREHOUSES": SENSORY, SHORT-TERM, AND LONG-TERM

How many sights do you see in a single day? How many sounds do you hear? If you tried to assimilate all the sensory inputs that flood your brain daily, you would suffer from information overload. How does your brain sort out the stimuli you need or want to remember, and where does this material go when you're not using it? Information-processing theorists visualize memory as consisting of at least three different but linked "storehouses" (see Figure 5-1): *sensory memory,* the system's initial entry point; *working memory* for short-term storage and manipulation of information; and *long-term memory* for virtually permanent storage.*

Sensory Memory: Initial Storage

Sensory memory, the first of the mind's three "storehouses," temporarily registers incoming information: whatever you see, hear, smell, taste, or touch. This brief storage is called *echoic memory* for sounds and *iconic memory* for sights. But without some kind of processing, sensory memories fade quickly. The "echo" of the initial impression lasts only seconds, or fractions of a second (Lovelace, 1990).

Sensory memory apparently declines very little with age. Despite the visual losses that typically accompany aging, iconic memory (the part of sensory memory on which the most significant findings have been reported) seems to hold up fairly well. Differences in the ability of younger and older adults to identify a

---

*Some researchers use the terms *primary memory* and *secondary memory* for short-term storage of information after it leaves sensory memory. In this system of classification, the term *tertiary memory* refers to long-term memory.

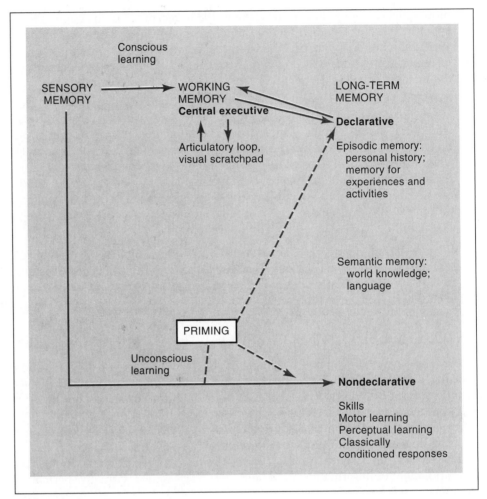

FIGURE 5-1

An information-processing model. Declarative memories generally reach long-term memory via an explicit (effortful) channel, which involves short-term storage and processing in working memory, controlled by the central executive. The central executive can also retrieve information from long-term memory for conscious use. Nondeclarative memories may take the implicit (unconscious) channel, bypassing working memory, and may also be recalled without conscious effort.

(SOURCE: Adapted from Lovelace, 1990.)

series of letters that flash on a screen are quite small. Any slight loss of sensory memory probably plays an insignificant role in problems older people have with learning and retrieval (Poon, 1985), though some researchers speculate that slight losses in sensory memory might lead to larger deficits in short-term and long-term memory (Craik & Jennings, 1992).

Working Memory: Intermediate, Short-Term Storage

When you look up a telephone number and try to remember it before dialing, it goes from sensory memory into *working memory,* an intermediate, short-term "storehouse" or "workbench" for active files—the information your mind is currently encoding or retrieving.

Working memory can normally hold only about five to nine separate chunks of information (such as numbers, letters, or words) at a time (G. A. Miller, 1956). But it's possible to increase the amount of material held in working memory by grouping items into larger chunks. For example, you can more easily remember a telephone number like 2-9-7-5-3-8-4 by mentally combining the digits into 297-53-84, making three chunks instead of seven. Even then, a telephone number or any other item will remain in working memory only about 30 seconds unless you engage in *rehearsal*—conscious repetition—or some other purposeful effort. Rehearsal is a simple device to maintain information in working memory.

According to a widely used model, a *central executive* controls the processing of information in working memory (Baddeley, 1981, 1986). The central executive can expand the capacity of working memory by moving information into subsidiary systems. When verbal information is to be remembered "as is," the central executive may send it to an *articulatory loop* for rehearsal. (For example, you can repeat a telephone number over and over while thinking about what you want to discuss during the call.) A *visual scratch pad* serves a similar purpose, keeping visual images "on hold" while the central executive is occupied with other tasks.

The central executive can order information prepared (encoded) for transfer to *long-term memory,* a "storehouse" of virtually unlimited capacity that holds information for very long periods of time. The central executive also retrieves information, as needed, from long-term memory. Rehearsed information, if repeated often enough, can be transferred to long-term memory. More sophisticated strategies to encode information for long-term storage are (1) *organization,* categorizing the information or arranging it into some sort of coherent pattern; and (2) *elaboration,* finding a relationship between items you are trying to remember, such as *tea* and *cup,* or *hot* and *cold;* or making associations with something you already know.

The capacity of working memory to hold and process information is widely believed to shrink with age. Some researchers assess age effects by asking people to repeat longer and longer sequences of digits (such as, 4-9-7; 5-3-7-1-8-2-9; 6-9-1-4-3-8-2-5-7-3-1). *Digit span*—the number of digits a person can recall in the order presented—seems to be only slightly affected by age, though it may take an older person a bit longer to respond (Craik & Jennings, 1992; Poon, 1985; Wingfield & Stine, 1989). But when asked to repeat *backward* several strings of numbers of increasing length, older adults generally do not do as well as younger ones, though the difference is not dramatic (Craik & Jennings, 1992; Lovelace, 1990).

A key factor seems to be the complexity of the task—how much effort it requires (Kausler, 1990; Wingfield & Stine, 1989). Tasks such as rehearsal, which require only passive holding of information, show very little decline. Tasks that require reorganization, elaboration, or other mental manipulation show the greatest falloff (Craik & Jennings, 1992). For example, if you are asked to repeat a series of items (such as "Band-Aid, elephant, newspaper") in order of increasing size ("Band-Aid, newspaper, elephant"), you must call to mind your previous knowledge of Band-Aids, newspapers, and elephants (Cherry & Park, 1993). Similarly, if material needs to be reorganized, more mental effort is needed to keep it "in mind," using more of the limited capacity of working memory. Some researchers have suggested that as people get older they have less mental energy, or *attentional resources,* to focus on a task (Craik, 1994; Craik & Byrd, 1982; Wingfield & Stine, 1989). Perhaps for that reason, among others we'll discuss later, older adults tend not to use organization and elaboration, even though those are generally considered the most effective encoding strategies (Craik & Jennings, 1992; Salthouse, 1991).

Then, too, motivation may be a factor. Older people may be less attentive to certain kinds of material because they don't see any need to remember it and don't want to expend energy on the task (Craik & Byrd, 1982; see Figure 5-2). Albert Einstein, one of the fathers of nuclear physics, when asked how many feet are in a mile, reportedly said, "I don't know. Why should I fill my head with things like that when I could look them up in any reference book in 2 minutes?"

FIGURE 5-2

Which is the real penny? Most people can't tell, no matter how many times they have seen and held pennies, because they don't pay attention to minor details. Particularly as people age, they tend to conserve mental resources by reserving attention for things they consider important.

(SOURCE: Nickerson & Adams, 1979.)

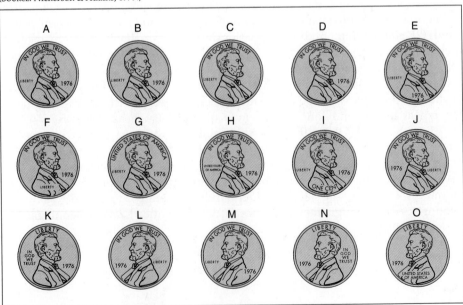

TABLE 5-1   EXAMPLES OF DIFFERING CONTENTS OF DECLARATIVE AND NONDECLARATIVE MEMORY

Declarative	*Nondeclarative*
Facts What is bread made of?	*Habits* Biting your nails
Language What is the plural of *ox*?	*Motor skills* Playing Ping-Pong
Social customs How can you get money in a strange city?	*Perceptual skills* Remembering where you left your car
Personal episodes What dessert did you have at your last birthday party?	*Conditioned responses* How do you react if you see a snake next to your foot?

Long-Term Memory: Inactive Storage

Although long-term memory is believed to have nearly unlimited storage space, not all of its contents are equally accessible. Why is it easy to remember how to ride a bicycle, even after long periods of disuse, while names of people we haven't seen for years, or facts we rarely use, tend to escape us? One likely answer is that long-term memory is divided into "rooms" with different kinds of contents (see Table 5-1 and refer back to Figure 5-1), and aging affects them differently. The two chief divisions are *declarative memory* and *nondeclarative memory.*

Names, dates, definitions of words, recollections of experiences, and many other kinds of information that can be brought to mind and "declared" belong to **declarative memory.** Declaration need not be verbal; it may consist of a mental image, such as a face, a place, or the scent of a rose. Either way, there is a feeling of familiarity, a sense that this is something you have seen, heard, touched, tasted, or smelled before (Squire, 1992, 1994). Declarative memory is often assessed by tests of recognition and recall.

Remembering how to ride a bicycle is an example of **nondeclarative memory** (sometimes called *procedural memory*). This part of long-term memory contains information generally pertaining to skills, habits, or ways of doing things. Much of this information apparently reaches long-term memory directly from sensory memory, largely or completely bypassing working memory and the control of the central executive. In simplest terms, declarative memory is knowing *that . . .* ; nondeclarative memory is knowing *how* (Lovelace, 1990; Schacter, 1992; Squire, 1992).

Recently, researchers have paid increasing attention to apparent differences in how these components of long-term memory are processed. **Explicit memory** refers to conscious or intentional recollection. **Implicit memory** refers to remembering that is unconscious and unintentional (Ashcraft, 1994; Craik & Jennings, 1992; Schacter, 1992). Declarative material, such as knowledge of facts, names, and events, usually requires explicit recall; by contrast, much nondeclarative (procedural) information seems to be processed implicitly. It may be encoded or retrieved without conscious effort—it is simply there when you need it.

AGING AND LONG-TERM MEMORY: STABILITY OR DECLINE?

If older adults have deficiencies in working memory, we might expect them to have more trouble remembering declarative information (facts, names, events) than nondeclarative information (skills and procedures), which may bypass working memory (Kausler, 1990; Lovelace, 1990). In general, that has been found to be true, but the picture is not entirely simple. Let's look more closely at some specific contents of declarative and nondeclarative memory. Then we'll discuss *priming,* an unconscious process that may be involved in remembering both kinds of information.

Declarative Memory: Episodic and Semantic

Do you remember what you had for breakfast this morning? Did you lock your car when you parked it? Did you feed the cat today? Personal experiences, activities, and events such as these—linked to specific times and places, or *episodes*—are stored in *episodic memory,* one of the two main subdivisions of declarative memory. The other main subdivision is *semantic memory:* general knowledge of historical facts, geographic locations, social customs, meanings of words, and the like. Episodic memory is what we generally mean when we say "I remember"; semantic memory is what we mean when we say "I know" (Lovelace, 1990). Semantic memory grows out of episodic memory. When you encounter information often enough, it becomes part of your general knowledge, or *knowledge base* (Camp, 1989).

Of these two components of declarative memory, age generally seems to have a greater effect on episodic memory. Older adults are less likely than younger ones to recall specific events, even in their personal lives—perhaps because they encode less information about the context of an event (where it happened, who else was there) and so have fewer connections to jog their memory (Kausler, 1990; Lovelace, 1990). Older people have had so many similar experiences that individual ones may run together in their minds. A similar phenomenon may be behind older people's tendency to "recall" things that never occurred, or to be uncertain whether something occurred (Cohen & Faulkner, 1989). ("I'm sure I took my medicine today!" "Did I sign the check before mailing it?") Or they may tell the same story over and over to the same people without realizing that they've told it before. But when older people perceive an event as distinctive or novel, they can remember it as well as younger ones (Camp, 1989; Cavanaugh, Kramer, Sinnott, Camp, & Markley, 1985; Kausler, 1990).

Semantic memory, the other main component of declarative memory, takes several forms, none of which depend on remembering when and where something was learned. One is *world knowledge.* What is the capital of France? How many days does a leap year have? Is New York east or west of California? This is

(Alan Carey/The Image Works)

Games like Trivial Pursuit draw on world knowledge, a component of semantic memory. Although young adults may retrieve this knowledge more quickly, older adults tend to do well at such games because they have accumulated more general knowledge through the years.

the sort of information featured in trivia games and television quiz shows. Older adults generally do well in games like Trivial Pursuit because they have accumulated a large quantity of factual knowledge during the course of a lifetime. And older adults seem to be able to retrieve this knowledge efficiently, even though younger adults may do it more quickly in some instances (Camp, 1989; Horn, 1982b; Lachman & Lachman, 1980).

Often, older adults are especially strong in a second type of world knowledge: *social knowledge,* or awareness of behavior appropriate to a situation. How long should a widow or widower remain in mourning? What should you do if a guest insults you at a dinner party? Older people are transmitters of such culturally sanctioned customs and values. In some cultures, they are explicitly recognized as keepers of social knowledge and preside over ceremonies that accompany life transitions, such as puberty and marriage (Mergler & Goldstein, 1983).

Language, too, is part of semantic memory. How many synonyms for *fat* can you list? What is the plural of *child?* What is the difference between *lying down* and *laying down?* Vocabulary and knowledge of linguistic rules, like world knowledge, generally do not decline and may even increase across adulthood (Camp, 1989; Horn, 1982b). However, older adults often have more trouble with some other aspects of linguistic memory. We've all had "tip-of-the-tongue" experiences, when we fumble for a word, or know something but can't quite express it, or (like Laurence Olivier in later life) can't recall someone's name—the last being the most troublesome memory problem for adults of all ages (West, 1985). Older adults, even though their knowledge is greater, seem to have more of these experiences than younger ones, perhaps in part because of problems in working memory (Heller & Dobbs, 1993; Light, 1990; Schonfield, 1974; Schonfield & Robertson, 1960, as cited in Horn, 1982b).

Nondeclarative Memory: Motor, Perceptual, and Conditioned

If nondeclarative memory—the ability to *do* something rather than to recollect something—is a result of unconscious processing, it should be relatively unaffected by age-related problems in working memory. And in general, any deficiencies older people show in nondeclarative memory tend to be negligible or small (Kausler, 1990).

Researchers have learned much about unconscious learning by studying people with amnesia, Alzheimer's disease, and some types of brain damage, which severely impair memory. These patients often retain certain memory functions, which, by inference, must be independent of conscious control. Let's look more closely at several types of unconscious learning and how age affects them.

MOTOR MEMORY   Vladimir Horowitz, considered by many music lovers the greatest piano virtuoso of his time, gave sold-out, critically acclaimed performances up to his death at 85—4 days after he had completed his last recording and a month before two scheduled recitals in Germany (Schonberg, 1992). Another brilliant keyboard artist, Arthur Rubinstein, gave his farewell recital at 89, having put off his retirement for almost a year after he began to go blind (Rubinstein, 1980). These are but a few of many examples of the persistence of motor learning into very old age.

The fact that motor memory involves unconscious processing can be inferred from studies such as one in which amnesiacs and patients with Alzheimer's disease were successfully taught to hold a stylus to a rotating disk (Heindel, Butters, & Salmon, 1988). Such a feat would appear to be impossible if remembering how to perform a learned motor task required conscious recall. So would driving a car while talking to a passenger or listening to the radio. In fact, deliberately trying to remember how to do something can worsen performance. As Yogi Berra, a catcher for the New York Yankees baseball team, is said to have remarked, "How can you think and hit the ball at the same time?"

Unconscious processes involved in motor activity may also aid in recall of declarative information. In Liberia, Kpelle people had trouble recalling traditional epic songs—except when they were actually singing and dancing (Lancy, 1977). You may have experienced a similar effect: not being able to remember a familiar phone number except by tapping it out on a touch-tone phone. Your fingers "know" the number, even though your conscious mind draws a blank.

Motor memory seems to hold up well throughout adulthood, though older adults may need to compensate for the general slowing that occurs with age. Older people who are expert typists can copy a document as fast as younger ones; apparently they look farther ahead to give their minds more time to process the material they haven't yet come to (Salthouse, 1985). And although young adults can write faster than older ones, practice and familiarity with the material can reduce the difference in speed (Dixon, Kurzman, & Friesen, 1993).

PERCEPTUAL MEMORY   Approximately how many times has the term *encoding* been used so far in this chapter? Is the answer closer to two or twelve? Which was mentioned first, *sensory memory* or *articulatory loop*?

(AP Photo by Jeff Bradley/Wide World)

At age 92, Zhu Jingda of Canton had not forgotten his tennis form, which he learned at age 10. Motor memory, which involves unconscious processing, seems to hold up well throughout adulthood.

Such questions call on *perceptual skills:* the ability to judge and reconstruct in your mind the physical features, frequency or order of occurrence, or location of something in relation to something else. With unconscious processing, you may be able to file such perceptual impressions in memory while focusing on a conscious encoding task (such as trying to remember what you are reading). Later, you can consciously retrieve and assess your perceptions (Kausler, 1990; Lovelace, 1990).

If their encoding is indeed unconscious, we might expect perceptual skills to remain relatively constant with age. Estimation of frequency has been found to decline very little, and only after the middle years. However, memory of order and location fall off earlier and more sharply. In one study, which included large samples of young, middle-aged, and elderly adults, middle-aged people were as accurate in assessing word frequency as the younger ones, and elderly ones only slightly less so. By contrast, deficits in remembering order and location were fairly pronounced in middle-aged participants and even more so in older ones. In fact, the older people did just about as poorly in reconstructing the order of words and activities as they did in remembering word pairs, a declarative task (Salthouse, Kausler, & Saults, 1988, as cited in Kausler, 1990). Thus a distinction between conscious processing and unconscious processing may not fully account for whether or not age deficits appear in some forms of nondeclarative memory.

CONDITIONED RESPONSES   Another form of unconscious learning that is generally believed to enter nondeclarative memory is **classical conditioning.** A *conditioned response* is one that a person has learned to make automatically to a certain stimulus by association with another stimulus that normally elicits the response. Perhaps the earliest and probably the most famous example of classical conditioning was an experiment in which the Russian physiologist Ivan Pavlov (1927) trained dogs to salivate at the sound of a bell by feeding them whenever the bell rang.

When rabbits and humans were conditioned to blink in response to a tone by blowing a puff of air into their eyes immediately after the tone was sounded, younger adults acquired the conditioned eyeblink much faster than older ones (Woodruff-Pak, 1990). But a current cross-sectional study of adults age 20 to 90 found that age-related deficits in the acquisition of conditioned responses leveled off after the forties (Woodruff-Pak & Jaeger, in preparation). And in a recent longitudinal study in which older adults were followed for 2 or 3 years, cognitively normal participants—even among the oldest old—showed no significant change in ability to be classically conditioned. Those in the old-old group who did show declines in this ability were likely to be near death or to develop dementia (Ferrante & Woodruff-Pak, 1995). Thus earlier reports of large decrements in older adults' ability to be classically conditioned (Solomon, Pomerleau, Bennett, James, & Morse, 1989) may have been overstated or may have been related to illness rather than to normal aging.

Priming

Let's play "Wheel of Fortune." Can you guess the winning word by filling in the blanks?

$$P\_\_\_A\_\_\_\_U\_\_\_\_$$

If you are playing along at home, this might be hard to guess. But suppose, at the end of the show, the answer *peanut* flashes on your television screen. If you later see the same program again, in reruns, you may come up with the answer more easily. Much as priming a surface prepares it for the next coat of paint, the previous encounter has primed your memory to produce the information.

Priming is an increase in ability to do a previously encountered task or to remember previously encountered material. Both declarative and nondeclarative memory can show effects of priming (refer back to Figure 5-1). For example, you may be able to summon up factual knowledge to answer a test question more quickly if you've already seen the question and answer on a list for review. In one study of effects of priming on motor and perceptual memory (Benzing & Squire, 1989), amnesiacs who had lifted weights with one hand were better able to judge the weight of objects lifted with the other hand, even though they had extreme difficulty remembering that they had lifted the weights before.

Priming is an unconscious, automatic process. It can occur whether or not a person remembers where the information was first encountered, or even whether it was previously encountered at all (Ashcraft, 1994; Heindel, Salmon, & Butters, 1989, 1991; Squire, 1992). It's possible, of course, in our "Wheel of Fortune" example, that you would not only be able to give the answer *peanut* but might also remember having seen it on the first run. Similarly, you might remember having previously run across a test question. But whether or not you recall having seen information before will not affect priming. The amnesiacs in the weight-lifting experiment, who lacked episodic memory, showed what Roediger (1990) calls "retention without remembering": knowing something on the basis of prior experience, without remembering the experience itself (Lovelace, 1990). Likewise, during stem completion exercises (such as "Complete the word S - T - R -__ -__ -__") amnesiacs tend to come up with words they were shown earlier, even though they have no recollection of having seen them (Camp & McKitrick, 1992; Schacter, 1992; Squire, 1992).

Speed is one indication that priming has occurred. Both normal adults and people with Alzheimer's disease can more rapidly identify pictures they have previously seen (Camp & McKitrick, 1992). For priming to be effective, earlier and later stimuli should be as close to identical as possible; showing a different picture of an object, or a name instead of a picture, reduces priming effects (Squire, 1992).

Priming seems to be equally efficient in younger and older adults; normal older people whose episodic memory has weakened can benefit as much from priming as younger ones (Lovelace, 1990). In one study, 48 young adults and 48 older adults were shown a group of pictures and then were asked to choose the same pictures from among others they hadn't yet seen. The tests were repeated 1 day, 1 week, and 3 weeks later. Approximately equal numbers of older and younger adults were better able to select the familiar pictures, and to do so more quickly, even though the older people were less able to say which pictures they had seen before (Mitchell, Brown, & Murphy, 1990).

SUMMING UP: MEMORY AND AGE

Information-processing theory and research suggest that memory is a highly complex set of processes and storage systems, and a number of questions remain to be answered. Still, we can draw several conclusions about effects of aging on memory (see Table 5-2).

Age seems to have little or no effect on sensory memory. Aging *does* negatively affect the capacity of working memory to process certain kinds of declarative information and to access it in long-term memory. Older adults may have less attentional resources to focus on manipulating information and may not use the most effective strategies for encoding it. After years of living, recollection of specific episodes begins to fade and events tend to run together in memory. On the other hand, the ability to call on general knowledge *increases*, though the ability to express it verbally may not. Unconscious remembering, usually of skills or procedures, generally holds up well with age.

TABLE 5-2 RELATIONSHIP BETWEEN AGING AND PERFORMANCE IN VARIOUS TYPES OF MEMORY

Memory	Increases with Age	No Change or Small Decline	Moderate to Large Decline
Sensory		X	
Working			
Digit span forward		X	
Digit span backward		X	
Organization			X
Elaboration			X
Long-term			
Declarative			
Episodic			
Memory for experiences and activities			X
Personal history			X
Semantic			
World knowledge	X		
Vocabulary	X		
Word finding			X
Nondeclarative			
Skills		X	
Perceptual abilities		X	
Motor learning		X	
Classical conditioning		X	

BIOLOGICAL APPROACH: HARDWARE OF MEMORY

▼

If older adults have difficulty encoding information and retrieving certain kinds of memories, an explanation may lie in underlying changes in the "hardware," or "machinery," of memory: the brain. Like a machine, the brain has electrical circuits, "input" and "output" channels, and specific parts that seem to be involved in processing particular kinds of information. It may be that the reason people never forget how to ride a bicycle, for example, is that the muscular commands become "hard-wired" into brain cells or their connections, just as a computer's operating commands are permanently stored in its wiring. We need to keep in mind, however, that this analogy with computers is valid only up to a point. The brain is a living biological system. It needs adequate sleep and nutrition, as well as oxygen (see Box 5-2). If injured, it has some capacity to repair itself.

THE ART OF AGING

The Best Memory Aid: A Healthy Lifestyle

Have you ever tried to take a test after cramming all night or eating a heavy meal? If so, you may have learned—the hard way—the connection between what you do with your body and what you can do with your mind. For example, cigarette smoking apparently has negative effects on complex problem solving that makes high demands on working memory and long-term memory (Spilich, June, & Renner, 1992). On the other hand, getting enough sleep and eating the right foods can make a positive difference in how well memory works across the adult lifespan.

Sleep

Burning the midnight oil can interfere with the transfer of information to long-term memory. Avi Karni (Karni, Tanne, Rubenstein, Askenasy, & Sagi, 1994), a neuropsychologist with the National Institutes of Health, made that discovery while studying how people acquire a specific visual skill: pinpointing the location of shapes on a computer screen. Noticing that participants did better the day *after* a training session, he and his colleagues reasoned that something happens during sleep to strengthen neural connections in the brain and facilitate learning.

The researchers observed the participants during sleep and awakened them at various times during the night. Those who were awakened from light sleep (when the body is relaxed, the eyes move slowly, and brain waves are somewhat erratic) could remember the next morning what they had learned the previous day. But those who were awakened from *REM sleep*—the deeper stage when dreams occur, characterized by rapid eye movements and more regular brain waves—did not retain the

(Shirley Zeiberg)

Drinking diet soda during all-night cramming for an examination may impair memory and thus worsen test performance.

new knowledge. Karni concluded that REM sleep is an important time for consolidation of new learning.

This finding has implications for young adults, who often put work, study, or social demands ahead of their need for sleep. It may also help explain some memory problems in older adults (especially men), who tend to sleep more lightly, wake more frequently, dream less, and have fewer periods of deep sleep than in their earlier years (Webb, 1987; Woodruff, 1985).

Nutrition

"You are what you eat" is as true of memory as of other mental and physical capacities. Specific foods can improve or impair memory.

The brain's chemical energy comes mainly from *glucose* extracted from starches in food. When you put unusual demands on your brain, it needs to draw extra glucose from the bloodstream. To test the effects of glucose on memory, one group of researchers (Manning, Hall, & Gold,

(CONTINUED)

BOX 5-2

CONTINUED

1990) on 2 successive days gave healthy older adults lemonade sweetened with glucose and then with an artificial sugar substitute. On the day they drank the glucose, the participants did better on declarative memory tasks, such as remembering a story and a list of words. Those who had poor glucose regulation—who tended to retain high levels of glucose in their blood—performed especially poorly after drinking the substitute, suggesting that (as with diabetics, who tend to show impaired memory) not enough glucose was getting to the brain. Glucose supplements might help in such cases.

Not all sugars are brain food. *Fructose*, used to sweeten many foods and drinks, can supply energy to bodily tissues but not to the brain. A better way to get a quick mental boost is to eat an apple or crackers. Both are rich in carbohydrates, which break down into sugars when digested.

Aspartame, a chemical used in diet drinks and artificial sweeteners, contains *phenylalanine*, the amino acid involved in *phenylketonuria (PKU)*,

an enzyme disorder that can cause mental retardation. Even in normal people, too much diet soda can impair mental performance—especially when accompanied by cake or other sweets, which make it easier for phenylalanine to get into the brain. Eating protein-rich foods such as peanuts or cheese with diet drinks can offset the effects of phenylalanine.

Zinc is crucial to nerve cells in the cortex that control memory and high-level thinking. Classic signs of zinc deprivation are wounds that heal slowly, white spots on the fingernails, poor vision in dim light, and deadened taste or smell. Anyone with these symptoms should consult a doctor promptly. Zinc deficiency can be treated with diet supplements; but changing your own diet can be dangerous, as *too much* zinc can be toxic and may be associated with Pick's disease, a serious brain malfunction.

NOTE: Unless otherwise noted, material in the section on "Nutrition" is based on Chafetz, 1992.

As we've already discussed, studies of brain-damaged people in whom certain memory functions remain intact point to the existence of more than one storehouse of memory. Now, recent research, some of it made possible by such high technology as *magnetic resonance imaging* (MRI) and *positron emission tomography* (PET), has directly confirmed that there are indeed multiple memory systems, which "are anatomically distinct, and . . . are involved in acquiring and storing fundamentally different kinds of information" (Squire, 1992, p. 214). Scientists today are getting an increasingly clear picture of which physical structures of the brain control which aspects of memory and how these brain structures change with age.

STRUCTURES CONTROLLING CONSCIOUS MEMORY

Some of the most solid findings to date concern two areas of the brain that together play a major role in explicit, or conscious, memory: the *hippocampus* and nearby structures, and the *frontal lobes* (see Figure 5-3 on page 180).

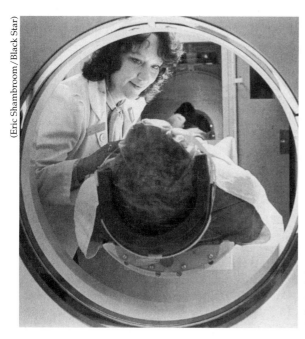

(Eric Shambroom / Black Star)

Brain scans and other high-tech procedures have confirmed the existence of several anatomically distinct memory systems, used to acquire and store different kinds of material.

Hippocampus

The *hippocampus,* a seahorse-shaped structure deep in the central portion of the brain (the medial temporal lobe), appears to be critical to memory for declarative information.[*] Without the hippocampus, unconscious learning generally continues to function; conscious learning does not (Moscovitch & Winocur, 1992).

The hippocampus, together with related structures in the cortex, apparently acts like a switchboard, controlling the ability to remember many kinds of declarative information, from word pairs to life events. So long as you are looking at something (say, the information on this page) or keeping it in mind, your mental image of it remains intact. As soon as you shift your attention to something else (move on to another section of the text, for instance), your recall of that information depends on cortical connections activated by the hippocampal system. Without the hippocampus, these connections are not made and the memory cannot be stored. In terms of information processing, the hippocampus is vital to the encoding functions of working memory.

But the role of the hippocampus seems to be only temporary. It is involved in the creation and immediate retrieval of *new* memories, but eventually those are consolidated and permanently stored in another part of the brain, probably in the cortex, where they can be retrieved without the help of the hippocampus. (That's why amnesiacs who have suffered recent damage to the hippocampus may recall long-ago events but not recent ones.)

[*]Unless otherwise noted, this discussion is based on Squire (1992).

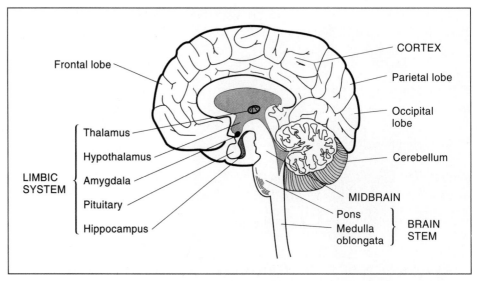

FIGURE 5-3

Simplified side view of the human brain. The hippocampus and frontal lobes of the cortex (the outer layer) appear to play key roles in the formation, initial storage, and retrieval of declarative memories. The frontal lobes seem to be involved in strategic aspects of memory. Various types of implicit (unconscious) memory are controlled by other structures.

(SOURCE: Adapted from Sagan, 1977.)

The hippocampus, which loses an estimated 20 percent of its nerve cells with advancing age (Ivy, MacLeod, Petit, & Markus, 1992), may be a key to understanding why many older adults have trouble assimilating new declarative information. The location and arrangement of arteries supplying the hippocampus make it particularly vulnerable to injury from changes in blood pressure that often occur during adulthood (Horn, 1982b). If older adults suffer hippocampal deterioration, the alertness, concentration, and organizational abilities needed to process new information efficiently may decline; but recall of *prior* learning, which is apparently independent of the hippocampus, may improve as a result of the growing complexity of neural connections in the cortex.

High levels of stress hormones in the bloodstream may play a part. In some older adults, the regulatory "switch" for production of stress hormones seems to be constantly "on": a continuous stream of hormones appears to affect the hippocampus, reducing performance on tests of attention and memory (Sapolsky, 1992). These, along with changes in other, related structures—particularly the frontal lobes—may make adults gradually less able to store new material in long-term memory.

Frontal Lobes

When a name or a fact escapes you, how can you jog your memory? The ability to think up strategies for encoding and retrieval seems to be one function of the brain's **frontal lobes**—the front portions of the *cerebral cortex*, the brain's outer layer, which controls higher-level thinking (Shimamura, Janowsky, & Squire, 1991). Current research suggests that the frontal lobes play a role in both normal and pathological memory changes.

Since both the frontal lobes and the hippocampus appear to be involved in conscious memory, what is the relationship between them? According to one model (Moscovitch & Winocur, 1992), the actual encoding, storage, and retrieval of memories is the job of the hippocampus and its associated structures, under the supervision and control of the frontal lobes. The hippocampus encodes consciously perceived information rapidly, almost automatically, and without organization. It also can retrieve apparently associated information from long-term memory. But the hippocampus lacks "intelligent" discrimination. The information it comes up with (much like the data you may find when doing a key-word search by computer) may or may not be relevant. How, then, do you select the right "file drawer" for a piece of information, or come up with the right answer to a question?

According to this model, the frontal lobes give the hippocampus direction. They coordinate, interpret, and elaborate information to provide proper instructions for encoding and retrieval. It is the operations of this strategic frontal system, not the operations of the hippocampus or its associated structures, that you are aware of in searching your memory. The frontal lobes constantly evaluate the output of the hippocampal system: *Does this answer make sense? Which answer is the best one?* or *I need more information.* In other words, the frontal lobes seem to play a role similar to that of the central executive in working memory.

Growing evidence implicates the frontal lobes in selective declines in normal cognitive functioning (Parkin & Walter, 1992). The ability to remember when and where you learned something (episodic memory) seems to be related to the functioning of the frontal lobes (Craik, Morris, Morris, & Loewen, 1990). So does learning that requires organization and elaboration. But damage to the frontal lobes usually does *not* hamper learning of information that can be encoded without creating new categories or associations (Shimamura et al., 1991). Commonly observed deficits in working memory in older adults may be due to a large (as much as 50 percent) loss of nerve cells in the frontal lobes, which help focus attention and inhibit irrelevant responses (H. Brody, 1955, 1970; Shimamura et al., 1991). However, it is possible that the brain may compensate in part for this loss by adding new connections (see Chapter 4).

STRUCTURES CONTROLLING UNCONSCIOUS MEMORY

Since nondeclarative memory for skills, habits, and procedures survives damage to the hippocampus, other brain structures must be responsible for them. A number of structures appear to control various kinds of implicit, or unconscious, learning (refer back to Figure 5-3).

Perceptual and motor skills seem to depend on the *neostriatum,* a subcortical structure above the hippocampus, which controls motor activity (Squire, 1992). Patients with Huntington's disease, which involves destruction of the neostriatum, lose the ability to learn these skills; patients in the early stages of Alzheimer's disease, whose neostriatum is not yet affected, do not (Heindel et al., 1991).

Muscular conditioning—such as the eyeblink response described earlier, or changes in heart rate due to conditioned fear—appears to be linked to the *cerebellum*, the brain's coordinating center for muscular activity, which lies below the cortex near the back of the head. While simple conditioning can occur in both humans and other animals independently of the hippocampus, the hippocampus may contribute to more complex conditioning that is affected by surrounding sights, sounds, or smells (Penick & Solomon, 1991).

Emotional conditioning seems to be located in the *amygdala*, an almond-shaped structure near the hippocampus, adjoining the temporal lobe (Squire, 1992). An example of emotional conditioning can be seen when amnesiacs or persons with Alzheimer's disease learn to dislike a person who hurts or angers them, even if they don't recognize the person or remember the incident that provoked the emotional response (Camp et al., 1993).

Direct (repetition) priming—the simplest kind, in which the answer called for is identical with the stimulus initially presented—apparently results from changes in perceptual processing systems in the rear of the cortex. These changes occur in the early stages of processing, before any analysis of meaning or any involvement of the hippocampal system; thus amnesic and normal people benefit equally. Other priming functions seem to involve different cortical regions in either the right or the left hemisphere; for vision alone, as many as 30 specific areas that may contribute to priming have been identified (Squire, 1992).

NEW DIRECTIONS FOR RESEARCH

▼

In keeping with the lifespan developmental approach, it is becoming increasingly obvious that memory development cannot be properly studied from a single perspective. More and more, researchers studying "software" and "hardware" of memory are communicating and cooperating, either to confirm theories or to generate new ones. A new discipline called *neuroscience* draws on biology, neuropsychology, cognitive psychology, neurology, and related disciplines. In the future, information-processing research on memory functioning and biological research on brain structures will be more closely linked. Recent technological advances allow researchers to peer into the brain while it is actively processing information, so that relationships between brain functions and brain structures can be tested directly.

The lifespan approach also suggests that cognitive abilities such as memory can be influenced by a variety of factors outside the brain: health, education, lifestyle, personality. In one series of studies (Moscovitch & Winocur, 1992), institutionalized older adults consistently did worse on neuropsychological measures than a carefully matched control group living in the community, who were more active and felt more in control of their lives. Among the institutionalized group, those who were better adjusted tended to do better on tests of learning and memory; and changes in their activity level and perceived control correlated with changes in cognitive performance.

Do gender and culture influence changes in memory? Although complaints of memory problems and inability to concentrate are frequently mentioned as associated with menopause, research so far is sparse on effects of lowered estrogen levels on memory. In one study comparing memory in 19 women immediately before and 2 months after surgical removal of the ovaries, women who received estrogen injections did as well as or better than before on a variety of memory tasks. Women who received a placebo (sesame oil) showed a decline in recall of word pairs but not in several other functions, such as digit span and recall of pictures. It is possible, then, that estrogen may affect rote verbal recall or the ability to learn new associations (Phillips & Sherwin, 1992).

A recent cross-cultural study of three cultures—mainland Chinese, mainstream American, and American Deaf—found a link between memory changes in older adults and cultural attitudes toward aging. Memory performance among young adults in the three cultures was identical. But among mainstream Americans, who held the most negative attitudes toward aging, older participants did worse than those in either of the other two cultural groups in the memory tasks, which involved explicit recall of new information. Older Chinese, whose culture seemed to promote the most positive view of aging, performed best, about as well as younger Chinese (Levy & Langer, 1994). These findings seem to confirm what the lifespan developmental approach would predict: social and psychological as well as biological forces influence how well memory holds up.

Future research needs to target a wide range of biological, functional, environmental, and psychosocial influences on memory development throughout adulthood. True lifespan studies may yield valuable knowledge, not only about why and how memory changes, but about what adults can do to prevent, compensate for, and perhaps even reverse memory losses.

ASPECTS OF MEMORY AND FORGETTING IN ADULTHOOD

Why do older adults embellish stories? Why do they often have trouble remembering things they plan to do? Why do they tend not to use the most effective strategies for learning? Do younger adults have more understanding of how their memory works? What memory aids are most helpful to adults at various ages? Why do adults forget—and what would happen if they didn't? Although study of some of these aspects of memory is relatively new, some tentative conclusions have emerged.

INTRUSION ERRORS: REMEMBERING WHAT DID NOT HAPPEN

How often have you heard someone relate an incident over and over, each time piling on additional (and often inaccurate) details? Such "tall tales" may be the unwitting result of *intrusion errors:* extraneous information coming into working memory through associations retrieved from long-term memory. These errors often show up on tests when people "remember" relevant or irrelevant information that wasn't originally presented. In one study (Pompi & Lachman, 1967), young adults read the following passage:

> Chief Resident Jones adjusted his face mask while anxiously surveying a pale figure secured to the long gleaming table before him. One swift stroke of his small sharp instrument and a thin red line appeared. Then an eager young assistant carefully extended the opening as another pushed aside glistening surface fat so that vital parts were laid bare. Everyone present stared in horror at ugly growth too large for removal. He now knew it was pointless to continue. (pp. 144-145; punctuation added)

After reading this paragraph, participants were shown a list of words and were asked to identify those that had appeared in the story. Many "remembered" words like *doctor, blood,* and *scalpel,* which were not in the text.

Older adults, with their extensive accumulation of experience, are particularly prone to intrusion errors, especially when retelling stories (Hasher, 1992). Their vast knowledge plays tricks on them, making them "recall" things that didn't happen. Some researchers believe that a tendency to be distracted by extraneous information may help explain difficulties with tasks involving working memory (Craik & Jennings, 1992; Hasher & Zacks, 1988).

On the other hand, older adults may be more interesting storytellers precisely *because* they embellish (Hasher, 1992). Oral transmission of stories about long-ago events or moral values is a role played by elders in many nonwestern cultures (Mergler & Goldstein, 1983). Contemporary South American Indians have a saying, "When an old man dies, a whole library burns" (Cole & Scribner, 1974). Older people can also be good at brainstorming, because they are less likely than younger ones to reject ideas that "come out of left field" (Hasher, 1992).

An Aboure chief tells a legend to boys in the village of Yaou on the Ivory Coast of Africa. Older adults are often interesting storytellers because they add fresh details.

(Marc and Evelyne Bernheim/Woodfin Camp and Associates)

(Frank Siteman/Monkmeyer)

Posting a grocery list on the refrigerator is a common explicit external memory aid.

Explicit Internal Aids

At age 31, the journalist Georgie Ann Geyer, then a foreign correspondent in Cuba, unexpectedly found herself face to face with Fidel Castro. Unfortunately, she had left her notebook at the hotel, but she couldn't let the opportunity to interview the revolutionary leader slip by. "So," she later wrote, "I began to work out a certain method I later perfected. I learned to focus—virtually to set my mind on—certain important phrases as he uttered them. I had the conscious feeling of a hand coming out of my mind and grasping them and freezing them for a moment. I found that with this method I could keep quotes perfectly for at least three days" (Geyer, 1983, pp. 81-82).

The method Geyer evolved is a form of *mental imaging.* A more common use of visual images is in remembering names; for example, you might picture Mary Gates hopping merrily over a gate (West, 1985). Older adults are less likely than younger adults to use such imaging strategies spontaneously; when they do, the images tend to be relevant to their experience rather than arbitrary, "made-up" ones (Camp, Markley, & Kramer, 1983).

Have you ever found yourself able to remember who was at a meeting by picturing where each person sat? An ancient Greek named Simonedes is credited with originating this **method of loci,** another form of mental imaging. The idea is to identify a series of places associated with items you want to remember, and then mentally or physically revisit those places during recall. The method also works for prospective actions: you can associate things you want to remember to do with specific locations (such as rooms in your house), so that the desired actions will come to mind as you visualize or go to each place. Older adults have been trained to remember grocery lists this way (Camp, 1988; West, 1985).

Rehearsal, organization, and *elaboration* are verbal explicit internal aids. While elaboration and organization are more effective for encoding, information learned through elaborative techniques—such as rhyming, forming words or phrases from initial letters, and making up stories incorporating the information to be learned—will not be retained for any length of time without occasional rehearsal. Also, to use mnemonics effectively, the strategies themselves must be practiced frequently (West, 1985).

Since explicit internal strategies take conscious effort on the part of working memory, they tend to be more useful to younger adults than to older ones. Although both younger and older people can be trained to use these skills, older trainees show less improvement, especially for difficult tasks. Also, older adults, unless given periodic monitoring and support, tend to stop using the techniques, perhaps because the effort seems too great (Anschutz et al., 1987; Baltes, 1993; Camp, 1988; Camp et al., 1993; Scogin & Bienias, 1988; Verhaeghen, Marcoen, & Goossens, 1992).

Implicit Internal Aids

Implicit memory aids can be effective for older adults—especially those with memory impairments, whose unconscious memory functioning is likely to be relatively intact (Howard, 1991).

Spaced retrieval, which may involve elements of priming or classical conditioning, is a training method to help normal or demented older adults recall information for longer and longer periods. If they miss, they are given the right answer and then retested after a shorter interval. People who ordinarily cannot associate a face with a name for more than 1 minute have been trained to remember such associations for as long as 5 weeks (Camp & Stevens, 1990). This technique has proved effective with Alzheimer's patients (Camp & McKitrick, 1992; Riley, 1992), even in a prospective memory task (McKitrick, Camp, & Black, 1992).

Another technique utilizing *classical conditioning* was demonstrated at a day care center for impaired older adults, where a group of demented women were constantly heaping verbal abuse on an African American man who triggered their remembered racial prejudice. Because of their dementia, they were unable to explicitly encode instructions from the staff to "be nice" to this man. But when he was given the task of handing out rewards and honors, they quickly became conditioned to associate him with positive feelings, and their verbal abuse diminished—though they couldn't explain why they liked him now, nor could they remember having abused him (Camp et al., 1993).

Implicit External Aids

Three-dimensional puzzle maps of foreign cities like Paris, sold in novelty shops, allow prospective travelers to internalize knowledge of the shapes and locations of major landmarks such as the Eiffel Tower and the Louvre. Putting these puzzles together gives people a cognitive map, which primes them to recognize landmarks. If and when they visit the city and see the actual structures, they may have an "O" experience: a flash of recognition that they already know this information (Camp et al., 1993). Such *tactile-visual cues* offer promise for improving implicit memory in older adults, especially those with memory impairments.

Combined Aids

When Mark Twain found that his grandchildren were having trouble remembering the names and dates of reigns of English monarchs, he invented a painless method to make the information stick. Along the roadway on his farm, he pounded stakes in the ground at intervals proportional to the length of each monarch's reign. On each stake, he wrote the appropriate name and dates. As he and his grandchildren walked around the farm, the youngsters unconsciously absorbed a sense of the relative length of these reigns (implicit external aid). At the same time, the labels on the stakes served as explicit external aids. As a special motivator, Twain added a challenge to perceptual learning: he would throw an apple down the road, and the child who correctly estimated in whose "reign" the apple fell would get to eat it (Twain, 1963). In devising this highly creative mnemonic aid, Twain wisely recognized that (1) learning can and should be fun, and (2) the most powerful memory tools often combine more than one mnemonic strategy (West, 1985).

FORGETTING AND ITS SURPRISING BENEFITS

A middle-aged man who, in his childhood, had been a highly successful quiz show contestant remarked, only partly in jest, "I am absolutely cursed with a good memory. I really do not know how to forget" (R. D. Feldman, 1982, p. 278).

It may seem strange to talk about forgetting as something a smart person would want to know how to do. From an information-processing perspective, forgetting is a breakdown of memory—either decay of stored material or inability to retrieve it. A computer, unless it's malfunctioning, does not delete information from its own memory. But the human mind can. An important difference between human beings and computers, then, is the ability to forget.

A novel way to think of memory is as a dynamic, ever-changing synthesis of remembering and forgetting, a unified system in which the two components must be in balance (Camp & McKitrick, 1989). Memory gives continuity and stability; forgetting clears the way for freshness, creativity, and innovation (Klass, 1986). Memory obviously has become dysfunctional when forgetting dominates remembering, as in Alzheimer's disease and other forms of dementia (Camp & McKitrick, 1989). But what if remembering dominates? Wouldn't it be nice never to forget a name, a face, a fact, or an appointment? Are there penalties to inability to forget?

Forgetting is the mind's overflow valve. In a cautionary tale by an Argentinian writer (Borges, 1964), a man who can't forget ends up drowning in his memories. A short-order cook who couldn't forget would be overwhelmed by orders he or she had already filled and wouldn't be able to remember the new ones (W. Epstein, 1977).

One clinical neuropsychologist called forgetting "an essential component of a memory system, preventing the mind from being cluttered by outdated and useless information" (Kihlstrom, 1983, p. 73). A mind that couldn't forget would contain an indiscriminate jumble of the important and unimportant, the relevant and irrelevant. A person with such a mind would very likely be a colossal bore, perpetually digressing into endless trivialities.

A person who couldn't forget details would have great difficulty generalizing (Camp, 1988; Camp & McKitrick, 1989). A famous memory whiz called "S.," who was studied by the noted Russian neuropsychologist Luria (1968), could recall a list of 50 words, years after seeing them only once. But he had trouble recognizing a face! Why? He remembered each fleeting expression but couldn't form a composite mental image of the person. Perhaps the eminent philosopher and psychologist William James had such a phenomenon in mind when he observed a century ago, "if we remembered everything, we should on some occasions be as ill off as if we remembered nothing" (1890, p. 680).

Can older adults forget more or less easily than younger ones? Two studies found no significant age differences in *intentional forgetting*—ability to forget when instructed to do so (Camp, Markley, & Spenser, 1987; Pavur, Comeaux, & Zeringue, 1984). But while younger and older adults seem equally able to forget in the laboratory, older people may be more likely to do it in everyday life. In fact, the idea of forgetting as an ability in its own right may put memory "losses" usually associated with aging in a different light.

Perhaps older people's reluctance to use certain strategies for remembering, even when taught, is a sign that those strategies are not suited to their needs. Older people may shift to a strategy of selective forgetting so they can use their mental energy and attention more efficiently for the tasks that matter at their time of life. Rather than trying to remember specific details, they may be more interested in discerning patterns and principles. By culling nonessential information, they may be better able to find meaning in things they consider worth remembering. From a lifespan perspective, forgetting may be the price for a developmental change that enables wisdom to emerge (Camp, 1988; Camp & McKitrick, 1989).

SUMMARY

▼

STUDYING MEMORY SYSTEMS

- Information-processing researchers study the processes involved in forming, retaining, and recovering memories, both in the laboratory and in everyday life.
- Biological researchers study the physical brain structures involved in memory.

INFORMATION-PROCESSING APPROACH: SOFTWARE OF MEMORY

- Memories are processed by encoding, storage, and retrieval. Difficulties in any of these processes may impair memory.
- Recall of newly encountered information seems to drop off with age. Recall is more affected by age than recognition is.
- The information-processing model includes three interacting storage systems: sensory memory, short-term (working) memory, and long-term memory.
- Sensory memory seems virtually unaffected by age.

- Working memory handles effortful processing and retrieval.

- The capacity of working memory is limited and seems to decline with age, especially for complex tasks and strategies. Attention and motivation may affect its efficiency.

- Methods of encoding material for long-term storage include rehearsal, organization, and elaboration.

- Long-term memory contains both declarative and nondeclarative material. Most declarative information is processed effortfully (explicitly); nondeclarative information may be processed unconsciously (implicitly), bypassing working memory.

- Because individual memories become less distinctive with age, the episodic component of declarative memory is more affected than the semantic component.

- Most forms of unconscious learning—motor learning, some kinds of perceptual learning, classical conditioning, and priming—decline very little with age.

BIOLOGICAL APPROACH: HARDWARE OF MEMORY

- The hippocampus, under direction by the frontal lobes of the cortex, initially encodes and retrieves declarative memories. Other brain structures appear to control various kinds of unconscious learning. Retrieval of long-term memories may be independent of the hippocampus.

NEW DIRECTIONS FOR RESEARCH

- There is a trend toward interdisciplinary research involving the biological and information-processing approaches and incorporating environmental, lifestyle, and psychosocial factors.

ASPECTS OF MEMORY AND FORGETTING IN ADULTHOOD

- Although older adults are subject to intrusion errors, some of these intrusions may be beneficial.

- The stability of prospective memory depends largely on the task and on availability of external cues or aids.

- Production deficiencies in encoding strategies may be remedied by training, but older adults seem to have more limited potential for improvement than younger adults.

- Older adults' overall assessment of their world knowledge may be affected by stereotypes about aging. It is not clear whether or to what extent metamemory is involved in production deficiencies.

- A variety of mnemonic devices—external or internal and explicit or implicit—can help enhance memory for adults of varying ages and circumstances.

- Lifestyle factors (sleep and nutrition) can affect memory.

- Memory may be viewed as a synthesis of remembering and forgetting; if either dominates, memory may become dysfunctional.

- Forgetting prunes out unneeded memories, prevents mental congestion, and permits generalization. The ability to forget seems unaffected by age, but older adults may be more likely to forget selectively in everyday life.

KEY TERMS

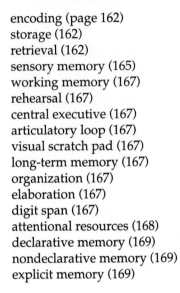

encoding (page 162)
storage (162)
retrieval (162)
sensory memory (165)
working memory (167)
rehearsal (167)
central executive (167)
articulatory loop (167)
visual scratch pad (167)
long-term memory (167)
organization (167)
elaboration (167)
digit span (167)
attentional resources (168)
declarative memory (169)
nondeclarative memory (169)
explicit memory (169)

implicit memory (169)
episodic memory (170)
semantic memory (170)
classical conditioning (173)
priming (174)
hippocampus (179)
frontal lobes (180)
intrusion errors (183)
prospective memory (185)
production deficiency (185)
developmental reserve (187)
metamemory (188)
mnemonics (189)
E-I-E-I-O model (190)
method of loci (191)
spaced retrieval (194)

CHAPTER **6**

INTELLIGENCE AND CREATIVITY

CHAPTER 6

INTELLIGENCE AND CREATIVITY

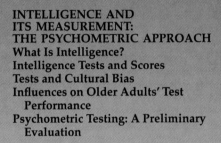

**INTELLIGENCE AND
ITS MEASUREMENT:
THE PSYCHOMETRIC APPROACH**
What Is Intelligence?
Intelligence Tests and Scores
Tests and Cultural Bias
Influences on Older Adults' Test
 Performance
Psychometric Testing: A Preliminary
 Evaluation

**INTELLECTUAL DEVELOPMENT
IN ADULTHOOD: BASIC ISSUES**
Is Intelligence One Ability or Many?
Does Intelligence Grow or Decline
 during Adulthood?
Do Changes in Intelligence Vary?
Does Intelligence Show Plasticity?
Summing Up: Intelligence and Age

CREATIVITY
What Is Creativity?
Studying and Measuring Creativity
Creativity and Age

BOXES
6-1 The Multicultural Context:
 Is Intelligent Behavior the Same
 in All Cultures?
6-2 The Cutting Edge: Are Intelligence
 Tests the Best Predictors of Job
 Performance?
6-3 The Art of Aging: Creativity Takes
 Hard Work at Any Age

Few of us make the most of our minds. The body ceases to grow in a few years; but the mind, if we will let it, may grow almost as long as life lasts.

John Lubbock, *The Pleasures of Life*

FOCUS: AKIRA KUROSAWA

(UPI/Bettmann)

The Japanese filmmaker Akira Kurosawa,* who wrote and directed such classics as the Academy Award-winning *Rashomon* (1951) and *Seven Samurai* (1954), has been called a cinematographic genius. Kurosawa, who tried painting before going into filmmaking, uses the screen as his canvas. Artistic intelligence—an unerring sense of composition, form, color, and texture— pervades his scenes.

During his primary (elementary) school days, according to a schoolmate who later became his scriptwriting collaborator, he was "not the little-genius type who merely gets good grades" but a natural leader, a "commanding" figure (Richie, 1965, p. 10). He was president of his class as well as valedictorian. As a young adult, he continued to show leadership. As an assistant to the great film director Kajiro Yamamoto, he invariably brought Yamamoto and everyone else working on a production around to his way of thinking.

Kurosawa was in his mid-twenties when he won an apprenticeship with Yamamoto at the studio later known as Toho. During the oral examination, he displayed unusual breadth and depth of knowledge and well-reasoned opinions. On the job, he was a quick study. Assigned to write scenarios, the talented novice polished off the first few and came up with idea after idea for more. He picked up editing with equal ease. He learned to look for visual solutions to dramatic problems, and he experimented with dubbing sound onto images. "He is completely creative," said Yamamoto (Richie, 1965, p. 12).

*Sources of biographical information about Akira Kurosawa are Goodwin (1994), Kurosawa (1981), and Richie (1965).

In his directorial debut, *Sanshiro Sugata* (1943), Kurosawa broke with Japanese tradition by borrowing tension-building techniques from western action movies. This film, adapted from a novel about the rise of judo as a martial art, portrayed the physical and spiritual development of a fighter. Kurosawa, a descendant of medieval warriors (*samurai*), wrote the screenplay at one sitting. Its "innovative exuberance, original imagery, and intuitive approach place *Sanshiro* in the company of inspired debut films" (Goodwin, 1994, p. 43).

"From the beginning," said Yamamoto, "Kurosawa was completely engrossed in separating what is real from what is false. He . . . holds out until everything is just the way that he sees it" (Richie, 1965, p. 13). For *The Most Beautiful* (1944), a story of women leaving home to work in a wartime factory, Kurosawa made the actors sleep in a real factory dormitory, trained them on the shop floor, and filmed the production line right there. In *Red Beard* (1965), his dedication to historical detail—which extended to creating "age stains" on teacups that would never be seen onscreen—dragged out the filming for 2 years.

By that time Kurosawa, who had left the Toho studio in protest following a labor dispute, had returned and formed his own production unit there. Now the arrangement fell apart. Kurosawa blamed the studio system for stifling social criticism and expressed regret that he had bowed to demands to limit his exposure of official corruption (*The Bad Sleep Well*, 1960). He had chafed under censorship; some of his films had been cut or never shown. *The Men Who Tread on the Tiger's Tail*, a commentary on a decaying feudal, militaristic society, filmed just as American occupation troops entered Japan after World War II, had not been released until 1952, 7 years later.

When dwindling movie audiences caused Japanese studios to stop financing his films, he hit a low point and, in 1971, became ill and attempted suicide. Since then, he has attracted support from foreigners, including the American producer-directors Steven Spielberg, George Lucas, and Francis Ford Coppola.

Always a keen social observer, Kurosawa has tackled such topics as the civil service bureaucracy (*Ikiru*, 1952) and, more recently, threats to the environment (*Dreams*, 1990) and atomic bomb survivors (*Rhapsody in August*, 1991). Today, in his eighties, he is working on *Not Ready Yet*, about the last phase of a writer's career. The title, a chant from the children's game of hide and seek, echoes his own refusal to retire. In the sixth decade of his career, he "remains passionately engaged in [its] creative challenges" (Goodwin, 1994, p. 56).

The story of Akira Kurosawa touches on several themes of this chapter. One of these themes is the relationship between intelligence and creativity, and their influence on adult accomplishments. A second theme concerns various forms or aspects of intelligence—for example, artistic, verbal, practical, and interpersonal. A third theme is the role of personality, motivation, experience, and social context in intellectual achievement. A fourth theme is how age may affect productivity.

Do adults' minds continue to grow, though their bodies do not? Do some intellectual abilities, like some physical abilities, begin to falter and decline? Do adults develop new kinds of abilities as they get older? To answer such questions, we need to consider others. What are intelligence and creativity? How do they differ? How can they be measured? Are most highly creative people (like Kurosawa) highly intelligent, and vice versa? Can a person be creative but not intelligent, or intelligent but not creative? Does an ability to answer factual questions mean that a person is smarter than someone whose memory for facts is not as good? What about the ability to write a well-reasoned essay? To seize an opportunity? To get along with others? To cope with setbacks?

In this chapter, we discuss, in turn, intelligence and creativity throughout adulthood. In Chapter 7, we look at special features of mature thought, at wisdom, and at moral reasoning.

INTELLIGENCE AND ITS MEASUREMENT: THE PSYCHOMETRIC APPROACH

▼

WHAT IS INTELLIGENCE?

For years, psychologists argued about whether intellectual ability is inherited or acquired. Today there is general agreement that both factors play an important part, though their relative influence may be hard to determine. Still unresolved, however, are more basic questions about what intelligence is and how to measure it.

At a symposium in 1921 sponsored by the *Journal of Educational Psychology*, more than a dozen eminent psychologists tried to agree on a definition of intelligence but couldn't manage to do it (Sattler, 1988). A later attempt to pick up where the 1921 conference left off failed as well (Sternberg & Detterman, 1986).

While it's hard to define what intelligence *is*, there's a fair amount of agreement on what it *does*. **Intelligent behavior** is generally considered to be both *goal-oriented* (conscious and deliberate rather than automatic or accidental) and *adaptive* (aimed at identifying and solving problems). When more than 1,000 experts in psychology, education, sociology, and genetics were asked to rate important elements of intelligent behavior, nearly all checked three of the thirteen choices: reasoning, capacity to acquire knowledge, and problem-solving ability (Snyderman & Rothman, 1987). But even this consensus may break down when we look at cross-cultural research, since some cultures have divergent views of intelligent behavior (see Box 6-1).

INTELLIGENCE TESTS AND SCORES

Given the difficulty of defining intelligence, it's not surprising that the question of how to assess it is highly controversial. In everyday life, of course, people frequently make informal judgments about intelligence. Such remarks as "Juan is smarter than Philippe" and "Margaret is not very bright" imply that intelligence

BOX 6-1

THE MULTICULTURAL CONTEXT

Is Intelligent Behavior the Same in All Cultures?

How would you answer the following test question?

> In the far north all bears are white. Novaya Zemlya is in the far north. What color are the bears there? (Luria, 1976)

Most educated western adults would say that bears in Novaya Zemlya are white. But the Russian psychologist Alexander Luria, who did research in rural areas of central Asia, found that unschooled peasants often failed to answer such questions correctly. Older adults in western cultures who have had less education than younger ones also tend to give wrong answers (Botwinick, 1978; Denney, 1974). Does this mean that the peasants and older adults are incapable of logical thought? Some researchers have made that inference.

But a closer look at Luria's findings reveals that many of the peasants simply *refused* to try to solve the problem about the bears in Novaya Zemlya. They said, for example, "You should ask the people who have been there and seen them" or "We don't talk about what we haven't seen." One investigator (Scribner, 1979), analyzing Luria's data, called such responses evidence of a "concrete bias," which could be corrected with

(Steve Maslowski/Photo Researchers)

If all bears in the far north are white, what color are the bears in a particular far northern province? Most educated western adults would answer, "White." Uneducated peasants of central Asia refused to answer—not because they couldn't think logically, but because they hadn't seen the bears.

is something quantifiable, something individuals possess in greater or lesser amounts. And, indeed, this is the basic assumption of the *psychometric approach*, which has dominated the study of intelligence since the late nineteenth century. *Psychometric* literally means "measuring the mind." Psychometric tests seek to measure intelligence through questions or tasks that serve as indicators or predictors of intellectual functioning in such areas as verbal comprehension, mathematical computation, and reasoning, as well as certain nonverbal performance skills.

formal education; and indeed Luria found that to be true. Moreover, even unschooled peasants occasionally took a more "theoretical" approach to the question and did get the right answer.

Why, then, did these peasants often perform differently from educated western adults on tasks involving formal logic?

We may find a clue in a study of the Kpelle (people from central Liberia in Africa). When Kpelle adults were asked to sort 20 objects, they consistently did so on the basis of "functional" categories (that is, knife with orange or potato with hoe). Western psychologists associate functional sorting with a low level of thought, but the Kpelle kept saying that this was the way a "wise man" would do it. Finally, the experimenter asked, "How would a fool do it?" He then received the "higher-order" categories he had originally expected—four neat piles with food in one, tools in another, and so on (Glick, 1975, p. 636).

Gisela Labouvie-Vief (1985), a psychologist at Wayne State University, suggests that people in different cultures may define problems differently on the basis of their prior experience and knowledge, and their way of approaching a problem may be *correct* in that context. To illustrate, she cites another example from Luria's work. Three peasants in Uzbekistan were shown pictures of a saw, a hammer, and an ax. They then were shown a picture of a log and were asked whether it belonged in the same category with

the other three (tools). They said it did—and proceeded to explain why:

> *Peasant 1:* . . . We make all sort of things out of logs—handles, doors, and the handles of tools.
> *Peasant 2:* We say a log is a tool because it works with tools to make things.
> *Experimenter:* But one man said a log isn't a tool since it can't saw or chop.
> *Peasant 3:* Yes you can—you can make handles out of it! . . .
> *Experimenter:* Name all the tools used to produce things. . . .
> *Peasant 1:* We have a saying: take a look in the fields and you'll see tools. (Luria, 1976, pp. 94–95)

Luria saw this exchange as evidence that the peasants were unable to classify. But Labouvie-Vief suggests a different interpretation. What if the experimenter and the peasants were simply on different cultural wavelengths, with the experimenter rigidly trying to guide them toward the "correct" definition of *tools*, while the peasants banteringly argued for a more flexible definition?

Similarly, Labouvie-Vief observes, older western adults may have their own way of looking at a problem. And they are more likely than younger adults to question the validity of a task if they don't see the point of it. We need to be cautious, then, about making assumptions about intellectual "deficits" that may actually represent differences in outlook.

Intelligence test scores are based on comparisons with *standardized norms*, standards derived from scores of a large representative sample of people who took the same test. Because the early intelligence tests were designed for children, Alfred Binet—who, with his colleague Theodore Simon, introduced the first such test, the Binet-Simon Scale, in 1905—developed the concept of *mental age* to indicate a child's intellectual level (Binet & Simon, 1905, 1908). A child (regardless of chronological age) with a mental age of 9 is one who has scored about the same as the average 9-year-old.

(Science Museum, London)

ANTHROPOMETRIC
LABORATORY
For the measurement in various ways of **Human Form and Faculty**.

Entered from the Science Collection of the S. Kensington Museum.

This laboratory is established by Mr. **Francis Galton** for the following purposes:—

1. For the use of those who desire to be accurately measured in many ways, either to obtain timely warning of remediable faults in development, or to learn their powers.

2. For keeping a methodical register of the principal measurements of each person, of which he may at any future time obtain a copy under reasonable restrictions. His initials and date of birth will be entered in the register, but not his name. The names are indexed in a separate book.

3. For supplying information on the **methods, practice, and uses of human measurement.**

4. For **anthropometric experiment and research,** and for obtaining data for statistical discussion.

Charges for making the principal measurements:
THREEPENCE each, to those who are already on the **Register.**
FOURPENCE each, to those who are not:— one page of the Register will thenceforward be assigned to them, and a few extra measurements will be made, chiefly for future identification.

The Superintendent is charged with the control of the laboratory and with determining in each case, which, if any, of the extra measurements may be made, and under what conditions.

FIGURE 3-1. An Announcement for Galton's Laboratory. Reproduced by permission of the Photo Science Museum, London, England.

A pioneer in psychometric testing was Francis Galton, a nineteenth-century English physician who established a laboratory to measure individual differences in such abilities as judging weights and hearing high-pitched sounds. Galton's measurements were forerunners of today's psychometric intelligence tests.

But if, say, an 8-year-old and a 12-year-old both have a mental age of 9, are they equally intelligent? Plainly not. To more readily compare children of different ages, William Stern (1911), a German psychologist, came up with a "mental quotient," which, with further refinement, became the *intelligence quotient (IQ)*. IQ was obtained by dividing mental age by chronological age and then multiplying by 100 to eliminate the decimal point. An IQ of 100 would mean that a child's mental age and chronological age were the same. A 10-year-old with an IQ of 120 would have a mental age of 12. IQ was found to remain fairly constant throughout childhood.

Measuring adults' intelligence presented a special problem. As a rule, adults (unlike children) do not show steady, age-linked improvement on tested tasks. Thus, a method for calculating adults' intelligence needed scoring techniques divorced from mental age. The solution was the *deviation IQ.* Now used for children as well as for adults, deviation IQ is based on the distribution of raw scores and the *standard deviation from the mean* (see Figure 6-1). David Wechsler (1939), who developed the Wechsler-Bellevue Intelligence Scale, assigned an IQ of 100 to the mean, or average, score at each age level, with higher and lower IQs determined by their distance from the mean.

The *Wechsler Adult Intelligence Scale (WAIS)*—like the Wechsler tests for children—has subtests that yield separate scores. Items are not graduated by age. An emphasis on nonverbal performance (identifying the missing part of a picture, copying a design, or mastering a maze) gives the test less bias toward verbal abilities than some other psychometric tests. The eleven subtest scores are combined into a verbal IQ and a performance IQ, and, finally, a total IQ. (Figure 6-2 shows examples of items like those on WAIS.)

Many people think an IQ score represents a fixed, inborn quantity of intelligence. What it actually tells is how well a person does certain tasks at a particular time and place in comparison with other test takers. Thus, if intelligence tests measure aptitude, they do so only indirectly. Furthermore, performance on tested tasks almost inevitably reflects learned information and skills. It is, therefore, impossible to separate measured intelligence from achievement, which depends on memory, schooling, and other influences. For example, in one study of identical twins raised in different homes, differences in IQ were directly related to the number of years of education each twin had had (Bronfenbrenner, 1979). Furthermore, although scores of both school-age children and adults tend to be fairly stable, some individuals show marked change—further evidence that something beyond innate ability is being measured (Kopp & McCall, 1982). Of course, innate intelligence (even if it could be measured directly) is only one ingredient of competence, and not necessarily the most important one in a particular situation. Others include motivation or goals, education, and life experience.

FIGURE 6-1
"Deviation IQ" is based on a bell-shaped curve with the average IQ (100) at its center. The farther a score deviates from this average, or mean, the fewer people make that score. More than two-thirds of test-takers score within 15 points on either side of 100—in other words, between 85 and 115. Fewer than 5 percent score below 70 or above 130.
(SOURCE: R. S. Feldman, 1993.)

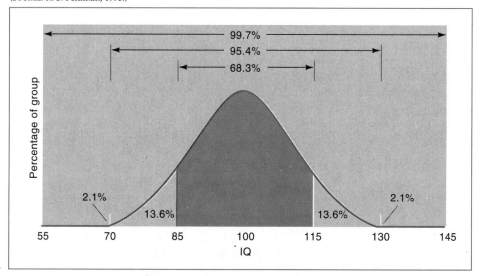

VERBAL SCALE

Information

On what continent is the Taj Mahal?

Comprehension

Explain the meaning of this saying:"A journey of 1,000 miles begins with a single step."

Arithmetic

A pair of shoes that normally sells for $70 has been reduced 20 percent. How much do the shoes cost now?

Similarities

In what way are a radio and a television alike?

PERFORMANCE SCALE

1	2	3	4
<	)	:	~

1	4	2	3	4	3	1	2	3	1

Digit symbol (match symbols to numbers using the key).

Picture completion (identify what is missing).

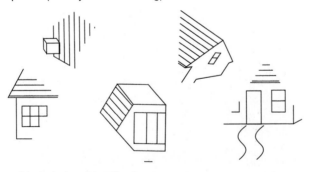

Object assembly (put pieces together).

FIGURE 6-2

Examples of items like those on the verbal and performance sections of the Wechsler Adult Intelligence Scale, revised version (WAIS-R).

(SOURCE: Adapted from R. S. Feldman, 1993.)

(National Archives)

Education can affect results on intelligence tests. When army recruits were tested during World War I, southern white soldiers did better than southern black soldiers, who had gone to poor-quality segregated schools. But black soldiers who had attended integrated northern schools scored higher, on average, than white soldiers from some southern states. The longer the black soldiers had lived in northern cities, the higher their scores (Kottak, 1994).

TESTS AND CULTURAL BIAS

While there are undoubtedly real differences in intellectual ability among individuals, there are serious questions about how accurately psychometric tests assess those differences. Members of certain ethnic groups do better than others on intelligence tests, for reasons that have been hotly debated. For example, there is a 15-point difference between average IQ scores of black and white Americans (E. B. Brody & Brody, 1976; Reynolds, 1988). Although it has been argued that the cause is largely genetic (Herrnstein & Murray, 1994; Jensen, 1969), this IQ gap is more commonly attributed to influences of income, education, and culture (Kottak, 1994; Miller-Jones, 1989), including living conditions and environmental stimulation, which can affect self-esteem and motivation as well as academic performance (Kamin, 1974, 1981).

Some analysts claim that the poorer showing of minority groups on intelligence tests reflects a failure of the tests to screen out such influences. Because psychometric tests infer abilities from knowledge, it is argued that they may be subject to *cultural bias:* a tendency to include questions that have content or call for skills more familiar or meaningful to people from some cultural groups than others (Sternberg, 1985a, 1987). Other scholars find the evidence for cultural bias unconvincing (Herrnstein & Murray, 1994).

In any case, so far it has not proved possible to develop tests that are free of any cultural content or that include only content common to all cultures (Anastasi, 1988; Kottak, 1994; Miller-Jones, 1989; Sternberg, 1985a). Then, too, it is almost impossible to screen for culturally fostered values and attitudes. As we pointed out earlier, in Box 6-1, the Kpelle of Liberia customarily classify according to functional relationships; for example, *animal* with *eat*. In the United States, people who grow up in lower-class homes, where tasks and roles are less differentiated than in upper-class families, tend to classify more like the Kpelle than like upper-class Americans (Miller-Jones, 1989). Also, Americans in lower socioeconomic groups tend to value rote memory, while middle- and upper-class people value reasoning (Sternberg, 1985a, 1986; Sternberg, as quoted in Quinby, 1985). People from nonindustrial cultures, which place less emphasis on speed and competition than American culture, may be at a disadvantage on timed tests (Kottak, 1994). So, for different reasons, may older adults.

INFLUENCES ON OLDER ADULTS' TEST PERFORMANCE

We've all had the experience of doing the same task better at one time than another. Health, comfort, energy, anxiety, motivation, study habits, and skill in taking tests can affect test scores. Some of these influences become accentuated as adults age. A number of physical and psychological factors that tend to lower older people's test scores can lead to underestimation of their intellectual ability. Their performance may be improved by attempting to control or alter some of these conditions:

- *Physical health.* The Seattle and Duke longitudinal studies, among others, found that adults who do best on intelligence tests are physically fit and well rested. They have few indicators of neurophysiological problems and a relatively low incidence of cardiovascular problems, which can restrict blood flow to the brain (Botwinick, 1984; Manton, Siegler, & Woodbury, 1986; Palmore, Burchett, Fillenbaum, George, & Wallman, 1985; Schaie, 1990a).

- *Vision and hearing.* Older adults may have trouble understanding test instructions and doing the tasks.

- *Speed, coordination, and mobility.* The time limits on most intelligence tests are particularly hard on older people. Because both physical and psychological processes, including perceptual abilities (Schaie, 1994), tend to slow with age, older adults do better when they are allowed as much time as they need (Hertzog, 1989; J. L. Horn & Cattell, 1966; Schaie & Hertzog, 1983). If, as some psychologists claim, it is misleading to equate intelligence with speed (Sternberg, 1985a, 1987), then timing a test may inaccurately depict older people as less intelligent than younger ones. However, other psychologists argue that because speed is a function of the central nervous system, it is a true indicator of intellectual functioning. And some studies suggest that even when tests are not timed, older people do not do as well as younger ones (Botwinick, 1984).

- *Attitudes toward a testing situation.* Test anxiety is common among older adults, particularly if they are unfamiliar with the testing situation and have not taken tests for a long time. They may lack confidence in their ability to solve test problems, and the expectation that they will do poorly may become a self-fulfilling prophecy. Fear of failing memory may make them skip questions when they are not sure they know the answers (Cavanaugh & Morton, 1989). Or they may lack motivation: doing well may not mean much to them unless they are, for example, taking the test to qualify for a job or for some other important purpose.

PSYCHOMETRIC TESTING: A PRELIMINARY EVALUATION

Psychometric testing has a long and useful history. Its critics, while many or all of their objections may be well taken, have yet to come up with substitute methods that approach its sophistication. In addition, individual intelligence tests, the kind most often used with adults, can yield much useful information beyond simply a number that represents an ability. They are, in effect, clinical interviews that can reveal a great deal about how a person handles stress, failure, and success, as well as many other aspects of personality and personal history. Reports of IQ tests administered by psychologists generally include descriptions of physical appearance, level of anxiety, motivation, socioeconomic status, educational and occupational background, family history, reasons for having the test conducted, and other valuable data.

We do need to be conscious of the limitations of psychometric testing of adults. These tests have proved to be reasonably effective for the purpose for which they originally were designed: predicting academic success. They give reasonably accurate measurements of verbal and mathematical abilities, and they are fairly dependable predictors of performance in jobs that call for the specific skills they measure. But psychometric tests, as they are currently designed and used, may paint an unduly bleak picture of cognitive abilities in older adults. Furthermore, the picture may be incomplete; the tests may overlook certain abilities, particularly those abilities that may emerge or become more important in the adult years.

As we look now at basic issues concerning intellectual development in adulthood—and, in Chapter 7, as we focus on possible qualitative changes in intellectual functioning—we will continue to consider the appropriateness of psychometric tests of adults' intelligence.

INTELLECTUAL DEVELOPMENT IN ADULTHOOD: BASIC ISSUES

▼

Four basic issues concerning the nature of intelligence are central to the study of intellectual development during adulthood (Dittman-Kohli & Baltes, 1990) and to the lifespan developmental approach (Baltes, 1987). Is intelligence one ability or many? Does it grow or decline, or both? Do these changes vary among individuals? Can intelligence be improved?

IS INTELLIGENCE ONE ABILITY OR MANY?

Whether intelligence consists of a single ability or multiple abilities has been debated for more than a century. This question is not merely academic or semantic: the answer can affect what we seek to measure when we devise tests that may be used to decide who gets what educational and job opportunities (see Box 6-2). Tests that yield a single IQ reflect a unitary view of intelligence; tests that yield scores in several categories, such as abstract reasoning and practical problem solving, reflect a multidimensional view. There is also disagreement about how closely related various abilities are. Obviously, a single IQ of, say, 110, gives a very different picture from separate scores of, say, 90 for verbal abilities and 130 for nonverbal ones.

The issue is particularly important to a study of adult development and aging. A multidimensional view of intelligence allows for the possibility of simultaneous advances and declines; a unitary view does not.

Factor Analysis: The Quest for Statistical Confirmation

Beginning in the late 1920s with the work of Charles E. Spearman (1863-1945), psychometric researchers have used a method called *factor analysis* to try to determine statistically which of these two views is correct. Factor analysis seeks to identify underlying factors common to a group of tests on which the same people score similarly. For example, if adults with high scores on reading tests also have high scores on vocabulary tests, this correlation may suggest an underlying verbal ability. The trouble with factor analysis is that it can be quite subjective. The investigator's point of view may affect selection of data, statistical procedures, and designation of factors. As a result, factor analysis has furnished ammunition for both camps in the battle over whether intelligence is general or specialized.

Spearman (1927) proposed that a general factor (g) underlies the specific (s) factors measured by various kinds of tests that require complex mental effort (such as mathematical reasoning, verbal comprehension, and hypothesis testing). On the other hand, Louis L. Thurstone (1938), who developed the Primary Mental Abilities Test, maintained that intelligence comprises a group of eight "primary" abilities, each more or less independent of the others: for example, verbal comprehension, inductive and deductive reasoning, perceptual speed, and rote memory. However, later analysis showed that these factors were not as independent as Thurstone had first thought. Joy Guilford (1956, 1959, 1967, 1982) constructed a complex model of the "structure of intellect," with 150 separate though cross-linked factors.

The debate continues today (Box 6-2). One pair of analysts (Kranzler & Jensen, 1991a, 1991b) claim that g is the product of at least four independent underlying processes; another investigator (Carroll, 1991a, 1991b), applying a different method of analysis to the same data, claims that the results more appropriately support a unitary g. Because of its inherent subjectivity, then, factor analysis cannot definitively tell us whether intelligence is one ability or many.

Two contemporary thinkers—Robert Sternberg, a psychologist at Yale University; and Howard Gardner, a neuropsychologist and educational researcher at Harvard University—are leaders in a growing trend toward viewing intelligence as multidimensional. Both claim that traditional psychometric tests fail to measure important mental abilities, and both have proposed theories and done research aimed at developing more comprehensive methods of assessment.

Sternberg's Triarchic Theory: Three Aspects of Intelligence

Alix, Barbara, and Courtney applied to graduate programs at Yale. Alix had an almost straight-A college transcript, scored very high on the Graduate Record Examination (GRE), and had excellent recommendations. Barbara's grades were only fair, and her GRE scores were low by the university's high standards, but her letters of recommendation enthusiastically praised her exceptional research and creative ideas. Courtney's grades, GRE scores, and recommendations were good but not among the best.

Alix and Courtney were admitted to the graduate program. Barbara was not admitted but was hired as a research associate and took graduate classes on the side. Alix did very well for the first year or so, but less well after that. Barbara confounded the admissions committee by doing work as outstanding as her letters of recommendation had predicted. Courtney's performance in graduate school was only fair, but she had the easiest time getting a good job afterward (Trotter, 1986).

What explains these outcomes? According to Sternberg (1985a, 1987), Barbara and Courtney were strong in two aspects of intelligence that psychometric tests miss: creative insight and practical intelligence. Unlike traditional psychometric researchers, Sternberg is less interested in the structure of the mind than in the processes that underlie intelligent behavior. His *triarchic* (three-part) *theory of intelligence* embraces three elements of information processing that are useful in different kinds of situations:

1. *Componential element—how efficiently people process information.* This is the *analytic* aspect of intelligence. It tells people how to solve problems, how to monitor solutions, and how to evaluate results. Alix was strong in this area; she was good at taking intelligence tests and finding holes in arguments.

BOX 6-2

THE CUTTING EDGE

Are Intelligence Tests the Best Predictors of Job Performance?

Today, tests to screen prospective employees are common. But can the same kind of test accurately predict success in such varied kinds of work as bricklaying and data processing?

Two Texans—Malcolm James Ree, a psychologist at St. Mary's University; and James A. Earles, a mathematician in San Antonio—say yes. Ree and Earles (1992) touched off a controversy with their claim that tests of general intelligence (*g*, as researchers call it) are the best predictors of performance on any job, and that measures of specific aptitudes—verbal, quantitative, spatial, or mechanical—add little. The claim was based on a statistical review of a number of large-scale studies, many done in the armed services.

The article, published in *Current Directions in Psychological Science*, a journal of the American Psychological Society, provoked so much reaction that the journal devoted a special section to the subject. In a rebuttal entitled "The *g*-ocentric View of Intelligence and Job Performance Is Wrong," Robert Sternberg (whose multifactorial theory of intelligence we discuss in this chapter) and his colleague Richard K. Wagner compared the idea that all abilities revolve around general intelligence to the discredited belief that the earth is the center of the universe. Sternberg and Wagner (1993) argued that intelligence tests predict

(Joseph Nettis/Photo Researchers)

Is a test of general intelligence the best predictor of success in such diverse kinds of work as architectural drafting and building construction? Some psychologists say yes; some say no.

job performance less reliably than school performance because real-life and academic problems require different kinds of intelligence. Academic problems, unlike those in real life, are well-defined, have one right answer and one method of obtaining it, and provide the solver with all needed information.

2. ***Experiential element***—*how people approach novel or familiar tasks*. This is the *insightful* aspect of intelligence. It allows people to compare new information with what they already know and to come up with new ways of putting facts and ideas together—in other words, to think originally. Automatic performance of familiar operations (such as recognizing words) facilitates insight, because it leaves the mind free to tackle unfamiliar tasks (such as decoding new words). Barbara was strong in this area.

Other contenders weighed in on both sides. One (Jensen, 1993) argued that *g* is not limited to academic intelligence and that, although there *is* considerable variance between actual job performance and what the tests predict, such factors as personality, motivation, interests, and values are more likely than specific abilities to account for the difference. Another (McClelland, 1993) criticized the omission of such factors as gender, race, education, and social class: "Being white, male, better educated, and from an advantaged background often correlate with better job performance, particularly as measured by a supervisor's ratings. Any of these correlations . . . may predict job performance better than intelligence" (p. 6). The authors of the original article, replying to their critics (Ree & Earles, 1993), pointed to well-documented relationships between *g* and other job qualifications, such as motivation, leadership, and social skills. An applicant selected for general intelligence, they maintained, is likely to show these other characteristics as well.

The heated exchange skirted a troubling aspect of the modest relationship between test scores and job performance. White adults referred for jobs on the basis of a battery of tests used by state employment agencies tend to perform less well after being hired than their scores would predict, while African Americans do better on the job than on the tests. This situation led to the controversial practice—later outlawed—of "race-norming, " ranking scores within racial categories to avoid screening out capable minority applicants. It also led to calls for revision of the tests to eliminate cultural bias, and pleas to employers to rely less on the tests in hiring. Ree and Earles (1992) gave passing recognition to this problem, suggesting the substitution of "content-free" tests designed to measure *g* through such basic cognitive indicators as speed of information processing; but there is dispute over whether such tests could legitimately be related to job performance.

One question we should ask in weighing findings about job performance is just what they are measuring. If findings refer to occupational level—the difficulty or complexity of a job, which Ree and Earles (1992) used as one index of job performance—it is hardly surprising that an engineer has a higher IQ than a lumberjack; but is a mediocre engineer a better performer than a competent, industrious lumberjack? How does a finding that engineers have (and presumably need) higher measured intelligence than lumberjacks support the conclusion that intelligence tests can select the best performers in *any* field?

Much more thought and study need to go into the issue of how much weight should be given to intelligence (however measured) in employment decisions and what other factors, if any, should be taken into consideration to make predictions of performance more reliable for employers and fairer to applicants.

3. *Contextual element—how people deal with their environment.* This is the *practical* aspect of intelligence. It is the ability to size up a situation and decide what to do: adapt to it, change it, or find a new, more comfortable setting. Courtney was strong in this area.

Sternberg's theory is of special interest to students of adult development because it focuses on aspects of intelligence that may become increasingly valuable in adult life.

In our example, for instance, Alix's componential ability helped her sail through college examinations. But in graduate school, where original thinking is expected, it was Barbara's superior experiential intelligence—her fresh insights and innovative ideas—that began to shine. Courtney was strongest in practical, contextual intelligence—"street smarts." She knew her way around. She chose "hot" research topics, submitted papers to the "right" journals, and knew where and how to apply for jobs.

A major component of contextual, or practical, intelligence, is *tacit knowledge*—"inside information" or "savvy," which is not formally taught or openly expressed. Getting ahead in a career, for instance, often depends on tacit knowledge (knowing how to win a promotion or cut through red tape). Sternberg's method of assessing tacit knowledge is to compare a person's chosen course of action in hypothetical, work-related situations with the choices of experts in the field and with accepted "rules of thumb." Tacit knowledge, measured in this way, seems to be unrelated to IQ and predicts job performance moderately well (Sternberg & Wagner, 1993; R. K. Wagner & Sternberg, 1986). Further research is needed to determine how and when tacit knowledge is acquired, why some people acquire it more efficiently than others, and whether it can be taught directly or is best picked up by observing mentors.

Gardner's Theory: Multiple Intelligences

As a child, Brian was in an automobile collision that left him with severe damage to the left hemisphere of the brain. He cannot speak and does not seem to understand when spoken to. Yet he can draw, sing, and compose music. What explains a case like Brian's? And what about Loretta, a gifted lawyer who has trouble figuring out how to fit luggage into the trunk of a car?

Howard Gardner once believed that intelligence is a single quality measurable by written tests. But cases like these have convinced him that intelligence is plural (Gardner, 1983). He has identified seven autonomous "intelligences" or talents, which enable people to solve problems and do productive work in various fields: *linguistic* (writers, editors, translators), *logical-mathematical* (scientists, business people, doctors), *musical* (musicians, composers, conductors), *spatial* (architects, mechanics, city planners), *bodily-kinesthetic* (dancers, athletes, surgeons), *interpersonal* (teachers, actors, politicians), and *intrapersonal* (counselors, psychiatrists, spiritual leaders).

High intelligence in one of these seven areas is not necessarily accompanied by high intelligence in any of the others. A person may be extremely gifted in art (a spatial ability), precision of movement (bodily-kinesthetic), social relations (interpersonal), or self-understanding (intrapersonal), but not have a high IQ. In fact, only a few of the "intelligences"—linguistic, logical-mathematical, and, to some extent, spatial—are tapped by conventional intelligence tests. But is someone who is good at analyzing paragraphs and making analogies necessarily more intelligent than someone who has perfect musical pitch, or someone who can organize a closet or a group project, or someone who can pitch a curve ball at the right time?

(AP/Wide World Photos)

The physicist Albert Einstein had a different kind of intelligence from that of an equally able poet or musician, according to Howard Gardner's theory of multiple intelligences.

According to Gardner, brain research strongly supports the existence of multiple intelligences, since different parts of the brain seem to process different kinds of information. Thus the scientist Albert Einstein, the poet T. S. Eliot, and the cellist Pablo Casals may have been equally intelligent, each in a different area (Kirschenbaum, 1990).

Talents, says Gardner, develop into "competencies" through training and practice, often revealing themselves in a "crystallizing moment" in which a person discovers an unsuspected ability. Environment plays an important part in this process. People tend to develop competencies that their families and culture value and encourage. A person who does not hear music, for example, is unlikely to develop competency in that field.

Gardner's ideas show how closely the issue of unitary versus multidimensional intelligence is tied to the other three issues we're about to discuss: growth versus decline, individual variability, and plasticity. According to Gardner, the various intelligences develop and change throughout the lifespan, often at different rates. For example, logical-mathematical ability tends to develop earlier and to decline more quickly than interpersonal ability. But these patterns vary from one person to another, and furthermore, they may be modifiable. Rather than try to measure inborn ability, Gardner would judge each intelligence by its products (competencies): how well a person can tell a story, remember a melody, or get around in an unfamiliar area. Assessments based on extended observation would be used to reveal an individual's strengths and weaknesses for purposes of guiding further development, rather than to compare individuals (Scherer, 1985). Defenders of psychometric tests object to such unquantified assessments as too subjective and too prone to observer bias (Sattler, 1988).

DOES INTELLIGENCE GROW OR DECLINE DURING ADULTHOOD?

Does intelligence (like physical strength) peak in early or middle adulthood and then diminish? During the 1970s, that question became a major issue among psychologists. In one camp were those who challenged the "myth" of general intellectual decline in late life (Baltes & Schaie, 1974, 1976; Schaie & Baltes, 1977). In the other camp were those who dismissed this more positive view as too rosy (J. L. Horn & Donaldson, 1976, 1977). However, the findings of these two groups of investigators were not truly contradictory. Their differences lay mainly in emphasis and interpretation, and their positions have drawn closer with time. It is becoming clearer and clearer, in examining the results of intelligence tests given to adults of various ages, that while some abilities may decline, others remain stable or even improve throughout most of adult life.

Adult IQ: The Classic Pattern

Older adults, as a group, do not perform as well as younger adults on the Wechsler Adult Intelligence Scale (WAIS). But when we look at scores on the component subtests of WAIS, it becomes plain that the decline is almost entirely in nonverbal performance. On the five subtests making up the performance scale, scores drop with age; however, on the six tests making up the verbal scale—particularly tests of vocabulary, information, and comprehension—scores fall only slightly and very gradually (see Figure 6-3). This is called the *classic aging pattern* (Botwinick, 1984).

What might account for this pattern? For one thing, the verbal items that hold up with age are based on straightforward knowledge; unlike the performance tests, they do not require the test taker to figure out or do anything new (Schonfield & Robertson, 1968, as cited in Botwinick, 1984). In addition to processing new information, the performance tasks involve speed and perceptual and motor skills. Part of the age difference in performance on this type of task is attributable to muscular and neurological slowing (Storandt, 1976).

Fluid and Crystallized Intelligence: Biology versus Culture

Another influential line of research that has found a divergence between two types of abilities is that of John L. Horn (1967, 1968, 1970, 1982a, 1982b) and Raymond B. Cattell (1965). On the basis of a variety of tests, these researchers proposed a distinction between *fluid intelligence* and *crystallized intelligence*: between forms of intelligence largely determined by genetic and physiological factors (primarily the state of the brain and nervous system), which decline with age, and forms of intelligence largely affected by cultural experience, which hold their own or even improve.

Fluid intelligence is the capacity to process novel information (for example, to follow diagrammed instructions for folding a paper square into a swan). It is the ability to apply mental powers to situations that require little or no previous knowledge (J. L. Horn, 1982a, 1982b). This kind of intelligence is based on per-

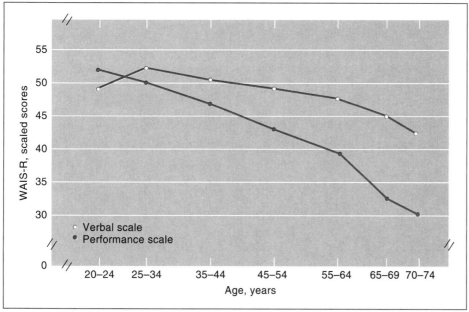

FIGURE 6-3

Classic aging pattern on the revised version of the Wechsler Adult Intelligence Scale (WAIS-R). Scores on the performance subtests decline far more rapidly with age than scores on the verbal subtests.

(SOURCE: Botwinick, 1984.)

ception of complex relationships, implications, and inferences. It is unique to an individual and largely uninfluenced by prior learning. Psychologists measure fluid intelligence by such tests as the Raven Progressive Matrices, which includes such tasks as selecting the pattern that best completes a larger one (see Figure 6-4 on the following page).

Crystallized intelligence is the ability to apply learned information and experience—knowledge acquired over a lifetime. It depends on education and cultural background and, of course, on memory. Adults show crystallized intelligence in a wide range of situations that call for skills based on semantic memory (see Chapter 5), such as language comprehension, mathematical reasoning, and application of knowledge of facts, social customs, and values (J. L. Horn, 1982a, 1982b). Crystallized intelligence depends on well-learned, automatic information processing, especially in such complex tasks as reading, which call on many mental operations. Psychologists measure crystallized intelligence by tests of vocabulary, general information, analogies, word associations, and responses to social situations and dilemmas. In some tasks, both fluid and crystallized intelligence may be used.

Fluid and crystallized intelligence peak at different times (see Figure 6-5). Fluid intelligence begins to decline in young adulthood, perhaps because of changes in the brain. But crystallized intelligence typically improves through middle age and often until near the end of life. In fact, up to ages 55 to 65, the

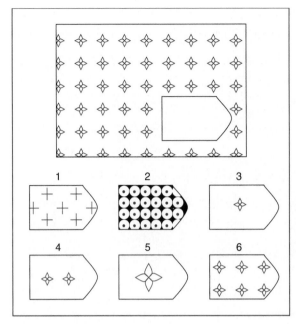

FIGURE 6-4
Left: Item from the Raven Progressive Matrices Test. This task is a measure of fluid intelligence, not dependent on previous knowledge.
(SOURCE: Raven, 1983.)

FIGURE 6-5
Below: Changes in fluid intelligence and crystallized intelligence over the lifespan. Although fluid abilities (largely biologically determined) decline after young adulthood, crystallized abilities (largely culturally influenced) increase until late adulthood.
(SOURCE: J. L. Horn & Donaldson, 1980.)

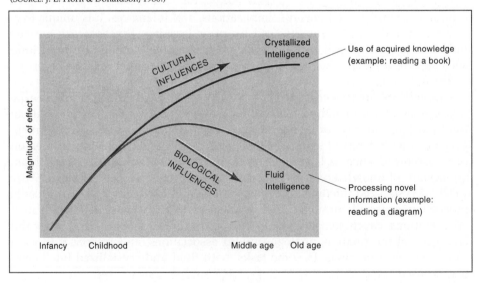

improvement in crystallized intelligence is about equal to the decline in fluid intelligence. Verbal abilities sharpen, especially when used regularly (J. L. Horn, 1982a, 1982b; J. L. Horn & Donaldson, 1980).

As in the classic aging pattern on WAIS, then, we see two kinds of intelligence that follow different paths. In the classic aging pattern, however, the trend in both verbal and performance scores is downward throughout most of adulthood; the difference, though substantial, is one of degree. Far more encouraging is the pattern of crystallized intelligence, which improves until fairly late in life, even though fluid intelligence declines.

The Dual-Process Model: Mechanics and Pragmatics of Intelligence

Age "adds as it takes away," the poet William Carlos Williams remarked in one of three books of verse written between his first stroke at age 68 and his death at age 79.

Baltes and his colleagues (1993; Baltes, Dittman-Kohli, & Dixon, 1984; Dixon & Baltes, 1986) have proposed a *dual-process model* of adult intellectual functioning, which builds on Horn and Cattell's work on fluid and crystallized intelligence. The dual-process model includes aspects of intelligence that are subject to deterioration, and also aspects that may continue to advance. The model identifies and seeks to measure two kinds of intellectual processes: *mechanics* and *pragmatics*.

Mechanics of intelligence are the basic, physiologically determined functions of the brain. They include speed and accuracy of processing sensory input, visual and motor memory, and such abilities as comparing and categorizing, which operate in working memory. Like fluid intelligence, these processes often decline with age. One example is a deterioration in the ability to ignore extraneous information, a problem similar to intrusion errors in memory (see Chapter 5).

Pragmatics of intelligence build on the mechanics. These processes involve a wide range of accumulated, culture-based knowledge and skills, such as reading, writing, language comprehension, practical thinking, specialized expertise, and occupational abilities—all potential growth areas. This dimension is similar to crystallized intelligence and depends greatly on long-term memory.

Middle-aged and older adults are likely to improve in the use of information and know-how they have garnered from education, work, and other experience. In fact, says Baltes, these pragmatic abilities often outweigh the brain's mechanical condition. To take an obvious example, an older adult who has learned to read can intellectually outperform a younger person who is in better shape neurologically but has not developed that pragmatic skill (Baltes, 1993).

Sequential Research: The Seattle Longitudinal Study

Most of the studies of adult intelligence we've discussed so far have been cross-sectional and thus may confound cohort with age. Younger adults may do better than older adults not because of an advantage conferred by youth, but because they are healthier and better nourished, have had more or better schooling, have gained more information from television, have jobs that depend on thinking rather than on physical labor, or have had more—and more recent—experience taking tests. Older people's poorer average showing may also reflect *terminal drop,* a sudden decrease in intellectual performance shortly before death (Botwinick, 1984; K. F. Riegel & Riegel, 1972; see Chapter 13).

In contrast with cross-sectional data, early longitudinal studies showed an increase in intelligence at least until the fifties (Bayley & Oden, 1955; W. A. Owens, 1966). But this research design may favor an older sample because of practice effects and *attrition,* a tendency of poorer scorers to drop out along the way (Botwinick, 1984).

The Seattle Longitudinal Study of Adult Intelligence, conducted by K. Warner Schaie and his colleagues over a span of more than three decades (Schaie, 1979, 1983, 1988a, 1988b, 1990a, 1994; Schaie & Hertzog, 1986), sought to overcome drawbacks of both cross-sectional and longitudinal research. Although this ongoing study is called *longitudinal,* it uses *sequential testing* (see Chapter 2), a combination of cross-sectional, longitudinal, and time-lag methods (Baltes, 1985; Schaie, 1979, 1983; Schaie & Hertzog, 1983; Schaie & Strother, 1968).

The study began in 1956 with 500 randomly chosen participants—25 men and 25 women in each 5-year age bracket from 20 to 70. Participants took a battery of timed tests of five primary mental abilities (see Table 6-1) originally identified by Thurstone (1938). Additional measures of intellectual abilities were added as the study progressed. Every 7 years, the original participants were retested and new participants were added; by 1994, about 5,000 people, forming a broadly diverse socioeconomic sample, had been tested. The researchers also took personal and health histories and administered psychological tests.

What has the study found? Most fairly healthy adults apparently experience no significant impairment in most abilities until after age 60. If they live long enough, most people's intellectual functioning will show some decline at some point, but not in all or even most abilities. On the average, participants showed intellectual gains until the late thirties or early forties, stability until the mid-fifties or early sixties, and then only small losses until the seventies. Even then, fewer than one-third at age 74, and fewer than half at age 81, had declined significantly during the previous 7 years. Although most people seem to lose some intellectual competence in their eighties and nineties, these losses show up mainly in unfamiliar, highly complex, challenging, or stressful circumstances (Schaie, 1990a, 1994).

One of the major findings, which supports Baltes's lifespan developmental approach, is that change is multidirectional: there is "no uniform pattern of age-related changes . . . [for] all intellectual abilities" (Schaie, 1994, p. 306). Virtually none of the participants declined on all fronts, and many improved in specific areas. Much as in Horn and Cattell's studies, fluid abilities began to decline in young adulthood, but crystallized abilities remained stable or increased into middle age and then began to show significant but not dramatic declines. These findings suggest that no single measure, such as IQ, can adequately describe either age changes in individuals or age differences among groups (Schaie, 1994).

TABLE 6-1   TESTS OF PRIMARY MENTAL ABILITIES GIVEN IN SEATTLE LONGITUDINAL STUDY OF ADULT INTELLIGENCE

Test	Ability Measured	Task	Type of Intelligence
Verbal meaning	Recognition and understanding of words	Find synonym by matching stimulus word with another word from multiple-choice list	Crystallized
Number	Applying numerical concepts	Check simple addition problems	Crystallized
Word fluency	Retrieving words from long-term memory	Think of as many words as possible beginning with a given letter, in a set time period	Part crystallized, part fluid
Spatial orientation	Rotating objects mentally in two-dimensional space	Select rotated examples of figure to match stimulus figure	Fluid
Inductive reasoning	Identifying regularities and inferring principles and rules	Complete a letter series	Fluid

SOURCE: Schaie, 1989.

Schaie (1990a) suggests that adults may optimize overall cognitive functioning by maintaining some abilities and letting other abilities slide—a concept that Baltes (1993; Baltes & Baltes, 1980, 1990), in his dual-process model, calls *selective optimization with compensation.* By capitalizing on pragmatic strengths, adults —particularly older ones—may be able to compensate for mechanical abilities that have weakened.

The concert pianist Arthur Rubinstein, who was still going strong in his eighties, once told a television interviewer how he managed to do it: he played fewer pieces, practiced each piece more often, and would slow down before a fast passage so that the audience would think he was playing it more rapidly than he actually was. As an octogenarian, the pianist Vladimir Horowitz also slowed his tempos and chose a less technically demanding repertoire; but his interpretations now showed extraordinary ripeness and finesse. A critic for the *New York Times* wrote of Horowitz: "Power does not necessarily diminish with age but simply changes its shape" (Schonberg, 1992, p. 288). Older adults—while they may take longer to do certain things and may no longer be as adept with unfamiliar material—can take advantage of mature judgment and insight developed from a lifetime of experience.

(UPI/Bettmann)

The pianist Vladimir Horowitz, who continued performing until his death at age 85, compensated for weakened mechanical abilities by choosing less technically demanding pieces, playing at slower tempos, and concentrating on interpretation.

DO CHANGES IN INTELLIGENCE VARY?

A striking feature of the Seattle Longitudinal Study is tremendous variation among individuals. For some people, intellectual abilities begin to decline during the thirties; for some, there is no decline until the seventies; and about one-third of people over age 70 score higher than the average young adult. Even in their eighties, more than half are maintaining their competence in at least four of the five primary areas. As a result, there is a wider range of ability among older adults than among younger ones. Some people remain relatively strong in one area, others in another (Schaie, 1990a, 1994).

Some researchers, therefore, are shifting attention from overall age differences and age changes to individual patterns of change and to variables that might help explain them (Schaie, 1990a, 1994). For example, people who have high scores in old age tend to be flexible and to have been satisfied with their accomplishments at midlife; not to have cardiovascular or other chronic diseases; to be relatively affluent and well-educated; to have stable marriages to intellectually keen spouses; to have done complex, nonroutine work and led active, stimulating lives; and to have maintained high perceptual processing speed (Dutta, Schulenberg, & Lair, 1986; Gribbin, Schaie, & Parham, 1980; A. Gruber & Schaie, 1986; Gruber-Baldini, 1991; Hertzog, Schaie, & Gribbin, 1978; Schaie, 1984, 1990a, 1994). One important factor, which we'll discuss later, is how, and how much, individuals use their abilities. Other factors have to do with gender and culture.

Gender Differences

Do men and women differ in how their intellectual abilities change with age? The answer is yes, though the differences are generally small and may reflect the kinds of skills men and women have been encouraged to develop.

In the Seattle Longitudinal Study, men's overall functioning eroded faster than women's. Terminal drop may be a factor: at any age, more men than women are close to death. Women seem to decline earlier in fluid abilities and men in crystallized abilities (Schaie, 1994). For example, spatial abilities such as figuring out directions from a map or assembling a bookcase ebb about twice as much in women as in men, who start out ahead and often remain stable in this area well into the eighties. On the other hand, women tend to retain their initial advantage in inductive reasoning (for instance, figuring out how often buses run from looking at a schedule), which declines at about the same rate in both sexes. Women also keep their edge in verbal memory (recalling word lists, for example), word fluency (thinking of words that start with *b*), and verbal comprehension (recognizing words they know), though comprehension does decline in the eighties—perhaps because at this age many women are living alone and have less opportunity for conversation (Foreman, 1994).

Some research indicates a possible neurological basis for women's overall superiority. A study of the kinds of errors made by each sex suggests that men's frontal lobes, which control strategic planning and management of tasks, begin to show functional losses in the seventies, about 10 years earlier than women's

With age, a woman's ability to figure out directions from a map is likely to decline more than a man's. But women remain stronger in verbal abilities.

(Joel Gordon)

frontal lobes (Hochanadel, 1991). A woman's brain has a thicker *corpus callosum*—the wide band of fibers connecting the two hemispheres. These denser interconnections may allow women to use their verbal strengths, concentrated in the left side of the brain, to compensate for spatial weaknesses in the right (Foreman, 1994).

Cultural and Cohort Effects

The Seattle Longitudinal Study found that health, work, and education influence intellectual performance across the adult years. If so, cultural factors such as availability and quality of health care and educational and job opportunities would seem to make a difference. Trends in health, education, and other lifestyle factors, as well as baby "booms" and "busts," technological advances, wars, plagues, famines, and other events, are part of the shared formative experience of different generations, or cohorts. And cohort differences can distort findings about effects of age.

In a factor analysis of WAIS scores done more than three decades ago, one team of investigators (Birren & Morrison, 1961) found that educational level played a much more significant role than age in *g* (general mental ability). Since at that time older cohorts had less schooling than younger ones, cross-sectional comparisons could be misleading unless effects of education were eliminated (Botwinick, 1984). If some of these early findings of apparently age-related declines actually reflected cohort differences, we would expect the differences to flatten out as young adults who have had the benefit of greater educational opportunity become older adults. Indeed, one more recent study of 20 college students and 20 college-educated older adults found no significant age differences in formal reasoning (Blackburn, 1984).

Health is a trickier factor because of its closer connection with age. Studies show that healthy older people do better on intelligence tests than older people who are in poor health (Botwinick, 1984). Does this mean that health, like education, should be factored out when studying effects of age? Or, since declining health often tends to accompany old age, would a study sample consisting only of healthy older people be artificially skewed? In any event, improvements in nutrition and medical care should, in time, diminish cohort differences due to health.

In the Seattle study, successive cohorts have—as we would expect—scored progressively higher at the same ages on inductive reasoning and verbal meaning. For example, the average 40-year-old in 1985 did better in both these areas than the average 40-year-old in 1971. But—again, as we would expect—this gain has leveled off. And performance in some other areas, particularly numerical skills, has actually declined among the most recent cohorts. Schaie (1990a) concludes that we may be reaching a point where older adults no longer are at much of a competitive disadvantage and, at least in numerical skills, may even outperform younger ones. On the other hand, he suggests, American society may be approaching a limit on the improvement possible for successive older cohorts as a result of education and healthy lifestyles.

(Spencer Grant/Photo Researchers)

This middle-aged woman taking a biology class at a community college in Massachusetts is an example of plasticity. *With study and training, older adults can develop new skills.*

DOES INTELLIGENCE SHOW PLASTICITY?

A key issue separating psychologists who have a relatively optimistic view of intellectual development in adulthood from those who have a less positive view is *plasticity,* or *modifiability:* whether or not intellectual performance can be improved during the middle to later years. Horn and Cattell, among others, stress the decline in fluid intelligence, which they view as biologically inevitable. Schaie, Baltes, and their colleagues stress the strong performance of crystallized or pragmatic abilities, along with the emergence of new abilities (discussed in Chapter 7); and they maintain that even fluid performance can be improved to some extent with training and practice.

Since plasticity is a key feature of Baltes's lifespan developmental approach, it is not surprising that he and his colleagues have been in the forefront of research on effects of training. Several of these studies have been based on the Adult Development and Enrichment Project (ADEPT), originated at Pennsylvania State University (Baltes & Willis, 1982; Blieszner, Willis, & Baltes, 1981; Plemons, Willis, & Baltes, 1978; Willis, Blieszner, & Baltes, 1981). A 7-year follow-up of ADEPT found that participants who received training declined significantly less than a control group (Willis, 1990; Willis & Nesselroade, 1990). In one study based on ADEPT, adults with an average age of 70 who received training in figural relations (rules for determining the next figure in a series), a measure of fluid intelligence, improved more than a control group who received no training. A third group who worked with the same training materials and problems, but without formal instruction, also did better than the control group, and this self-taught group maintained their gains better after 1 month (Blackburn, Papalia-Finlay, Foye, & Serlin, 1988). Apparently the opportunity to work out their own solutions fostered more lasting learning.

In *individual* training connected with the Seattle Longitudinal Study (Schaie, 1990a, 1994; Schaie & Willis, 1986; Willis & Schaie, 1986b), older people who had already shown declines in intelligence gained significantly in two other areas defined as fluid abilities: spatial orientation and, especially, inductive reasoning. In fact, about 4 out of 10 participants regained levels of proficiency they had shown 14 years earlier. Men improved more from training in inductive reasoning and women from training in spatial orientation, to the point of closing the gender gap in the latter. Also, trained participants retained an edge over an untrained control group, even after 7 years (Schaie, 1994). And gains measured with laboratory tasks showed substantial correlations with objective measures of everyday tasks (Willis, Jay, Diehl, & Marsiske, 1992; Schaie, 1994).

These findings suggest that intellectual deterioration may often be related to disuse (Schaie, 1994). Much as many aging athletes can call on physical reserves, older people who get training, practice, and social support seem to be able to draw on mental reserves. Adults may be able to maintain or expand this reserve capacity by engaging in a lifelong program of mental exercise. Taking up a musical instrument, learning to repair broken gadgets—almost any sort of mental challenge that involves new or unfamiliar tasks—can do the job (Golden, 1994). Old age need not be a time of intellectual decline if adults take steps to keep up or improve their mental powers throughout the lifespan (Dixon & Baltes, 1986).

SUMMING UP: INTELLIGENCE AND AGE

The four issues we've discussed—single versus multiple abilities, growth versus decline, variability, and plasticity—have generated intense controversy, and some dispute remains. However, most researchers and practitioners today believe that intelligence is made up of multiple abilities. Intelligence tests measure only some of these abilities.

Researchers tracking various intellectual abilities across adulthood have found that some—generally those that depend on the physical condition of the brain—decline with age (though at different rates); others, which depend on accumulated knowledge and skills, remain stable and may even increase. Differences—some of which are affected by gender and culture—exist among and within individuals. In fact, some older persons show no decline, or even improve, in abilities that typically diminish with age. Longitudinal findings on intellectual functioning, then, parallel results of recent research on internal biological systems (see Chapter 4), which, when measured longitudinally, range from marked decline to none.

Finally, research has demonstrated that it is possible for adults to improve their intellectual performance throughout the lifespan, even in tasks involving fluid intelligence. These findings parallel dramatic improvements in muscular strength and mobility achieved with weight-lifting programs for adults in their nineties (see Chapter 3). Still, research on memory (Chapter 5) suggests that, even for intellectual performance, biology may limit improvement in older adults more than in younger ones.

As Sternberg has noted, IQ tests tend to neglect the innovative and practical sides of intelligence. In the remainder of this chapter, we discuss creativity; in Chapter 7 we look at problem solving and other abilities that may emerge or deepen in mature adulthood.

CREATIVITY

▼

What is creativity? Can it be measured? If so, how? What causes it to bloom? Does it increase or decrease with age?

WHAT IS CREATIVITY?

Like intelligence, creativity defies exact definition. So says E. Paul Torrance (1988), who has spent a lifetime investigating it. As a graduate student at the University of Minnesota in 1958, Torrance (1988) began a systematic review of all the definitions of creativity he could find in the research literature. Each focused on products, attitudes, projects, abilities, or processes, and each raised further questions:

- *Production of something new*—a work of art, an advertising jingle, a chess move. But must the thing or idea be totally novel—something never seen before (Stein, 1953)—or new only to its creator (Stewart, 1950; Thurstone, 1952)?

- *Nonconformist attitude*—seeing and doing things in an unexpected, unusual, or out-of-the-ordinary way. But is creativity always nonconforming (Crutchfield, 1962; Lefrançois, 1982; Wilson, 1956), or do truly creative people feel free to conform or not, depending on the situation (Starkweather, 1976)?

- *Adventurous search for truth*—"getting away from the main track, breaking out of the mold, being open to experience, and permitting one thing to lead to another" (Bartlett, 1958, p. 103). But, again, does a creative mind recognize when the main track may be the right track?

- *Group of abilities*—to recognize problems, to transform customary thinking, and to generate a flow of diverse, innovative solutions (Guilford, 1956, 1959, 1960, 1986). But how do these abilities translate into concrete achievements?

- *Process*—perceiving or creating relationships (Spearman, 1930), thinking by analogy (Ribot, 1906), shaking things up and putting them together in a new way (Barchillon, 1961; Kubie, 1958), solving a sensed problem or meeting a felt lack or need (Wallas, 1926). But how, then, does creativity differ from *intelligent* problem solving? How much of it is conscious, and how much is unconscious? Is it primarily rational or nonrational? Does it involve analysis, synthesis, or both?

The creative process, as outlined by a number of investigators, has four steps, which may combine all these kinds of activity: (1) *Preparation*—sensing a problem and exploring and clarifying it. (2) *Incubation*—studying the problem, formulating possible solutions, and evaluating them critically. (3) *Illumination*—the burst of a new idea or insight. (4) *Revision*—testing and perfecting the solution, perhaps with input from others. One contemporary summation is: "find the *mess;* find the *facts;* find the *problem;* find the *ideas;* find the *solution;* find the *acceptance;* find the new *mess* " (Shaw, 1992b, p. 42).

As the foundation for his own work, Torrance (1965) adopted a process-based definition of creativity that emphasizes constructive response to an awareness of something missing, incomplete, or out of place. While directing research on a U.S. Air Force survival training program in the 1950s, he had observed fliers coming up with creative ways to survive extreme cold or heat, lack of food, water, or shelter, and capture by the enemy. Torrance (1957) concluded that creativity surfaces in the absence of a "learned or practiced solution to a problem." It "cannot be taught. . . . [It] must be self-discovered and self-disciplined" (Torrance, 1988, p. 57). Yet creativity builds on previous learning; it is the imaginative recombining of known pieces of information to resolve tension created by an immediate need.

What, then, is the difference between creativity and intelligence? Although the distinction is far from clear, creativity seems to involve a greater role for emotions, attitudes, unconscious thought processes, self-motivation, and offbeat, untutored methods. Still, as Torrance admits, the essence of the creative spark and the conditions that fan it into flame remain unclear. No one has yet been able to pinpoint what produces a Kurosawa or an Einstein and what precise processes enter into the creation of their works. And no one knows just what enables ordinary human beings to come up with innovative solutions to everyday problems. What, then, can we say about creativity? What lines of research have been pursued, and where have they led?

STUDYING AND MEASURING CREATIVITY

How can we compare the creativity of a distinguished artist, scientist, or filmmaker with the creative activities and abilities of ordinary people? One way to do this is to think of creativity as having five levels: (1) spontaneous expression, as in a child's scribblings; (2) producing artistic or scientific works; (3) inventing a new and useful object, method, or technique; (4) modifying a concept; and (5) originating a revolutionary new principle or movement (Taylor, 1959). Of course, the fifth level is rarely attained, and psychometric studies of creative behavior have therefore focused on the other four (Torrance, 1988). Much as intelligence tests attempt to measure abilities that predict success in school, psychometric tests of creativity attempt to measure abilities that predict creative productivity. Other investigators use biographical methods, case studies, or self-reports to identify sources and aspects of creativity in the lives and work of acknowledged innovators. Still other researchers use laboratory-based methods to identify elements of the creative process. Let's look at these three approaches.

The Psychometric Approach: Divergent Thinking

Some of the earliest psychometric research on creativity focused on its relationship to IQ. Although creative people tend to be fairly intelligent, the *most* academically gifted children or adults did not prove to be the most original thinkers

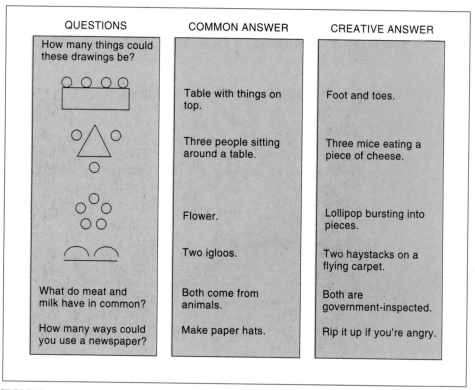

FIGURE 6-6
Tests of creativity seek to identify divergent thinking.
(SOURCE: Adapted from Wallach & Kogan, 1967.)

(Getzels, 1964, 1984; Getzels & Jackson, 1962; MacKinnon, 1962). More recent research suggests that the optimal IQ for creative development is only about 19 points above average for a particular field (Simonton, 1985).

If highly intelligent people are not the most creative, then creative thinking and scholastic success may require different abilities. Guilford (1956, 1959, 1960, 1986) distinguished between convergent and divergent thinking: *convergent thinking* seeks a single right answer (usually the conventional one); *divergent thinking* comes up with a wide array of fresh possibilities. Divergent thinking is not only fluent (able to generate many answers), but also flexible, original, and elaborative.

Unlike intelligence tests, which call for convergent thinking, tests of creativity call for divergent thinking (see Figure 6-6). The *Torrance Tests of Creative Thinking* (Torrance, 1966, 1974; Torrance & Ball, 1984), probably the most widely used psychometric tests of creativity, include such tasks as listing unusual uses for a common object (like a paper clip), completing a figure, and writing down what a sound brings to mind. Using these tests, Torrance has tried to learn what kind of person typically engages in creativity. He found that creative people tend to be courageous, independent, honest, tenacious, curious, and willing to take risks. Above all, like Akira Kurosawa, they have a passion for what they do.

Although tests such as Torrance's are fairly reliable (they yield consistent results), there is dispute over whether they have *construct validity*—that is, whether they identify people who are creative in real life (Anastasi, 1988; Mansfield & Busse, 1981; Simonton, 1990). Torrance's (1988) claim of validity rests on longitudinal studies of elementary and high school students, begun when the tests were in preparation (Torrance, 1972a, 1972b, 1981). Follow-up studies after intervals ranging from 7 to 22 years found that the tests had successfully predicted which youngsters would become creative achievers as adults. However, because these tests are given to adults less frequently than to children, we know very little about their predictive value across the adult lifespan. And, as Guilford recognized, divergent thinking is not the only factor in creativity; also important are sensitivity to problems and the ability to redefine or reinterpret them so as to obtain unique solutions.

The Biographical Approach: Studying Creative Achievers

The difficulty of defining and measuring creativity has led some investigators to turn to an earlier approach: studies of people, living or dead, who have been recognized as creative. Such investigators seek clues to the nature and workings of creativity by studying biographies and autobiographical writings or self-reports such as diaries and letters.

One current advocate of this approach is Howard Gardner, whose theory of multiple intelligences we've already discussed. Whereas psychometric researchers assume that creativity is the same for scientists, artists, and others, Gardner suggests that it is *multifactorial* and may operate differently in different fields. According to Gardner, creativity starts with a high degree of talent in one or more cognitive areas, but talent is not the whole story. Creativity is a web of biological, personal, social, and cultural forces.

Because creativity is so complex and because we know so little about it, Gardner (1986, 1988) has called for comprehensive interdisciplinary research enlisting the expertise of psychologists, cognitive scientists, historians, anthropologists, and neurobiologists to study the lives and work of acknowledged creative giants. Gardner has sketched preliminary outlines for such a study of the life of Sigmund Freud, based chiefly on the classic biography by Ernest Jones (1961).

Freud was highly talented in several of Gardner's realms of intelligence: linguistic, logical, intrapersonal (since he built his psychoanalytic theory on insights into his own psyche), and interpersonal (though he could repel as well as attract followers). But Jones believes that what raised Freud to the pinnacle of creative achievement was his ability to see in an isolated fact (such as his discovery of his previously submerged feelings toward his parents) a key to the forces motivating human behavior. This tendency sometimes made Freud jump to erroneous conclusions, however—for instance, he considered cocaine a cure for a variety of illnesses.

Freud himself attributed his success more to his personality than to his intellectual abilities. He depreciated his intellect and complained that he had no talent for science or mathematics. He felt that his strengths were compulsive curiosity, a

Sigmund Freud, the founder of
psychoanalysis, maintained that
creativity is a result of sublimated
sexual tension.

(Library of Congress)

bold adventurous nature, and a passion to conquer, combined with strong self-discipline, tenacity, perseverance, and an ability to withstand hostile criticism. He was a workaholic, often seeing patients until late at night and then writing into the early morning hours—a schedule he maintained almost until his death.

Creativity does not develop in a vacuum. Besides *cognitive gifts* and *personality traits,* a biographical study such as Gardner proposes would examine two environmental dimensions: the person's *field* of work and his or her *society.* Freud, of course, did not merely contribute to a field of knowledge; he created a new one. One avenue for biographical research would be to examine the state of knowledge at the time he began his work and then trace how his ideas changed at each step of the way, as the psychologist Howard Gruber (1981) did in his pioneering study of Charles Darwin's notebooks (see Box 6-3). It might then be possible to design computer simulations of Freud's mental processes. But such a study would still be incomplete without a historical analysis of conditions in Vienna at the turn of the century—a repressive society, but at the same time an unparalleled center of learning. Since the ultimate purpose would be to illuminate not merely the creative life of one individual but sources of creativity and conditions under which it develops, many such case studies would be needed to provide sufficient raw material for generalization.

Gardner (1988) suspects that tension serves as a springboard for creativity. The source of such tension may be a poor fit between two or more elements of a person's life: biological constitution, intellectual strengths and weaknesses, intellectual and personality styles, and chosen field. This tension motivates the individual "to strike out in a new direction and, ultimately, to fashion a creative product" (p. 320). In Freud's case, the problem of fit showed up in his search for a

BOX 6-3

THE ART OF AGING

Creativity Takes Hard Work at Any Age

At 48, the jazz singer Ella Fitzgerald began to record a 19-album series of nearly 250 popular classics; at 59, she finished it. Leonard Bernstein was 53 when he composed his *Mass* in memory of President John F. Kennedy. The British author William Golding produced 11 novels after *Lord of the Flies*, which came out when he was 43; he won Britain's prestigious Booker Prize for *Rights of Passage*, published when he was 69. The artist Marc Chagall designed the monumental mosaic *The Four Seasons* when he was in his late eighties and the stained-glass *America Windows* when he was 90. These are but a few examples of creative achievements in middle and old age.

What goes on in the minds of highly creative people? What enables some of them to remain productive beyond the usual peak years for their fields? We may find some clues in an intensive study the psychologist Howard Gruber did of the mental processes of Charles Darwin, who published his controversial theory of evolution at 50, well beyond the age when most scientists make their most important breakthroughs (Gardner, 1981).

Darwin's theory was based on his meticulously recorded observations of fossils, plants, animals, and rocks he had seen along the coast of South America and in the Pacific islands during a 5-year voyage of exploration two decades earlier.

(UPI/Bettmann)

Many creative accomplishments occur in middle age or later. In her forties, the jazz singer Ella Fitzgerald began recording a 19-album series of popular classics; she took 11 years to finish it.

Gruber pored over Darwin's notebooks to map the path of his thinking during the 18 months after his return from that voyage.

Gruber was struck by how long it took Dar-

field in which he could make his mark. Not until his late thirties did he begin to focus on the areas of investigation that would bear fruit in his life's work. In the case of Kurosawa, exposure to both eastern and western cultures produced a creative tension that enabled him to brilliantly reinterpret the themes of Shakespearean tragedies such as King Lear (*Ran*) and Macbeth (*Throne of Blood*) in the context of a breakup of the tightly ordered structure of traditional Japanese society.

win, then in his late twenties, to think through a new idea. Darwin had gone down at least one blind alley before he came upon an essay by the English economist Thomas Malthus, which described how natural disasters and wars keep human population increases under control. After reading Malthus's description of the struggle for survival, it occurred to Darwin that species whose characteristics were best adapted to their environment would tend to survive, and others would not. Even then, it took Darwin several months after reading Malthus's essay to develop his principle of natural selection, which explains how adaptive traits are passed on through reproduction. And it was not until more than 2 decades later that he finally published his theory and the supporting evidence.

Although each mind works somewhat differently, Gruber found some commonalities between Darwin's thought processes and those of other highly creative achievers in the arts and sciences:

- They work *painstakingly and slowly* to master the knowledge and skills they need to solve a problem. Darwin studied barnacles for 8 years, until he probably knew more about them than anyone else in the world.

- They constantly *visualize* ideas. Darwin drew one particular image—a branching tree—over and over, refining his theory of how more complex species evolve on the "tree" of nature.

- They are *goal-directed*; they have a strong sense of purpose and know where they want to go.

- They have *networks of enterprises*, often juggling several seemingly unrelated projects or activities.

- They are *able to set aside problems* they have too little information to solve and go on to something else, or adopt temporary working assumptions. Darwin did this when he got stuck on questions about heredity for which he had no reliable answers.

- They are *daring*. It took courage for Darwin to publish a theory that shattered the entrenched ideas of his day.

- Rather than work in isolation (as they are often thought to do), they *collaborate* or discuss their ideas with others, by choosing peers and designing environments that nurture their work.

- They *enjoy turning over ideas* in their minds. Darwin was reading Malthus's essay for amusement.

- Through hard work, they *transform themselves*, until what would be difficult for someone else seems easy for them.

In Gruber's view, creative growth in adults may be a developmental process that spans a period of years, much like children's cognitive growth. If that is true, then we need to study why this development seems to stop or slow down for some people in young adulthood, while in others it continues throughout the lifespan.

According to Freud, it is sexual tension that is at the root of creative endeavor; if a child's sexual curiosity is *sublimated,* or directed into socially acceptable channels, highly creative work may result. In one of his own biographical studies, Freud (1910/1957, 1947) suggested that the most famous painting by the Renaissance master Leonardo da Vinci—the *Mona Lisa*—was an expression of long-buried desire for the unwed mother from whom Leonardo had been torn in early childhood.

For Freud (1949), the act of creation arises from childlike dreams and fantasies tamed by the conscious, rational mind. Whether or not these processes originate in sublimated sexual drives, as Freud believed, alternation of spontaneous insights with conscious, rational effort is a recurrent theme in self-reports by noted artists and scientists. Jonas Salk, who developed the Salk polio vaccine, recalls that he used to try to picture what it would feel like to be a virus or a cancer cell. Jacob W. Getzels (1964), a pioneer in the study of creativity, observed that insights often flash into a creator's mind after such a period of idle daydreaming or seemingly fruitless struggle.

Getzels (1964, 1984) and others have identified *intrinsic motivation*—an urge to solve problems for the sake of solving them rather than for any external reward—as essential to creativity. One recent study, which confirmed the importance of intrinsic motivation, mapped thoughts and feelings of twelve internationally known scientists during various phases of the creative process. The study also found that *affect tolerance*—ability to tolerate negative feelings—is required for creative work (Runco & Albert, 1990; Shaw, 1992a, 1992b). Because the scientists understood that such feelings as anger, fear, sadness, shame, depression, anxiety, self-depreciation, and sensitivity to rejection are a necessary part of the process, they were able to cope with and surmount them (Shaw, 1989, 1992a, 1992b).

Laboratory Research: "Problem Finding"

> The formulation of a problem is often more essential than its solution, which may be merely a matter of mathematical or experimental skill. To raise new questions, new possibilities, to regard old questions from a new angle, requires imagination and marks real advance in science. (A. Einstein & Infeld, 1938, p. 92)

Einstein's comment foreshadowed an observation about the molecular biologist James D. Watson. Watson and Francis Crick won a Nobel prize for their discovery of the structure of DNA, the genetic substance that directs the functioning of all body cells. One of Watson's graduate students at Harvard University later remarked: "His greatest talent is an uncanny instinct for the important problem, the thing that leads to big-time results. He seems to . . . pluck it out of thin air" (Edson, 1968, pp. 29–31).

Still, widespread recognition of *problem finding*—the ability to identify and formulate novel and important problems—as a hallmark of creative thought awaited the completion of a classic longitudinal study of young adult art students, one of the first attempts to investigate creativity in the laboratory. Getzels and Mihaly Csikszentmihalyi (1968, 1975, 1976), another pioneer in the study of creativity, asked these art students to select and arrange objects for a still life. In doing so, the students set up their own artistic problems, which they then proceeded to solve. The students whose works were judged by art experts as best and most original, and who later proved to be most successful, were those whose "problems" had been most unusual and complex. The study was later replicated by another investigator, with similar results (Arlin, 1975, 1984).

This research supports Sternberg's suggestion that creativity may be linked to the development of mature thought. A shift in emphasis from problem solving to problem finding is sometimes described as characteristic of *postformal thought,* a mature way of thinking that we explore in Chapter 7.

CREATIVITY AND AGE

When a heart condition forced I. F. Stone to stop publishing his weekly news-letter of independent political reporting and commentary, the feisty journalist decided to undertake a project central to his lifelong political and philosophical outlook: a history of freedom of thought. His studies led him back to ancient Greece, the first society in which free expression flowered. But he was troubled by the trial of the philosopher Socrates, who was condemned to death for "corrupting" the youth of Athens with his teachings. This trial seemed to mock everything Athenian democracy stood for. Determined to get to the bottom of the paradox, Stone taught himself Greek so that he could translate original texts to see for himself what light they could shed. The result was *The Trial of Socrates* (1988)—one of the most original and insightful commentaries on that historic event—published when Stone was over 80. Stone even wrote a speech he felt Socrates should have made to win acquittal! In the acknowledgments, Stone wrote: "Finally, I pour a libation to my Macintosh word processor. Its large fat black 24-point Chicago Bold type enabled me to overcome a cataract and write the book" (p. 270).

The Age Curve

Stone's remarkable achievement flies in the face of the common belief that creativity diminishes in late life. To assess that belief, Dean K. Simonton (1990), a research psychologist at the University of California, reviewed findings from psychometric tests and lifespan studies. He found that the belief is largely true, with some *ifs, ands,* and *buts.*[*]

On psychometric tests of divergent thinking, age differences consistently show up. Whether the data are cross-sectional or longitudinal, scores peak, on average, around the late thirties. A similar age curve emerges when creativity is measured by variations in output (number of publications, paintings, or compositions). A person in the last decade of a creative career typically produces only about half as much as during the late thirties or early forties, though somewhat more than in the twenties.

However, the age curve varies significantly depending on the field. Poets, mathematicians, and theoretical physicists are most prolific in their late twenties or early thirties. Psychologists reach a peak around age 40, followed by a moderate decline. Novelists, historians, philosophers, and scholars become increasingly productive through their late forties or fifties and then level off. These patterns hold true across cultures and historical periods.

---

[*]Unless otherwise noted, the following discussion is based on Simonton (1990).

Quantity versus Quality

There are three ways to achieve a large lifetime output: (1) start early, (2) keep going, and (3) be unusually prolific. Not only are all three factors associated with high total production; the three factors are linked. Creative people who start producing early and maintain a large output generally continue to be highly productive in later life. Pablo Picasso, considered by many to be the greatest artist of the twentieth century, began painting in childhood and, up to his death in 1973 at the age of 91, produced more than 200 paintings and sculptures a year.

Of course, not everything a person creates is equally notable; even someone like Picasso is bound to produce some minor material. However, the **quality ratio**—the proportion of major works to total output—bears no relationship to age. The periods in which a person creates the largest number of memorable works also tend to be the ones in which he or she produces the largest number of forgettable ones. Thus the likelihood that a *particular* work will be a masterpiece has nothing to do with age. Irving Berlin, in a life that spanned 101 years, wrote more than 1,500 songs and 17 musical revues; some of his top hits were written in his fifties, sixties, seventies, and eighties. Songs he wrote in his sixties (such as "Count Your Blessings Instead of Sheep") were no more or less likely to prove immortal than songs he wrote in his early twenties (such as "Alexander's Ragtime Band").

Still, if we assess creativity in terms of sheer quantity of high-quality performance, the picture looks much like the general age curve. The more a creative person produces in, say, a 10-year period, the greater the chance that a large number (though not necessarily a large *proportion*) of those works will be major ones. Thus a person is likely to produce the greatest number of major works at peak periods of productivity (midlife or earlier, depending on the field). Kurosawa, for example, released three of his greatest films—*Rashomon, Ikiru*, and *Seven Samurai*—during a 3-year period within a decade when he was making about one film a year.

For the same reason, if we compare two equally creative people, the one who produces more work throughout an entire career is also likely to produce more noteworthy work; the most productive creators tend to make the most influential contributions overall. This is a key point because differences in productivity can be very great; the most productive scientists, for example, are about 100 times more productive than the least (Dennis, 1954, 1955). Thomas Alva Edison, inventor of the light bulb, held more than 1,000 patents.

Sometimes, though, losses in productivity may be offset by gains in quality. Maturity can change the tone and content of creative work. Age-related analyses of themes of ancient Greek and Shakespearean plays show a shift from youthful preoccupation with love and romance to more spiritual concerns (Simonton, 1983, 1986). And a study of the "swan songs" of 172 composers found that their last works—usually fairly short and melodically simple—were among their richest, most important, and most successful (Simonton, 1989).

A classic theory (Beard, 1874) offers a simple explanation for this phenomenon—and for why even *quantity* of production in such fields as philosophy and history often holds up until late in life. According to this theory, there are two factors in creativity: enthusiasm and experience. Enthusiasm peaks early, and thereafter production wanes. But experience continues to build, infusing later works—especially those requiring seasoned reflection—with mature insight and wisdom missing from the products of youth.

The German poet Rainer Maria Rilke (1984) wrote, "Ah! but verses amount to so little when one writes them young. One ought to wait and gather sense and sweetness a whole life long, and a long life if possible, and then, quite at the end, one might perhaps be able to write ten lines that were good." This growth of mature thought and wisdom—along with a parallel growth in moral reasoning—is the focus of Chapter 7, the third of our trilogy on intellectual development in adulthood.

SUMMARY

INTELLIGENCE AND ITS MEASUREMENT: THE PSYCHOMETRIC APPROACH

- Most psychologists agree that intelligent behavior is goal-oriented and adaptive and involves reasoning, acquiring knowledge, and solving problems.

- The psychometric approach assumes that individuals possess varying, measurable quantities of intelligence. Psychometric tests assess verbal comprehension, mathematical computation, reasoning, and nonverbal performance.

- Intelligence tests for adults are scored by comparison with standardized norms using the deviation IQ.

- Intelligence tests infer ability from performance and may be subject to cultural bias. Their appropriateness for mature adults has been questioned.

INTELLECTUAL DEVELOPMENT IN ADULTHOOD: BASIC ISSUES

- A multifactorial view of intelligence can accommodate simultaneous advances and declines; a unitary view cannot.

- Sternberg has proposed three elements of intelligence: componential, experiential, and contextual. The experiential and contextual elements (including tacit knowledge) may become more important in adulthood.

- Gardner has proposed seven independent "intelligences": linguistic, logical-mathematical, spatial, musical, bodily-kinesthetic, intrapersonal, and interpersonal.

- The classic aging pattern on WAIS shows a much larger and sharper decline in performance (nonverbal) tasks than in verbal tasks. Fluid intelligence has been found to decline with age, while crystallized intelligence remains constant or improves.

- According to Baltes's dual-process model, gains in the pragmatics of intelligence (crystallized) may compensate for losses in the mechanics of intelligence (fluid).

- The Seattle Longitudinal Study of Adult Intelligence, using a sequential design, found that intellectual development is multidirectional and shows great individual variability, small gender differences, and significant cohort effects.

- Training and practice can improve performance even of fluid tasks; declines may be largely related to lack of mental exercise.

CREATIVITY

- Creativity has been defined in terms of products, attitudes, projects, abilities, or processes. It is often considered a form of problem solving. Creativity has been studied by psychometric testing, by biographical studies, and by laboratory research.
- Biographical case studies may examine cognitive and personality factors, field of work, and cultural environment.
- Suggested sources and conditions of creativity include tension, intrinsic motivation, affect tolerance, problem finding, and an interplay of conscious and unconscious, rational and irrational thought.
- An age-related decline in creativity shows up in both psychometric tests and actual output. Peak ages and rates of decline vary by occupation.
- Individuals tend to produce the greatest number, though not necessarily the greatest proportion, of major works at peak periods of productivity (midlife or earlier, depending on the field).

KEY TERMS

▼

intelligent behavior (page 201)
psychometric approach (202)
intelligence quotient (IQ) (204)
deviation IQ (204)
Wechsler Adult Intelligence Scale (WAIS)
    (205)
cultural bias (207)
factor analysis (210)
componential element (211)
experiential element (212)
contextual element (213)
tacit knowledge (214)
classic aging pattern (216)
fluid intelligence (216)

crystallized intelligence (217)
dual-process model (219)
mechanics of intelligence (219)
pragmatics of intelligence (219)
terminal drop (220)
selective optimization
    with compensation (221)
convergent thinking (229)
divergent thinking (229)
Torrance Tests of Creative
    Thinking (229)
intrinsic motivation (234)
problem finding (234)
quality ratio (236)

CHAPTER 7

MATURE THOUGHT, WISDOM, AND MORAL INTELLIGENCE

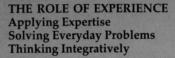

THE ROLE OF EXPERIENCE
Applying Expertise
Solving Everyday Problems
Thinking Integratively

POSTFORMAL THOUGHT: BEYOND PIAGET'S STAGES
How Postformal Thought Develops
Social Reasoning
   and Postformal Thought
Cultural Change
   and Postformal Thought
Criteria for Postformal Thought

A LIFESPAN MODEL OF COGNITIVE DEVELOPMENT

WISDOM
Wisdom in Folklore, Myth,
   and Philosophy
Psychological Concepts
   and Assessments
Summing Up: Wisdom and Age

MORAL DEVELOPMENT
Kohlberg's Theory: Moral Reasoning
Gilligan's Theory: Gender
   and Postformal Morality
Evaluating Kohlberg's and
   Gilligan's Theories

INTELLIGENCE, CREATIVITY, WISDOM, AND MORAL DEVELOPMENT: A LAST WORD

BOXES
7-1 The Multicultural Context:
   Postformal Thinking and
   Cultural Change
7-2 The Cutting Edge: Comparing
   Wisdom with Intelligence
   and Creativity
7-3 The Art of Aging: Moral Leadership
   in Middle and Late Adulthood

> *To accept all experience as raw material out of which the human spirit distills meanings and values is a part of the meaning of maturity.*
>
> Howard Thurman, *Meditations of the Heart*, 1953

FOCUS: NELSON MANDELA

(AP Photo by John Parkin/Wide World)

Nelson Mandela's[*] first name, Rolihlahla, means "stirring up trouble"— something he did throughout his long struggle to topple *apartheid,* South Africa's rigid system of racial separation and subjugation. But whereas the young Mandela has been described as passionate, hotheaded, and quick to anger, the 71-year-old man who, in 1990, emerged from 26 years of imprisonment was coolly reasonable and highly controlled. "I came out mature," he says (Stengel, 1994).

The historic accord that resulted in Mandela's election 4 years later as his country's first black president was the realization of a childhood dream—formed as young Mandela, born into a royal family, listened to elders recall a bygone era of peace, freedom, and equality. Later, suspended from college for participating in a student protest, Mandela in 1941 became one of thousands of young men from rural communities who headed for industrial Johannesburg looking for jobs. There he saw firsthand the effects of the color bar: squalid, crime-ridden shantytowns on the fringes of a prosperous city. He managed to find work, finish college by correspondence, and become a lawyer. Every day his office overflowed with people charged with violating unjust laws.

Meanwhile, Mandela had joined the African National Congress (ANC). He helped organize nonviolent demonstrations, which only brought violent repression, increasingly harsh laws, and police harassment. In 1952, after becoming a deputy

[*]Sources of biographical information about Nelson Mandela are Benson (1986), Goodrich (1995), Hargrove (1989), Mandela (1994), Meer (1988), Nelan (1994), Stengel (1994), P. Taylor (1994), and Watson (1994).

president of ANC, he, like many other militant blacks, was banned from attending meetings or traveling outside Johannesburg.

In December 1956, in a nighttime raid, he and 155 other ANC leaders were arrested and charged with conspiracy to overthrow the government. After a 4-year trial, during which police at one point opened fire on peaceful spectators, the defendants were acquitted. But ANC was banned, and so, as before, was Mandela. He went into hiding and organized a national 3-day work stoppage. The government, in an unsuccessful attempt to abort it, imprisoned more than 10,000 Africans, most without trial.

Mandela reluctantly concluded that the movement would have to meet force with force—but aimed at property, not people. He masterminded a bombing raid of 23 targets in major cities. "I did not plan it in a spirit of recklessness, nor because I have any love of violence," he said at his trial. "I planned it as a result of a calm and sober assessment of the political situation that had arisen after many years of tyranny, exploitation, and oppression of my people" (Benson, 1986, pp. 146–147).

Handed a life sentence in 1964 at age 45, Mandela continued to direct his people's struggle from his island prison. When he wasn't chopping rocks, he was educating himself and his jailmates in history, economics, and Afrikaans, the language of their white adversaries. He began a long dialogue with government officials, first by letter and then in secret meetings.

Supremely patient, confident, and resolute, Mandela planned to wear down the opposition. The longer he remained in prison—a man of justice caught in an unjust system—the more his moral authority grew. In 1985, he rejected an offer of release in exchange for a promise to refrain from violent or illegal action. Mandela—by then an international symbol of resistance—explained, in a statement to the African people, that his freedom was inseparable from theirs. Five years later, seeing the handwriting on the wall, South Africa's new president, F. W. de Klerk, released him, legalized ANC and other black political organizations, lifted discriminatory laws, and promised a nonracial constitution. ANC, in turn, gave up armed struggle. Despite the distrust between them, Mandela and de Klerk managed to reach agreement on a new constitution, set up free elections, and avoid all-out civil war. For these accomplishments, they received a Nobel Peace prize in 1993.

Since defeating de Klerk for president, Mandela at 75 has had the daunting task of reforming South Africa's political and economic system. He has approached it with the same cautious determination and moral courage he showed during his long imprisonment. Despite the hardships he and his people have suffered, he knows that bitterness will not help achieve his goals. In the name of cultural inclusiveness, he urges black South Africans to learn Afrikaans and to sing the old national anthem along with the new one. "We are starting a new era," he says, "of hope, of reconciliation, of nation building" (Nelan, 1994, p. 28).

Nelson Mandela is a gifted leader, a man of great intelligence and drive. In his youth, he was a man of action. In his middle and old age, he has also shown himself to be a man of disciplined thought and measured words. Did Mandela's experiences (as he suggests) shape a wiser, more mature way of thinking that helped him move South Africa from authoritarian white rule to a multiracial democracy? Do mature adults whose experience may be less unusual or dramatic than Mandela's develop new ways of thinking as well? Have you noticed any apparent changes in how your parents or grandparents think as they get older? And if mature cognition does show distinctive characteristics, what processes are involved?

Rather than focusing on *quantitative* changes in intellectual abilities (as we do, for the most part, in Chapter 6), a growing body of theory and research—arising chiefly from organismic and contextual perspectives—looks for *qualitative* changes, whether universal or individual, and their implications for the assessment of intelligence across the adult lifespan. In the first section of this chapter, we describe thought processes that capitalize on experience: expert and everyday problem solving and integrative thought. Next, we look at mature thought as a stage of cognitive development. Then we examine several meanings of *wisdom*. We go on to discuss moral development: how adults resolve moral dilemmas, from the purely personal to epochal issues such as those that confronted Nelson Mandela.

THE ROLE OF EXPERIENCE

According to Jean Piaget, cognitive progress from infancy through adolescence results from a combination of biologically programmed maturation and experience. What happens, then, in an adult? It would seem that experience should play an even greater role.

APPLYING EXPERTISE

Two young resident physicians in a hospital radiology laboratory examine a chest x-ray. They study an unusual white blotch on the left side. "Looks like a large tumor," one of them says finally. The other nods.

Just then, a longtime staff radiologist walks by and looks over their shoulders at the x-ray. "That patient has a collapsed lung and needs immediate surgery," he declares (Lesgold, 1983).

According to many studies, in mature adults the ability to solve novel problems (fluid intelligence) gradually diminishes, yet they show increasing competence in solving problems in their chosen fields. Why? The answer, according to William Hoyer and his colleagues (Hoyer & Rybash, 1994; Rybash, Hoyer, & Roodin, 1986), lies in specialized knowledge—a form of crystallized or pragmatic intelligence—which depends on accumulating and organizing a great deal of

Expertise in interpreting x-rays, as in many other fields, depends on accumulated, specialized knowledge, which continues to increase with age. Experts often appear to be guided by intuition and cannot explain how they arrive at conclusions.

very specific information about concepts and procedures, and on efficiently accessing this knowledge in memory. This expertise seems to be relatively independent of any declines in general intelligence and in the brain's information-processing machinery.

In one study (Ceci & Liker, 1986), researchers identified 30 middle-aged and older men who were avid spectators and bettors at a horse racing track. On the basis of skill in picking winners, the investigators divided the men into two groups: "expert" and "nonexpert." An IQ test found no significant difference in intelligence. But the "experts" were found to use a sophisticated method of reasoning, incorporating interpretations of much interrelated information about each horse; "nonexperts," by contrast, tended to use simpler, less successful methods. Again, this difference was not related to IQ—"experts" with low IQs used more complex reasoning than "nonexperts" with higher IQs.

The Hoyer group's explanation for this seeming paradox is that, with experience, information processing and fluid thinking become dedicated to specific knowledge systems. This process of *encapsulation* makes knowledge within the field of expertise easier to add to, access, and use. Indeed, there is a good deal of evidence that efficiency of information processing depends on the kind of material being processed (Hoyer & Rybash, 1994). Encapsulation is largely unidirectional and irreversible; adults, as long as they remain healthy and vigorous, continue to gain expertise. On the other hand, encapsulated abilities become less available for general use—for solving problems outside the specific field. Thus, despite a general loss in fluid intelligence, encapsulation "captures" or salvages fluid abilities for expert problem solving.

According to this model, encapsulation results in distinctively adult ways of thinking and knowing. Children and adolescents are better able to assimilate a wide variety of *new* knowledge; adults, however, concentrate on refining and broadening *existing* knowledge in a flexible, open-ended way that allows for application to ill-defined, multifaceted real-life situations, such as picking stocks or picking winners at the racetrack.

"Expert thinking" often seems automatic and intuitive. Because experts generally are not aware of the thought processes that lie behind their decisions (Dreyfus, 1993–1994; Rybash et al., 1986), they can't readily explain how they arrive at a conclusion or where a nonexpert has gone wrong. In our earlier example, the experienced radiologist might not see why the residents would even consider diagnosing a collapsed lung as a tumor; similarly, a chess master might not even consider moves a novice would mentally debate about. Nor do experts rely on rules; instead, they intuitively apply their accumulated experience—or what Sternberg calls *tacit knowledge* (see Chapter 6)—to particular cases (Dreyfus, 1993–1994). In one study, for example, novice nurses stuck to rules they had learned for taking care of babies; experienced nurses used intuition to guide them in deciding when it was better *not* to be bound by rules (Benner, 1984).

The encapsulation model is consistent with Baltes's lifespan developmental approach as a way of explaining increased competence in some areas despite measured losses in others. According to the encapsulation model, advances in expertise continue at least through middle age, before physiologically based deterioration may limit them.

SOLVING EVERYDAY PROBLEMS

If expertise allows adults to become better problem solvers in specialized fields, what about practical problems of daily living? Does experience make adults "experts" in everyday problem solving?

In one study (Denney & Palmer, 1981), 84 adults between ages 20 and 79 were given two kinds of problems. One kind was like the game "twenty questions." Participants were shown 42 pictures of common objects and were told to figure out which one the examiner was thinking of, by asking questions that could be answered "yes" or "no." Scoring was based on how many questions it took to get the answer and what percentage of questions eliminated more than one item at a time ("Is it an animal?") rather than only one item ("Is it a cow?"). The older the participants were, the worse they did on this part of the test.

The second kind of problem involved situations like the following: *your basement is flooding; you are stranded in a car during a blizzard; your 8-year-old child is 1½ hours late coming home from school.* Higher scores were given for responses that showed self-reliance and recognition of a number of possible causes and solutions. In this part of the test, the best practical problem solvers were people in their forties and fifties who based their answers on experiences of everyday living. There was a follow-up study, which tried to give the elderly an advantage by posing problems with which they would be most familiar (retirement, widowhood, and ill health); but people in their forties still came up with better solutions

(Akos Szilvasi/Stock, Boston)

What would you do if your car was stranded on a flooded highway? Ability to solve practical problems like this one seems to be high in middle and old age.

than either younger or older adults (Denney & Pearce, 1989). The implication was that the benefits of experience in dealing with problems reach a limit at some point during adulthood—perhaps in middle age.

Other researchers who studied everyday problem solving obtained different results, though (Cornelius & Caspi, 1987). These investigators constructed an inventory consisting of sample problems that younger, middle-aged, or older adults were likely to experience as consumers; in managing a home; in resolving conflicts with family members, friends, and coworkers; and in dealing with technical information. For each situation, four possible responses were presented. For example: You find out that you have been passed over for a better job. Would you: (a) try to find out why you didn't get it? (b) try to see the positive side of the situation? (c) accept the decision? (d) complain to a friend about the unfairness of the decision? A group of judges of various ages, most of whom had no formal training in psychology, rated the effectiveness of the responses. This time, everyday problem-solving capability (as defined by the judges) did *not* drop off after middle age, as fluid abilities do. Rather, like crystallized intelligence, performance on the inventory improved into late adulthood.

In an attempt to resolve the discrepancies in previous research, Camp, Doherty, Moody-Thomas, and Denney (1989) devised a study based in part on problems used in Denney's earlier studies and in part on real problems the participants had faced, such as marital quarrels, disputes with neighbors, health emergencies, loss of a job, and street violence. This time, the participants themselves generated the solutions, which were rated on *quality* rather than quantity. As in Cornelius and Caspi's study, older adults showed no age deficits. They did no worse than younger adults in solving their own problems and were more satisfied with their solutions. These findings are consistent with other evidence that older adults do not see themselves as declining in problem-solving ability and may even see this ability as increasing with age (Williams, Denney, & Schadler, 1983).

THINKING INTEGRATIVELY

The ability of mature adults to solve the kinds of problems they are familiar with may hinge on thinking *integratively*—integrating new experience with what they already know. Mature adults interpret what they read, see, or hear in terms of its meaning for them. Instead of accepting something at face value, they filter it through their own life experience and learning. This integrative characteristic of adult thought has implications for many aspects of life.

In one series of studies, college students and older adults were asked to recall and to summarize stories (Labouvie-Vief & Hakim-Larson, 1989). One (Labouvie-Vief, Schell, & Weaverdyck, 1982) was a fable about a wolf who promises to reward a crane for removing a bone stuck in the wolf's throat. The crane dislodges the bone with its beak—a maneuver that involves putting its head into the wolf's jaws—and then asks for the promised reward. The wolf replies that the crane's reward is to get away alive!

Both age groups could recall the story in detail, but they gave very different summaries. The students' summaries were longer and more detailed and were confined to material in the text. The summaries produced by older adults (whose average age was 74) tended to be shorter and more to the point. The older adults integrated the "moral" of the story with observations based on experience and real-world learning. For example, one older participant drew the moral that good deeds should be their own reward, but also noted "a certain shrewdness" on the part of the wolf, "who sought help in time of need, but was unwilling to give of himself even in a small way to show any appreciation" (p. 13). The thinking of the older adults was more flexible than that of the younger ones, whose attempts at summarizing were limited to step-by-step recall of the story.

Integrative thinking has emotional and social implications. The ability to interpret events in a mature way enables many adults to come to terms with childhood episodes that once disturbed them (Schafer, 1980). Research has shown, for example, that women's adjustment in adulthood is related not to what actually happened between them and their mothers but to how they view their mothers' behavior toward them (Main, 1987).

Society benefits from this integrative feature of adult thought. It is often mature adults who create inspirational myths and legends, who translate truths about the human condition into symbols to which younger generations can turn for guidance (Gutmann, 1977). People may have to be capable of integrative thought before they can become moral and spiritual leaders.

Intuition, integrative thinking, and subjective interpretation are important features of what some investigators have begun to see as a special, mature stage of intellectual development: postformal thought. We turn to this topic next.

POSTFORMAL THOUGHT:
BEYOND PIAGET'S STAGES

▼

According to Piaget, thinking begins in early childhood with manipulation of sensory information. It then progresses to concrete problem solving: for example, judging whether the amount of water in a flask changes when it is poured into a flask of a different shape. Many adolescents reach Piaget's highest stage, formal operations: They can think abstractly, systematically, and logically; they can make and test hypotheses about reality. (See Table 2-2 in Chapter 2 for a summary of Piaget's stages.)

Researchers during the late 1960s and early 1970s wanted to see how young, middle-aged, and older adults would do on the kinds of tasks Piaget used to measure cognitive development in children (Papalia, 1972; Papalia & Bielby, 1974; K. H. Rubin, 1973; K. H. Rubin, Attewell, Tierney, & Tumulo, 1973; Sanders, Laurendeau, & Bergeron, 1966; Tomlinson-Keasey, 1982). When some older adults gave answers similar to those of young children—saying, for example, that water poured from a thin flask into a wide one weighed more "because it's larger"—the researchers interpreted this as possible evidence of regression to an earlier stage of thought (Papalia, 1972). But later studies suggested that some older adults gave "wrong" answers because their thinking took more factors into account. For example, when asked whether there was the same amount of space in differently shaped houses made with the same number of blocks, one elderly woman said: "When you start getting fancy, you always lose some space because [you] have to have a hallway upstairs as well as downstairs, which takes away space" (Roberts, Papalia-Finlay, Davis, Blackburn, & Dellman, 1982, p. 191). Investigators thus began to wonder whether such "preformal" responses might actually represent an *advance* in cognitive development, a stage beyond formal operations.

Since the late 1970s, a number of researchers have suggested that mature thinking may be far richer and more complex than the abstract intellectual manipulations Piaget described. Thought in adulthood often appears to be flexible, open, adaptive, and individualistic. It relies on intuition as well as logic. It applies the fruits of personal experience to ambiguous situations that adults face every day. It can transcend a particular social system or system of thought. It is sometimes called *postformal thought,* and it is generally characterized by the ability to deal with uncertainty, inconsistency, contradiction, imperfection, and compromise (Arlin, 1984; Labouvie-Vief, 1985, 1986; Labouvie-Vief & Hakim-Larson, 1989; Sinnott, 1984).

HOW POSTFORMAL THOUGHT DEVELOPS

According to postformal theorists, people at the stage of formal operations are in the grip of polarized thinking. They do not see that there may be truth, logic, or validity in more than one point of view. When there is conflict, one side must be right and the other wrong. Polarized thinking often shows up in emotional clashes. Immature thinkers, when angered, blame the other person rather than accepting part of the responsibility (Blanchard-Fields, 1986; Labouvie-Vief, 1990a, 1990b; Labouvie-Vief, Hakim-Larson, DeVoe, & Schoeberlein, 1989). Polarized thinkers excel at structured problems with definite answers. They view any ambiguity as a result of muddled thinking. They see everything as black or white. Postformal thinkers see shades of gray (Labouvie-Vief, 1990a, 1990b).

Postformal thought may develop through experiences that open up a possibility of looking at things in unaccustomed ways. For many students of traditional college age, the academic and social challenges of college offer a chance to question childhood assumptions. The college experience undermines belief in absolute, eternal, objectively verifiable truths. Many students do a 180-degree swing and come to believe that "everything is relative"—all reality is subjective, all meaning tied to context. Eventually, though, they generally move beyond a totally relativist position and search for some means of assessing competing claims (Labouvie-Vief, 1990a, 1990b).

In a study that inspired much of the research on postformal thought, William Perry (1970) interviewed 67 Harvard and Radcliffe students throughout the undergraduate years. He found that their thinking progressed from rigidity to flexibility and ultimately to freely chosen commitments. First, said Perry, as students encounter a wide variety of ideas, they recognize the existence of several different points of view. They also accept their own uncertainty. They consider this stage temporary, however, and expect to learn the "one right answer" eventually. Next, they come to see all knowledge and values as relative. They recognize that different societies and different individuals have their own value systems. They now realize that their opinions on many issues are as valid as anyone else's, even those of a parent or teacher. But they feel abandoned and lost; they cannot find solid meaning or value in this maze of systems and beliefs. Order has been replaced by chaos. Finally, they achieve *commitment within relativism.* They make their own judgments and choose their own beliefs, values, and commitments despite uncertainty and the recognition of other valid possibilities.

Building on Perry's work, Gisela Labouvie-Vief (1982, 1990a, 1990b), a psychologist at Wayne State University, has proposed three levels of adult cognitive development:

1. *Intrasystemic level.* People at this level, which corresponds to Piaget's stage of formal operations, can reason within a single system of thought—for example, Euclidean or non-Euclidean geometry, capitalism or socialism, Christianity or Buddhism—but they cannot move outside it to reflect on it. Adolescents and entering college students are able to deal with only one logical system as "correct." While they may acknowledge that other people hold different opinions, it is hard for them to see that an alternative argument or system may be as valid as their own.

2. *Intersystemic level.* People become more aware of multiple, contradictory systems of thought. Although they can discuss and elaborate on these systems and are increasingly able to tolerate conflict, they still see the systems as distinct and irreconcilable.

3. ***Integrated level.*** This level is characterized by openness, flexibility, and responsible, autonomous reflection. People see change and diversity as positive, and they can draw on differing perspectives and value systems. Like Nelson Mandela, they choose their own principles and act on them—not haphazardly or arbitrarily, but by integrating subjectivity with a new, more mature form of objectivity. Truth is no longer seen either as absolute or as totally relative but is judged on the basis of rational, disciplined reflection and collective thought and discussion.

There is no set age for reaching any of these levels. While people generally do not achieve postformal thought until late adolescence or early adulthood, adults in their forties do not necessarily think more maturely than those in their twenties (Labouvie-Vief, Adams, Hakim-Larson, Hayden, & DeVoe, 1987).

SOCIAL REASONING AND POSTFORMAL THOUGHT

If such changes are characteristic of adult cognitive development, why doesn't Piaget's theory account for them? One obvious reason is that Piaget studied children, not adults. Then, too, he focused on problems involving the physical world, which require dispassionate, objective thinking. Adults are more likely to apply postformal thought to social dilemmas, which are less clearly structured and deal with human emotions. Social problems involve ***necessary subjectivity.*** They arise out of interactions in which each person's view of a situation inevitably affects the other and colors the situation as a whole—in which reality is partly "a creation of the knower" (Sinnott, 1984, p. 299).

In one study of the role of emotion in social reasoning (Blanchard-Fields, 1986), 20 adolescents, 20 young adults age 20 to 25, and 20 adults age 30 to 46 were given conflicting accounts of three situations. The first was a fictional war between "North Livia" and "South Livia," as reported by historians in each of these nations; the second was a description of a teenage boy's unwilling visit to his grandparents, told from his perspective and that of his parents; the third was the dilemma of a couple faced with an unintentional pregnancy, which the woman wanted to abort and the man did not. The task was to tell what each conflict was about and to answer probing questions about who was at fault, who won or lost, and how the conflict was resolved. Respondents were scored according to how well they could separate the *teller* from the *truth* of an account and could recognize the validity of multiple perspectives—two signs of postformal thought.

Immature thinkers were found to be more rigid and egocentric when dealing with emotionally charged situations than with emotionally neutral ones. In general, reasoning improved with age. Adolescents reasoned about as well as young adults in discussing the Livian war but scored lower than both adult groups when it came to the visit to the grandparents and the abortion dilemma—situations with which young people could identify emotionally. The more mature adults were aware of the interpretive bias in each account. They were able to explain each party's point of view and to recommend solutions based on understanding and mutual respect.

CULTURAL CHANGE AND POSTFORMAL THOUGHT

Does postformal thought occur in cultures where higher education is not common? Can cross-cultural contact facilitate postformal thought?

A study of women pig farmers in Honduras (described in Box 7-1) found that a shift to postformal thinking seems to occur when people's ideas, perceptions, or interpretations of reality "can no longer adequately make sense of the world" (L. Johnson, 1991, p. 62). The resulting tension may force them to open their minds to other ideas, perceptions, or interpretations that may work better in a changed situation (Sinnott, 1989). One way to identify the potential for development of postformal thought, then, is to look at groups undergoing highly stressful experiences while isolated from normal social contact.

An account of 45 Uruguayan travelers whose airplane crashed in the snow-covered Andes mountains in winter provides an example of how such a new social reality may develop (Read, 1974). Search parties had given everyone up for dead, but 10 weeks later two survivors managed to find their way down the mountain and get help for 14 others. An analysis of diaries kept by some of these survivors during the first month (Sinnott, 1984) reveals the levels of thinking on which various people operated.

BOX 7-1

THE MULTICULTURAL CONTEXT

Postformal Thinking and Cultural Change

In 1984, the Agency for International Development (AID) launched a program to "empower" women living on subsistence farms in Honduras: these women would be trained to start and run a cooperative business raising and marketing pigs. The project fundamentally challenged established customs in these rural communities; thus its success would depend on a major shift in cultural attitudes toward women's roles.

In the existing social system, women were subservient to men and had little or no experience with independent decisions or self-directed action. They often tended pigs tethered near their homes, but when a pig was ready for market, a man would take it and keep the money. In the new AID program, the women would be raising a different breed of pigs, imported from the

(Courtesy of Lynn Johnson)

Honduran farm women being trained to run cooperative pig farms were more successful when led by a facilitator who used postformal rather than formal operational thinking.

(CONTINUED)

BOX 7-1

CONTINUED

United States, which were larger and leaner than those usually raised in the area and required more care. Rather than raise a few pigs at home, the women were to be taught to operate pig farms; and they were to handle all phases of the operation, including marketing, themselves.

The administrators of the program realized that, to have any chance of success, the women would need a supportive environment. Before the program was introduced in a village, staff members met with village leaders and the husbands of the women who were to participate. They described how the project would operate and discussed the new behaviors that would be introduced into the social system. A village would not become part of the program unless the husbands and the village leaders accepted the women's new roles.

To give them role models for decision making, the women met regularly in small groups with a facilitator who was to guide them in dealing with problems that arose during the first year. The facilitators were to act as moderators, mentors, and agents of change. Each facilitator led two groups. Nine months after the project began, the two groups led by one of the facilitators were managing to keep pigs successfully; the other two were not.

What explains this result? According to a trained observer who regularly sat in on the groups (L. Johnson, 1991), the two facilitators showed markedly different levels of thinking. The facilitator of the two successful groups appeared to operate at a postformal level in her interactions with the rural women, and the women in her groups appeared better able to define and solve problems connected with the enterprise.

The unsuccessful facilitator, who appeared to be at the level of formal operations, dominated group discussions. She was rigidly moralistic, depreciated local customs, and tried to impose her own ideas. Because she seemed unable to move beyond her own way of thinking, she gave the women in her groups no model for moving beyond theirs and no assistance in bridging differing viewpoints. The successful facilitator acted on the assumption that local customs were different, but not necessarily inferior, to the way she was trying to teach. Using two-way, back-and-forth communication, she helped the women and the other villagers see that their old ways were not as well adapted to the new situation (raising the imported pigs). As a result, the women's own thinking expanded; they were able to think and behave in a new way.

The postformal facilitator encouraged cooperative problem solving and decision making. She enabled the women she worked with to learn how to solve problems in new ways, and, perhaps most important, to believe that they *could* acquire new knowledge, skills, and outlooks. When one of the groups began to argue about how money was being spent and accused the treasurer of appropriating funds for her own use, this facilitator explored possible causes of the problem from several viewpoints. She suggested more than one possible solution and ultimately focused on the one that seemed best suited to the situation: having the treasurer prepare a list of what had been spent for what purposes, with attached receipts, and in the future provide monthly financial reports—practices that were unfamiliar to these women. What would the other facilitator have done in such a situation? The observer's discussions with her suggest that she would have decided whether or not the treasurer was guilty and, if so, would have replaced her. By acting unilaterally and moving immediately to what she deemed the right solution, she would have deprived the women in her groups of experience with cooperative decision making and a chance to develop the confidence to function on their own.

Immediately after the crash, panic had reigned. After the first few moments, some survivors managed to calm the others down; but those who were operating at concrete or formal levels did not recognize that normal roles and behaviors would not work in this crisis situation. Attempts to "talk down" to those who were still hysterical only ended up with everyone upset. A month later, the diaries showed, the group had restructured itself. Relationships and roles had been drastically revised. Many people had raised their predominant level of thinking. Those who took a flexible, postformal approach had emerged as leaders. They could talk to anyone in the group on any intellectual level and could deal with people both in terms of their former social roles and in terms of their roles in this new society.

CRITERIA FOR POSTFORMAL THOUGHT

How can we tell when people are using postformal thought? On the basis of how men and women age 26 to 89 solved six problems, one theorist (Sinnott, 1984) identified several criteria:

- *Shifting gears.* Ability to shift back and forth from abstract reasoning to practical, real-world considerations. ("This might work on paper but not in real life.")
- *Multiple causality, multiple solutions.* Awareness that most problems have more than one cause and more than one solution, and that some solutions are more likely to work than others.
- *Pragmatism.* Ability to choose the best of several possible solutions and to recognize criteria used for choosing. ("If you want the most practical solution, do this; if you want the quickest solution, do that.")
- *Awareness of paradox.* Recognition that a problem or solution involves inherent conflict. ("Doing this will give him what he wants, but it will only make him unhappy in the end.")

According to another theorist (Arlin, 1984), postformal thinking contracts (shrinks) or expands the usual operations of formal logic. In *contracting* operations, postformal thinkers may focus on only certain aspects of a problem—the ones that seem most pressing or most important. Rather than methodically examining all possibilities, they may simplify a problem by ignoring complicating factors. In other words, they try to look at the forest, not the trees. In *expanding* operations, an adult may look beyond an immediate situation to find a larger problem. Problem finding makes use of multiple frames of reference and multiple sources of information. A marriage counselor, for example, must be able to hear a couple's often ill-defined concerns, demands, complaints, and desires and discern the overriding issues.

The literature on postformal thought challenges the basis for psychometric assessment of intelligence in adulthood. If the postformal theorists are right, it may be that mature adults do poorly on some tested tasks because the questions and answers do not adequately reflect their experience. If the purpose of intelligence is to deal with real-life problems, then the complex strengths of mature thought may compensate for—and even outweigh—any deficiencies.

Critics reply that the whole idea of postformal thinking has a thin research base. Because qualitative change does not readily lend itself to quantitative measurement, much of the supporting research has taken the form of extensive, time-consuming interviews, which are not easy to replicate; thus the validity of the conclusions cannot easily be tested. Future research may determine whether reliable, objective measures of postformal thinking can be developed.

A LIFESPAN MODEL
OF COGNITIVE DEVELOPMENT

One of the few investigators to propose a full lifespan model of stages of cognitive development from childhood through old age is Schaie (1977–1978), whose work on the Seattle Longitudinal Study is discussed in Chapter 6. Schaie describes intellectual development as proceeding according to changes in what is important to people and how they interpret and respond to their experiences. The five stages in his model (see Figure 7-1) represent transitions from acquisition of information and skills (*what* I need to know) through practical integration of knowledge and skills (*how* to use what I know) to a search for meaning and purpose (*why* I should know). The five stages are as follows:

1. *Acquisitive stage (childhood and adolescence).* Children and adolescents acquire information or a skill mainly for its own sake or as preparation for participation in society.

2. *Achieving stage (late teens or early twenties to early thirties).* Young adults no longer acquire knowledge merely for its own sake; they use what they know to become competent and independent.

3. *Responsible stage (late thirties to early sixties).* Middle-aged people are concerned with long-range goals and practical problems associated with their responsibilities to others (family members or employees).

4. *Executive stage (thirties or forties through middle age).* People in the executive stage, which may overlap with the achieving and responsible stages, are responsible for societal systems (such as governmental or business organizations) or, as in Mandela's case, social movements. They deal with complex relationships on several levels.

5. *Reintegrative stage (late adulthood).* Older adults, who may have let go of some social involvement and whose cognitive functioning may be limited by biological changes, are often more selective about what tasks they expend effort on. They focus on the purpose of what they do and concentrate on tasks that have meaning for them.

Again, if adults do go through stages such as these, then traditional psychometric tests, which use the same kinds of tasks to measure intelligence at all periods of

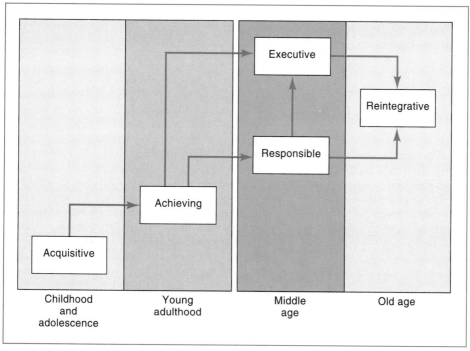

FIGURE 7-1
Stages of cognitive development in adults.
(SOURCE: Based on Schaie, 1977–1978.)

life, may be inappropriate for them. Tests developed to measure knowledge and skills in children may not be suitable for measuring intellectual competence in young and middle-aged adults, who use knowledge and skills to solve practical problems and achieve goals they set for themselves. If conventional tests fail to tap abilities central to adult intelligence, we may need measures that have what Schaie (1978) calls *ecological validity*—tests that show competence in dealing with real-life challenges, such as balancing a checkbook, reading a railroad timetable, or making informed decisions about medical problems.

Schaie's model also calls attention to an important cognitive development of late adulthood: a focus on tasks that have personal meaning. This may fit in with what is sometimes meant by *wisdom*—our next topic.

WISDOM

Wisdom (like *intelligence* or *creativity*) has many meanings but no precise definition; yet most people seem to think they know it when they see it (see Box 7-2 and Table 7-1). How can we describe wisdom? Is it intellectual, emotional, or spiritual, or all three? Do people become wiser as they get older, as is commonly believed, or is wisdom independent of age?

BOX 7-2

THE CUTTING EDGE

Comparing Wisdom with Intelligence and Creativity

"The processes of wisdom, intelligence, and creativity are the same," Sternberg (1990) asserts. "What differs is their use" (p. 153). On the basis of a series of studies designed to see how adults distinguish among the three attributes, Sternberg came up with a theoretical model of intelligence, creativity, and wisdom: three intellectual processes that, he says, differ only in their applications (see Table 7-1).

What do intelligent, wise, and creative people do with knowledge? Intelligent people recall, analyze, and use it effectively. Wise people excel in *metacognition,* or knowledge about knowledge. They probe inside knowledge to find its deeper meaning. They understand what they do and don't know, the limits of what can be known, and how knowledge affects their thinking. Creative people go beyond what is already known to create something new. Thus, "if we view existing knowledge as setting constraints, much like a prison, we might view the wise person as seeking to understand the prison and just what its boundaries are, the intelligent person as seeking to make the best of life in prison, and the creative person as seeking to escape from the prison" (p. 153).

A second difference has to do with how information is processed. An intelligent person uses automatic thought processes to deal efficiently with routine or familiar tasks. A creative person resists automatization, preferring to deal with what is novel and nonroutine. A wise person tries to understand how and why automatization works.

Intellectual style is the way people direct or govern their own mental functioning. Intelligent people are like executives; they apply rules and solve problems. Creative people are like legislators; they decide what to do and make up new ways of doing things. They are likely to answer test questions with answers the testmaker never thought of. Wise people are like judges; they are evaluative, though not rigidly judgmental. They are likely to size up a test questions and try to figure out why it is being asked.

Intelligence, creativity, and wisdom are associated with different attitudes toward ambiguity and obstacles. An intelligent person tries to eliminate ambiguity and get around obstacles within the problem as defined. A creative person sees ambiguity as a necessary evil and looks for a way to redefine the problem to avoid obstacles. A wise person is comfortable with ambiguity and simply wants to understand the obstacles and why they exist.

What are the goals of intelligent, wise, and creative behavior? The intelligent person is motivated to know and understand more and more things. The wise person seeks to understand deeply—to get at underlying meaning. The creative person "wants to see things in a way different from the way others see them" (p. 156).

Finally, each attribute is more likely to be valued in certain kinds of environments. A person who is considered intelligent in school may be viewed as naive or pretentious in some real-world settings. A person who is seen as creative in one environment may be considered an oddball in another. A person who is viewed as wise in one context may be called a fool or a dreamer in another.

Other research suggests that some of these distinctions may blur with age—that wisdom and creativity, for example, may become more integrated (Simonton, 1990). Problem finding has been identified as a characteristic of both creativity and postformal thought, or mature intelligence (Arlin, 1984). Perhaps, then, as people age, the connections among intelligence, wisdom, and creativity may become more complex and the differences less clear-cut.

TABLE 7-1 COMPARISON OF SIX ASPECTS OF WISDOM, INTELLIGENCE, AND CREATIVITY

Aspect	Wisdom	Intelligence	Creativity
Knowledge	Understanding of its presuppositions and meaning as well as its limitations	Recall, analysis, and use	Going beyond what is available
Processes	Understanding of what is automatic and why	Automatization of procedures	Preference for novel tasks
Primary intellectual style	Judicial	Executive	Legislative
Personality	Understanding of ambiguity and obstacles	Eliminating ambiguity and overcoming obstacles within conventional framework	Tolerance of ambiguity and redefinition of obstacles
Motivation	To understand what is known and what it means	To know and to use what is known	To go beyond what is known
Environmental context	Appreciation in environment of depth of understanding	Appreciation in environment of extent and breadth of understanding	Appreciation in environment of going beyond what is currently understood

Source: Sternberg, 1990.

WISDOM IN FOLKLORE, MYTH, AND PHILOSOPHY

Although the concept of wisdom is at least as old as civilization, only recently has it begun to be investigated systematically. In their investigations, modern psychologists have drawn on earlier concepts found in folklore, myth, and philosophy.

Folk wisdom is a collection of parables, proverbs, and stories reflecting special pragmatic knowledge or mastery of life. It has three major functions: practical, moral, and spiritual. It is a guide to living and a source or manifestation of spiritual growth. These sayings and tales often revolve around a person, such as King Solomon in the Bible, whose words and actions are seen as embodying seasoned judgment (Holliday & Chandler, 1986).

In ancient times, these tales were orally transmitted, often by elders, for the instruction and entertainment of listeners, both adults and children. (Nelson Mandela, in South Africa, absorbed such lore as a child while sitting in on communal councils.) When writing was invented, many of these stories were recorded by scribes. Ancient wisdom found in books such as the Bible and the Koran includes moral pronouncements and principles that form the basis of religious teachings.

Mythical writings in all cultures depict young heroes exploring and mastering the outer world. By contrast, tales about mature adults center on a search for wisdom (Chinen, 1985). The young warrior setting out on a hero's quest and the mature seeker of self-knowledge are examples of what the Swiss psychiatrist Carl Jung (1933) called *archetypes*. They represent recurrent ideas important in a culture's mythic tradition, which survives in its "collective unconscious." One such archetype, which appears in the Russian tale "Vasilisa the Wise," is about a girl's initiation into the use of her intuitive powers (Estés, 1992). Another is that of a wise elder who appears when a young hero needs help or advice. This archetypical image harks back to such ancient sources as the Greek tale of Mentor, the tutor who advised Odysseus's son Telemachus, to keep him out of danger. The word *mentor* came to mean a person who uses accumulated experience and wisdom to guide a young protégé.

A modern throwback can be seen in the movie *Star Wars*. Young Luke Skywalker is attempting to destroy the evil empire's monstrous Death Star spaceship. At first, he plans to aim his weapons by using the computer on his small fighter craft. Then he hears the voice of Obi Wan Kenobe, his counselor and teacher, telling him to turn off the computer and trust the "force." Luke does so, and the life force of the universe helps direct his fire to destroy the Death Star.

For the classical Greek philosophers, wisdom was a guide to right conduct. But rather than pithy sayings or allegorical legends, its source was reasoned reflection. For Socrates, wisdom lay in enlightened self-examination and moral behavior. For Plato, virtuous action was the product of rational thought. Aristotle distinguished between two sorts of wisdom: practical ethics and a quest for the nature and origins of the universe and human life. Thus wisdom began to be related to knowledge and learning (Holliday & Chandler, 1986).

While views of wisdom in western philosophy have focused largely on judgments about the external world and human behavior, some of the older eastern philosophical traditions look inward to the development of "higher," spiritual states of consciousness. According to the Vedas, sacred Hindu writings, wisdom lies in being fully attuned to the inner nature of the self and to the universal, underlying laws of nature (Alexander, 1982; Alexander, Kurth, Travis, Warner, & Alexander, in press-a; Alexander, Swanson, Rainforth, Carlisle, & Todd, in press-b). Spiritual development begins with detachment from both body and mind and their relationships with the outer world, "slowing down the flow of thought," and "going with the flow of life." Ultimately, one may experience "existence without thought"—a state of "nonpersonal consciousness" that rises above the narrow emotions, limited understanding, and self-centered consciousness of everyday life (Atchley, 1991b, pp. 3, 4). In some forms of Buddhism, too, wisdom is attained by "transcending the boundaries" of the self (Dittman-Kohli & Baltes, 1990, p. 68). The key elements of these and other eastern definitions of wisdom are rejection of logic as the basis of higher thought and ability to achieve a perspective beyond the self.

In contrast with western philosophy, eastern concepts of wisdom are based on higher, spiritual states of consciousness and harmony with the universe. Jainism stresses physical self-denial, reverence for all life, and good deeds as a path to nirvana, or extinction of the conscious self. This Jain pilgrim in India bows to a figure of Lord Bahūbali, revered as a saint, who is said to have stood, unmoving, in a yoga position for a full year while vines climbed up his arms.

PSYCHOLOGICAL CONCEPTS AND ASSESSMENTS

Today, with the graying of the planet, wisdom—regarded in many cultural traditions as largely the province of old age—has become an important topic of psychological research. Interest in wisdom has grown out of several lines of investigation, each of which reflects different aspects of its traditional meanings. The classical approach was to see wisdom as an aspect of late-life personality development. Today, some theorists, taking a more contextual perspective, describe wisdom as a cognitive ability. Others see wisdom as an integration of intellect and emotion. Another approach, which has roots in eastern philosophy, focuses on the spiritual domain. Let's look at each of these approaches.

Erikson: Wisdom and Late-Life Personality Development

For Erikson, wisdom is a "virtue" that results from successful resolution of the last of eight conflicts in personality development, that of *integrity versus despair* (see Chapter 11). Wisdom is the insight into life's meaning that can come to people contemplating the approach of death, an "informed and detached concern with life itself in the face of death itself" (Erikson, 1985, p. 61). Wisdom means accepting the life one has lived without major regrets. It involves accepting one's parents as people who did the best they could. It implies accepting death as the inevitable end of a life lived as well as one knew how to live it. In sum, it means a realistic acceptance of imperfection in oneself, in one's parents, and in life itself.

Clayton and Meacham: Cognitive Definitions

One of the first cognitive researchers to give an operational definition of wisdom was Vivian Clayton (1975, 1982), then at the University of Southern California. In contrast with *intelligence* (which she defined as an ability to think logically and abstractly), Clayton defined *wisdom* as an ability to grasp paradoxes, reconcile contradictions, and make and accept compromises. Because wise people weigh the effects of their acts on themselves and others, wisdom is particularly well suited to practical decision making in a social context. Whereas intelligence can figure out how to do something, wisdom asks whether it *should* be done. Wise people, then, are better than other people at solving social problems involving values—problems like easing racial tensions or deciding which divorcing spouse should have custody of the children.

Which is more likely to be wise: a child or an older person? John A. Meacham (1990), a psychologist at State University of New York in Buffalo, gives a surprising answer. He claims that wisdom is more likely to be an attribute of youth because older people know too much and are too sure of their knowledge.

The idea that humility is an important ingredient of wisdom goes back to Socrates, who was considered wisest of all the Greeks because he knew how much he did not know. According to Meacham (1982, 1990), wise people balance their acquisition of knowledge with a recognition of its inherent fallibility. Wise people don't know more than unwise people—they just use their information differently. They excel at asking questions and applying facts to real situations. Experience, rather than producing wisdom, "presents the greatest threat to our wisdom, particularly when it leads merely to the accumulation of information, to success, and to power" (Meacham, 1990, p. 209). Instead, wisdom comes from knowing less or becoming less positive about what one knows. It can be lost in old age unless a person is surrounded by supportive companions who allow the expression of doubts and challenge certainties.

Baltes: Toward an Empirical Definition

In contrast to Meacham, Baltes (1993) and his associates see wisdom as a special kind of expert knowledge. Since the late 1980s, they have been working out a definition that is empirically testable and consistent with the meanings ordinary people have historically attached to the term. And they have done extensive research to verify their definition.

Wisdom, for Baltes, is expert knowledge of the *fundamental pragmatics of life*, "permitting excellent judgment and advice about important and uncertain matters" (p. 586). The fundamental pragmatics of life consist of knowledge and skills that go to the heart of the human condition—the conduct, interpretation, and meaning of life. This factual and procedural knowledge of the fundamentals of living constitutes two basic criteria of wisdom.

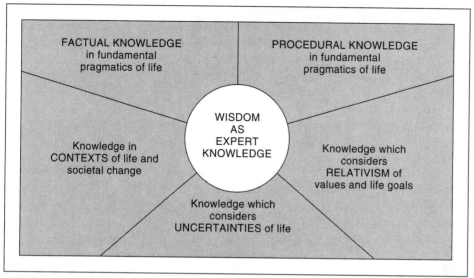

FIGURE 7-2
Five criteria of wisdom.
(Source: Baltes, 1993.)

Three other criteria are awareness of life's uncertainties; knowledge of the relativism of values, goals, and priorities; and understanding of the importance of context and societal change (Baltes, 1993; Staudinger, Smith, & Baltes, 1992; see Figure 7-2).

Wisdom, in Baltes's dual-process model (see Chapter 6), is part of the *pragmatics of intelligence,* a cognitive domain that remains stable and may even continue to improve into late adulthood (Baltes, 1993; Dittmann-Kohli & Baltes, 1990). Thus, whereas Clayton sees wisdom as distinct from intelligence, Baltes sees it as a component of intelligence (Blanchard-Fields, Brannan, & Camp, 1987). In effect, wisdom becomes the functional equivalent of expertise in a specialized field: knowledge of how to live well (Rybash et al., 1986).

Not everyone, of course, becomes wise, just as not everyone becomes an expert in chess or computers. In fact, Baltes suggests, wisdom can be expected to be fairly rare. Although wisdom may develop at any period of life, aging would seem to provide fertile soil for its growth. A longer life means more time for the development of favorable conditions such as general mental ability; education or training; practice in using the requisite skills; guidance from mentors; leadership experience; and professional specialization. Eventually, however, losses in the physiologically based mechanics of cognition may limit further refinement of wisdom.

To test the relationship between age and wisdom, Baltes's team did a series of studies comparing the responses of adults of various ages and professional backgrounds to hypothetical dilemmas. Responses were evaluated according to criteria similar to those in Figure 7-2; to be considered "wise," an answer had to score high in all five areas.

(Erika Stone)

Should a man who has been laid off stay home with his preschool children while his wife works? One team of researchers has attempted to assess wisdom by responses to such hypothetical dilemmas. This unhypothetical "househusband," whose wife is a physical therapist, sold his pet store to stay home and care for his 4-year-old daughter.

In one study (J. Smith & Baltes, 1990), 60 well-educated German professionals age 25 to 81 were asked to respond to four hypothetical dilemmas: (1) A 33-year-old professional woman is trying to decide whether to accept a major promotion or start a family. (2) A 63-year-old man whose company is closing the branch office where he works has been offered a choice between early retirement and a move to the main office for 2 or 3 years. (3) A laid-off mechanic can either move to another city to look for work or stay home with his preschool children while his wife continues the nursing career she has just gone back to. (4) A 60-year-old widow who has just finished a business course and opened her own firm now learns that her son has been left with two young children and wants her to help care for them. A panel of experienced human-services professionals rated the responses according to the five criteria. Of 240 solutions, only 5 percent were rated "wise." Older participants showed no more and no less wisdom than younger ones; the 11 "wise" responses were distributed nearly evenly among young, middle-aged, and older adults. Both younger and older participants showed more wisdom about decisions applying to their own stage of life; for example, the oldest group gave its best answers to the problem of the 60-year-old widow.

To see whether certain kinds of life experience lend themselves to the development of wisdom, the researchers set up a similar study of a group of distinguished middle-aged and older adults (their average age was 67) who had been identified by others as wise (Baltes, Staudinger, Maercker, & Smith, 1993). Nearly 60 percent of these people had published autobiographies, and more than 40 percent of them had been in the German resistance movement against the Nazis. When presented with two dilemmas—the one described above about the 60-

year-old widow and another about a phone call from a friend who intends to commit suicide—these participants outdid older clinical psychologists (who had previously performed best on such tasks) as well as control groups of older and younger adults with similar education and professional standing.

Perhaps the most significant contribution of Baltes and his associates to the study of wisdom is their attempt to study it systematically and scientifically. Their key finding is that wisdom, though not exclusively the province of old age, is one area in which older people, especially those who have had certain kinds of experiences, can hold their own—or better. A similar insight may be found in the following observation, made by a man in his sixties shortly before his death:

> Many people never reach any kind of maturity or wisdom at any age. Life experiences to many are not additive but simply repetitive. For others wisdom and maturity may occur early in life. There is, however, the unique quality some older and mature and hopefully wise people have, and that is the perspective of looking back over the years and seeing themselves in a way that younger, mature and wise people cannot do. (Shier, 1992)

Labouvie-Vief: Integrating Intellect and Affect

If the problems wise people solve best are value-centered, is intellect all that is needed to solve them? According to some theorists, solving value-laden problems requires a synthesis of intellect and affect (emotion). Labouvie-Vief (1990a, 1990b), one of the most prominent of these theorists, defines *wisdom* as an integration of two basic modes of knowing: *logos* (objective, analytic, and rational) and *mythos* (subjective, experiential, and emotional). She sees this integration as the major developmental task of a healthy adulthood. Full, mature mental functioning consists of a continuous dialogue between *mythos* and *logos,* in which "one mode [*mythos*] provides experiential richness and fluidity, the other [*logos*] logical cohesion and stability" (1990b, p. 53).

This wisdom does not necessarily come with advanced age; in fact, it appears to peak in middle age. Nor is it simply expertise. What makes people wise is not merely specialized knowledge, "but rather knowledge of issues that are part of the human condition. . . . Wisdom consists . . . in one's ability to see through and beyond individual uniqueness and specialization into those structures that relate us in our common humanity." If wisdom does have its own domain, says Labouvie-Vief, it must be broad enough to encompass morals and ethics, "understanding one's own emotions and inner life and differentiating them from those of others," and using that understanding rationally and reflectively (1990b, pp. 77–78). On this point, Baltes (1993) would presumably agree; indeed, he cites Labouvie-Vief's work as complementary to his own.

Wisdom and Spiritual Development

Many eastern cultures, rather than focusing on rationality and knowledge, seek detachment from the conscious mind as a path to inner spiritual growth (Atchley, 1991b). Some investigators, influenced by eastern philosophy, believe that wisdom is based on spiritual development and is likely to develop late in life.

According to one such definition (Achenbaum & Orwoll, 1991), wisdom has three interrelated facets: *intrapersonal wisdom* (self-examination, self-knowledge, and integrity); *interpersonal wisdom* (empathy, understanding, and maturity in human relationships); and *transpersonal wisdom* (capacity to transcend the self and strive for spiritual growth). Transpersonal wisdom—similar to the "nonpersonal consciousness" of the vedantic philosophy of Hindu India—is the key to the other two, since it provides a vantage point beyond the narrow concerns of self from which to observe oneself and one's relationships. Contemplation can foster all three facets of wisdom (Atchley, 1991b).

If wisdom is traditionally associated with age, then, it may be because contemplation and spiritual development are more likely to occur in later life. *Interiority*, a tendency toward introspection and concern with the inner life, which has been associated with aging (Jung, 1966; Neugarten, 1977), may serve as a stimulus. In one experiment, when 92 retired adults carried electronic pagers for 1 week, they reported that they voluntarily spent nearly half their waking time in solitude—often, absorbed in challenging, focused thought (R. Larson, Zuzanek, & Mannell, 1985). An older person, freed from youthful preoccupation with worldly goals and concerns, may be more open to "self-realization . . . the flowering of a world within that has hitherto been obscured by the drama of everyday life" (Atchley, 1991b, p. 5).

SUMMING UP: WISDOM AND AGE

So far, research findings on wisdom and age are not clear-cut. Baltes surmises that age may be conducive to wisdom but has not found confirming data—though certain kinds of "wisdom-producing" experience may give older people an edge. Labouvie-Vief's work suggests that wisdom is at its height in middle age. Why, then, do classic western literary traditions and eastern spiritual traditions describe wisdom as the province of old age?

One possible reason, which would be consistent with Labouvie-Vief's finding, is increased longevity. Ancient peoples may well have pictured the "wise elders" of myth and legend as being in their forties or even younger. Then again, the discrepancy may be a matter of definition. Research using other definitions of wisdom, or focusing on other features of it, might yield different results. If, for example, wisdom requires transcendence of the self, it may indeed take a very long time to acquire. Such a definition, however, would be difficult to test in the laboratory.

Self-transcendence may provide a way to view—and ameliorate—narrow, selfish thinking (Csikszentmihalyi & Rathunde, 1990). G. Stanley Hall (1922), a pioneer in the study of aging, saw such a role as especially suited to older adults, who, freed from anxiety about careers and capable of impartiality and breadth of vision, can take a fresh look at their society and its ills, offering a wisdom "which learning cannot give . . . . a kind of higher criticism of life" (pp. 410–411). Here we see one of the oldest functions of wisdom: moral guidance. But how does such moral development occur?

MORAL DEVELOPMENT

▼

A woman is near death from cancer. A druggist has discovered a drug that doctors believe might save her. The druggist is charging $2,000 for a small dose—10 times what the drug costs him to make. The sick woman's husband, Heinz, borrows from everyone he knows but can scrape together only $1,000. He begs the druggist to sell him the drug for $1,000 or let him pay the rest later. The druggist refuses, saying "I discovered the drug and I'm going to make money from it." Heinz, desperate, breaks into the man's store and steals the drug. Should Heinz have done that? Why or why not? (Kohlberg, 1969).

KOHLBERG'S THEORY: MORAL REASONING

"Heinz's" problem is the most famous example of Lawrence Kohlberg's approach to moral development. For more than 30 years, Kohlberg studied 75 young men, starting in the 1950s, when they were age 10 to 16. He told them stories, posing hypothetical dilemmas like Heinz's; at the heart of each was the concept of justice. By asking his respondents how they would resolve the problems, Kohlberg concluded that many people arrive at moral judgments independently; they do not simply adopt standards of parents, teachers, or peers.

Kohlberg was less interested in the answers people gave to his dilemmas than in the reasoning behind the answers. Two people who gave opposite answers to Heinz's dilemma could be at the same moral level if their reasoning was based on similar factors. On the basis of the thought processes shown by the responses, Kohlberg (1969) described three levels of moral reasoning that, in theory, roughly follow Piaget's cognitive stages of preoperational, concrete operational, and formal operational thought:

- *Level I: **Preconventional morality.*** People, under external controls, obey rules to avoid punishment or damage to people or property; or they act in their own self-interest, recognizing that others will do the same. This level is typical of children age 4 to 10.

- *Level II: **Morality of conventional role conformity.*** People have internalized the standards of authority figures. They are concerned about being "good," pleasing and caring for others, and maintaining the social order. This level is typically reached after age 10; many people never move beyond it, even in adulthood.

- *Level III: **Morality of autonomous moral principles.*** Morality is fully internal. People now recognize conflicts between moral standards and make their own moral judgments on the basis of principles of right, fairness, and justice. People generally do not reach this level of moral reasoning until at least age 13, or more commonly in young adulthood, if ever.

Each of the three levels is divided into two stages; Kohlberg later added a transitional level and a seventh stage. Table 7-2 gives descriptions of the levels and stages typically seen in adults.

TABLE 7-2   KOHLBERG'S LEVELS AND STAGES OF MORAL REASONING TYPICALLY SEEN IN ADULTS*

Levels	*Stages of Reasoning*
Level II: Conventional morality. Parental and social standards are internalized in the form of a desire to be seen as "good" or to follow accepted rules.	*Stage 3: Maintaining mutual relations and expectations.* Empathic viewpoint: it is right to fulfill one's expected role (i.e., daughter, brother, friend) and show mutual care and concern so as to appear "good" in the eyes of oneself and others. People evaluate an act by its motive or by putting themselves in another person's place (golden rule).

Stage 4: Maintaining social system and conscience. "Social contract" viewpoint: it is right to fulfill societal obligations, obey laws, and contribute to society in order to keep society going and to have a clear conscience. ("What if everyone did it?") An act is wrong if it violates a rule, except in extreme cases of conflict with other established duties or rights. |
| *Levels II-III: Postconventional but not yet principled morality.* At this transitional level, people recognize conflicting moral standards. They have moved beyond their society's moral system but have not yet developed their own system of moral principles. | *Stage 4 ½: Subjective emotional choice.* Arbitrary, relativist viewpoint: it is right to pick and choose among moral ideas or obligations on the basis of personal feelings, rather than being bound by societal standards. |
| *Level III: Morality of autonomous moral principles.* Moral decisions are based on internal, rationally derived principles that embrace fundamental values of justice and human welfare. | *Stage 5: Utilitarianism and fundamental rights.* "Prior to society" viewpoint: it is right to judge a social system by standards that exist prior to the establishment of a particular society. Laws should be based on rational calculation of the greatest good for the greatest number. Generally, laws should be obeyed, so as to treat people impartially and to fulfill the obligations of the social "contract." However, protection of certain fundamental values and rights outweighs majority rule.

Stage 6: Universal ethical principles. Absolutist viewpoint: it is right to be committed to universal, rationally valid principles, such as equality of human rights and respect for human dignity, whether or not these principles conflict with the laws of a particular society. |

Levels	Stages of Reasoning
	Stage 7: Cosmic perspective. Transcendental viewpoint: it is right to see oneself and one's conduct, not only as part of humanity, but as part of the universe. All parts of the universe are integrally connected, and an individual's actions impinge on the welfare of the whole. Human rights and ethical principles are based on the laws of nature (natural law).

*NOTE: Level I, Preconventional Morality, is typically seen in children under age 10.
SOURCES: Adapted from Kohlberg, 1969; Kohlberg & Ryncarz, 1990; Lickona, 1976.

"Live and Learn": Experience and Morality

Experience leads adults to reevaluate their criteria for what is right and fair. Some adults spontaneously offer personal experiences as reasons for their answers to moral dilemmas like Heinz's. People who have had cancer, or whose relatives or friends have had cancer, are more likely to condone a man's stealing an expensive drug to save his dying wife, and to explain this view in terms of their own experience (Bielby & Papalia, 1975). Such experiences, strongly colored by emotion, trigger rethinking in a way that hypothetical, impersonal discussions cannot, and are more likely to help people see other points of view.

Although cognitive awareness of higher moral principles develops in adolescence, most people do not commit themselves to these principles until adulthood, when turning points of identity often have to do with moral issues (Kohlberg, 1973). Two experiences that advance moral development in young adulthood are encountering conflicting values away from home (as happens in college or the armed services or sometimes in foreign travel) and being responsible for the welfare of other people (as in parenthood).

With regard to moral judgments, then, cognitive stages do not tell the whole story. Of course, someone whose thinking is still at Piaget's level of concrete operations is unlikely to make moral decisions at a postconventional level. But even someone who is at the stage of formal operations may not reach the highest level of moral thinking unless experience catches up with cognition. Many adults who are capable of logical reasoning do not break out of a conventional mold to make their own moral judgments unless, as in the case of Nelson Mandela, their experiences have prepared them for the shift.

In this and other respects, Kohlberg's work intersects the literature on postformal thought. Although Kohlberg himself equated postconventional morality with formal reasoning, its parallels with postformal thinking are striking—particularly the roles of experience, emotion, and individually chosen principles in resolving ambiguity and conflict. A connection between postformal thought and postconventional morality would also explain why many people do not fully achieve the postconventional level until adulthood, if at all.

(Thelma Shumsky/The Image Works)

The Native American chief Seattle exemplified Kohlberg's highest stage of ethical thinking in his response to the United States government's request to buy his tribe's lands.

A Seventh Stage: The Cosmic Perspective

At one point Kohlberg questioned his sixth stage, citing the difficulty of finding people at such a high level of moral development (Muuss, 1988). Yet shortly before his death Kohlberg was working on a seventh stage, which moves beyond considerations of justice and has much in common with self-transcendence in eastern tradition. In this seventh stage, adults reflect on the question, "*Why* be moral? Why be just in a universe that appears unjust?" (Kohlberg & Ryncarz, 1990, p. 192; emphasis added).

The answer, Kohlberg suggested, lies in achieving a *cosmic perspective:* "a sense of unity with the cosmos, nature, or God." This perspective enables a person to see moral issues "from the standpoint of the universe as a whole" (Kohlberg & Ryncarz, 1990, pp. 191, 207). It may or may not involve religious belief, but it parallels the most mature stage of faith the theologian James Fowler (1981) identified in interviews with about 400 people age 4 to 80. In that most developed stage of faith, "one experiences a oneness with the ultimate conditions of one's life and being" (Kohlberg & Ryncarz, 1990, p. 202).

In stage 7, ethics are grounded in *natural law*—principles based on human nature and embedded in the natural order of things. In experiencing oneness with the cosmos, a person comes to recognize that everything is connected. This means that one person's actions affect everything and everyone else, and the consequences reflect back on the doer.

In the mid-nineteenth century, the Native American chief Seattle eloquently expressed similar thoughts about people's intimate connections with one another and with all of nature. This is how he responded when the United States government tried to buy his tribe's lands:

> We are part of the earth and it is part of us. . . . What befalls the earth befalls all the sons of the earth. . . . All things are connected. . . . Man did not weave the web of life, he is merely a strand in it. Whatever he does to the web, he does to himself. . . . So, if we sell you our land, love it as we have loved it. Care for it as we have cared for it. . . . As we are part of the land, you too are part of the land. We *are* brothers after all. (Campbell & Moyers, 1988, pp. 34–35)

Cross-Cultural Research on Kohlberg's Theory

The American boys that Kohlberg and his colleagues followed into adulthood progressed through Kohlberg's stages in sequence, and none skipped a stage. Their moral judgments correlated positively with age, education, IQ, and socioeconomic status (Colby, Kohlberg, Gibbs, & Lieberman, 1983). Cross-cultural studies confirm this sequence—up to a point. Older people from countries other than the United States do tend to score at higher stages than younger people. But people from nonwestern cultures rarely score above stage 4 (C. P. Edwards, 1977; Nisan & Kohlberg, 1982; Snarey, 1985). It is possible that these cultures do not foster higher moral development, but it seems more likely that some aspects of Kohlberg's moral hierarchy may not fit the cultural values of some societies. Let's look at more closely at three cultures in which Kohlberg's dilemmas have been studied: China, Israeli kibbutzim, and India.

CHINA   The dilemma of Heinz, who could not afford a drug for his sick wife, was revised for use in Taiwan. In the revision, a shopkeeper will not give a man food for his sick wife.

This version would seem unbelievable to Chinese villagers, who in real life are more accustomed to hearing a shopkeeper in such a situation say, "You have to let people have things whether they have money or not" (Wolf, 1968, p. 21). Other cultural differences are involved as well (Dien, 1982). In Kohlberg's format, respondents make an either-or decision based on their own value systems. In Chinese society, people faced with such a dilemma discuss it openly, are guided by community standards, and try to find a way of resolving the problem to please as many parties as possible. The Chinese view is that human beings are born with moral tendencies whose development has to do with intuitive, spontaneous feelings supported by society, rather than with analytical thinking, individual choice, or personal responsibility. In the west, even good people may be harshly punished if, under the force of circumstances, they break a law. The Chinese are unaccustomed to universally applied laws; they prefer to abide by the sound decisions of a wise judge. Whereas Kohlberg's philosophy is based on justice, the Chinese ethos leans toward conciliation and harmony.

How, then, can Kohlberg's theory, rooted in western values and reflecting western ideals, be applied to moral development in an eastern society that works along very different lines? Some say that an alternative view is required, which measures morality by the ability to make judgments based on norms of reciprocity, rules of exchange, available resources, and complex relationships (Dien, 1982).

ISRAELI KIBBUTZIM   People born and raised on a kibbutz (collective farm) in Israel are imbued with a socialist perspective. How do such people score on a problem such as Heinz's dilemma, which weighs the value of human life against a druggist's right to charge what the traffic will bear?

Interviewers using Kohlberg's standardized scoring manual ran into trouble in trying to classify such responses as the following:

> The medicine should be made available to all in need; the druggist should not have the right to decide on his own. . . . The whole community or society should have control of the drug.

> I believe everyone has the right . . . to reach happiness. . . . People are not born equal genetically and it is not fair that one who is stronger physically should reach his happiness by whatever means at the expense of one who is weaker because the right to happiness is a basic human right of everyone, equal to all. (Snarey, 1985, p. 222)

These responses were coupled with statements about the importance of obeying the law and thus were confusing to the interviewers, who estimated them as fitting in with conventional stage 4 reasoning or as being in transition between stages 4 and 5. However, from the perspective of an Israeli kibbutz, such responses may represent a postconventional moral principle missing from Kohlberg's description of stage 5. If membership in a kibbutz is viewed as a commitment to certain social values, including cooperation and an equal right to happiness for all members of a society, then concern about upholding the system may be not merely for its own sake, but to protect those principles (Snarey, 1985).

INDIA   When asked whether Heinz should steal the drug to save his pet's life (instead of his wife's), a 50-year-old Indian found such an action commendable because it recognized the oneness of all life (Vasudev, 1983, pp. 7–8). This principle, characteristic of Indian philosophical, spiritual, and religious thought, was missing from Kohlberg's system until his preliminary exploration of stage 7.

When Kohlberg's dilemmas were tested in India, participants displayed all of Kohlberg's modes of moral reasoning, but not all Indian modes of moral reasoning were reflected in Kohlberg's scheme (Snarey, 1985). Thus, Buddhist monks from Ladakh, a Tibetan enclave in India, scored lower than laypeople. Apparently Kohlberg's model, while capturing the preconventional and conventional elements of Buddhist thinking, was inadequate for understanding postconventional Buddhist principles of cooperation and nonviolence (Gielen & Kelly, 1983). Kohlberg's scoring methods also broke down when Indian participants responded to probing questions by telling stories from which the listener was supposed to draw a lesson—a common form of moral discourse in that country (Shweder, personal communication, 1984, as cited in Snarey, 1985).

GILLIGAN'S THEORY: GENDER AND POSTFORMAL MORALITY

Are there differences between men's and women's moral development? Because Kohlberg's original studies were done on boys and men, some critics have questioned whether his analysis of morality applies to women. Carol Gilligan (1982, 1987) has argued that Kohlberg's system gives a higher place to "masculine" values (justice and fairness) than to "feminine" values (compassion, responsibility, and caring), and that it does not address a woman's central moral dilemma: the conflict between her own needs and those of others. While our society typically expects from men assertiveness and independent judgment, it expects from women self-sacrifice and concern for others.

Gilligan examined women's reasoning about the control of fertility by interviewing 29 women who were deciding whether to terminate or continue their pregnancies. These women saw morality in terms of selfishness versus responsibility—an obligation to exercise care and to avoid hurting others. Gilligan concluded that women think less about abstract justice and fairness than men do and more about their responsibilities to specific people (see Table 7-3, on the following page, for Gilligan's proposed levels of moral development in women). In more recent research, however, Gilligan has described moral development in *both* men and women as evolving beyond abstract reasoning to compassion and care.

If both justice and caring are moral imperatives, what happens when they conflict? Consider an example. A male college student (whom we'll call "the philosopher") had an affair with a married woman. He felt it was only fair to inform her husband, as he himself would have wanted to be told if he were in the husband's place. But the woman was going through a difficult time and couldn't face the additional stress. So, out of concern for her, "the philosopher" refrained from doing what he felt was right. While the woman was waiting for an opportune time to tell him, the husband found out anyway. This episode shook "the philosopher's" moral foundations. He felt morally compromised by his failure to act. But he also saw that there are times when absolute truth may be incompatible with compassion. Indeed, he began to entertain the notion that truth itself might depend on the situation. He could see more than one side to the problem, and he recognized that the "right" solution might not necessarily work out best in the real world (Gilligan, Murphy, & Tappan, 1990).

According to Kohlberg's scale of moral reasoning, the young man in this example—who had attained stage 5, the first stage of postconventional morality—apparently slipped back to an earlier stage in which moral choices are arbitrary rather than principled.

Gilligan had a different explanation, however. She saw the apparent "regression" as actually showing progress from formal reasoning to more mature, postformal thought. Gilligan interpreted the student's thinking as a sign of "a new, more integrated and encompassing moral understanding" in a world of complex relationships and choices (Gilligan et al., 1990, p. 218). For Kohlberg, the highest moral principles were universal and absolute; for Gilligan, a shift from absolute to relativistic thinking represented an advance in maturity.

TABLE 7-3   GILLIGAN'S LEVELS OF MORAL DEVELOPMENT IN WOMEN

Stage	Description
Level 1: Orientation of individual survival	The woman concentrates on herself—on what is practical and what is best for her.
Transition 1: From selfishness to responsibility	The woman realizes her connection to others and thinks about what would be the responsible choice in terms of other people (such as the unborn baby), as well as herself.
Level 2: Goodness as self-sacrifice	This conventional feminine wisdom dictates sacrificing the woman's own wishes to what other people want—and will think of her. She considers herself responsible for the actions of others, while holding others responsible for her own choices. She is in a dependent position, one in which her indirect efforts to exert control often turn into manipulation, sometimes through the use of guilt.
Transition 2: From goodness to truth	The woman assesses her decisions not on the basis of how others will react to them but on her intentions and the consequences of her actions. She develops a new judgment that takes into account her own needs, along with those of others. She wants to be "good" by being responsible to others, but also wants to be "honest" by being responsible to herself. Survival returns as a major concern.
Level 3: Morality of nonviolence	By elevating the injunction against hurting anyone (including herself) to a principle that governs all moral judgment and action, the woman establishes a "moral equality" between herself and others and is then able to assume the responsibility for choice in moral dilemmas.

SOURCE: Adapted from Gilligan, 1982.

Gilligan's research on real-life moral dilemmas found that many people in their twenties become dissatisfied with the limitations of pure logic. They begin to broaden their sights to allow themselves to live with moral contradictions, such as not telling a truth that may hurt someone.

Moral development, for Gilligan, is not black and white; it takes place in the many gray areas of life. It is a matter of learning the often painful and puzzling lessons of experience and of taking responsibility for one's inevitable mistakes.

EVALUATING KOHLBERG'S AND GILLIGAN'S THEORIES

Kohlberg's work has had a major impact. His theory has enriched our thinking about how morality develops, has supported an association between cognitive maturity and moral maturity, and has stimulated much research and other theories of moral development.

One practical problem in evaluating Kohlberg's system is its time-consuming testing procedures. The standard dilemmas need to be presented to each subject individually and then scored by trained judges. One alternative is the Defining Issues Test (DIT), which can be given quickly to a group and scored objectively (Rest, 1975). DIT has 12 questions about each of 6 moral dilemmas; its results correlate moderately well with scores on Kohlberg's traditional tasks.

A more serious criticism is that Kohlberg's theory does not establish a clear relationship between moral reasoning and behavior. Studies suggest that people at postconventional levels of thought do not necessarily *act* more morally than those at lower levels (Colby & Damon, 1992; Kupfersmid & Wonderly, 1980; see Box 7-3).

Gilligan initially challenged the applicability of Kohlberg's theory to women. What has research found on this point? Some studies of moral reasoning in adulthood have shown differences in the levels achieved by men and women—differences that consistently favored men. However, large-scale studies comparing results from many experiments found no significant differences in men's and women's responses to Kohlberg's dilemmas across the lifespan (L. J. Walker, 1984). Under Kohlberg's definitions and scoring guidelines, men reached no higher stages of moral reasoning than women. In the few studies in which men scored slightly higher, the findings were not clearly gender-related, since the men generally were better educated and had better jobs than the women. Thus the weight of evidence does not appear to back up either of Gilligan's original contentions: a male bias in Kohlberg's theory or a distinct female perspective on moral decisions. Furthermore, Gilligan's own later work suggests that men, as well as women, may place a high value on caring. It seems that if the "different voice" in Gilligan's earlier research reflected an alternative value system, it was not gender-based.

Gilligan does deserve credit for introducing some practical, real-world considerations to the study of moral development. She has made an important contribution in calling attention to the value of caring and to the need, at times, to live with contradictory moral principles.

The theories of Kohlberg and Gilligan have evolved to a point of much greater agreement. Gilligan now places less emphasis on differences between men and women. And, with the inclusion of his seventh stage, Kohlberg's theory now places caring for the universe and all its components at the highest level of moral thought.

THE ART OF AGING

Moral Leadership in Middle and Late Adulthood

What makes a single mother of four young children, with no money and a tenth-grade education, dedicate her life to religious missionary work on behalf of her equally poor neighbors? What leads a pediatrician to devote much of his practice to poor children instead of to patients whose parents could provide him with a lucrative income?

In the mid-1980s, two psychologists, Anne Colby and William Damon, sought answers to questions like these. They embarked on a two-year search for people who showed unusual moral excellence in their day-to-day lives. The researchers eventually identified 23 "moral exemplars," interviewed them in depth, and studied how they had become moral leaders (Colby & Damon, 1992).

To find moral exemplars, Colby and Damon worked with a panel of 22 "expert nominators," people who in their professional lives regularly think about moral ideas—philosophers, historians, religious thinkers, and so forth. The researchers drew up five criteria: sustained commitment to principles that show respect for humanity; behavior consistent with one's ideals; willingness to risk self-interest; inspiring others to moral action; and humility, or lack of concern for one's ego.

The chosen exemplars varied widely in age, education, occupation, and ethnicity. There were 10 men and 13 women, age 35 to 86, of white, African American, and Hispanic backgrounds. Education ranged from eighth grade up through M.D.s, Ph.D.s, and law degrees; and occupations included religious callings, business, teaching, and social leadership. Areas of concern included poverty, civil rights, education, ethics, the environment, peace, and religious freedom.

The research yielded a number of surprises, not least of which was this group's showing on Kohlberg's classic measure of moral judgment. Each exemplar was asked about "Heinz's dilemma," and about a follow-up dilemma: how the man should be punished if he does steal the drug. Of 22 exemplars (one response was not scorable), only half scored at the postconventional level; the other half scored at the conventional level. The major difference between the two groups was level of education: those with college and advanced degrees were much more likely to score at the higher level,

INTELLIGENCE, CREATIVITY, WISDOM, AND MORAL DEVELOPMENT: A LAST WORD

There is a limit to . . . progress in intelligence; but the development of the qualities of the heart knows no bounds. (M. K. Gandhi, as quoted in Kumar & Puri, 1983)

Caring was at the core of life for Mohandas Karamchaud Gandhi, known as Mahatma, or "great soul." Gandhi struggled for decades to achieve an independent India free of British domination, in which Hindus, Muslims, and all other

and no one who had only a high school diploma scored above the conventional level. Clearly, it is not necessary to score at Kohlberg's highest stages to live an exemplary moral life.

How does a person become morally committed? The 23 moral exemplars did not develop in isolation, but responded to social influences. Some of these influences, such as those of parents, were important from childhood on. But many other influences became significant in later years, helping these people evaluate their capacities, form moral goals, and develop strategies to achieve them.

These moral exemplars had a lifelong commitment to change: they focused their energy on changing society and people's lives for the better. But they remained stable in their moral commitments, in what they felt was important in determining their actions. At the same time, they kept growing throughout life, remained open to new ideas, and continued to learn from others.

The processes responsible for stability in moral commitments were gradual, taking many years to build up. They were also collaborative: leaders took advice from supporters, and people noted for independent judgment drew heavily on feedback from those close to them—both those people who shared their goals and those who had different perspectives.

Along with their enduring moral commitments, certain personality characteristics seemed to remain with the moral exemplars throughout middle and late adulthood: enjoyment of life, ability to make the best of a bad situation, solidarity with others, absorption in work, a sense of humor, and humility. They tended to believe that change was possible, and this optimism helped them battle what often seemed like overwhelming odds and to persist in the face of defeat.

While their actions often meant risk and hardship, these people did not see themselves as courageous. Nor did they agonize over decisions. Since their personal and moral goals coincided, they went ahead and did what they believed needed to be done, not calculating personal consequences to themselves or their families, and not feeling that they were sacrificing or martyring themselves.

Of course, there is no "blueprint" for creating a moral giant, just as it does not seem possible to write directions to produce a genius in any other field. What studying the lives of such people can bring is the knowledge that ordinary people can rise to greatness and that openness to change and new ideas can persist throughout adulthood.

peoples could live in harmony. He believed that violence is never justified, even in the noblest causes. Although often imprisoned for his activities, he did not waver in his beliefs or goals. When India finally attained independence in 1947, and a separate Muslim state of Pakistan was created, Gandhi—then in his late seventies—went on a hunger strike in an effort to stop the ensuing violence. This moral weapon accomplished what, according to the *London Times*, "several divisions [of troops] could not have done." Moved by Gandhi's act of self-sacrifice, both Hindus and Muslims laid down their arms. Another hunger strike, in Delhi in January 1948, led to cooperative efforts to secure protections for the Muslim minority. But 12 days after breaking his fast, Gandhi—then 78—was shot and killed on his way to a prayer meeting. The assassin was a fellow Hindu who could not accept Gandhi's vision of brotherhood.

(AP/Wide World Photos)

Mahatma Gandhi's philosophy of nonviolence was a formidable moral weapon in India's struggle for independence from Britain. Gandhi is shown here on his release from one of many periods of imprisonment.

Gandhi's philosophy of nonviolence profoundly influenced other great leaders, among them Nelson Mandela and Martin Luther King. Gandhi himself exemplifies the ability to deal with almost intractable problems through a creative fusion of intellect and emotion, spirituality and moral suasion. In his efforts to defuse conflicts and inspire cooperation, he showed great wisdom—wisdom grounded in a transcendent moral vision.

Few of us reach the heights of intelligence, creativity, and wisdom or achieve the moral and spiritual leadership Gandhi did, and few of us have such influential careers. But caring and concern for others are important qualities in any adult, as is the work to which one chooses to devote one's life. We turn to these aspects of the social world of adulthood in Part Three.

SUMMARY

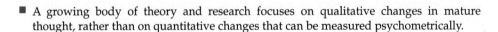

- A growing body of theory and research focuses on qualitative changes in mature thought, rather than on quantitative changes that can be measured psychometrically.

THE ROLE OF EXPERIENCE

- According to Hoyer's model, adults maximize their intellectual functioning through encapsulation of fluid abilities within specialized fields of expert knowledge.
- Everyday problem solving improves in middle age and may remain stable or continue to improve in old age.
- Mature adults integrate new experience with existing personal knowledge and interpret information or events in terms of their own life experience.

POSTFORMAL THOUGHT: BEYOND PIAGET'S STAGES

- Several investigators have proposed a postformal stage of adult thinking—beyond Piaget's highest stage, formal operations.

- A shift to postformal thought is said to occur in college, when students are exposed to ambiguities and opposing viewpoints, and their thinking typically progresses from rigidity to flexibility to freely chosen commitments.

- Labouvie-Vief has proposed three levels of adult cognitive development: intrasystemic, intersystemic, and integrated.

- Criteria for postformal thought include shifting gears, awareness of multiple causes and solutions, pragmatism, awareness of paradox, and contractions and expansions of formal thinking.

A LIFESPAN MODEL OF COGNITIVE DEVELOPMENT

- Schaie has proposed five stages of age-related cognitive development: acquisitive (childhood and adolescence), achieving (young adulthood), responsible and executive (middle adulthood), and reintegrative (late adulthood).

- This model suggests a need to develop new kinds of intelligence tests that are ecologically valid for adults.

WISDOM

- Sternberg, on the basis of studies of adults' views of creativity, intelligence, and wisdom, distinguishes the three concepts on the basis of automaticity of information processing, approach to knowledge, styles of mental regulation, personality factors, fundamental motivations, and supportive environments.

- Modern psychologists who investigate wisdom have drawn on folk, mythic, and philosophical traditions.

- According to Erikson, wisdom is a virtue emerging from the final crisis of human personality development, *integrity versus despair*. It permits acceptance of one's life and approaching death.

- Among cognitive definitions of wisdom, that of Baltes has been empirically tested. Baltes sees wisdom as expertise in "fundamental pragmatics of life."

- For Labouvie-Vief, wisdom is a synthesis of reason with emotion, or subjective experience, and appears to peak in middle age.

- Some investigators, influenced by eastern philosophy, see wisdom as a product of spiritual development or self-transcendence.

MORAL DEVELOPMENT

- Kohlberg's theory of moral reasoning holds that people reason out moral principles; thus moral development is related to cognitive development.

- Many adults remain at Kohlberg's conventional level of morality; some advance to a postconventional level of autonomous moral principles.

- Gilligan has criticized Kohlberg's emphasis on justice as a predominantly male value and has proposed a theory of women's moral development centered on caring and responsibility.

- Gilligan's recent work suggests that many adults, both men and women, reach a stage of relativist morality that reflects postformal thought.

KEY TERMS

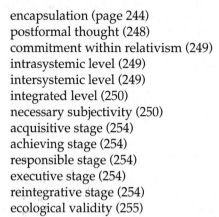

encapsulation (page 244)
postformal thought (248)
commitment within relativism (249)
intrasystemic level (249)
intersystemic level (249)
integrated level (250)
necessary subjectivity (250)
acquisitive stage (254)
achieving stage (254)
responsible stage (254)
executive stage (254)
reintegrative stage (254)
ecological validity (255)

metacognition (256)
archetypes (258)
fundamental pragmatics of life (260)
intrapersonal wisdom (264)
interpersonal wisdom (264)
transpersonal wisdom (264)
preconventional morality (265)
morality of conventional role
    conformity (265)
morality of autonomous moral
    principles (265)
cosmic perspective (268)

D ecisions, decisions—adulthood is one long series of decisions. What kind of work to do and how to prepare for it, whether to marry and have children or to establish other kinds of intimate relationships, where and how to live, what recreations to pursue, whether and when to retire and what to do afterward, how to deal with adult children and aging parents—these and other lifestyle choices, all made within a social context, shape the course and direction of adult life. As adults take on social roles—worker, spouse, "significant other," parent, grandparent—those roles affect how they think and act; and how they think and act affects how they play those roles.

Adults set priorities every day, often involving role conflicts. A college senior struggling to prepare for medical school neglects to write home to the parents who are paying for his education. A lawyer works 80 hours a week while trying to find time to see her fiancé and her friends, run 5 miles a day, and occasionally relax. A middle-level management executive feels defensive when his boss questions his career commitment because he leaves work early enough to have dinner with his children. A single mother is overwhelmed by the stress of trying to raise a baby alone and make ends meet. A man in his late fifties worries about whether he can keep his job long enough to retire on the pension he and his wife have been counting on. A recently widowed woman in her eighties, who walks with a cane and has failing eyesight, debates about whether to stay in her home, move in with her daughter's family, or go into an assisted-care facility.

In Chapter 8, we discuss activities that structure a large part of adults' waking hours: education, work, leisure, and retirement. In Chapter 9, we examine intimate relationships involving friendship, love, and sexual attraction, which generally form the core of personal lifestyles. In Chapter 10, we look at the mature relationships of adult children, parents, and siblings; at grandparenthood and great-grandparenthood; and at living arrangements for aging adults who need family and community care and support.

PART THREE

THE
SOCIAL
WORLD

CHAPTER **8**

EDUCATION, WORK, LEISURE, AND RETIREMENT

EDUCATION
College
Lifelong Learning
Adult Illiteracy

WORK AND LEISURE
Vocational Choice
  and Career Development
Changing Occupational Patterns
Age and Job Performance
Occupational Stress
Unemployment
Work, Leisure, and Intellectual Growth

RETIREMENT AND
OTHER LATE-LIFE OPTIONS
To Retire or Not to Retire
Financing Retirement
Preparing for Retirement
How Do Retired People Use Their Time?
How Does Retirement Affect
  Well-Being?
How Does Retirement Affect Society?

BOXES
8-1 The Art of Aging: Computer
    Training—Teaching Older Adults
    New Tricks
8-2 The Cutting Edge: Age
    Discrimination and Public Safety
8-3 The Multicultural Context:
    Work and Retirement in China

What am I
But an unfinished poem
I am constantly working on?

Rita Duskin, "My Portrait,"
in *The Frugal Chariot*, 1970

FOCUS: JIMMY CARTER

(Michael O'Neill)

James Earl ("Jimmy") Carter, Jr.,* was one of the most unpopular presidents of the United States in the twentieth century. Yet a little more than a decade after having been turned out of office, he is one of the most active and most admired ex-presidents in modern American history, "pursuing lost and neglected causes with a missionary's zeal"—and an amazing degree of success (Nelson, 1994).

As a boy in tiny, rural Plains, Georgia, Carter helped with chores on the family farm, sold peanuts and cotton, and absorbed his parents' traditional values: education, hard work, religious faith, and public service. His career choice, influenced by an uncle who was a radioman in the Pacific fleet, was to be a naval officer. He won an appointment to the U.S. Naval Academy and served as engineering officer of the first nuclear-powered submarine under Captain Hyman G. Rickover. Rickover "had a profound influence on my life," Carter later wrote. ". . . He expected the maximum from us, but he always contributed more" (*1977 World Book Yearbook*, p. 53).

Carter's career took a new turn after his father's death. He resigned from the Navy and returned to Plains to run the family farm and peanut warehouse. An outspoken foe of racial segregation, he was narrowly elected to the Georgia Senate in 1962 and to the governorship in 1970. As governor, he streamlined the state government and pushed through legislation to equalize state aid to rich and poor school districts, establish community centers for retarded children, and protect the environment. He initiated merit selection of judges and state officials and greatly increased the number of black appointees and employees.

*Sources of biographical information on Jimmy Carter are Bird (1990), Carter (1975), Carter Center (1995), J. Nelson (1994), *1977 World Book Yearbook*, Wooten (1995), and various newspaper articles.

In 1976, in the wake of the Watergate scandal that toppled President Richard M. Nixon, Carter, previously little known outside Georgia, won the Democratic nomination on the first ballot after sweeping 18 primary elections. He went on to become the first southerner in the twentieth century to be elected president. His appeal was as an outsider who would clean up government and restore a moral tone. But despite such historic achievements as peace between Israel and Egypt and a treaty relinquishing control of the Panama Canal, he became bogged down in the interminable Iranian hostage crisis and took the blame for high fuel prices, gasoline lines, and a sagging economy. After a devastating defeat by Ronald Reagan in the 1980 election, he retired from political life.

Or so it seemed. Just look at what Carter has done since then:

He helps build and renovate houses for low-income families through the nonprofit organization Habitat for Humanity.

Between 1980 and 1990, he raised more than $150 million for the Carter Center in Atlanta, which sponsors programs in human rights, education, preventive health care, and international conflict resolution. The center has spearheaded a successful campaign to eliminate Guinea worm disease from villages with contaminated water supplies in Africa, India, and Pakistan. The center also monitors human rights cases around the world and has worked quietly to secure the release of hundreds of political prisoners. In 1991, in a blunt speech in Beijing, Carter pressed China to release prisoners taken during the 1989 protest in Tiananmen Square.

He acts as a roving peacemaker and guardian of freedom. In 1989, he twice flew to Africa to attempt to mediate the 29-year-old Ethiopian civil war. He oversaw the Nicaraguan elections that ousted the Sandanistas, and he persuaded their leader, Daniel Ortega, to accept the result. He has traveled to the middle east to nudge the peace process along. He monitored presidential elections in Paraguay in 1993. His visit to North Korea in 1994 reduced tension over that country's refusal to dismantle its nuclear weapons program and paved the way for a nonproliferation treaty. Also in 1994, having earlier helped set up Haiti's first democratic election, he averted an American invasion by obtaining the withdrawal of the military regime that had removed the elected president, Jean-Bertrand Aristide. And, 2 months after his seventieth birthday, he brokered a 4-month cease-fire between Bosnian Muslims and Serbs in their civil war and secured pledges from both sides to resume peace negotiations. For these activities he was nominated for the Nobel Peace Prize—for the sixth time.

It has been said that Carter "used his presidency as a stepping stone to higher things" (Bird, 1990, p. 564). Freed from the pressures of politics, he has risen to the role of elder statesman, using the passion for detail that often was his undoing in the White House to fight for the humane causes he has always believed in.

Jimmy Carter's "forced retirement" was more publicized than most, and few adults have the resources and opportunities of an ex-president. But Carter is far from unique in using his retirement years productively. He is one of many older adults whose late-life activism is leading to a new view of how life can be structured throughout adulthood.

The typical life structure in industrialized societies is *age-differentiated:* roles are based on age (as in the left side of Figure 8-1). Young people's primary role is that of students. Young and middle-aged adults are predominantly workers. Older adults organize their lives around retirement and leisure. Yet, as Matilda Riley (1994), a senior social scientist at the National Institute on Aging, observed:

> . . . these structures fail to accommodate many of the changes in people's lives. After all, does it make sense to spend nearly one-third of adult lifetime in retirement? Or to crowd most work into the harried middle years? Or to label as "too old" those as young as 55 who want to work? Does it make sense to assume that . . . physically capable older people—an estimated 40 million of them in the next century—should expect greater support *from* society than they contribute *to* society? . . . Surely, something will have to change! (p. 445)

Age-differentiated roles are a holdover from an earlier era, when life was shorter and social institutions were less diverse. The result is a *structural lag:* increasing numbers of older adults are able to contribute to society, but opportunities to use and reward their abilities are inadequate. Also, by devoting themselves to one aspect of life at a time, people do not enjoy each period of life as much as they might and may not prepare themselves adequately for the next phase. For example, by concentrating on work, adults may forget how to play; then, when they retire, they may not know what to do with a sudden abundance of leisure time.

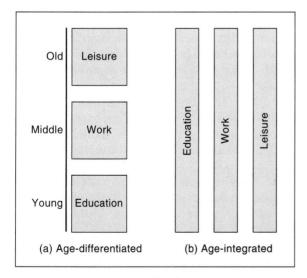

(a) Age-differentiated   (b) Age-integrated

FIGURE 8-1
Contrasting social structures.
(a) Traditional age-differentiated structure, typical of industrialized societies. Education, work, and leisure roles are largely "assigned" to different phases of life.
(b) Age-integrated structure which would spread all three kinds of roles throughout the adult lifespan and help break down social barriers between generations.
(SOURCE: M. W. Riley, 1994, p. 445.)

In an *age-integrated* society (as in the right side of Figure 8-1), all kinds of roles—learning, working, and playing—would be open to adults of all ages (Bolles, 1979; Riley, 1994). They could intersperse periods of education, work, and leisure throughout the lifespan. Things seem to be moving in that direction. College students may take work-study programs or "stop out" for a while before resuming their education. Middle-aged and older adults may go back to school or take, say, a year off work to pursue a special interest. A person may have several careers in succession, each requiring additional education or training. People may retire earlier or later than in the past, or not at all. Retirees may devote time to study or to a new line of work.

As we discuss education, work, leisure, and retirement, keep in mind that much of the research reflects the older, age-differentiated model of social roles, and the cohorts whose lives it describes. With "age integration" emerging in many societies, future cohorts may have very different experiences and attitudes.

EDICATION

▼

One of the last drawings by the Spanish artist Francisco de Goya—made in his eighties—is a sketch of an old man hobbling on a crutch and a cane. On it, Goya wrote *Aún aprendo:* "I keep learning" (D. B. W. Lewis, 1968). Although formal education traditionally ends in young adulthood, people continue to learn from the school of life. And today more and more adults of all ages are enrolling in educational programs, to gain degrees, learn new skills, pursue interests, improve literacy, or keep up with the challenges and opportunities of the world of work—or simply because they enjoy learning.

COLLEGE

Today's college and university classrooms look much different from those of a generation ago. Of nearly 14.2 million students enrolled in American institutions of higher learning, an increasing proportion are age 35 and older (National Center for Education Statistics, 1989, 1991). Since 1970, the number of students age 25 and up has more than doubled to nearly half the total enrollment (U.S. Department of Education, cited in Haas, 1989). Young women are more likely than young men to go to college and about as likely to aim for advanced degrees. Fifty-five percent of all college students and about 58 percent of students of non-traditional ages are women. The latter include married or divorced women who need to increase their income, "empty nesters" seeking midlife careers, and women inspired by feminist goals of becoming independent and self-supporting (Haas, 1989; National Center for Education Statistics, 1989, 1991). More than half of the bachelor's and master's degrees awarded during 1990 and 1991, and about 40 percent of doctoral and professional degrees, were awarded to women (National Center for Education Statistics, 1991). But according to the National Research Council, only slightly more than 4 percent of the Ph.D. degrees awarded to American citizens in 1993 went to African Americans.

Many colleges make it easy for students to take leaves of absence or to earn credit for independent study or work done at other institutions, and some actively seek mature students who may have dropped out years before. Most colleges give credit for life experience and previous learning. They also attempt to accommodate the practical needs of students of nontraditional age through part-time matriculation, Saturday and night classes, independent study, on-campus child care, financial aid, free or reduced-tuition courses, and "distance learning" via computers or closed-circuit broadcasts. Adults who choose to go back to school tend to be more motivated than younger students. What they may lack in academic skills they make up for in the richness and variety of their life experience (Datan, Rodeheaver, & Hughes, 1987; Haas, 1989).

LIFELONG LEARNING

Qian Likun, a star student who walks to his classes on health care and ancient Chinese poetry, took part in a 2.3-mile foot race. This might not seem unusual, until you learn that Qian is 102 years old, one of thousands of students in China's network of "universities for the aged." More than 800 of these schools have been founded since the 1980s, showing China's commitment to its elderly population—and older people's willingness and ability to learn everything from basic reading and writing to esoteric subjects (Kristof, 1990). China's program exemplifies a trend toward *lifelong learning*—organized, sustained study by adults of all ages.

Educational programs specifically designed for mature adults are booming in many parts of the world. Elderhostel, for example, is an international network of 1,600 colleges and other educational institutions in 40 countries, offering low-cost, noncredit 1- or 2-week residential minicourses in Shakespeare, geography, early American music, and other subjects for adults over 60 and their spouses or companions.

Since the mid-1960s the government of Japan has planned and implemented a system of continuing education for its growing population of older adults (Nojima, 1994). *Kominkans* (community educational centers) offer classes in child care, health, traditional arts and crafts, hobbies, exercise, and sports. A newer 2-year advanced studies program is designed to train community leaders who have studied 1 year at a kominkan or have done extensive community work.

In the United States, educational opportunities for older adults have mushroomed since the mid-1970s (Moskow-McKenzie & Manheimer, 1994). In one category are free or low-cost classes, taught by professionals or volunteers, at neighborhood senior centers, community centers, religious institutions, or department stores. These classes generally have a practical or social focus. A second category consists of college- and university-based programs with education as the primary goal. Many regional community colleges and state universities, as well as a few private universities, offer special programs for older adults. Some vocational programs give special attention to the needs of older women who have never worked for pay but now must do so.

Why do mature adults go to school? A review of the literature (Willis, 1985) identified five common goals:

BOX 8-1

THE ART OF AGING

Computer Training: Teaching Older Adults New Tricks

At a college in New Orleans that offers free mini-courses for people age 65 and older, by far the most popular offering is computer training. Each semester more than 100 students enroll, and the waiting list is equally long. Work training programs of the American Association of Retired Persons (AARP) cannot begin to accommodate all the requests for introductory or advanced courses in using computers and word processing.

Why do so many older adults want to learn to use computers? Some are just curious. Some need to acquire new job skills or update old ones. Some want to keep up with the latest technology: to communicate with children and grandchildren who are computer-literate, or to emulate friends who are on the information highway.

Initially, there were indications that some older adults had less positive attitudes toward computers than younger ones—that they considered computers dehumanizing (Brickfield, 1984; Nickerson, 1981). A randomized telephone survey in 1981 found that use of computers decreased with age (from 40 percent among 45- to 54-year-olds down to 19 percent among people 65 and older) but was also related to socioeconomic status and educational level. The survey found similar patterns for other technological innovations: electronic calculators, video recorders,

(Beringer-Dratch/The Image Works)

Computer courses are popular among older adults, either to upgrade work skills or for personal enjoyment.

video games, and electronic teller machines (Brickfield, 1984).

If a similar survey were done today, when computers have become a familiar part of everyday life, it would almost certainly show smaller age differences, and any such differences undoubtedly will continue to flatten out as better-educated cohorts enter old age. Indeed, studies during the 1980s that compared attitudes of college students with attitudes of highly educated older adults (Ansley & Erber, 1988) or retirees attending a senior center program on computers (Krauss & Hoyer, 1984) found no age differences. However, men were more positively

1. *To gain adaptive knowledge and skills,* often to keep up with new developments in their fields, move up the career ladder, or prepare to go into business for themselves. In the United States, almost two-thirds of adults who take part-time classes do so for job-related reasons (U.S. Department of Education, 1986).

2. *To train for new occupations* when their old ones become obsolete or when their needs and interests change. Some middle-aged women who have

disposed toward computers than women (Krauss & Hoyer, 1984)—a finding that still holds true, apparently, since 95 percent of the users of Internet, the world's largest computerized information network, are men, according to a 1994 report by *Time* magazine.

Research consistently shows that older adults can be trained to become computer-literate (Garfein, Schaie, & Willis, 1988; Hartley, Hartley, & Johnson, 1984); but they may take longer than younger people to master skills, and they may need more help (Charness, Schumann, & Boritz, 1992; Elias, Elias, Robbins, & Gage, 1987; Zandri & Charness, 1989). Well-educated older adults who went through 2 weeks of training in desktop publishing ended up more comfortable and more confident about their abilities (Jay & Willis, 1992). A recent study in Ontario, Canada, found that, for both younger and older adults, anxiety before training in word processing did not affect final performance. The researchers observed, "If older adults can be persuaded to seek retraining, despite any initial negative attitudes, their success in training will be more a function of their training program than their attitudes" (Charness et al., 1992, pp. 103–104). One caution: The participants in this research were volunteers, who wanted to learn word processing and presumably believed they could do it. The findings may not apply to people who are required to undergo computer training in job situations.

Do older people need special training techniques? In general, the answer is no: the most effective methods for younger adults are also best for older adults (Charness et al., 1992). For example, modeling the use of a computer along with a tutorial program is more effective than a tutorial alone (Gist, Rosen, & Schwoerer, 1988); and having an instructor and a manual is better than totally computer-based training. In the Canadian study discussed above, a self-paced method worked better than fixed pacing for both age groups. However, the pace of training can be more critical for older learners than for younger ones (Charness et al., 1992).

The following suggestions, which reflect a need to be sensitive to biological and cognitive changes that commonly occur with advancing age (Charness et al., 1992; Zandri & Charness, 1989), can facilitate computer instruction for older adults:

- Offer slower or self-paced instruction, and expect older learners to take longer than younger ones.

- Do hands-on training, perhaps in pairs or in small groups.

- Have an instructor available to answer questions about unfamiliar concepts and terms.

- Give older learners more help with novel problems.

- Monitor progress to forestall any problems that might sap confidence.

devoted their young adult years to homemaking and parenthood are taking the first steps toward reentering the job market.

3. *To understand and cope with technological and cultural change,* such as the use of computers (see Box 8-1).

4. *To understand their own aging processes,* particularly changes in memory and other aspects of cognition, and to learn strategies for making the most of their abilities.

5. *To develop new and satisfying retirement and leisure roles;* for example, studying a foreign language to prepare for travel abroad. People who are close to retirement often want to explore interests they didn't have time to pursue earlier in life.

With the increase in longevity, there will be a growing interest in educational programs that can make retirement more meaningful and enjoyable. And with the disparity in life expectancy between men and women, there is a growing need for educational programs for widows, focusing on independent living, management of personal finances, and development of new relationships.

It seems clear that in today's complex society, education is never finished. Getting a college degree in one's early twenties will not be enough for most adults in the future (Willis, 1985). Expanding technology and shifting job markets will require a lifespan approach to education. Individuals must be prepared to have several careers, each perhaps quite different from the others. And as some occupations become obsolete and others emerge or require new skills, retraining will become more and more essential.

Older adults can learn new skills and information most readily when the materials and methods take into account the physiological, psychological, and intellectual changes they may be experiencing (Chapters 3 to 7). One special need of many adults of all ages is literacy training.

ADULT ILLITERACY

Ed is a 29-year-old silkscreen printer, a trade he learned in high school. Because he's quick-witted, personable, and determined, his employers and coworkers do not realize, at first, that he cannot read beyond a fourth- or fifth-grade level. "I've lost lots of jobs because of my reading problem," he says (Feldman, 1985).

Ed is one of an estimated 90 million Americans who are functionally illiterate—who cannot read, write, or do arithmetic well enough to handle many everyday tasks (Kirsch, Jenkins, Jungeblut, & Kolstad, 1993). The estimate comes from the National Adult Literacy Survey, which was given to more than 26,000 people age 16 or older in 1992. Participants were rated on their ability to do such tasks as finding information in a newspaper article and filling out a bank deposit slip. More than 20 percent showed limited skills. More than 4 out of 10 at the lowest level of skills were poor, 1 out of 4 were immigrants, and 6 out of 10 had not completed high school. Two out of 10 had visual problems. Adults over 65 did worse than other age groups, and young adults did worse than in a 1985 survey (Kirsch et al., 1993).

According to Madeleine M. Kunin, Deputy Secretary of Education, "we simply are not keeping pace with the kinds of skills required in today's economy" (Ludmer-Gliebe, 1994, p. 19). At the turn of the century, a fourth-grade education was considered enough for "literacy"; today, a high school diploma is barely adequate. Even a college degree does not guarantee a high level of literacy: about half of college graduates can't decipher a bus schedule, and only 13 percent can do math problems involving several steps (Barton & Lapointe, 1995).

Globally, illiteracy is more widespread among females than males. In 1985, an estimated 889 million adults throughout the world—1 in 4—were illiterate (UNESCO, 1989), and nearly two-thirds of them were women. Of the 116 million children under age 11 who do not go to school, two-thirds are girls (Sticht & McDonald, 1990). Illiteracy varies widely from one region of the world to another: more than half of adult Africans are illiterate, as compared with 36 percent of Asians and only 17 percent of Latin Americans (UNESCO, 1989).

In 1990, the United Nations declared an International Literacy Year and launched informal educational programs in such places as Bangladesh, Nepal, and Somalia (Linder, 1990). In 1991 the United States Congress passed the National Literacy Act, which requires the states to establish literacy centers with federal funding assistance. The goal is to wipe out illiteracy by the year 2000. Since literacy is a fundamental requisite for participation in a modern, information-driven economy, expansion of literacy programs—the most basic form of adult education—is a pressing need.

WORK AND LEISURE

"What do you do?" is often the first question one adult asks when meeting another. What work adults do is central to who they are. Work is entwined with all aspects of development. Intellectual, physical, social, and emotional factors affect our work; and our work can affect every other area of our lives.

First, let's define some terms that are used, sometimes interchangeably, to describe work. A *job* can be any activity performed for pay, but this term typically refers to employment by someone or some organization other than oneself. A job may be temporary or transient. The term *occupation*, by contrast, refers to a regular, relatively permanent field of work or means of livelihood. The term *vocation* usually refers to a chosen field. A *profession* is an occupation or vocation that generally requires college or postgraduate training and involves a good deal of independent judgment and control. The word *career* has a dynamic quality; it is a developmental path of achievement, which, if followed to its natural conclusion, may represent a life's work.

Leisure is discretionary use of time. Leisure time is free time, when people are not gainfully employed and can do whatever they wish. The line between work and leisure is not always easy to draw. The same type of activity—say, photography—may be work for one person and a leisure pursuit for another, and both may enjoy it equally. Leisure activities normally have no monetary reward; but what about a Sunday painter who occasionally sells a canvas at an art fair, or a homeowner who picks up pocket money by having a garage sale?

Only in modern, developed societies is leisure a significant aspect of adult life, and not until after retirement does it become a central focus. The United States in the 1930s adopted an 8-hour, 5-day work week for most of the population; paid vacations also became standard. Still, many workers who are starting or running businesses or trying to get ahead in their careers have little leisure time.

In this section, let's look at how people choose vocations and develop careers. Then we'll describe changing occupational patterns. We'll consider how age affects work performance. We'll discuss stress and burnout. Finally, we'll examine the interaction of work, leisure, and intellectual growth. In the next section, we'll discuss how adults use leisure time in retirement.

VOCATIONAL CHOICE AND CAREER DEVELOPMENT

What influences decisions about vocation? How do adults progress along their chosen career paths? Why do some people have stable careers, while others go through one or more changes? Let's look at several classic theories and how they have withstood the test of changing social conditions.

Holland: Personality and Vocation

John Holland (1985) matched six personality types—investigative, social, realistic, artistic, conventional, and enterprising—with corresponding occupations or work environments. According to Holland's theory, people with predominantly *investigative* personalities are likely to become scientists or detectives; *social* types may choose mental health or teaching; *realistic* people may be mechanics or electricians; *artistic* people become writers, artists, or musicians; *conventional* people go into accounting or banking; and *enterprising* people enter sales or management. Women tend to show artistic, social, and conventional traits and to go into corresponding occupations. Job satisfaction is highest when a personality type matches the work environment, and the worker is most likely to stay in that position. Of course, neither people nor work environments can be described in terms of a single "pure" trait; the question is which type is predominant.

Holland's theory has been influential, particularly in the development of personality inventories used in vocational guidance. But it has several important limitations. First, some jobs require a mix of traits and skills, and some people are happiest in such jobs. Second, Holland's theory does not deal with environmental or cultural forces that limit or influence career choices. What jobs are available at a given time and place will depend in part on the physical environment and its exploitation. A person living in a coal-mining area is more likely to become a miner than is a person growing up in a major urban center. Socioeconomic differences, including educational opportunities, often limit vocational choice. Gender, too, makes a difference. Even in the United States today, after four decades of "women's liberation," female airline pilots and male nurses remain quite rare. More men gravitate toward jobs involving risk and physical abilities; more women go into nurturing professions.

Finally, Holland's theory fails to explain *how* the choice of a career—the vital match-up between personality and work environment—occurs, or how careers develop across the adult lifespan. The work environment itself can be an agent of change; for example, an electrician hired to help with lighting in a theater might discover an artistic bent and begin to specialize in theatrical lighting. The interaction between person and environment is dynamic.

Does personality determine occupational choice? One theory says yes. Gender makes a difference, even after four decades of the women's movement; for instance, the vast majority of nurses are women.

Super: Stages in Career Planning and Development

Some theorists who take an organismic perspective have proposed that vocational choice and career development occur in stages.

Donald Super's (1957, 1985) influential theory encompasses eight stages of career exploration and development from puberty through adulthood, which evolve along with a person's maturing self-concept. These stages are: (1) crystallization, (2) specification, (3) implementation, (4) establishment, (5) consolidation, (6) maintenance, (7) deceleration, and (8) retirement. (George Vaillant and Daniel Levinson, whose theories of personality development we discuss in Chapter 11, describe somewhat similar stages of career development.)

During the *crystallization stage,* in early adolescence, a person has only vague, general ideas about a career. According to Erikson's theory of personality development (see Table 2-2 in Chapter 2), identity confusion is typical of the teenage years. As young people begin to develop a firm sense of self, they develop a concept of occupation as a defining feature of the self.

In the *specification stage,* from late adolescence into the college years, young people learn more about various occupations and about what goes on in the workplace. They begin to focus on specific career tracks and recognize that choosing one vocation requires abandoning other possibilities.

The *implementation stage* begins in the early twenties. Young adults try out one or more entry-level jobs or start professional training. Coming face to face with the actual world of work may lead to changes of mind before making a final career choice.

In the *establishment stage*, which starts in the mid-twenties, young adults have made a commitment to a career goal—advancement along a chosen path. They now see their work as an intrinsic part of their self-concept.

On the basis of expertise developed during the establishment stage, adults in the mid-thirties move into the *consolidation stage*. They strive to move up in their fields as fast and as far as possible, continually consolidating their gains as a firm footing for the next step up the ladder.

By middle age, career goals either have been met or are now seen as out of reach, and the urge to advance slackens. During the *maintenance stage*, which generally begins in the mid-forties, middle-aged people focus on maintaining, rather than acquiring, prestige, authority, and responsibility.

People may reduce their workload as they gradually shift into the *deceleration stage* in the late fifties, when they face the need to retire in the not-too-distant future and gradually begin to distance themselves from their work, both physically and emotionally. Those whose self-concept is too deeply enmeshed in work may have difficulty letting go.

Finally, the *retirement stage*, which traditionally begins at age 65, brings formal separation from the job and requires adjustment to lack of a career as a defining feature of the self.

Super's theory, then, sees career decisions as based on a rational, realistic understanding of the self and the world of work. However, critics question the idea that a clear self-concept guides career development and point out that career paths often do not proceed in such an orderly, reasoned manner; they are often more a result of luck or emotional factors. Nor does the theory take account of constraints on the freedom to make career decisions (Neff, 1985).

Super's theory was developed at a time when fewer women worked outside the home, and decisions made in the late teens or twenties often shaped a man's entire working life. Today many people start second, third, or even fourth or fifth careers at some point during adulthood, and retirement at 65 no longer is as typical as it was during the 1950s. A universal set of stages does not seem to adequately explain the many ways careers develop.

Ginzberg: Stable and Shifting Career Patterns

In the 1950s, Eli Ginzberg proposed a three-stage model similar to Super's, based on research with predominantly white male college students. In 1972, Ginzberg revised his model. After examining the occupational histories of women, and also of men from a wider variety of backgrounds, he saw that career decisions are often open-ended. Rather than settling for what initially seems achievable, people seek to progressively improve the match between their abilities and expectations and what they are getting out of their work. This constant process of reevaluation can lead to a change of career—sometimes a radical change. Ginzberg noted that women's career paths tend to be less continuous than men's; they may take time out for motherhood and then resume employment, possibly in a new occupation. When we look at career paths in the United States today, Ginzberg's theory, as amended, seems to provide a more accurate description than Super's of how people make vocational decisions.

Career paths fall into two basic patterns: *stable* or *shifting*. People with stable career patterns and many years of accumulated expertise often reach positions of power and responsibility. Middle-aged men with stable careers tend to be either "workaholics" or "mellowed" (Tamir, 1989). Workaholics work at a frenzied pace, either in a last-ditch effort to reach financial security before they retire or because they find it hard to relinquish authority. "Mellowed" people have come to terms with their level of achievement, even if they have not gone as far as they had hoped. The best adjusted among them have a sense of relaxation rather than failure. They are often happier, less cynical, and steadier in temperament than their more successful counterparts. Although these men want to do challenging work, they do not pin their emotional well-being on their jobs as much as they used to (Bray & Howard, 1983).

Because fewer middle-aged and older women have worked throughout adulthood, they are less likely to exhibit the stable career pattern. And changing economic and social conditions are making that pattern less common among men as well. Although people may change careers anytime during adulthood, middle age is a common time to do it. With longer life expectancies, many middle-aged people do not want to keep doing the same thing for the next 20 years. Personal, family, and lifestyle changes that often occur at this time of life may lead to a change of careers. The emptying of the nest may alter a woman's orientation from family to career and may give a man a new sense of freedom to experiment. Divorce or widowhood may create a need for more income. People who have paid off the mortgage or put the last child through college may look for an easier workload, a job that pays less but is more satisfying, or a business venture that is risky but exciting. Others realize that they are ill-prepared for retirement and focus on accumulating a nest egg.

Of course, career-changers are often influenced by factors having to do with the job situation itself. Some are forced by unemployment or technological change to seek new careers. Some, thwarted in the desire to move up the career ladder, strike out in new directions, seeking more personal and intellectual challenge or more opportunity for advancement. People who choose to make a change are often considered particularly valuable employees, since they tend to be highly motivated and ambitious (Schultz & Schultz, 1986).

Raynor: Motivation and Career Paths

Why do some people stay on the same career path while others switch? Why do some people keep striving to advance, while others hit a dead end? Joel Raynor's *achievement motivation* theory (J. N. Atkinson & Raynor, 1974; Raynor & Rubin, 1971) takes a contextualist perspective, emphasizing differences among people and occupations, and how they interact.

According to Raynor, people's motivation to strive for success is influenced by their perception of what kind of career path they are on—*contingent* or *noncontingent* (see Figure 8-2). People on **contingent career paths** see their future success as determined by their own actions. A worker seeks knowledge and skill, expecting that this effort will bring higher income and status and that failure to make the effort will cut off opportunity for advancement. People on **noncontingent career**

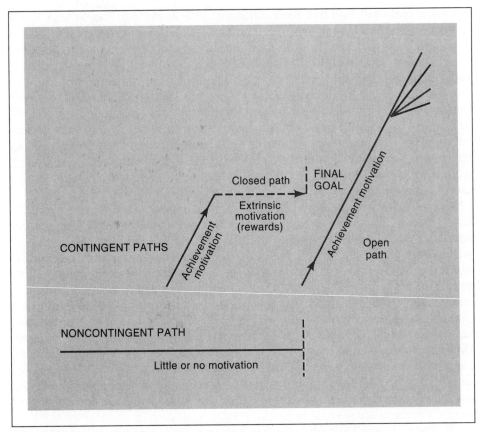

FIGURE 8-2

Raynor's model of career paths. Adults who perceive advancement as contingent on their own efforts are more motivated to strive for success than those who do not. On closed paths leading to a fixed goal (such as retirement), motivation shifts from intrinsic to extrinsic rewards (such as bonuses and pensions) as the goal comes within reach. On open paths, where new opportunities keep appearing, people continue to be motivated to achieve.

paths lack motivation for achievement because they see themselves in dead-end jobs with no hope of advancement or significant improvement. Eventually they either quit and look for better jobs or resign themselves to a hopeless situation.

Contingent career paths can be seen as either *closed* or *open*. A closed path has specific steps leading to a final goal, such as becoming a top-level executive or reaching retirement. The closer people get to that goal, the less they are motivated toward achievement for its own sake and the more they look to external rewards, such as bonuses and retirement benefits. In an open career path, there is no fixed endpoint. New opportunities appear along the path, sustaining the motivation to achieve. Adults on an open career path tend to keep updating their skills and acquiring new ones. Again, it is the worker's *perception* of the career path, not an outsider's objective description, that affects motivation.

Raynor's theory recognizes that people and their work situations differ. However, it does assume a universal motivation toward career advancement. Thus it fails to account for a person who simply gets fed up with the rat race or tires of doing the same work and wants to try something new.

No one theory fully explains how people choose their vocations and how their careers develop; and all these theories may be less applicable outside of developed western cultures. Still, each can offer insights as we explore today's world of work.

CHANGING OCCUPATIONAL PATTERNS

The structure of the American work force is changing profoundly. For the first time, there are more people in executive, professional, and technical jobs (nearly 1 out of 3 workers) than in manufacture or transport of goods (1 in 5). The number of white-collar jobs jumped 38 percent from 1980 to 1990, while the number of skilled blue-collar jobs declined. Only 4 percent of the work force have unskilled jobs (U.S. Bureau of the Census, 1990). One result has been a sharp decline in job opportunities and wages for less educated workers (Eisenberg, 1995).

As work shifts from manufacturing to service and information, many organizations are restructuring and downsizing. In the future, less work (only 20 percent, according to one knowledgeable prediction) will be done by full-time salaried employees and more by outside contractors, specialized consultants, and part-time or temporary help. More and more adults will be self-employed, working at home, or spreading their services among several employers (Handy, 1991). In the past, white males were the mainstay of the work force. Today a greater proportion of women are in the labor force than ever before: 57 percent in 1992 (H. Hayghe, U.S. Department of Labor, personal communication, March 1992). Between now and the year 2000, most people entering the labor force for the first time will be women, members of minority groups, or both (A. Kaplan, personal communication, 1993; Wharton, 1993). Will a changing economy be able to provide enough jobs for them?

Gender in the Workplace

The increase in women's employment is a global phenomenon (see Figure 8-3). A longer lifespan means that women no longer spend most or all of their adult lives raising children (Eisenberg, 1995). Trends toward later marriage, later childbearing, and smaller families, as well as flexible schedules and job sharing, have made it easier for women in some countries to pursue occupational goals. The typical European woman spends most of her life in the work force, with time out for childbearing and child raising (Jallinoja, 1989). Worldwide, 40 percent of women are involved in economic activity (United Nations, 1991), and the proportion is expected to reach 60 percent by the year 2000 (Nuss, Denti, & Viry, 1989). Women throughout the world tend to have clerical, sales, and service jobs, especially during the childrearing years (O'Grady-LeShane, 1993). And because their work is often part time and low-status, women the world over earn less than

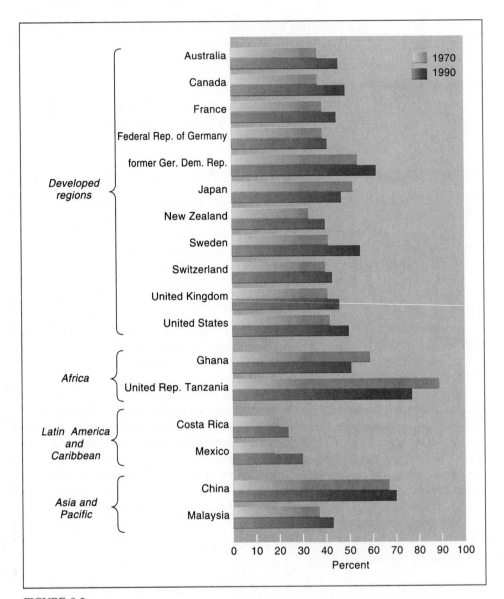

FIGURE 8-3

Economic activity rates of women in selected countries, 1970 and 1990. Women's participation in the work force has increased in developed regions, except for Japan. The dramatic increase in Mexico is due to greater opportunities for employment. The decline in Africa is due to poor economic growth.

(SOURCE: United Nations, 1991, table 8, reprinted in O'Grady-LeShane, 1993, p. 28.)

men (Bruce, Lloyd, & Leonard, 1995; United Nations, 1991). The gap is widest in Japan and narrowest in Tanzania.

In the United States, gender has far less to do with vocational choice than before. Today, 46 percent of American economists, 33 percent of computer analysts, and 28 percent of mail carriers—though only 15 percent of scientists, mathematicians, and engineers—are women (U.S. Department of Labor, 1992). More than 6 million women are executives, administrators, or managers—nearly twice as many as in 1980 (U.S. Bureau of the Census, 1990). But while there are more American women in business, government, and the professions than in the past, the top ranks are still male-dominated. Many younger women in middle-management positions complain of a "glass ceiling."

Laws mandating equal opportunity in employment are designed to give both sexes equal rights in hiring, pay, and promotion. But reality still falls far short of this ideal. For every dollar men earn, women who work full time earn only about 71 cents (U.S. Department of Labor—Women's Bureau, 1994). The gap between women's earnings in high executive positions and those of their male counterparts has widened from 21 percent to 35 percent in the past decade (C. Scott, 1993). However, the gap has narrowed for college-educated women as a whole; in an otherwise weakening wage structure, their earnings (adjusted for inflation) have risen 15 percent since 1979, while college-educated men's real earnings declined 3 percent (Mishel & Bernstein, 1994).

Minorities in the Workplace

In the United States in 1991, two-thirds of white and Hispanic people age 16 and older, but only about 63 percent of African Americans, were in the labor force; inclusion of 16- to 24-year-olds brought down these rates (Schick & Schick, 1994).

Employment rates and wages of African Americans have fallen in comparison with those of white people, despite the strides made by blacks since 1940 in education. About 80 percent of young adults of both races now finish high school, and differences in standardized test scores have narrowed. But more white people still go to college and qualify for better-paying jobs. The shrinkage of well-paid manufacturing jobs and the shift to lower-paid service positions has been particularly disastrous for young African American men (Bernstein, 1995); 46 percent of them held good blue-collar jobs in 1974, but only half as many by 1986 (Eisenberg, 1995).

Furthermore, the wage gap between white and African American male college graduates has widened even more than for those with less education (Bernstein, 1995). Foreign-born professionals earn approximately $4,000 more than native-born professionals of the same race. Among professionals, native-born black people have the lowest median salary, a little more than $26,000. Only 2 percent of African American professionals earn more than $100,000, compared with 44 percent of white, 41 percent of Asian, and 13 percent of Hispanic professionals (Bouvier & Simcox, 1994). Eight out of 10 female African American professionals work either in government or for nonprofit agencies (Berrios, 1993).

AGE AND JOB PERFORMANCE

Does age affect performance on the job? Findings of an analysis of more than 185 studies are mixed (Rhodes, 1983). Studies on absenteeism give conflicting results. Apparently that is because younger workers have more avoidable absences than older workers (possibly owing to a lower level of commitment), while older workers have more unavoidable absences (probably owing to poorer health and slower recovery from accidents).

When we look at how well adults do their work, the picture again is not clearcut. A key factor may be experience rather than age. When older people perform better, it may be because they have been on a job longer; and people in older cohorts may have changed jobs less than younger people. In general, age differences seem to depend largely on how performance is measured and on the demands of a specific kind of work. A job requiring quick reflexes is likely to be done better by a young person; a job that depends on mature judgment may be better handled by an older person.

A recent comprehensive study commissioned by the United States Congress found that, even in such highly demanding, responsible work as policing and firefighting, age in and of itself does not appear to be an accurate predictor of job performance (see Box 8-2). Many older workers are not only experienced and skilled but dependable, loyal, and respectful of authority (AARP, 1989b; Barth, McNaught, & Rizzi, 1993; Rix, 1994). Yet managers tend to assume that older workers are less energetic, less efficient, less flexible, and unwilling or unable to adapt to change; therefore, companies are less likely to invest in their training. In hard times older workers tend to be first to be laid off or pushed into retirement ("Negative Stereotypes," 1995; "Older Workers," 1993).

"Although psychologists have made substantial progress in dispelling age stereotypes, it is abundantly clear that there is work left to do. This is especially true in the workplace," writes Frank J. Landy (1994, p. 10), director of the Center for Applied Behavioral Sciences at Pennsylvania State University. The Age Discrimination in Employment Act (ADEA), as amended in 1986, protects most workers age 40 and older from being denied a job, fired, paid lower wages, or forced to retire because of age. The law applies to firms with 20 or more employees. ADEA has eliminated some blatant practices, such as help-wanted ads that specify "age 25 to 35." But, as Landy (1994, p. 10) observes, "many employers have been reluctant to recognize" the protections against age discrimination built into ADEA. Complaints of unfair terminations and pay and promotional policies and unequal availability of training are increasing; and, with a growing backlog of cases, the Equal Employment Opportunity Commission is averaging nearly 1 year to investigate each. Furthermore, age discrimination can often be very difficult to prove. A worker has to establish that it was age, not some other reason the employer may come up with, which actually motivated an action. A review of almost 700 cases filed between 1970 and the mid-1980s (C. J. Snyder & G. V. Barrett, 1988) found that the employer had won about two-thirds of the time.

BOX 8-2

THE CUTTING EDGE

Age Discrimination and Public Safety

Should the police, firefighters, prison guards, and others doing dangerous work essential to public safety be required to retire at age 65?

When the United States Congress amended the Age Discrimination in Employment Act (ADEA) in 1986 to outlaw mandatory retirement, it left an exception for public safety officers, pending study of whether older workers could be counted on to protect the public. The exception was to expire at the end of 1993.

An interdisciplinary task force commissioned by Congress spent almost 2 years reviewing more than 5,000 research articles and collecting data from more than 500 cities. The chair was Frank Landy (1992, 1994), professor of psychology and director of the Center for Applied Behavioral Sciences at Pennsylvania State University. The task force examined effects of age on critical abilities, as well as the probability that a disabling medical emergency, such as a heart attack or stroke, would occur on the job, endangering the public.

The research team uncovered some interesting facts. The age at which public safety officers were required to retire in various places ranged from 55 to 72. Only 30 percent of an officer's time was spent on tasks that directly involved public safety; the rest of the time, a firefighter, for example, might be cleaning equipment, cooking meals, inspecting dwellings for smoke detectors, or giving tours of the firehouse to schoolchildren.

The study, echoing lifespan psychologists, found that physical fitness and mental abilities varied increasingly with age and differed more within age groups than between age groups. In fact, 60- to 65-year-old public safety officers were more fit overall than 45- to 55-year-olds, probably because those who are not fit leave such jobs early. Any decline in abilities critical to perform-

(Grantpix/Monkmeyer)

Public safety officers tend to be more physically and mentally fit at 65 than at 45, perhaps because those who are not fit don't stay on the job that long.

ing public safety tasks was slight, on average, and was not uniform; some people declined faster than others, some not at all, and some improved with age, depending largely on lifestyle, nutrition, exercise, and health.

The conclusion? Tests of specific psychological, physical, and perceptual-motor abilities can predict job performance far better than a person's age. Furthermore, the likelihood is very small that a disabling medical emergency such as a heart attack or stroke will jeopardize performance of a critical task. In a 500-member police department, such an episode might occur only once in 25 years. And since many tasks directly involving public safety are done in teams, a partner could take over in such a rare event. The task force

(CONTINUED)

BOX 8-2

CONTINUED

noted that older officers often move into safe desk jobs, where they can share their knowledge with younger workers. The researchers recommended replacing the mandatory retirement age with tests (which already exist) to assess the ability of particular individuals to perform on the job. The bottom line? There are no grounds for the idea that older workers *as a group* endanger public safety.

However, that is not the end of the story. During the Congressional debates, unions representing public safety officers attacked the methods, procedures, results, and even the goals and motives of the study. They opposed forcing older workers to undergo periodic fitness tests, a proposal they had consistently fought in contract negotiations. The unions also feared that the report, in downplaying the risks and stress of public safety work, would call into question their members' large pension benefits (Landy, 1994). But the mandatory retirement provision lapsed, despite attempts in the House of Representatives to make it permanent; thus forced retirement of public safety officers is now unlawful.

Political fallout aside, the task force established a benchmark that will have an influence beyond this specific legislation. Its findings and recommendations have already begun to be cited in court cases. Landy (1994) concludes that there is "a clear recognition now of the scientific foundation for eliminating this last vestige of age discrimination" (p. 20).

OCCUPATIONAL STRESS

The Japanese have a word for it: *karoshi*, "death from overwork." One survey found that 40 percent of Japanese workers are afraid of literally working themselves to death.

Occupational stress—stress that is job-related—has become a worldwide epidemic, and not only in the executive suite. It affects waitresses in Sweden and bus drivers in continental Europe. It strikes in developing countries, where assembly-line workers must cope with the unfamiliar strains of industrialization (United Nations International Labor Organization, UNILO, 1993). In the United States, estimated costs of stress-related injuries and diseases have reached $200 billion a year in soaring worker's compensation claims, medical expenses, health insurance, absenteeism, and loss of productivity (UNILO, 1993). In Japan, 40 percent of teachers have health problems that may be stress-related. Table 8-1 lists some important sources of stress for women on the job.

A combination of high-pressure demands with little autonomy or control and little pride in the product is a major pattern of stress (UNILO, 1993; Williams, 1991). Studies of 30- to 60-year-old men in a range of occupations found that men experiencing these conditions were 3 times more likely than other men to have high blood pressure and to show changes in heart muscles that often precede heart attacks (Schnall et al., 1990). The studies controlled for smoking, alcohol, type A behavior, and several other factors. Stress is particularly prevalent among older industrial workers, who may have trouble—or may fear they will have trouble—keeping up physically with the faster pace of new equipment (DeCarlo & Gruenfeld, 1989).

Another major cause of stress on the job is conflict with supervisors, subordinates, and coworkers (Bolger, DeLongis, Kessler, & Schilling, 1989). Dissension at work may be especially trying because people tend to suppress their anger instead of expressing it. Most self-reported incidents of stress have to do with work overload—in the case of women, both at home and on the job.

Women and members of minority groups often feel special pressures in the workplace, especially in corporations, where their superiors generally are white men. Many companies have programs to help women develop positive ways to cope with occupational stress. One high-technology company established training opportunities and support groups for women; under conditions of safety and trust, women workers feel supported by management and can work more productively (A. Kaplan, personal communication, 1993). Another approach is to train female workers to become more assertive and task-oriented, behave more impersonally, and think more analytically. A third suggested approach, based on qualities commonly thought to be women's strengths, is to offer workshops for both male and female employees on how people can work together more effectively (I. Stiver, personal communication, 1993).

TABLE 8-1   SOURCES OF STRESS FOR WOMEN ON THE JOB

Rank	Stressor
1	Lack of promotions or raises
2	Low pay
3	Monotonous, repetitive work
4	No input into decision making
5	Heavy work load or overtime
6	Supervision problems
7	Unclear job descriptions
8	Unsupportive boss
9	Inability or reluctance to express frustration or anger
10	Production quotas
11	Difficulty juggling home and family responsibilities
12	Inadequate breaks
13	Sexual harassment

NOTE: Working conditions are listed in the order in which they were reported by 915 female office workers. In most cases the stressors are similar to those reported by workers in general, but there are some differences. Whereas these women rank low pay as the second greatest source of stress, this item is generally eighth or ninth in importance to men. Sexual harassment is almost always a woman's problem. One surprise is the low ranking for "juggling work schedule with home and family responsibilities," below elements of work life itself.
SOURCE: Adapted from Working Women Education Fund, 1981, p. 9.

(Frank Siteman/Stock, Boston)

Sexual harassment on the job can be a source of stress, but it can be difficult to distinguish from normal behavior between the sexes. To constitute illegal harassment, an incident must be part of a severe, pervasive pattern creating a work environment that a reasonable person would find hostile and abusive.

Sexual harassment is a stressor that is getting much attention these days. The psychological pressure created by unwelcome sexual overtures, particularly from a superior, can be extremely distressing. But distinguishing between harassment and normal behavior between the sexes has been a vexing problem. The United States Supreme Court has held that to constitute *sexual harassment,* behavior must be so "severe and pervasive" as to create a working environment that "a reasonable person would find hostile or abusive," whether or not the victim suffers actual psychological harm. A hostile or abusive environment is not merely offensive; it is one that may interfere with performance, impede advancement, or affect psychological well-being—for example, a workplace "permeated with 'discriminatory intimidation, ridicule, and insult'" (Equal Employment Opportunity Commission, 1994, p. 7166). Sexual harassment is a violation of Title VII of the Civil Rights Act; complaints can be filed with the Equal Employment Opportunity Commission.

Burnout may be a result of work-related stress; it involves emotional exhaustion, a feeling of being unable to accomplish anything on the job, and a sense of helplessness and loss of control. It is especially common among people in the helping professions (such as teaching, medicine, therapy, social work, and police work) who feel frustrated by their inability to help people as much as they would like to. Burnout is usually a response to long-term stress rather than a reaction to an immediate crisis. Its symptoms include fatigue, insomnia, headaches, persistent colds, stomach disorders, abuse of alcohol or drugs, and trouble getting along with people. A burned-out worker may quit a job suddenly, may pull away from family and friends, and may sink into depression (Briley, 1980; Maslach & Jackson, 1985).

UNEMPLOYMENT

Perhaps the greatest work-related stressor is sudden, unexpected loss of a job. The usual official unemployment rate in the United States is about 7 percent of the work force. In 1991, about 13 percent of black women and 12 percent of black men in the work force were unemployed, as compared with approximately 6 percent of whites and 10 percent of Hispanics (Schick & Schick, 1994).

Research on unemployment since the 1930s (concentrating almost entirely on men) has linked it to physical and mental illness (such as heart attack, stroke, depression, and anxiety); to marital and family problems; to health, psychological, and behavior problems in children; and to suicide, homicide, and other crimes (Brenner, 1991; Merva & Fowles, 1992; Voydanoff, 1990). Stress comes not only from loss of income and the resulting financial hardships, but also from the effect of this loss on the unemployed person's self-concept. Workers who derive their identity from their work, men who define manhood as supporting a family, and people who define their worth in terms of the dollar value of their work lose more than their paychecks when they lose their jobs. They lose a piece of themselves and their self-esteem (Voydanoff, 1987, 1990).

Women are as likely as men to feel upset over loss of a job. In a study of former employees of a plant in Indiana that closed in 1982, the unemployed of both sexes reported headaches, stomach trouble, and high blood pressure, and felt less in control of their lives (Perrucci, Perrucci, & Targ, 1988).

A sense of control has been identified as crucial to coping with unemployment. A study of 190 unemployed workers found that those who believed they had some influence on their circumstances were less anxious and depressed, had fewer physical symptoms, and had higher self-esteem and life satisfaction than those who believed external forces were in control (Cvetanovski & Jex, 1994).

Those who cope best with unemployment have some financial resources to draw on, often savings or earnings of other family members. Rather than blaming themselves for losing their jobs, or seeing themselves as failures, they assess their situation more objectively. They have the support of understanding, adaptable families and friends (Voydanoff, 1990). People who can look at loss of a job as a challenge for growth may develop emotionally and professionally. They may change not only jobs but the entire direction of their careers.

WORK, LEISURE, AND INTELLECTUAL GROWTH

Do people change as a result of what kind of work they do and how they use their leisure time? Some research says yes.

A combination of cross-sectional and longitudinal studies (Kohn, 1980) revealed a reciprocal relationship between the *substantive complexity* of work— the degree of thought and independent judgment it requires—and a person's flexibility in coping with intellectual demands. People with more complex work tend to become more flexible thinkers; and flexible thinkers are likely to continue doing more complex work. Why is the complexity of work tied so closely to intellectual growth? One reason may be that, in a society in which work plays a central role in people's lives, mastery of complex tasks gives people confidence in their ability to handle problems. It also may open their minds to new experience and stimulate them to become more self-directed.

Nor does growth stop at the end of the work day; what kind of work people do affects and is affected by what they do in other areas of life. People with substantively complex work "come to engage in more intellectually demanding leisure-time activities. In short, the lessons of work are directly carried over to nonoccupational realms" (Kohn, 1980, p. 204).

This idea of a link between work and leisure—because learning is carried over from one to the other (the *spillover hypothesis*) or because of personality factors that affect both—is one of several ways of looking at the two domains. Three other hypotheses are: (1) *Compensation hypothesis*—Leisure activities make up for what is missing in work (Wilensky, 1960). People who do dull work look for stimulating leisure activities; people who do challenging work let down and relax during their time off. (2) *Resource provision-depletion hypothesis*—Work promotes or constrains certain kinds of leisure activities by providing or depleting resources of time, energy, and money (Staines, 1980). (3) *Segmentation hypothesis*—Work and leisure are independent; choices in one area have no relationship to the other (Dubin, 1956; Kabanoff, 1980).

A follow-up to the initial research on substantive complexity of work explored more deeply the relationship between work and intellectual aspects of leisure (Miller & Kohn, 1983). The key finding, supporting the spillover hypothesis, was that the substantive complexity of work—more than any other aspect of a job situation—strongly influences the intellectual level of leisure activities for both men and women, regardless of income and educational level.

For many adults, it seems, work and leisure are two sides of the same coin; choices in one facet of life affect the other. If so, then the kind of work people do should make a difference in how they spend their time after retirement. And, in a society in which work is increasingly complex and leisure options are more sophisticated, we can expect to see continuing intellectual gains in late life.

RETIREMENT AND OTHER LATE-LIFE OPTIONS

▼

Retirement is a relatively new idea. It took hold in many industrialized countries during the late nineteenth and early twentieth centuries; but in less developed countries, most people still work until they are no longer physically able.

In the United States, the economic depression of the 1930s was the impetus for the social security system—which, together with company-sponsored pension plans negotiated by labor unions, opened the door to almost universal retirement at age 65. But retirement, like many other aspects of adult development, has become far more complicated than it once was. With mandatory retirement virtually outlawed as a form of age discrimination, adults have far more choices, among them early retirement, retiring from one career to start another, working part time to keep busy or to supplement income, going back to school, doing volunteer work, pursuing other leisure interests—or not retiring at all.

(UPI/Bettmann)

At 87 the comedian George Burns vowed never to retire. He was still going strong in his late nineties.

TO RETIRE OR NOT TO RETIRE

"I get shivers thinking about not working. I'd hate to sit in a park. . . . Retirement is death."

"I can't wait. . . . It should be as delightful as the rest of my life has been, just a different way of investing my activity."

These contrasting comments exemplify the wide range of feelings adults in the latter part of middle age have about the prospect of retirement. One researcher (Karp, 1989) interviewed 72 white professional men and women in their fifties about their work and their attitudes toward retirement. The respondents fell into three groups: (1) those who were so attached to their work that they did not want to imagine retiring; (2) those who were looking forward to retirement as an opportunity to do things they hadn't had time for; and (3) a middle group who had mixed feelings or simply hadn't yet thought much about retirement. In general, those who were in good health, were very happy at work, were still striving to achieve unfinished career goals, or felt financially insecure had the most negative attitudes toward retirement.

Nowadays there are plenty of role models for continuing to work in old age. "I—will—never—retire!" wrote the comedian George Burns (1983, p. 138) at age 87. "I firmly believe that you should keep working as long as you can." Burns, who was still performing in his late nineties, is one of a considerable number of late-life achievers who keep their minds and bodies active doing the work they love. The actress Jessica Tandy, at 81, won an Academy Award for her starring role in the film *Driving Miss Daisy* and went on to another Oscar nomination for

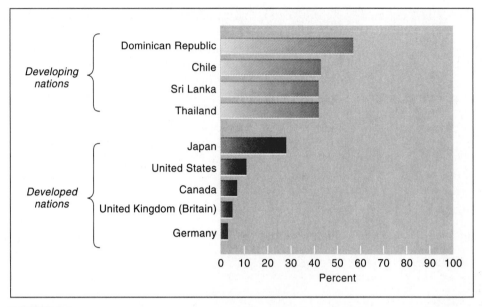

FIGURE 8-4

Percentage of older adults in the work force, selected countries.

NOTE: Percentages for developing nations are for people age 60 and over; percentages for developed nations are for people age 65 and older.

(SOURCES: Commonwealth Fund, 1992; Kaiser, 1993.)

Fried Green Tomatoes. When she died at 85 in 1994, she was up for an Emmy award. At 91, Armand Hammer headed Occidental Petroleum (Wallechinsky & Wallace, 1993). Julia Child was still writing cookbooks at 80. During the 10 years before his death at 80, Jonas Salk was working on an AIDS vaccine (Bronte, 1993; Schmeck, 1995). Many other people without famous names quietly go to work each day as typists, lawyers, nurses, or cashiers.

Still, most adults who can retire do retire. Among industrialized countries, the working elderly range from only 3 percent of all older adults in Germany to 28 percent in Japan (Commonwealth Fund, 1992; see Figure 8-4). In the United States, the proportion of older men in the labor force has fallen steadily. In 1900, 2 out of 3 men age 65 and over were working; in 1950, almost 1 in 2; and today, only about 1 in 6, or 16 percent (AARP, 1994; Quinn, 1993). For older women, the pattern has been different. Their participation in the labor force increased slightly in the first half of the twentieth century, then fell again, and has now stabilized at around 8 percent (AARP, 1994; U.S. Bureau of the Census, 1992b; Schick & Schick, 1994).

Men who continue to work after age 65 tend to be better educated than those who retire. They are more likely to be in good health, and they may have wives who are still working. Not surprisingly, they strongly want to work and do *not* want to retire, whereas retired men show little or no interest in working. The fundamental difference seems to be whether or not men view paid work as necessary to self-fulfillment (Parnes & Sommers, 1994).

In most of the developing world, large numbers of older adults continue to work for income: more than 40 percent in Sri Lanka, Thailand, and Chile and 57 percent in the Dominican Republic, according to a United Nations study (Kaiser, 1993). However, their main means of support is not work but aid from their children—except in Chile, where pensions are sizable. In all four countries, older adults remain economically and socially useful, engaging in household tasks and family and community functions such as teaching, counseling, negotiating marriages, and leading religious rituals; still, more than 90 percent cannot or can barely meet their basic needs. Although the great majority say they are satisfied with their lives, it is questionable how much real choice they have, in comparison with older adults in developed nations such as the United States.

FINANCING RETIREMENT

Why do people retire? Poor health is a factor in some decisions (Sammartino, 1987), but usually not the most important factor (Parnes & Sommers, 1994). More important is financial security, which usually depends on some sort of public or private retirement plan.

In many parts of the world, adults contemplating retirement can look forward to variations on one or more of four kinds of government-sponsored old age protection. Workers in most industrialized countries, including the United States, get *social insurance.* Lifetime benefits, based on prior contributions by employers, employees, or both, depend on how long a person worked and how much he or she earned. A few developed countries have *universal pensions* for all citizens as a matter of right, independent of prior earnings; and a few have a combination of the two systems. Some, such as the United Kingdom and the United States, also have *voluntary pension plans* encouraged by tax deferrals or other devices. Some developing countries have government-run *provident funds,* compulsory savings plans funded by employer and employee. At retirement, a worker gets the money in a lump sum. Often certain groups, such as agricultural workers, are not covered, and the funds are frequently inadequate for long-term protection (O'Grady-LeShane, 1993; Schulz, 1993b; see Table 8-2).

In most developing countries, social insurance programs have had a spotty record. Often a majority of the population, especially workers in the "informal sector" and in rural areas, are left out, and mismanagement is common (Schulz, 1993c, p. 70; see Box 8-3). A new system in Chile—a variation on the provident fund, combined with public regulation and financial guarantees—may represent a meaningful alternative. While preliminary results are promising, there are questions about whether the plan can survive downturns in investment markets and provide enough income for future retirees (Schulz, 1993c).

In the United States, many workers can retire and live relatively comfortably. (See Figure 8-5 for a breakdown of older adults' sources of income.) Between 1968 and 1987, partly because of cost-of-living adjustments and increases in social security benefits, the poverty rate for older Americans was reduced from 28.5 percent to 12.2 percent (Monk, 1994). However, with a growing elderly population and proportionately fewer workers contributing to the social security system, it seems likely that benefits—in real dollars—will not continue to rise and

TABLE 8-2   TYPES OF OLD-AGE PROTECTION SYSTEMS IN VARIOUS PARTS OF THE WORLD

Country	Universal Pension	Social Insurance	Provident Fund
Developed regions			
Australia*	X		
Canada	X	X	
France		X	
Germany		X	
Japan		X	
New Zealand	X		
Sweden	X	X	
Switzerland		X	
United Kingdom		X	
United States		X	
Africa			
Ghana			X
United Rep. Tanzania			X
Latin America and Caribbean			
Costa Rica			X
Mexico			X
Asia and Pacific			
China†			
Malaysia			X

*The age pension is a flat-rate, means-tested benefit funded from general revenues.
†China has an employment-related system for employees in state-run enterprises and a separate program for government and party officials.
NOTE: Some countries have more than one social protection system.
SOURCES: O'Grady-LeShane, 1993, p. 29; based on data from Organization for Economic Cooperation and Development, 1988, p. 17; Tracy & Pampel, 1991, pp. xi–xix; USDHHS, 1988.

may even decline. As for private pensions, a shift from defined benefit plans that guarantee a fixed retirement income to riskier defined contribution plans, in which benefits depend on returns from invested funds, is making the financial future less certain for many workers (Rix, 1994).

Between 1950 and 1990, the median retirement age in the United States dropped from 67 to 63 (Farrell, Palmer, Atchison, & Andelman, 1994). About 3 out of 4 American workers, both men and women, now retire before age 65—many in their late fifties (Monk, 1994). Many companies are downsizing and are therefore offering strong incentives to encourage early retirement. Often private pension plans penalize employees who continue to work past the early sixties (Quinn, 1993). However, for those who live long enough, social security can have the opposite effect, penalizing early retirement. The trend toward early retirement among men appears to have leveled off. Among women, it has been offset by a rise in midlife careers (Quinn, 1993).

BOX 8-3

THE MULTICULTURAL CONTEXT

Work and Retirement in China

Karl Marx, the father of communism, hoped to dignify workers—and end exploitation of the working class—through communal ownership of all property and means of production. Today the People's Republic of China is the last major communist power in the world. Its economy has unique characteristics, some of which are influenced by the country's long cultural history.

How do China's workers fare? The answer depends on whether they live in urban or rural areas (Hayward & Wang, 1993).

In cities such as Shanghai, almost 80 percent of the population work for large state-owned enterprises. Pay is set by a national wage scale according to occupation and seniority, regardless of profit or individual productivity. Workers get free medical care and disability pay.

Because of chronic unemployment among young urban dwellers, China in 1978 instituted retirement policies to ensure regular turnover. Employers can require workers to retire, generally at age 60 for men and age 50 for women. A special feature of the system is that a worker who retires can let his or her child take over the job. After this policy went into effect, as many as 80 percent of new retirees were replaced by their children (Davis-Friedmann, 1983).

Pension benefits range from 60 to 75 percent of a worker's latest income. Pensions are not automatic, however; they are granted by a government agency, which reviews the applicant's work history, health, finances, and political record. Thus, the state, as well as the employer, is directly involved in individual retirement decisions. Some workers are not allowed to retire, others are called back to work after retirement, and some are required to do neighborhood maintenance or public service work, paid or unpaid.

Retirees can continue to work in industry and earn money—supposedly, no more than before retirement, but this proviso is often ignored. In China—by contrast with many western countries—skilled older urban workers, who tend to be better educated and better trained than younger workers, are often at an advantage in the job market, especially since the rise of small, privately owned businesses. Thus, healthy older adults can earn more after retirement than before. Their pension funds together with their potential earning power make them central to the economic life of the multigenerational family, reversing the traditional pattern of kinship obligations in which children supported the older generation (Davis-Friedmann, 1985).

However, the picture is very different for rural workers—almost 80 percent of the Chinese labor force. The land is owned by the people, not the state. Between 1949 (the year of the communist revolution) and 1978, farmers were organized in communal households and had to meet government production quotas (Davis-Friedmann, 1983). Now, in most areas, farm production is controlled by family households, which contract with state grain production offices. As a result of this decentralized system, there is little government management of day-to-day work (Gui, 1989). Few farm workers receive government pensions; and for those who do, the income may amount to one-fourth or less of what urban workers get.

Retirement in rural communities typically means, not stopping work, but a shift in the type of work a person does. Older men turn over the most laborious aspects of farm work to their sons but continue to do less strenuous tasks into their seventies. Older women confine themselves to household chores. Parents usually live in the home of the oldest married son. Lacking adequate pensions, they must depend on their children (Davis-Friedmann, 1983). However, declining fertility and the exodus of young adults to urban areas are eroding this tradition.

As rural areas become more developed, the state can be expected to take a more active role in providing for elderly workers. In better-off regions, social security systems similar to those for urban workers are likely to emerge. In impoverished communities, public welfare and family support (already showing signs of strain) must somehow be made to serve the needs of older adults until economic development takes place.

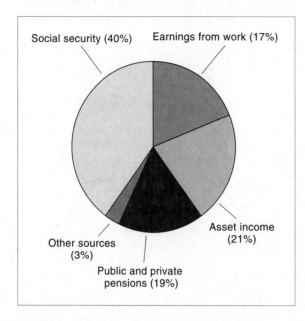

Social security (40%)   Earnings from work (17%)

Other sources
(3%)

Public and private
pensions (19%)

Asset income
(21%)

FIGURE 8-5
Sources of income of older Americans.
(SOURCE: AARP, 1994.)

PREPARING FOR RETIREMENT

"Being useful is essential to my sense of who I am," says a librarian who "slid" into retirement and has mixed feelings about the decision. "My job gave my life structure. It was the thing around which everything else revolved."

Retirement is an important transition. Preparation can be a key to making that transition successful and rewarding. Ideally, retirement planning should begin by middle age.

How well are today's middle-aged adults planning for retirement? In a recent study of 45- to 59-year-olds, 4 in 10 respondents said they had saved too little or nothing at all for retirement, and 2 out of 3 expected to have serious problems living on their retirement incomes (Rix, 1994). The "baby boom" generation, who will start retiring early in the twenty-first century, as a group are better educated and have higher incomes than their parents; and many couples will have social security and pension benefits from two wage-earners rather than one. But it has been estimated that—short of selling their homes—they would need to triple their current savings rate to maintain their present living standard after retirement (Farrell et al., 1994). And if social security and pension benefits do not keep pace with cost of living, many "boomers"—especially minorities, single women, and the poorly educated, who will depend heavily on social security—may suffer real hardships (Farrell et al., 1994; Rix, 1994).

Planning for retirement should include not only providing for financial needs, but structuring life to make it enjoyable and productive after retirement, anticipating physical or emotional problems, and discussing how retirement will affect a spouse. Assistance can come from preretirement workshops, self-help books, and company-sponsored programs.

HOW DO RETIRED PEOPLE USE THEIR TIME?

"Most people I know who are retired are so busy that they don't know how they found time to work," says a retired speech therapist.

Someone who retires does not become a new person overnight; lifelong habits and attitudes generally continue to influence behavior (J. R. Kelly, 1994). The work ethic by which many people have lived throughout their adult lives may translate into what has been called a *busy ethic*—a need to keep busy and active so as not to appear or feel lazy or useless (Ekerdt, 1986). Thus one study found that the most satisfied retirees are physically fit people who are using their skills in part-time paid or volunteer work (Schick, 1986). Let's look at three ways of using time after retirement: paid work, volunteerism, and leisure activities.

Paid Work after Retirement

Some people are not happy unless they are gainfully employed. Some retirees find part-time or new full-time jobs; some (who may call themselves "semi-retired") keep doing what they were doing before but cut down on their hours and responsibilities. Self-employed men are less likely to make an abrupt switch from full-time work to complete retirement (Burkhauser & Quinn, 1989). A longitudinal study of men originally identified as gifted in childhood found that those who had been self-employed at any time before retirement were more likely to do some type of part-time work after retirement (Elder & Pavalko, 1993).

Volunteerism

Since the late 1960s, the proportion of older adults doing volunteer work has nearly quadrupled, from 11 percent to about 40 percent; this figure includes nearly 1 out of 3 people over 75 (Chambre, 1993). Most older volunteers work alongside adults of all ages, more than half in churches or synagogues. Countless community-based programs are built specifically around older volunteers. Government-sponsored services include retired executives who advise small businesses, retired accountants who help fill out tax returns, senior companions who visit frail elderly people in their homes, and foster grandparents who for a small stipend provide social and emotional support to neglected or autistic children, teenage parents, and substance abusers.

What accounts for this increase in volunteerism? One reason is a changing public image of older adults and their capabilities—a recognition that older people can be active, healthy, contributing members of a community. Then, volunteer work itself has taken on higher status. Finally, today's better-educated older population has more to contribute and more interest in contributing (Chambre, 1993).

In less developed nations, such as India, Cameroon, and Malta, older adults regularly make useful, informal, unpaid contributions, such as looking after children, working with local officials and civic organizations to solve community problems, and checking on elderly neighbors who may be ill or in need of help (S. C. Taylor, 1993). Finding ways to use older volunteers most effectively will be a worldwide challenge in coming years.

(Joel Gordon)

Many retired people find satisfaction in sharing skills and experience accumulated over a lifetime. Gwendolyn Stanley volunteers in a prison nursery on Rikers Island, where she teaches mothers parenting skills and helps them care for their infants.

Leisure during Retirement

For many retirees, life in some ways is not much different from before. There is simply more time for the same kinds of leisure activities they always enjoyed.

Interviews with 25 "unexceptional" men and women of modest means, who had retired from routine jobs at a midwestern food-processing plant, revealed more continuity than change in lifestyles. These people, none of whom were college-educated, were "aging in place" in the homes they had lived in before. Most had made only vague plans for what they wanted to do. After taking one or two car trips and perhaps doing a few projects around the house, they had settled into new yet familiar routines. The important difference was a new sense of freedom ("I can do what I want to do when I want to do it") and relief from pressure, fatigue, and ringing alarm clocks (J. R. Kelly, 1994, p. 490). Their activities were generally accessible and low-cost and revolved around family, home, and companions: conversation, watching television, visiting with family and friends, informal entertaining, going to inexpensive restaurants, playing cards, or just doing "what comes along" (J. R. Kelly, 1994, p. 491).

Interestingly, none of these retirees participated in activities for senior citizens. One explanation for this often-observed phenomenon is the concept of the *ageless self*—the idea that people tend to see themselves as the same person regardless of how old they get (Kaufman, 1986). Because many older adults do not think of themselves as fundamentally different from before, they may avoid activities that redefine them as "old."

The *family-focused lifestyle* of the former factory workers was one of two common patterns of retirement activity identified in an earlier study by the same researcher (J. R. Kelly, 1987). The other pattern—*balanced investment*—was typical of more educated people who allocated their time more equally among family, work, and leisure. These patterns may change with age. Younger retirees who were most satisfied with their quality of life were those who traveled regularly and went to cultural events; after 75, family- and home-based activity yielded the most satisfaction (J. R. Kelly, Steinkamp, & Kelly, 1986). A Canadian study (Mannell, 1993) found that retirees who were extraordinarily satisfied with their lives engaged in *serious leisure*—activity that "demands skill, attention, and commitment" (J. R. Kelly, 1994, p. 502). Sunday painters, amateur carpenters, and others who have made an effort to become good at something they love often use their expanded leisure time during retirement to make this interest the central focus of their lives.

An ethnic perspective on leisure comes from a nationwide survey of nearly 1,700 older Americans. Fewer than 1 in 4 older African Americans engage in outdoor sports—such as boating, bird watching, golf, or tennis—compared with 85 percent or more of older whites, Hispanics, and Native Americans. Most older African Americans do things that produce something useful, such as sewing, gardening, and fishing. Perhaps because poverty and racial discrimination have shut them out of many leisure activities throughout their lives, they may not think of doing things just for fun. Or they may continue to lack the resources to do so (M. B. Brown & Tedrick, 1993).

There are many paths to enjoying retirement, but they have two things in common: doing satisfying things and having satisfying relationships. For most older people, both "are an extension of histories that have developed throughout the life course" (J. R. Kelly, 1994, p. 501).

HOW DOES RETIREMENT AFFECT WELL-BEING?

A familiar saying, "It's better to be rich and healthy than poor and sick," sums up many people's feelings about retirement. Not surprisingly, retirees who are financially secure and feel well are happier in retirement than those who miss their income and do not feel well enough to enjoy their leisure (Barfield & Morgan, 1974, 1978; Bossé, Aldwin, Levenson, & Workman-Daniels, 1991). A common fear is that retirement may erode financial security and health, as well as supportive social contacts.

Becoming Poor in Retirement

Married couples rarely become poor after retirement, especially if they have pension benefits. When a husband dies, however, his widow is 4 times as likely as a married person to fall below the poverty line (Burkhauser, Holden, & Feaster, 1988). Older women are almost twice as likely to be poor as older men (15 percent as compared with 8 percent), and older people who live alone or with nonrelatives are about 4 times as likely to be poor as older persons who live with family members (AARP, 1994).

Because many jobs typically held by minority-group workers are not covered by social security, these workers are more likely than others to end up on Old Age Assistance. More than one-fourth of older African American adults and one-fifth of elderly Hispanics are poor, compared with only 11 percent of older white adults (AARP, 1994).

Money and health are the main worries of retired people, and the cost of long-term health care is one of the most significant worries of all. To allay the risk of poverty resulting from long-term illness, many people believe there is need for a government-sponsored, self-supporting insurance program (Hurd, 1989).

Physical and Mental Health

Retirement itself generally has little effect on physical health (Herzog, House, & Morgan, 1991; Palmore, Fillenbaum, & George, 1984), but does it affect mental health? The answer may depend on when and why people retire. An analysis of data from six longitudinal studies—three national and three local—found that although retirement generally has little effect on morale, early retirement, which is often a result of poor health, tends to lead to greater declines in health and in satisfaction (Palmore et al., 1984). Among 1,516 older men surveyed in the cross-sectional Boston Veterans Administration Normative Aging Study, retirees were more likely than workers to report depression, obsessive-compulsive behavior, and physical symptoms with no organic cause. Those who had retired early (before age 62) or late (after age 65) reported the most symptoms (Bossé, Aldwin, Levenson, & Ekerdt, 1987). It's possible, then, that retirement did not bring on their mental problems, but rather that they retired when they did because they were having problems. A study of 200 men in the same sample who had retired in the previous year suggested that "those who are forced to retire unexpectedly or involuntarily, for reasons of health, plant closings, etc., or who experience health or financial declines after retirement may experience greater retirement stress than those whose retirement is voluntary, on schedule, and not financially burdensome" (Bossé et al., 1991, p. P13).

A study that looked directly at the effects of voluntary versus involuntary retirement found that, at least for people age 65 and older, those who had control over the decision were more satisfied with their lives and had less cognitive impairment than those who did not (Herzog et al., 1991). These findings are consistent with earlier research that found negative effects of unexpected or involuntary retirement (Beck, 1982).

Unexpected or involuntary retirement may affect women especially severely (Matthews & Brown, 1988). Interviews with 124 women and 176 men who had been retired about 8 years and were living in an urban area of Ontario, Canada, found that although retirement was not traumatic in general, the strongest predictor of its effect on morale was whether or not people retired at a time of their own choosing. Women were more likely than men to have to retire for reasons having to do with other people—for example, the retirement or infirmity of a spouse or some other family member.

During retirement, leisure-time friends may replace coworkers as sources of social support.

Social Support

For most adults, work is a convenient source of social contact; and social contact can be an important source of support, especially as people age. Does the loss of these extensive, regular contacts with coworkers (who may also be friends and confidants) affect people's well-being after retirement?

Cross-sectional comparisons have found that older adults who have been retired for a long time have fewer social contacts than more recent retirees or those who continue to work at least part time. But, while the extent of the social network and the frequency of contacts declines, the quality of support—having people to rely on in times of crisis—apparently does not. A 3-year longitudinal study of 1,311 relatively healthy older men in the Boston Normative Aging Study confirmed this finding (Bossé, Aldwin, Levenson, Spiro, & Mroczek, 1993). Two lifespan developmental explanations for this phenomenon are *convoy theory* and *selectivity theory.*

Convoy theory, proposed by Robert Kahn and Toni Antonucci (1980), distinguishes relationships in terms of their relative intimacy. Only a person's outer circles of social contact are significantly affected by retirement. Coworkers in these circles tend to drop away, to be replaced by new leisure friends or by more time spent with other friends and acquaintances. But, regardless of what happens to these relatively casual friendships, retirees still have a stable inner circle of close friends and family members and thus do not feel a loss of social support or well-being.

Laura Carstensen's (1991) *selectivity theory* focuses on changes in how social contacts function in adult life. According to this theory, social interaction has three functions: (1) it is a source of information; (2) it helps people develop and maintain a sense of self; and (3) it is a source of pleasure or emotional well-being. The first two functions—information and identity—decline, because they are needed less as time goes on; but the emotional function, which depends on the quality of social support, becomes central. Retired people become more selective about their social interactions so as to maintain a high quality of dependable social support—people they truly enjoy and can count on in time of need. Thus, far from diminishing well-being, limitations on an aging person's social support network can be positive and adaptive.

HOW DOES RETIREMENT AFFECT SOCIETY?

Whether and when people retire affects not only themselves and their immediate families but society as a whole. Almost all industrialized countries are concerned about the cost of supporting their growing older populations. In the United States, massive federal deficits have raised serious doubts about the ability to continue to fund social security entitlements (Crown, 1993). One response has been to encourage older adults to keep working, by eliminating mandatory retirement and raising the age for collecting full social security benefits (slated to rise from 65 to 67 in 2003). On the other hand, unemployment and high labor costs for experienced workers create pressures for policies to nudge (or push) older people out of the work force, as is done in France, Germany, and the Netherlands.

The social impact of retirement is closely linked to the *dependency ratio:* the comparative size of the productive and dependent parts of a population. With older adults living longer and growing in numbers, the portion of the population in the productive years (age 18 to 64) will diminish relative to the portion presumed to be dependent (age 65 or older). In the United States this ratio is expected to drop from 5.5 in 1980 to 2.5 in 2040 (Adamchak & Friedmann, 1983), suggesting that in the future there may not be enough workers to support the aging population. But older people are not the only "dependent" group. As the number of older Americans increases, the number of children and teenagers will decline, keeping *total* dependency below what it was in 1960, when the "baby boomers" were growing up (Adamchak, 1993). An important question, then, is how willing working adults will be to assume more of a burden for supporting the older generation instead of the younger generation.

In actuality, of course, some older adults and some people under 18 work, while many people of "working age" do not. Thus a more realistic (though more difficult) way to calculate a dependency ratio is to look at who actually is and is not in the labor force. Studies that attempted to do this have concluded that the total burden on the working segment of the population is likely to *decrease* because there will be more workers, including more women and minorities, to share the load (Adamchak & Friedmann, 1983; Crown, 1993). This will be especially true if a large proportion of older adults in future cohorts remain in the work force.

Dependency calculations are only as good as the assumptions on which they are based—assumptions about birth, immigration, and unemployment rates, who participates in the labor force, when people retire, social policies and programs, patterns of aging, cultural attitudes, and other factors that are subject to change and hard to anticipate. Since all these factors vary considerably from one country to another, so will the costs and challenges of supporting a graying population. Above all, Crown (1993) argues, "the affordability of an aging population will be dictated largely by future economic growth" (p. 36). If workers' incomes in industrialized countries rise faster than tax rates to fund programs for the elderly, the dependency burden will be lighter.

We also need to recognize that adults, particularly women, who are not "working" often spend a considerable amount of time caring for their children, their grandchildren, their parents, and each other—a significant economic contribution that is not figured into dependency calculations or, usually, into pensions (O'Grady-LeShane, 1993). A United Nations (1991) report observed that if housework and family care were included in calculations of national productivity, the total world output would rise by 25 to 30 percent. Women's advocates argue that we need to redefine work to include caregiving functions that are still the central tasks of many women the world over, and that we need to find ways to compensate women for that work during their productive years and beyond (O'Grady-LeShane, 1993).

For both economic and psychological reasons, some experts, pointing to examples of productive aging in less developed cultures as well as in our own, are predicting an "end of retirement as we know it" (S. C. Taylor, 1993, p. 32). They do not mean a return to the harsh system of yesteryear—"work until you drop"—but a proliferation of options for productive activity that can benefit older adults and society as a whole. As M. W. Riley (1994) suggested, the later years could be made more satisfying by restructuring the course of life. Today, young adults generally plunge into education and careers, middle-aged people use most of their energy earning money, and some older people have trouble filling their time. If people at all ages wove more balanced proportions of study, work, and leisure into their lives, young adults would feel less pressure to establish themselves early, middle-aged people would feel less burdened, and older people who want to and are able to continue doing productive work would be more stimulated and would feel—and be—more useful.

SUMMARY

■ Increased longevity and changing social institutions may herald a change from age-differentiated to age-integrated roles.

EDUCATION

■ A large proportion of today's college students are of nontraditional age; a majority are women. Many dropped out and have returned to complete their education.

■ Lifelong learning is an important trend. Adult education takes a wide variety of forms, from college-level courses to programs that are practically or socially oriented.

■ Goals of older learners are to gain adaptive knowledge and skills, to train for new occupations, to understand and cope with technological and cultural change, to understand their own aging processes, and to develop new and satisfying retirement and leisure roles.

■ Adult illiteracy is a worldwide problem. In complex societies, functional literacy requires an increasing level of skill.

WORK AND LEISURE

■ According to Holland's theory, vocational choice is based on a match between personality type and work environment.

■ Super's theory traces eight stages of career development tied to the maturing self-concept.

■ Ginzberg's theory describes two basic career paths: stability and change.

■ Raynor's theory of career development emphasizes interaction between achievement motivation and people's perception of its effect on their career paths.

■ Significant changes in the American work force include a shift from manufacturing and transport to service and information, from blue-collar to white-collar work, from full-time salaried positions to independent contracting and part-time or temporary jobs, and from a preponderance of white males to an increasing number of women and minorities.

■ An increase in women's employment is occurring worldwide. Women tend to have part-time, low-status jobs and to earn less than men; but that pattern is changing in the United States, where gender discrimination in the workplace is illegal.

■ In the United States, African Americans have the highest rates of unemployment. Among professionals, African Americans have the lowest earnings.

■ Apparent age differences in job performance seem to depend on experience, on how performance is measured, and on the demands of the job.

■ Causes of occupational stress include a combination of high pressure and low autonomy; interpersonal conflict; work overload; and tensions affecting women and minorities.

■ Unemployment has both physical and psychological effects for men and for women.

■ People who do more complex work tend to engage in more intellectually demanding leisure activities.

RETIREMENT AND OTHER LATE-LIFE OPTIONS

- Most adults in industrialized countries retire. Many older adults in less developed countries work but cannot meet their basic needs.

- Finances rather than health will usually determine the decision to retire.

- Most American workers retire before age 65, but the trend toward early retirement has leveled off.

- Options for use of time after retirement include paid work, volunteerism, and leisure activities. Lifestyle after retirement tends to be related to the things a person enjoyed doing before.

- Widows, minorities, and people with long-term illnesses are most likely to become impoverished after retirement.

- Although the quantity of social contacts diminishes after retirement, the quality of social support networks generally does not.

- The societal impact of retirement has to do with the dependency ratio. Studies suggest that the total burden of dependency is not likely to increase, but economic growth will be a key factor in keeping the burden bearable.

- With increased longevity, a shift from retirement to "productive aging" may be under way.

KEY TERMS

▼

age-differentiated (page 283)
age-integrated (284)
lifelong learning (285)
crystallization stage (291)
specification stage (291)
implementation stage (291)
establishment stage (292)
consolidation stage (292)
maintenance stage (292)
deceleration stage (292)
retirement stage (292)
contingent career paths (293)
noncontingent career paths (293)

burnout (302)
substantive complexity (303)
spillover hypothesis (304)
compensation hypothesis (304)
resource provision-depletion
    hypothesis (304)
segmentation hypothesis (304)
family-focused lifestyle (313)
balanced investment (313)
serious leisure (313)
convoy theory (315)
selectivity theory (316)
dependency ratio (316)

CHAPTER 9

INTIMATE RELATIONSHIPS AND LIFESTYLES

FOUNDATIONS OF INTIMATE RELATIONSHIPS
Friendship
Love
Sexuality

NONMARITAL LIFESTYLES
Single Life
Homosexual Relationships
Cohabitation

MARITAL AND POSTMARITAL LIFESTYLES
Marriage
Divorce and Remarriage
What Makes Marriages Succeed?

FAMILY LIFE
Changing Family Structures
Parenthood Today
Parenthood as
  a Developmental Experience
When Children Leave:
  The "Empty Nest"
Parenthood, Role Changes,
  and Marital Satisfaction
Remaining Childless

BOXES
9-1 The Art of Aging: How Dual-Earner
    Couples Cope
9-2 The Multicultural Context: Divorce
    in France—A Two-Track System
9-3 The Cutting Edge: Motherhood
    after Menopause

Relationship is life, and this relationship is a constant movement, a constant change.

J. Krishnamurti, *You Are the World*, 1989

FOCUS: LOUISE ERDRICH AND MICHAEL DORRIS

(James Woodcock/Courtesy of HarperCollins)

Louise Erdrich and Michael Dorris* have been married since 1981 and have six children. After they married, Louise adopted Michael's three children, and they have had three more children together. They live in an old farmhouse in New Hampshire.

Louise and Michael have some experiences in common with many other contemporary adults who are committed to long-term relationships. For one thing, they have had to meet the challenge of a dual-career blended family. In certain ways, though, their relationship is unique. Both are best-selling authors who have won national awards for their writing on Native American themes. (Louise is part Chippewa, and Michael is part Modoc.) It was their love of writing that initially drew them to each other; and it was Michael who found Louise a publisher for her prize-winning first novel, *Love Medicine* (1984). Since then, they have written a novel together (*The Crown of Columbus*, 1991).

They met and became friends at Dartmouth College. Louise was a member of the first class of women admitted to this formerly all-male college. Michael, an anthropology instructor, had just been hired to start a program in Native American studies.

The year before, at age 26, Michael had become one of the first unmarried men in the United States to adopt a child, a 3-year-old Sioux boy named Abel. Single parenthood was nothing new to him; his two grandfathers and his father had died early in life, leaving widows to raise their children. Michael wanted a child of his own,

*Sources of biographical material about Louise Erdrich and Michael Dorris are Dorris (1989), Erdrich (1984), D. Foster (1991), Getlin (1994), Passaro (1991), and Schumacher (1991).

and the fact that Abel had been diagnosed as mentally retarded did not deter him. Later—as Michael relates in *The Broken Cord* (1989), which was made into a television movie—he discovered that the child (called "Adam" in the book) was a victim of fetal alcohol syndrome.

After Louise's graduation, she and Michael kept in touch but did not meet again until 4 years later. By then Louise was beginning to establish herself as a writer, and Michael had adopted two more children. Michael attended a reading Louise gave of her work and was stunned by its power.

Although marriage crossed their minds that evening, they had to part for 9 months while Michael went to New Zealand on a research fellowship. But his renewed contact with Louise had reawakened his earlier interest in writing. They corresponded, sending each other drafts of their work. When he returned, their friendship blossomed into love and marriage.

Louise not only married Michael; she "married" his children as well. She shared in the responsibility of caring for Abel until, at age 20, he moved into a supervised home. In a foreword to *The Broken Cord*, she writes movingly of the mixture of love and frustration entailed in being a stepparent to Abel.

In the course of their married life, Michael and Louise have developed an unusual degree of personal and professional communication. As one interviewer observed, "They will finish each other's thoughts, embellish or clarify ideas, banter back and forth—all in a way that makes their answers to a question seem to come from one person" (Schumacher, 1991, p. 28). Each is intimately involved in every stage of the other's work, and each has learned to accept the other's criticism. "Marriage," says Louise, "is a process of coming to trust the other person over the years, and it's the same thing with our writing" (Schumacher, 1991, p. 31). They regard each volume, no matter whose name is on the cover, as their joint product. "As we've worked on more and more books together," says Michael, "it's become harder to separate one or another's contributions. . . . In a way, these books are like our children" (Schumacher, 1991, p. 30).

The story of Louise Erdrich and Michael Dorris touches on several topics we will cover in this chapter: friendship, love, marriage, parenthood, adoption, stepparenthood. Of course, no one story can encompass today's wide range of intimate relationships and lifestyles. In many societies, people are no longer simply expected to get married, stay married, have children, and maintain distinct roles for men and women (Eisenberg, 1995; O'Grady-LeShane, 1993; Thornton, 1989). Adults can decide whether and when to marry, divorce, or remarry and whether, when, and how to become parents. Some choose an unwed partnership with someone of the same or the other sex. Some remain single and live alone or in group settings. Some couples decide to remain childless; some delay parenthood until their thirties or even until middle age. An increasing number become single parents—either by choice, as Michael Dorris initially did, or through divorce or widowhood. In this chapter, as we discuss intimate relationships and lifestyle patterns, you may gain insights into your own relationships and find useful information about an important and perplexing aspect of adult development: dealing with people who are as complicated as yourself.

FOUNDATIONS OF INTIMATE RELATIONSHIPS

According to Erikson, developing intimate relationships is the crucial task of young adulthood. Traditionally, this is the time when people establish relationships that may continue for much of their adult lives—relationships based on friendship, love, and sexuality. But in many societies, chronological age is no longer as important as social age. In a highly mobile society, friendships may come and go. In a freer society, so may marital and sexual partners. And in a society that is taking a more realistic look at older people and their needs and desires, it's virtually never too late for romance and sexual satisfaction.

Still, some patterns do exist. What can research tell us about how friendship, love, and sexuality develop and change throughout adult life? Let's begin with friendship.

FRIENDSHIP

Michael Dorris and Louise Erdrich were close friends before they became lovers, and they continue to be both. How does friendship differ from love? According to 150 adults—two-thirds of whom were college students and one-third no longer in school—a friendship involves trust, respect, enjoyment of each other's company, understanding and acceptance of each other, willingness to help and to confide in one another, and spontaneity, or feeling free to be oneself (K. E. Davis, 1985). Romantic bonds have these aspects too—plus sexual passion and extreme caring. The participants in this study saw "best friendships" as more stable than ties to a spouse or lover. Most people's close and best friends were of the same sex; but 27 percent listed members of the other sex as best friends.

Young adults who are building careers and caring for babies may have limited time to spend with friends. Middle-aged people, too, are busy with family and work and may be engrossed in building up security for retirement. Still, friendships do persist throughout middle age and are a strong source of emotional support and well-being (Baruch, Barnett, & Rivers, 1983; House, Landis, & Umberson, 1988). What midlife friendships lack in quantity, they often make up for in quality. People turn to friends for emotional support and practical guidance—for example, to help them deal with maturing children and aging parents. At this time, chronological age is less of a factor than social age or similarity in life stage in making new friends (Troll, 1975). A woman who has delayed parenthood until her late thirties or her forties may become friendly with other mothers who are several years younger than she is, as well as with professional colleagues who are several years older.

The fact that people *choose* their friends may be especially important to older people, who often feel control over their lives slipping away (R. G. Adams, 1986). This element of choice may help explain why most older people have close friends, and why those who have an active circle of friends are happier and healthier (Babchuk, 1978–1979; Lemon, Bengtson, & Peterson, 1972; Steinbach, 1992). Important aspects of friendships among the elderly include common interests, social involvement, and mutual help (R. G. Adams, 1986). Especially for people living in retirement communities or senior housing, friends and neighbors often take the place of faraway family members (Cantor, 1980). Intimacy is important to older adults, who need to know that they are still valued and wanted despite physical and other losses. This is especially true for formerly married women (Essex & Nam, 1987). Well into old age, women continue to see their friends at least as often as in the past. Older men see friends less, see them more in groups rather than one to one, and consider friendship less important (Field & Minkler, 1988).

Friends can be a bulwark against the impact of stress on physical and mental health (Cutrona, Russell, & Rose, 1986). People who can confide in friends and can talk about their worries and pain deal better with the changes of aging (Genevay, 1986; Lowenthal & Haven, 1968). They also seem to extend their lives (Blazer, 1989; Steinbach, 1992). Many widowed people become closer to their friends and find friends more helpful than relatives (Lund, Caserta, Van Pelt, & Gass, 1990). For most older people, morale depends more on how often they see their friends than on how often they see their children (Glenn & McLanahan, 1981).

Apparently older people enjoy time spent with friends more than time spent with family. In one study (Larson, Mannell, & Zuzanek, 1986), 92 retired women and men between ages 55 and 88 wore beepers for 1 week. When paged, at approximately 2-hour intervals, they filled out reports on what they were doing, with whom, and what they were thinking and feeling. These people were generally more alert, excited, and emotionally aroused with friends than with family members, including their spouses. One reason may be that older people spend more active leisure time with friends, and the lightheartedness and spontaneity of friendships help them rise above daily concerns. The relative brevity and infrequency of time spent with friends may add to its special savor. Still, according to this study, spending time with friends does not appear to improve *overall* life satisfaction, as spending time with a spouse does.

Adults older than 85 maintain friendships and even make new friends, often calling a friend someone who formerly would have been considered merely an acquaintance. Because disabilities may hamper face-to-face contact, friendships may be maintained by telephone or mail and tend to be less intimate than in earlier years (C. L. Johnson & Troll, 1994).

LOVE

For most adults, a loving relationship with a partner, of the same or the other sex, is a pivotal element of their lives. According to Robert J. Sternberg's *triangular theory of love* (1985b; Sternberg & Barnes, 1985; Sternberg & Grajek, 1984), love has three faces, or elements: intimacy, passion, and commitment. *Intimacy,* the emotional element, involves self-disclosure, which leads to connection, warmth, and trust. *Passion,* the motivational element, is based on inner drives that translate physiological arousal into sexual desire. *Commitment,* the cognitive element, is the decision to love and to stay with the beloved. The degree to which these three elements are present determines what kind of love people feel (see Table 9-1), and mismatches can lead to problems in relationships. Some research suggests that trust, which is essential to intimacy with a lover, depends on the security of earlier attachments—attachments to parents or caregivers in infancy and childhood (DeAngelis, 1994).

Do opposites attract? Not as a rule. Research has found a tendency toward *assortative mating:* just as people choose friends with whom they have something in common, they tend—like Michael Dorris and Louise Erdrich—to fall in love with and marry someone much like themselves (E. Epstein & Gutmann, 1984). Lovers often resemble each other in physical appearance and attractiveness, mental and physical health, intelligence, popularity, and warmth. They are likely to be similar in the degree to which their parents are happy as individuals and as couples, and in such factors as socioeconomic status, race, religion, education, and income (Murstein, 1980). Husband and wife often have similar temperaments, too; risk takers tend to marry other risk takers—though they may be risking early divorce (Zuckerman, 1994)!

Of course, love doesn't always last. Among college students who were asked to recall how or why they fell in and out of love with a previous partner, the students who could explain why their earlier relationships ended were more satisfied with their current partners than those whose earlier relationships appeared to be unresolved (Clark & Collins, 1993).

SEXUALITY

Sexual development has a physical side (Chapter 3). But it also has a social side. In the United States today there is far more openness in discussing and expressing sexuality than there was in the past, and greater acceptance of sexual activity as normal, healthy, and pleasurable. One major change is greater acceptance of premarital or nonmarital sex, particularly in a loving, monogamous relationship. A related change is a decline in the *double standard,* the code that traditionally gave males more sexual freedom than females. Another ongoing change is in attitudes toward *sexual orientation*—the tendency to be consistently attracted to the other sex (*heterosexual*), the same sex (*homosexual*), or both sexes (*bisexual*). There is less stigma on homosexuality, which has now been deleted from the American Psychiatric Association's official list of emotional disorders. Still another social force that may be changing sexual behavior is the threat of AIDS.

TABLE 9-1 PATTERNS OF LOVING

Type	Description
Nonlove	All three components of love—intimacy, passion, and commitment—areabsent. This describes most of our personal relationships, which aresimply casual interactions.
Liking	Intimacy is the only component present. This is what we feel in truefriendship and in many loving relationships. There is closeness, understanding, emotional support, affection, bondedness, and warmth. Neither passion nor commitment is present.
Infatuation	Passion is the only component present. This is "love at first sight," a strong physical attraction and sexual arousal, without intimacy or commitment. This can flare up suddenly and die just as fast—or, given certain circumstances, can sometimes last for a long time.
Empty love	Commitment is the only component present. This is often found in long-term relationships that have lost both intimacy and passion, or in arranged marriages.
Romantic love	Intimacy and passion are both present. Romantic lovers are drawn to each other physically and bonded emotionally. They are not, however, committed to each other.
Companionate love	Intimacy and commitment are both present. This is a long-term, committed friendship, often occurring in marriages in which physical attraction has died down but in which the partners feel close to each other and have made the decision to stay together.
Fatuous love	Passion and commitment are present, without intimacy. This is the kind of love that leads to a whirlwind courtship, in which a couple make a commitment on the basis of passion without allowing themselves the time to develop intimacy. This kind of love usually does not last, despite the initial intent to commit.
Consummate love	All three components are present in this "complete" love, which many of us strive for, especially in romantic relationships. It is easier to reach it than to hold onto it. Either partner may change what he or she wants from the relationship. If the other partner changes, too, the relationship may endure in a different form. If the other partner does not change, the relationship may dissolve.

SOURCE: Sternberg, 1985b.

Premarital Sex

Do you think your parents or grandparents were sexually active before marriage? How would you react if your children had premarital sex? According to one report, 61 percent of men but only 12 percent of women born before 1910 admit to premarital sex. By the 1980s, women had nearly as much sexual experience before marriage as men did (T. W. Smith, 1994).

In 1972, 62 percent of women age 30 and older considered premarital sex "always" or "almost always" wrong. By 1986, only 45 percent held that view; and a similar change had occurred among men (Thornton, 1989). In one study, 82 percent of never-married women in their twenties had had intercourse, and 53 percent were currently sexually active (Tanfer & Horn, 1985). The later people marry, the less likely they are to be virgins on the wedding day.

Sexual Orientation

Homosexuality has been accepted as normal in many societies (Evans-Pritchard, 1970; Ford & Beach, 1951; Herdt, 1981, 1987; Schieffelin, 1976), or even as preferable to heterosexuality (R. C. Kelly, 1976; van Baal, 1966); and its incidence seems to be similar in a number of cultures (Hyde, 1986). In the United States, although homosexuality has become more visible in recent years, only 2.8 percent of men and 1.4 percent of women in a major, nationally representative survey identified themselves as homosexual or bisexual. However, 5 percent of men and 4 percent of women reported at least one homosexual encounter as adults. Homosexual identification was more prevalent (9 percent for men and 3 percent for women) in the largest cities (Michael, Gagnon, Laumann, & Kolata, 1994).

What causes sexual orientation? Freud believed that it is determined by parenting styles; learning theorists claim that (like any other behavior) it is learned through imitation and reinforcement. So far, neither of these perspectives is strongly supported by research.

A review of a large number of recent studies indicates that biology may play an important role in sexual orientation (Gladue, 1994). A man or woman who is the identical twin of a homosexual has about a 50 percent probability of being homosexual himself or herself; by comparison, the figure for a fraternal twin is only about 20 percent, and the figure for an adopted sibling is 10 percent or less. Furthermore, genetic analysis suggests that male homosexuality may run in some families. In addition, certain differences in brain anatomy, in responses to hormones, and in psychological abilities such as spatial skills—similar to known differences between heterosexual men and heterosexual women—have been found between heterosexual and homosexual men (though not, thus far, between lesbians and heterosexual women). We can't, of course, be sure that a correlation between sexual orientation and brain structure or functioning indicates a causal relationship. Still, while not all men and women may achieve their sexual orientation in the same way, it appears increasingly likely that the process is a complex one in which genes may interact with certain critical hormonal and environmental events.

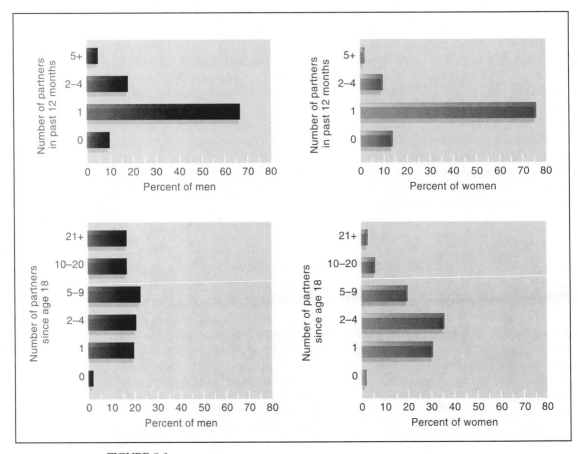

FIGURE 9-1

Number of sex partners in past 12 months and since age 18.

(SOURCE: Data from Michael, Gagnon, Laumann, & Kolata, 1994.)

AIDS and Sexual Behavior

The threat of AIDS has led some 3 in 10 adult Americans, especially those who have multiple sex partners, to modify their sexual behavior—by having fewer partners (see Figure 9-1), selecting partners more carefully, or using condoms. In fact, according to a major, nationally representative study, about 11 percent say they are abstaining from sex altogether (Michael et al., 1994). Similarly, in a nationally representative sample of 15- to 44-year-old unmarried, sexually experienced women, one-third had changed their behavior, most often by limiting the number of partners (McNally & Mosher, 1991).

Safer sex practices have become prevalent among homosexuals, many of whom have come to view promiscuity without regard for possible consequences as irresponsible (King, Camp, & Downey, 1991). Fear of AIDS may explain the fact that fewer than 2 percent of sexually active men and women say they have had homosexual relations, and fewer than 1 percent report bisexual activity, within the previous year (T. W. Smith, 1994).

However, a telephone survey of more than 10,000 married and unmarried Americans age 18 to 75 found that many adults, including those especially at risk, do not take precautions against AIDS. Only 17 percent of heterosexuals with multiple partners, and only 13 percent of those with high-risk partners, use condoms whenever they have sex (Catania et al., 1992). A small recent study of women who sought HIV testing and counseling (but tested negative) found that only one-fourth adopted safer sex practices afterward (Ickovics et al., 1994). There is a widespread—but false—impression that AIDS is primarily a "homosexual disease," and this may lull many heterosexuals into complacency.

NONMARITAL LIFESTYLES

A sexual "evolution" since the 1960s has made a variety of adult lifestyles other than traditional marriage more socially acceptable. In this section, we'll look at single life, homosexual lifestyles, and cohabitation. In the next section, we'll discuss changing marital and postmarital patterns.

SINGLE LIFE

One reflection of the sexual "evolution" is a dramatic increase in the percentage of young Americans who have not yet married—more than 3 out of 5 women and approximately 4 out of 5 men age 20 to 24 (see Table 9-2). A growing number never marry at all. About 5 percent of women and 4 percent of men 65 years and older have never married, and the percentage is twice as big in more recent cohorts (U.S. Bureau of the Census, 1992b, 1993). The trend started earlier among African Americans, with the result that black men and women age 55 to 64 are twice as likely to have remained single as whites of the same age, and 1.5 times as likely as blacks older than 84 (U.S. Bureau of the Census, 1991a, 1991b). Worldwide, the percentage of never-married women has increased since 1970 (United Nations, 1991).

Why do heterosexual adults opt for single life? Some stay single so that they can be freer to take risks—to move across the country or across the world, to make career changes, to further their education, or to do creative work, without having to worry about how their quest for self-fulfillment affects another person. Some value sexual freedom. Others just like being alone. And others postpone or avoid marriage for fear that it will end in divorce (P. C. Glick & Lin, 1986b). Postponement may make sense, since, as we'll see, the younger people are when they first marry, the likelier they are to split up.

By and large, single young adults like their status. They are busy and active and feel secure about themselves. Most of the never-married participants in a study of 400 never-married, divorced, and remarried Ohioans were not lonely, and fewer than 20 percent had multiple sexual partners (Cargan, 1981). A small

TABLE 9-2 PERCENT OF MEN AND WOMEN NEVER MARRIED AT VARIOUS AGES, 1970–1992

Men	1970	1980	1992
20–24 years	54.7	68.8	80.3
25–29 years	19.1	33.1	46.7
30–34 years	9.4	15.9	29.4
35–39 years	7.2	7.8	18.4
Women	**1970**	**1980**	**1992**
20–24 years	35.8	50.2	65.7
25–29 years	10.5	20.9	33.2
30–34 years	6.2	9.5	18.8
35–39 years	5.4	6.2	12.6

SOURCE: U.S. Bureau of the Census, 1993.

study of single middle-aged women in Pennsylvania found that more than half gave marriage a low priority; they were interested in marriage only on an egalitarian basis, were not confident about finding such a relationship, and made little effort to do so so (N. M. Brown, 1993). Never-married older women do not become lonely with the loss of friends and family, but they do feel lonely if they lose their health (Essex & Nam, 1987). Poor health undermines their sense of self-reliance and may force them into dependence on relatives they would rather not be with.

Many older singles, like younger ones, date people of the other sex—primarily for companionship, not to seek a mate. A national survey of more than 1,400 previously married single adults age 55 to over 75 (R. A. Bulcroft & Bulcroft, 1991) found that older men are much more likely to date than older women, perhaps because of the greater availability of women in this age group. Nearly half of the daters of both sexes call their relationships "steady." Most elderly daters are sexually active but do not expect to marry. Among both whites and African Americans, men are more interested in romantic involvement, while women may fear getting "locked into" traditional gender roles (K. Bulcroft & O'Conner, 1986; Tucker, Taylor, & Mitchell-Kernan, 1993).

HOMOSEXUAL RELATIONSHIPS

Homosexual relationships take many forms, including anonymous contacts, nonexclusive group living, "open" couples, and roommates who may or may not be lovers. But most homosexuals (like most heterosexuals) seek love, companionship, and sexual fulfillment through a relationship with one person, usually about their own age.

Lesbians tend to have stable, monogamous relationships; gay men (like heterosexual men) are more likely to "cruise," looking for multiple partners (Berger & Kelly, 1986). Still, a study of 112 homosexual men age 40 and over found that 7 out of 10 had a primary sexual relationship with another male at some time (Berger, 1982). In a study of 18 homosexual men and women age 40 to 72, all but one had present or past lovers; most of these relationships had lasted several years. Several participants had engaged in *serial monogamy*—a pattern (also common among heterosexuals) of involvement in one sexually exclusive relationship after another (Berger, 1984). The notion that partners in homosexual relationships typically play "masculine" and "feminine" roles has been discredited by research on thousands of male and female homosexuals, both young and old (Berger, 1984; Berger & Kelly, 1986).

Older homosexual couples, like heterosexual couples, place importance on a good sex life. In one study (Berger, 1984), such couples reported having sex anywhere from daily to every other month. When asked how their sex lives had changed since their youth, men referred to frequency of sex; women responded in terms of the quality of the relationship.

Because there was pervasive prejudice against homosexuality when they were young adults, many older homosexuals did not "come out" (acknowledge and accept their sexual identity) until after years of struggle and self-doubt, sometimes after marriage and parenthood. Often these heterosexual marriages were the result of strong social pressure. Many homosexuals have experienced discrimination (sometimes compounded by age discrimination) in employment or housing, and some have lost custody of their children (Berger, 1984; Berger & Kelly, 1986).

(Mimi Forsyth/Monkmeyer)

Lesbians tend to have stable, monogamous relationships. An estimated 8 to 10 million American children are living with homosexual parents.

Today, homosexuals in the United States are seeking the legal recognition of their unions that already exists in some countries (Kottak, 1994), and the right to adopt children or raise their own. They also are pressing for an end to discrimination in employment, housing, and other areas. A recent (and controversial) trend is the inclusion of unmarried domestic partners—homosexual or heterosexual—in health insurance, pension plans, and bereavement leave.

COHABITATION

Cohabitation is an increasingly popular lifestyle in which an unmarried couple involved in a sexual relationship live together. Almost half the population of the United States who are in their early thirties have cohabited, and about 4 percent of the population is cohabiting at a given time (Bumpass & Sweet, 1988). Such consensual relationships, which may produce children, are common in many countries (United Nations, 1991). In Sweden in 1992, for example, there were twice as many new consensual unions as new marriages (Eisenberg, 1995).

Why do heterosexual couples cohabit? For one thing, young people in industrialized societies with relatively high standards of health and nutrition now reach sexual maturity earlier than in previous generations (Chumlea, 1982; Eveleth & Tanner, 1976), and more of them pursue advanced education. These trends combine to create a longer span between physiological maturity and social maturity. Many young adults want close romantic and sexual relationships but are not ready for marriage—and may never be. More women today are self-supporting, and there is less social pressure to marry. Some older couples cohabit to avoid losing pension or social security benefits from a previous marriage.

Some research shows that couples who live together before getting married have lower-quality marriages, less commitment to marriage, and greater likelihood of divorce. Wives who have cohabited tend to see marriage as a relationship in which each partner is free to do as he or she wishes (Thomson & Colella, 1992; Bumpass & Sweet, 1988). Differences between couples who cohabit and couples who "wait for marriage," however, may reflect the kinds of people who choose each alternative rather than effects of cohabitation itself. And these differences have diminished as cohabitation has become more common (Schoen, 1992).

MARITAL AND POSTMARITAL LIFESTYLES

▼

Marriage doesn't have the same meaning everywhere. In some Himalayan cultures a woman may marry a set of brothers (Kottak, 1994). In west Africa, a working woman who is married to a man may also take a "wife" to care for her home and children (Amadiume, 1987). But the universality of some form of marriage throughout history and around the world (Kottak, 1994) shows that it meets a variety of fundamental needs. Marriage is usually considered the best way to ensure orderly raising of children. It provides for division of labor within a consuming and working unit. Ideally, it offers intimacy, friendship, affection, sexual fulfillment, and companionship. In the United States, despite a decline in the marriage rate, marriage (though not necessarily "till death do us part") remains the lifestyle of the vast majority of adults; and many whose first marriages fail try again. Let's look at changing patterns of marriage, divorce, and remarriage, and at why some marriages last and some do not.

MARRIAGE

The typical "marrying age" varies greatly across cultures (Bianchi & Spain, 1986). In eastern Europe, people tend to marry early; in Hungary, for example, 70 percent of women and 33 percent of men age 20 to 24 have already married. Industrialized nations are seeing a trend toward later marriage as young adults take time to pursue educational and career goals or to explore relationships. In Scandinavia, 85 percent of women and 95 percent of men age 20 to 24 have not yet married (though most eventually will marry), and cohabitation is common among young adults. Japan, too, has a high proportion of unmarried young adults, but rather than cohabiting they tend to live with their parents. In the United States, the median age of first-time bridegrooms in 1991 was 26.3 years; that of first-time brides was 24.1 years—an increase of about 2 years for both sexes since 1980 (U.S. Bureau of the Census, 1992b).

Nine out of 10 American women, but only 3 out of 4 African American women, eventually marry. For both black and white women, this figure is down from about 95 percent before the late 1970s (Norton & Miller, 1992). The dramatically lower marriage rate among African Americans today may be due in part to high unemployment among black men and greater economic independence among black working women. Also, the lower life expectancy of black men, and their tendency to marry much younger women, reduces marital prospects for older black single women (Tucker, Taylor, & Mitchell-Kernan, 1993).

Marriage and Happiness

National surveys have shown that marriage is the most important factor in happiness—more important than work, friendships, or anything else. But while more married people than never-marrieds call themselves "very happy," the gap has narrowed dramatically—among 25- to 39-year-olds, from 31 percentage points in the early 1970s to 8 points in 1986, according to surveys done by the National Opinion Research Center (Glenn, 1987). Apparently, never-married people (especially men) are happier today, while married people (especially women) are less happy. And unmarried people tend to be happier than people who are unhappily married.

One possible explanation for the change is that some benefits of marriage are no longer confined to wedlock. Single people can get both sex and companionship outside of marriage, and marriage no longer is the sole (or even the most reliable) source of security for women. Since most married women now continue to work, and most husbands do not share the burdens of homemaking and child care equally (see Box 9-1), marriage may increase rather than decrease women's stress.

BOX 9-1

THE ART OF AGING

How Dual-Earner Couples Cope

The growing number of marriages in which both husband and wife are gainfully employed represents a major change from traditional family patterns. A big advantage, of course, is financial. A second income raises some families from poverty to middle-income status and makes others affluent. It makes women more independent and gives them a greater share of economic power in a marriage; and it reduces the pressure on men to be providers. On average, American wives who work full time contribute 40 percent of family income (L. A. Gilbert, 1994), and many women who work in mills and factories contribute almost half (Thompson & Walker, 1989). Less tangible benefits may include a more equal relationship between husband and wife, better health for both, greater self-esteem for the woman, and a closer relationship between a father and his children (L. A. Gilbert, 1994).

But this way of life also creates stress. Working couples face extra demands on their time and energy, conflicts between work and family roles, possible rivalry between spouses, and anxiety and guilt over meeting children's needs. Husband and wife are part of three role systems—the wife's work system, the husband's work system, and the joint family system. Each role makes greater or lesser demands at different times, and partners have to decide which should take priority when. The family is most demanding when there are young children. Careers are especially demanding, and especially stressful, when a worker is getting established or being promoted. And both kinds of demands frequently occur around the same time, in young adulthood.

While men's participation in household tasks, especially parenting, has been increasing since 1970, society often reinforces traditional gender roles (L. A. Gilbert, 1994). Men, on average, earn much more than their wives and have more powerful positions. Studies done in the late 1980s found employed women doing almost 80 percent of the housework (Berardo, Sheehan, & Leslie, 1987) and 90 percent of the child care (Lamb, 1987).

More recent research suggests that "the inevitability of a 'second shift' for wives is overstated" (L. A. Gilbert, 1994). Dual-career families fall into three patterns: conventional, modern, and role-sharing. In a *conventional* marriage, both partners consider household chores and child care "women's work." The husband may "help,"

The two sexes often have different expectations about marriage. To women, marital intimacy entails sharing of feelings and confidences. Men tend to express intimacy through sex, practical help, companionship, and doing things together (Thompson & Walker, 1989). Many men are uncomfortable talking about feelings, or even listening to their wives talk about theirs. Since women are more likely to do things that matter to men, men often get more of what is important to them, while wives are left feeling dissatisfied. Perhaps that helps explain why the association between marriage and psychological well-being is more pronounced for men (C. E. Ross, Mirowsky, & Goldsteen, 1990).

but his career takes precedence; he is usually more ambitious, earns more than his wife, and sees it as "her choice" to add a career to her primary domestic role. In the *modern* pattern, husband and wife share parenting, but the wife does more housework. The man's active fathering may stem not from egalitarian principles but from wanting to be involved with his children. The *role-sharing* pattern, the most egalitarian, occurs in at least one-third of heterosexual dual-career families. Both husband and wife are actively involved in household and family responsibilities as well as careers (L. A. Gilbert, 1994). But even among couples highly committed to dual-career lifestyles, tasks tend to be gender-typed: wives buy groceries and husbands mow the lawn (Apostol et al., 1993).

Unequal roles are not necessarily seen as inequitable. What spouses perceive as fair may depend on the size of the wife's financial contribution, whether she thinks of herself as a coprovider or merely as adding a second income, and the meaning and importance both she and her husband place on her work. Whatever the actual division of labor, couples who agree on their assessment of it are more satisfied than those who don't. And partners are less likely to sense any unfairness when they enjoy a harmonious, caring, involved family life (L. A. Gilbert, 1994).

Still, an unequal division of work may contribute to the higher degree of marital distress reported by wives in a recent study of 300 mostly managerial and professional dual-earner couples. Interestingly, couples without children experienced more distress than those with children, as did couples with higher-prestige jobs (Barnett et al., 1994). Another study found that women's personal activities tend to suffer more than men's, perhaps reflecting the time they put into domestic work. Women's greater willingness to compromise may help keep the dual-earner lifestyle afloat, but the resulting stress may weaken the marriage (Apostol et al., 1993).

The strains experienced by dual-earner families could be alleviated by various societal changes. Such changes include more part-time, flex-time, and shared jobs and more at-home work (without loss of fringe benefits); more affordable high-quality child care; and tax credits or other assistance to let new parents postpone returning to work (Eisenberg, 1995). One encouraging change was the Family Leave Act of 1993, which requires businesses with 50 or more workers to offer 12 weeks of unpaid leave for the birth or adoption of a child—although this still falls far short of (for example) the 6-month paid leave offered to new parents in Sweden.

Marital and Extramarital Sexual Activity

Americans apparently have sex less often than images in the media suggest, but married people have it more often than singles who are not cohabiting. Comprehensive face-to-face interviews with a random sample of 3,432 men and women age 18 to 59 found that about one-third have intercourse two or more times a week: 40 percent of married couples, more than 50 percent of cohabiting couples, and fewer than 25 percent of those who do not live with a sex partner (Michael et al., 1994).

BOX 9-2

THE MULTICULTURAL CONTEXT

Divorce in France: A Two-Track System

Most western countries and all American states now have no-fault divorce laws. Under the older adversarial system of divorce, one partner had to accuse the other (sometimes falsely) of some form of misconduct, such as adultery or mental cruelty. In most places where no-fault divorce has been adopted, it replaced this adversarial system. Not so, however, in France—a country that is still traditional in many ways.

In France, divorce reform—adopted in 1975—created a two-track system. The new law instituted three types of no-fault divorce for couples who agree to it, while preserving the old system of adversarial proceedings and legal sanctions for those who don't (Mazel, 1984). In effect, the reform created a vast nationwide quasi experiment. It made possible comparisons of divorce data, not only before and since reform, but among couples who chose fault and no-fault options.

The two main forms of no-fault divorce are: (1) mutual consent, with no need to give a reason for terminating the marriage; (2) an uncontested request by one party (usually stating that life together is no longer possible or tolerable). A third option—separation for 6 years or more—is used mainly when one spouse has become mentally incapacitated.

As in other countries that have adopted no-fault laws, the number of divorces in France has risen. In 1971 about 40,000 divorce decrees were issued; in 1975, the year the law was passed, more than 53,000; and in 1981, nearly 82,500. From 1976 to 1981, the proportion of no-fault divorce increased from 11 percent to more than 50 percent of all divorces.

The choice appears to be influenced by age and socioeconomic status. Younger couples are more likely than older couples to use no-fault proceedings. Professionals tend to choose a form of no-fault divorce, while working-class couples stick with the traditional fault option; artists, merchants, and owners of small businesses are equally divided between the two. A likely explanation is that upper-class professionals, thanks to their educational and cultural background, have a good chance of maintaining their social status after divorce and therefore may be more willing to agree to it than working-class people, especially working-class women, for whom divorce can mean a significant drop in income and social standing.

Monetary awards are an important factor. The ex-wife receives such an award in 41 percent of fault divorces, but in only 6 percent of mutual-consent cases and 21 percent of uncontested cases. Most of this money is designated as child support, since (as in the United States) the new law virtually eliminated alimony. Not surprisingly, then, only 10 percent of divorces involving children are by mutual consent, and almost no couples with large families choose no-fault divorce. Ironically, however, awards tend to be higher in no-fault situations, owing to the greater earning power of the party paying child support (usually the man).

Perhaps the most significant change is in who initiates divorce. Between 1971 and 1981, the proportion of cases in which only one party sought to end the marriage dropped from almost 60 percent to less than 35 percent. In other words, nearly 2 out of 3 divorces were requested by both parties. In France, then, the option of divorce without a finding of fault has allowed more couples to agree to end their marriages rather than staying together to avoid the bitterness of the adversarial process.

Most couples have sexual relations more frequently during the first year of marriage than ever again. And the more sexually active they are during that first year, the more active they are likely to be in the future. One study found that, among couples married less than 2 years, 83 percent make love at least once a week and 45 percent three times a week or more; after 10 years of marriage, the comparable figures drop to 63 percent and 18 percent (Blumstein & Schwartz, 1983). Because of physical changes in sexual capacity (see Chapter 3), most older married couples have sex less frequently but still may find it intensely pleasurable.

Some married people seek sex outside of marriage, especially after the first few years, when the excitement and novelty of sex with the spouse wear off or problems in the relationship surface. According to recent surveys, extramarital sex is much less common than is generally thought. Only about 21 percent of men and 11.5 percent of women who have ever been married report having had extramarital relations. Young adults are more likely to engage in extramarital activity than those born before 1940 (T. W. Smith, 1994). More than 3 out of 4 Americans think extramarital affairs are always wrong, and 14 percent think they are almost always wrong (Michael et al., 1994).

DIVORCE AND REMARRIAGE

Divorce rates reflect differences among cultures. Divorce has increased dramatically in such countries as the United States, the United Kingdom, Australia, Sweden, France (see Box 9-2), and the former Soviet Union. This increase has accompanied the passage in most western countries, mainly in the 1960s and 1970s, of more liberal divorce laws, which eliminate the need to find one partner at fault. Japan, a more traditional society, had a lower, more stable divorce rate than any of these countries between 1948 and 1988 (A. Burns, 1992). Countries such as Italy (see Figure 9-2) and Ireland, where religious opposition to divorce is strong, have not experienced appreciably higher rates. In fact, the Irish constitution still prohibits divorce, although surveys show that most citizens favor legalizing it.

The United States has one of the highest divorce rates in the world (Bruce, Lloyd, & Leonard, 1995; A. Burns, 1992; U.S. Bureau of the Census, 1992b; again, see Figure 9-2). The rate seems to have leveled off since 1980, after having risen for two decades. Still, about 1 out of 2 marriages dissolved during the 1980s. Divorce is most prevalent among women of the "baby boom" generation (Norton & Miller, 1992). Although dissolution of marriage is largely a phenomenon of young adulthood, the divorce rate has gone up for middle-aged couples, too. Current rates suggest that the first marriage of about 1 woman in 8 will end in divorce after she reaches age 40 (Uhlenberg, Cooney, & Boyd, 1990). The increase in divorce is especially striking among African Americans; the proportion of black women age 55 to 64 who are divorced is about 15 times as high as for those age 85 and over (U.S. Bureau of the Census, 1991b). Divorce in late life is rare; couples who take this step usually do it earlier.

Contrary to common belief, research suggests that no-fault laws, at least in most parts of the United States, are not significantly responsible for the rise in

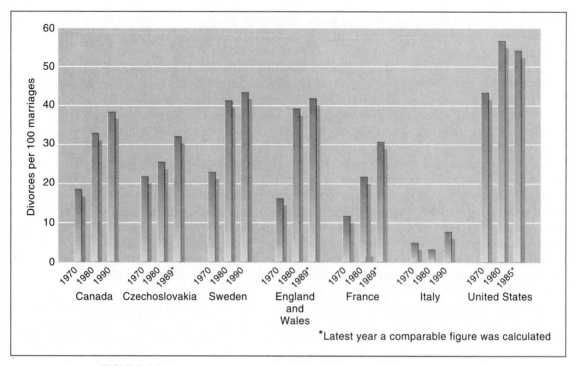

FIGURE 9-2
Divorce rates have risen since 1970 in many developed countries; but rates remain relatively low in Italy, where religious opposition remains strong.
(SOURCE: Bruce, Lloyd, & Leonard, 1995, p. 20; based on data from Monnier & Guibert-Lamoine, 1993.)

divorce. It appears that changes in the old, stiffer laws (which were widely evaded) were more a response to a greater demand for divorce than a cause of the demand (Marvell, 1989; G. C. Wright & Stetson, 1978).

Several societal developments underlie the increase in divorce. Women who are more financially independent of their husbands may be less likely to stay in bad marriages. Instead of staying together "for the sake of the children," spouses may be more likely to conclude that staying in an unhappy, conflict-filled marriage may do greater psychological damage. Of course, for the increasing number of childless couples, it's easier to return to a single state (Berscheid & Campbell, 1981; Eisenberg, 1995). Perhaps most important, while most people today *hope* their marriage will endure, fewer *expect* this.

Age at marriage is a major predictor of whether the marriage will last. Teenagers have high divorce rates; people who wait until their late twenties or later to marry have the best chances for success. Also more likely to divorce are women who drop out of high school or college (Norton & Miller, 1992). Marriage burnout may be related to career burnout. Occupational stress can lead to unrealistic demands on a spouse to make up for boredom, lack of recognition, or hassles at work (Pines, 1991). Table 9-3 summarizes other factors in divorce.

TABLE 9-3 PERSONAL FACTORS ASSOCIATED WITH PROBABILITY OF DIVORCE

Factor	Remarks
Premarital cohabitation	This factor has been explained as a result of the fact that people who live together are less conventional. As this lifestyle becomes more common, it should exert less influence. And in fact, for recent cohorts the effect is weaker.
Young age at marriage	This is the strongest predictor of divorce in the first 5 years of marriage.
Bearing a child before marriage	Premarital pregnancy of itself does not seem to increase the risk of divorce.
Having no children	Having at least one child reduces the risk of divorce, especially if that child is a boy. Fathers tend to be more involved with sons than with daughters, and greater involvement of the father in child care reduces risk of divorce.
Stepchildren in the home	The presence of children from a previous marriage brings additional stresses and divided loyalties.
Divorce of own parents	This is still an important risk factor, even now that it is more common to have divorced parents.
Being African American	This difference still exists when socioeconomic status, fertility, sex ratios, and age at marriage are controlled.

SOURCES: Schoen, 1992; L. K. White, 1990.

Economic Consequences of Divorce

Despite highly publicized celebrity settlements—for example, the $100 million the Hollywood producer Steven Spielberg paid his ex-wife, Amy Irving, in 1989—most women are worse off after divorce. Changes such as the sharp curtailing of spousal maintenance, or alimony, were intended to treat both spouses as equals. But in most marriages, husbands and wives do not have equal economic resources or equal bargaining power (Seltzer & Garfinkel, 1990).

Alimony is now awarded to either spouse in only about 1 out of 7 cases, and then for only 2 to 5 years. Expecting a middle-aged woman who has not worked for pay or whose income is significantly less than her ex-husband's to rapidly become self-supporting can create obvious hardships. Women's power is further reduced by the fact that most states now allow one spouse to obtain a divorce without the other's consent (Sitarz, 1990). A requirement of mutual consent would give a dependent wife leverage to press for better terms (Becker, 1992).

Because the woman usually has custody of the children, and child support—if awarded at all—is generally inadequate and often evaded, many women and their families have to make a major financial adjustment after divorce. Including earnings from employment, the average divorced woman receives only 70 percent of her former income in the year following the divorce; 5 years afterward, her economic position has not appreciably improved. More than 40 percent of divorced women have their incomes cut by more than half. Meanwhile, the man's standard of living tends to rise because he is allocating a smaller proportion of his income to support of his family. The result is a dramatic increase in poverty rates for women and children involved in divorce or separation (Duncan & Hoffman, 1985; Seltzer & Garfinkel, 1990). More than half of poor families in the United States are headed by single mothers, 4 out of 5 of whom were once married (Weitzman, 1985). Worldwide, female-headed households, which are increasing in number, tend to be poorer than households headed by men (Brocas, Cailloux, & Oget, 1990; United Nations, 1991).

Wives who have the least income of their own tend to obtain the least favorable property settlements (Seltzer & Garfinkel, 1990). In states that require equal division of property after divorce, the court may order the house (frequently the main asset) to be sold and the proceeds divided between the ex-spouses, leaving the woman and children unable to find comparable housing (Weitzman, 1985). If a woman does get the home, it is often encumbered with a mortgage, while the man typically gets the liquid assets (Illinois Task Force, 1990). On the other hand, in most states the unpaid contributions a homemaker made to the marriage are now considered in the property settlement (Sitarz, 1990).

In many countries, such as Canada, Australia, New Zealand, and the United

A divorce mediator tries to help a couple reach a fair agreement acceptable to both. For some couples, mediation can be more amicable, quicker, and less expensive than negotiating through attorneys and can result in better compliance with the terms of the decree.

(Jim Whitmer/Stock, Boston)

States, no-fault divorce has been accompanied by increased use of mediation to resolve issues regarding the divorce settlement (Davidson, 1985; Foy, 1987). Rather than having the parties negotiate through their attorneys, a neutral third party—the mediator—guides them in sorting out their rights and responsibilities. The goal is to reach a fair agreement acceptable to both sides. Full and frank disclosure of all assets is essential, as is confidentiality (Ferstenberg, 1992; Payne & Overend, 1990).

Mediation can be more amicable, less time-consuming, and less expensive than adversarial negotiations, and because the agreement is voluntary, mediation can result in better compliance. It also may help a couple to cooperate in dealing with the needs of the children (Ferstenberg, 1992; Lemmon, 1983). Couples who are not under severe financial pressure and are coping well with the breakup of their marriage are most likely to reach a mediated settlement and to be satisfied with the process (Irving & Benjamin, 1988).

Emotional Adjustment to Divorce

Ending even an unhappy marriage can be extremely painful, especially when there are children. Divorce can bring feelings of failure, blame, hostility, and self-recrimination.

Reactions to stress may show up in poor health. Separated and divorced people have elevated rates of illness and death (Kitson & Morgan, 1990). Another common reaction is difficulty in performing ordinary social activities—a problem that, according to some research, affects divorced women more than widows (Kitson & Roach, 1989).

Adjustment depends partly on how people feel about themselves and their ex-partners, and on how the divorce was handled. The person who takes the first step to end a marriage often feels a mixture of relief, sadness, guilt, apprehension, and anger. Nonetheless, the initiating partner is usually in better emotional shape in the early months of separation than the other partner, who feels the additional pain of rejection, loss of control, and powerlessness (J. B. Kelly, 1982; Pettit & Bloom, 1984). Anger, depression, and disorganized thinking and functioning are common after divorce. So are relief and hope for a fresh start (J. B. Kelly, 1982).

An important factor in adjustment is emotional detachment from the former spouse. People who still argue with their former mates or have not found a new lover or spouse experience more emotional distress. For both sexes, an active social life helps cut the emotional ties to the ex-spouse (Tschann, Johnston, & Wallerstein, 1989).

Divorce can be especially traumatic for middle-aged and older people, who expect their lives to be relatively settled. People who divorce after age 50, particularly women, tend to have more trouble adjusting and less hope for the future (Chiriboga, 1982). Older divorced and separated men are less satisfied with friendships and leisure activities than married men. For both sexes, rates of mental illness and death are higher, perhaps because social support networks for older divorced people are inadequate (Uhlenberg & Myers, 1981).

(Joel Gordon)

Most divorced people— especially men—remarry.

Remarriage after Divorce

Remarriage, said Samuel Johnson—an eighteenth-century scholar, essayist, and poet—"is the triumph of hope over experience." An estimated three-quarters of divorced women in the United States remarry, and men are even likelier to remarry than women. A woman is more likely to remarry if her first marriage was brief, if she was young when it ended, if she has no children, if she is white and non-Hispanic, if she has a high school education, and if she lives in the west. Remarriages tend to be less stable than first marriages; 37 percent of remarriages fail within 10 years, compared with 30 percent of first marriages (Bumpass, Sweet, & Martin, 1990).

Despite the increase in divorce during the past 20 years, very few people over age 65—6 percent of women and 5 percent of men—are divorced and not remarried. Given the high divorce rates for younger age groups in recent decades, the proportion of divorced older people is likely to rise in the future, and the gap between the sexes will probably widen (Uhlenberg et al., 1990). (We discuss remarriage after widowhood in Chapter 13).

WHAT MAKES MARRIAGES SUCCEED?

Divorce has become so common that social scientists are studying why some marriages do *not* break up. In one study of 300 couples who had been happily married for at least 15 years, both men and women tended to give reasons such as a positive attitude toward the spouse as a friend and a person, commitment to marriage and belief in its sanctity, and agreement on aims and goals. Happily married couples spent much time together and shared many activities (Lauer & Lauer, 1985). Similarly, in an in-depth study of 15 couples who had been married more than 30 years, the factors that emerged most consistently were enjoyable relationships and commitment—both to the idea of marriage and to the partner. Another key factor was intimacy balanced with autonomy, which in turn either affected or was affected by good communication, similar perceptions of the relationship, and religious orientation (L. C. Robinson & Blanton, 1993).

Other studies have found that success in marriage is closely associated with how partners communicate, make decisions, and deal with conflict. In long-lived marriages, spouses tend to work out problems together rather than letting them fester (Brubaker, 1983, 1993). How couples handle disagreements and fights may predict the course of a marriage. Whining, defensiveness, stubbornness, and withdrawal (walking away or not talking to the spouse) are signs of trouble. But arguing and showing anger (as a form of communication) seem to be good for a marriage (Gottman & Krokoff, 1989). In one study that followed 150 couples through the first 10 years of marriage, those who learned to "fight fair" were 50 percent less likely to divorce (Markman, Renick, Floyd, Stanley, & Clements, 1993).

FAMILY LIFE

What is often called the *traditional family*—a husband, a wife, and their biological children—is far from universal. In Brazil, for example, a marriage does not create a new family. The man and woman continue to belong to their separate families of origin, and their children belong to both (Kottak, 1994). Family life throughout the world is highly diverse and rapidly changing (O'Grady-LeShane, 1993).

Particularly in the United States and western Europe, dramatic changes have occurred in families' size, composition, structure, and living arrangements (Eisenberg, 1995; Gilliand, 1989). What do today's families look like? Why, when, and how do adults become parents, and how does parenthood influence their development? Why do some people choose not to become parents? As we look at what has happened to the American family, keep in mind that similar trends are taking place elsewhere.

CHANGING FAMILY STRUCTURES

In 1991, barely half of American children lived in families with both biological parents—about 56 percent of white children but only 26 percent of African American children and 38 percent of Hispanic children (Furukawa, 1994). Between 1960 and 1991, the percentage of families headed by a single parent more than tripled, to nearly 29 percent (see Figure 9-3). Single parenthood is usually a result of divorce but is sometimes a matter of choice. There are almost 6 times more single mothers raising children than single fathers. Still, families headed by single fathers are one of the fastest-growing elements of the population (Outtz, 1993); the number of such families with children under 18 nearly doubled between 1980 and 1991 (U.S. Bureau of the Census, 1991a).

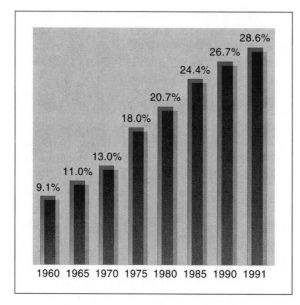

FIGURE 9-3
*Single-parent families. Since 1950,
the percentage of American families
headed by a single parent has more
than tripled.*
(Source: U.S. Bureau of the Census, 1991a.)

Divorce and remarriage have resulted in a growing number of blended families; according to one estimate, 14 percent of young children living with two parents are stepchildren. An estimated 8 to 10 million children live with homosexual parents. And, as we discuss in Chapter 10, as of 1991 more than 1 million children were being raised by grandparents (Outtz, 1993). The official definition of *family* now used by the U.S. Bureau of the Census is "two or more persons . . . residing together, and related by birth, marriage, or adoption" (1991a, p. 22).

Another important change in family life is that most mothers now work for pay, in or outside the home. In the United States, fewer than 1 in 5 families—or, according to one frequently cited estimate, fewer than 1 in 10—has a working father and a mother who is a full-time homemaker (J. Gardner, 1994; Outtz, 1993). More than 6 out of 10 married women with children under 18, and 8 out of 10 single mothers, are in the work force (K. A. Matthews & Rodin, 1989; Outtz, 1993). An estimated 1 million or more fathers stay home while their wives work—something almost unheard of when these men were growing up (Perricone, 1992). But the proportion of mothers who are employed may be leveling off, as many educated, professional women quit work and stay home to raise their babies.

PARENTHOOD TODAY

At one time, a blessing offered to newlyweds in the Asian country of Nepal was, "May you have enough sons to cover the hillsides!" Today, Nepali couples are wished, "May you have a very bright son" (B. P. Arjyal, personal communication, February 12, 1993). While sons still are preferred over daughters, even boys are not wished for in such numbers as in the past.

In preindustrial societies, large families were a necessity: children helped with the family's work and would eventually care for aging parents. The death rate in childhood was high, and having many children made it more likely that some of them would reach maturity. Today, because of technological progress, fewer workers are needed; because of modern medical care, more children survive; and because of government programs, some care of the aged is provided. Now overpopulation and hunger are major problems in some parts of the world, and children have become an expense rather than an economic asset.

One response to these changes in developing countries such as Nepal, as well as among more educated adults in industrial countries like the United States, is greater interest in limiting family size and in spacing children farther apart. In 1990, the average American woman had two children—half as many as in 1900 (Eisenberg, 1995). A United Nations population conference held in Cairo, Egypt, in September 1994 adopted a new strategy for controlling world population growth—which has been projected to double to 12.5 billion by the year 2050—by encouraging member nations to improve women's reproductive health care and give them more power to make their own reproductive choices (Cowell, 1994).

Still, the desire for children is almost universal. This urge is not limited to married people—which may be one reason that a growing number of single women have children.

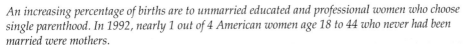

An increasing percentage of births are to unmarried educated and professional women who choose single parenthood. In 1992, nearly 1 out of 4 American women age 18 to 44 who never had been married were mothers.

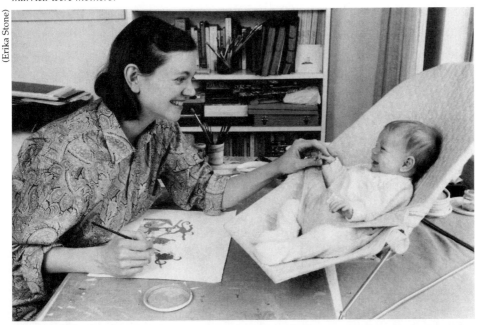

(Erika Stone)

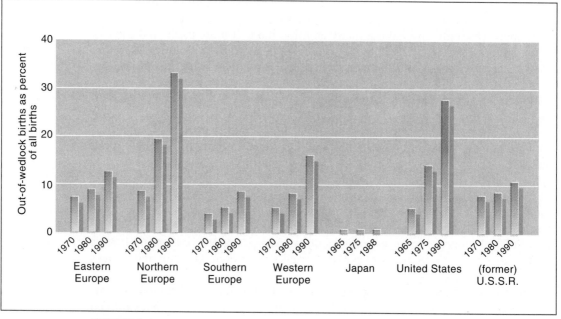

FIGURE 9-4
Out-of-wedlock births are increasing in the United States, Europe, and the former Soviet Union, but not in Japan.

NOTE: Years reported vary in some cases.

(SOURCE: Bruce, Lloyd, & Leonard, 1995, p. 73. Based on data from Council of Europe, 1993; United Nations, 1992; and U.S. Department of Health and Human Services, 1993b.)

Motherhood without Marriage

Between 1940 and 1990, births in the United States that were out of wedlock climbed from fewer than 4 percent of all births to 28 percent—a sevenfold jump in 50 years (National Center for Health Statistics, 1994). Out-of-wedlock births have also increased dramatically in other countries, especially Denmark and Sweden (Gilliand, 1989; United Nations, 1991)—though not in Japan (see Figure 9-4). In Sweden half of all births are to unmarried women; but unlike unwed mothers in the United States, these Swedish mothers generally are living in consensual unions (Eisenberg, 1995).

Nearly 25 percent of never-married American women between ages 18 and 44 were mothers in 1992, as compared with 15 percent in 1982. The change is particularly marked among educated and professional women (who tend to marry later nowadays, or not at all, and to be financially and emotionally independent) and is occurring across racial lines—although poor, uneducated, and minority women are still far more likely to become unwed mothers (Bachu, 1993). Of all black babies born in 1991, about 68 percent were born to unmarried women, compared with 22 percent of white babies and 38 percent of Hispanic babies (Eisenberg, 1995). One factor in the rise of single black mothers since the mid-1960s has been a sharp decrease in the number of marriageable black men who can support a family (W. J. Wilson, 1987).

Homosexual Parenting

Although many heterosexuals do not think children should live with openly homosexual parents, this attitude seems to be declining. In 1994, a *Newsweek* poll found that 65 percent of Americans were opposed to such family arrangements—down from 75 percent found in 1989 in polls by *Time* magazine and Cable News Network.

Opposition to homosexuals' raising children is usually based on a belief that homosexuals are more likely to abuse children or that growing up in such a family will cause children to develop a homosexual orientation or psychological problems. In actuality, abuse by homosexual parents is rare; most abusive acts are committed by heterosexual parents (R. L. Barrett & Robinson, 1990; Cramer, 1986). Openly homosexual parents usually have positive relationships with their children (Turner et al., 1985). Children raised by homosexual parents are as likely to be heterosexual as children raised by heterosexual parents (King, 1996) and no more likely to have psychological problems (Patterson, 1992). This evidence lends support to the view that sexual orientation is more influenced by biological factors than by environmental factors.

Delayed Parenthood

By and large, adults in industrialized countries today have children later in life than before. Between 1970 and 1987, the percentage of American women who had a first child after age 30 quadrupled, though most births were still to women in their twenties (National Center for Health Statistics, 1990; see Figure 11-4 in Chapter 11). In England and Wales, the birthrate among women age 35 to 39 increased by 44 percent in the 1980s, while births to women in their twenties declined by 19 percent (P. Brown, 1993). More educated women have babies later; educational level is the most important predictor of the age at which a woman will bear her first child (Rindfuss, Morgan, & Swicegood, 1988; Rindfuss & St. John, 1983). However, the trend toward motherhood after 30 appears to have peaked, at least in the United States, in part because more women who wait that long are choosing to remain childless (National Center for Health Statistics, 1994).

The risks of delayed childbearing appear to be less than previously believed. There is a greater chance of miscarriage after age 35, and more likelihood of chromosomal abnormalities or birth-related complications. But most risks to the baby's health are only slightly greater (Berkowitz, Skovron, Lapinski, & Berkowitz, 1990; P. Brown, 1993).

Infertility and New Ways to Parenthood

One risk in waiting to have children is failure to conceive. About 11 percent of American couples experience *infertility*—inability to conceive after 12 to 18 months of trying (Mosher & Pratt, 1990). The chance of infertility rises from 5 percent when a man or woman is in the early twenties to about 15 percent a decade later (R. B. Glass, 1986; Menken, Trussell, & Larsen, 1986). Sometimes drug treatment can correct the problem ("Assisted Reproduction," 1995).

BOX 9-3

THE CUTTING EDGE

Motherhood after Menopause

While many women in their fifties and sixties are enjoying their grandchildren, some women in this age group still want to bear their own children. A woman past menopause may be able to bear a child by "borrowing" ova from a younger woman.

This procedure already has been used widely with women in their thirties and forties, past what is usually considered childbearing age. A donated ovum is fertilized with sperm from the woman's husband. The resulting embryo, grown in the laboratory, is implanted in the mother-to-be, who has been given hormones to prepare her uterus for pregnancy (Lutjen et al., 1984). A research team led by Mark V. Sauer, an obstetrician and gynecologist at the University of Southern California in Los Angeles, has found this procedure as effective with women 40 to 44 years old as with women under 35 (Sauer, Paulson, & Lobo, 1990).

Now, Sauer and his colleagues have shown that women over age 50 also can have babies this way. Eight of 14 postmenopausal women treated with the technique became pregnant; one had a miscarriage, four gave birth to healthy infants, and three were still pregnant when the report was published (Sauer, Paulson, & Lobo, 1993). According to Sauer, these rates are as good as those normally obtained with 30-year-olds ("Brave New Biology," 1993). One caution, based on experience in Britain, is that *in vitro* mothers have a greater chance of multiple births (P. Brown, 1993).

Why would a woman past 50 want to have a baby? Some of the women in Sauer's study were already mothers (and even grandmothers) but had remarried and wanted to start a second family with the new spouse. Some had been too busy with their careers to have children earlier. Some couples who had already raised children simply wanted more. All were screened psychologically before being allowed to participate.

The number of older women who take advantage of this new technology is likely to remain small, in part because of the need to find donors. But what if young women could ensure their future fertility by freezing and storing their *own* ova, or sections of productive ovarian tissue, for later use? Already, four babies have been born from ova that were frozen and then thawed. Scientists in London, Melbourne, and Edinburgh are refining preservation techniques through research on mice and other animals and are also experimenting with mice as incubators for transplanted ova (P. Brown, 1993).

Such research holds out a promise of giving women greater control over their reproduction. As the editors of the British journal *New Scientist* observed: "Removing the pressure to become a mother before middle age is potentially as revolutionary a step for women as the right to vote or equal pay" ("Mind and Body," 1993).

But the prospect of postmenopausal births troubles some observers. Is there any upper limit to the age at which a woman can have a baby with the aid of science? And, just because older women *can* have babies, *should* they? Is it fair to give birth to a child knowing that there's a strong chance of not being able to see the job of parenting through?

Infertility burdens a marriage emotionally. Women, especially, often have trouble accepting the fact that they cannot do what comes so naturally and easily to others. Spouses may become angry with themselves and each other and may feel empty, worthless, and depressed (Abbey, Andrews, & Halman, 1992). Their sexual relationship suffers as sex becomes a matter of "making babies, not love" (Sabatelli, Meth, & Gavazzi, 1988). Such couples may benefit from professional counseling or support from other infertile couples.

Some infertile adults remain childless. Some, as we'll discuss in a moment, adopt children. Others avail themselves of new "high-tech" solutions, such as *artificial insemination* (injection of sperm directly into the woman's cervix), *in vitro fertilization* (fertilization of an ovum outside the mother's body and later implantation in her uterus), and *ovum transfer* (implantation of an ovum donated by a fertile woman). The congressional Office of Technology Assessment estimates that Americans spend $1 billion a year on infertility treatments, many or most of which are unsuccessful. A success rate of 12 live births for every 100 in vitro fertilizations is considered par for the course (de Lafuente, 1994). Some couples, therefore, turn to *surrogate motherhood:* impregnation of a fertile woman with the prospective father's sperm. She then bears the baby and surrenders it to the man and his wife.

New and unorthodox means of conception raise a number of ethical questions. Must people who use them be infertile, or should people be free to make such arrangements simply for convenience? Should single people and homosexual couples have access to these methods? What about women past menopause (see Box 9-3)? Should the children know about their parentage? Should chromosome tests be performed on prospective donors and surrogates? What happens if a couple who have contracted with a surrogate divorce before the birth?

Surrogate motherhood is in legal limbo, partly as a result of the "Baby M" case, in which a surrogate mother changed her mind and wanted to keep the baby (Hanley, 1988a, 1988b; Shipp, 1988). She was not granted custody of the child, but she did receive visiting rights. The American Academy of Pediatrics (AAP, 1992) recommends that surrogate parenting be considered a tentative, pre-conception adoption agreement in which, before birth, the surrogate mother is the sole decision maker. AAP also recommends a prebirth agreement on a period of time in which the surrogate may assert her parental rights. Perhaps the most objectionable aspect of surrogacy, aside from the possibility of forcing the surrogate to relinquish the baby, is the payment of money (up to $30,000, including fees to a "matchmaker"). The idea of a "breeder class" of poor and disadvantaged women who carry the babies of the well-to-do strikes many people as wrong. Still, one thing seems certain: as long as there are people who want children and who are unable to conceive or bear them, human ingenuity will come up with ways to satisfy the need.

Adoption

Since 1970, more Americans—including single people, older people, working-class families, and homosexual couples—have become adoptive parents. Adults

Diane Papalia (center, one of the authors of this textbook), her husband Jonathan, and their adopted daughter, Anna. Adoptive parents face special risks and challenges, such as the need to explain the adoption to the child.

adopt children for various reasons. Among African Americans, for example, adoption is related less to infertility than to a wish to provide a family for a known child, often a relative (Bachrach, London, & Maza, 1991). Because advances in contraception and legalization of abortion have reduced the number of adoptable healthy white American babies, many children available for adoption are disabled, are beyond infancy, or are of foreign birth.

Although adoption is accepted in the United States, there are still prejudices and mistaken ideas about it. One mistaken belief is that adopted children are bound to have problems because they have been deprived of their biological parents. Actually, a recent federally funded study of 715 families with teenagers who had been adopted in infancy found that nearly 3 out of 4 saw their adoption as playing only a minor role in their identity. However, adoption did contribute to identity problems in some cases (Bemon & Sharma, 1994). In another study of 85 adopted children, most of them viewed adoption positively—though teenagers saw it less positively than younger children (D. W. Smith & Brodzinsky, 1994).

Adopting a child does carry special risks and challenges. Besides the usual issues of parenthood, adoptive parents need to deal with acceptance of their infertility (if this is why they adopted), awareness that they are not repeating their own parents' experience, the need to explain the adoption to their children, and possible discomfort about their children's interest in the biological parents.

Blended Families

With today's high rate of divorce and remarriage, families made up of "yours, mine, and ours" are becoming more common. In 1987 there were 4.3 million such families and about 6 million stepchildren in the United States (P. C. Glick, 1989). These families face special challenges.

A *blended family* (also called a *stepfamily, reconstituted family,* or *combined family*), results from the marriage or cohabitation of adults who already have children. It is different from a "natural" family. First, it usually has a larger supporting cast, including former spouses, former in-laws, and absent parents, as well as aunts, uncles, and cousins on both sides. It is, in short, burdened by much baggage not carried by an "original" family, and it cannot be expected to function in the same way. A welter of family histories can complicate present relationships. Previous bonds between children and their biological parents or loyalty to an absent or dead parent may interfere with forming ties to the stepparent—especially when children move back and forth between two households. Disparities in life experiences are common, as when a father of adolescents marries a woman who has never had a child (Visher & Visher, 1983).

Stepfamilies have to deal with stress from losses (due to death or divorce) undergone by both children and adults, which can make them afraid to trust or love. Stepparents need to have realistic expectations and to allow time for loving relationships to develop. Stepfamilies need to see what is positive about their differences: to welcome diversity instead of resisting it. They can build new traditions and develop new ways of doing things that feel right for them. For people who have been bruised by loss, a blended family can provide the same benefits as any family that cares about all its members (Berman, 1981; Visher & Visher, 1983, 1989).

PARENTHOOD AS A DEVELOPMENTAL EXPERIENCE

Whether or not a child is a biological offspring, and whether or not the parents are married, parenthood is a developmental experience. As children develop, parents do too.

The coming of a child marks a major transition in parents' lives. Both women and men often feel ambivalent about the emotional and financial responsibilities and the necessary commitment of time and energy. About one-third of mothers find parenting both enjoyable and meaningful, one-third find it neither, and one-third have mixed feelings (Thompson & Walker, 1989). Husbands consider having children more important and are more apt to want them than wives do (Seccombe, 1991); but once the children come, fathers enjoy looking after them less than mothers do.

While fathers generally believe they should be involved in their children's lives, most are not nearly as involved as mothers are (Backett, 1987; Boulton, 1983; LaRossa, 1988; LaRossa & LaRossa, 1981). A recent study of parents of 4-year-olds in 10 European, Asian, and African countries and the United States found that fathers think they are contributing more than they actually are. Internationally, fathers average less than 1 hour a day in sole charge of their children during the work week. When men do supervise their children, it is usually with the mother. American fathers spend only 1 hour a day in such shared child care, as compared with 3 hours for Belgian and Thai fathers. American mothers, on the other hand, spend an average of nearly 11 hours each weekday caring for preschoolers—more than mothers in any of the other 10 countries (Olmsted & Weikart, 1994).

Ultimately, parenthood is a process of letting go. From the moment of birth, children's normal course of development leads toward independence. This process reaches its climax as children move through adolescence.

It is ironic that people at the two times of life most popularly linked with emotional crises—adolescence and midlife—often live in the same household. It is usually middle-aged adults who are the parents of adolescent children. While dealing with their own special concerns, parents have to deal daily with young people who are undergoing great physical, emotional, and social changes. Sometimes parents' own long-buried adolescent fantasies resurface as they watch their children turning into sexual beings. Seeing their children at the brink of adulthood makes some parents realize even more sharply how much of their own life is behind them. They may become resentful and jealous and may overidentify with the child's fantasies (Meyers, 1989).

Although recent research contradicts the stereotype of adolescence as a time of inevitable turmoil and rejection of parental values, some rebellion against parental authority is necessary for the maturing youngster to achieve independence (Offer, 1982, 1987; Offer & Schonert-Reichl, 1992). An important task for parents is to accept children as they are, not as what the parents had hoped they would be. Parents must realize that they cannot make children into carbon copies or improved models of themselves. Children may choose directions very different from those the parents want them to follow.

WHEN CHILDREN LEAVE: THE "EMPTY NEST"

For years, people have talked about the *"empty nest"*—a supposedly difficult transition or crisis, especially for women, when the last child leaves home. Actually, although most parents like to see their children frequently, they like not living with them (L. White & Edwards, 1990).

While some women who have a heavy investment in mothering do have problems at this time, they are far outnumbered by those who find it liberating not to have children at home anymore (Barnett, 1985; Mitchell & Helson, 1990; L. B. Rubin, 1979). For many women, the empty nest is a relief from the "chronic emergency of parenthood" (Cooper & Gutmann, 1987, p. 347). They can now express such qualities as assertiveness, aggression, and self-determination, which they may have repressed for the sake of harmony in the home during their years of active mothering.

The empty nest may be harder on fathers, who may regret that they did not spend more time with their children when they were younger (L. B. Rubin, 1979). This stage also appears to be hard on parents whose children do not become independent when the parents expect them to (Harkins, 1978) and on women who have not prepared for it by reorganizing their lives through work or other involvements (Targ, 1979).

The empty nest does not signal the end of parenthood; it is merely a transition to a new stage—the relationship between adult children and their parents (which we discuss in Chapter 10). Parents' ties to children may recede in importance once the children become adults, but these ties normally last as long as parent and child live.

PARENTHOOD, ROLE CHANGES, AND MARITAL SATISFACTION

A couple's joint responsibilities as parents inevitably affect their own relationship. Today, with the rise in both life expectancy and divorce, about 1 marriage in 5 lasts 50 years (Brubaker, 1983, 1993). What happens to the quality of longtime marriages as the partners deal with changing roles and patterns of childrearing, work, and retirement?

In general, marital satisfaction seems to follow a U-shaped curve. From an early high point, it declines until late middle age and then rises again through the first part of late adulthood (S. A. Anderson, Russell, & Schumm, 1983; Gilford, 1984; Glenn, 1991; Gruber & Schaie, 1986). The least happy time is the period when most couples are heavily involved in childrearing and careers. Positive aspects of marriage (such as cooperation, discussion, and shared laughter) follow the U-shaped pattern. Negative aspects (such as sarcasm, anger, and disagreement over important issues) decline from young adulthood through age 69 (Gilford, 1984; Gilford & Bengtson, 1979)—perhaps because many conflict-ridden marriages end along the way.

In one study of 175 couples, which confirmed the U-shaped curve, the researchers followed 22 couples for 30 years and the rest for shorter lengths of time. An intriguing finding was that the longer a couple were married, the more they resembled each other in their outlook on life and way of thinking—even in mathematical skills. This tendency toward likemindedness halted temporarily with the drop in marital satisfaction during the childrearing years (Gruber & Schaie, 1986). In another study of 17 marriages that lasted 50 to 69 years, nearly three-fourths were described—on the basis of interviews and observations over 50 years—as following one of two patterns: either the U-shaped curve or a fairly consistent level of happiness. None of the marriages showed either a continuous increase or a continuous decline in satisfaction (Weishaus & Field, 1988).

Let's look more closely at three sections of the curve: the early years (when parenthood usually begins), the middle years, and the later years.

The Early Years

For most couples, when children come the honeymoon is over. One research team followed 128 middle- and working-class couples from the first pregnancy until the child's third birthday. Although some marriages improved, many suffered overall, especially in the eyes of the wives. Many spouses loved each other less, became more ambivalent about their relationship, argued more, and communicated less. This was true no matter what the sex of the child and whether or not the couple had a second child by the time the first was 3 years old. But when the researchers looked not at the overall quality of the marriage, but at such specific measures as love, conflict, ambivalence, and effort put into the relationship, at least half of the sample showed either no change or a small improvement (Belsky & Rovine, 1990).

What distinguished marriages that deteriorated after parenthood from those that improved? In deteriorating marriages, the partners were more likely to be younger and less educated, to have less income, and to have been married for a shorter time. One or both partners tended to have low self-esteem, and husbands were likely to be less sensitive. The mothers who had the hardest time were those whose babies had difficult temperaments. Surprisingly, couples who were most romantic "pre-baby" had more problems "post-baby," perhaps because they had unrealistic expectations. Also, women who had planned their pregnancies were unhappier, possibly because they had expected life with a baby to be better than it turned out to be.

One often-violated expectation involves division of chores. If a couple share such chores fairly equally before the baby is born and then, after the baby's birth, the burden shifts to the wife, marital happiness tends to decline, especially for nontraditional wives (Belsky, Lang, & Huston, 1986).

The Middle Years

The U-shaped curve hits bottom during the first part of the middle years, when many couples have teenage children. Identity issues of midlife appear to affect wives' (though not husbands') feelings about their marriages; women become less satisfied with the marriage as childrearing makes fewer demands and their feelings of personal power and autonomy increase (Steinberg & Silverberg, 1987).

Communication between partners can often mitigate the stress caused by physical signs of aging, loss of sex drive, changes in work status or satisfaction, and the death of parents, siblings, or close friends. Many couples report that hard times have brought them closer (Robinson & Blanton, 1993).

In a good marriage, the departure of grown children may usher in a "second honeymoon." In a shaky marriage, though, the "empty nest" may pose a personal and marital crisis. With the children gone, a couple may realize that they no longer have much in common and may ask themselves whether they want to spend the rest of their lives together.

The Later Years

Couples in their sixties are more likely than middle-aged couples to call their marriage satisfying. Many say that their marriage has improved over the years (Gilford, 1986). Spouses who are still together late in life are likely to have worked out their differences and to have arrived at mutually satisfactory accom-

(Billy E. Barnes/Stock, Boston)

The years of middle age, when parents are likely to be raising teenage children, tend to be stressful in a marriage. Women especially, often become less satisfied.

modations. However, people may say that their marriage is happy as a conscious or unconscious justification for having stayed in it so long.

The ability of married people to handle the ups and downs of late adulthood with relative serenity may well result from mutual supportiveness, which reflects three important benefits of marriage: intimacy (sexual and emotional), interdependence (sharing of tasks and resources), and the partners' sense of belonging to each other (Atchley, 1985; Gilford, 1986). Marital satisfaction may also depend on a couple's ability to adjust to the freedom that results from shedding the roles of breadwinner and childrearer (Zube, 1982). The couple may find more interest in each other and more enjoyment in each other's company. On the other hand, as the husband becomes less involved with work and more interested in intimacy, the wife may be more interested in personal growth and self-expression. In changing roles, couples may argue over who does what. Retirement-age husbands spend less than 8 hours a week, on average, on household chores, while their wives spend nearly 20 hours a week more and do more than three-fourths of the housework (Rexroat & Shehan, 1987).

People over 70 consider themselves less happily married than those age 63 to 69. Women, who generally expect more warmth and intimacy from relationships than men do, tend to be less satisfied with marriage at this age. Advancing age and physical ills may aggravate strains on a marriage. People who have to care for disabled partners may feel isolated, angry, and frustrated, especially when they are in poor health themselves (Gilford, 1986). Caring for a spouse with dementia is especially demanding (as we discuss in Chapters 10 and 12). Caregiving spouses who are optimistic and well-adjusted to begin with, and who stay in touch with friends, do best (Hooker, Monahan, Shifren, & Hutchinson, 1992; Skaff & Pearlin, 1992).

REMAINING CHILDLESS

"When are you going to have a baby?" This question is heard less often these days, as society has moved away from the attitude that all married couples who *can* have children *should* have them (Thornton, 1989). According to a projection by the U.S. Bureau of the Census, 16 percent of "baby boom" women will not become mothers—about twice as many as in their mothers' generation (O'Connell, 1991).

About 5 to 7 percent of American couples are childless by choice (Bloom & Pebley, 1982). Some decide before marriage never to have children. Others keep postponing conception, waiting for the "right time," until they decide that the right time will never come.

Some childless couples want to devote their time and energy to social causes or careers. Some feel more comfortable with adults or think they would not make good parents. Some want to retain the untrammeled intimacy of the honeymoon. Some enjoy the freedom to travel or to make spur-of-the-moment decisions (F. L. Campbell, Townes, & Beach, 1982). But some people who want children are discouraged by the costs and the difficulty of combining parenthood with employment. Better child care and other support services might help more couples make truly voluntary decisions (Bloom & Pebley, 1982).

In general, older people without children are no lonelier, no more negative about their lives, and no more afraid of death than those with children (C. L. Johnson & Catalano, 1981; Keith, 1983; Rempel, 1985). However, widowed mothers have higher morale than childless widows (O'Bryant, 1988). Some older women express regret at not having had children; the older they are, the more intense their regret (B. B. Alexander, Rubinstein, Goodman, & Luborsky, 1992).

Whether an adult remains single, forms homosexual relationships, cohabits, marries, divorces, remarries, has children or not—all are choices that involve the establishment (or nonestablishment) of intimate relationships. Ties with parents, with grandchildren, and with siblings are different. People do not form these bonds; they are simply part of their lives. But these relationships, too, evolve and change during adulthood, as we discuss in Chapter 10.

SUMMARY

FOUNDATIONS OF INTIMATE RELATIONSHIPS

- Intimate relationships based on friendship, love, and sexuality develop and change throughout adulthood; they may be affected more by social age than by chronological age.

- Across the adult lifespan, friends can be an important source of emotional support. Older people may enjoy being with friends more than with family members. Very old people maintain friends and make new ones, but they may define friendship more broadly than before.

- According to Sternberg's triangular theory of love, the relative presence or absence of intimacy, passion, and commitment determines the nature and quality of love.

- Major changes in attitudes toward sexuality in the United States include a decline in the double standard and greater acceptance of premarital and nonmarital sex and of homosexuality.

- Research on causes of sexual orientation has found little support for environmental theories. Recent evidence points to a genetic cause or predisposition. Interaction among genetic, hormonal, and environmental events may be crucial.

NONMARITAL LIFESTYLES

- The percentage of adults who remain single has increased dramatically.

- Lesbians are more likely than male homosexuals to have stable, monogamous relationships. Homosexuals today are seeking societal recognition of their unions, as well as other rights.

- Cohabitation is increasingly accepted, in part because of the increased span between sexual and social maturity.

MARITAL AND POSTMARITAL LIFESTYLES

- The "marrying age" varies across cultures. In the United States, it tends to be later than in the past.

- Married people tend to be happier than singles, but the gap has narrowed dramatically and is less evident in women than in men.

- Divorce rates have risen sharply in many western countries. The rate in the United States is one of the highest in the world but has now leveled off.

- Societal developments contributing to the increase in divorce include greater financial independence of women, less willingness to put up with an unhappy marriage, and decreased expectations about the permanence of marriage. The economic impact of divorce is most likely to be negative for women and children.

- Most divorced people remarry. Men are more likely to remarry than women.

- Spouses in long-time marriages attribute their success to such factors as enjoyment and commitment.

FAMILY LIFE

- Families have undergone dramatic changes: single-parent households; working mothers; children raised by stepparents in blended families, by homosexual parents, or by grandparents.

- Out-of-wedlock births are increasing, especially among educated and professional women.

- Adults today in industrialized countries have fewer children and have them later.

- Infertility has new solutions: some infertile couples still adopt, but others use technologically assisted methods to conceive and bear children.

- Children raised by homosexual parents show no greater tendency toward homosexuality than other children.

- Blended families are becoming more common because of high rates of divorce and remarriage.

- Parenthood is a developmental experience: the coming of a child marks a major transition in parents' lives.

- Once grown children leave, the "empty nest" is liberating to many mothers; it may be harder on fathers who now regret not having spent more time with their children.

- Marital satisfaction generally declines during the childrearing years, then rises until age 69, then undergoes another dip.

- Remaining childless has become more socially accepted. Research has found few important drawbacks to childlessness in late life.

KEY TERMS

▼

triangular theory of love (page 325)
assortative mating (325)
sexual orientation (325)
heterosexual (325)
homosexual (325)
bisexual (325)
serial monogamy (331)
cohabitation (332)

infertility (347)
artificial insemination (349)
in vitro fertilization (349)
ovum transfer (349)
surrogate motherhood (349)
blended family (351)
empty nest (352)

MATURE KINSHIP TIES AND LIVING ARRANGEMENTS

CHAPTER 10

MATURE KINSHIP TIES AND LIVING ARRANGEMENTS

THE ADULT FAMILY: CHANGING ROLES AND RELATIONSHIPS
Young Adult Children
  and Middle-Aged Parents
Middle-Aged Children
  and Elderly Parents
Siblings
Multigenerational Late-Life Families

GRANDPARENTHOOD AND GREAT-GRANDPARENTHOOD
The Grandparent's Role
The Great-Grandparent's Role
Raising Grandchildren
  and Great-Grandchildren

LIVING ARRANGEMENTS, CAREGIVING, AND COMMUNITY SUPPORT
Adult Children at Home:
  The Not-So-Empty Nest
Living Arrangements for Older Adults
Family Caregiving
Care of the Old-Old:
  An International Perspective

BOXES
10-1 The Multicultural Context:
     The Extended-Family Household
     in Hispanic Cultures
10-2 The Cutting Edge: Establishing
     Mature Relationships with Parents
10-3 The Art of Aging:
     Choosing Living Arrangements

FOCUS: MARIAN ANDERSON

(UPI/Bettmann)

The African American contralto Marian Anderson,[*] had—in the words of the great Italian conductor Arturo Toscanini—a voice heard "once in a hundred years." She was also a pioneer in breaking racial barriers. Turned away by a music school in her home town of Philadelphia, she studied voice privately and in 1925 won a national competition to sing with the New York Philharmonic. She performed in European capitals throughout the 1930s but was often forced to put up with second-class treatment at home. When she was refused the use of a concert hall in Washington, D.C., Eleanor Roosevelt—who was then First Lady—arranged for her to sing on the steps of the Lincoln Memorial. The unprecedented performance on Easter Sunday, 1939, drew 75,000 people and was broadcast to millions. Several weeks later, Marian Anderson was the first black singer to perform at the White House. But not until 1955, a year after the Supreme Court outlawed segregated public schools, did Anderson, at age 57, become the first person of her race to sing with New York's Metropolitan Opera.

A remarkable story lies behind this woman's "journey from a single rented room in South Philadelphia" (McKay, 1992, p. xxx). It is a story of nurturing kinship ties—bonds of mutual support that extended from generation to generation.

Marian Anderson was the eldest child of John and Annie Anderson. Two years after her birth, the family left their one-room apartment to move in with her father's parents and then, after two more baby girls came along, into a small rented house nearby. John Anderson peddled coal and ice, and Annie Anderson took in laundry.

[*]The chief source of biographical material about Marian Anderson and her family is Anderson (1956, 1992). Some details come from Kernan (1993) and from obituaries published in *Time* (April 19, 1993), *People Weekly*, *The New Yorker,* and *Jet* (April 26, 1993).

The family maintained close contact with their relatives. When 6-year-old Marian showed interest in music and joined the junior choir at church, her father brought home a piano that had been sitting unused in her uncle's house. Her aunt sang duets with her and arranged for her to do a benefit concert.

When John Anderson died, the family again moved in with his parents, his sister, and her two daughters. Marian Anderson's grandfather had a steady job. Her grandmother took care of all the children, her aunt ran the house, and her mother worked as a cleaning woman to contribute to household expenses. Years later, the singer had vivid memories of her grandmother: "What she said was law. Everyone knew she was the boss, and if she wanted any of us at any time we came flying. . . . There was an old-fashioned organ in Grandmother's parlor, and I remember that she occasionally played it, her body swaying to the rhythmic pressure of her feet on the pedals. We would sit and listen quietly, knowing better than to disturb her. . . . Grandmother loved children and always had scads of them living in her house. . . . Grandmother saw to it that we each had our little jobs to do. . . . And there were useful things for us to learn, . . . how to share a home with others, how to understand their ways and respect their rights and privileges" (Anderson, 1992, pp. 17–18).

But the most important influence in Marian Anderson's life, even during her adult years, was the counsel, example, and spiritual guidance of her hardworking, unfailingly supportive mother. When her first major recital in New York's Town Hall was a financial and critical failure, her mother advised her: "Whatever you do in this world, no matter how good it is, you will never be able to please everybody. All you can strive for is to do the best it is humanly possible for you to do" (Anderson, 1992, p. 76).

Anderson and her mother had bought a small house across the street from her grandmother's, using a modest inheritance and the singer's savings from her early tours. Anderson's mother, who lived to be 89, insisted on remaining in that house even when her daughter—by then a world-renowned concert star—offered to buy her a bigger one. Annie Anderson shared the house with one of her other two grown daughters; the third daughter lived next door with her son, James DePriest.

"It is the pleasantest thing in the world to go into that home and feel its happiness. . . ." Marian Anderson wrote in 1956. "They are all comfortable, and they cherish and protect one another. . . . I know that it warms [Mother] to have her grandson near her as he grows up, just as I think that when he gets to be a man, making his own life, he will have pleasant memories of his home and family" (1992, p. 93).

The singer and her husband, an architect, never had a child of their own. During the summer, their nephews would come to stay with them on their Connecticut country estate. In 1992, Marian Anderson—widowed and frail at age 95—went to live with her nephew, DePriest, then music director of the Oregon Symphony. She died of a stroke at his home the following year.

Marian Anderson "lived through momentous changes in America and the world" and in African American life (McKay, 1992, p. xxiv). But one thing that never changed was the strong, supportive network of intergenerational and intragenerational relationships that sustained her and her family.

Relationships with family members continue to be important into very old age (C. L. Johnson & Troll, 1992). Among these important relationships are ties to the family in which one grew up—to parents, brothers, and sisters—and to new families created by one's grown children. This complex interweaving of kinship ties, extending to distant relatives, is what is meant by an *extended family.*

In less developed countries, people customarily live in multigenerational extended-family households (see Box 10-1). But that pattern is changing (Gorman, 1993). In Ghana, for example, where old age was traditionally regarded as a blessing and older adults were venerated, young adults willingly undertook their care. Now modernization, industrialization, migration to urban centers, and the coming of western religions are undermining extended family life and respect for the elderly (N. M. Brown, 1990).

In the United States and other industrialized countries, the *nuclear family*—a two-generation family made up of parents and their growing children—is the usual household unit. Adult children and parents generally want to be independent of each other. But at times—especially among minority families like Marian Anderson's—adults do live with adult relatives. This most often happens when a son or daughter has trouble getting established financially, needs a place to live after the loss of a spouse, or has other problems; or when a parent is too frail, infirm, or poor to live alone.

In this chapter, we look at ties between adults and their families of origin—their parents and siblings—and at how these roles and relationships develop and change throughout life. We discuss grandparenthood and great-grandparenthood, including special issues that may arise after adult children divorce and when grandparents are confronted with the challenge of raising their grandchildren. We also look at a variety of living arrangements, particularly in late life; at problems that arise when adults become caregivers for aging parents or other relatives; and at community support programs, both in the United States and in other societies.

THE ADULT FAMILY: CHANGING ROLES AND RELATIONSHIPS

▼

Elliott Roosevelt, a son of President Franklin Delano Roosevelt, used to tell this story: At a state dinner, Elliott's mother, Eleanor Roosevelt, who was seated next to him, leaned over and whispered in his ear. A friend later asked Elliott, then in his forties, what she had said. "She told me to eat my peas," he answered.

Even after the years of active parenting are over and the children have left home, parents are still parents. Yet the parent-child relationship does change with advancing age. So, too, do relationships with adult sisters and brothers.

BOX 10-1

THE MULTICULTURAL CONTEXT

The Extended-Family Household in Hispanic Cultures

In the colorful novels of Latin American authors such as Isabel Allende, Gabriel García Márquez, and Mario Vargas Llosa, households throb with the lively doings of grandparents, parents, and children, as well as uncles and aunts. Although these novelists infuse their stories with brilliant imaginative elements, their picture of multigenerational life in one household is rooted in fact.

Most elderly Latin Americans live in extended-family households. In Colombia, Costa Rica, the Dominican Republic, Mexico, Panama, and Peru, the proportion of extended-family households ranges from just over half (52 percent) in Mexico to almost two-thirds (64 percent) in the Dominican Republic (de Vos, 1990). In all six countries, unmarried people are more likely than married people to live in extended-family households. Overall, two-thirds of unmarried people live in extended-family households, compared with about one-half of married people. As in the United States, two married couples rarely live together, unless one couple is very old or

very young. But in the United States, unlike Latin America, unmarried older people tend to live alone rather than with family.

Since gender is even more important in Latin America than in North America in determining social roles, it is not surprising that women are more likely than men to live in extended-family households. This finding may reflect women's greater life expectancy, their closeness to their children, or their greater financial need. On the other hand, neither the age of an older person nor residence in a rural or urban setting affects the likelihood of living with relatives (de Vos, 1990).

The importance of the extended family in these cultures is reflected in Hispanic communities in the United States. Among Hispanic families, older people have traditionally received a great deal of respect. In these families (as in African American families), grandparents have played an important role in childrearing and have exerted considerable influence over family decisions. In recent years, this pattern has been breaking down, so that relations between the generations are becoming more like those in the population as a whole. Still, Hispanic people show a strong extended-family pattern, with active helping networks, and the position of the elderly remains relatively high.

(Elliot Varner Smith/International Stock Photo)

Extended-family households, like this Ecuadorian family of Otavalo Indians, are prevalent in Latin America. Women and single elderly people are more likely than men or married people to live in such households.

YOUNG ADULT CHILDREN AND MIDDLE-AGED PARENTS

Do your parents sometimes treat you like a child? Do you relate to them differently from when you were growing up? Young adults need to establish an autonomous identity and a mature relationship with their parents, and this need raises new issues and calls for new attitudes and behaviors on the part of both generations (see Box 10-2). Many parents have difficulty treating their offspring as adults, and many young people have difficulty accepting their parents' continued concern about them.

Still, young adults and their parents generally enjoy each other's company and get along well. Most parents of children age 16 or over express satisfaction with their parenting role—85 percent in one nationwide survey of more than 3,000 people. Four out of 5 parents are happy with how their children turn out, though more than 3 out of 4 are bothered or upset about them at times (Umberson, 1992). Sore points may include conflicts in values and parents' desire for their children to be like them. Some families maintain harmony by avoiding touchy intergenerational issues—they create "demilitarized zones" in which certain topics are simply off limits (Hagestad, 1984).

Young newlyweds (especially women) tend to maintain close ties with their middle-aged parents, who often help them financially, with baby-sitting, and with setting up their first homes. Parents and adult children visit frequently, and young couples spend a great deal of time talking with and about their parents. Parents generally give their children more than they get from them (Aldous, 1987; Troll, 1986, 1989; Troll, Miller, & Atchley, 1979). Their continuing support probably reflects the relative strength of middle-aged adults and the continuing needs of young adults, who are experiencing stress as they establish careers and families (Pearlin, 1980). This balance may shift as parents grow older.

MIDDLE-AGED CHILDREN AND ELDERLY PARENTS

"My mother is my best friend," says a 45-year-old woman. "I can tell her anything." A 50-year-old man visits his retired father every evening, bringing him news and asking his opinions about problems in the family business. A 40-year-old divorced mother sees her parents more often now than she did during her 15 years of marriage and needs their help more now than at any time since her teens. A couple in their early sixties find that the time they had hoped to spend traveling and playing with their grandchildren is being spent instead caring for their widowed mothers.

The bond between middle-aged children and their elderly parents is strong, growing out of earlier attachment and continuing through the rest of their lives (Cicirelli, 1980, 1989b; Rossi & Rossi, 1990). According to a study done in 1984, 4 out of 5 older adults have living children, and 2 out of 3 live within 30 minutes of at least one child. Six out of 10 see their children at least once a week, and 3 out of 4 talk on the phone that often (AARP, 1994). Older people in better health have more contact with their families than those in poorer health and report feeling closer to family members (Field, Minkler, Falk, & Leino, 1993).

BOX 10-2

THE CUTTING EDGE

Establishing Mature Relationships with Parents

When does a person become an adult? According to one study, this transition usually occurs in the late twenties—at least for white middle-class high school graduates. A dramatic shift in psychological maturity typically occurs between ages 24 and 28; it can be tracked by measuring a young adult's relationship with his or her parents. Men and women mature differently, but whether a person is married or unmarried does not seem to matter.

These conclusions emerged from interviews with 150 high school graduates from a midwestern suburb: 78 women and 72 men between ages 22 and 32 (S. J. Frank, Avery, & Laman, 1988). Participants were assessed according to 11 aspects of maturity. Five of the measures evaluated autonomy, including how well the young adults could make decisions and take responsibility for their own lives. Another five measures evaluated relationships between the generations—how close they were, how they communicated, and how the young people felt about their parents.

The researchers found six major patterns:

1. *Individuated.* Young adult (YA) feels respected by parents, freely seeks their advice and help, acknowledges their strengths, enjoys being with them, and has few conflicts with them. Yet YA feels separate from parents and is aware of (and untroubled by) a lack of intensity and depth in the relationship.

2. *Competent-connected.* YA is strongly independent, with life views that differ radically from parents' beliefs, but feels more empathic toward parents than individuated YA and often helps parents resolve their own problems of health, drinking, or relationships. The mother may be seen as demanding and critical, but YA understands her limitations, keeps conflicts within limits, and stays close to her.

3. *Pseudoautonomous.* YA pretends not to care about conflicts with parents and disengages rather than confronting parents openly. Fathers are often seen as uninterested and mothers as intrusive; both are seen as unable to accept YA for himself or herself.

Mothers and daughters are more likely to stay in close contact than any other combination of family members (G. R. Lee, Dwyer, & Coward, 1993; Troll, 1986). Daughters who have a good relationship with their parents are more likely than those with a poor relationship to report a sense of well-being and less likely to suffer anxiety or depression (Barnett, Kibria, Baruch, & Pleck, 1991). Among African Americans, adult children are more likely to visit their mothers than their fathers, and the mother-daughter relationship is especially strong (Spitze & Miner, 1992).

At midlife many people can look at their parents more objectively than before, neither idealizing them nor blaming them for mistakes and inadequacies. It becomes possible to see parents as individuals with both strengths and weaknesses. Something else happens during these years: one day a son or daughter looks at a mother or father and sees an old person. The middle-aged child real-

4. *Identified.* In this unusually open and intimate relationship, YA accepts parents' values and outlook on life, seeks advice on most major decisions, and feels secure in the parents' availability. There is little tension, and parents are seen as nonjudgmental and supportive.

5. *Dependent.* YA cannot cope with ordinary life situations without parents' help, feels troubled by this but unable to change, and sees parents as overbearing and judgmental or emotionally detached and preoccupied with themselves. YA either goes along with parents' wishes or gets into childish power struggles.

6. *Conflicted.* This pattern emerged only with fathers. YA sees the father as hot-tempered and incapable of a close relationship, feels constantly under attack, is ashamed of the father's inadequacies, and longs to be closer to him.

Young women were most likely to be "competent-connected" with their mothers and "identified" or "conflicted" with their fathers. Men were most often "individuated" with both parents or "pseudoautonomous" with their fathers. And women were somewhat more likely than men to be "dependent" on their mothers. For both sexes, age was important. About half of those over 28 felt that they could cope with most aspects of life without asking their parents for help, and only 1 in 5 had serious doubts that they could manage on their own. For people under 24, however, these proportions were reversed: only 1 in 5 felt that they could cope with most aspects of life independently, and half had serious doubts that they could manage on their own.

If findings like these are borne out by broader research, developmentalists will need to take a new look at the timetable for the end of adolescence and the beginning of adulthood, and what this means for education, career planning, and relationships between the generations. However, we need to look closely at the populations involved. This new schedule for achieving adulthood probably reflects the fact that middle-class young people remain dependent on their parents for support longer today than they did in the past. Adulthood may come sooner for less affluent young people, who become economically independent at earlier ages. We have to guard against drawing sweeping conclusions from a relatively small, limited sample.

izes that the parent is no longer a pillar of strength but is starting to lean on the child. Older adults, for their part, may look at a middle-aged child who is at a peak of achievement with new, more respectful eyes.

Of course, many parents continue to show concern about their children. Elderly parents whose children have serious problems are more likely to be depressed themselves (Pillemer & Suitor, 1991). In one study (Greenberg & Becker, 1988) more than half of the elderly mothers and one-third of the fathers experienced significant stress because of their children's problems—in the fathers' case, more because of their wives' reactions than because of the problems themselves. For mothers, the most stressful relationships were those in which a daughter had broken off contact with the family; for fathers, the most stressful relationships were with sons who continued to depend on their parents emotionally or financially.

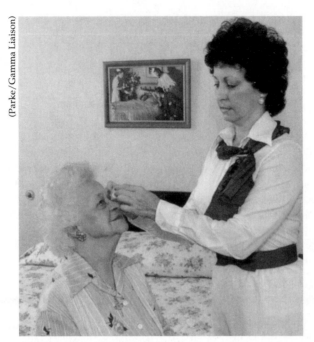

(Parke/Gamma Liaison)

The bond between middle-aged children and elderly parents is strong and generally continues as long as both parent and child live. Mothers and daughters usually remain closer than any other combination of family members. This middle-aged daughter putting drops in her mother's eyes realizes that her mother is no longer a tower of strength but instead is beginning to lean on her.

Older adults help their children in various ways, and when they need help their children are the first people they turn to and the ones likely to do the most (Field & Minkler, 1988). Middle-class parents generally "give more services and money to their children throughout their life, and children give more emotional support, household help, and care during illness" (Troll, 1986, p. 23). Among working-class families, money is more likely to flow from child to parent (Troll et al., 1979).

Many older adults resume a more active parenting role when their children need help. Single adult children receive more financial assistance from elderly parents than married ones do; divorced children are more likely to get emotional support and help with child care and housework. Unhappily married, divorced, and widowed adults often get from parents the emotional support they do not get from spouses. Parents of divorced children see them more often than before and may take them into their homes. Many parents of alcoholics and drug abusers support their children financially as well as emotionally. Parents of mentally ill, moderately retarded, or physically disabled children often maintain their protective roles as long as they live (Aldous, 1987; Greenberg & Becker, 1988). Today many parents serve as caregivers for adult children with AIDS (Brabant, 1994).

Help goes the other way, as well. Although most older adults are physically fit, vigorous, and independent, some seek their children's assistance in making decisions and may even depend on them for daily tasks and financial support. If older people become ill or infirm, their children may be faced with managing their lives.

People in American society do not fall naturally into a pattern common in many other societies, in which older people expect to live and be cared for in their children's homes, just as the parents once cared for the children. Such institutional supports as social security, Medicare, and Medicaid have shifted responsibilities from the shoulders of adult children. Still, most are conscious of their obligations to their parents and often expect more of themselves than the parents do of them. In a study of 144 parent-child pairs, both generations gave top ranking to the same three filial responsibilities: helping parents understand their resources, giving emotional support, and talking over matters of importance (see Table 10-1). Both generations gave less weight to adjusting work or family schedules to help parents. The children felt that they should give money to their parents, but most of the parents did not. More children than parents considered it important to make room for a parent in their homes in an emergency, to care for parents when they were sick, and to sacrifice personal freedom (Hamon & Blieszner, 1990).

TABLE 10-1 EXPECTATIONS OF ADULT CHILDREN AND THEIR PARENTS REGARDING FILIAL RESPONSIBILITY

Item	Adult children		Parents	
	Percent	Rank	Percent	Rank
Help understand resources	99.3	1	97.2	2
Give emotional support	97.2	2	95.7	3
Talk over matters of importance	96.5	3	98.6	1
Make room in home in emergency*	94.4	4	73.0	7
Sacrifice personal freedom*	93.7	5	81.0	6
Give care when sick*	92.4	6	64.3	9
Be together on special occasions	86.0	7	86.7	5
Give financial help*	84.6	8	41.1	13
Give parent advice	84.0	9	88.7	4
Adjust family schedule to help*	80.6	10	57.4	10
Feel responsible for parent*	78.2	11	66.4	8
Adjust work schedule to help*	63.2	12	42.1	12
Parent should live with child*	60.8	13	36.7	15
Visit once a week	51.4	14	55.6	11
Live close to parent	32.2	15	25.7	16
Write once a week	30.8	16	39.4	14

NOTES: (1) Ranking reflects percentage of respondents who "strongly agreed" or "agreed" with each item on the Hamon Filial Responsibility Scale. (2) Asterisk indicates significant differences in proportion of endorsement for children and parents. SOURCE: Adapted from Hamon & Blieszner, 1990, p. P111.

SIBLINGS

For most people, relationships with brothers and sisters are the longest-lasting. Many adult siblings (especially sisters) stay in touch and stand ready to help each other. Sibling relationships over the lifespan generally take the form of an hourglass, with the largest amount of contact at the two ends: childhood and middle to late adulthood. Marriage often means less contact (the slim neck of the hourglass), though it rarely affects the emotional quality of the sibling relationship. The arrival of children may bring siblings closer together, as do such negative events as divorce, widowhood, or the death of a family member (Connidis, 1992).

Sibling Relationships in Middle Age

After establishing their own identities through career and family, middle-aged siblings often make special efforts to renew ties, and earlier rivalry tends to be replaced by intimacy and affection (Cicirelli, 1980; H. G. Ross, Dalton, & Milgram, 1980; J. P. Scott & Roberto, 1981). More than two-thirds of people with living siblings—some 85 percent of middle-aged Americans—feel close or very close to their brothers and sisters and have good relationships with them; more than three-fourths say that they get along well or very well (Cicirelli, 1980). Closeness—both emotional and geographic—and a sense of responsibility for each other's welfare are the most important influences on how often brothers and sisters see each other (T. R. Lee, Mancini, & Maxwell, 1990). Siblings usually get together at least several times a year—in many cases, once a month or more. It is unusual for them to lose touch completely (Cicirelli, 1980).

Issues sometimes arise over the care of elderly parents and over inheritance, especially if the sibling relationship has not been good. In one study of 140 sibling pairs who were caring for one or both parents, many of the participants felt they were doing more for their parents and deriving more satisfaction from helping them than their siblings were. The closer the siblings, the more they agreed in assessing their respective contributions (Lerner, Somers, Reid, Chiriboga, & Tierney, 1991). Among 95 married daughters caring for parents with dementia, siblings were a strong source of support—but also the most important source of interpersonal stress (Suitor & Pillemer, 1993).

Sibling Relationships in Late Life

Elizabeth ("Bessie") and Sarah ("Sadie") Delany both lived to be over 100; their father was a freed slave who became an Episcopalian bishop. Bessie overcame racial and gender discrimination to become a dentist, and Sadie became a high school teacher. The sisters never married. Determined to be independent, for three decades they lived together in Mount Vernon, New York. Although their personalities were as different as sugar and spice—and had been since childhood—the two women were best friends, sharing a sense of fun and the values their parents instilled in them (Delany, Delany, & Hearth, 1993).

(Jacques Chenet/Gamma Liaison)

Bessie and Sadie Delany, daughters of a freed slave, were best friends all their lives—more than 100 years—and wrote two books together about the values they grew up with and the story of their long, active lives. Elderly siblings are an important part of each other's support network, and sisters are especially vital in maintaining family relationships.

More than 75 percent of Americans age 65 and older have at least one living sibling, and brothers and sisters play important roles in the support networks of older people (Scott & Roberto, 1981). Elderly siblings see each other as often as in middle age and are just as involved (Field & Minkler, 1988). The nearer people live to their siblings and the more siblings they have, the more likely they are to confide in them (Connidis & Davies, 1992). Sisters are especially vital in maintaining family relationships (Cicirelli, 1989a). Among a national sample of bereaved adults in the Netherlands, those coping with the death of a sister experienced more difficulty than those who had lost a spouse or a parent (Cleiren, Diekstra, Kerkhof, & van der Wal, 1994).

For people who have only one or two children, or none, relationships with siblings in late life may be increasingly important as a source of emotional support and practical help (Cicirelli, 1980; Rubinstein, Alexander, Goodman, & Luborsky, 1991; Scott & Roberto, 1981). Both brothers and sisters and their children provide such support to never-married women (Rubinstein et al., 1991).

Looking back, older people who feel close to their brothers or sisters express a sense of peace with life and with themselves, whereas those who are estranged from their siblings often feel upset, as if they have failed to live up to expectations. Siblings who have reestablished ties generally feel that they have accomplished something important (H. G. Ross et al., 1980).

MULTIGENERATIONAL LATE-LIFE FAMILIES

While the family remains the primary source of emotional support for older adults, the late-life family has certain special characteristics (Brubaker, 1983, 1990). First and foremost, it often spans four or five generations. Today an increasing number of adults play the roles of grandparent and grandchild at the same time. For the first time in history, most adults live long enough to see their grandchildren grow up, and most grandchildren have a chance to know at least two and often three or all four grandparents (Cherlin & Furstenberg, 1986b).

The presence of so many family members can be enriching but can also create special pressures. As we'll see in the next section, the role of grandparent is not as clear as it used to be. Divorce and remarriage can interfere with grandparent-grandchild relationships. On the other hand, despite sagging energy, some grandparents and even great-grandparents step in and raise grandchildren.

In addition, more "young-old" people have at least one parent who has lived long enough to have several chronic illnesses and whose care may be physically and emotionally draining. Many women today spend more of their lives caring for parents than for children (Abel, 1991). Now that the fastest-growing group in the population is age 85 and over, many people in their late sixties or beyond—whose own health and energy may be faltering—find themselves in this position. The *parent-support ratio*—the number of people 85 and over for every 100 people age 50 to 64—tripled (from 3 to 10) between 1950 and 1993; it may triple again by 2053 (U.S. Bureau of the Census, 1995).

In Japan, whose population is aging more rapidly than that of any other industrialized country, the problem will be particularly acute. By 2020, Japan will have the oldest *age structure*—that is, the largest percent of aged people—of any society on earth, and half of its elderly population will be 75 or older. It is predicted that the number of bedridden or demented elderly people—who, under Japanese tradition, are expected to live in the home of the eldest son—will approximately double to 3 million by 2010 (Nishio, 1994). (We discuss family caregiving later in this chapter.)

GRANDPARENTHOOD
AND GREAT-GRANDPARENTHOOD

In some African communities, grandparents are called "noble." In Japan, grandmothers wear red as a sign of their status (Kornhaber, 1986). Although most western societies have no badges or titles of honor, becoming a grandparent can be an extremely important event in a person's life.

Adults in the United States usually become grandparents for the first time in middle age—women, on average, at 50 and men at 52 (Troll, 1983). African Americans of both sexes generally become grandparents earlier than whites (Strom, Collinsworth, Strom, & Griswold, 1992–1993). More than 75 percent of older Americans are grandparents, and more than 40 percent are great-grandparents (Menninger Foundation, 1994).

Today's busy, active grandparents often are torn between personal, work, and family needs. Still, they can be an important influence on their grandchildren's development. Most grandparents fall into a companionate style: they do not intervene in the children's upbringing unless the need arises but enjoy frequent, casual companionship.

With increased longevity, most people spend more of their lives as grandparents than in past generations (Cherlin & Furstenberg, 1986b). But they have fewer grandchildren. Because young adults have smaller families, and a growing number remain childless, the average 60-year-old grandparent today has only 3 grandchildren, compared with 12 to 15 around the turn of the century (Uhlenberg, 1988). Men and women whose adult children have postponed or decided against parenthood often feel disappointed and somehow cheated. Some become foster grandparents or volunteer in schools or hospitals (Porcino, 1983, 1991).

THE GRANDPARENT'S ROLE

Today's grandparents are likely to be designing rocking chairs rather than sitting in them, marketing cookies rather than baking them, and wearing jogging suits instead of aprons. The changes grandparents have lived through have resulted in lifestyles and roles very different from those of previous generations.

In families like Marian Anderson's, grandparents were an essential part of the family's economic and emotional health. In some cultures, they still are. In a United Nations study of four developing countries—Chile, the Dominican Republic, Sri Lanka, and Thailand—66 to 90 percent of older adults were involved in major family decisions, and 19 to 49 percent gave financial support to grandchildren (Kaiser, 1993). But in most developed countries, the predominance of the nuclear family and other social changes have made the grandparent's role more peripheral.

Grandparenthood, especially when families were large, used to be seen as a natural extension of parenthood; the youngest child was barely launched, or still at home, when the eldest began having babies. Today, there is a gap between the emptying of one generation's nest and the filling of the next, and this is a time when many middle-aged parents spread their own wings and make important life changes. Like young adults, they may move wherever their inclinations or aspirations take them. And rising living standards, together with social security, have made the generations less financially dependent on each other (Cherlin & Furstenberg, 1986b; Kornhaber & Woodward, 1981).

Active grandparents like Marian Anderson's grandmother can still be an important influence on their grandchildren's development. They are a link to the extended family. Grandparent and grandchild know each other intimately, on many levels. The grandparent serves as teacher, caretaker, role model, and sometimes negotiator between child and parent. But how prevalent is this kind of grandparenting? Interviews with 300 grandchildren, age 5 to 18, and 300 grandparents suggest that only 15 percent of children have this "vital connection" (Kornhaber, 1986; Kornhaber & Woodward, 1981).

Today's busy, lively grandparents face a conflict between personal and family needs (Cherlin & Furstenberg, 1986b; Kornhaber & Forsyth, 1994). Many feel that they have raised their children and now are entitled to pursue their own interests. Yet they may have an uneasy feeling that they are missing out on something important: intimacy with their grandchildren (Kornhaber, 1986; Kornhaber & Woodward, 1981).

While grandparenthood has changed, the role can still be positive and significant. A major study of a three-generational, nationally representative sample found that "grandparents play a limited but important role in family dynamics" and that many have strong emotional ties to their grandchildren (Cherlin & Furstenberg, 1986a, p. 26). The researchers found three styles of grandparenting: remote, companionate (the predominant style), and involved. *Remote* grandparents (29 percent) see their grandchildren so infrequently that the relationship is more symbolic than real. *Companionate* grandparents (55 percent) do not intervene directly in the children's upbringing but enjoy frequent, casual companionship. Only 16 percent of grandparents are *involved* to the extent of disciplining or correcting their grandchildren, giving advice, discussing the child's problems, being consulted on important decisions concerning the child, and exchanging help with errands, chores, and projects. (Figure 10-1 shows the most frequent grandparent-grandchild activities.) Younger grandparents, those who see their grandchildren almost every day, and those who have a close relationship with the child's mother are more likely to be involved.

Grandparenting styles may differ with different grandchildren, and at different times in a child's life. Grandparents are likely to be more involved during a child's preadolescent years (Cherlin & Furstenberg, 1986b). However, satisfaction with grandchildren stays high into very old age, even though the generations see each other less often as children grow up (Field & Minkler, 1988).

One prominent researcher (Troll, 1980, 1983) sees grandparents as family "watchdogs." They stay on the fringes of their children's and grandchildren's

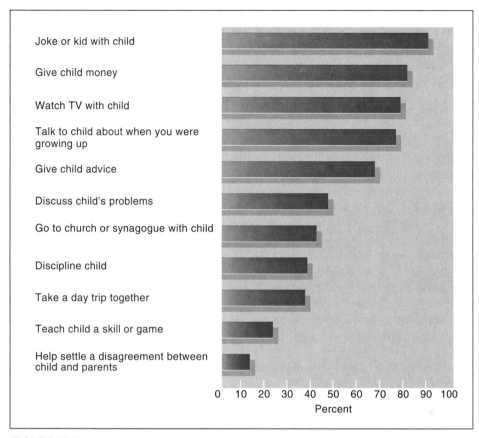

FIGURE 10-1

What grandparents do with their grandchildren: proportions of grandparents in a nationally representative sample who had engaged in various activities with their grandchildren in the previous 12 months.

(SOURCE: Cherlin & Furstenberg, 1986b, p. 74.)

lives, watching to be sure that things are going well, but rarely play a strong role unless they need to. In a crisis—after a divorce, for example, or during illness or money troubles—they may step in and become more active (Cherlin & Furstenberg, 1986a, 1986b). Some grandparents do even more. In 1987, nearly 14 percent of preschool children of employed mothers were under a grandparent's care in the daytime (U.S. Bureau of the Census, 1990). And some grandparents, as we will see, raise a grandchild when the parents cannot or will not do it.

Gender and Racial Differences

Grandmothers tend to have closer, warmer relationships than grandfathers with their grandchildren and to serve more often as surrogate parents. The mother's parents are likely to be closer to the children than the father's parents and are more likely to become involved during a crisis (Cherlin & Furstenberg, 1986a,

1986b; Hagestad, 1978, 1982; B. Kahana & Kahana, 1970). Grandmothers tend to be more satisfied with grandparenting than grandfathers are (J. L. Thomas, 1986). However, grandfathers may be more nurturing and more physically demonstrative with their grandchildren than they were with their own children; they may regard grandparenthood as a "second chance" to make up for their failings as parents (Kivnick, 1982). Grandfatherhood may be more central for African American men than for white men (Kivett, 1991). African American grandparents are more likely to become involved in raising their grandchildren, even when there is no crisis (Cherlin & Furstenberg, 1986a, 1986b; Strom et al., 1992–1993).

A recent study (Strom et al., 1992–1993) compared 204 black and 204 white grandparents' perceptions about grandparenting. The researchers also compared how 295 black and 175 white grandchildren, age 7 to 18, assessed their grandparents. (These youngsters were not related to the grandparents who participated in the study.) While both groups of grandparents rated their performance favorably, black grandparents scored themselves significantly higher than white grandparents. The children's answers were more mixed. Black children rated their grandparents higher in overall success and in teaching about right and wrong, good manners, the importance of learning, and caring about the feelings of others. (Black grandparents, too, saw teaching as their greatest strength, even though they had less formal education than their white counterparts.) White children gave their grandparents higher ratings in coping with difficulty, managing frustration, and understanding what it is like to grow up today.

An apparent factor in the success of black grandparents is their investment of time. Black grandparents are more than twice as likely as white grandparents to spend at least 5 hours a month with their grandchildren. Not surprisingly, grandparents of both races who spent more time with their grandchildren considered themselves more effective, and the grandchildren agreed. The races had different perspectives on the effect of a grandparent's age. Black grandparents age 60 and over rated themselves as more effective than younger grandparents; again, the grandchildren agreed. The opposite was true for white grandparents. Black children said older grandparents had more of an influence on them; white children found younger grandparents more supportive. Black grandparents' strengths—teaching, willingness to spend time with grandchildren of all ages, acceptance of family responsibilities regardless of distance, and effectiveness during old age—make them "a powerful influence in the lives of grandchildren," the study concluded (p. 266).

Grandparenting after Divorce and Remarriage

Because ties with grandparents are so important to children's development, since 1965 every state in the United States has passed legislation giving grandparents (and in some states, great-grandparents, siblings, and others) the right to seek court-enforced visitation after divorce or the death of a parent. Such visitation is not automatic; a judge must find it in the best interest of the child. The decision may depend on what kind of relationship the grandparents and grandchild have had, and whether or not the visits seem likely to interfere with the parent-child relationship or otherwise upset the child (Edelstein, 1990–1991; Lake, 1989).

Such laws, important though they are, cannot obscure the fact that divorce changes relationships, not only among a father, mother, and children, but with grandparents as well. In intact families, both sets of grandparents generally have about the same access and involvement. But after a divorce, since the mother usually has custody, her parents tend to have more contact and stronger relationships with their grandchildren, while the paternal grandparents tend to have less (Cherlin & Furstenberg, 1986b). Paternal grandparents may suffer grief, disappointment, anger, and a sense of loss (Myers & Perrin, 1993). Even if the children's mother does not break contact, it may be awkward for the father's parents to keep it up if their son has dropped out of his children's lives (Cherlin & Furstenberg, 1986b).

A mother's remarriage generally reduces the need for support from her parents, but not their contact with their grandchildren. However, it may increase the likelihood that the paternal grandparents will be displaced or that the family will move away, making contact more difficult (Cherlin & Furstenberg, 1986b). A new union usually brings a new set of grandparents into the picture, and often additional grandchildren as well.

Middle-aged and older adults may also become stepgrandparents after their own remarriage. One-third of the grandparents in the national three-generational survey discussed above (Cherlin & Furstenberg, 1986b) had at least one stepgrandchild. When families "multiply by dividing," the web of connections becomes complex (T. S. Kaufman, 1993, p. 226). Stepgrandparents may find it hard to establish close relationships with their new stepgrandchildren, especially older children and those who do not live with the grandparent's adult child (Cherlin & Furstenberg, 1986b; Myers & Perrin, 1993). Such issues as birthday and Christmas presents for a "real" grandchild's half- or stepsiblings, or which grandparents are visited or included at holidays, can generate tension. Still, a combined family can offer expanded opportunities for love and nurturing when grandparents are determined to build bridges rather than walls (T. S. Kaufman, 1993).

THE GREAT-GRANDPARENT'S ROLE

When Dorothy Bernstein died at age 86, six great-grandchildren under age 6 were at her funeral. Her three adult grandchildren spoke of how proud she had been of becoming a great-grandmother, and how—even during her final illness—her eyes had lit up when the little ones came to visit her (R. D. Feldman, personal observation, March 6, 1994).

When grandchildren grow up and become parents, grandparents move into a new role: great-grandparenthood. Because of age, declining health, and the scattering of families, great-grandparents tend to be less involved than grandparents in a child's life. And because four- or five-generation families are relatively new, there are few generally accepted guidelines for what great-grandparents are supposed to do (Cherlin & Furstenberg, 1986b).

Still, most great-grandparents find the role emotionally fulfilling. When 40 great-grandfathers and great-grandmothers, age 71 to 90, were interviewed, 93 percent were enthusiastic. More than one-third (mostly women) were close to their great-grandchildren; the others had less contact. The ones who were close to the children were likely to live nearby and to be close to the children's parents and grandparents. They often helped out with loans, gifts, and baby-sitting (Doka & Mertz, 1988).

Both grandparents and great-grandparents can be important to their families. They are sources of wisdom, companions in play, links to the past, and symbols of the continuity of family life. As Erikson has observed (see Chapter 11), they express a natural longing to transcend mortality by investing themselves in the lives of future generations.

RAISING GRANDCHILDREN AND GREAT-GRANDCHILDREN

"We hadn't had children in our home for years; suddenly they were there almost 24 hours a day," said Mary Etta Johnson (Larsen, 1990–1991, p. 32). Johnson and her husband, Albert, took their two preschool-age grandchildren into their home after their daughter and son-in-law became involved with drugs and divorced. About 1 year later, the Johnsons obtained permanent custody.

An increasing number of American grandparents and great-grandparents from their late thirties to their late seventies—anywhere from 551,000 to 3 mil-

June Sands of Los Angeles hugs her 5-year-old daughter, Victoria, as her mother—Victoria's guardian, Elaine Sands—smiles fondly. Elaine and her husband, Don Sands, are among a growing number of grandparents raising grandchildren, temporarily or permanently. Elaine and Don took over Victoria's care while June was overcoming a 20-year drug addiction. June Sands had been in jail and in withdrawal when her daughter was born, but she had been drug-free for a year when this picture was taken. She lived near her parents, worked as a baby-sitter in a health club, and visited her daughter regularly.

(Eugene Richards/Magnum Photos)

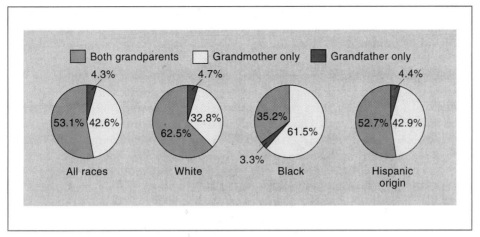

FIGURE 10-2

Grandparents maintaining families with grandchildren present, by gender and race, 1991, percent.
When grandparents raise grandchildren, the grandmother is almost always present. The
grandmother is more likely to raise grandchildren alone in black families than in others.
(SOURCE: Schick & Schick, 1994.)

lion, by various estimates—are serving as "parents by default" for children
whose parents are addicted to drugs or alcohol, divorced, dead, physically or
mentally ill, unwed, underage, unemployed, abusive, neglectful, or in jail, or
who have simply abandoned them (Chalfie, 1994; Landers, 1992a). Census figures show a 16 percent increase in **kinship care**—children growing up in homes
of relatives without their parents—during the 1980s (Landers, 1992b). A 17
percent rise in the number of grandchildren raised by grandparents occurred in a
single year, from 1992 to 1993 (Chalfie, 1994). Many of these children have behavioral or learning problems as a result of a parent's abuse of alcohol or drugs
(Landers, 1992a). Most grandparent caregivers (68 percent) are white; 29 percent are black. Of those who are single, 93 percent are women (Chalfie, 1994; see
Figure 10-2).

This phenomenon is occurring elsewhere as well. During war, famine, or other
disasters, young adults in less developed countries may go off in search of food
or safety, leaving the grandparents to care for the young (Gorman, 1993). In many
parts of Africa, the older generation are giving double care—first for adult children with AIDS and then for *their* orphaned children.

Unplanned "parenthood" of this nature can be a physical, emotional, and
financial drain on middle-aged or older adults (Burton, 1992; Minkler & Roe,
1992). They may have to quit their jobs, shelve their retirement plans, and drastically reduce their leisure pursuits and social life to deal with the rigors of childrearing. Most grandparents don't have as much energy, patience, or stamina as
they once had, and sorely needed social services such as respite care are generally unavailable (Crowley, 1993). Financial ruin may become a real threat. More
than 40 percent of grandparent caregivers are poor or nearly poor. Their median
annual income is $18,000, half that of a two-parent family (Chalfie, 1994).

Most grandparents who take on this responsibility do it because they love the children and do not want them placed in foster homes with strangers. Two-thirds of custodial grandparents, according to one study, report a greater sense of purpose in life (Jendrek, 1994). But many are ambivalent. The age difference between grandparent and grandchild can become a barrier; and both generations may feel cheated out of their traditional roles. At the same time, grandparents often have to deal with grief, anger, and pain; with a sense of guilt and failure because the adult children they raised have failed their own children; and with rancor between themselves and their adult child. For some caregiver couples, the strains may produce tension in their own relationship (Crowley, 1993; Larsen, 1990–1991). If parents later resume their normal role, the grandparent may find it emotionally wrenching to return the child (Crowley, 1993).

Grandparents who do not become foster parents or gain custody have no legal status and no more rights than unpaid baby-sitters; they face many practical problems, from getting medical insurance for the child to enrolling the child in school or qualifying for public housing. Obtaining legal custody can be difficult, time-consuming, and expensive, and custody can be taken away if a parent later challenges it. Custody laws vary from state to state. Grandparents' rights activists are urging national custody standards, as well as other legal remedies such as allowing a primary caregiver's insurance to cover a child. Some family advocates propose a new legal category called *kinship adoption*, which would allow the birth parent to retain a limited role, with the right, for example, to visit the child and to see school records (Crowley, 1993; Landers, 1992a).

LIVING ARRANGEMENTS, CAREGIVING, AND COMMUNITY SUPPORT

Living independently is a hallmark of adulthood in the United States. Sometimes, however, circumstances limit choices. Let's look at what happens when adult children do not leave their parents' household, or when they return to it. Then we'll examine where older adults live and with whom, the role of community support, and what happens when aging adults need long-term care.

ADULT CHILDREN AT HOME: THE NOT-SO-EMPTY NEST

What if a nest does not empty when it normally should, or is refilled by young adults returning home to live? This unanticipated situation—like that of grandparents raising grandchildren—may lead to tension (Lindsey, 1984).

In recent decades more young adults are returning to their parents' homes (Glick & Lin, 1986a). Jobs are harder to get, housing costs have climbed, couples have postponed marriage, and divorce and unwed parenthood have risen (Clemens & Axelson, 1985; Glick & Lin, 1986a). Those most likely to come "home" are never-married people and, to a lesser extent, divorced or separated people (Ward, Logan, & Spitze, 1992). Most parents express satisfaction with the arrangement, especially when it is temporary and when the adult child is under age 22 (Clemens & Axelson, 1985). Parents appreciate help with household chores and with caring for younger children, and they enjoy sharing leisure activities. Usually everyone is active and healthy.

But serious conflicts may arise, especially when a young adult child is unemployed and financially dependent. Disagreements may center on household responsibilities and the child's lifestyle: dress, sex, alcohol, drugs, and choice of friends. The young adult is likely to feel isolated from peers and to have trouble establishing intimacy, while the parents may have to postpone renewing their own intimacy, exploring personal interests, and resolving marital issues. The most difficult situation for parents seems to be the return of divorced or separated children with their own children (Aquilino & Supple, 1991). The return of an adult child works best when parent and child negotiate their roles and responsibilities, acknowledging the child's full adult status and the parents' right to their own privacy and independence.

When an adult child moves into the home of elderly parents, the parents report that the generations get along quite well (Suitor & Pillemer, 1987, 1988). Reported conflict is lowest in households with older adult children and households in which parent and child have the same or similar marital status. It may be that people who get along well are those most likely to choose to live together.

LIVING ARRANGEMENTS FOR OLDER ADULTS

About 95 percent of Americans age 65 and older, including 79 percent of those who are disabled, live in the community, not in institutions (AARP, 1994; U.S. Department of Health and Human Services, USDHHS, 1995). More than two-thirds of the noninstitutionalized elderly—82 percent of men and 57 percent of women—live with family members. Most live with a spouse; about 13 percent live with children or other relatives (AARP, 1994; see Figure 10-3). Elderly men are more likely than women, and white people are more likely than black people, to live with a spouse (AARP, 1994; U.S. Bureau of the Census, 1991a). About 30 percent live alone—41 percent of the women, though only 16 percent of the men.

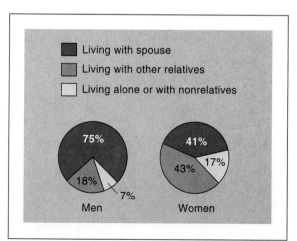

FIGURE 10-3

Living arrangements of noninstitutionalized persons age 65 and older, 1992.

(SOURCE: AARP, 1994; based on data from U.S. Bureau of the Census.)

THE ART OF AGING

Choosing Living Arrangements

Three friends in their late sixties bought a big old house and turned it into a "geriatric commune" with shared kitchen and dining room. "It takes a lot of the stress out of aging to know you have a place that's yours and people who will care," they say (Porcino, 1993, pp. 28, 30).

This is but one of an almost bewildering range of choices in living arrangements available to older adults today (see Table 10-2). Let's see how various options match up with specific lifestyles and needs.

Many aging couples and single adults who can manage on their own or with minimal help stay in the homes or apartments they have lived in for years. "Aging in place" makes sense for those who have an adequate income or a paid-up mortgage, can manage the upkeep, are happy in the neighborhood, and want to be near friends, adult children, or grandchildren.

Older adults who don't want to maintain a large house, don't have a family nearby, or prefer a different locale or climate may decide to move into low-maintenance or maintenance-free townhouses, condominiums, or cooperative or rental apartments. Or they may buy mobile homes so that they can travel and visit far-flung family members.

Those who want or need a higher level of amenities, services, or care without sacrificing independence or dignity may want to consider the following options:

- *Retirement hotel.* Hotel or apartment building remodeled to meet the needs of independent older adults. Typical hotel services (switchboard, maid service, message center) are provided.

- *Retirement community.* Large, self-contained development with owned or rental units or both. Support services and recreational facilities are often available.

- *Shared housing.* Housing can be shared informally by adult parents and children or by friends. Sometimes social agencies match people who need a place to live with people who have houses or apartments with extra rooms. The older person usually has a private room but shares living, eating, and cooking areas and may exchange services such as light housekeeping for rent.

The likelihood of living alone increases with age. Two percent of women and 3 percent of men live with nonrelatives (AARP, 1994; U.S. Bureau of the Census, 1995).

Most older people want to live in the community. Those who do feel better than those in institutions, even when their health is about the same (Chappell & Penning, 1979). But living arrangements can become a major problem as people age. A person may no longer be able to manage three flights of stairs. A neighborhood may deteriorate, and helpless-looking older people may become prey to young thugs. Mental or physical disability may make living alone impractical.

Most older people do not need much help; those who do need help can usually remain in the community if they have at least one person to depend on. The single most important factor keeping people out of institutions is being married

- *Accessory apartment* or *ECHO (elder cottage housing opportunity) housing.* An independent unit created so that an older person can live in a remodeled single-family home or in a portable unit on the grounds of a single-family home—often, but not necessarily, that of an adult child. These units offer privacy, proximity to caregivers, and security.

- *Congregate housing.* Private or government-subsidized rental apartment complexes or mobile home parks designed for older adults. They provide meals, housekeeping, transportation, social and recreational activities, and sometimes health care. One type of congregate housing is called a *group home.* A social agency that owns or rents a house brings together a small number of elderly residents and hires helpers to shop, cook, do heavy cleaning, drive, and give counseling. Residents take care of their own personal needs and take some responsibility for day-to-day tasks.

- *Assisted-living facility.* Semi-independent living in one's own room or apartment. Similar to congregate housing, but residents receive personal care (bathing, dressing, and grooming) and protective supervision according to their needs and desires. *Board-and-care homes* are similar but smaller and offer more personal care and supervision.

- *Foster-care home.* Owners of a single-family residence take in an unrelated older adult and provide meals, housekeeping, and personal care.

- *Continuing care retirement community.* Long-term housing planned to provide a full range of accommodations and services for affluent elderly people as their needs change. A resident may start out in an independent apartment; then move into congregate housing with such services as cleaning, laundry, and meals; then into an assisted-living facility; and finally into a nursing home. *Life-care communities* are similar but guarantee housing and medical or nursing care for a specified period or for life; they require a substantial entry fee in addition to monthly payments.

(Health Care Finance Administration, 1981; C. L. Johnson & Catalano, 1981). As long as a couple are in relatively good health, they can usually live fairly independently and care for each other. The issue of living arrangements becomes more pressing when one or both become frail, infirm, or disabled, or when one spouse dies.

People who are not living with a spouse most often get help from a child, usually a daughter. Those who cannot call on a spouse or child usually get help from friends (Chappell, 1991). Social activities, such as going to church or temple or a senior center, or doing volunteer work, help people stay in the community (Steinbach, 1992). And an emerging array of housing options and community support programs are making it easier for older people to live with some degree of independence (see Box 10-3 and Table 10-2).

TABLE 10-2 OPTIONS FOR LIVING ARRANGEMENTS

	Financing			Amenities										Restrictions				
	Own	Rent	Extra fees/dues	Home health care	Housekeeping services	Laundry services	Meals provided	Nursing care	Property maintenance	Recreational facilities	Resident governance	Social activities	Transportation	Age	Waiting list	Rules/regulations	Children allowed	Pets allowed
Accessory apartment	■	■												▲				
Apartment		●	▲		▲	▲			●	■	■	■		▲	■	■	■	■
Assisted-living facility/ board-and-care home		●		●	●	●	●	■	●	■	■	●		■	■	■	●		■
Congregate housing		●	●	■	●	●	●	▲	●	●	■	●	●	●	■	■	▲	■
Continuing-care retirement community	■	■	●	●	●	●	●	●	●	●	●	●	●	●	■	●	▲	■
Cooperative housing		●	▲	▲	▲	▲	▲	●	■	●	■	▲		■	■	■	●	■	■
ECHO housing	■	●												■				
Foster-care home		●		●	●	●	●	▲	●	■	▲	●		■	●	■	●	■	■
Manufactured (mobile) home	●	■		▲	▲	▲	▲	▲	●	■	■	■	▲	■	■	■	●	■
Retirement community	■	■	■				■	■	■	●	■	●	■	■	■	●		■
Retirement hotel		●	●	▲	●	●	●	▲	●	■	▲	■	▲	●	●	■	●	▲	▲
Shared housing	■	■	■	▲	■	■	■	▲	■	▲	●	■	■	■	■	■	■	■
Single-family residence	●	■																
Townhouse/ condominium	●	■	●	▲	▲	▲	▲	▲	■	■	●	■		▲	▲	●	■	■

NOTE: ● = usually; ■ = sometimes; ▲ = rarely
SOURCE: *Modern Maturity*, April–May 1993, pp. 32–33.

Living Alone

A growing number of older Americans live alone and like it. Between 1980 and 1993, the percentage of older people living alone increased by 32 percent. Of the 9.4 million older people who live alone, 7.4 million are women (AARP, 1994). Eighty percent are widowed, and almost 50 percent have either no children or none living nearby. They are older and poorer on the average than elderly people who live with someone else. Yet almost 90 percent value their independence and prefer to be on their own. Fewer than 1 percent say they would rather live with their children (Commonwealth Fund, 1986; U.S. Bureau of the Census, 1992b).

Ethnic factors seem to influence this choice. Among elderly Americans of European ancestry, those whose roots are in southern, central, or eastern Europe are more likely than people from northwestern Europe to live with relatives. These patterns hold no matter how many generations have been in the United States (Clarke & Neidert, 1992).

African American men and women age 65 to 74 are significantly more likely to live alone than white men and women, though that is not true among older cohorts (USDHHS, 1992). Increases in divorce and single life began showing up earlier among African Americans who now are entering late adulthood. Also, because of the low life expectancy of black men and their tendency to marry younger women, their wives are likely to be widowed at an early age. Women in general are less likely than men to remarry after being widowed, and that is especially true of black women—perhaps because of their relative economic independence and their disinclination to have to care for an elderly man. An analysis of data from a nationally representative survey of African Americans found that as black women age they are increasingly less likely than men to be married, romantically involved, or interested in a romantic relationship. Unmarried women were better off financially than married ones (Tucker, Taylor, & Mitchell-Kernan, 1993).

Still, the increasing tendency for older African American women to live alone may put them at risk. Of older women living alone, black women are 3 times as likely as white women to have incomes below the poverty level (U.S. Bureau of the Census, 1991b). And women living alone are more likely to end up in institutions. Since elderly black women are expected to outnumber older black men almost 2 to 1 by the year 2000, they may need to rely more heavily on kinship and community support (Tucker et al., 1993).

"Aging in Place"

Once a week, a county home health aide rings the doorbell of 92-year-old Harold Mills in Cedar Rapids, Iowa. She cleans his house, rubs his back, and takes him shopping for groceries. Other agencies send helpers to cut his grass, shovel snow, and deliver hot meals, as well as a social worker to check on him (R. Lewis, 1992).

A growing number of older Americans—85 percent, according to a recent survey (AARP, 1993b)—say they want to stay in their own homes indefinitely. Gerontologists call this phenomenon *aging in place.* Older adults usually want to remain in a familiar neighborhood, to be independent, to have privacy, and to maintain social contacts (Gonyea, Hudson, & Seltzer, 1990). For many homeowners, a paid-up mortgage and the possibility of a reverse mortgage for monthly income make aging in place an attractive option.

Most older people do not need or want to have their lives totally managed for them, but some have impairments that make it hard to get along entirely on their own. Relatively minor support—such as meals, transportation, and home health aides—can often help them stay put (E. M. Brody, 1978; Lawton, 1981). So can ramps, grab bars, and other modifications within the home. Private or community-based geriatric care managers can arrange for such services as visiting nurses, escort services, meals on wheels, home care, help with paying bills and budgeting, crisis intervention, and counseling (Leonard, 1992–1993). In Iowa, which has the greatest concentration of people over age 85 in the United States (12 percent of the state population), a new program coordinates in-home services of 32 public and private agencies for people with health conditions that would otherwise force them into nursing homes. The sliding-fee plan is tailored to each client's needs and resources. Those who can't stay in their homes even with such assistance may be moved to private boarding homes and assigned visiting nurses, transportation to medical care, and help with financial affairs (R. Lewis, 1992).

Aging in place may mean one thing in a suburban community and another in an inner-city neighborhood. Because of the flight from the cities after World War II, there are now many aging suburbanites who may find it more and more difficult to live in homes built for young families and in communities designed around the automobile (Hare, 1993). From 1960 to 1980, the number of older adults in the suburbs nearly doubled (Fitzpatrick & Logan, 1985; Gonyea, Hudson, & Seltzer, 1990). How long will they be able to climb stairs, drive cars, and maintain their aging dwellings? Suburban communities could be made more age-appropriate by permitting convenience stores in residential areas, by creating pedestrian-friendly traffic patterns, and by encouraging pooled transportation. Unused space in "empty-nest" homes could be remodeled into apartments to provide additional income, companionship, enhanced security, and assistance with home chores (Hare, 1993).

In inner cities, where minorities predominate and more than 1 out of 10 residents are elderly, aging in place may occur by default. Like the suburbs, many inner city neighborhoods that have become "retirement communities" were not designed for that purpose and lack convenient shopping and transportation. Unlike the suburbs, these neighborhoods are often unsafe, but their elderly residents cannot simply decide to move. Low incomes, segregated housing (particularly for African Americans), and ageism create barriers to free movement and perpetuate dependence on longstanding social networks (Skinner, 1993). The frail urban elderly often are isolated, fearful, and virtual prisoners in their homes—not just aging in place but "stuck in place" (Skinner, 1993, p. 93). One of their fears is being forced to move to make way for gentrification. A study in Manhattan found that 65 percent of older adults do not know where they would go if they were displaced (Singelakis, 1990).

Living Semi-Independently

When Wilma Bingham could no longer manage to live in her home, she wanted a place where she could have help with housekeeping chores—and keep her cat. Her daughter found a solution: a one-bedroom apartment in an assisted-living facility, where she could keep her independence and dignity (and her pet) while getting the services she needed (Glasheen, 1993).

In recent years, creative social planning has enabled more and more older Americans in Wilma Bingham's position to remain in the community. Box 10-3 (earlier in this chapter) describes a number of options—some traditional and some innovative—for older people who can and want to be partially self-sufficient. Besides assisted living, these alternatives include retirement communities, housing shared by friends or relatives, group homes run by social agencies, accessory housing in or on the grounds of a private residence, and congregate housing—apartments clustered around a central dining room, with housekeeping, recreation, and transportation services. One promising trend is the development of continuing-care or life-care communities, where an aging person can stay as needs change (Gonyea et al., 1990; Hare & Haske, 1983–1984; Lawton, 1981; Porcino, 1983, 1991, 1993; Steinbach, 1992).

Living with Adult Children

Most older people—even those in difficult circumstances—do not want to live with adult children or other relatives. They are reluctant to burden their families and to give up their own freedom. It can be inconvenient to absorb an extra person or two into a household, and everyone's privacy—and relationships—may suffer. Parents living with their children's families may feel useless, bored, and isolated from their friends. If the adult child is married and parent and spouse do not get along well, the marriage may be threatened (Shapiro, 1994).

Despite these concerns, more than 1 million older Americans live with their adult children, and the proportions increase with age. Fourteen percent of men and 26 percent of women over age 85 live with an adult child (Shapiro, 1994). Older black people who have functional impairments are more likely than older white people to live with a child or someone else, and to rely on informal caregiving (Soldo, Wolf, & Agree, 1990; Worobey & Angel, 1990).

The success of such an arrangement depends largely on the quality of the relationship that has existed in the past and on the ability of both generations to communicate fully and frankly. The decision to move an adult parent into a child's home should be mutual and needs to be thought through carefully and thoroughly. When parents and children respect each other's dignity and autonomy and accept their differences, it is easier to resolve the inevitable conflicts and to work out such practical details as who uses the bathroom, kitchen, or television when (Shapiro, 1994). It's best, of course, if the parent can have his or her own room. Some adult children who can afford it remodel their homes or build additions to give parents their own quarters, sometimes with a separate entrance. It's important for both generations to maintain their interests, activities, and social life, and for the older person to have some responsibility for household chores.

(Susan Lapides/Design Conceptions)

Only 5 percent of older adults in the United States live in institutions at any one time, but the probability of spending time in a nursing home increases dramatically with age. A good nursing home offers stimulating activities and companionship, as well as a full range of social, therapeutic, and rehabilitative services.

Living in Institutions

Although at any given time only 5 percent of people over 65 in the United States (mostly women) live in institutions, the lifetime probability of spending time in a nursing home is much higher. The probability increases markedly with age: 1 percent at ages 65 to 74, 6 percent at 75 to 84, and 24 percent at 85 and over (AARP, 1994; U.S. Bureau of the Census, 1995).

Most older people do not want to live in institutions, and most of their families do not want them to. Older people often feel that placement in an institution is a sign of rejection; and children usually place their parents reluctantly, apologetically, and with great guilt. Sometimes, though, because of an older person's needs or a family's circumstances, such placement seems to be the only solution. The elderly at highest risk of institutional living are those living alone, those who do not take part in social activities, those who perceive their health as poor, those whose daily activities are limited by poor health or disability, and those whose caregivers are overburdened (McFall & Miller, 1992; Steinbach, 1992). Almost three-fourths of the 1.7 million nursing home residents are women (most of them widows), less than half can get around by themselves, about 60 percent are mentally impaired, and one-third are incontinent (AARP, 1986; Center on Elderly People Living Alone, 1995b; Moss & Halamandaris, 1977; Ouslander, 1989; U.S. Bureau of the Census, 1992b; Wolinsky & Johnson, 1992a, 1992b).

The difference between good and inferior nursing home care can be very great. A good nursing home has an experienced professional staff, an adequate government insurance program, and a coordinated structure that can provide various levels of care (Kayser-Jones, 1982). It is lively, safe, clean, and attractive. It offers stimulating activities and opportunities to spend time with people of both sexes and all ages. It provides privacy—among other reasons, so that residents can be sexually active. And it offers a full range of social, therapeutic, and rehabilitative services. The best-quality care seems to be available in larger, nonprofit facilities with a high ratio of nurses to nursing aides (Pillemer & Moore, 1989). One essential element of good care is an opportunity for residents to make decisions and exert some control over their lives (E. Langer & Rodin, 1976).

Federal law (Omnibus Budget Reconciliation Act, OBRA, 1987, 1990) sets tough requirements for nursing homes and gives residents the right to choose their own doctors; to be fully informed about their care and treatment; and to be free from physical or mental abuse, corporal punishment, involuntary seclusion, and physical or chemical restraints. Institutions must provide a written assessment and plan of care for each resident and must keep a registry of nursing aides who have satisfactorily completed training and evaluation, including any documented findings of neglect or abuse. Some states, such as Illinois, train volunteer ombudsmen to act as advocates for nursing home residents, to explain their rights, and to resolve their complaints about such matters as privacy, treatment, food, and financial issues.

As the population ages, and women's life expectancy continues to increase faster than men's, the number of nursing home residents is expected to grow rapidly. It is estimated that 52 percent of women and 33 percent of men who turned 65 in 1990 will spend some time in nursing homes (Center on Elderly People Living Alone, 1995b). This trend will require more nursing homes and new ways to finance care. In 1993, the cost of such care averaged $39,000 a year; because of gaps in both private and governmental health insurance, about one-third of this cost fell directly on patients and their families. Medicare paid for less than 9 percent of all expenditures on nursing home care. Although Medicaid covers more than half of such expenditures, it is available only to people who have virtually exhausted their own resources (Center on Elderly People Living Alone, 1995a, 1995c).

FAMILY CAREGIVING

Caregiving is informal, unpaid care of a person whose independence is physically, mentally, emotionally, or economically limited (Lund, 1993a). It may include errands, chauffering, help with finances or housework, or complete physical care. The work is confining, often distressing, and usually continuous.

Of the nearly 13 million Americans who need long-term care, only about 2½ million live in institutions (Center on Elderly People Living Alone, 1995c). With the high cost of nursing homes and most older people's reluctance to enter and stay in them, many dependent elders receive home care, sometimes for years. Care may take place in the older person's home or in the caregiver's. Four out of 5 elderly people who require care get it from family members (Barnhart, 1992).

TABLE 10-3 CAREGIVERS IN THE UNITED STATES	
Category	*Percent Who Provide Care*
Gender	
Female	75
Male	25
Age	
Under 35	28
35–49	29
50–64	26
65 and older	15
Marital status	
Married	66
Not married	34
Current employment	
Full-time	42
Part-time	13
Retired	16
Not employed or homemaker	27

NOTE: A survey of 750 households found this profile of the people who provide unpaid care for an elderly relative or friend.
SOURCES: AARP, 1989a; Center on Elderly People Living Alone, 1995c; "Juggling Family, "1989.

Women are most likely both to give and to receive care (see Table 10-3). When an adult child provides care for a parent, the arrangement most commonly involves a daughter and mother. Often the need arises when a husband dies, leaving a widow who cannot manage on her own. Because women tend to marry older men and to outlive them, they are more likely to end up in need of care and to have to rely on a child (Lee et al., 1993). Daughters are the ones who generally take on the responsibility for aging, ailing mothers (Troll, 1986), though many grandchildren serve as caregivers as well (Barnhart, 1992). While daughters are more likely than sons to provide care for either parent, the likelihood is far greater when the recipient is the mother. Perhaps because of the intimate nature of the contact and the strength of the mother-daughter bond, mothers may prefer a daughter's care (Lee et al., 1993).

Not all caregiving is for older adults. About 40 percent of Americans requiring long-term care are adults under age 65 with chronic disorders or severe physical and mental disabilities (Center on Elderly People Living Alone, 1995c). Their caregivers are more likely to be living with them and, according to one study, experience even greater financial, physical, and emotional strain than caregivers for older people (Scharlach & Fredriksen, 1994).

Burdens and Strains of Caregiving

Adult children and parents get along best while the parents are healthy and vigorous. When older people become infirm, especially if they suffer from mental deterioration or personality changes, the burden of caring for them may strain the relationship.

Caregiver burnout is physical, mental, and emotional exhaustion that affects many adults who care for aged relatives (Barnhart, 1992). The strains created by incessant, heavy demands can be great—sometimes so great as to lead to abuse, neglect, or even abandonment of the dependent elderly person (see Chapter 12). Even the most patient, loving caregiver may become frustrated, anxious, or resentful under the constant strain of meeting an older person's seemingly endless needs—especially if there is no one else to turn to.

Some studies show that adults who care for patients with Alzheimer's disease or some other form of dementia are under more stress than the patients (Barnhart, 1992). The uncertainty of a diagnosis of Alzheimer's may produce even more stress than the disease itself (Garwick et al., 1994). Strains tend to affect the whole family, including the caregiver's adult children and their spouses (Fisher & Lieberman, 1994). Often, related emotional issues—such as conflicts with siblings who do not provide their expected share of help—aggravate the strain (Strawbridge & Wallhagen, 1991).

Not all caregivers experience significant stress, however; it depends on their age, circumstances, relationship to the patient, and available resources (Harper &

An adult who cares for a spouse or another family member with Alzheimer's disease may suffer more stress than the patient. This woman stays by her husband's bedside all night because he requires constant monitoring. Physical, mental, and emotional exhaustion often lead to caregiver burnout.

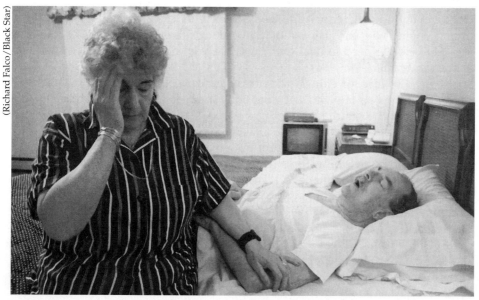

(Richard Falco/Black Star)

Lund, 1990). In one study, more than half of the adult children surveyed felt some strain, and one-third reported substantial strain, in connection with helping their parents. The strain most often showed up as physical or emotional exhaustion and a feeling that the parent was impossible to satisfy (Cicirelli, 1980).

How a person reacts to the demands of caregiving is likely to be affected by other responsibilities and stresses. Caregivers who feel their burden most keenly are those who work full time, are raising young children, lack support and assistance, and have limited financial resources. Burdens are exacerbated if the caregiver does not feel close to the person who is receiving the care, and if that person is aggressive or violent (Lund, 1993a). African American daughters report less strain than white daughters; but for both, conflict between caregiving and personal and social life leads to emotional strain. In one group of black caregivers, women in poor health with other conflicts in their lives and no respite from caregiving were most likely to feel strain (Mui, 1992). White caregivers but not African Americans feel more strain when their relationship with their parents is not good and when they are having conflicts at work (Mui, 1992; Walker, Martin, and Jones, 1992).

The unavoidable demands and strains of caregiving are often complicated by deep feelings about the parent-child relationship and other aspects of the caregiver's life. Adult children who care for aging parents may be torn between love and resentment; between their duty to their parents and their duty to their spouses and children; between wanting to do the right thing and not wanting to change their lives.

The needs of aging parents seem to fall into the category of nonnormative, unanticipated demands. New parents expect to assume the full physical, financial, and emotional care of their babies, with the assumption that such care will gradually diminish as children grow up. Most people do *not* expect to have to care for their parents; they ignore the possibility of their parents' infirmity and rarely plan ahead for it. When their elderly parents' dependency becomes undeniable, many adult children are shocked, grief-stricken, and angry. They have trouble coping with the changes they see taking place (Barnhart, 1992), and they may perceive the need to deal with these changes as interfering with other obligations and plans.

The need to care for elderly parents often arises at a time when middle-aged adults are trying to launch their own adolescent or young adult children. This "generation in the middle," sometimes called the "sandwich generation," must allocate time, money, and energy to both. Caregivers who have full-time jobs may have to quit or cut back to part-time work in order to devote a large portion of their time to caring for parents, sometimes for years on end. The caregiver's marriage may suffer, and sometimes even end in divorce (Lund, 1993a). Adults who have been looking forward to the end of responsibility for their children—and who now sense keenly that their own remaining years are limited—may feel that caring for their parents will deprive them of any chance to fulfill their dreams. Perhaps the greatest loss involved in caregiving is loss of a sense of control over one's life (J. Evans, 1994). The feeling of being tied down, of not being able to take a vacation or make other plans, is, for some adult children, the hardest thing about caring for elderly parents (Robinson & Thurnher, 1981).

A common source of negative feelings is the disappointment, anger, or guilt many adults feel when they realize that they, rather than their parents, now have to be the strong ones. Anxiety over the anticipated end of their parents' lives may be tinged with worry about their own mortality (Cicirelli, 1980; Troll, 1986). When caregiving ends because of a parent's death, adult children must come to terms with feelings that are often ambivalent.

Reducing the Strains: Community Support

> He or she grows weaker, you take over, nobody sees. Whatever he can no longer do, you do. . . . The loss of control over his body frustrates him and he tries to exert control over yours. His wish is your command. . . . Most everybody identifies with him. "How is he doing?" At first, that's all you cared about, too. Now you sometimes wonder why no one asks about you. . . . You start to feel that you don't exist. (Strong, 1988, p. 75)

Caregivers need care, too. Often families and friends fail to recognize that caregivers have a right to feel discouraged, frustrated, and put upon. Caregivers need to give themselves permission to care for *themselves* by taking some time for activities that give them a life outside of the loved one's disease (J. Evans, 1994).

In addition, there is an urgent need for more community support to reduce the strains of caregiving and prevent burnout. Expanded support programs for caregivers could reduce or postpone the need for institutionalization. Such support services may include free or low-cost daytime activity programs; transportation and escort services; in-home services providing meals, housekeeping, and home health aides; and, most important, respite care—letting caregivers get away for a day, a weekend, or a week.

Flexible work schedules and leave provisions can benefit working adults with dependents who need care. The Family and Medical Leave Act, adopted in 1993, guarantees workers a period of unpaid leave to care for a spouse, parent, or child. Some large corporations are already providing time off for caregiving.

Adult day care centers, which provide stimulating activities and care while caregivers are at work, are a growing trend; about 3,000 such centers have opened across the country. Researchers at the University of Utah have developed a series of videotapes for use by caregivers, as well as in adult day care centers and nursing homes. The tapes are designed to engage the attention of patients with Alzheimer's disease, giving the caregiver or professional staff an uninterrupted respite of 20 to 60 minutes (D. Lund, personal communication, November 1994).

Counseling, support, and self-help groups enable caregivers to share problems, gain information about community resources, and improve caregiving skills. One such program helped daughters recognize the limits of their ability to meet their mothers' needs and the value of encouraging their mothers' self-reliance. This understanding lightened the daughters' burden and improved their relationship with their mothers, with the result that the mothers became less lonely (Scharlach, 1987). In one longitudinal study, caregivers who had adequate community support reported many dimensions of personal growth. Some had become more empathic, caring, understanding, patient, and compassionate,

A nurse in an adult day care center in San Francisco leads an exercise group. Such centers can provide stimulating activities and care for older adults while giving caregivers a respite.

closer to the person they were caring for, and more appreciative of their own good health. Others felt good about having fulfilled their responsibilities. Some had "learned to value life more and to take one day at a time," and a few had learned to "laugh at situations and events" (Lund, 1993a).

Legal Intervention

When parents can no longer handle their own financial and practical affairs, a son or daughter may have to step in (Porcino, 1983). Parents who are mentally competent (that is, capable of making decisions and understanding the consequences) may agree to put money into a bank account held jointly with an adult child, a living trust, or a trust account with automatic inheritance by surviving adult children. A power of attorney, which can be withdrawn at any time, can give an adult child the power to make financial decisions for the parent.

A much more serious step is to have an older adult declared legally incompetent. In that case, the older adult becomes the ward of a guardian or conservator (usually an adult child or other relative, a friend, or a financial institution). A person placed under guardianship loses, permanently, the right to conduct business, to sign contracts, to vote, or even to decide where to live. The guardian controls not only the ward's property but his or her *person* and can place the ward in an institution or make any other decisions on her or his behalf. To make sure that the guardian acts in the best interests of the older person, some courts appoint a second type of guardian, called a guardian *ad litem*. Because of the potential for abuse, it is a good idea for all adults to specify in advance (usually in a will) the person they want to act as guardian in case they become mentally incompetent.

CARE OF THE OLD-OLD:
AN INTERNATIONAL PERSPECTIVE

Other industrialized nations are struggling with issues similar to those that have emerged in the United States regarding care of the frail elderly. In several European countries, notably England and the Netherlands, there was a shift to less restrictive residential facilities and to home and day care in the 1980s (Davies, 1993). A stated goal of government policy in Great Britain is "to enable persons as far as possible to live in their own homes or in a homelike environment in the local community" (Cm. 849, 1989, paragraph 1.8). Neighborhood volunteers are used extensively as home helpers (Nishio, 1994). However, aging in place is not seen as a panacea; English policy encourages the most suitable and cost-effective solution for each individual (Davies, 1993).

Although the goal of moving away from institutionalization is not new, changes in the balance of spending between residential and community-based care have been slow to come. Concern over cost containment and efficient use of public funds is widespread, even in countries such as the Netherlands, Sweden, and Australia, which are strongly committed to a welfare state (Davies, 1993). A recent trend toward diversification of care has been particularly marked in Australia. Between 1986 and 1991, along with a 25 percent increase in funding, government financial incentives induced a partial shift from nursing home care toward hostels, a semi-independent living arrangement operated either privately or not for profit. Hostels typically offer a single room with private or shared bath; staff members are available 24 hours a day for nonmedical care (Borkowski & Ozanne, 1993).

Efforts are growing to relieve the burdens of family and other nonprofessional caregivers, without whom agencies and institutions would be badly understaffed. There is more official recognition of the value of informal caregivers' contributions and of their right to be consulted in assessments and decisions (Davies, 1993). Sweden, which currently has the world's proportionally largest elderly population, has made sizable public expenditures to employ home helpers (Nishio, 1994). Family caregivers, in addition to qualifying for up to 30 days of insured sick leave, get allowances for doctor-approved care and can be paid at the same rates as professional home care workers if they must give up their jobs to perform it (Davies, 1993).

In Japan, where the aged population is growing faster than in other industrialized nations, reliance on family care remains strong. Only 10 percent of Japanese elderly people live alone (compared with 30 percent in Sweden), and only 1.5 percent live in homes for the aged or other institutions (compared with 6 to 7 percent in Sweden). More than 4 out of 5 Japanese families with feeble, dependent elderly members keep up the tradition of three-generational households. When one elderly spouse becomes bedridden, both typically move in with the family of the eldest married son. Thus, in contrast with American custom, daughters-in-law rather than daughters are most likely to become primary caregivers (see Figure 10-4). As in the United States, both patient and caregiver are usually women: a Japanese daughter-in-law is more than twice as likely to care for a mother-in-law as for a father-in-law (Nishio, 1994).

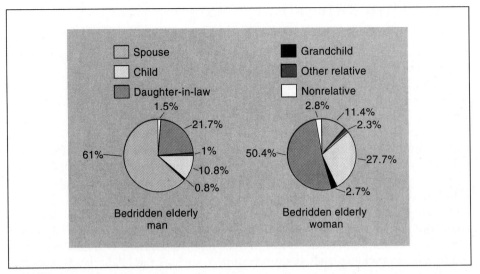

FIGURE 10-4

Caregivers for bedridden elderly people in Japan. As in the United States, a spouse is more likely to be the primary caregiver if the bedridden person is a man. But daughters-in-law are more likely to be caregivers in Japan than in the United States, especially for a woman.

(SOURCE: Nishio, 1994, p. 257; based on data from Japanese Social Welfare Association, 1990.)

Eventually, Japan's exploding older population will overstrain family-based care. Accordingly, the number of nursing homes, infirmaries, and other institutions is rapidly increasing; since 1990 there has been a tenfold rise in facilities serving remote areas. However, the official strategy is to limit the need for hospitalization and institutionalization by broadening and professionalizing home care, promoting preventive programs, and enhancing the general quality of life. Social work and care specialities have been recognized as official positions, with qualifying examinations. Japan plans to add 100,000 paid home helpers, 50,000 hospital beds for short stays, 10,000 day care centers, and 10,000 home care support centers to assist caregivers. Other proposals are to pay families for providing care and to train young-old people for that purpose (Nishio, 1994).

In the developing nations of Asia, Africa, and Latin America, institutions for the elderly are rare. Family care is still the norm, even though migration to cities and the consequent breakup of the extended family make it less feasible. Any residential care tends to be funded by religious groups and other nonprofit organizations with limited resources (Gorman, 1993).

In China, government policies reinforce traditional customs. The family and the local community are expected to provide medical and long-term care; the role of the central government is minimal (Olson, 1994). In rural areas, most care is in the home; only limited supplementary medical services are available. County-operated hospitals are for acute or short-term illnesses only. Families can hire semiskilled nursemaids to care for bedridden patients in the hospital as well as at home; otherwise, family members are expected to stay at the bedside. For people with no children to care for them, village committees in some rural communities make agreements with neighbors, schools, or other entities to deliver groceries, medicine, and coal. The Chinese government has begun to prod rural townships to establish homes for the aged—independent living facilities with communal baths and a common dining and recreation room. A town committee decides when it is time for a childless elderly person to enter such a home.

In urban areas, too, primary responsibility rests with the family, community, and work unit, not the central government. For most urban workers, health insurance continues into retirement but normally does not cover long-term care. Local committees identify older people who need in-home care and assign a trained person to visit them, run errands, prepare meals, and contact doctors when needed. Those not ill enough to need hospitalization receive drug therapy, physical therapy, medical examinations, and traditional Chinese treatments in their homes. Childless people may be able to live in one of the few government-operated social welfare institutes, which provide both assisted living facilities and complete, continuous care for the bedridden.

Policies regarding long-term care are still evolving. Policymakers in developed and developing nations may be able to learn from each other's experience as they seek ways to care for dependent older people with dignity—to avoid warehousing on the one hand and exploitation of family caregivers on the other.

Despite the challenging needs of frail older adults and their families, the vast majority of older people lead active, fulfilling lives. It's sometimes tempting, even for professionals who deal with problems and issues of aging, to focus on numbers and categories, to lose sight of the fact that the journey through adulthood is highly personal. Now that we've explored the social contexts of adult life, let's turn—in Part Four—to the world within: the world of personality and mental health, including ways of coping with losses that occur throughout the adult lifespan.

SUMMARY

- Extended-family households are common in Asia and Latin America. In the United States, where independence is a primary value, parents and adult children generally live together only when one or the other is in need of help.

THE ADULT FAMILY: CHANGING ROLES AND RELATIONSHIPS

- Young adults need to establish their own identity and a mature relationship with their parents; this need calls for new attitudes and behaviors on the part of both generations.

- Contact between middle-aged children and older parents (especially daughters and mothers) remains high, and mutual help continues. Parents may resume an active parenting role for a child who needs special help.

- Sibling relationships are the longest-lasting in most people's lives. Sibling contact throughout the lifespan follows an hourglass pattern; middle-aged siblings often renew or strengthen ties after their children leave home.

GRANDPARENTHOOD AND GREAT-GRANDPARENTHOOD

- Although most American grandparents today are less intimately involved in grandchildren's lives than in the past, they often play a more active role when problems arise.

- Women tend to be closer to their grandchildren than men are, but men may be more attentive to their grandchildren than they were to their children.

- African American grandparents tend to be more involved in their grandchildren's lives, and are perceived as more successful grandparents overall, than white grandparents.

- Divorce and remarriage of an adult child often affect grandparent-grandchild relationships and create new stepgrandparenting roles.

- The great-grandparent's role is less clear and less involved than that of grandparents, but most great-grandparents find it emotionally fulfilling.

- An increasing number of children are being raised by grandparents and great-grandparents. This unplanned role can create physical, emotional, and financial strains.

LIVING ARRANGEMENTS, CAREGIVING, AND COMMUNITY SUPPORT

- Recently, more young adults are returning to live in the parents' homes for such reasons as financial need and divorce.

- Most older adults want to—and do—live in the community, not in nursing homes; and alone or with a spouse, not with adult children.

- Most older adults who live alone are widowed women, who tend to be older, poorer, and more vulnerable than other older adults, and are more likely to end up in institutions.

- A wide range of alternatives now exists for older adults who can live semi-independently: these include assisted living, retirement communities, shared housing, group homes, accessory housing, congregate housing, and continuing-care or life-care communities.

- When older adults live with adult children, the success of the arrangement depends on their relationship and on their ability to communicate.

- Although only about 5 percent of older adults live in nursing homes, people are much more likely to spend time in an institution as they get older.

- For many infirm older adults, family care is an alternative to institutionalization. Women are more likely than men to need care and to become caregivers. Adult day care centers, in-home services, and support groups are among community programs that can help ease caregivers' burdens.

- When older adults cannot manage their affairs, legal intervention may be necessary. Such measures may range from a power of attorney to court appointment of a guardian.

- There is a trend toward less institutional care and more home- or community-based care in many industrialized countries. In addition, some of these countries are instituting policies to help caregivers.

KEY TERMS

extended family (page 363)
nuclear family (363)
age structure (372)
kinship care (379)

aging in place (385)
caregiving (389)
caregiver burnout (391)

"One of the pleasantest things in the world," wrote the eighteenth-century English essayist William Hazlitt, "is going [on] a journey; but I like to go by myself."

The journey through the world of adulthood is a journey of the unique self. It is a journey that involves hardships, pressures, and disappointments, as well as the thrill of accomplishment, the warmth of human contact, and the sheer enjoyment of living. It is a journey that inevitably ends, sooner or later, in death.

In the first three parts of this book, we explore the worlds of body and mind and the social world of roles and relationships. In Part Four, we turn our focus inward to the world of the feeling, experiencing, striving, responding self—a world so deeply personal that its outlines may at times seem indistinct, its shadowy depths hard to fathom. What light can scientific theory and research shed?

We begin in Chapter 11 by attempting to define personality. How can we study it? How and when does it form, and how much does it change during adulthood? Can we discern any general patterns in something so individual? In Chapter 12 we look at mental health and at how people cope with the ups and downs of life and the challenges of aging. In Chapter 13, we approach the last boundary—death—and see how people face the end of the journey for themselves and their loved ones.

The journey through the world within will not always be easy, but it may reward us with a clearer view of ourselves and of others who are making such journeys.

PART FOUR

THE WORLD WITHIN

CHAPTER 11

PERSONALITY DEVELOPMENT

DEFINING AND STUDYING PERSONALITY
What Is Personality?
Measuring Personality
Origins of Personality:
   Inheritance and Experience

MODELS OF ADULT PERSONALITY: STABILITY OR CHANGE
Trait Models
Self-Concept Models
Stage Models
The Timing-of-Events Model

GENDER AND PERSONALITY
Gender Stereotypes, Gender Roles,
   and Gender Identity
Women's Personality Development:
   The Mills Studies

SYNTHESIZING APPROACHES TO ADULT PERSONALITY DEVELOPMENT

BOXES
11-1 The Cutting Edge: Can Personality
      Patterns Cause Disease?
11-2 The Art of Aging: Navigating
      the Midlife Crossing
11-3 The Multicultural Context:
      Druze Men—New Roles
      in Late Middle Age

FOCUS: EVA PERÓN

(AP/Wide World Photos)

María Eva Duarte de Perón* was a controversial figure, a woman of myth and mystery who (as would later be dramatized in Andrew Lloyd Webber's musical *Evita*) rose from tawdry origins to become first lady of Argentina. During her 6-year "reign," she was both adored and hated. Her followers saw her as a selfless friend of the downtrodden and a champion of women's rights. Her enemies saw her as power-hungry, manipulative, and ruthless. On one point all agree: she was a beautiful woman. And she knew how to use her beauty to advantage.

Eva (affectionately known as Evita) began life in 1919 in the small, dusty village of Los Toldos. She was the fifth illegitimate child of a poor uneducated peasant woman and a married man from a nearby town. Eva and her brother and sisters were shunned by respectable people; when their father died, his wife's family tried to bar them from the funeral. Eva's destitute mother moved in with a man who had a modest restaurant; they also took in lodgers, but the family remained very poor. It was these early experiences, common among the Argentinian underclass, that Eva Perón had in mind when, later, she called herself a "woman of the people."

Eva was an intense, frail child, given to tantrums and driven by dreams of glory. She attended school only through the primary grades. Her real schooling was in her mother's tempestuous household, where, one journalist observed, the little girl learned "that life was a struggle for survival in which the prizes went to the toughest and the most unscrupulous" and men were to be used for a woman's ends (Flores, 1952, p. 22).

*Sources for biographical information on Eva Perón are Barager (1968), Blanksten (1953), Flores (1952), Perón (1951), and J. M. Taylor (1979).

At age 15, during the Great Depression, Eva migrated to the capital, Buenos Aires, where she pursued an acting career. She was not very talented, but by 1943 she was starring in a radio series and had begun to develop a popular following. At that time, a new military government seized power, and Eva became the mistress of Colonel Juan Domingo Perón, a widower twice her age. Perón quickly advanced from undersecretary of war to secretary of labor, minister of war, and vice-president. He made Eva head of the officially recognized union of radio workers, gave her an office near his, and appointed her friends to government posts.

Perón's growing support from labor, and Eva's influence, disturbed his military colleagues. In October 1945, he was arrested and imprisoned. At one point, an angry mob dragged Eva from a car and beat her. On October 17, however, in a "spontaneous" demonstration that Eva (as she later claimed) had actually helped organize, thousands of workers marched on the government house and successfully demanded Perón's restoration.

Perón and Eva were married immediately, and the following year he became president of the "new Argentina." Eva, by now a political force in her own right, worked tirelessly, putting in 18-hour days and receiving as many as 26 delegations daily. She toured Europe, met with heads of state, and signed treaties—though her trip was marred in Rome, where she was the object of a bomb threat, and in Switzerland, where demonstrators opposed to Perón's fascist regime threw tomatoes at her.

By 1948, she owned three newspapers in Buenos Aires and had a daily bylined column. She persuaded her husband to push through a women's suffrage law, and she herself organized a women's branch of the Peronist party. She also established the multimillion-dollar Eva Perón Foundation, funded by mandatory contributions from workers and by donations that her opponents claimed were extorted. The foundation built hospitals, clinics, and schools, distributed toys, dispatched emergency aid, and bought arms for a workers' militia. As Eva Perón became an international figure, she combed her hair back and put away her flamboyant clothes; she wore sober suits or sweaters and slacks, saving her resplendent gowns and jewels for formal occasions.

Juan Perón always insisted he had made Eva what she was, but many observers thought otherwise: "She lacked formal training, but not political intuition; she was impetuous, domineering, and spectacular. . . . She accepted ideas [from Perón], but she added passion and courage. . . . She was a fiery little thing—indomitable, aggressive, spontaneous, at times barely feminine" (Barager, 1968, pp. 230–231). Humorless and unforgiving, she often demanded the resignations of those who crossed her.

Eva made a bid for the vice presidency in 1951 but retreated under pressure from military leaders. When she developed cancer, she kept up her frantic pace; during her husband's second inaugural parade in June 1952, she stood at his side in an open car, supported by a contraption of wire and plaster. When she died the following month at age 33, the line of mourners stretched for 35 blocks. For a time, she was worshipped as a saint, and the dates of her birth and death became national observances. Three years later, however, when Perón was overthrown, mobs tore down her statues and burned items bearing her name.

Eva Perón was an enigma. Who, really, was she? In a few years, she transformed herself from an illegitimate, outcast waif to one of the most powerful women of all time. But even the basic facts of her life are open to question, for she destroyed whatever records she could and intimidated interviewers into silence or flattery; and even less clear are the motives and attitudes that shaped her behavior. Was she a "Lady Bountiful dedicating her life to humble folk" (Flores, 1952, p. 14)? A loyal, devoted wife? A vicious, conniving shrew? The real power behind her husband's "throne"? Or—as some claim—a naive girl whose husband used the common people's devotion to her to bind them closer to him?

To what extent was she a product of family background and societal conditions? Her early experiences may well have fueled her hatred for the establishment, her will to be heard, her fight for women's rights, her disregard for normal channels of authority, her need for control, and her hunger for her people's love—themes that run consistently through her short life. But did success change her, or did her character remain essentially the same throughout her meteoric rise? Of course, she did not live long enough to experience a midlife crisis or to cope with the challenge of aging. She did not witness the fall of Perón in 1955, his brief return to power in 1972, or his death in 1974. How might Eva Perón—and history—have been affected had she lived through those times? What if she, rather than Perón's third wife, Isabel, had succeeded him as president?

Not many personalities are as paradoxical as Eva Perón's, but her story raises fundamental questions we can ask about every adult. Is an adult's personality a product more of inborn tendencies or of experience? How, and how much, does personality change during adult life? How much is it influenced by culture? By gender? In this chapter, we discuss important issues in the study of adult personality and describe several lines of theory and research that attempt to explain it.

DEFINING AND STUDYING PERSONALITY

How often have you heard comments such as "She has a lot of personality," or, "He has as much personality as a wet dishrag"? In everyday conversation, *personality* often seems to refer to something that a person has more or less of. In reality, personalities differ not so much in quantity as in quality. When we speak of your personality, we are talking about your basic nature—what kind of person you are: brave or fearful, stingy or generous, cheerful or gloomy. But even this may not be quite accurate. You may be brave at one time and fearful at another, or perhaps both fearful and brave at once.

Personality, like intelligence, is complex—hard to define and measure. Indeed, according to some psychologists the influences on personality are so haphazard and so idiosyncratic that we cannot make any general statements at all about it. What is personality? How does somebody get one? How can something so intangible be measured? Let's begin with the problem of definition.

WHAT IS PERSONALITY?

There are almost as many definitions of *personality* as there are investigators in the field. But one concept seems to underlie virtually all of them: that personality is the essence of a *person*—a unique, recognizable individual.

Personality is hard to define because we can't see, hear, or touch it; we have to infer it from behavior. Behaviorists, such as B. F. Skinner, see no point in making such inferences; they simply define personality as observable behavior. However, most psychologists think of personality as including not just overt behavior, but also some sort of inner structure of mind and emotions that lies behind what people say and do (Hjelle & Ziegler, 1992). Although this structure is constantly developing, it is generally assumed to be responsible for attitudes and behavior patterns that are fairly consistent. Suppose a friend suddenly begins to act "different." One day he or she is shy, the next day gregarious; one moment passive, the next moment aggressive. You'd probably find such shifts strange and unsettling. You might say your friend "isn't himself" or "isn't herself."

Adaptation—adjustment to the events, circumstances, and conditions of life— is an important function of personality. People may adapt by changing something about themselves, their surroundings, or both. But the ways in which a person adapts show continuity. One prominent researcher has suggested that people develop "generalizations" which they apply consistently to different situations (Block, 1993). For example, one student who fails a test may complain that it was unfair; another may blame himself or herself for not studying harder. If these two students were involved in an automobile accident, each would be likely to react in the same characteristic way. To sum up, then, *personality* is a set of "distinctive patterns of behavior, . . . thoughts and emotions . . . that characterize each individual's adaptation to the situations of his or her life" (Mischel, 1986, p. 4)— that is, a person's unique and relatively consistent way of feeling, thinking, and behaving.

MEASURING PERSONALITY

Longstanding research confirms the essential continuity of personality. For the most part, bubbly junior high schoolers grow up to be cheerful 40-year-olds, complaining adolescents turn into querulous adults, assertive 20-year-olds become outspoken 30-year-olds, and people who cope well with problems of youth are equally able to handle problems of later life (Block, 1981; Costa & McCrae, 1980; Eichorn, Clausen, Haan, Honzik, & Mussen, 1981; Haan & Day, 1974; Livson, 1976; Noberini & Neugarten, 1975). Attitudes shown in young adulthood even seem to affect physical health in middle age (see Box 11-1). However, some aspects of personality do soften with maturity. Although impulsive children usually grow up to be restless, impatient adults, as adults they are less impulsive than they were earlier (M. A. Stewart & Olds, 1973).

How do researchers make such determinations, and how valid are they? To study personality scientifically, psychologists need some way to measure it. One common method is a *personality inventory*—a psychometric test that asks people to rate themselves or others on traits such as thoroughness, confidence, and irritability; to report on activities they do or don't enjoy; or to give opinions on a

THE CUTTING EDGE

Can Personality Patterns Cause Disease?

How do you explain bad things that happen to you? Do you usually blame them on yourself ("It's all my fault") or on other people or circumstances ("My parents are so unreasonable!")? Do you generally see these unwelcome and uncontrollable events as having a broad effect ("It's going to ruin my life!") or a limited effect ("I've still got my friends and my health")? Do you see such things as transient ("It's just a passing thing") or long-lasting ("I'll never get over this")?

A 35-year longitudinal study (Peterson, Seligman, & Vaillant, 1988) suggests that how people react to misfortune may affect their health. The study found that people's habitual *explanatory style* in young adulthood—their way of explaining bad events such as illness—may lead to sickness in later years.

The researchers analyzed open-ended questionnaires that had been filled out in 1946 by participants in the Grant Study of Harvard men (discussed in this chapter). Among men who, at age 25, were equally healthy physically and emotionally, those whose explanatory style was most pessimistic—who blamed bad events on themselves and believed those events to have broad, long-lasting effects—were most likely to have health problems in middle age. The relationship between explanatory style and health did not become significant until age 40, perhaps because health and lifestyle become more variable at midlife. The correlation peaked at age 45 (20 years after the men had responded to the questionnaire). After that, it fell off somewhat, though it remained strong at age 60.

What accounts for these findings? Perhaps people who feel helpless in the face of adversity tend to be fatalistic about illness; thus they may (1) become passive when they get sick and not seek or follow medical advice; (2) neglect basic health care; (3) be poor problem solvers and fail to "nip a crisis in the bud" (Peterson et al., 1988, p. 26); (4) be lonely and withdrawn, lacking social contacts that can help in dealing with illness; (5) be depressed, and thus at increased risk of disease; or (6) have a weakened immune system, a typical effect of stress and helplessness.

Of course, the sample in this research was not representative. It included no women, and the men were a highly privileged, college-educated group. All of them were healthy to begin with. Also, the results at various ages were interdependent, since a participant who became unhealthy was more likely to remain so. Still, the possibility that some people may literally talk themselves into poor health is provocative. It seems consistent with evidence that people who believe they have control over what happens to them are less likely to have stress-related illnesses (see Chapter 4).

variety of topics. By comparing ratings taken from adults of different ages—either the same people or different people—researchers attempt to gauge how much personality changes over time.

Another basic technique is the *Q-sort*. A person is given a deck of cards. On each card is a statement or an adjective referring to a personality characteristic. A card may say "I am often lonely" or "I solve problems easily," or simply "energetic," "anxious," or "friendly." The person is asked to sort the cards into categories, depending on how closely they describe him or her. A variation, which can be used to measure results of therapy, is to have a person do Q-sorts for both the *real self* (who he or she actually is) and the *ideal self* (who he or she would like to be), and then to compare the results on successive occasions.

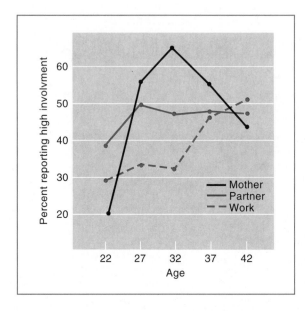

FIGURE 11-1
Women's role changes from college to midlife. In a longitudinal study, 105 alumnae of Mills College reported that their involvement in mothering reached a height at age 32 and then declined sharply, while involvement in work roles rose. Involvement in the role of spouse or partner remained relatively stable.
(SOURCE: Helson & Moane, 1987, p. 182.)

A number of other techniques have been devised. For example, Ravenna Helson and her associates, whose longitudinal studies of Mills College alumnae we discuss later in this chapter, have asked women to graph their involvement in the roles of mother, partner, and worker at various times in their lives (see Figure 11-1).

Each of these methods can be affected by observer bias (see Chapter 2) or subjectivity. Other methods, such as interviews and self-reports, are not only subjective but often open-ended, and thus somewhat harder to reliably quantify and compare. Indeed, it has been argued that any data based on fallible human judgment and intuition cannot be accurate or reliable (L. Ross, 1977; L. Ross & Nisbett, 1991).

Still, considerable research has demonstrated that human judgment, while imperfect, can provide information as useful as other kinds of data psychologists collect. Numerous studies show strong correlations between different people's judgments of someone's personality (Kenrick & Funder, 1988). Judgments of personality also stand up well against observations, predictions, and experimental findings about behavior. Today, most psychologists acknowledge not only that personality is coherent enough to merit study, but that human judgments can describe it reasonably well (Block, 1993; Funder, 1993).

ORIGINS OF PERSONALITY: INHERITANCE AND EXPERIENCE

Despite its essential continuity, personality is not fixed at birth: it is an "evolving process subject to a variety of internal and external influences" (Hjelle & Ziegler, 1992).

From infancy on, some people seem to be constitutionally able to adapt more easily than others. *Temperament,* or disposition—an important shaper of personality—is a person's characteristic, biologically based emotional style of approaching and reacting to people and situations. Whether a person is, for example, flexible and easygoing, resistant to new experiences, or slow to warm up appears to be largely determined by heredity (Braungart, Plomin, DeFries, & Fulker, 1992; Emde et al., 1992; A. Thomas & Chess, 1984). Researchers have found evidence for varying degrees of genetic influence on a wide range of personality characteristics (McGue, Bacon, & Lykken, 1993), from shyness (Daniels & Plomin, 1985; Kagan, 1989) to leadership (Tellegren et al., 1988).

But genes do not tell the whole story. One group of investigators (Eaves, Eysenck, & Martin, 1989) reviewed a large amount of research involving identical twins (who have exactly the same heredity), fraternal twins (who, like any other siblings, share many, but not all, hereditary traits), and other family members in Great Britain, Australia, Sweden, and the United States at various periods of life. Environmental influences accounted for fully half the measured variations in personality. Such influential experiences are unique even for people who grow up in the same household at the same time. This may help explain why Eva Perón, and not one of her sisters, became the first lady of Argentina.

The uniqueness of early experience may reflect temperamental differences. Children's behavior may evoke responses, such as a parent's smiling back at a smiling baby, which reinforce the inborn disposition that produced the behavior (Caspi, 1993; Lytton, 1990). As children grow up, they often seek out environ-

Studies of identical twins, who share exactly the same heredity, have found significant environmental as well as genetic influences on personality, reflecting the uniqueness of early experience even in the same household.

(Thomas Wanstall/The Image Works)

ments that strengthen their genetic tendencies; for example, by selecting friends and eventually mates who are like themselves (Caspi, 1993). Some genetically influenced differences between fraternal twins seem to increase during adulthood, perhaps because of such new, reinforcing experiences (Eaves et al., 1989). Thus an interaction of inheritance and experience affects personality at all ages (Bates & Wachs, 1994).

Sorting out the sources of personality and their complex interrelationships is a formidable task. Much research remains to be done before we can fully understand how personality develops. Further study of how heredity and environment interact throughout life could make an important contribution.

MODELS OF ADULT PERSONALITY: STABILITY OR CHANGE

▼

The two quotations at the beginning of this chapter represent the extremes of a debate over stability versus change in adult personality. Is personality "set like plaster" in early adulthood, or can adults keep "giving birth" to themselves? Different investigators—representing conflicting metatheoretical perspectives and often using different definitions, assumptions, and measuring tools—have come up with differing answers.

- *Trait models* focus on mental, emotional, temperamental, and behavioral traits, or attributes. Trait models are somewhat mechanistic: they attempt to reduce personality and behavior to basic elements, and they assume that traits fairly predictably influence behavior. Studies based on these models find that adult personality changes very little.

- *Self-concept models* are concerned with how people view themselves. These models describe people as actively regulating their own personality development by means of processes similar to those in organismic theories such as that of Piaget. Such models incorporate both stability and change.

- *Stage models*, which are more clearly organismic, portray a typical sequence of age-related development that continues throughout the lifespan. Studies framed in this way find significant, predictable changes in adult personality.

- The *timing-of-events model* is contextual. Researchers who take this approach find that change is related not so much to age as to the varied circumstances and events of life.

Not surprisingly, researchers representing these differing perspectives often come out with results that are difficult to reconcile or even to compare. One leading team of trait researchers (Costa & McCrae, 1994) has attempted to make sense of this diversity by mapping six interrelated elements that "make up the raw material of most personality theories" (p. 23). These elements are (1) *basic tendencies*, (2) *external influences*, (3) *characteristic adaptations*, (4) *self-concept*, (5) *objective biography*, and (6) *dynamic processes*.

Basic tendencies include not only personality traits, but physical health, appearance, gender, sexual orientation, intelligence, and artistic abilities. These tendencies, which may be either inherited or acquired, interact with external (environmental) influences to produce certain characteristic adaptations: social roles, attitudes, interests, skills, activities, habits, and beliefs. For example, it takes a combination of musical inclination (a basic tendency) and exposure to an instrument (an external influence) to produce musical skill (a characteristic adaptation). Basic tendencies and characteristic adaptations, in turn, help shape the *self-concept,* or sense of self, which bears only a partial resemblance to the objective biography, the actual events of a person's life. Thus a woman may think of herself as having more musical ability than she has objectively demonstrated, and her behavior may be influenced by that self-image. *Dynamic processes* link the other five elements; one such process is learning, which enables people to adapt to external influences (for example, to become accomplished in playing a musical instrument).

Various theorists emphasize one or another of these elements. Trait models focus on basic tendencies, which are the least likely to change. Self-concept models deal with the sense of self. Stage models and the timing-of-events model highlight universal or particular aspects of the objective biography. Let's look more closely at each of these approaches.

TRAIT MODELS

Are you cheerful? Are you generally persistent? Are you easily irritated? Cheerfulness, persistence, and irritability are three examples of personality traits. Some researchers have grouped related traits into categories called *personality dimensions.* They seek to identify constellations of attributes that define an individual and to determine how much or how little these dimensions change. According to one influential trait model, the answer is: not much after age 30.

Costa and McCrae: The Five-Factor Model

A trait model that has substantially influenced the study of personality across the adult lifespan is that of Paul T. Costa and Robert R. McCrae, gerontology researchers with the National Institute on Aging. Their *five-factor model* (as the term implies) has five dimensions, or domains: (1) *neuroticism,* (2) *extraversion,* (3) *openness to experience,* (4) *conscientiousness,* and (5) *agreeableness.* Each comprises several associated traits (see Figure 11-2).

Neuroticism is a cluster of six negative traits: anxiety, hostility, depression, self-consciousness, impulsiveness, and vulnerability. Highly neurotic people are nervous, fearful, irritable, easily angered, and sensitive to criticism. They may feel sad, hopeless, lonely, guilty, and worthless. We can speculate that Eva Perón would have had high scores on some facets of this dimension.

Extraversion also has six facets: warmth, gregariousness, assertiveness, activity, excitement-seeking, and positive emotions. Extraverts are sociable, take-charge types who have close, compassionate relationships and like attention. They keep busy and active; they are constantly looking for excitement, and they enjoy life. Extraversion, too, seems to describe Eva Perón's personality.

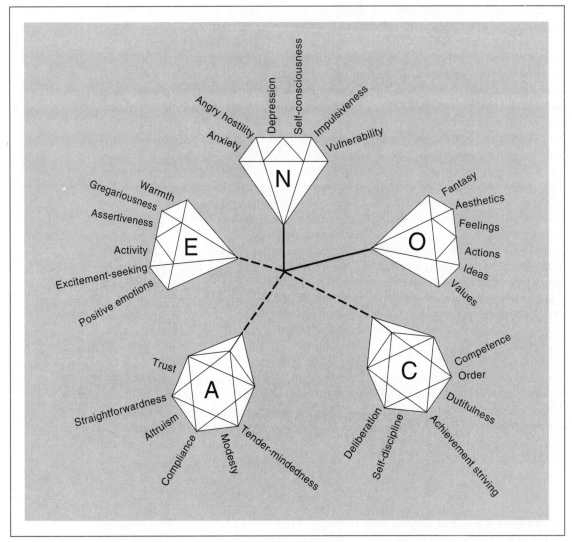

FIGURE 11-2

Costa and McCrae's five-factor model. Each factor, or domain of personality, represents a cluster of related traits or facets. N = neuroticism, E = extraversion, O = openness to experience, A = agreeableness, C = conscientiousness.

(SOURCE: Adapted from Costa & McCrae, 1980.)

People who are *open to experience* are willing to try new things and embrace new ideas. They have a vivid imagination and strong feelings. They appreciate beauty and the arts and question traditional values. Eva Perón would probably have scored high on this dimension.

Conscientious people are achievers: they are competent, orderly, dutiful, deliberate, and disciplined. Most of these characteristics could be identified with Eva Perón.

Agreeable people are trusting, straightforward, altruistic, compliant, modest, and easily swayed. Eva Perón would have had a low score on this dimension.

By analyzing a combination of cross-sectional, longitudinal, and sequential data from several large samples, including their own Baltimore Longitudinal Study of Aging, Costa and McCrae (1980, 1988, 1994a, 1994b; Costa et al., 1986; McCrae & Costa, 1984; McCrae, Costa, & Busch, 1986) have found a remarkable degree of stability in all five dimensions. Their samples consisted of men and women ranging in age from the twenties to the nineties. Their methodology included personality inventories, structured interviews, ratings by spouses and peers, and other measures.

Because the Baltimore Longitudinal Study was limited to predominantly white, college-educated volunteers, it could be open to sampling bias. Costa and McCrae therefore compared their findings on neuroticism, extraversion, and openness with ratings of the same traits in a nationwide cross-sectional sample of more than 10,000 people age 32 to 88. The differences were quite small and confirmed the stability, on average, of all three dimensions. This was true even for the midlife period, which some investigators—as well as many writers in the popular press—have described as a time of psychological upheaval. However, Costa and McCrae (1994b) did find age-related differences in cross-sectional comparisons of college students with young and middle-aged adults.

"Somewhere between age 21 and age 30 personality appears to take its final, fully developed form," Costa and McCrae (1994a) conclude. Their findings, together with similar data from other trait-based research, make a powerful case for that view. But some psychologists—for example, Helson (1993)—have criticized trait research in general, and Costa and McCrae's work in particular, as too limited, since it does not appear to account for aspects of personality that have been found by other research to change. Costa and McCrae (1994a) argue that even what may seem to be drastic changes actually reflect stable tendencies. For example, people who make dramatic career changes in midlife are likely to have a basic tendency to be open to experience.

Personality Dimensions in Late Life

Research on personality development in late life has had mixed results. In a longitudinal study of 74 Californians between ages 69 and 93, which used a trait model somewhat different from Costa and McCrae's, some dimensions of personality did show change. Over 14-year periods, *agreeableness* increased, especially in the oldest old, while *extraversion* (including talkativeness, frankness, and excitability) and *activity, energy, and health* decreased. The most stable dimension was *satisfaction*, including self-esteem, cheerfulness, satisfaction with oneself and one's circumstances, and little tendency to worry or be restless. Another highly stable dimension was *intellect*, comprising cognitive functioning and openmindedness (Field & Millsap, 1991).

However, the most extensive research in this area (Schaie & Willis, 1991), a sophisticated cross-sequential study of more than 3,000 older adults, found very little longitudinal change over 7 years. Instead, it found cohort differences. As a group, older people today seem to be more flexible and adaptable and less socially responsible than previous generations. These findings suggest that age differences found in cross-sectional studies may reflect culturally influenced differences among cohorts more than change within individuals.

(James H. Simon/The Picture Cube)

Cross-cultural differences in personality may diminish in a world in which adolescents like these Japanese teenagers dance to the same music and wear the same kind of clothing as American teenagers.

Culture and Personality

On a Sunday afternoon in the town of Frobisher Bay on Baffin Island in Canada, Eskimo (Inuit) boys and men age 7 to 47 played baseball. The teams were of different sizes, and players joined and quit at will. There was no umpire, and nobody kept score. No one struck out; each batter kept swinging until he hit the ball, then ran clockwise around the bases (opposite to the usual direction) while opponents threw the ball at him or tried to tag him out. One team batted until all its players were out; then the other team was up. The game would go on until dark, or until too many players wandered away.

An American observer might have remarked that this game had no rules, but the observer would have been wrong. The game did have rules, but they were few, flexible, and informal. In this, the game was like other aspects of traditional Eskimo culture, which encouraged individual, noncompetitive achievement. Thus a player was, for instance, more interested in proving how well he could dodge the ball than in trying to score for his team. When Eskimo culture began to change through contact with European and Canadian cultures, and the town itself took on a more formal organization and laws, Eskimos began playing baseball "by the book" (Honigmann, 1967).

The differences between traditional Eskimo baseball and the game with which you are probably familiar reflect different cultural values. Cultural values also influence personality traits such as competitiveness and flexibility. As it did in this case, cross-cultural contact frequently leads to cultural changes. Anthropologists often study isolated cultures, like the traditional Eskimo, to observe "pure" cultural traits.

As the world becomes a global village, in which people listen to the same music, eat the same foods, and wear the same clothing, will we see a "global personality"? Researchers who administered questionnaires to nearly 6,000 adolescents in 10 countries (Japan, Israel, Hungary, West Germany, Italy, Australia, Turkey, Bangladesh, Taiwan, and the United States) found remarkably little variation (Offer, Ostrov, Howard, & Atkinson, 1988). The "universal adolescent," it appears, is happy, self-confident, caring, sociable, and able to cope with life's problems. It will be interesting to see whether this cross-cultural similarity in personality traits continues in adulthood.

Laypeople's Views about Personality Change

How would you describe your personality? Do you think it has changed much in the past 10 years? How much do you think it will change by the time you are, say, 10 years older?

Much of the trait research we have described is based on self-ratings. Longitudinal research compares people's assessments of their own personality attributes—say, agreeableness or impatience—at different times. Cross-sectional research, which is more common, compares self-assessments of people of different ages at the same time. From these comparisons, researchers make inferences about stability or change.

Trait researchers rarely ask people how stable or changeable they *believe* personality to be. But a team of German researchers (Krueger & Heckhausen, 1993) did ask that and found noticeable perceptions of change.

Their 180 participants, evenly distributed by age and sex, rated themselves on 91 desirable and undesirable traits. They also indicated how much they believed each trait increases or decreases during each decade from the twenties through the eighties. The traits were classified by five dimensions (some of which are the same as Costa and McCrae's): *extraversion, agreeableness, conscientiousness, emotional stability,* and *intellect.*

As in other cross-sectional trait research, young, middle-aged, and older adults showed little or no difference in current self-ratings, except that older people rated themselves less harshly on undesirable traits. However, when asked about personality change, the respondents—regardless of gender or education—described modest change in almost all traits across the decades, with positive change predominating from early adulthood through the sixties (see Figure 11-3). Older adults were more optimistic than younger ones about the direction of change in late life.

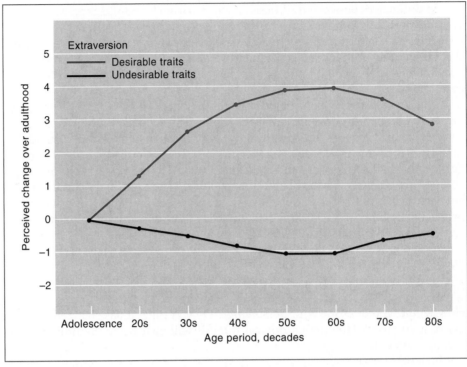

FIGURE 11-3

Subjective perceptions of personality change. According to a study done in Germany, most adults believe that people change significantly across adulthood. For most trait groupings (such as extraversion, shown here), the participants saw increases in positive (desirable) traits and decreases in negative (undesirable) traits until the sixties.

(SOURCE: Based on data in Krueger & Heckhausen, 1993.)

Apparently, adults of different ages have remarkably similar "theories" about how personality changes across most of the adult lifespan. These findings suggest that people may "expect and experience similar kinds of change" (Krueger & Heckhausen, 1993, p. 106), which may not be captured by standard trait research.

SELF-CONCEPT MODELS

"Who in the world am I? Ah, *that's* the great puzzle," said Alice in Wonderland, after her size had abruptly changed—again. Solving Alice's "puzzle" is a lifelong process of getting to know our developing selves.

According to self-concept models, our view of ourselves is the core of personality. Although the sense of self might seem the most personal thing imaginable, many psychologists see it as a *social* phenomenon, which grows out of interaction with others. People peer into a mirror created by their social world and blend the image they see reflected there with the picture they already have of themselves.

Self-concept theorists are concerned with the cognitive side of personality: what people think about who they are. The self-concept, they say, is made up of *schemas*—working models, or constructs, of reality around which behavior is organized. (For instance, a person's self-concept may include a schema for musicianship.) The self-concept includes knowledge of what a person has been and done, and it guides that person in deciding what to be and do in the future (Markus & Cross, 1990; Markus & Nurius, 1986). Thus it includes both self-understanding and self-regulation.

Schemas, like scientific theories, are only tentative; people continually revise them to conform with experience (Bowlby, 1973; S. Epstein, 1990; Tomkins, 1986). But interpretations of experience are subjective; a schema may filter out information that challenges one's beliefs about oneself (Caspi, 1993; Darley & Fazio, 1980; Greenwald, 1980; Markus, 1977; M. Snyder, 1987; Swann, 1983, 1987). Thus the self-concept is caught in constant dynamic tension between stability and change.

One current self-concept model is that of Susan Krauss Whitbourne (1987; Whitbourne & Primus, in press). It focuses on the development of *identity styles:* characteristic ways of confronting, interpreting, and responding to experience. According to Whitbourne, identity is made up of accumulated images of the self, both conscious and unconscious. Perceived personality traits, such as sensitivity and stubbornness, form part of that identity. These self-images normally remain stable unless contradicted by changes in life circumstances or roles. Even then, such changes do not shatter the personality's fundamental continuity but are incorporated into a modified, restabilized image of the self.

In Whitbourne's model, self-perceptions are confirmed or revised through two continuing processes of interaction with the social environment (similar to those Piaget described for children's cognitive development): *identity assimilation* and *identity accommodation.* **Identity assimilation** is an attempt to fit new experience into an existing self-concept. Most people will go to great lengths to confirm a favorable view of the self. A woman who thinks of herself as a proud and loving mother will see her interactions with her children in a positive light. If her relationship with one of the children begins to sour, she is likely to dismiss the problem as a temporary "phase" or to find a specific reason for an upsetting encounter. However, if something happens that she cannot satisfactorily explain to herself (for example, if her child is constantly stealing from her), she will be forced to adjust her self-image and her view of the relationship. This **identity accommodation,** though painful, is necessary for effective adaptation.

Overuse of either assimilation or accommodation is unhealthy. People who constantly assimilate are blind to reality; they see only what they are looking for. People who constantly accommodate are weak and easily swayed. A balance between the two processes is vital. Where a person generally strikes that balance determines his or her identity style.

Whitbourne's model, then, incorporates into an essentially stable concept of personality a mechanism for dealing flexibly with new experience in a way unique to the individual. However, this model does not as yet have a strong research base.

TABLE 11-1 FOUR STAGE MODELS OF ADULT PERSONALITY DEVELOPMENT

Approximate Age	Erikson	Vaillant	Levinson	Helson
20s	Crisis 6: Intimacy versus isolation	Establishment	Novice phase of early adulthood (entry life structure)	Bad self, bad partner
30s		Consolidation	Age 30 transition	Struggle for independent identity
			Culminating phase of early adulthood (culminating life structure)	
40s	Crisis 7: Generativity versus stagnation	Midlife transition	Midlife transition	Unpleasant consequences of independence
			Entry life structure for middle adulthood	Troubling relationships; overload
50s		Tranquil 50s	Age 50 transition Culminating life structure for middle adulthood	Prime of life
60s	Crisis 8: Integrity versus despair		Late adult transition	

STAGE MODELS

Stage models attempt to describe *normative personality change:* age-related patterns of personality development common to most members of a population. These changes emerge in successive periods, often marked by emotional "crises." Stage models do not suggest that everyone's life follows exactly the same course; but they do portray a common core of "life tasks" that occur in a certain sequence at approximately the same ages (Levinson, 1980, 1986). If these tasks are not accomplished, development in the next stage may be weakened.

A classic normative-crisis model is that of Erik Erikson, who broke with Freud in part because of his conviction that personality is not frozen at puberty—that people grow and change throughout adult life. Let's look at Erikson's stage model and at two others that were influenced by it: those of George Vaillant and Daniel Levinson. All three models are summarized in Table 11-1, along with another model (Helson's) that we discuss later in this chapter.

Erikson: Balancing Positive and Negative Tendencies

For Erikson (1950, 1985; Erikson, Erikson, & Kivnick, 1986), personality develops through a balancing of positive and negative tendencies at eight critical stages across the lifespan (see Table 2-2 in Chapter 2). Successful resolution of a crisis results in the emergence of a particular "virtue."

The sixth crisis, *intimacy versus isolation,* is the major issue of young adulthood. Young adults who have developed a strong sense of self are ready to fuse their identity with that of another person. Not until a person is ready for intimacy can "true genitality" occur—mutual orgasm in a loving, male-female relationship. Young adults who cannot, or are afraid to, make deep commitments to others may become isolated and self-absorbed. However, adults do need a certain amount of isolation to think about their lives. Resolution of the conflicting demands of intimacy and isolation results in the "virtue" of love: devotion between partners who have chosen to share their lives, to have children, and to help those children achieve their own healthy development. Critics object that people may acquire the virtue of love in a wide variety of lifestyles other than heterosexual marriage that produces children.

Erikson's sixth "crisis," intimacy versus isolation—the major issue of young adulthood—is successfully resolved by a commitment to share one's life with a beloved. According to Erikson, young adults who do not make such a commitment may become isolated and self-absorbed.

(Jean-Claude Lejeune/Stock, Boston)

(Elizabeth Crews/Stock, Boston)

According to Erikson, middle-aged adults like this teacher's aide may express generativity—*a concern for guiding the next generation—by teaching or being mentors to young people, as well as through relationships with their own children and grandchildren. People who do not find a satisfying outlet for generativity may become self-absorbed, self-indulgent, and stagnant.*

Erikson's seventh crisis, *generativity versus stagnation,* occurs in middle age. Although Erikson did not invent the term *midlife crisis* (see Box 11-2), he did see the years around age 40 as a critical time, when adults develop *generativity:* a concern for establishing and guiding the next generation. Looking ahead to the waning of their own lives, mature adults need to participate in life's continuation. The generative impulse is not necessarily limited to a person's own children and grandchildren; although Erikson (1985) believed that people who have not been parents cannot easily fulfill it, his view is considered narrow by many psychologists today. Erikson did say that generativity can be expressed through teaching or mentorship, through productivity or creativity, and through "self-generation," or self-development. The "virtue" of this period is care: "a widening commitment to *take care of* the persons, the products, and the ideas one has learned *to care for*" (1985, p. 67). People who do not find a satisfying outlet for generativity become self-absorbed, self-indulgent, and stagnant. As in all of Erikson's stages, it is the balance that is important; even the most generative person goes through fallow periods.

In Erikson's final crisis, *integrity versus despair,* older adults need to accept the way they have lived in order to accept their approaching death. They struggle to achieve a sense of integrity, a sense of the coherence and wholeness of their lives, rather than give way to despair over the impossibility of going back and doing things differently (Erikson et al., 1986). People who succeed in this final task gain a sense of order and meaning in life. The "virtue" that develops during this stage is wisdom (see Chapter 7). People who do not achieve wisdom—acceptance—are overwhelmed by despair when they realize that time is too short to follow other paths. Some despair is inevitable, Erikson maintained; people need to mourn, not only for their own misfortunes and lost chances but for the vulnerability and transience of the human condition. Yet he also believed that late life is a time to play, to recapture a childlike quality. Although the time for procreation is over, creation can take place. Even as physical functions weaken, people can enjoy enriched experiences of body and mind.

Vaillant: Relationships and Life Adjustment

An important longitudinal study that supported a progression of normative stages was the Grant Study of Harvard University graduates. The 268 men selected for the study, which began in 1938 when they were still in college, were self-reliant and emotionally and physically healthy. Retesting them in middle age, Vaillant (1977; Vaillant & Vaillant, 1990) concluded that people's lives are shaped by important sustained relationships. Of the men who at age 47 were considered best adjusted, 93 percent had established stable marriages before age 30 and were still married at 50.

With some variations, Vaillant (1977) saw a typical pattern. At age 20, many of the men were still dominated by their parents—a finding that has appeared again in later research (S. J. Frank, Avery, & Laman, 1988). During their twenties, and sometimes their thirties, they established themselves: achieved autonomy, married, had children, and deepened friendships. Somewhere between the twenties and the forties, these men entered a stage of *career consolidation*. They worked hard at strengthening their careers and devoted themselves to their families. They followed the rules, strove for promotions, and accepted "the system," rarely questioning whether they had chosen the right woman or the right career. The excitement, charm, and promise they had radiated as students disappeared; now they were described as "colorless, hardworking, bland young men in gray flannel suits" (Vaillant, 1977, p. 217).

The stage of career consolidation ends, according to Vaillant, when "at age 40—give or take as much as a decade—men leave the compulsive, unreflective busywork of their occupational apprenticeships, and once more become explorers of the world within" (Vaillant, 1977, p. 220). The midlife transition may be stressful because of new demands, such as changing the parenting role to meet the needs of teenage children. Many men reassess their past, come to terms with long-suppressed feelings about their parents, and reorder their attitudes toward sexuality.

Still, as troubling as these middle years sometimes were for the men in the Grant Study, the transition rarely amounted to a crisis. They were no more likely at midlife than at any other time during the lifespan to get divorced, to become disenchanted with their jobs, or to become depressed. By their fifties, the best-adjusted men in the group saw the years from 35 to 49 as the happiest in their lives. The best-adjusted men also were the most generative, as measured by their responsibility for other people at work, their gifts to charity, and their children, whose academic achievements equaled those of the fathers (Vaillant, 1989).

The fifties were a generally mellower and more tranquil time of life than the forties. Vaillant noted tendencies that also have been observed by others: a lessening of sexual differentiation with advancing age and a tendency for men to become more nurturant and expressive.

THE ART OF AGING

Navigating the Midlife Crossing

Changes in personality and lifestyle during the early to middle forties are often attributed to a *midlife crisis*, a stressful period triggered by review and reevaluation of one's life, which may herald the onset of middle age. The term was coined by the psychoanalyst Elliott Jacques (1967) and burst into public consciousness in the 1970s, with the popularization of the normative stage theories of Erik Erikson and Daniel Levinson. It has become a trendy catchphrase, which may pop up as an explanation for an episode of depression, an extramarital affair, or a career change.

According to Jacques, what brings on the midlife crisis is awareness of mortality. The first part of adulthood is over; its tasks are largely done. Time has become shorter, and many people now realize that they will not be able to fulfill all the dreams of their youth, or they realize that ful-fillment of their dreams has not brought them satisfaction.

According to the Swiss psychologist Carl Jung (1966), the need to acknowledge eventual mortality and to give up youthful self-images are two necessary tasks of middle age. These tasks require a gradual shift from an outward orientation, a concern with finding a place in society, to an introspective preoccupation with the inner life (Jung, 1966), which the gerontologist Bernice Neugarten (1977) calls *interiority*. Because the tasks of midlife and the inner dialogue they call for involve threatening ideas, this can be a stressful period. Questioning their goals, people may temporarily lose their sense of direction.

Today the idea of a universal, psychologically necessary midlife crisis is in doubt. Although Ravenna Helson (1992) found evidence of it in her studies of Mills College alumnae, other research has failed to support it (Costa & McCrae, 1980; Costa et al., 1986; Lacy & Hendricks, 1980; Vaillant, 1977). Instead, many psychologists now talk about a *midlife transition*, which, while some-

The researchers again examined the physical and mental health of 173 of the men at age 65 (Vaillant & Vaillant, 1990). The best adjusted 65-year-olds had been rated in college as well organized, steady, stable, and dependable; and they continued to show these traits. But some other characteristics linked with good adjustment in young adulthood, such as spontaneity and making friends easily, no longer influenced adjustment.

Levinson: Building and Changing Life Structures

Levinson (1978, 1980, 1986) and his colleagues at Yale University conducted in-depth interviews and personality tests with 40 men age 35 to 45, equally divided among four occupations: industrial workers, business executives, biologists, and novelists. From this study, as well as from biographical sources and from other research, Levinson formed a theory of personality development in adulthood.

At the heart of Levinson's theory is an evolving *life structure*—"the underlying pattern or design of a person's life at a given time" (1986, p. 6), which is built

times stressful, does not necessarily amount to a crisis (Brim, 1977; Chiriboga, 1989; Haan, 1990; Rossi, 1980).

How a man handles the midlife transition may reflect his place in society (Farrell & Rosenberg, 1981). In one study, only 12 percent of 300 middle-aged men in a socioeconomically diverse sample experienced a full-blown midlife crisis, though about two-thirds had some adjustment problems. Unskilled laborers were much more likely to show stress than professional men or middle-class executives, but the lower-class men were more likely to deny or avoid their problems or to express them through authoritarian attitudes.

Studies of nearly 300 women between ages 35 and 55 with diverse incomes and lifestyles (Barnett, 1985; Baruch, Barnett, & Rivers, 1983) found no evidence of midlife crisis. The two key factors in healthy adjustment, regardless of age, were a sense of mastery over one's life and the amount of pleasure derived from living. Paid work was the single best predictor of mastery; a positive experience with husband and children, including a good sex life, was the best predictor of pleasure; and the single best key to general well-being was a challenging job that paid well and offered opportunities to use skills and make decisions. The women who scored highest overall on both mastery and pleasure were employed married women with children; the lowest scorers were unemployed, childless married women.

For many people, then, entering middle age may be just one more of life's many transitions. Whether a transition turns into a crisis may depend on particular circumstances and how a particular person deals with them: "One person may go from crisis to crisis while another . . . experience[s] relatively few strains" (Schlossberg, 1987, p. 74). And timing of life events may play a part. In a study by Taguiri and Davis (Baruch et al., 1983), men in their thirties who had achieved success quite young were struggling with questions usually thought to be characteristic of midlife: "Was it worth it?" "What next?" and "What shall I do with the rest of my life?"

around whatever a person finds most important. Most people build a life structure around work and family. Levinson's stages, which he calls *phases* (refer back to Table 11-1), are linked by transitional periods when people reappraise their life structure. Indeed, Levinson says, people spend nearly half their adult lives in transitions, which may involve crises. Each phase has its own tasks, whose accomplishment becomes the foundation for the next life structure.

In the *novice* phase of early adulthood (ages 17–33),[*] a man[†] needs to leave his parents' home and become financially and emotionally independent. He forms relationships, usually leading to marriage and parenthood, and chooses an occupation. Two important tasks are forming a dream and finding a mentor. A *dream* usually has to do with a career: a vision of, say, winning a Nobel Prize. A *mentor* is a slightly older man who offers guidance and inspiration and passes on wisdom, moral support, and practical help in both career and personal matters.

[*]All ages are approximate in Levinson's model.
[†]Levinson (1986) claims that his conclusions also apply to women, with some variations.

(Walter Silver/The Picture Cube)

According to Levinson, one important task for a young adult like this dental student (left) is to find a mentor: an older man, like this dental school dean (right), who can offer career guidance, inspiration, and practical help.

In the *culminating* phase (ages 33–45), after the age-30 transition, a man settles down. He sets goals (a professorship, for instance, or a certain level of income) and a time for achieving them (say, by age 40). He anchors his life in family, occupation, and community. At the same time, he chafes under authority; he wants to speak with his own voice. He may discard his mentor and be at odds with his wife, children, lover, boss, friends, or coworkers.

Life structures change appreciably at midlife. The realization that a cherished dream will not come true may bring on an emotional crisis. Four out of 5 of the men in the study often felt upset and acted irrationally between ages 40 and 45. Levinson maintains that such turmoil is inevitable as people question their previously held values. Reevaluation helps people come to terms with their youthful dreams, to emerge with a more realistic self-image, and to substitute more attainable goals.

Between ages 45 and 50, men carve out new life structures, possibly by taking a new job or a new wife. Those who make no changes lead a constricted life in middle age. They may be busy and well-organized but unexcited. Often those who do change their life structures find middle age the most fulfilling and creative time of life. Although Levinson and his colleagues did not follow their sample into the fifties and sixties, they made projections for those years (refer back to Table 11-1).

Evaluating Stage Models

The participants in the classic normative studies were, for the most part, fairly small samples of privileged white men born in the 1920s or 1930s. The resulting models cannot readily be generalized to people of other races or socioeconomic levels.

Furthermore, these models have been criticized for taking male development as the norm. In Erikson's model, intimacy follows achievement of a stable identity, which is supposed to take place in late adolescence. But according to Erikson, a woman achieves identity and intimacy at the same time, defining herself by the man she will marry. In one study, which tested the relationship between identity and intimacy (Kahn, Zimmerman, Csikszentmihalyi, & Getzels, 1985), researchers measured the "identity strength" of sophomore and junior art students. Eighteen years later, 60 percent of the sample responded to a questionnaire about their marital status, as an indication of how successfully they had achieved intimacy in young adulthood. The results showed dramatic gender differences. The men who had shown strong identity in their student days were much more likely than other men to be married, but no more or less likely to have stable marriages. With women, it was just the opposite: those who had a strong identity in their youth were no more or less likely to have married; but if they had married, they were far more likely to have stayed married. Findings like these, which suggest differences in the meaning and development of intimacy for men and women, have led some researchers to insist on models that focus specifically on women's development (Gilligan, 1982). Later in this chapter we'll report on one such model.

Another problem with classic normative models is that cohorts with different experiences may develop differently. These studies were done before, and thus do not reflect, the dramatic increase in career changes, dual-earner marriages, and openly heterosexual and homosexual cohabitation. Nor have these theories been tested in other cultures, some of which have very different concepts of life's stages.

In traditional Hinduism—the religion that dominates much of the culture of India—men go through four stages of development (Zimmer, 1956). These resemble the stages of western models in some ways but are quite different in other ways. (Again, studies of personality development in other cultures have often focused on male development.) Unlike normative models in western culture, which attempt to describe actual stages in personality development, the Hindu stages represent a spiritual ideal that few people will ever fully achieve. The stages, which apply to all but the lowest caste, correspond roughly to youth, young adulthood, middle adulthood, and late adulthood. There are no transitional periods and, presumably, no crises; each stage is viewed as preparation for the next.

The first stage is that of the *obedient pupil* receiving knowledge from his spiritual teacher, or guru. This mentor-like relationship is exclusive and all-encompassing. Sexual relations are forbidden and severely punished.

When the student stage is over, the young man is suddenly thrust into married life. His parents having chosen a wife for him, he becomes a *householder*—the second stage—and supports his family by taking over his father's craft, business, or profession.

The third stage, *departure to the forest,* which begins in the latter part of middle age, is another abrupt change. Up to now, the man has dutifully played socially imposed roles. Now he throws off his social "mask," withdraws from family life and material concerns, and lets his sons take over the "joys and burdens of the

(Peter Menzel/Stock, Boston)

The final stage of the Hindu life path is that of a wandering holy beggar, who strips himself of everything that defines his past identity and seeks to enter a state of perfect bliss and harmony with all existence.

world" as he retreats from everyday life "to enter upon the path of the quest for the Self" (Zimmer, 1956, p. 157). This period of meditation and self-discovery prepares him for the fourth and final stage.

The fourth stage is that of the *wandering holy beggar*. The man casts off everything that defines and limits him—his clothing, memories, emotions, habits, likes, and dislikes. He thinks neither of the present nor of the future, neither of his mind nor of his body. His goal now is to strip away the personal self, to identify with all existence and enter a state of perfect harmony and bliss.

The Gusii, a polygamous society in western Kenya (Levine, 1980), have a "life plan" with well-defined expectations, which is very different from either the Hindu life path or the classic western normative models. The Gusii have no words meaning "adolescent," "young adult," or "middle-aged." People continue to reproduce as long as they are biologically able. A man is circumcised sometime between ages 9 and 11 and will become an "elder" when his first child marries. Between these two events, he goes through only one recognized stage of life—*omomura*, or "warrior." The *omomura* phase may last anywhere from 25 to 40 years, or even longer. Women have an additional middle stage—*omosubaati*, or "married woman"—because of the greater importance of marriage in a woman's life.

In Gusii society, then, transitions depend not on age but on life events. Status is linked to circumcision, marriage (for women), having children, and becoming a parent of a married child and thus a prospective grandparent. The Gusii do have a **social clock,** a set of norms or expectations for when these events should occur. People who marry late or do not marry at all, and people who have their first child late or have no children, are ridiculed and ostracized.

Although the Gusii have no recognized midlife transition, some of them do reassess their lives around the time they are old enough to be grandparents.

Awareness of mortality and of waning physical powers can bring on something resembling a midlife crisis, from which a man or woman may emerge as a ritual healer. The quest for spiritual powers has a generative purpose, too: elders are responsible for ritually protecting their children and grandchildren from death or illness.

Stage models have captured both the professional and the public imagination, largely because of their main message: that adults continue to change, develop, and grow. Whether or not people grow in the particular ways suggested by these models, they have challenged the notion that hardly anything important happens to personality after adolescence.

THE TIMING-OF-EVENTS MODEL

In childhood, internal maturational events signal transitions from one developmental stage to another. A baby says the first word, takes the first step, loses the first tooth. The body changes at the onset of puberty. But although age may be fairly indicative of children's development, individual circumstances or life events may be more significant for adults.

The *timing-of-events model,* supported by Bernice Neugarten and others (Neugarten, Moore, & Lowe, 1965; Neugarten & Neugarten, 1987), views major life events as markers of development. According to this model, people develop in response to the times in their lives when key events do or do not occur. Life events are of two types. Events people expect because they happen to most adults are called *normative life events;* examples are parenthood and retirement. Unusual events that cannot be expected are called *nonnormative life events;* examples are a traumatic accident, an unanticipated promotion, or a lottery prize.

(Erika Stone)

In the timing-of-events model, the impact of an event like parenthood depends on whether it is "on time" or "off time" according to the social clock. According to this model, having a baby in the forties is more likely to cause stress than having a baby in the twenties. But with more American women delaying parenthood, one study found no age differences in adjustment.

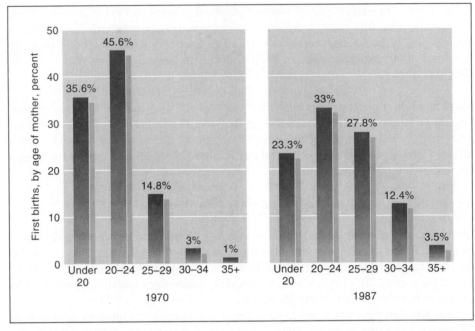

FIGURE 11-4

Changes in age of first childbirth, 1970–1987. Today, women tend to have children later in life than their mothers did. More women now have a first child after age 30.
(SOURCE: National Center for Health Statistics, 1990.)

Whether or not an event is normative—and therefore expected—often depends on its timing. Events that are normative when they are "on time" (according to the social clock) become nonnormative when they are "off time"—that is, early or late. Marrying at 14 or 41 or retiring at 41 or 91 would be a non-normative event. People are usually keenly aware of their own timing and describe themselves as "early," "late," or "on time" in marrying, having children, settling on careers, or retiring. Normative events that come "on time" are generally taken in stride; "it is the events that upset the expected sequence and rhythm of the life cycle that cause problems" (Neugarten & Neugarten, 1987, p. 33).

Crises are caused, then, not by reaching a certain age, but by the expected or unexpected occurrence and timing of life events. If events occur as expected, development proceeds smoothly. If not, stress can result. Stress may occur in response to an unexpected event (such as losing a job), an event that happens earlier or later than expected (being widowed at age 35, having a first child at 45, being forced to retire at 55), or the failure of an expected event to occur at all (never being married, or being unable to have a child).

The typical timing of some events, such as marriage, varies from culture to culture (Bianchi & Spain, 1986) and from one generation to the next. One illustration is the recent rise in the average age when adults first marry in the United States (U.S. Bureau of the Census, 1992b); another is the trend toward delayed first childbirth (see Figure 11-4). Since the mid-twentieth century, American society has become less age-conscious; the feeling that there is a "right time" to do certain things is less widespread (Neugarten & Hagestad, 1976; Neugarten & Neugarten, 1987). Today people are more accepting of 40-year-old first-time parents and 40-year-old grandparents, 50-year-old retirees and 75-year-old workers, 60-year-olds in blue jeans and 30-year-old college presidents—as well as a president of the United States in his mid-forties. Major events that once characterized a certain time of life, such as marriage, the first job, and the birth of children and grandchildren, are now less predictable. According to the timing-of-events model, we should expect this uncertainty to produce stress (Neugarten & Neugarten, 1987).

However, rapid social change tends to undermine the predictability which the timing-of-events model assumes. Today, for example, American couples who delay becoming parents until ages 28 to 37 seem to adjust no better and no worse than younger parents with similar demographic characteristics (Roosa, 1988). Does this finding suggest that the timing-of-events model is wrong about the effects of not being "on time," or does it merely reflect a current "blurring of traditional life periods" (Neugarten & Neugarten, 1987, p. 32)?

The timing-of-events model has made an important contribution to our understanding of adult personality by emphasizing the importance of the individual life course and challenging the idea of universal, age-related change. Yet ultimately its usefulness, like that of the classic stage theories, may well be limited to cultures and historical periods in which norms of behavior are stable and widespread.

GENDER AND PERSONALITY

▼

Do women's personalities develop differently from men's across the adult lifespan? Theorists and researchers who have explored that topic have come up with almost as many questions as answers.

GENDER STEREOTYPES, GENDER ROLES, AND GENDER IDENTITY

Are women the "weaker sex"? Are men "strong and silent"? *Gender stereotypes*—exaggerated generalizations about differences between men and women—pervade many cultures (Williams & Best, 1982). Although not all individuals conform to them, these stereotypes often form a part of a society's *gender roles:* cultural norms or expectations for appropriate male or female behavior, interests, attitudes, abilities, and personality traits.

In most cultures women have been expected to care for the household and children and to make sure that the family functions smoothly, while men are protectors and providers. Such gender roles, transmitted through socialization in early childhood, are incorporated into an individual's *gender identity:* awareness of what it means to be male or female (Huyck, 1990). As part of their socially sanctioned gender roles, men are generally expected to be active, aggressive, autonomous, and achievement-oriented; women are regarded as more nurturing, deferential, dependent, empathic, and concerned with relationships. Both in everyday speech and in psychological measurement, the first group of characteristics traditionally have been called *masculine* and the second group *feminine.*

However, apart from aggression, which does seem to be stronger in men (Frieze, Parsons, Johnson, Ruble, & Zellman, 1978), measured differences in these attributes are not consistently sex-related (Huyck, 1990). Differences within either sex are greater than average differences between the sexes, which are statistically small and are valid for large groups but not necessarily for individuals. Still, although measurable cognitive and personality differences between the sexes generally are small, both males and females believe themselves to be more different than they actually are (Matlin, 1987).

Gender identity is an integral part of the sense of self; and, like other aspects of the self-concept, it may represent a filtered view of reality. Men and women who absorb gender stereotypes into their self-concept may deny their natural inclinations and force themselves into ill-fitting academic, vocational, or social molds. Stereotypes can affect the simplest everyday tasks as well as far-reaching life decisions. A man may be "all thumbs" when it comes to preparing a baby's bottle or mending a button; a woman "can't" nail boards together or bait a fishhook (Bem, 1976).

Many psychologists today recognize that "masculinity" and "femininity" are not polar opposites. People of both sexes have a mixture of "masculine" and "feminine" personality characteristics. Some people are ***androgynous***—that is, they are high in both "masculine" and "feminine" characteristics. Some people are ***undifferentiated***—low in both. Some people are high in one or the other. Sandra Bem (1974, 1976), a leader in the study of gender roles, maintains that the androgynous personality is the healthiest. An androgynous person may be assertive, self-reliant, and dominant, as well as compassionate, sympathetic, and understanding.

Bem's Sex Role Inventory (1974) places people in one of four categories—masculine, feminine, androgynous, or undifferentiated—by asking them to rate themselves according to a list of adjectives or phrases. This and similar instruments can be used to study whether men and women become more or less "masculine" or "feminine" across the adult lifespan. Before we turn to such research, let's look at some theories of how gender identity develops and whether and how it can change.

How Do Gender Roles and Gender Identity Develop?

There are a number of theories—many of them conflicting—about how gender roles and gender identity develop in childhood, and each has specific consequences for later life.

In classical Freudian psychoanalytic theory, boys and girls achieve permanent gender identity by identifying with the parent of the same sex and repressing or giving up the idea of possessing the parent of the other sex.

According to ***self-in-relation theory***, proposed by Jean Baker-Miller (1976), a feminist psychotherapist, men and women develop gender identity differently,

(Claire Rydell/The Picture Cube)

According to social-learning theory, young children—like this boy following in his father's footsteps—learn gender roles by observing and imitating the parent of the same sex.

and this difference explains much about adult personality development. While masculine identity requires a distancing from the mother, feminine identity does not; a girl's tie with her mother widens to include nurturant relationships with others as well. Self-in-relation theory holds that men, too, have a primary desire for connection with other people. When that desire is frustrated by a culturally induced pursuit of autonomy and avoidance of close attachments, the result may be a sense of emptiness, loneliness, and depression in midlife (S. J. Bergman, 1991; J. B. Miller, 1991). In this view, a woman's "weaknesses"—vulnerability, dependence, and emotionality—are actually strengths: "valuable attributes that foster connection, intimacy, and growth" (R. Weiss, 1994, p. 3).

According to *social-learning theory,* of which Albert Bandura is the most prominent advocate, young children learn to identify with and act like the parent of the same sex. They learn gender roles the same way they learn other kinds of socially approved behavior: through observation, imitation, and reinforcement from parents and society. ("Don't be a sissy!" "Girls don't climb trees!") Since gender identity and gender roles are learned, they can later be modified through selection and imitation of new models, or through reinforcement of different kinds of behavior.

Other psychologists, such as Kohlberg (1966), have proposed *cognitive-developmental theories.* Rather than depending on adults as models or dispensers of reinforcement, these theorists hold, children learn about gender (and other aspects of their world) by actively thinking about their experience. They organize their behavior around these perceptions, adopting behaviors they see as consistent with their identity as male or female. One cognitive-developmental model (Pleck, 1975; Rebecca, Hefner, & Oleshansky, 1976) proposes that people learn about gender roles in four stages. In childhood, they move from vague notions (stage 1) to rigid ideas (stage 2) of what males and females are and do. In adulthood, their self-concept becomes more flexible and androgynous (stage 3). In stage 4, *gender-role transcendence,* gender roles become irrelevant and people do whatever is most adaptive in a situation.

Bem's (1981, 1983, 1985) **gender-schema theory** combines elements of the social-learning and cognitive-developmental approaches. According to Bem, people develop *gender schemas,* patterns of behavior organized around gender, which help them sort out their observations of what it means to be male or female. They pick up these schemas in childhood as they see how society classifies people and behavior. As in social-learning theory, learned schemas can be modified; but modification may require altering culturally ingrained attitudes, which are highly resistant to change.

As early as 1910, for instance, the founders of kibbutzim (communal settlements) in Israel tried to do away with special roles for men and women by changing family structure and assigning chores without regard to sex. Later, however, people on kibbutzim reverted to traditional gender roles, with men doing agricultural and mechanical work and women cooking, laundering, and caring for children (Tiger & Shepher, 1975). In the United States, although the past several decades have brought major changes in how men and women think, feel, and act with regard to gender, many people still view certain activities as unmasculine or unfeminine.

Do Gender Roles Change during Adulthood?

There is considerable evidence that people may become more androgynous in midlife. Costa and McCrae (1980), in keeping with their findings of stability in other areas of personality, have questioned the significance of such data. However, a number of studies have found that middle-aged men tend to be more open about feelings, more interested in intimate relationships, and more nurturing than younger men; while middle-aged women are more assertive, active, self-confident, and achievement-oriented (Chiriboga & Thurnher, 1975; Cooper & Gutmann, 1987; Cytrynbaum et al., 1980; Helson & Moane, 1987; Huyck, 1990; Neugarten, 1968). Some social scientists attribute these apparent developments to the hormonal changes of menopause and the male climacteric (Rossi, 1980); others offer psychological and cultural explanations.

One of the earliest and most influential theorists to describe normative changes in gender roles across the adult lifespan was the Swiss psychologist Carl Jung, whose work, like that of Erikson, departed from Freudian theory. Jung (1953, 1969) held that healthy development calls for a balance or integration of conflicting parts of the personality. Until about age 40, adults concentrate on obligations to family and society and develop those aspects of personality that will help them reach these external goals. According to Jung, women emphasize expressiveness and nurturance; men are primarily oriented toward achievement. Men suppress their feminine aspects; women suppress their masculine aspects. At midlife, when careers are established and children are grown, men and women seek a "union of opposites" by expressing their previously "disowned" aspects.

(Beringer/Dratsch/The Image Works)

The emptying of the nest when grown children go off to college or establish their own households may signal a reversal of conventional gender roles. A middle-aged man may become more concerned with intimacy while his wife becomes more dominant and independent.

The psychologist David Gutmann (1975, 1977, 1985), who reviewed a large number of cross-cultural studies, suggests that traditional gender roles evolved to ensure the security of the young and the well-being of the growing family. After child raising is over, says Gutmann, there is not just a balancing of roles but often a reversal of roles. Men are now free to explore their previously repressed "feminine" side and thus become more passive (see Box 11-3); women become more dominant and independent.

Such changes may be most characteristic of societies or cohorts with relatively conventional gender roles. For example, in American society many middle-aged men have become more interested in intimacy at a time when women have been entering the workplace or exploring other facets of their personalities. This mismatch between men's and women's needs may help explain why midlife has been found to be the low point in marital satisfaction, and why many men seem to regret the "empty nest" while many women welcome it (see Chapter 9). Now that most younger women combine paid work with parenthood, and some younger men are more active in childrearing, we may no longer see such dramatic switches in gender roles at midlife. Indeed, a recent time-sequential comparison (Hyde, Krajnik, & Skuldt-Niederberger, 1991), which used a modified version of Bem's Sex Role Inventory, found more "masculine" women age 21 to 40 and more androgynous men at all ages than in a similar sample 10 years before.

With regard to late life, the current sample, like the earlier one, had more androgynous men and more "feminine" women in the oldest group (61 to 86) than in younger groups. This finding suggests that both older men and older women may become more "feminine," reflecting increased dependency (Hyde et al., 1991). Such comparisons do not, of course, establish whether individuals actually change. For that, we need longitudinal research.

BOX 11-3

THE MULTICULTURAL CONTEXT

Druze Men: New Roles in Late Middle Age

The Druze are an Islamic sect in the middle east; they live in isolated highland farming villages. Although similar to other Muslim peoples in language and most other aspects of lifestyle, in one respect they are unique. The Druze broke with the rest of Islam on doctrinal grounds more than 800 years ago, and since then they have lived as an often oppressed, highly self-sufficient minority. They will fight to the death any threat to their beliefs and traditions.

To protect their religion and their identity, the Druze operate as a secret society within the Islamic world and even within their own villages. Their sacred texts, which control their culture, are open only to men; and even men are generally given access to this hidden knowledge only in late middle age and only after living an exemplary life. Younger men "are not instructed in the religion or even told that they are Druze until they reach the age of discretion" (Gutmann, 1974, p. 235).

Once accepted into the inner circle of *Aqil* ("those who know"), Druze men radically change their lifestyle. They shave their heads, put on special clothing, stop smoking and drinking, and spend much of their time in prayer. The initiate "is expected to devote himself to good and pious thoughts and to forget the errors and stupidities of his life before he was introduced to true knowledge" (p. 235).

Despite these highly specific features of Druze life, the psychologist David Gutmann (1974, 1977), who studied the Druze of Israel and the Golan Heights, found parallels with changing gender roles of aging men in other cultures. When Druze men were given a projective personality test, their responses were similar to those of Navajo and Mayan men, as well as to an urban sample from Kansas City. In all four cultures, older men's interpretations of pictures were less aggressive and competitive than those of

Could such changes be related more to life events than to chronological age? One research team (B. Abrahams, Feldman, & Nash, 1978; S. S. Feldman, Biringen, & Nash, 1981; Nash & Feldman, 1981) examined people at successive stages in the family life cycle and found that the prospect and advent of parenthood intensified "masculinity" and "femininity." A number of studies have found that both women's and men's concepts of gender identity are affected by their life situation, social context, and social roles (Blanchard-Fields & Abeles, in press). For example, a recent finding that older people are more sensitive than younger people (Blanchard-Fields, Suhrer-Roussel, & Hertzog, 1994) may reflect not an age-related increase in androgyny but an increase in emotional expressiveness related to grandparenthood or other role changes (Blanchard-Fields & Abeles, in press).

WOMEN'S PERSONALITY DEVELOPMENT: THE MILLS STUDIES

The issue of how similarly or differently men and women develop takes us back to a major criticism of classic stage models: their use of male samples and norms, which may not be generalizable to women. Let's look at some longitudinal

younger men. For example, when shown a picture of a man climbing (or perhaps descending) a rope, a younger man would describe the man in the picture as demonstrating strength and boldness, competing against other climbers, training for competition, or perhaps escaping from prison. An older man was more likely to see him as playing, resting, or diving into water; as fleeing from danger; as struggling against his own weakness; or as exhausted and clinging desperately to the rope. Older men were also likely to give magical or imaginative interpretations, perhaps seeing the man on the rope as impaled by a spear, or the rope as a snake.

According to Gutmann, such reactions reveal an age-related shift from *active mastery* to *passive mastery*. In many agrarian, preliterate societies, "young men are expected, through their *own* energies, to wrest resource and power from physical nature, from enem[ies] or from both; older men are expected . . . to coax power from the [gods]" (1977, p. 305). Older Druze men show passive or "feminine" leanings not in outward behavior, but in their spiritual life. While they retain positions of prestige and involvement in society, often "laying down the law" to their grown sons and other younger relatives, in their relationship to God they are humble, docile, and unquestioningly subservient. They believe that this passivity enables them to tap into the power of the supernatural world to safeguard and increase the production of children, flocks, and crops. The *Aqil*, then, "relinquishes his own productivity" to become "the bridge between the community and the productive, life-sustaining potencies of Allah, . . . carr[ying] forward the moral rather than the material work of the community" (1974, p. 244).

Thus, says Gutmann, the Druze religion seems to provide a useful role for older men undergoing personality changes common to their age, which have no comparable, constructive outlet in modern secular societies—a role suited to a stage of life when the tasks of parenthood and physical productivity are over.

---

research that has sought to correct this imbalance and to track changes in women's roles.

One of the most comprehensive longitudinal studies of women's personality development is that of Ravenna Helson and her associates, who for more than three decades have followed 140 women from the classes of 1958 and 1960 at Mills College in Oakland, California. Using a combination of psychological ratings and open-ended questions, Helson and her colleagues found three types of systematic personality change that correspond roughly to stage, life events, and trait approaches: *normative change,* which applied to the sample as a whole; change associated with *role patterns and paths;* and change associated with particular *personality patterns.*

Normative Changes

The Mills studies suggest a progression of stages different from those of the men in Vaillant's and Levinson's studies (refer back to Table 11-1). But, like the men in those studies, these women do appear to have gone through periods of reorganizing their perceptions to bring new meaning to their "life stories."

(Bobbe Wolf)

The prime of life for a woman is the early fifties, according to Helson's research on graduates of Mills College. At this age, a woman generally is young enough to be in good health and old enough to have launched her children and to be financially comfortable. The energy that went into raising children now is redirected to her partner, her work, or herself.

Helson (1992) asked 88 Mills alumnae in their early fifties to identify the "most unstable, confusing, troubled, or discouraged time in your life since college—the one with the most impact on your values, self-concept, and the way you look at the world" (p. 336). The early forties turned out to be the time of greatest turmoil for the largest number of women, supporting the notion of a female midlife crisis. The outcome of this struggle was a "revision of the life story," giving "the plot of their lives a self-chosen new direction" (p. 343).

Crises also appeared at other times of life. Many of them could be categorized by themes which were often age-related, though motherhood tended to delay these critical times. Typical themes among women in their early to mid-twenties were *bad self* and *bad partner.* The "bad self" theme was characterized by feeling lonely, isolated, unattractive, inferior, and often passive. The "bad partner" theme often revolved around a husband who was a substance abuser, suicidal, or exploitive.

A theme common enough to be considered a stage in women's development was a struggle for *independent identity,* status, and power, and the desire to achieve control over one's life. This theme, which often arose around age 30 to 40, might involve graduate training, a career, or a love affair (heterosexual or lesbian).

As the participants moved into middle age, between ages 36 and 46, these women's stories involved themes of *unpleasant consequences of independence and assertiveness:* rebuffs at work, for instance, or abandonment by their husbands. Later midlife themes, between ages 47 to 53, often focused on *troubling relationships* with partners, parents, or children; or on *overload,* sometimes caused by the demands of other people, sometimes by economic strain or heavy responsibilities at work.

When is the prime of life? Among nearly 700 Mills alumnae age 26 to 80 who were studied in 1983, women in their early fifties most often described their lives as "first-rate." In 1989, women in the original Mills longitudinal sample, then in their early fifties, also rated their quality of life as high (Mitchell & Helson, 1990). Generally, these women were young enough to be in good health and old enough to have launched all their children and to be well off financially. Life at home was simpler; the energy that had gone into childrearing was redirected to partners, work, community, or themselves. They had developed greater confidence, involvement, security, and breadth of personality. The women with the most positive outlook were optimistic; they had good relationships, a favorable self-concept, a feeling of control over their lives, and active interests; and they were managing their lives sensibly. They were likely to be caring for others—the generativity described by Erikson.

The normative changes these women experienced seem to bear out the idea proposed by Jung, Gutmann, and others "that young adult roles increase women's femininity but that women become more confident and assertive around midlife" (Helson, 1993, pp. 101–102). The highest quality of life was associated, not with a reversal of gender roles, but with an androgynous balance of "masculine" autonomy and "feminine" involvement in an intimate relationship.

Further evidence for change in gender roles is provided by self-reports and personality ratings. On a standard measure of gender-related characteristics, the California Psychological Inventory, traits associated with femininity—sympathy and compassion combined with a sense of vulnerability, self-criticism, and lack of confidence and initiative—increased during the twenties and then declined across middle age (see Figure 11-5). Between ages 21 and 43, the women developed more self-discipline and commitment, independence, confidence, and coping skills (Helson & Moane, 1987); from ages 43 to 52, they continued to grow in independence and self-confidence. They became more decisive, dominant, and self-affirming and less self-critical (see Table 11-2). This normative personality change was unrelated to such typical midlife events as the empty nest, menopause, or caring for aging parents (Helson & Wink, 1992).

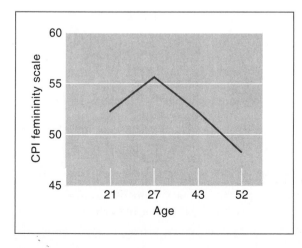

FIGURE 11-5

Changes in femininity with age. In a sample of 79 Mills College women who took the California Psychological Inventory (CPI) at ages 21, 27, 43, and 52, traits associated with femininity became stronger between ages 21 and 27, then weaker at midlife and into the early fifties.

(SOURCE: Adapted from Helson, 1993, p. 101.)

TABLE 11-2   SELECTED FEELINGS ABOUT LIFE BY WOMEN IN THEIR EARLY FIFTIES

	More True Now	Less True Now
Identity questioning and turmoil:		
Excitement, turmoil about my impulses and potential	21	56
Searching for a sense of who I am	28	47
Anxious that I won't live up to my potential	25	47
Coming near the end of one road and not finding another	27	45
Assurance of status:		
Feeling established	78	11
Influence in my community or field of interest	63	24
A new level of productivity	70	11
Feeling selective in what I do	91	2
A sense of being my own person	90	3
Cognitive breadth and complexity:		
Bringing both feeling and rationality into decisions	76	1
Realizing larger patterns of meaning and relationship	72	7
Appreciating my complexity	69	10
Discovering new parts of myself	72	11
Present rather than future orientation:		
Focus on reality—meeting the needs of the day and not being too emotional about them	76	6
More satisfied with what I have; less worried about what I won't get	76	11
Feeling the importance of time's passing	76	10
Adjustment and relational smoothness:		
Feeling secure and committed	71	12
Feeling my life is moving well	74	15
Feeling optimistic about the future	58	20
A new level of intimacy	53	30
Doing things for others and then feeling exploited	14	56
Feeling very much alone	26	45
Feelings of competition with other women	7	63
Feeling angry at men and masculinity	14	52
Awareness of aging and reduced vitality:		
Looking old	70	15
Being treated as an older person	64	14
Reducing the intensity of my achievement efforts	44	26
Liking an active social life	27	52
Being very interested in sex	19	64

NOTE: The women judged whether each item was more applicable to them now than in their early forties, less applicable now than then, or about the same.
SOURCE: Helson & Wink, 1992.

As with the classic normative studies of male samples, of course, the experience of these Mills graduates has to be considered in terms of their socioeconomic status, cohort, and culture. They are a group of educated, predominantly white, upper-middle-class American women who lived through a time of great change in women's roles brought about in part by the women's movement, by economic changes, by changing patterns of family life, and by new patterns in the workplace. The Mills women were undoubtedly influenced by these factors.

Thus the normative changes found in the Mills research are not necessarily the same as maturational changes, which would occur regardless of class, cohort, and culture. For example, on a measure designed to show women's psychological dependence on their husbands, the Mills women at age 52 scored significantly lower (that is, showed less dependence) than their mothers had at the same age (Wink & Helson, 1993). Today's young women, in turn, may be developing differently from the women in the Mills sample. As Helson and Moane (1987) observe, "If a substantial number of women continue to launch careers in their 20s and have children in their 30s, the pattern of normative change may take a different form" (p. 185).

Change Associated with Role Patterns and Paths

Certain aspects of personality development in the Mills women seemed to be related to life events. Some women, for example, followed the expected pattern for their generation—marrying and starting families in young adulthood—and by age 43 continued to maintain their traditional roles. These women did not exhibit the gains in dominance and independence that the rest of the sample showed. They also became increasingly "overcontrolled," a pattern some theorists have noted in women who place others' needs before their own (Helson & Picano, 1990).

Still, more than one kind of lifestyle seemed to foster positive development. Women who committed themselves during their twenties to career, family, or both developed more fully than women who had no children and who chose work beneath their capabilities. Between age 27 and the early forties, women who had faced the challenges of career or parenthood became more disciplined, independent, hard-working, and confident and improved their "people skills." Compared with women who had made neither commitment, they were more dominant, more motivated to achieve, more emotionally stable, more goal-oriented, and more interested in what was going on in the world (Helson & Moane, 1987). Of course, this was not a controlled experiment, and so these correlations can only suggest—not establish—causal relationships.

Changes Associated with Personality Patterns

The Mills researchers found certain changes related to specific personality patterns. For example, by means of a prototype of the Q-sort technique some women were identified as *willful*—a form of what Freud called a *narcissistic*, or excessively self-absorbed, personality. These women became more effective, happier, more sociable, and more confident between ages 21 and 27. But, as Freudian theory would predict, they became more maladjusted by midlife. They tended to have problems with drugs, relationships, and careers (Wink, 1991, 1992).

The Mills studies are notable for their eclectic combination of research tools and their attempt to combine several approaches to the study of adult personality development. This research avoids a simplistic, either-or approach and points toward further synthesis that needs to be done.

SYNTHESIZING APPROACHES TO ADULT PERSONALITY DEVELOPMENT

▼

Advocates of stability and advocates of change often defend their positions zealously. Still, it seems plain, as the historian C. Vann Woodward (1989) has observed, that "there would be no history at all without some of both." The same is true of adult personality. As we noted at the beginning of this chapter, the search for evidence of stability began in response to claims "that personality is largely an illusion, that behavioral outcomes depend on particularities of situations" (Helson, 1993, p. 94). In the 1970s, theories of normative change took center stage, only to yield to the timing-of-events model. Since then, Costa and McCrae have redirected attention to the essential stability of personality.

Recently, there have been efforts to pull these diverse approaches together. One, mentioned earlier in this chapter, is the broad conceptual framework developed by Costa and McCrae (1994) to embrace interactions among basic tendencies, external influences, self-concept, and life events. Perhaps even more promising, and more fully developed, is Helson's use of techniques for exploring personality from several theoretical perspectives, acknowledging the roles of gender, class, cohort, and culture. The Mills College studies found that "personality does change from youth to middle age in consistent and often predictable ways" (Helson & Moane, 1987, p. 185). But there were important areas of stability as well. For example, certain persistent traits, such as optimism, affected quality of life at various ages (Mitchell & Helson, 1990).

Recognizing that Costa and McCrae have made a strong case for the stability of basic traits, Helson (1993) emphasizes the importance of longitudinal research to discover how adults do and do not change. More sophisticated instruments will be required to permit comparisons among longitudinal studies that have used different methods and often small, disparate samples. Such methods might uncover specific processes that promote continuity or change. Of course, we need to remember that continuity and change often go hand in hand. A personality dimension that is basically stable may manifest itself differently at different times (Costa & McCrae, 1994a). For example, an extraverted 25-year-old shoe salesman may, at 70, be lobbying against cuts in social security.

The study of adult personality embodies several features of the lifespan developmental perspective. The entire lifespan contributes to the shaping of personality. We can see the multidirectionality of development in, for example, men's greater need for intimacy in middle age, when women show increased independence. History and context—that is, cohort and culture—are essential in considering normative versus nonnormative change. Indeed, it may be impossible to develop any theory of personality development that is entirely culture-free. And the interdisciplinary nature of the field can be seen in the efforts of geneticists, anthropologists, sociologists, psychologists, and others who are involved in the study of personality.

An important function of personality, as we mentioned at the beginning of this chapter, is adaptation. In Chapter 12, we look more closely at how people cope with difficult circumstances and particularly at how they adapt to the challenge of aging.

SUMMARY

DEFINING AND STUDYING PERSONALITY

- Common themes in definitions of personality include uniqueness or individuality, attitudinal and behavioral continuity, and characteristic adaptive patterns.
- Commonly used instruments for measuring personality include the personality inventory, the Q-sort, and interviews or self-reports.
- Interacting genetic and experiential influences contribute to personality development throughout life.

MODELS OF ADULT PERSONALITY: STABILITY OR CHANGE

- A major issue in the study of adult personality is stability versus change. In general, trait theories find stability, stage and life-events theories describe change, and self-concept theories seek to account for both.
- In Costa and McCrae's five-factor model, all dimensions of personality appear to remain stable after about age 30. According to other trait research, differences in late life seem to reflect cohort effects. Cultural change can influence personality.
- Self-concept models focus on the self-image and its cognitive interaction with the social environment. In Whitbourne's model, identity styles represent a balance between identity assimilation (stability) and identity accommodation (change).
- Stage models, such as the classic models of Erikson, Vaillant, and Levinson, portray normative personality changes as a series of stages across the adult lifespan, with critical transitions. Levinson maintains that midlife turmoil is inevitable, but Vaillant and a number of other researchers have found little evidence of it. Normative personality development may be influenced by socioeconomic status, gender, cohort, and culture.
- The timing-of-events model, supported by Neugarten and others, focuses on the impact of the timing of important life events.

GENDER AND PERSONALITY

- Gender roles, often stereotyped, are incorporated into men's and women's gender identity and may influence their attitudes and behavior as adults.

- The Bem Sex Role Inventory has identified four categories of gender roles: masculine, feminine, androgynous, and undifferentiated.

- Theories of how gender identity develops, such as Freudian theory, self-in-relation theory, social-learning theory, cognitive-developmental theories, and gender-schema theory, have different implications for personality development in adulthood.

- Several prominent theorists and researchers have noted a balancing or reversal of gender roles in middle age.

- The Mills College studies of women have found normative changes that differ from those previously identified for men. This research has also found changes associated with particular role paths and personality patterns.

SYNTHESIZING APPROACHES
TO ADULT PERSONALITY DEVELOPMENT

- Recently there have been attempts to synthesize various approaches to adult personality development.

KEY TERMS

▼

adaptation (page 406)
personality (406)
personality inventory (406)
explanatory style (407)
Q-sort (407)
real self (407)
ideal self (407)
temperament (409)
self-concept (411)
personality dimensions (411)
five-factor model (411)
schemas (417)
identity styles (417)
identity assimilation (417)
identity accommodation (417)
normative personality change (418)
generativity (420)
midlife crisis (422)

interiority (422)
life structure (422)
dream (423)
mentor (423)
social clock (426)
timing-of-events model (427)
normative life events (427)
nonnormative life events (427)
gender stereotypes (429)
gender roles (429)
gender identity (429)
androgynous (430)
undifferentiated (430)
self-in-relation theory (430)
social-learning theory (431)
cognitive-developmental theory (431)
gender-schema theory (432)

CHAPTER 12

MENTAL HEALTH, COPING, AND ADJUSTMENT TO AGING

MODELS OF COPING
Environmental Models
Behavioral Models
Coping-Style Models
Cognitive-Appraisal Model

"SUCCESSFUL AGING"
Normative Models
Balance Models
Laypeople's Views
  about Successful Aging

**DESTRUCTIVE
BEHAVIOR PATTERNS**
Substance Use Disorders
Partner Abuse
Child Abuse and Neglect
Abuse of the Elderly

**MENTAL HEALTH IN LATE LIFE:
A LIFESPAN DEVELOPMENTAL
APPROACH**
Mental Health and Life Satisfaction
Mental Disorders
Assessing Strengths

BOXES
12-1 The Cutting Edge: Both Job and
     Family Roles Affect Men's
     Psychological Well-Being
12-2 The Multicultural Context:
     Coping with Economic Change
     in Rural Malaysia
12-3 The Art of Aging: Religion and
     Emotional Well-Being in Late Life

FOCUS: ARTHUR ASHE

(Mike Theiler / Reuters / Bettmann)

The tennis champion Arthur Ashe* was one of the most respected athletes of all time. He was known for his quiet, dignified manner on and off the court; he did not dispute calls, indulge in temper tantrums, or disparage his opponents.

On April 8, 1992, Ashe called a press conference and announced to the world that he had AIDS. It was the latest and worst in a series of what to many people would have been crushing blows, beginning at age 6 with the loss of his mother.

Ashe, an African American, was born in segregated Richmond, Virginia. Tennis—the game he loved to play—was almost the exclusive province of white people, and so he became a special target for bigotry. His father taught him always to maintain his composure, to behave better than his oppressors, and to channel his aggressive impulses into the game itself.

For Ashe, tennis became a means of combating racial prejudice. Though he was twice refused a visa to play in the South African Open, he was finally allowed to compete in 1973, and again in 1974 and 1975. Despite South Africa's rigid apartheid system, he insisted that there be no segregated seating at his matches. During one tournament, a young black boy kept following him around. Ashe asked him why. The child replied that Ashe was the first free black man he had ever seen.

Ashe continued to work against apartheid, for the most part quietly, behind the scenes. Once, he was accused of being an "Uncle Tom" by angry militants who shouted him down while he was giving a speech. He politely rebuked them: "What do

*Sources of biographical information on Arthur Ashe are Ashe and Rampersad (1993), Finn (1993), and Witteman (1993).

you expect to achieve when you give in to passion and invective and surrender the high moral ground that alone can bring you to victory?" (Ashe & Rampersad, 1993, pp. 117, 118). Years later, he felt tremendous pride when he saw Nelson Mandela, the symbol of opposition to apartheid, freed from prison and riding in a ticker-tape parade in New York City. But Ashe would not live to see Mandela become president of South Africa.

In 1979, at age 36, while still engaged in a brilliant career that had included winning the United States Open, the Australian Open, and Wimbledon, Ashe suffered the first of several heart attacks and had quadruple bypass surgery. Forced to retire from tennis, he had to figure out how to move on with his life. A book by Daniel Levinson, which his wife gave him, prompted him to try a brief period of psychotherapy to gain insight into his troubled feelings.

Ashe now embarked on a new phase of his career, serving for 5 years as captain of the United States Davis Cup tennis team. Before one crucial match, he told John McEnroe—an uninhibited and rambunctious player—that another outburst would cause Ashe to forfeit the match. McEnroe listened in silence and went on to win a grueling 5-set match—quietly. Yet Ashe also learned to admire McEnroe, whose flare-ups represented a different way of dealing with powerful emotions.

After two consecutive Davis Cup victories, Ashe in 1983 watched his team lose in the first round, underwent a double bypass operation, and returned to lead the team into the finals, only to lose to Sweden. When he was criticized for not being a forceful enough leader, he began to realize that there are times when bold action is required—and not only on the tennis court. In 1984, the same year in which he was replaced as captain of the team, he was arrested in a protest outside the South African embassy in Washington, D.C.

One summer morning in 1988, Ashe woke up and could not move his right arm. He was given two options: immediate brain surgery, or wait and see. He opted for action. Preparatory blood tests showed that he was HIV-positive, probably from a blood transfusion during his heart surgery 5 years earlier. The surgery revealed a parasitic infection linked to AIDS, and the virus had progressed to AIDS itself. Like an athlete who is outscored but still in the game, Ashe refused to panic or to give up. Relying on the best medical knowledge, he chose to do all he could to fight his illness. He also chose to keep quiet about it.

In 1992, Ashe learned that *USA Today* planned to reveal that he had AIDS. Reluctantly, he went public first—but he then used the opportunity to become a leader in the movement for AIDS research. He established a foundation, launched a $5 million fund-raising campaign, and worked tirelessly for the cause until his death.

Arthur Ashe died of AIDS-related pneumonia in 1993, at age 49. Shortly before, he had summed up his situation in his usual style: "I am a fortunate, blessed man. Aside from AIDS and heart disease, I have no problems" (Ashe & Rampersad, 1993, p. 328).

Arthur Ashe's characteristic way of coping with trouble was to meet it as he did an opponent on the tennis court: with grace, determination, and coolness under fire. He managed to keep his head to the end, under conditions that might have driven some people to drink, depression, or worse. Again and again, he turned adversity into opportunity.

Mental health has been defined as an "attempt to live meaningfully, in a particular set of social and environmental circumstances, relying on a particular collection of resources and supports"—in other words, trying "to do the best we can with what we have" (Kivnick, 1993, p. 15). It involves developing inner strengths and using external resources to compensate for weaknesses and deficits. Efforts toward self-development—thriving rather than merely surviving—are signs of a healthy personality (Butler, Lewis, & Sunderland, 1991; E. Sherman, 1993). Mental health may include how people see themselves, how they integrate various roles and aspects of the self (see Box 12-1), and whether or not they strive for growth. It may also include identification with, and commitment to, something

---

BOX 12-1

THE CUTTING EDGE

Both Job and Family Roles Affect Men's Psychological Well-Being

Traditionally, women's mental health has been assessed in terms of family, and men's in terms of work. In recent years, however, researchers have paid more attention to the neglected aspects of both men's and women's lives. A number of studies have emphasized the importance of work in women's lives (see Box 11-2 in Chapter 11), and recent research has shown the importance of family connections to men's well-being.

In one study (Barnett, Marshall, & Pleck, 1992), researchers asked 300 employed husbands, age 25 to 40, who were part of two-earner couples, to evaluate their work, marital, and parental roles, noting both rewards and concerns. For example, in terms of work, the men were asked how rewarding it was "to have a variety of tasks" and how much of a concern "lack of job security" was. For the marital role, they rated such rewards as "enjoying the same activities" and such concerns

as "your partner's being critical of you." For the parental role, rewards included "seeing your children mature and change," and concerns included "having too many arguments and conflicts with them." Each man received a "quality" score for each role (his "reward score" minus his "concern score"). The men also were assessed for anxiety and depression.

The study's main finding was surprising: the widely held view that work is the main determinant of mental health for men turned out not to be so. Apparently, men's family roles are just as important, and their various roles are related. Good relationships with wife and children can make up for a poor experience on the job. When both job and family roles are unsatisfactory, the result is often psychological distress. One difference between men and women is that for working women merely being a parent often offsets job concerns; whereas for men what is important is not parenthood itself, but how rewarding the parental role is. Being a father may be less central to a man's sense of self than motherhood is to a woman, but rewards from parenthood are just as important to fathers as to mothers.

beyond the self—family, community, nation, culture, religion, or a cause, such as the fight against racial prejudice or AIDS (Jahoda, 1958; E. Sherman, 1993). A correlate of mental health is *life satisfaction*, which is sometimes defined as *morale*, or as how a person judges the quality of his or her life (R. Schulz, 1985). A favorable self-image and high self-esteem enhance morale. So do autonomy and a sense of mastery (E. Sherman, 1993). On all these counts, Arthur Ashe, even as his physical health deteriorated, was in extremely good mental health.

Many people, of course, have dealt with threats to mental health, with varying degrees of success. Some succumb to mental disorders that interfere with normal cognitive functioning or social roles. Almost half of all American adults have experienced a mental disorder, mild or severe, at some time in their lives. Most common is major depression, followed by alcohol dependence and phobias (Blazer, Kessler, McGonagle, & Swartz, 1994; Kessler et al., 1994). Poorly educated, low-income urban dwellers are most susceptible to mental illness. Men are more likely to abuse drugs or to have antisocial behavioral disturbances; women are more prone to anxiety and depression (Robins et al., 1984; Wykle & Musil, 1993). Younger adults tend to be subject to emotional problems, anxiety, and substance abuse; older adults, especially men, are more likely to have severe cognitive impairment (Regier et al., 1988; Wykle & Musil, 1993). Perhaps because mental illness has traditionally been stigmatized, fewer than 40 percent of all victims seek treatment; but many adults manage to overcome their conditions without professional help (Blazer et al., 1994; Kessler et al., 1994).

In this chapter, we discuss both positive and negative aspects of mental health throughout the adult lifespan, and its biological, psychological, and social roots. Let's begin by looking at how adults cope with stress, including the challenge of aging—one match Arthur Ashe never got to finish.

MODELS OF COPING

Stress is an inevitable part of life. As a leading researcher has said, "Complete freedom from stress is death" (Selye, 1980, p. 128). The question is how—and how well—someone copes with it.

Coping is adaptive thinking or behavior aimed at reducing or relieving stress that arises from harmful, threatening, or challenging conditions. Psychologists and laypeople alike recognize coping as an important aspect of mental health. Let's look briefly at three traditional approaches to the study of coping: *environmental*, *behavioral*, and *coping-style* models. Then we'll take a closer look at the newer *cognitive-appraisal* model.

ENVIRONMENTAL MODELS

One of the earliest approaches to the study of coping was quantitative. Researchers asked 5,000 hospital patients about important life events that had preceded their illness—both negative events (such as the death of a spouse) and

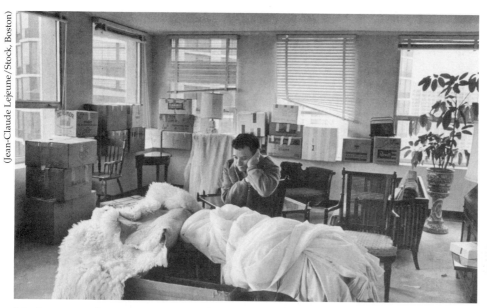

Moving to a new home is a stressful experience. People cope with such stress in different ways and with varying degrees of success. According to the environmental-press model, a person's comfort depends on the match between competence and demands made on it.

positive events (such as the birth of a child)—and how much adjustment each required (Holmes & Rahe, 1976). On the basis of these reports, the investigators assigned numerical values called "life change units" (LCUs) to each type of event (see Table 4-3 in Chapter 4). About half the people with 150 to 300 LCUs in a year, and about 70 percent of those with 300 or more LCUs, had become ill within the next 1 or 2 years. In other words, the more major changes a person faced within a given time, the harder it was to cope with them.

Such an approach represents an *environmental model* of coping, and it is essentially mechanistic. Human beings are considered *reactors* rather than *actors*; size and frequency of environmental demands determine how well a person can cope. Too many stressors (sources of stress), or a single major stressor (such as the death of a spouse), can overwhelm a person's ability to cope—much as putting too much stress on machinery can cause overload and can damage the operating parts.

An environmental model has several shortcomings. First, it does not consider how an individual interprets an event. Second (as we discuss in Chapter 11), the timing of an event may make a difference. Third, stress also may result from *lack* of change—boredom, inability to advance at work, or unrewarding personal relationships. Fourth, several studies suggest that both physical and mental health are more likely to be affected by ongoing irritations and strains of everyday life than by major, isolated events (George, 1980; Lazarus, 1981; Pearlin, 1980; Pearlin, Lieberman, Menaghan, & Mullan, 1981). Fifth, the model ignores individual differences. Why does one person break down under the stress of a deadline or emergency, while another rises to the occasion?

(Jean-Claude Lejeune/Stock, Boston)

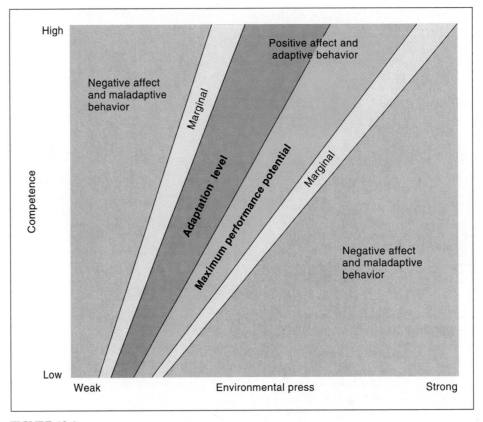

FIGURE 12-1

Environmental-press model. The more competent the individual, the wider the range of environmental situations in which a sense of comfort will be experienced and behavior will be adaptive (top of figure). Less competent individuals (bottom of figure) are more likely to feel stress as a result of environmental demands.

(SOURCE: Lawton & Nahemow, 1973, p. 661.)

Two environmental models attempt to solve one or more of these problems. The **congruence model** (Kahana, 1982) recognizes that people's needs differ, and environments differ in how they meet those needs. Levels of life satisfaction or stress depend on congruence—the match—between person and environment. For example, placing an older adult who has a strong need for independence in a nursing home is likely to increase stress.

The **environmental-press model** (Lawton, 1982; Lawton & Nahemow, 1973) emphasizes differences in demands that environments make (*environmental press*) and in individuals' *competence*—their ability to meet those demands. As shown in Figure 12-1, when both press and competence are relatively high or relatively low, people are comfortable in their environment and tend to take it for granted—they are at their normal *adaptation level*. When moderately pressed by the environment, they reach their maximum potential. But when environmental press is too low or too high, people become uncomfortably aware of the environment, perceiving it as boring or overwhelming.

The environmental-press model has implications for aging. If environmental press increases (for example, when an older person's city neighborhood becomes unsafe) or competence diminishes (for example, when an older adult living in a suburb can no longer drive), that person will fall below the adaptation level and feel stress. To restore an adaptive fit, ways must be found either to reduce environmental demands or to increase the individual's competence.

These two models, then, offer reasons why different situations may be more or less stressful for different people. But, like other environmental models, they do not tell us *how* people cope.

BEHAVIORAL MODELS

Behavioral models of coping give the individual a somewhat more active role. These models, based on animal studies, seek to explain behavior in terms of classical or operant conditioning, or both. From a behavioral perspective, coping involves learned adaptations to environmental stressors, leading to a reduction of perceived stress. An animal confronted by an enemy, or a person confronted by a stressor, generally has three options: flee to a safer place, fight and attempt to master the situation, or stay put and try to endure it. When escape or avoidance is impossible and attempts at mastery fail or are punished, organisms adapt through **learned helplessness.** Over a period of time they learn to live with what originally was an extremely stressful situation and give up trying to change it (Ursin, 1980). We can see learned helplessness in battered spouses who stay with their mates, or in citizens who stay home on election day because they do not believe their vote means anything.

COPING-STYLE MODELS

A third, more complex, approach to coping is based on the psychoanalytic tradition. It focuses more on thoughts and attitudes than on outward behavior. From this perspective, coping is a form of problem solving, and individual *coping strategies* or *styles*, like personality traits, tend to be fairly stable.

Some researchers attempt to rank coping styles according to effectiveness. One such model came out of the longitudinal Grant Study of Harvard University men, described in Chapter 11. Vaillant (1977) identified four kinds of **adaptive mechanisms**—characteristic ways of coping or interacting with the environment: (1) *mature* (such as using humor or helping others); (2) *neurotic* (such as repressing anxiety, or saying the opposite of what one feels); (3) *immature* (such as fantasizing, or experiencing imaginary aches and pains); and (4) *psychotic* (distorting or denying reality). Men who used mature adaptive mechanisms were happier and mentally and physically healthier than others; they got more satisfaction from work, enjoyed richer friendships, made more money, and seemed better adjusted. In midlife the best-adjusted men were 4 times more likely to cope with life events in "mature" rather than "immature" ways (Vaillant, 1989). Likewise, at age 65, those who used "mature defense mechanisms"—who handled problems without blame, bitterness, or passivity—showed the healthiest adjustment (Vaillant & Vaillant, 1990).

Richard Lazarus and his colleagues, proponents of the cognitive-appraisal model (to be discussed next), make several criticisms of coping-style models (Lazarus & Folkman, 1984). First, coping styles may fail to capture the multidimensionality of human behavior. A middle-aged man who must deal simultaneously with, for example, (a) a threatened layoff, (b) a wife who has breast cancer, (c) a homosexual son who has just come out of the closet, and (d) the care of an aging mother may not cope in the same way with all four situations. And a particular coping style may not work equally well for all adults. Second, these models do not distinguish between coping and other forms of adaptive behavior that do not involve effort. When you are driving a car, you do many things that enable you to get to your destination in one piece: stopping at a red light, yielding the right-of-way, and so on. These learned responses are so automatic that you hardly have to think about them. However, you must call on your coping skills if you suddenly find your car sliding on a patch of ice or about to collide with another vehicle. Third, models that evaluate coping styles in terms of outcomes tend to confuse the process with the product. Coping is struggle, not success; management, not mastery.

COGNITIVE-APPRAISAL MODEL

In the *cognitive-appraisal model* (Lazarus & Folkman, 1984), coping is an evolving process, which occurs only in situations that a person sees as taxing or exceeding his or her resources and thus demanding unusual effort. According to this contextual model, people choose coping strategies on the basis of their cognitive appraisal of a situation. Coping includes anything an individual thinks or does in trying to adapt to stress, regardless of how well it works. Because the situation is constantly changing, coping is dynamic, not static; choosing the most appropriate strategy requires constant reappraisal of the relationship between person and environment (see Figure 12-2). Arthur Ashe, for instance, made significant reappraisals and changed his coping strategies at several points in his adult life.

The choice and effectiveness of a coping strategy are influenced by personal resources and by personal and environmental constraints, as well as by how great the threat appears to be. *Personal resources* include health, energy, beliefs about personal control or supernatural control, commitments and motivations, social skills and problem-solving skills, social support, and material resources (money, goods, and services). Use of personal resources may be limited by *personal constraints:* psychological problems, such as fear of failure, or attitudes reflecting societal norms, such as gender roles. *Environmental constraints* might be, for example, competing demands for the same resources, or institutions that thwart coping.

To identify characteristic coping strategies, cognitive-appraisal researchers try to get people to recall what they actually felt and did in stressful situations. Most of the time, people strike a balance between two modes of coping: *problem-focused* and *emotion-focused*. Which one predominates depends on the situation, the person, and the available options (Monat & Lazarus, 1985).

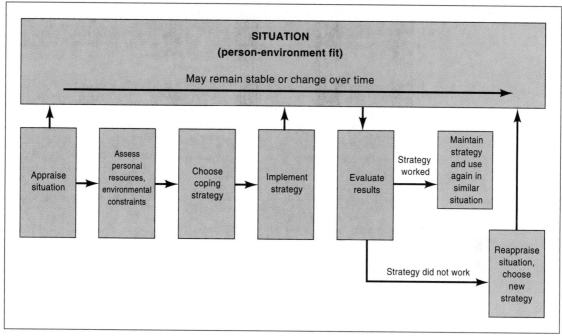

FIGURE 12-2
Cognitive-appraisal model of coping.
(SOURCE: Based on Lazarus & Folkman, 1984.)

Problem-focused coping is directed toward eliminating, managing, or improving a stressful condition. It generally predominates when a person sees a realistic chance of effecting change. *Emotion-focused coping,* sometimes called *palliative coping,* is directed toward "feeling better"—managing the emotional response to a stressful situation to relieve its physical or psychological impact. This form of coping is likely to predominate when a person concludes that little or nothing can be done about the situation itself. Some emotion-focused strategies divert attention from a problem; others consciously or unconsciously reinterpret the situation—for example, by giving in to it or pretending it doesn't exist. Box 12-2 describes an emotion-focused strategy used by factory workers in Malaysia to cope with stress caused by economic and social change.

Emotion-focused strategies generally rank low on coping-style hierarchies; denying a problem, for example, is seen as merely putting off something that may become harder to deal with. The cognitive-appraisal model, however, does not view any strategy as inherently good or bad. Effectiveness depends on the context. As Arthur Ashe observed, denial may be harmful if it keeps a person with chest pains from seeing a doctor; but "good denial"—"refusal to dwell on the idea of death," or to accept the idea that death is imminent, can allow a person who is terminally ill to "go calmly on with . . . life" for the time that remains (Ashe & Rampersad, 1993, pp. 328, 327). People must cope—if nothing else, by managing their emotions in the face of the inevitable.

BOX 12-2

THE MULTICULTURAL CONTEXT

Coping with Economic Change in Rural Malaysia

In the former British crown colony of Malaysia in the south Pacific Ocean, industrialization is transforming rural life. Since 1970, Japanese, western European, and American corporations seeking to cut labor costs have moved hundreds of factories producing food, clothing, and electronics to Malaysia, where poverty has forced thousands of farm families off the land.

How do rural Malays cope with this radical change of lifestyle? One study (Ong, 1987) focused on a newly industrialized area, where young, poor, unmarried peasant women from neighboring villages assemble components for transistors and capacitors. The electronics factories have a hierarchy based on ethnicity and gender. Top management positions are filled by Japanese men. Production supervisors are Chinese or Malay men. At the bottom are the female Malay workers, wearing overalls and rubber gloves instead of their traditional tunics and sarongs.

Malay communities cooperate in providing this work force. The Japanese management makes concerted efforts to stay on good terms with the villagers, donating money for village events and assuring parents that their daughters are well cared for. Village schools train future workers by insisting on order, obedience, and hard work.

Assembling electronics is grueling work; it requires constant, close concentration and frequent overtime. Lives that were formerly based on seasonal cycles of planting and harvesting are now regulated by factory shifts and schedules. Women who were once in charge of their own work now must deal with rigid shop routines, production quotas, and constant supervision. The male bosses, said one woman, "exhaust us very much, as if they do not think that we too are human beings" (Ong, 1987, p. 202). The women work for low wages, which they are often expected to turn over to their families. Without unions, there is no job security. Many workers last only a few years.

A common response to these exploitative, dehumanizing conditions is "possession by spirits." First one worker, then another, then another will see "spirits," which are believed to have come for vengeance because a factory has been built on a traditional burying ground. These "displaced spirits" are said to throng onto the shop floor and enter the women, who begin to sob, laugh hysterically, scream, and curse. A hundred or more workers may be affected at one time. The bosses may call in ritual healers to keep the spirits away by sacrificing chickens and goats, but still the "possession" continues.

How does "possession" help these Malay women cope? It can be seen as an unconscious or symbolic protest against factory discipline and male control—a form of rebellion that the bosses cannot easily stop because it is considered acceptable in Malay society. Since this behavior does nothing to improve working conditions, it is an *emotion-focused* rather than *problem-focused* strategy. In fact, it may help maintain the status quo by providing a socially acceptable outlet for the tensions of factory life (Ong, 1987).

In general, older adults do more emotion-focused coping than younger ones (Folkman, Lazarus, Pimley, & Novacek, 1987; Prohaska, Leventhal, Leventhal, & Keller, 1985). Is that because older people are less able to focus on problems or because they are more selective about when to focus? In a recent study (Blanchard-Fields, Jahnke, & Camp, 1995), 70 adolescents, 69 young adults, 74 middle-aged adults, and 74 older adults wrote essays on how to solve each of 15 problems. Regardless of age, participants most often recommended problem-focused strategies, especially in situations that were not highly emotional, such as returning defective merchandise. But age differences showed up in problems that were more emotional, such as moving to a new town or taking care of an older parent. In such situations, older adults chose more emotion-regulating strategies than younger adults did.

These findings, along with several other studies, suggest that with age, people may be more able to control their emotions when a situation calls for it (Blanchard-Fields & Irion, 1987; Folkman & Lazarus, 1980; Labouvie-Vief, Hakim-Larson, & Hobart, 1987), and this style of coping can be quite adaptive. For many people, especially older ones, religious behavior seems to be an effective coping strategy (see Box 12-3 and Table 12-1).

Of course, one unavoidable condition adults must cope with is aging itself. How do they do it? Some theories and studies have dealt specifically with that question.

"SUCCESSFUL AGING"

▼

"Successful aging"—what the heck does that mean? . . . Is our society so achievement-oriented that it is now possible to fail at growing old? By encouraging the definition of a right and a wrong way to age, you are discouraging attempts to treat ourselves with kindness. (D. King, 1993, p. 14)

This letter to a magazine from an indignant reader challenges a concept that gerontologists have been studying and arguing about for nearly half a century. Are some adaptations to aging more successful—psychologically healthier—than others? Is "successful aging" the same for everyone? Or is the only relevant definition a personal one? Let's look at several theoretical models of successful aging, and then at what a group of ordinary adults had to say about it.

NORMATIVE MODELS

For normative theorists, adults age successfully when they complete the normal psychological tasks of each period of life in an emotionally healthy way. Erikson saw the critical tasks of middle and late adulthood as generativity and integration. Jung and Levinson spoke of a need to balance the masculine and feminine sides of one's nature and to turn from striving for worldly success to explore the inner life. Three classic models focus specifically on adaptation to aging.

BOX 12-3

Religion and Emotional Well-Being in Late Life

Their health isn't what it was, they've lost old friends and family members, and they don't earn the money they once did. Their lives keep changing in countless stressful ways. Yet in general, older adults have fewer mental disorders and are more satisfied with life than younger ones. What accounts for this remarkable ability to cope?

In one study, interviewers asked 100 well-educated white men and women—age 55 to 80, about evenly divided between working class and upper middle class, and 90 percent Protestant—to describe the worst events in their lives and how they had dealt with them (Koenig, George, & Siegler, 1988). The respondents described 289 stressful events and 556 coping strategies.

Heading the list of strategies (see Table 12-1) were behaviors associated with religion, cited by 58 percent of the women and 32 percent of the men. Almost three-fourths of these religious strategies consisted of placing trust and faith in God, praying, and getting help and strength from God. Other religious sources of help included friends from church, church activities, the minister, and the Bible.

The next most common strategy was taking one's mind off a problem by keeping busy—for example, in work-related, social, recreational, and family activities; by reading or watching television; or by working at hobbies.

The third and fourth strategies involved acceptance—and other people. Many respondents were helped by the philosophy expressed in the "serenity prayer": "God grant me the serenity to accept things I cannot change, the courage to change those I can, and the wisdom to know the difference." These people would think about a problem and do everything they could to resolve it—but then would accept the situation, if necessary, and get on with their lives. Support and encouragement from family and friends also helped; when asked, most people said that others had helped them through bad times. Relatively few respondents had turned to a health worker; when they did, that person was 4 times more likely to be a personal physician than a mental health professional.

Other research has confirmed the supportive role of religion for the elderly, especially for women, African Americans, and the oldest old. An analysis of data from four national surveys confirmed earlier findings that black elderly people are more involved with religion than whites, and women are more involved than men (Levin, Taylor, & Chatters, 1994). Possible explanations include the social support offered by religion, the perception religion offers of a measure of control over life through prayer, and faith in God as a way of interpreting stresses—for example, belief that one is part of a larger plan.

In a study of 836 older adults from two secular and three religiously oriented groups, morale was positively associated with three kinds of religious activity: *organized* (going to church or temple and taking part in the activities), *informal* (praying, reading the Bible), and *spiritual* (personal cognitive commitment to religious beliefs). The more religious people had higher morale and a better attitude toward aging and were more satisfied and less lonely. Women and people over 75 showed the strongest correlations between religion and well-being (Koenig, Kvale, & Ferrel, 1988).

The church always has been important to African Americans. At all ages, black women are more religious than black men. But involvement in religion is high among men too, and the gender difference narrows or even reverses in the oldest groups (Levin & Taylor, 1993). Elderly black people who feel supported by their church tend to report high levels of well-being; and the more religious older black people are, the more satisfaction they report with life (Coke, 1992; Walls & Zarit, 1991). For all ages and both sexes, the most common religious activity is personal prayer (Chatters & Taylor, 1989).

Since almost all research on religion in the lives of older Americans has been cross-sectional, it is possible that turning toward religion in old age is a cohort effect rather than a result of aging. It is also likely, however, that as people think about the meaning of their lives and about death as the inevitable end, they may focus more on spiritual matters.

TABLE 12-1   SPONTANEOUSLY REPORTED EMOTION-REGULATING COPING STRATEGIES USED BY OLDER ADULTS

Rank Order	Frequency of Mention	
	Number	(%)
Religious	97	(17.4)
Kept busy	84	(15.1)
Accepted it	63	(11.3)
Support from family or friends	62	(11.1)
Help from professional	34	(6.1)
Positive attitude	31	(5.6)
Took one day at a time	29	(5.2)
Became involved in social activities	19	(3.4)
Planning and preparing beforehand	15	(2.7)
Optimized communication	13	(2.3)
Limited activities, didn't overcommit	11	(2.0)
Sought information	8	(1.4)
Exercised	8	(1.4)
Helped others more needy	7	(1.3)
Realized that time heals all wounds	7	(1.3)
Avoided situation	6	(1.1)
Experience of prior hardships	5	(.9)
Carried on for others' sake	5	(.9)
Ingested alcohol, tranquilizers	5	(.9)
Carried on as usual	4	(.7)
Took a vacation	3	(.5)
Realized others in same situation or worse	3	(.5)
Released emotion (cried or cursed)	3	(.5)
Lowered expectations or devaluated	3	(.5)
Miscellaneous	31	(5.6)
Totals	556	(100.6)

NOTES: 100 older adults reported 556 coping behaviors for 289 stressful experiences. Percentages add up to more than 100 because of rounding.
SOURCE: Koenig et al., 1988, p. 306.

Peck: Personality Adjustments of Middle and Late Adulthood

One of the earliest attempts to specify factors in successful aging was that of Robert Peck (1955). Expanding on Erikson's concepts, Peck identified seven psychological developments he saw as necessary to healthful adaptation to aging: four in middle age and three in old age.

Peck's critical adjustments of middle age represent a shift from physical prowess to mental and emotional flexibility. None of these developments need wait until middle age; but according to Peck, if they do not take place by middle age, successful adjustment is doubtful.

- *Valuing wisdom versus valuing physical powers. Wisdom,* defined as the ability to make the best choices in life, depends on a broad range of life experience and more than makes up for diminished strength and stamina and the loss of youthful appearance.
- *Socializing versus sexualizing in human relationships.* People come to value the men and women in their lives as unique individuals, as friends, and as companions rather than primarily as sex objects.
- *Emotional flexibility versus emotional impoverishment.* As children grow up and become independent, and as parents, spouses, and friends die, the ability to shift emotional investment from one person to another and from one activity to another becomes crucial.
- *Mental flexibility versus mental rigidity.* By midlife, many people have worked out a set of answers to life's important questions. But unless they continue to seek new answers, they can become set in their ways and closed to new ideas.

Peck's necessary adjustments of late life allow people to move beyond concerns with work, physical well-being, and mere existence to a broader understanding of the self and of life's purpose.

- *Broader self-definition versus preoccupation with work roles.* As retirement approaches, people who have defined themselves by their work need to redefine their worth and give new structure and direction to their lives by exploring other interests and taking pride in personal attributes.
- *Transcendence of the body versus preoccupation with the body.* As physical abilities decline, people adjust better if they focus on relationships and activities that do not demand perfect health. Throughout life, adults need to cultivate mental and social powers that can grow with age.
- *Transcendence of the ego versus preoccupation with the ego.* Probably the hardest, and possibly the most crucial, adjustment for older people is to move beyond concern with themselves and their present lives to acceptance of the certainty of death. They need to recognize the lasting significance they have achieved through what they have done—children they have raised, contributions they have made to society, and personal relationships they have forged. Rather than becoming preoccupied with their own needs, they can continue to contribute to the well-being of others.

According to activity theory, an older person who remains busy and involved in community life—like this foster grandfather in a day care center in Minneapolis—is aging more successfully than one who disengages from social roles.

Disengagement Theory versus Activity Theory

Which is a healthier, or more adaptive, adjustment to aging: tranquilly watching the world go by from a rocking chair or keeping busy from morning till night? Two contrasting models have been proposed: disengagement theory and activity theory. According to ***disengagement theory***, aging normally brings a gradual reduction in social involvement and greater preoccupation with the self. According to ***activity theory***, the more active people remain, the better they age.

Disengagement theory was one of the first influential theories in gerontology. Its proponents (Cumming & Henry, 1961) argued that disengagement is a universal condition of aging—that declining physical functioning results in an inevitable, gradual withdrawal from social roles, ultimately leading to death. More than three decades later, there have been few independent empirical findings to support disengagement theory, and it has "largely disappeared from the empirical literature" (Achenbaum & Bengtson, 1994, p. 756). It is now viewed as fundamentally flawed. David Gutmann (1974, 1977, 1992), for example, has argued that "disengagement" in traditional cultures, such as Druze society (see Box 11-3 in Chapter 11), is only a transition between the roles of middle age and late adulthood, and that true disengagement occurs only in societies in which elderly people are left without established roles appropriate to their stage of life.

Activity theory arose as an alternative to disengagement theory. Its proponents, chiefly Bernice Neugarten and her associates (Neugarten, Havighurst, & Tobin, 1968), disagreed with the idea that older adults are more satisfied with life when they disengage from social roles, and that encouraging them to remain active is therefore pointless. According to activity theory, continued activity is crucial to successful aging. An adult's roles (worker, spouse, parent, and so on) are seen as the major source of satisfaction; the greater the loss of roles through retirement, widowhood, distance from children, or infirmity, the less satisfied a person will be. People who are aging successfully keep up as many activities as possible and find substitutes for lost roles.

When Neugarten and her associates looked at aging adults' personalities, activity, and satisfaction with life (Neugarten et al., 1968), they found four major styles of aging. (1) *Integrated* people were functioning well, with a complex inner life, intact cognitive abilities, and a high level of satisfaction. (2) *Armor-defended* people were achievement-oriented, striving, and tightly controlled. (3) *Passive-dependent* people were apathetic or sought comfort from others. (4) *Unintegrated* people were disorganized, had little control over their emotions, showed poor cognitive and psychological functioning, and had problems coping. For the most part, integrated and armor-defended people were more active than the other two groups, and more activity was generally associated with more satisfaction.

However, some studies found that activity in and of itself bears little relationship to satisfaction with life (Lemon, Bengtson, & Peterson, 1972). Later studies suggested that the *kind* of activity matters: informal activities with friends and family are more satisfying than formal, structured, group activities or solitary activities such as reading, watching television, and hobbies (Longino & Kart, 1982). But a subsequent analysis indicated that people's attitude about life is affected only slightly, if at all, by *any* kind of activity (Okun, Stick, Haring, & Witter, 1984). Further, an analysis of the effect of activity on mortality among 508 older Mexican Americans and "Anglos" over an 8-year period found that whether people died earlier or later was totally unrelated to how active they had been, once other factors such as age, health, and gender were taken into account (D. J. Lee & Markides, 1990). Thus although activity theory has not, so far, been discarded (Marshall, 1994), some gerontologists have come to view it as simplistic.

BALANCE MODELS

According to normative models, people adapt to aging through a series of typical personality changes. But aging, particularly in developed societies, has lost some of its normative character, in part because of advances in health and fitness and wide variations in whether and when people retire. Two recent models emphasize interaction between individual and environment, suggesting that "successful aging" is a balance between stability and change, and that the right balance may not be the same for everyone.

Atchley: Continuity Theory

According to **continuity theory**, which has been proposed by the gerontologist Robert Atchley (1989), people who age successfully are able to maintain some continuity, or connection with the past, in both internal and external structures of their lives. *Internal structures* include knowledge, self-esteem, and a sense of personal history, or what Erikson called "ego integrity." *External structures* include roles, relationships, activities, and sources of social support, as well as the physical environment.

It is normal, Atchley suggests, for aging adults to seek a satisfactory balance between continuity and change in their life structures. Too much change makes life too unpredictable; too little change makes life too dull. Thus although some change is both desirable and inevitable, there is an internal drive for consistency: a need to avoid a total break with the past. This drive is socially reinforced, since others tend to expect a person to think and act about the same as always.

"Successful aging," then, may mean different things to different people. In this view, activity is important not for its own sake, but to the extent that it represents a continuation of a person's lifestyle. For older adults who always have been active and involved in social roles, it may be important to continue a high level of activity. Others, who have been less active in the past, may be happier in the proverbial rocking chair. This idea gains support from research (reported in Chapter 8) showing that many retired people are happiest pursuing work or leisure activities similar to those they have enjoyed in the past.

When aging brings physical or cognitive changes, it may be hard to maintain continuity in the external environment. An older adult may become dependent on caregivers and may have to make new living arrangements. Successful adaptation may depend on support from family, friends, or social institutions to help compensate for losses and to minimize discontinuity. This idea is in line with the growing trend in many countries to try to keep older adults out of institutions and in the community, and to help them live as independently as possible (see Chapter 10).

Continuity theory may help explain findings that—contrary to widespread belief—homosexuals tend to adapt to aging with relative ease. It has been suggested that, since they have generally had practice in dealing with one kind of stigma, they may be better prepared to cope with another—the stigma of aging. And their sexual orientation may make them comfortable with flexible, androgynous roles (Berger & Kelly, 1986). Thus shocks of aging may be cushioned by continuity in certain areas. Homosexuals who are best adjusted in the later years—most satisfied with their lives, least self-critical, and least prone to psychosomatic problems—are highly satisfied with their sexual orientation; they tend to have gone through a period of sexual experimentation earlier in life, which may have helped them adjust to the implications of being homosexual (Adelman, 1991).

Whitbourne: Identity Styles and Adaptations to Aging

According to Whitbourne's (1987; Whitbourne & Primus, in press) model of personality development (introduced in Chapter 11), people cope with aging much as they have coped with earlier challenges. Physical, mental, and emotional changes associated with aging can be unsettling to the self-concept and must be assimilated, accommodated, or both. Identity style—how a person generally strikes a balance between assimilation (continuity) and accommodation (change)—is likely to determine how someone adapts to aging.

Both assimilation and accommodation have benefits and costs. People whose style is predominantly assimilative are likely to maintain a youthful, positive self-image and to deny any negative changes. They may deplete their psychological energy trying to keep up this optimistic outlook and may fail to take measures that might help compensate for losses. People whose style is predominantly accommodative are likely to see themselves—perhaps prematurely—as old. Although more secure in their definition of themselves, they may become overly preoccupied with symptoms of aging and disease. People with a more evenly balanced identity style may be able to make a more realistic adjustment. They can take steps to control what can be controlled and strive to accept what cannot.

Currently, in line with the growing recognition of both stability and change in personality throughout the adult lifespan, balance models—particularly continuity theory—are attracting more interest than the older normative models. It will be interesting to see whether these newer models can develop a stronger research base. Ultimately, theories of "successful aging" must stand or fall on how accurately they can describe "normal" behavior in late life. It may be, however, that no grand, universal theory can be devised to describe normal aging—that "successful aging" may be different for each society, each successive cohort, or even each individual.

LAYPEOPLE'S VIEWS ABOUT SUCCESSFUL AGING

How would *you* define "successful aging"? One researcher (Ryff, 1989) asked a group of middle-aged and older adults. Unlike theorists who emphasize self-oriented factors, such as self-knowledge and self-acceptance, participants in both age groups defined "successful aging" mostly in terms of relationships: caring about and getting along with others.

However, differences between the two age groups showed up when they were asked what they were unhappy about and what they would change if they could. Middle-aged people were most unhappy about family problems. They wished they could change some aspect of themselves or accomplish more in schooling or careers. Older people most commonly said that they were unhappy about nothing and would change nothing except health. The fact that middle-aged people emphasized continued growth and older people emphasized acceptance is reminiscent of Erikson and Peck, and suggests that "successful aging" may take on a different meaning near the end of life.

Unfortunately, not everyone at any age copes successfully with the many stresses of living. In the next section we'll deal with destructive behavior patterns. We'll conclude the chapter with a look at mental health in late life: how satisfied older adults are with their lives; mental disorders that sometimes occur; and inner strengths developed in the course of living that can be unique resources for coping with aging.

DESTRUCTIVE BEHAVIOR PATTERNS

When Nicole Simpson called the police in a frantic attempt to get her husband, O. J. Simpson, to stop beating her, the football hero told the officers to go home; he said it was just a private matter. But destructive behavior—whether directed at oneself or at others—is not just a private matter. As Michael Dorris discovered (see Chapter 9), people who abuse alcohol or drugs not only hurt themselves and those around them but often do irreparable damage to their children. People who abuse domestic partners or children do harm that can have long-lasting repercussions, even for future generations, since victims of abuse often become abusers themselves. And people who abuse the aged and infirm contribute to a climate in which everyone's safety and dignity is imperiled.

SUBSTANCE USE DISORDERS

Elvis Presley, Janis Joplin, John Belushi, River Phoenix—there is a long list of celebrities who have succumbed to substance use disorders. *Substance abuse* means harmful use of alcohol or other drugs. It is defined as a maladaptive behavior pattern, lasting more than 1 month, in which a person continues to use a substance after knowingly being harmed by it or uses it repeatedly in a hazardous situation, such as driving while intoxicated (American Psychiatric Association, APA, 1994). Abuse can lead to *substance dependence,* or addiction, which may be physiological, psychological, or both. A person who meets three of the following criteria is considered dependent: increased tolerance (needing more of the substance to achieve the same effect); experiencing withdrawal symptoms when taken off the substance; taking more of the substance, or for a longer time, than intended; wanting but being unable to cut down or control its use; spending a great deal of time and effort to obtain the substance or to recover from its effects; giving up or reducing important social, occupational, or recreational activities because of use of the substance; continuing to use it even though it is causing or worsening persistent or recurrent physical or psychological problems (APA, 1994). Substance use disorders tend to run in families and may result from a combination of genetic factors, vulnerable personality, and environmental influences (Irons, 1994).

The extent of substance problems among older adults is often underestimated. Since many older people live alone or have limited social contacts, a problem may go undetected. Family members sometimes ignore or cover up evidence of substance abuse. Even in hospitals, substance disorders in this age group are often unrecognized, unreported, or not referred for treatment, perhaps because of a mistaken notion that these are not problems of the elderly or that not much can be done about them (R. M. Atkinson, Ganzini, & Bernstein, 1992). Table 12-2 on the following page shows factors that increase the risk of substance abuse in an older adult.

TABLE 12-2   FACTORS INCREASING RISK OF SUBSTANCE ABUSE IN OLDER ADULTS

Demographic factors
Male gender (alcohol, illicit substances)
Female gender (sedative-hypnotics)

Substance-related factors
Prior substance abuse
Family history (alcohol)

Increased biological sensitivity
Drug sensitivity
Medical illnesses associated with aging
Cognitive loss
Cardiovascular disease
Metabolic disorders

Medically induced factors
Prescription-drug dependence
Drug-drug and alcohol-drug interactions
Caregiver overuse of *as needed* medication
Physician advice or permission to use alcohol

Psychosocial factors
Loss and other major stresses
Discretionary time, money
Social isolation
Family collusion

Psychiatric factors
Depression
Dementia
Subjective symptoms of chronic illness

SOURCE: Adapted from Atkinson et al., 1992, p. 520.

Cohort Effects

Imagine what would happen if marijuana, cocaine, and heroin were legalized in the United States tomorrow, as they have already been in some countries. Almost overnight, you would begin to see advertisements for these products, and they would soon become readily available in many stores. If this happened, would your attitude toward the use of such drugs change? Would your children's attitudes be different from yours if they grew up in a society in which these drugs were legal?

One drug, alcohol, was illegal for a time in the United States but then was legalized again. Most readers of this text cannot remember a time when there were, for instance, no beer commercials, but many older adults can. People who grew up between 1920 and 1933, when it was illegal to sell or distribute alcohol (though the prohibition was widely disobeyed), may well have different attitudes toward drinking from younger age groups.

Use or abuse of specific substances has less to do with age than with cohort and context; and habits and attitudes are usually set by early adulthood (Atkinson et al., 1992). Middle-aged adults who grew up in the 1960s, when adolescents' use of marijuana and other illegal drugs was at its peak, are far more likely to use those drugs today than their parents were at the same time of life (Rosenburg, in press). In one longitudinal study, when more than 1,000 high school sophomores and juniors were interviewed again at age 24 or 25, most of those who had begun using a certain drug in their teens were still using it (Kandel, Davies, Karus, & Yamaguchi, 1986).

Alcohol Abuse and Dependence

Alcoholism has been called the "major mental health problem of the century" (Horton & Fogelman, 1991, p. 302). Nearly 14 million Americans—constituting more than 7 percent of the population—abuse alcohol or are dependent on alcohol (B. S. Grant et al., 1994). It has been estimated that a majority of homicides (APA, 1994) and half of all rapes and automobile accidents involve alcohol. Alcohol abuse is especially a male problem; it is the most commonly diagnosed mental illness among men age 18 to 64 and third most common among men age 65 and older, after affective disorders and other kinds of substance abuse (B. S. Grant, personal communication, July 6, 1995; Horton & Fogelman, 1991). Alcoholism is the leading mental health problem among Native Americans (Stanford & Du Bois, 1992).

Although older adults are less likely to abuse alcohol than other age groups, the most common substance problems in this age group involve alcohol. Older adults are more likely to abuse alcohol than other drugs, especially illegal drugs (Atkinson et al., 1992). Some data suggest that about 1 in 10 older persons living in the community and 1 in 5 living in nursing homes are alcoholic (Horton & Fogelman, 1991). Other estimates for the institutionalized elderly range as high as 60 percent, though there are no studies on actual rates of alcohol abuse in long-term care (Lichtenberg, 1994). Older men are 2 to 6 times likelier than older women to have documented alcohol problems. Two clinical studies suggest that alcoholism may be more prevalent among older African Americans than among other racial or ethnic groups (Blum & Rosner, 1983; McCusker, Cherubin, & Zimberg, 1971).

Two-thirds of elderly alcoholics began drinking before or during their early twenties and typically showed a lifelong pattern of addictive behavior. However, some started drinking heavily after age 50, generally in response to stressors such as bereavement, retirement, loneliness, physical illness, or pain. Contrary to a common misconception, elderly alcoholics in both categories respond well to treatment (Horton & Fogelman, 1991; Lichtenberg, 1994)—sometimes even better than younger alcoholics (Atkinson et al., 1992). Table 12-3 on the following page deals with other common beliefs and mistaken beliefs about alcohol problems, particularly in later life.

Alcohol is likely to become a more serious problem for older adults in the future (Atkinson et al., 1992). Although cross-sectional research shows less alcohol use among older adults than among younger adults, this may well be a cohort effect limited to the generation that lived through Prohibition. Two large longitudinal studies (Dufour, Colliver, Stinson, & Grigson, 1988; Glynn, Bouchard, LoCastro, & Laird, 1985) found no change in use of alcohol for any age group. Thus future generations of older adults are likely to maintain their current higher levels of alcohol consumption.

Substance addiction is not just an individual problem. It can affect a whole family, and it is often associated with domestic violence and family conflict (Irons, 1994).

TABLE 12-3 COMMON BELIEFS ABOUT ALCOHOL PROBLEMS	
Belief	*True or False, and Why*
"It is easier to detect an alcohol problem in an older adult than in a younger one."	*False.* Alcohol abuse in later life is often hidden and consequently overlooked. Older people's drinking isn't as likely to be detected through problems at work or arrests for drunk driving, and many drink only in private.
"Medications usually reduce effects of alcohol in older people."	*False.* Medications intensify alcohol's effects, thereby intensifying its dangers.
"Women with alcohol problems tend to be more secretive about their drinking than men."	*True.* Society places a greater stigma on women who abuse alcohol than on men, so women may hide their drinking more and feel greater shame and guilt.
"In older people, the central nervous system is very sensitive to the depressant effect of alcohol."	*True.* The central nervous system is quite sensitive to alcohol, and its effects may be mistaken for dementia.
"Signs of alcohol problems in older persons are easy to detect."	*False.* Alcohol dependence can resemble many medical conditions, and medical problems can mask alcohol dependence.
"Older adults are more likely than younger ones to admit to having an alcohol problem."	*False.* An alcohol problem is often a strong moral issue for older adults, and denial may be stronger in this group.
"Alcohol problems in later life increase the chance of suicide."	*True.* Risk of suicide is very high for older white males with a history of alcohol abuse who live alone.
"Alcohol is a stimulant and makes older persons feel younger and more energetic."	*False.* Alcohol is a depressant and impairs thinking, memory, judgment, and coordination.
"A person must want to stop drinking before he or she can be helped to stop."	*False.* Alcoholics usually cannot recognize the severity of their problem, but many can be persuaded to seek treatment.
"The same amount of alcohol has a greater effect on older adults than on younger ones."	*True.* Alcohol is metabolized and excreted more slowly in older adults, resulting in higher blood alcohol levels and more rapid intoxication.

SOURCE: Adapted from Pratt, Wilson, Benthin, & Schmall, 1992.

PARTNER ABUSE

The cases of Nicole Simpson and of Lorena Bobbitt, who cut off her husband's penis with a kitchen knife after 4 years of alleged sexual and physical abuse, have focused public attention on *partner abuse*—violence against a spouse, a former spouse, or an intimate partner.

In the United States, more than 90 percent of the victims of partner abuse are women (Bureau of Justice Statistics, 1994). Abuse typically begins with shoving or slapping and then escalates into beatings that leave some women living in terror, some critically injured, and some dead. Once a woman has been abused, she is likely to be abused again—in about 1 in 5 cases, at least twice more within 6 months (Bureau of Justice Statistics, 1994).

The actual extent of violence between intimate partners is unknown: such violence generally occurs in private, and victims often do not report it because they are ashamed or afraid of reprisal. More than 570,000 women each year are victims of *reported* domestic violence, and more than 1,400 women are killed by their intimate partners (Bureau of Justice Statistics, 1994). The most likely victims of partner abuse are women who are young, poor, and uneducated, and women who are divorced or separated (Bureau of Justice Statistics, 1994). Violence often starts early in a relationship (O'Leary et al., 1989).

It is hard to compare partner abuse across cultures because of differing beliefs about what constitutes abusive behavior. In societies where women are treated as men's property, the concept of spouse abuse may be nonexistent.

Abusers and Victims

Men who abuse women tend to be social isolates, to have low self-esteem, to be sexually inadequate, to be inordinately jealous, to minimize or deny the frequency and intensity of their violence, and to blame the woman (Bernard & Bernard, 1984; Bouza, 1990). Wife battering is most frequent in marriages with a dominant husband and least frequent in egalitarian marriages. It is fairly frequent in marriages with a dominant wife; a frustrated husband may see hitting his wife as the only way to exert power over her (Yllo, 1984).

Why do women stay with men who abuse them? Some have low self-esteem and feel that they deserve to be beaten. Also, victims of aggression often minimize its importance. They may attribute it to alcohol, frustration, and stress. They may interpret it as a sign of love or of masculinity and may deny that their mates really mean to hurt them. As many as one-fourth of women and one-third of men with aggressive spouses do not consider themselves unhappily married (O'Leary et al., 1989). Financially dependent wives are especially vulnerable; battered wives who return to their husbands are usually not employed and feel they have nowhere else to go (Kalmuss & Straus, 1982; Strube & Barbour, 1984). Some women are afraid to leave. Constant ridicule, criticism, threats, punishment, and psychological manipulation can undermine their self-confidence (NOW Legal Defense and Education Fund & Chernow-O'Leary, 1987). Also, their abusers isolate them from family and friends. If they try to end the relationship, or call the police, they simply get more abuse (Geller, 1992).

(Mark Antman/The Image Works)

Shelters where battered women can go for refuge and counseling are one response to the problem of domestic violence.

Can a violent relationship be turned around? Sometimes. Programs are springing up to help abusive men stop their violent behavior, usually through group counseling (Bernard & Bernard, 1984; Feazell, Mayers, & Deschner, 1984). Family therapy, which treats the entire family together, can sometimes stop mild to moderate abuse before it becomes dangerous (Gelles & Maynard, 1987). Effective intervention may depend on understanding the cycle of abuse—what sets it off and what keeps it going (M. J. Kirschenbaum, 1994).

Abusers who recognize their problem the first or second time it arises and seek help are most likely to change. Also, many of those who get court-ordered treatment can be taught to modify their behavior. Men who are arrested for family violence are less likely to continue to abuse their families, and an increasing number of communities are adopting this approach (Bouza, 1990; L. W. Sherman & Berk, 1984; L. W. Sherman & Cohn, 1989). However, some hard-core abusers see nothing wrong with what they do. They are the ones least amenable to rehabilitation and most likely to kill (Geller, 1992). The federal Violence Against Women Act, passed in 1994, provides for tougher law enforcement, funding for shelters, a national domestic violence hotline, and educating judges and court personnel, as well as young people, about domestic violence.

Abused Older Women

When we think of wife beating, we may think of a young woman, often with children. Yet studies show that about 1.4 million American women age 45 to 64 and an estimated 500,000 women age 65 and older are abused by a husband or male partner (Older Women's League, 1994). In interviews with a random sample of 2,000 older adults in the Boston area, 58 percent of women who had been subjected to violence accused their spouses (Pillemer & Finkelhor, 1988).

Why do older men abuse their mates? Conflict that has gone on throughout a marriage may break out more virulently when something happens to upset the equilibrium. A retired man who feels a loss of manhood may try to reassert it by striking his wife; a man who was abusive to coworkers and subordinates may now turn on his wife as the only handy target (AARP, 1993c). If a woman becomes infirm, her partner may crack under the stress of caregiving.

Special pressures tend to keep an older abused wife in an abusive relationship. The economic and psychological jolt of leaving a home of many years and disrupting long-established relationships with friends, family, and neighbors can be formidable. It may be next to impossible for an older woman to find a job. Most shelters and other services are geared to younger women. And adult children often refuse to believe what has happened or blame the mother (McLeod, 1994).

CHILD ABUSE AND NEGLECT

Partner abuse and *child abuse*—maltreatment of a child involving physical injury—often go together. In half of all American families in which women are beaten, children are beaten too (NOW Legal Defense and Education Fund & Chernow-O'Leary, 1987), and more than 90 percent of all child abuse occurs at home (Bergman, Larsen, & Mueller, 1986; Browne & Finkelhor, 1986; Child Welfare League of America, 1986). In the late 1980s and early to mid-1990s, more than 2 million children in the United States were reported to be victims of abuse or of *neglect*—the withholding of adequate care.

Abuse may be followed by killing. According to the Department of Justice, parents were charged in 57 percent of murders of children under 12 years old in large urban areas in 1988; and in 8 out of 10 cases the parent had abused the child (Dawson & Langan, 1994). Sometimes a child's killer is the mother's boyfriend, and the mother fails to intervene or tries to cover up. Sometimes the woman is abused and is too intimidated to protect the child.

Why do adults hurt children? More than 9 out of 10 abusers are not psychotic and do not have criminal personalities; but many are lonely, unhappy, depressed, angry, dissatisfied, isolated, and under great stress. Some have health problems that impair their ability to raise their children. Often they were themselves mistreated as children and felt rejected by their parents (Trickett & Susman, 1988). The power they exert over their children through abuse may be a misplaced effort to gain control over their own lives (Schmitt & Kempe, 1983; Wolfe, 1985). By contrast, parents who neglect children are likely to be irresponsible and apathetic and to ignore the child (Wolfe, 1985).

Abusers often hate themselves for what they do and yet feel powerless to stop. It may be that the strains of caregiving are just too much for them. Often they do not know how to be good parents, and they may lose all control when they cannot get children to do what they want them to do—stop crying, for example, or use the toilet at an unrealistically early age. Furthermore, they often expect their children to take care of them, and they become abusive when this does not happen. They have more confrontations with their children than nonabusive parents do, are less effective in resolving problems, and use punishment more (Reid, Patterson, & Loeber, 1982; Trickett & Kuczynski, 1986; Wolfe, 1985).

Abusive parents are more likely than other couples to have marital problems and to fight physically with each other. They have more children and have them closer together, and their households are more disorganized. They experience more stressful events than other families (Reid et al., 1982). The arrival of a new man in the home—a stepfather or the mother's boyfriend—may trigger abuse. Unemployment, dissatisfaction at work, and chronic financial hardship are closely correlated with both child and spouse abuse (Wolfe, 1985).

Abusive and neglectful parents tend to lack normal social relationships. Abusive parents cut themselves off from neighbors, family, and friends. Consequently, there is no one to turn to in times of stress and no one to see what is happening. Neglectful parents are isolated within the family and tend to be emotionally withdrawn from spouse and children (Wolfe, 1985).

To prevent child abuse and neglect, overwhelmed parents may need help: community educational and support programs, subsidized day care, volunteer homemakers, and temporary "respite homes" or "relief parents" who take over the children when the parents feel too burdened (Wolfe, 1985). One of the most effective ways to stop child abuse, like partner abuse, is to treat it as a crime; people who are arrested for family violence are less likely to continue the maltreatment (Sherman & Berk, 1984).

ABUSE OF THE ELDERLY

Consider the following scenario: A middle-aged woman drives up to a hospital emergency room in a middle-sized American city. She lifts a frail, elderly woman (who appears somewhat confused) out of the car and into a wheelchair, wheels her into the emergency room, and quietly walks out and drives away, leaving no identification (Barnhart, 1992). "Dumping" is one form of *elder abuse*—maltreatment or neglect of dependent older persons or violation of their personal rights. Each year, an estimated 100,000 to 200,000 geriatric patients are abandoned in emergency rooms throughout the United States by caregivers who feel they have reached the end of their rope (Lund, 1993a).

A study in the Boston area suggests that only 1 case of elder abuse in 14 reaches public attention (Pillemer & Finkelhor, 1988). There may be 2 million victims each year (AARP, 1993c). The American Medical Association (1992) has issued guidelines to assist in identification and reporting (see Table 12-4).

Elder abuse most often happens to frail elderly people living with spouses or children. The abuser is more likely to be a spouse, since more older people live with spouses (see Figure 10-3 in Chapter 10); the risk is greater when the caregiver is depressed (Paveza et al., 1992; Pillemer & Finkelhor, 1988). Many older men are abused, but more women are injured by abuse. Rates of violence are high in families with an older person suffering from dementia (Paveza et al, 1992).

Few studies have looked directly at elder abuse among minorities, and among those that have, the results are contradictory. Some studies found no differences in incidence of abuse between white people and minorities; others reported either more or less abuse among minorities. It may be that elderly people in various ethnic groups have different ideas of what constitutes abuse or may, for cul-

TABLE 12-4   SIGNS OF ELDER ABUSE

Type of Abuse	*Specific Indications*
Physical abuse	Pushing, hitting, pinching Force-feeding Improper use of restraints Improper use of medication
Physical neglect	Failure of caregiver to provide necessities (such as food, drinks, eyeglasses, and hearing aids)
Psychological abuse	Causing mental anguish through berating, intimidating, or threats of punishment or isolation
Psychological neglect	Failure to provide social stimulation Prolonged isolation Ignoring or giving silent treatment
Financial or material abuse	Stealing money or possessions Coercing signature on contracts
Financial or material neglect	Failure to use available funds and resources to sustain or restore health and well-being
Violating personal rights	Denying right to privacy Denying right to make own personal and health decisions Forcible eviction or forcible placement in nursing home

SOURCE: Adapted from American Medical Association, 1992.

tural reasons, be less likely to complain about it. In one study, researchers presented 13 scenarios to 30 African American, 30 white, and 30 Korean American women age 60 to 75 (Moon & Williams, 1993). Korean Americans were far less likely than the other two groups to identify certain situations as abusive or to say that they would seek help. For example, in one scenario, an unemployed man who lives with his 78-year-old widowed mother throws a frying pan at her when she burns the food. All the African Americans and all but one of the white respondents, but only 60 percent of the Korean Americans, called this behavior abusive. Many Korean Americans expressed reluctance to seek help because that would mean disclosing "family shame" or creating family conflict.

Elder abuse should be recognized as a type of domestic violence. Both abused and abuser generally need treatment (Hooyman, Rathbone-McCuan, & Klingbeil, 1982; Pillemer & Finkelhor, 1988). Neglect by family caregivers is usually unintentional; many don't know how to give proper care or are in poor health themselves. Most physical abuse can be quickly resolved by counseling and provision of needed services (AARP, 1993c). Abusers need treatment to recognize what they are doing and assistance to reduce the stress of caregiving. Self-help groups may help victims acknowledge what is happening, recognize that they do not have to put up with mistreatment, and find out how to stop it or get away from it.

MENTAL HEALTH IN LATE LIFE: A LIFESPAN DEVELOPMENTAL APPROACH

▼

Contrary to stereotype, decline in mental health is not typical in late life. In a 1-year study of 1,300 older adults, about 7 out of 10 maintained or improved their mental health (Haug, Belkgrave, & Gratton, 1984). In fact, mental illness is less common among older adults than younger adults. In the United States, fewer than 14 percent of older women and fewer than 11 percent of older men have any mental disorders (Wykle & Musil, 1993), though among older people admitted to nursing homes, an estimated 43 to 60 percent do (Gatz & Smyer, 1992).

Emphasis on the multidirectionality of change—growth as well as decline—is an important feature of the lifespan development perspective. Adults become more different than alike as they age, and mental status is no exception. Other features of the lifespan approach—recognition of the context of development and its multiple causes—apply to mental health as well.

Mental disorders often have a physical basis. A person who has trouble getting around because of arthritis may become depressed unless special efforts are made to maintain social contact. A person who loves crossword puzzles but can no longer write without pain may need to look for new sources of intellectual stimulation. A person who has had a heart attack may be afraid to resume sexual activity; and if this concern is not communicated and dealt with, it may strain the marital relationship and affect the mental health of both spouses.

Personality can also play a role. People high in a dimension called *neuroticism* (see Chapter 11) may be vulnerable to mental disorders in old age. Common personality developments that have been identified with aging, such as interiority and preoccupation with bodily changes, may lead to disturbance if carried to extremes. Where a person lives and with whom—the presence or absence of a spouse or some other intimate companion—can make a difference (Lebowitz & Niederehe, 1992).

Plasticity is another feature of the lifespan approach. Contrary to Freud's belief that older people's mental processes are too rigid and that they have too little time left to make therapy worthwhile (Whitbourne, 1989), gerontologists find that the aged can respond successfully to treatment.

Let's look first at the positive side of mental health, then at mental disorders in late life, and finally at a way of assessing strengths and resources of older adults.

MENTAL HEALTH AND LIFE SATISFACTION

Many factors, including physical health, psychological adjustment, socioeconomic status, life events, and social support, can affect an older person's mental health (Wykle & Musil, 1993). Similar factors have been identified as important in life satisfaction (R. Schulz, 1985). A sense of personal control is vital (Hooker & Kaus, 1994; M. E. Lachman, 1986).

In 1981, a Harris poll found that the vast majority (87 percent) of older Americans agreed with the statement, "As I look back on my life, I am fairly well satis-

TABLE 12-5	LIFE SATISFACTION OF OLDER ADULTS: RESPONSES TO A HARRIS POLL		
	Percentage Agreeing	*Percentage Disagreeing*	*Percentage Not Sure*
Positive statements			
As I look back on my life, I am fairly well satisfied	87	11	2
Compared to other people my age, I make a good appearance	84	7	8
I've gotten pretty much what I expected out of life	81	14	5
The things I do are as interesting to me as they ever were	69	27	4
As I grow older, things seem better than I thought they would be	53	38	9
I have gotten more of the breaks in life than most people I know	62	31	6
I would not change my past life even if I could	64	29	6
I expect some interesting and pleasant things to happen to me in the future	62	28	11
I am just as happy as when I was younger	48	48	4
I have made plans for things I'll be doing a month or year from now	49	47	4
These are the best years of my life	33	60	7
Negative statements			
I feel old and somewhat tired	45	51	3
My life could be happier than it is now	55	40	5
In spite of what some people say, the lot of the average person is getting worse, not better	48	39	13
When I think back over my life, I didn't get most of the important things I wanted	36	59	4
This is the dreariest time of my life	27	70	3
Most of the things I do are boring or monotonous	21	76	3
Compared to other people, I get down in the dumps too often	18	78	5

SOURCE: Belsky, 1984; reprinted from National Council on the Aging, 1981.

fied," and one-third called their older years the best years of their lives (Belsky, 1984, p. 10; see Table 12-5). Older black and Hispanic adults, who tended to have financial and health problems, were less satisfied than whites. However, other research has found that elderly black people are *more* satisfied with their lives than whites (Deimling, Harel, & Noelker, 1983; Ortega, Crutchfield, & Rushing,

1983), primarily because of their greater participation in religion. African Americans who are in good health, have children, and have more education tend to be the most satisfied (Ward & Kilburn, 1983); elderly blacks who live in rural areas are less satisfied than rural whites (Revicki & Mitchell, 1990). Elderly Native Americans, despite their generally deprived socioeconomic status, have a fairly high average level of life satisfaction (64 percent), but their scores range widely (F. L. Johnson et al., 1986). Older Hispanics, many of whom are poor and illiterate (Sanchez, 1992), show the least satisfaction and the poorest mental health of all these ethnic groups (F. L. Johnson et al., 1988).

MENTAL DISORDERS

When Hugh Downs—a well-known figure on television—brought his aging father to live with him and his family in Arizona, they suspected that the elderly man was developing Alzheimer's disease. But his lapses of memory and his tendency to get lost turned out to be combined effects of several types of drugs prescribed to counter the side effects of medication for high blood pressure. With a change of medications, his behavior returned to normal; he even began to look younger. For the next 10 years, until he died at 83, he worked in his son's and daughter-in-law's companies and built up a small estate by investing the income (Downs, 1993).

Many older people and their families mistakenly believe that they can do nothing about mental and behavioral problems. Actually, some 100 such conditions—including about 15 percent of dementia cases—can be cured or alleviated. The most common, besides drug intoxication, are depression, delirium, metabolic or infectious disorders, malnutrition, anemia, alcoholism, low thyroid functioning, emotional problems, and minor head injuries (National Institute on Aging, 1980, 1993; Wykle & Musil, 1993). But many older adults, especially those in minority groups and those who live in rural areas, do not get the help they need (Fellin & Powell, 1988; Roybal, 1988), whether because they do not realize their symptoms are treatable, because they are too proud or too fearful to admit they need help, or because they think they cannot afford it. Private treatment can be expensive; not every community offers low-cost mental health services, and not enough programs reach out to find those in need. Although it has been estimated that close to 8 percent of noninstitutionalized older adults need psychiatric services, only about 5 percent get treatment from either mental health professionals or primary physicians (B. Burns & Taub, 1990).

Older people may be afflicted with the same mental illnesses that strike younger people, except that *schizophrenia*—loss of contact with reality, involving hallucinations, delusions, and other thought disturbances—rarely begins in old age (Butler, 1987b). Let's look more closely at three mental disorders popularly believed to be most common in late life: depression, dementia, and hypochondriasis.* As we'll see, this seems to be true only of dementia.

---

*Diagnostic criteria for all three conditions come from the American Psychiatric Association's *Diagnostic and Statistical Manual of Mental Disorders, Fourth Edition* (APA, 1994).

(Joel Gordon)

Depression in older adults may be underdiagnosed because physicians attribute the symptoms to physical illness or to aging, or because older people tend not to complain of feeling depressed. Men are less likely than women to see doctors or report health problems.

Depression

Art Buchwald is a Pulitzer prize-winning author whose humorous columns appear in some 550 newspapers; he has made millions of Americans laugh for four decades. In private life, however, Buchwald has struggled for years with depression so serious that twice he came close to suicide (Buchwald, 1994). Barbara Bush, the former First Lady, has told of a 6-month episode she experienced in 1976, when she fought off depression that had led her to thoughts of suicide (Bush, 1994).

Everyone feels "blue" at times; an occasional low mood does not necessarily signify clinical depression. A *major depressive episode,* the most severe form of clinical depression, is one that continues for at least 2 weeks, during which a person shows extreme sadness or loss of interest or pleasure in life, as well as at least four other symptoms, such as changes in weight or appetite; insomnia; agitation; fatigue; feelings of worthlessness or inappropriate guilt; inability to think, concentrate, or make decisions; and thoughts of death or suicide. The symptoms must not be due to drug abuse, medication, a medical condition, or recent bereavement and must cause significant distress or impairment in social, occupational, or other functioning (APA, 1994). Other forms of clinical depression are either severe but transient, or continuing or chronic but milder ("Depression," 1995).

About 15 to 17 percent of Americans, two-thirds of them women, have experienced some form of clinical depression, 10 percent within a given year (Blazer et al., 1994; "Depression," 1995; Kessler et al., 1994). Anywhere from 50 to 65 percent of depressed people—including a disproportionate number of older adults—go untreated, in part because of a mistaken belief that depression is a sign of weakness or that it will lift by itself. Actually, in 1 out of 5 cases depression becomes chronic, and it may indeed lead to suicide ("Depression," 1995; "Listening to Depression," 1995).

A common belief is that older people, because of their physical and emotional losses, are particularly subject to depression. Older adults do show more symptoms of mood disturbance than younger ones. But, surprisingly, they are less likely to be diagnosed as depressed (Gallo, Anthony, & Muthen, 1994). Only an estimated 1 to 2 percent of noninstitutionalized elderly people meet the diagnostic criteria for clinical depression, though about 10 percent have some symptoms (Jefferson & Greist, 1993). Epidemiological studies find that major depression is 3 times as prevalent in younger adults (George, Blazer, Winfield-Laird, Leaf, & Fischbach, 1988). Why is this?

It is possible that depression tends to be milder among older adults. Or it may be underdiagnosed; doctors may tend to attribute its symptoms to physical illness or to aging (George, 1993). Since depression often accompanies such medical conditions as Parkinson's disease, stroke, thyroid disorder, and certain vitamin deficiencies, it may be hard to sort out which is which (Jefferson & Greist, 1993). Standard diagnostic criteria may fail to detect some cases of depression in older adults. This may also be true of members of racial and ethnic minorities whose poverty would seem to put them at high risk of depression but who do not seem to become clinically depressed any more frequently than white people do (George, 1993; Stanford & Du Bois, 1992). Perhaps the simplest explanation, which is supported by a large-scale study in Baltimore and the Durham-Piedmont region of North Carolina, is that older adults are less likely than younger ones to *say* they feel depressed (Gallo et al., 1994).

One indication that depression may be underdiagnosed in older adults is the prevalence of suicide in this age group. Suicide rates are high among older adults (see Figure 13-3 in Chapter 13), particularly among white men and people with chronic ailments (Wykle, Segal, & Nagley, 1992). In 1988, 21 percent of suicides in the United States were committed by older people, although older people are only 12.4 percent of the population (McIntosh, 1992). Physicians often fail to identify suicidal older patients, because an older person may complain of physical symptoms rather than mental distress (Wykle & Musil, 1993; we discuss suicide in more detail in Chapter 13).

According to national and international epidemiological studies, older women are almost twice as likely as older man to be clinically depressed (Bebbington, 1990; Regier et al., 1988). But other sources suggest that rates of depression among women and men even out after age 65 (Jefferson & Greist, 1993). An explanation for this discrepancy may be that women are more likely to see doctors and to report physical problems, which often accompany depression (Wykle & Musil, 1993).

(Jim West/Impact Visuals)

Wilhelmina Driver of Detroit, age 80, holds some of the medications she must take daily. Elderly people who take a number of medicines— some over-the-counter or prescribed by different doctors without each other's knowledge—may be at risk of overmedication, which can produce depression and other problems.

Depression can have various causes, which may act together. Some people may be genetically predisposed to it through a biochemical imbalance in the brain. Failure to maintain a healthful lifestyle with adequate exercise can contribute to it. Stressful events or loneliness can trigger it (Jefferson & Greist, 1993; "Listening to Depression," 1995). Nearly half of all caregivers of Alzheimer's patients suffer from it ("Alzheimer's and Stress," 1994). A strong network of family and friends can help older people ward off depression or cope with it.

Depression can be a side effect of certain medications, such as tranquilizers, sedatives, sleeping pills, and drugs prescribed for high blood pressure, especially when accompanied by excessive drinking (Jefferson & Greist, 1993). An older person may take a dozen or more different medicines, some of them nonprescription ("over the counter"). Because physicians do not always ask what medications a patient is already taking, they may prescribe drugs that interact harmfully. And because of age-related changes in metabolism, a dosage that would be right for a 40-year-old may be an overdose for an 80-year-old.

Antidepressant drugs can treat depression by restoring the chemical balance of neurotransmitters in the brain, but they can have some unwanted side effects, including inhibition of sexual functioning (Jefferson & Greist, 1993; "Listening to Depression," 1995; "Sexual Side Effects," 1994). *Electroconvulsive therapy (ECT),* also called *shock therapy,* may be necessary to treat severe depression. Usually, electric shocks are administered 3 times a week for about 3 weeks. Because it works more quickly than antidepressant drugs, ECT is sometimes preferred when there is a high risk of suicide.

Psychotherapies have also been effective in treating older persons with depression. These include *cognitive therapy* (teaching patients to recognize and correct negative thinking), *behavior therapy* (using positive and negative reinforcement), and *brief dynamic therapy* (creating a genuine, nonmanipulative working alliance between therapist and client). Cognitive-behavioral approaches seem to work best and most quickly for older adults, often in only 15 to 20 sessions (Koenig & Blazer, 1992). A promising new cost-effective intervention is *music therapy:* learning how to reduce stress by listening to music. A homebound person can learn the techniques with only a weekly visit or phone call from a therapist (Hanser & Thompson, 1994).

Dementia

Dementia—development of multiple cognitive deficits including memory impairment—is not one illness but a dozen or more that have similar symptoms but different causes. Dementias may be due to one or a combination of medical conditions, most commonly Alzheimer's disease. Dementia may also be caused by other conditions, such as cardiovascular disease, Parkinson's disease, and substance abuse; but not all people who have those conditions develop dementia.

Dementia can come on gradually or suddenly. People with dementia lose their ability to learn new information, remember old information, or both. In addition, they become impaired in at least one of the following areas: speech and writing; motor activities; recognition of objects and people; and planning, executing, and monitoring their own behavior (usually a function of the frontal lobes). To constitute dementia, these impairments must be severe enough to cause problems at work, in daily activities, or in social relationships. People with dementia may have trouble packing a suitcase; show poor judgment (for example, they may drive in a blizzard); become violent or suicidal; stumble and fall frequently; make crude jokes, stop bathing, and disregard other social conventions; or accuse family members of stealing their belongings. Often, they are oblivious of their condition and make plans that are completely unrealistic, such as deciding to run for president.

Dementia is uncommon even in late life, but (except for dementia caused by HIV, the AIDS virus) it is more likely to occur in late life than at any other time. A large British study (Paykel et al., 1994) found that the rate of dementia doubles approximately every 5 years after age 75, from slightly more than 2 percent of people age 75 to 79 to about 8.5 percent at ages 85 to 89. Minimal dementia, which involves milder impairment, rises more steeply, from about 3 percent at age 75 to almost 30 percent after age 90.

In the past, dementia was defined by a progressive pattern of deterioration. Today, diagnosis is based simply on the presence of the deficits described above, whether or not they get worse. Whether dementia can be arrested or reversed depends on the underlying cause and also on the timeliness and effectiveness of treatment.

(Bob Adelman)

When Parkinson's disease robbed the artist Joe Dawley of his fine motor control, he became dangerously depressed. But a switch from realistic painting to an impressionistic style, with broader brushstrokes that he could still execute, gained him increased sales and recognition and lifted his spirits.

The most common form of dementia among older adults is *dementia of the Alzheimer's type* (described in Chapter 4). The onset of this progressive, degenerative dementia is gradual. The next most common form among older adults is *vascular dementia* (formerly called *multi-infarct dementia*), a syndrome in which the brain is damaged by a series of small strokes or any of a wide variety of other vascular diseases, including arteriosclerosis. Chronic abnormalities of blood pressure—both low and high—can lead to vascular dementia and to cognitive impairment. With increasing age, adults are more and more likely to experience dementia of the Alzheimer's type along with vascular dementia (Emery & Oxman, 1994).

Vascular dementia is thought to be more prevalent in men than in women. In this type of dementia, rapid changes are more common than a slow progression, and the pattern of deficits may depend on what areas of the brain are affected. As with other irreversible dementias, treatment is aimed at arresting or controlling the progress of the disease or ameliorating its symptoms. Treatment for vascular dementia usually focuses on controlling hypertension and taking other steps to reduce the risk of a massive stroke.

Parkinson's disease is a slowly progressive neurological disorder characterized by tremor, stiffness, slowed movement, and unstable posture. Anywhere from 20 to 60 percent of people with Parkinson's disease suffer from dementia. The physical symptoms of the disease can be treated with drugs designed to increase the level of the neurotransmitter dopamine or to slow its loss.

Since victims of major depression often show cognitive losses, including memory lapses and difficulty in thinking and concentrating, it can be difficult—particularly in older persons—to pinpoint the cause as dementia, depression, or both. The standard term for cognitive impairment due to major depression is *pseudodementia* (APA, 1994). Some researchers, however, prefer to use the term *transitory dementia* (Emery & Oxman, 1994), since people who are treated for depression sometimes improve for a while and then regress. In some longitudinal studies, dementia associated with depression has evolved into degenerative, or irreversible, dementia. This suggests that real deterioration does occur in depressive dementia, though at present the factors associated with such a progression are not known.

Hypochondriasis

People who complain of aches and pains that seem to have no medical basis are often dismissed as hypochondriacs. Many laypersons and even some physicians do not realize that *hypochondriasis* is a mental illness, defined as "preoccupation with fears of having, or the idea that one has, a serious disease based on a misinterpretation of one or more bodily signs or symptoms" (APA, 1994, p. 462). This belief continues even though the patient is reassured that his or her concern is medically unwarranted or exaggerated. To be diagnosed as hypochondriasis, the condition must have lasted for at least 6 months; must not be limited to concerns about appearance; and must cause significant problems in social life, occupation, or other aspects of everyday living—for example, causing the person to stay home from work or to stay away from family gatherings. Cultural factors may need to be taken into consideration; in some cultural groups a physician's reassurances may not carry as much weight as the opinion of a traditional nonmedical healer.

The common belief that older people are more likely to be hypochondriacs is mistaken. Hypochondriasis can start at any age, and in fact it is believed to begin most often in young adulthood. Because it is a chronic condition, it becomes in effect part of the personality structure. Thus older adults who show such a "trait" may simply be acting as they have acted for years. People who have had (or whose family members have had) serious illnesses, particularly as children, are more likely to become hypochondriacs. So are people who have experienced severe psychosocial stress, such as bereavement. In some cases hypochondriasis accompanies other mental disorders, particularly anxiety and depression (APA, 1994).

ASSESSING STRENGTHS

Instead of thinking about old age primarily in terms of compensating for deficits, we must learn . . . to think also in terms of maximizing human resources. And we must broaden our notion of elders' resources to include the vitality, the grit, the underlying commitment to values that constitute the infinite resources of the human spirit. (Kivnick, 1993, p. 13)

(Peter Southwick/AP/Wide World Photos)

Rose Kennedy (shown here at her ninety-second birthday party with her fourth son, Senator Edward Kennedy) coped with a series of tragic events—including the institutionalization of a mentally retarded daughter, the death of her eldest son during World War II, and the assassinations of her next two sons, President John F. Kennedy and Senator Robert Kennedy—and still could manage to smile.

A 92-year-old woman with near-crippling arthritis—a descendant of a slave—keeps her longtime clerical job and remains active in her church. Two middle-aged professional women keep up their morale and that of the 85-year-old mother-in-law they care for, who has lost her eyesight and has had to be moved from her southern farm community to their northern city. How can people like these do what they do? According to Helen Q. Kivnick (1993), who worked extensively with Erik Erikson, the answer lies in the dynamics and strength of the human spirit.

According to Kivnick, those who deal with this age group should not focus merely on remediating or compensating for mental health problems. Rather, older people should be helped to identify, use, and build on the unique strengths they have displayed during the course of their lives, not only for their own benefit but as resources for society. On the basis of Erikson's theory of personality development, Kivnick has created a guide for assessing "life strengths" of older adults. This guide can be used by care managers or family members in talking with older people about their needs and desires. It can also help older people reflect on their own situation and help younger people anticipate and prepare for old age.

The suggested questions are designed to discover individual strengths that have evolved out of Erikson's eight "crises," or stages of life. Table 12-6 offers a sampling of questions addressing issues of each stage. Three fundamental questions underlie all the others: *What is it about your life that is most worth living for? What makes you feel most alive? What makes you feel most like yourself?* As you read the questions, think about how you would answer them today. Do you think you are likely to answer them in the same way when you grow older? How would your parents and grandparents have answered these questions? (If you don't know, and if they are still alive, why not ask them?)

TABLE 12-6   LIFE STRENGTHS INTERVIEW GUIDE

Stage 1: Trust versus mistrust
1. What is it in your life that gives you hope?
2. How do moral beliefs and values fit into your life?
3. What is it in your life that gives you a sense of security?

Stage 2: Autonomy versus shame and doubt
1. What parts of your life is it most important that you stay in charge of?
2. Do you get to use the phone, listen to the radio, watch TV, decorate, spend money as you wish?

Stage 3: Initiative versus guilt
1. What do you do for fun these days?
2. What have you done, in your life, which makes you proudest?
3. What do you want to do, most of all, with the rest of your life?

Stage 4: Industry versus inferiority
1. What have you worked hard at?
2. What kinds of things have you always been good at?

Stage 5: Identity versus confusion
1. When people describe you, what do they say? What would you like them to say?
2. What is the image that you carry around inside, about who you are in the world?

Stage 6: Intimacy versus isolation
1. Whom do you count on these days? Who counts on you?
2. Who, in which relationships, has brought out the best in you?

Stage 7: Generativity versus self-absorption
1. How do you show your caring?
2. What is there about yourself and your life that you want to make sure people remember?

Stage 8: Integrity versus despair
1. What strategies have you used for coping with fear?
2. Are you afraid of dying? Do you know what you are afraid of?
3. What are your thoughts about your own death? How you'd like to die? Where you'd like to die? Who should be there with you?

NOTE: Questions are grouped under the stages of Erikson's theory of personality development to which they relate.
SOURCE: Adapted from Kivnick, 1993, pp. 18–19.

Many younger adults (and some older ones) may never have truly addressed the last group of questions—questions about their attitude toward their own death. This is, to a large extent, a reflection of the way American society deals with (or, more typically, refuses to deal with) death and dying. Yet living and dying are intertwined, and confronting death is a critical issue for mental health in adulthood. In Chapter 13, we discuss death and bereavement, and how people in various cultures cope with these inevitable events.

SUMMARY

- Mental health can be defined in terms of self-concept, self-development, and satisfaction with life.

- Almost half of American adults have had a mental disorder, most commonly major depression.

- Young adults are more susceptible to emotional illness, anxiety, and substance abuse; older adults are more susceptible to severe cognitive impairment.

MODELS OF COPING

- Three traditional approaches to the study of coping are environmental, behavioral, and coping-style models.

- Environmental models emphasize quantitative change based on the magnitude of environmental demands.

- Behavioral models place more emphasis on active responses to stress.

- Coping-style models emphasize individual strategies of problem solving.

- The cognitive-appraisal model views the choice of appropriate coping efforts as the result of constant reappraisal of a situation.

"SUCCESSFUL AGING"

- Three classic normative models of successful aging are Peck's personality adjustments of middle and late adulthood, disengagement theory, and activity theory.

- According to Atchley's continuity theory, aging adults seek a balance between continuity and change.

- According to Whitbourne's model of personality development, identity style can predict adaptation to aging.

- Research on ordinary adults' concepts of successful aging points to the importance of relationships, of growth for middle-aged people, and of acceptance for older people.

DESTRUCTIVE BEHAVIOR PATTERNS

- The extent of substance abuse among older adults is often underestimated.

- Habits and attitudes regarding substance use are generally established by young adulthood and have more to do with cohort than with age.

- Alcoholism is a major mental health problem, especially among men. Older adults are more likely to abuse alcohol than other drugs.

- The overwhelming majority of victims of partner abuse are women. Abused women often stay with their abusers out of vulnerability, fear, and a lack of alternatives. Older abused wives face special problems.

- Abusive and neglectful parents show specific characteristics and behavior patterns.

- Elder abuse, which may be significantly underreported, most often happens to a frail elderly person living with a spouse who is his or her caregiver.

MENTAL HEALTH IN LATE LIFE:
A LIFESPAN DEVELOPMENTAL APPROACH

- Except among nursing home residents, mental illness is less common in late life than among younger adults.

- A lifespan developmental perspective on mental health emphasizes tendencies toward both growth and decline, the context and multiple causation of mental status, and responsiveness to treatment even in late life.

- Most older Americans seem to be fairly satisfied with life, although satisfaction is lower among some ethnic groups.

- Nearly half of older adults who need treatment for mental conditions that can be cured or alleviated do not get it.

- For many reasons, depression may be underdiagnosed in older adults and therefore go untreated.

- Dementias, which may be due to one or a combination of conditions, are most likely to occur in late life. Some dementias can be reversed with treatment.

- Common forms of progressive dementia are those caused by Alzheimer's disease, vascular disease, and Parkinson's disease.

- Hypochondriasis is a chronic condition that can begin at any age.

- Assessing the life strengths of older adults can help them and society to make the most of the inner resources they have developed.

KEY TERMS

coping (page 448)
congruence model (450)
environmental-press model (450)
learned helplessness (451)
adaptive mechanisms (451)
cognitive-appraisal model (452)
problem-focused coping (453)
emotion-focused coping (453)
disengagement theory (459)
activity theory (459)
continuity theory (460)
substance abuse (463)
substance dependence (463)
partner abuse (467)

child abuse (469)
neglect (469)
elder abuse (470)
schizophrenia (474)
major depressive episode (475)
antidepressant drugs (477)
electroconvulsive therapy (ECT) (477)
cognitive therapy (478)
behavior therapy (478)
brief dynamic therapy (478)
music therapy (478)
Parkinson's disease (479)
pseudodementia (480)
hypochondriasis (480)

CHAPTER 13

DEALING WITH DEATH AND BEREAVEMENT

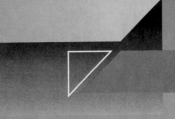

**CHANGING PERSPECTIVES
ON DEATH AND DYING**
Biological, Social, and Psychological
　Aspects of Death
The Study of Death: Thanatology
　and Death Education
Hospice Care

FACING DEATH
Attitudes toward Death and Dying
Approaching Death

FACING BEREAVEMENT
Forms and Patterns of Grief
Surviving a Spouse
Losing a Parent
Losing a Child

CONTROVERSIAL ISSUES
Suicide
Euthanasia

**FINDING MEANING AND PURPOSE
IN LIFE AND DEATH**
Reviewing a Life
Overcoming Fear of Death
Development: A Lifelong Process

BOXES
13-1　The Cutting Edge:
　　　Near-Death Experiences
13-2　The Multicultural Context:
　　　Postponing Death
13-3　The Art of Aging: Evoking
　　　Memories for a Life Review

FOCUS: LOUISA MAY ALCOTT

(The Bettmann Archive)

One of the most moving parts of Louisa May Alcott's classic nineteenth-century novel *Little Women* is the chapter recounting the last year in the life of gentle, home-loving Beth, the third of the March sisters (the others being Meg, Jo, and Amy). Beth's life and her death at age 18 are based on those of Alcott's own sister Elizabeth (Lizzie), who wasted away and died at 23 (Elbert, 1984; MacDonald, 1983; Stern, 1950). Despite its dated language and what some may consider sugar-coated sentimentality, Alcott's fictionalized account of her family's growing intimacy in the face of tragedy has struck an empathetic chord in generations of readers, many of whom have never actually seen a person die.

In the novel, realizing that Beth's illness was terminal, "the family accepted the inevitable, and tried to bear it cheerfully. . . . They put away their grief, and each did his or her part toward making that last year a happy one.

"The pleasantest room in the house was set apart for Beth, and in it was gathered everything that she most loved. . . . Father's best books found their way there, mother's easy chair, Jo's desk, Amy's finest sketches; and every day Meg brought her babies on a loving pilgrimage, to make sunshine for Aunty Beth. . . .

"Here, cherished like a household saint in its shrine, sat Beth, tranquil and busy as ever. . . . The feeble fingers were never idle, and one of her pleasures was to make little things for the school-children daily passing to and fro . . ." (Alcott, 1929, pp. 533–534).

As Beth's illness progressed, the increasingly frail invalid put down the sewing needle that had become "so heavy." Now "talking wearied her, faces troubled her, pain claimed her for its own, and her tranquil spirit was sorrowfully perturbed by the ills that vexed her feeble flesh," while "those who loved her best were forced to see the thin hands stretched out to them beseechingly, to hear the bitter cry, 'Help me, help me!' and to feel that there was no help." But with "the wreck of her frail body, Beth's soul grew strong." Jo stayed with Beth constantly (as Alcott herself stayed with her sister Lizzie), sleeping on a couch by her side and "waking often to renew the fire, to feed, lift, or wait upon the patient creature" (pp. 534–535). Beth finally drew her last quiet breath "on the bosom where she had drawn her first"; and "mother and sisters made her ready for the long sleep that pain would never mar again" (p. 540).

The sequence of events described in *Little Women* is strikingly close to reality, as outlined by one of Alcott's biographers: "In February, Lizzie began to fail rapidly from what Dr. Geist labeled consumption. With aching heart Louisa watched while her sister sewed or read or lay looking at the fire. . . . Father had come home from the West to hear from Dr. Geist that there was no hope. . . . Anna [Alcott's older sister] did the housekeeping so that Mother and Louisa could devote themselves to Lizzie. The sad, quiet days stretched on in her room, and during endless nights Louisa kindled the fire and watched her sister. . . . The farewells were spoken. . . . At last . . . Lizzie became unconscious, quietly breathing her life away. . . . With her mother, Louisa dressed Lizzie for the last time . . ." (Stern, 1950, pp. 85–86).

Alcott herself wrote at the time, "Our Lizzie is *well* at last, not in this world but another where I hope she will find nothing but rest from her long suffering. . . . Last Friday night after suffering much all day, she asked to lie in Father's arms & called us all about her holding our hands & smiling at us as she silently seemed to bid us good bye. . . . At midnight she said 'Now I'm comfortable & so happy,' & soon after became unconscious. We sat beside her while she quietly breathed her life away, opening her eyes to give us one beautiful look before they closed forever" (Myerson, Shealy, & Stern, 1987, pp. 32–33).

Human beings are individuals. They undergo different experiences and react to them in different ways. But one unavoidable part of everyone's life is its end. The better people can understand this inevitable event and the more wisely they can approach it, the more fully they can live until it comes.

People's attitudes toward death are shaped by the time and place in which they live. Louisa May Alcott's (and the fictional Jo's) tender care of a beloved, dying sister around whom the entire household revolved for a full year represents a common experience not only in the nineteenth-century United States but in many contemporary rural cultures. Looking death in the eye, bit by bit, day by day, Alcott and her family absorbed an important truth: that dying is part of living, and confronting the end of life can give deeper meaning to the whole of life. Such an experience is less common in American society today.

The stark biological fact of death, then, is far from the whole story. Its meaning and impact are profoundly influenced by what people feel and do, and people's feelings and behavior are greatly affected by how their culture deals with death.

In this chapter, we look at the intertwined biological, social, and psychological aspects of death (the state) and dying (the process), and at changing societal views and customs related to both. We note differences in how adults of different ages think and feel about dying. We examine changes adults undergo in the face of death and how they deal with the death of those they love. We compare mourning patterns in different cultures and various forms grief can take. We discuss such controversial issues as assisted suicide and euthanasia ("mercy killing"). Finally, we see how facing death can help people find meaning and purpose in life.

CHANGING PERSPECTIVES ON DEATH AND DYING

Before modern times, in a typical year some 50 people out of every 1,000 died; and during plagues or natural disasters, the death rate might reach 40 percent. More than one-third of all babies died in infancy, and half of all children died before their tenth birthday. People saw relatives and friends succumb to fatal illnesses at an early age, and they expected some of their own children to die young (Lofland, 1986). Death was a normal, expected event, sometimes even welcomed as a peaceful end to suffering.

Advances in medicine and sanitation during the twentieth century brought about a "mortality revolution" in developed countries (Lofland, 1986, p. 60). Death rates fell to less than 9 percent. Infant mortality dropped below 1 percent in the United States (though it is about twice as high for African American babies), and even lower in much of Europe (Centers for Disease Control and Prevention, 1994; USDHHS, 1995; Wegman, 1992). Today, as compared with a century ago, children are more likely to reach adulthood, adults are more likely to reach old age, and older people can overcome illnesses they grew up regarding as fatal. In the United States, only AIDS is an exception to the general pattern of declining mortality (Centers for Disease Control and Prevention, 1994).

As death increasingly became a phenomenon of late adulthood, it became "invisible and abstract" (Fulton & Owen, 1987–1988, p. 380). The urbanized "baby boom" generation born after World War II was the first to reach adulthood with only a 5 percent chance of having experienced the death of anyone in the immediate family. Many old people lived and died in retirement communities or nursing homes. Care of the dying and the dead, a familiar aspect of family life in rural societies, became largely a task for professionals. People went to hospitals to die, and undertakers prepared their bodies for burial. More than 2 out of 3 deaths in the United States occurred somewhere other than at home. Many people went through most of their lives without thinking much about their own death (Fulton & Owen, 1987–1988; Lofland, 1986).

Today, though, things are again changing. Violence, drug abuse, poverty, and—above all—the spread of AIDS make it hard to deny the reality of death.

Because of the prohibitive cost of extended hospital care that can do nothing to save the terminally ill, many more deaths are occurring at home (Techner, 1994). Hospice care is helping patients and their families face death and bereavement more openly and supportively. Still, it generally takes an airplane crash, a series of suicides, or an epidemic to bring death to the forefront of public awareness.

BIOLOGICAL, SOCIAL, AND PSYCHOLOGICAL ASPECTS OF DEATH

There are at least three aspects of death and dying: *biological*, *social*, and *psychological*.

Although the legal definition varies, *biological* death is generally considered to be the cessation of bodily processes. A person may be pronounced dead when breathing and heartbeat stop for a significant time or when all electrical activity in the brain ceases. Criteria for death have become more complex with the development of medical apparatus that can prolong basic signs of life, sometimes indefinitely. People in a deep coma can be kept alive for years. A person whose brain has completely stopped functioning—and who, therefore, is by definition dead—can be maintained by mechanical devices that artifically sustain heartbeat and respiration.

These medical developments have raised agonizing questions about whether or when life supports, such as respirators and feeding tubes, may be withheld or removed, and whose judgment should prevail. Sometimes humanitarian or practical considerations conflict with religious beliefs or professional standards. Many of these issues have ended up in court, and some are still unresolved.

Biological aspects of death are becoming harder to disentangle from some of its *social* aspects: attitudes toward death, care of and behavior toward the dying, where death takes place, and efforts to postpone or hasten it. Other social aspects of death include disposing of the dead, mourning customs and rituals, and the transfer of possessions and roles.

Many social aspects of death and dying are governed by religious or legal prescriptions that reflect a society's view of what death is and what happens afterward. In Malayan society, for instance (as in many other preliterate societies), death was seen as a gradual transition. A body was at first given only provisional burial. Survivors continued to perform mourning rites until the body decayed to the point where the soul was believed to have left it and to have been admitted into the spiritual realm. The ancient Egyptian *Book of the Dead* gave instructions for sacrifices and rituals to help a dying or deceased person achieve a rightful place in the community of the dead (Kastenbaum & Aisenberg, 1972).

Some modern social customs have evolved from ancient beliefs and practices. Embalming goes back to a practice common in ancient Egypt and China: mummification, preserving a body so the soul can return to it. A traditional Jewish custom is never to leave a dying person alone, even for an instant (Gordon, 1975; Heller, 1975). Anthropologists suggest that the original reason for this may have been a belief (widespread among ancient peoples) that evil spirits hover around a dying person, trying to enter the body (Ausubel, 1964).

The sarcophagus of King Tutankhamon, whose body was preserved by mummification, a forerunner of the contemporary custom of embalming. Such social conventions reflect cultural beliefs about death: the ancient Egyptians preserved the body so that the soul later could reenter it.

Such social conventions, and the attitudes they reflect, are closely linked with *psychological* aspects of death: how people feel about their own death and about the death of those close to them. Rituals give people facing a loss something important to do at a time when they otherwise would feel helpless. Some rituals allow for extended interaction with the dying or dead person and affirm the strength and efficacy of the community (Kastenbaum & Aisenberg, 1972). The Jewish deathbed vigil not only provides spiritual solace to the dying but helps alleviate any guilt survivors might feel (Gordon, 1975; Heller, 1975).

An Orthodox Jewish funeral is designed to help the bereaved confront the reality of death. The simple coffin (often a plain pine box) is kept closed. At the cemetery, mourners shovel dirt into the grave. After the funeral, all who attend are invited to the home of the nearest relative, where, throughout the week of *shiva*—a period of intense mourning following a death—mourners vent their feelings and share memories of the deceased. During the following year, the bereaved are gradually drawn back into the life of the community (Gordon, 1975; Heller, 1975).

By contrast, many people in contemporary American society have a great deal of trouble coming to terms with death. Avoidance or denial has been fostered by social conventions that contrast sharply with those of Orthodox Judaism and of Louisa May Alcott's era: isolation of dying persons in hospitals or nursing homes; refusal to openly discuss their condition with them; and reluctance to visit, thus leaving them to cope with dying alone.

THE STUDY OF DEATH: THANATOLOGY AND DEATH EDUCATION

Thanatology, the study of death and dying—or "the study of life with death left in" (Kastenbaum, 1993, p. 76)—is arousing a great deal of interest as people come to recognize the importance of integrating death into life.

How can people prepare for their own death, or the death of those they love? How much should terminally ill patients be told about their situation? These are among the questions dealt with in *death education:* programs to teach people about death and to help them deal with it personally and professionally. Such programs are offered to students, social workers, doctors, nurses, and other professionals who work with dying people and survivors, and to the community. Goals include allaying death-related anxieties; helping people to develop their own belief systems, to see death as a natural end to life, and to prepare for their own death and the death of those close to them; teaching humane ways to treat the dying; providing a realistic view of health care workers and their obligations to the dying and their families; offering an understanding of the dynamics of grief; helping suicidal people and those around them; and helping consumers decide what kinds of funeral services they want (Leviton, 1977).

HOSPICE CARE

Along with the growing tendency to face death openly and honestly, movements have arisen to make dying more humane. These include hospice care and support groups for dying people and their families.

Hospice care is warm, personal, patient- and family-centered care for the terminally ill, focused on relief of pain, control of symptoms, and quality of life. It can be given in a hospital or another institution, at home, or through some combination of home and institution.

The hospice movement began in London in 1968 in response to a need for special facilities and special care for dying patients. A typical hospital is set up to treat acute illness, with the goal of curing patients and sending them home well. As a result, dying patients in a hospital often receive needless tests and useless treatments, are given less attention than patients with better chances of recovery, and are constrained by rules that are not relevant to them. And hospital care for an extended terminal illness has become enormously expensive.

Today there are about 2,000 hospice programs nationwide, and more than 1 million patients have used their services. More than 8 out of 10 hospice patients have cancer; most of the rest have AIDS or heart disease. Medicare and some health insurance policies will pay for hospice services (National Hospice Organization, undated).

The hospice philosophy is summed up in the words of its founder, Cicely Saunders: "You matter to the last moment of your life, and we will do all we can, not only to help you die peacefully, but to live until you die" (National Hospice Organization, undated, p. 6). The emphasis is on *palliative care,* on relieving pain and suffering and allowing patients to die in peace and dignity. Doctors, nurses, social workers, psychologists, aides, clergy, friends, and volunteers work

(Grantpix/Monkmeyer)

An elderly cancer patient hugs her visiting grandchildren in a hospice in West Covina, California. Hospice care is personalized and patient-centered; family members often take an active part in care.

together to treat symptoms, to keep patients as comfortable and alert as possible, to show interest in and kindness to them and their families, and to help families deal with the illness and ultimately with bereavement. Family members themselves often take an active part in the patient's care.

In a study in which terminally ill cancer patients were randomly assigned either to standard hospital care or to hospice care, the hospice patients and the family members most involved with their day-to-day care were more satisfied than the hospital patients and their relatives. The difference in satisfaction seemed to reflect the greater time spent by the hospice teams in helping patients and their families cope with impending death (Kane, Wales, Bernstein, Leibowitz, & Kaplan, 1984). As a leading thanatologist has written, "The most profound social value actualized by successful hospice programs is perhaps the simplest: the community has not retreated from death and loss" (Kastenbaum, 1993, p. 81).

FACING DEATH

All deaths are different, just as all lives are different. The experience of dying is not the same for an accident victim, a patient with terminal cancer, a person who commits suicide, and someone who dies instantaneously of a heart attack. Nor is the experience of loss the same for their survivors. The timing-of-events model (see Chapter 11) suggests why death does not mean the same thing to an 85-year-old man with excruciatingly painful arthritis, a 56-year-old woman at the height of a brilliant legal career who discovers she has leukemia, and a 20-year-old who dies of an overdose of drugs. Nor, as contextual theorists would point out, is death the same for a Brahman in India as for a homeless person in New York. Cohort also plays a role. Among older first-generation Japanese Americans, acceptance of the inevitable may reflect Buddhist teachings; but third-generation Japanese Americans have been found to be less accepting, not only because they are younger but because they have grown up with the American belief in the ability to control one's destiny (Kalish & Reynolds, 1976).

Yet, all people are human, and just as there are commonalities in adults' lives, there are similarities in the way adults face death at different ages. Let's look first at how young, middle-aged, and older adults feel about dying, and then at changes that may occur as death approaches.

ATTITUDES TOWARD DEATH AND DYING

Do you ever think about your own death? Do you think about it as much as your parents or grandparents? How do adults of different ages cope with the knowledge that they must die?

Young Adulthood

Most young adults avoid thinking about death. Of course, they understand in an abstract way that it does occur. Adolescents are influenced by the *personal fable*— an egocentric belief that they are unique or special, are not subject to the natural rules that govern the rest of the world, and can take almost any kind of risk without danger (Elkind, 1984). This belief fades as young adults take on sobering occupational and family responsibilities, but young adults still do not like to think that death can happen to them (Kastenbaum, 1977).

Those who have finished their education or training and have embarked on careers, marriage, or parenthood are eager to live the lives they have been preparing for. If they are suddenly taken ill or badly injured, they are likely to feel more intensely emotional about imminent death than people in any other period of life (Pattison, 1977). They are extremely frustrated: they have worked terribly hard—for nothing. Their frustration turns to rage, and that rage often makes young adults troublesome hospital patients.

Homosexuals (and others) who develop AIDS in their twenties or thirties must face issues of death and dying at an age when they would normally be dealing with such issues of young adulthood as establishing an intimate relationship. Rather than having a lifetime of losses as a gradual preparation for the final loss of life, "the gay man may find his own health, the health of his friends, and the fabric of his community all collapsing at once" (Cadwell, 1994, p. 4).

Middle Adulthood

It is in middle age that most people realize they are indeed going to die. As they read the obituary pages—which they are likely to do more regularly than before—they find more and more familiar names, and they may compare the ages with their own. Their bodies send them signals that they are not so young, agile, and hearty as they once were; and they may become more introspective (see Chapter 11). Often—especially after the death of both parents—there is a new awareness of being the "older generation" (Scharlach & Fredriksen, 1993).

Middle-aged people perceive time in a new way. Previously, they thought in terms of how many years they had been alive; now they think of how many years are left until death, and of how to make the most of those years (Neugarten, 1967). The realization that death is certain and that the time remaining is limited may be an impetus for a major life change. When Saul Alinsky, a community organizer in Chicago, was asked what had made him decide to devote his life to organizing working-class people, he recalled a time when he had been gravely ill: "I realized then that I was going to die. I had always known that in some abstract sense, of course, but for the first time I really knew it deep inside me. And I made up my mind that before I died I would do something that would really make a difference in the world" (S. Alinsky, personal communication, 1966).

Even people who outwardly continue their previous patterns of living often make subtle shifts and more conscious choices. Awareness that time is shortening may lead them to take stock of careers, marriages, relationships with children, friendships, values, and how they spend their time and energy (see Box 11-2 in Chapter 11).

Late Adulthood

In general, older people are less anxious about death than middle-aged people (Bengtson, Cuellar, & Ragan, 1975). They are more likely to use emotion-focused coping strategies (see Chapter 12). Through the years, as people lose friends and relatives, they gradually reorganize their thoughts and feelings to accept their own mortality. Physical losses and other problems of old age may diminish their pleasure in living.

According to Erikson (see Chapter 11), people in late adulthood must deal with the last of eight crises: *integrity versus despair*. Those who resolve this final crisis achieve a wisdom that enables them to accept both what they have done with their lives and their impending death. Peck's adjustments of old age (see Chapter 12) may help people cope. People who feel that their lives have been meaningful are usually better able to face death.

Some, though, have complex feelings—like 82-year-old Rita Duskin, the mother of one of the authors of this book, who wrote the following lines shortly before her second, fatal, heart attack:

> I refuse to believe I am a piece of dust scuttering through uncaring space. I believe I count—that I have work to do—that there is need of me. I have a place. I want to live. The moment is Now—Now is my forever. I am still somebody—somebody on whom nothing is lost. With my last breath, I sing a psalm. (R. Duskin, personal communication, February 1986)

Thus acknowledgment of death may be mixed with a poignant affirmation of the preciousness of the life that is slipping away.

According to Erikson, people in the last stage of life must deal with the personality crisis of integrity versus despair. The outcome may be wisdom that enables them to accept their coming death, as well as the way they have lived their lives.

APPROACHING DEATH

What kinds of changes do people undergo shortly before death? How do they come to terms with its imminence?

Physical and Psychological Changes

Psychological changes often begin to take place even before there are overt physiological signs of dying. In Chapter 6, we noted that a terminal drop in intellectual functioning often appears at this time (Kleemeier, 1962; K. F. Riegel & Riegel, 1972). Terminal drop is sometimes attributed to chronic ailments that sap mental energy and motivation. It affects abilities that are relatively unaffected by age, such as vocabulary (N. White & Cunningham, 1988), and it is seen in people who die young as well as those who die at a more advanced age.

Terminal drop may predict which individuals in a tested group are within a few years of death (Palmore, 1982). One research team (Siegler, McCarty, & Logue, 1982), using data from the Duke Longitudinal Study, compared scores on intelligence and memory tests of people who died within 1 year of testing with scores of people who died 8 to 13 years afterward and people who died 14 or more years afterward or were still alive. Those who survived longest, regardless of age, tended to have had the highest scores on both verbal and nonverbal items (see Figure 13-1).

Personality changes also show up during the terminal period. In one study, 80 people age 65 to 91 were given psychological tests. Afterward, the researchers compared the scores of those who died within 1 year with the scores of those who lived an average of 3 more years. The people who died within 1 year had lower scores on cognitive tests, indicating terminal drop; and on the whole, they also were less introspective and more docile. Individual differences had to do with what was going on in people's lives at the time of testing. Those who were dealing with a crisis and were close to death were more afraid of and more preoccupied with death than those facing similar crises who were not close to death; but those close to death whose lives were relatively stable at the time showed neither special fear of death nor preoccupation with it (Lieberman & Coplan, 1970). These observations suggest a psychosomatic relationship, in which psychological changes are related to physiological changes in the body, and vice versa. The changes cannot simply be effects of a single episode of disease, since people who later recovered from acute illnesses did not show the same pattern of decline as those who later died from the same kinds of illnesses.

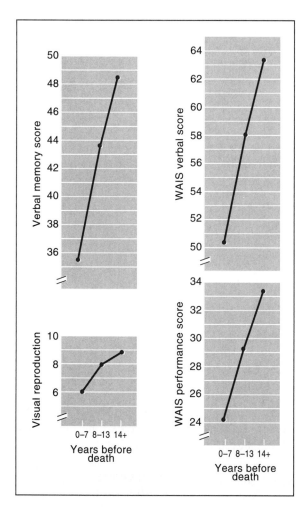

FIGURE 13-1

Effects of terminal drop on memory and intelligence. People closer to death performed worse on verbal and visual memory tests and on the verbal and nonverbal performance sections of the Wechsler Adult Intelligence Scale (WAIS).

(SOURCE: Siegler et al., 1982, fig. 2.)

BOX 13-1

THE CUTTING EDGE

Near-Death Experiences

When the psychoanalyst Carl Jung had a heart attack in 1944, he had a vision in which he entered the antechamber of a gigantic stone temple floating in space. A Hindu clothed in white robes sat silently on a stone bench before the gate to the temple, which was surrounded by burning candles, "and," Jung (1961) later wrote, "I knew that he expected me." But before Jung could enter the temple, the figure of his doctor floated up from the earth below. Mutely, the doctor informed him that he had been sent to say that Jung must return. "I was profoundly disappointed," Jung's report continues, "for now . . . I was not to be allowed to enter the temple, to join the people in whose company I belonged. . . . Suddenly the terrifying thought came to me that Dr. H. would have to die in my stead." On the day Jung was able to sit up for the first time since his attack, "Dr. H. took to his bed and did not leave it again. . . . Soon afterward he died of septicemia [blood poisoning]" (pp. 289–293).

Many people who have come close to death from drowning, cardiac arrest, or other causes have described *near-death experiences*—profound, subjective events that sometimes result in dramatic changes in values, beliefs, behavior, and attitudes toward life and death (Greyson, 1993). These experiences often include a new clarity of thinking, a feeling of well-being, a sense of being out of the body, and visions of bright lights or mystical encounters. Such experiences have been reported by an estimated 30 to 40 percent of hospital patients who were revived after coming close to death (Ring, 1980; Sabom, 1982) and by about 5 percent of adult Americans in a nationwide poll (Gallup & Proctor, 1982).

Near-death experiences have been explained as a response to a perceived threat of death (a *psychological* theory); as a result of biological states that accompany the process of dying (a *physiological* theory); and as a foretaste of an actual state of bliss after death (a *transcendental* theory). A recent study of such experiences, both in people who actually did come close to death and in others who only thought they were close

Some people who have come close to death have had visions or other experiences that are sometimes interpreted as a result of physiological or psychological changes on the brink of death (see Box 13-1).

Kübler-Ross: Stages of Dying

Elisabeth Kübler-Ross, a psychiatrist who works with dying people, is widely credited with having inspired the current interest in the psychology of death and dying. She found that most patients welcome an opportunity to speak openly about their condition, and that most are aware of being close to death even when they have not been told how sick they are.

After speaking with some 500 terminally ill patients, Kübler-Ross (1969, 1970) outlined five stages in coming to terms with death (see Table 13-1 for a fuller description and illustration of each). The stages are (1) denial (refusal to accept the reality of what is happening); (2) anger; (3) bargaining for extra time (see Box 13-2); (4) depression; and (5) ultimate acceptance. She also proposed a similar progression in the feelings of people facing imminent bereavement (Kübler-Ross, 1975).

to death, found some support for all three theories (J. E. Owens, Cook, & Stevenson, 1990). Researchers studied the medical records and personal accounts of 28 hospital patients who would have died if doctors had not saved them, and of 30 who mistakenly thought they were dying. The two groups of patients had very similar sensations, a finding that lends support to the psychological theory. But those who had actually been near death were more likely to report certain aspects of the near-death experience—evidence for the physiological theory. And the researchers saw support for the transcendental theory in the fact that the dying patients reported clearer thinking, despite the likelihood that their brain functioning was in fact diminished.

Near-death experiences may be classified as cognitive, affective, paranormal, or transcendental, depending on what elements appear to predominate (Greyson, 1993). *Cognitive* elements are changes in thought processes. Time seems to slow down, thoughts speed up, and people may feel a sudden sense of understanding as their whole life seems to pass before them in instanta-

neous, panoramic review. *Affective* elements are changes in emotional state: overwhelming feelings of peace, painlessness, joy, love, and oneness with the universe, often emanating from an encounter with a diffuse being of light. *Paranormal,* or psychic, elements include heightened sensations, extrasensory perception, visions of the future, and observation of one's body from an outside vantage point. *Transcendental* elements may include journeys to a higher realm (such as Jung experienced), encounters with angels or spirits of the dead, and a barrier, or point of no return to the material world.

Near-death experiences are sometimes said to offer a reassuring, or even romanticized, preview of death. If so, such experiences might be expected to encourage thoughts of suicide, but studies show a paradoxical decrease in suicidal thoughts. One suggested explanation is that a near-death experience enhances the "sense of meaning and purpose in life, a view of problems that transcends the individual, and a sense of belonging to something greater than the self" (Greyson, 1992–1993, p. 87).

Kübler-Ross's model has been criticized and modified by other professionals who work with dying patients. They point out that Kübler-Ross's "stages" are not true stages, as in organismic theories. Although the emotions that Kübler-Ross describes are common, not everyone goes through all five stages, and people may go through the stages in different sequences. A person may go back and forth between anger and depression, for example, or may feel both at once. Instead of the orderly progression in the theoretical model, dying people may show "a jumble of conflicting or alternating reactions running the gamut from denial to acceptance, with a tremendous variation affected by age, sex, race, ethnic group, social setting, and personality" (Butler & Lewis, 1982, p. 370). Unfortunately, some health professionals assume that these stages are inevitable and universal, and others feel that they have failed if they cannot bring a patient to "the ultimate goal, the big number 5—'acceptance' of death" (Leviton, 1977, p. 259).

Dying, like living, is an individual experience. For some people, denial or anger may be a healthier way to face death than calm acceptance. Thus Kübler-Ross's description—useful as it is in helping us understand the feelings of people who are facing the end of life—should not be held up as a model or a criterion for a "good death."

TABLE 13-1   KÜBLER-ROSS'S STAGES OF DYING

Stage	Explanation	Example
Denial	Most people respond with shock to the knowledge that they are about to die. Their first thought is, "Oh, no, this can't be happening to me." When people around the patient also deny reality, he or she has no one to talk to and, as a result, feels deserted and isolated. When allowed some hope along with the first announcement and given the assurance that they will not be deserted no matter what happens, people can drop the initial shock and denial rather quickly.	Mrs. K., 28, a mother of two young children, was hospitalized with a terminal liver disease. After visiting a faith healer, she told the hospital chaplain, "It was wonderful. I have been healed. I am going to show the doctors that God will heal me. I am all well now" (1970, p. 43). Eventually, she showed that she was no longer denying her illness when, holding the doctor's hand, she said, "You have such warm hands. I hope you are going to be with me when I get colder and colder" (1970, p. 45).
Anger	After realizing that they are dying, people become angry. They ask, "Why me?" They become envious of those around them who are young and healthy. They are really angry not at these people but at the youth and health they themselves do not have. They need to express their rage to get rid of it.	Mr. O., a successful businessman who had been a dominant, controlling person all his life, became enraged as Hodgkin's disease took away his control over his life. His anger dissipated somewhat after his wife and the hospital nurses gave him back a measure of control by consulting him on time and length of family visits and times for various hospital procedures.
Bargaining	The next thought may be, "Yes, it's happening to me—*but*." The *but* is an attempt to bargain for time. People may pray to God, "If you just let me live to see my daughter graduated . . . *or* my son married . . . *or* my grandchild born . . . I'll be a better person . . . *or* I won't ask for anything more . . . *or* I'll accept my lot in life." These bargains represent the acknowledgment that time is limited and life is finite. When people drop the *but*, they are able to say, "Yes, me."	A woman in great pain was very sad at the thought that she would not be able to attend the wedding of her oldest and favorite child. With the aid of self-hypnosis, she controlled her pain; and during the period before the wedding she promised that she would ask no more if she could live only long enough to be there. She did attend, a radiant mother of the groom, and when she returned to the hospital, despite her fatigue she told the doctor, "Now don't forget I have another son!" (1970, p. 83).

Stage	Explanation	Example
Depression	In this stage, people need to cry, to grieve for the loss of their own life. By expressing the depths of their anguish, they can overcome depression much more quickly than if they feel pressured to hide their sorrow.	Mr. H., who had enjoyed singing in the choir, teaching Sunday school, and doing other church and community work, was no longer able to carry out these activities because of his illness. He said, "The one thing that makes life worthless right now is the fact that I look upon myself . . . as not ever being able to go back to these things" (1970, p. 103). Other elements in his depression were his feeling that his wife did not appreciate his involvement in these nonpaying activities that he considered valuable, and the fact that he had never completed the mourning process for his parents and a daughter who had died. After he reviewed his feelings with the doctor and the chaplain and his wife reassured him that she did appreciate him, his depression lifted.
Acceptance	Finally, people can acknowledge, "My time is very close now, and it's all right." This is not necessarily a happy time, but people who have worked through their anxieties and anger about death and have resolved their unfinished business end up with a feeling of peace with themselves and the world.	Mrs. W., 58, was facing the pain and the knowledge of abdominal cancer with courage and dignity—until her husband begged the surgeons to do an operation that could prolong her life. She changed radically, becoming restless and anxious, asking often for pain relief, and screaming and hallucinating in the operating room so that the surgery did not take place. After husband and wife spoke separately with the doctor, it became clear that Mrs. W. was ready to die but felt that she could not until her husband was able to accept her illness and let her go. When he finally saw that his need to keep her alive conflicted with her need to detach herself from the world (including him) and die, both partners were able to share their feelings and accept her death.

SOURCE: Kübler-Ross, 1969, 1970.

BOX 13-2

THE MULTICULTURAL CONTEXT

Postponing Death

President Thomas Jefferson died on the Fourth of July, the anniversary of the Declaration of Independence, of which he had been the principal author. Jefferson's last words were "Is it the Fourth?"

Is there such a thing as a will to live? Can people postpone their own death so that they can celebrate a birthday, an anniversary, a grandchild's wedding, or another significant event?

Studies have examined death rates around two important holidays—Passover and the Harvest Moon festival—each identified with, and meaningful to, a certain ethnic group and not to others, who thus can serve as comparison groups. On the Jewish feast of Passover, more than 75 percent of American Jews attend a *seder* (a ceremonial dinner), usually at home with close family members (Phillips & King, 1988). During the Chinese Harvest Moon festival, the senior woman of the house directs a ceremonial meal there (Phillips & Smith, 1990); this holiday emphasizes the symbolic importance of older women and is more important to them than to young women or to men of any age. Passover usually falls near Easter (the last supper of Jesus and the disciples is said to have been a seder), and the Harvest Moon festival takes place in autumn. But the date of each changes from year to year by as much as 4 weeks.

In two California studies, death rates from natural causes were found to be lower just before each of these two holidays for people of Jewish and Chinese extraction, respectively, and higher just afterward. For Jewish people, the "Passover effect" was strongest if the festival fell on a weekend, when more people tend to celebrate it; it was not affected by the specific date of the holiday.

The effect was especially strong among Jewish men, who usually lead the seder. It was not found in African Americans, in Asians, or in Jewish infants, none of whom celebrate Passover (Phillips & King, 1988). Similarly, the "Harvest Moon effect" did not appear among Jewish people or the general population, or among elderly Chinese men or younger Chinese women. It appeared only among Chinese women over age 75, the group to whom this holiday means the most. Their death rate was unusually low before the Harvest Moon festival and unusually high afterward. The pattern held for the three leading causes of death in the elderly: heart disease, cancer, and stroke (Phillips & Smith, 1990).

How might such effects work? It is not likely that stress or overeating causes high death rates after these holidays; these factors would not explain the very much lower death rates before the holidays. Perhaps psychosomatic processes allow some people to postpone death until they have reached an occasion important to them. They may will themselves to live just a little while longer, putting forth every ounce of psychological and physical strength so as to experience just one more celebration.

Conversely, research suggests that people with a mystical, fatalistic belief that they will soon die do in fact die sooner than those who do not have such a belief (Phillips, Ruth, & Wagner, 1993). A dual effect based on gender showed up in a study of more than 2 million deaths from natural causes. A woman was more likely to die in the week after her birthday than at any other time, but a man was more likely to die just before his birthday (Phillips, 1992). It may be that birthdays serve as an anticipated social event for women, but a discouraging stock-taking for men.

FACING BEREAVEMENT

Bereavement is the loss of someone to whom one feels close, and the process of adjustment to it. Bereavement can affect practically all aspects of a survivor's life, often starting with a change in status and roles—for example, from a wife to a widow or from a son or daughter to an orphan. *Grief* is the emotional response experienced in the early phases of bereavement; it can take many forms, from rage to a feeling of emptiness. Although bereavement and grief are universal experiences, they also have a cultural context. *Mourning* refers not to feelings but to behavior—the ways, usually culturally accepted, in which the bereaved and the community act while adjusting to a death. Examples of mourning include the all-night Irish wake, at which friends and family toast the memory of the dead person; and flying a flag at half-mast after the death of a public figure (Lund, 1993b).

Traditional cultures help people deal with bereavement through customs that have well-understood meanings and provide a reassuring anchor amid the turbulence of loss. These customs vary greatly from culture to culture. In Japan, religious rituals encourage survivors to maintain contact with the deceased. Families keep an altar in the home dedicated to their ancestors; they talk to their dead loved ones and offer them food or cigars (Stroebe, Gergen, Gergen, & Stroebe, 1992). Alex Haley, in *Roots* (1976), observed that in Gambia the dead were still

(AP/Wide World Photos)

Mourning customs vary greatly across cultures. In Mexico, young and old alike sit on tombs of relatives, keeping an all-night vigil on the nationwide Day of the Dead. Family members clean the graves, plant flowers, light candles, and even offer the deceased person's favorite foods.

considered part of the community. For example, at his graduation, 10-year-old Kunta Kinte felt proud not only of his family sitting in the front row but of his ancestors buried beyond the village, especially his beloved grandmother. By contrast, among Native Americans, the Hopi try to forget a dead person as quickly as possible. They believe that death brings pollution and that the spirits of the dead are to be feared; therefore, they do not keep photos or other reminders of someone who has died. Muslims in Egypt express grief through deep sorrow; Muslims in Bali are encouraged to laugh, be joyful, and suppress sadness (Stroebe et al., 1992).

There is no one "best" way to cope with loss. What works for one culture or one family may not work for another. In helping people handle grief, counselors need to take both ethnic traditions and individual differences into account.

Let's look next at forms and patterns of grief. Then we'll focus on how people adjust to one kind of bereavement that happens to many adults, especially as they grow older: loss of a spouse. Finally, we'll discuss two other particularly difficult losses: death of a parent and death of a child.

FORMS AND PATTERNS OF GRIEF

Grief is a highly personal experience. Recent research has challenged earlier notions of a single, "normal" pattern of grieving and a "normal" timetable for recovery. For example, a widow talking to her late husband might once have been considered emotionally disturbed; now this is recognized as a very common and helpful behavior (Lund, 1993b). And while some people recover fairly quickly after bereavement, others never completely get over it.

Anticipatory Grief

The family and friends of a person who has been ill for a long time often prepare themselves for the loss through *anticipatory grief*, symptoms of grief experienced while the person is still alive. Anticipatory grief may help survivors handle the actual death more easily (J. T. Brown & Stoudemire, 1983). Women who can prepare themselves for widowhood psychologically and in practical terms—for example, by discussing pensions and insurance with their husbands—may make a more positive adjustment, though they may be no less distressed after the loss (O'Bryant, 1990–1991). In other cases, however, preparation seems to have little impact on adjustment. One study found that elderly widows who had expected their husbands' deaths and "rehearsed" for widowhood by thinking and talking about the future were no better or worse adjusted than women whose husbands had died unexpectedly (Hill, Thompson, & Gallagher, 1988).

Grief Work: A Three-Stage Pattern

Perhaps the most common and most widely studied pattern of grief after death is that the bereaved person accepts the painful reality of the loss, gradually lets go of the bond with the dead person, readjusts to life without that person, and develops new interests and relationships. This process of *grief work* generally takes place in three phases—though, as with Kübler-Ross's stages, they may vary (J. T. Brown & Stoudemire, 1983; R. Schulz, 1978):

1. *Shock and disbelief.* This first phase may last several weeks, especially after a sudden or unexpected death. Immediately following a death, survivors often feel lost and confused. Their shock, and their inability to believe in the death, may protect them from more intense reactions. Shortness of breath, tightness in the chest or throat, nausea, and a feeling of emptiness in the abdomen are common. As awareness of the loss sinks in, the initial numbness gives way to overwhelming feelings of sadness, which are commonly expressed by frequent crying.

2. *Preoccupation with the memory of the dead person.* The second phase may last 6 months or longer. The survivor tries to come to terms with the death but cannot yet accept it. Frequent crying continues, and often insomnia, fatigue, and loss of appetite. A widow may relive her husband's death and their entire relationship. From time to time, she may be seized by a feeling that her dead husband is present: she will hear his voice, sense his presence in the room, even see his face before her. She may have vivid dreams of him. These experiences diminish with time, though they may recur—perhaps for years—on such occasions as the anniversary of the marriage or of the death.

3. *Resolution.* The final phase has arrived when the bereaved person renews interest in everyday activities. Memories of the dead person bring fond feelings mingled with sadness, rather than sharp pain and longing. A widower may still miss his dead wife; but he knows that life must go on, and he becomes more active socially. He gets out more, sees people, picks up old interests, and perhaps discovers new ones.

Most bereaved people eventually are able, with the help of family and friends, to come to terms with their loss and resume normal lives. For some, however, *grief therapy*—treatment to help the bereaved cope with their loss—is indicated (R. Schulz, 1978). Professional grief therapists help survivors express sorrow, guilt, hostility, and anger. They encourage clients to review the relationship with the deceased and to integrate the fact of the death into their lives so that they can be free to develop new relationships and new ways of behaving toward friends and relatives.

Varied Reactions to Loss

How universal is the pattern described above? Recently, researchers have found that grieving does not necessarily follow a straight line from shock to resolution. Instead, it may be a succession of emotional ups and downs of varying lengths, which may eventually subside but never completely flatten out (Lund, 1993b). Furthermore, there are considerable differences in reactions to bereavement. Some people mourn intensely for a very long time: Queen Victoria of England wore black and mourned her husband, Prince Albert, for the last 40 years of her life. Others, apparently, hardly mourn at all.

One team of psychologists (Wortman & Silver, 1989) reviewed studies of reactions to major losses: in some cases, the death of a loved one; in other cases, loss of a person's own mobility as a result of spinal injury. The psychologists found some common assumptions to be more myth than fact. Five common beliefs about loss are: (1) Everyone who suffers a severe loss will be distraught and probably depressed. (2) People who do not show such distress will have psychological problems later on. (3) A bereaved person has to "work through" a loss by focusing on it and trying to make sense of it. (4) The intense distress of mourning will come to an end within a fairly short time. (5) People will eventually accept a loss, both intellectually and emotionally. According to these researchers, none of these beliefs is valid for everyone.

First, they say, depression is far from universal. From 3 weeks to 2 years after their loss, only 15 to 35 percent of widows, widowers, and victims of spinal cord injury showed signs of depression. *Second*, failure to show distress at the outset does not necessarily lead to problems; in fact, the people who were most upset immediately after a loss or injury were likely to be most troubled up to 2 years later. *Third*, not everyone needs to work through a loss or will benefit from doing so; some of the people who did the most intense grief work had more problems later. *Fourth*, not everyone returns to normal quickly. Studies have found that parents of children killed by drunk drivers are likely to be functioning poorly up to 7 years later, and that more than 40 percent of widows and widowers show moderate to severe anxiety up to 4 years after the spouse's death, especially if it was sudden. *Fifth*, people cannot always resolve their grief and accept their loss. Parents and spouses of people who die in car accidents often have painful memories of the loved one even after many years (Wortman & Silver, 1989).

Rather than a single three-stage pattern, this research found three main patterns of grieving. In the expected pattern, the mourner goes from high to low distress. In a second pattern, the mourner does not experience intense distress immediately or later. In a third pattern, the mourner remains distressed for a long time (Wortman & Silver, 1989).

The finding that grief takes varied forms and patterns has important implications for helping people deal with loss. It may be unnecessary and even harmful to urge or lead mourners to "work through" a loss, or to expect them to follow a set pattern of emotional reactions—just as it may be unnecessary and harmful to expect all dying patients to experience Kübler-Ross's stages. Respect for differing patterns of grief can help the bereaved deal with loss without making them feel that their reactions are abnormal.

SURVIVING A SPOUSE

Widowhood is one of the greatest emotional challenges that can face any human being. It means not only the loss of a life partner but the disruption of virtually every aspect of the survivor's life. In a classic ranking of stressful life events, the event identified as requiring the most adjustment was death of a spouse (see Table 4-3 in Chapter 4). Yet widowhood can also be seen as a developmental experience.

(Julian Calder/Woodfin Camp and Associates)

Widowhood is a tremendous emotional challenge—not only because of the loss of a life partner, but because it changes almost all aspects of the survivor's life. Women, who tend to live longer than men, are more likely to be widowed.

Because women tend to live longer than men, and tend to be younger than their husbands, they are more likely to be widowed (O'Bryant, 1990–1991). They also are more likely to be stronger for the experience (Umberson, Wortman, & Kessler, 1992), though worse off economically. In the United States, nearly 49 percent of women over age 65 are widowed and have not remarried, as compared with only 14 percent of men over 65. Among those over 85, 80 percent of women but only 43 percent of men are widowed and have not remarried. The average white woman is widowed at age 56, the average African American woman at 49, and the average Hispanic woman at 48 (U.S. Bureau of the Census, 1990).

Adjustments

Aside from grieving, how does losing a husband or wife affect day-to-day life? A survivor of a long marriage generally faces many emotional and practical problems. A good marriage can leave a gaping emotional void: the loss of a lover, a confidant, a good friend, and a steady companion. Even with a bad marriage, a loss may be felt.

For one thing, the survivor no longer has the *role* of spouse. This loss may be especially hard for a woman who has structured her life and her identity around caring for her husband (Saunders, 1981). It also affects working people of both sexes who no longer have a partner to come home to, and retirees who have no one to talk to—or argue with.

Social life changes, too. Friends and family usually rally to the mourner's side immediately after the death; but then they go back to their own lives. Married friends, uncomfortable with the thought that bereavement could happen to them too, may avoid the widowed person. Both widowed men and women often feel like a "fifth wheel" with couples who have been longtime friends (Brubaker, 1990). However, both widows and widowers see friends more often than married people do, perhaps because they have more time and more need for social contact; and, although most widowed people make new friends, most of their friends continue to be old ones (Field & Minkler, 1988). Widowed men are more likely to seek the companionship of women. Women—especially middle-aged and older ones—usually make friends with other widows but have a hard time meeting and forming relationships with men (Brecher & Editors of Consumer Reports Books, 1984; Lopata, 1977, 1979).

Economic hardship can be a major problem. On average, family income drops 44 percent after the death of a spouse (J. Healy, 1983). When the husband has been the main breadwinner, his widow is deprived of his income; when the husband is widowed, he has to buy many of the services his wife provided. When both spouses have been employed, the loss of one income can be a blow (Lopata, 1977, 1979).

Not surprisingly, widowed people of both sexes have higher rates of mental illness, especially depression, than married people (Balkwell, 1981). Widowed men tend to be more vulnerable to depression than widowed women, perhaps because they are less likely than women to have formed other intimate relationships. Among women, a primary factor in depression seems to be financial strain; among men, the stress of managing a household (Umberson et al., 1992).

Although it takes time for the pain of loss to heal, most bereaved spouses eventually rebuild their lives. They may not get over the loss, but they get used to it. Loneliness and sadness give way to confidence in the ability to manage on their own. The people who adjust best are those who keep busy, take on new roles (such as new paid or volunteer work), or become more deeply involved in ongoing activities. They see friends often (which helps more than frequent visits with their children), and they may take part in support groups for widows. Social support—including being encouraged to express feelings without being given unsolicited advice—is especially important in the first few months; survivors who cope well during that period usually do better than others in the long run. Quality of relationships may be more important than frequency of contact (T. B. Anderson, 1984; Balkwell, 1981; C. J. Barrett, 1978; Lund, 1989, 1993b; Vachon, Lyall, Rogers, Freedmen-Letofky, & Freeman, 1980).

Many studies have found older adults to be better adjusted to widowhood than younger adults. A common interpretation is that loss of a spouse is more traumatic in young adulthood, when it is less expected (DiGiulio, 1992). However, the reason may be that younger widowed people in these studies were more recently bereaved. One study did control for how long people had been widowed; it found that the age at which bereavement occurs has little long-term effect on morale: losing a husband or wife is no easier or harder at an earlier or a later age. Older widows and widowers did tend to have somewhat higher morale than younger ones; a crucial factor may be greater availability of companions, especially widowed peers (Balkwell, 1985).

In the short term, younger widows do have more psychological problems (Parkes & Weiss, 1983). Burdened with full responsibility for breadwinning and

(Marty Lederhandler/AP/Wide World Photos)

Stephen Schattman, age 96, and Sylvia Herman, age 82, celebrated their engagement at breakfast in a New York City diner. The couple, who first met 55 years earlier, came together again after both lost their spouses. Remarriages of widowed older adults, who often knew each other before, tend to be calmer than marriages earlier in life.

parenthood, and often with a drastically reduced standard of living, they may lack the time or energy to develop a new social life. They may find themselves resenting their children and feeling guilty about their resentment (DiGiulio, 1992). Physical health, however, is more likely to be adversely affected when loss occurs in middle age (Perkins & Harris, 1990; Wolinsky & Johnson, 1992a, 1992b).

In general, though, age is not a major factor in the grieving process; coping skills are. People who have had practice in coping with loss and have developed effective coping strategies are better able to deal with bereavement (Lund, 1993b).

Remarriage

Elderly widowers are more likely to remarry than widows, much as men of any age are more likely than women to remarry after divorce (P. C. Glick & Lin, 1986b). Men have more potential partners. And men usually feel more need to remarry; women more frequently can handle their own household needs, are sometimes reluctant to give up survivors' pension benefits, or do not want to end up caring for an infirm husband.

In one study of 24 older couples who had remarried when both partners were over 60, most had been widowed. Most of them had known each other during their first marriages or had been introduced by friends or relatives (Vinick, 1978). Why had they decided to marry again? Men tended to mention companionship and relief from loneliness; women tended to mention their feelings toward the new husband or his personal qualities. Almost all these people, who had been remarried for 2 to 6 years, were happy. Their marriages were calmer than marriages earlier in life; the partners had a "live and let live" attitude.

LOSING A PARENT

Problems of widowhood are much discussed; so are effects of caring for an aging parent (Chapter 10). Less attention has been paid to the impact on an adult child of the death of a parent. Yet that loss can be hard to bear: "Not only is there the loss of the oldest and one of the most important (yet ambivalent) relationships in one's life, but there [may be] the trauma of breaking up a household in which one may have grown up and of losing the older buffer between oneself and death" (Dainoff, 1989, p. 64). This connection may be stronger today than ever before, since, with longer life expectancies, it is not unusual for a parent to remain alive during the first 50 years or more of a child's life (Umberson & Chen, 1994). Half of all children become orphans by their mid-fifties and 3 out of 4 by their early sixties (Winsborough, Bumpass, & Aquilino, 1991).

A survey of 220 bereaved adult children found that 1 out of 4 still suffered social and emotional problems 1 to 5 years after the parent's death (Scharlach, 1991). In-depth interviews with 83 volunteers, age 35 to 60, found a majority still experiencing emotional distress—ranging from sadness and crying to depression and thoughts of suicide—after 1 to 5 years, especially following loss of a mother. Close to half of those who had lost either parent reported continuing physical reactions, such as illness, fatigue, and a general decline in health (Scharlach & Fredriksen, 1993). While psychological distress generally surfaces quickly, health problems may show up considerably later (Umberson & Chen, 1994).

On a deeper level, the death of a parent can be a maturing experience. From an organismic perspective, it can push adults into resolving important midlife developmental issues: achieving a stronger sense of self and of personal choice, along with a greater sense of responsibility, commitment, and attachment to others and a more pressing, realistic awareness of their own mortality (M. S. Moss & Moss, 1989; Scharlach & Fredriksen, 1993). The 83 respondents mentioned above, while not a representative sample, reported changes dramatic enough to serve as "evidence of the potential importance of parental death as a developmentally significant event in midlife" (Scharlach & Fredriksen, 1993, p. 317). Let's look at some of those changes.[*]

Changes in the Self

Eight years after the distinguished actor Michael Redgrave died, his daughter, the actress Lynn Redgrave (then 50), wrote and performed a one-woman show, *Shakespeare for My Father*. In it, she finally came to terms with the hurt and frustration her father's coldness had caused her as a child. "It was a privilege to be my father's daughter," she told an interviewer. "But with it went a great price. I paid that price, and I'm stronger for it" (Ryan, 1993).

Many middle-aged adults who lose a parent experience some effect—generally positive—on their sense of self (see Table 13-2). Many feel themselves becoming more self-assertive, autonomous, self-confident, and responsible—in short,

---

[*]The discussion in the remainder of this section is largely indebted to M. S. Moss and Moss (1989) and Scharlach and Fredriksen (1993).

TABLE 13-2 SELF-REPORTED PSYCHOLOGICAL IMPACTS OF A PARENT'S DEATH

Impacts	Death of Mother (Percent)	Death of Father (Percent)
Self-concept		
More "adult"	29	43
More self-confident	19	20
More responsible	11	4
Less mature	14	3
Other	8	17
No impact	19	12
Feelings about mortality		
Increased awareness of own mortality	30	29
More accepting of own death	19	10
Made concrete plans regarding own death	10	4
Increased fear of own death	10	18
Other	14	16
No impact	17	23
Religiosity		
More religious	26	29
Less religious	11	2
Other	3	10
No impact	60	59
Personal priorities		
Personal relationships more important	35	28
Simple pleasures more important	16	13
Personal happiness more important	10	7
Material possessions less important	5	8
Other	20	8
No impact	14	36
Work or career plans		
Left job	29	16
Adjusted goals	15	10
Changed plans due to family needs	5	6
Moved	4	10
Other	13	19
No impact	34	39

SOURCE: Scharlach & Fredriksen, 1993, table 1, p. 311.

more mature—when their parents die. As one adult who had lost a mother said, "I can't call her up if I need advice anymore" (Scharlach & Fredriksen, 1993, p. 310). Orphaned middle-aged adults often feel strengthened as they review the parent's life in relation to their own. For the first time they may be able to accept and forgive the parent's failures, especially toward themselves. They also may be prompted to review their own lives and to revise their goals and activities— change jobs, go back to school, or retire. Many now place more importance on personal relationships, simple pleasures such as enjoying nature, and personal happiness, and less emphasis on material possessions. Some experience a surge of creativity as they deal with the loss by editing a parent's diary or memoirs, or (like Lynn Redgrave) writing their own. But some, especially those whose identity has been intertwined with the parent, may worry about the future, despair over their lack of self-fulfillment, and shy away from responsibility for managing their own lives.

A parent's death is a reminder of one's own mortality. It removes a "buffer" against death and may leave the adult child feeling older and unprotected. Yet sometimes it brings a less anxious acceptance of death, along with a greater sense of purpose about the time remaining. Often the loss of a parent leads people to prepare for death in concrete ways, such as making funeral arrangements or a will. Many people, especially those whose parents died young, consider the parents' age at death significant for their own lifespan. One man threw a large party for his fiftieth birthday, celebrating the fact that he had lived longer than his father. Some people make special plans for their "bonus" years. Some alter their lifestyle. "I don't want to die like my father," said one woman. "I'm on a stringent exercise program to make sure I stay healthy" (Scharlach & Fredriksen, 1993, p. 310).

Changes in Relationships

The death of a parent often brings changes in other relationships—either more intimacy or more conflict. A bereaved adult child may assume more responsibility for the surviving parent and for keeping the family together. The intense emotions of bereavement may draw siblings closer, or they may become alienated over differences that arose during the parent's final illness.

If an adult child has been taking care of a parent, the parent's death may free him or her to spend more time and emotional energy on relationships that have been temporarily neglected, such as those with a spouse or partner or with children or grandchildren. Or the death may free a middle-aged person to shed a relationship that was being maintained to meet the parent's expectations.

Recognizing the finality of death and the impossibility of saying anything more to the deceased parent, some people are motivated to resolve any conflicts in their ties to the living while there is still time. Sometimes siblings who have been estranged realize that the parent who provided a link between them is no longer there, and they try to mend the rift. People may also be moved to reconcile with their own adult children.

For many people, the bond between parent and child—powerful in life—persists after death. "Death ends a life but it does not end a relationship" (R. Anderson, 1980, p. 110). Even very old people often mention their parents as the most influential persons in their lives, and a dead parent can be an ongoing presence in a son's or daughter's life (Troll & Smith, 1976).

LOSING A CHILD

When King David, in the Bible, hears that Absalom, the favorite son who has tried to dethrone him, is dead, the king weeps: "O my son Absalom, my son, my son Absalom! Would I had died for you, O Absalom, my son, my son!" (2 Samuel, 19:1).

There is no English word for a parent who has lost a child. A person who has lost a spouse is a *widow* or *widower;* a person who has lost both parents is an *orphan*. But a person whose child has died is bereft even of an identity. A person may be somewhat emotionally prepared for the death of a spouse or a parent, but not for the death of a child.

In earlier times, it was more common for a parent to bury a child. Today, with medical advances and the increase in life expectancy in industrialized countries, a child who survives the first year of life is far more likely to live to old age, and infant mortality has reached record lows—in the United States, 8.5 deaths per 1,000 live births (Centers for Disease Control and Prevention, 1994; USDHHS, 1995). The death of a child, therefore, no matter at what age, comes as a cruel, unnatural shock, an untimely event that, in the normal course of things, should not have happened (Raphael, 1983). The parents may feel they have failed, no matter how much they loved and cared for the child, and they may find it hard to let go.

If a marriage is strong, the couple may draw closer together, supporting each other in their shared loss. But the death of a child can weaken and destroy a marriage. One spouse may blame the other. Or the husband and wife may simply have different ways of grieving and of rebuilding their lives. Unresolved issues stemming from a child's death may lead to a divorce, even years later (Brandt, 1989).

Although each mourner must cope with grief in his or her own way, some bereaved parents have found that plunging into work, interests, and other relationships, or joining a support group of bereaved parents, helps ease their pain. Some well-meaning friends tell bereaved parents not to dwell on their loss. But remembering the child in a meaningful way may be exactly what parents need to do. At the 1992 Democratic National Convention, Elizabeth Glaser, the wife of the television actor and director Paul Michael Glaser, told how, in 1981, she had contracted the HIV virus from a blood transfusion and unknowingly passed it on to her infant daughter, Ariel, in her breast milk. After Ariel died of AIDS at age 7, Elizabeth Glaser launched a crusade to increase public awareness of pediatric AIDS. By the time of her own death in 1994 at the age of 47, the foundation she established had raised more than $30 million for research and education (Kennedy, 1994).

CONTROVERSIAL ISSUES

▼

Do people have a right to take their own life? If so, under what circumstances? What should be the legal liability, if any, of someone who helps a person commit suicide? Should a doctor prescribe a medicine for a terminally ill patient that will relieve pain but may shorten the patient's life? What about giving a lethal injection to end the patient's suffering? Who decides that a life is not worth prolonging? Who decides when to stop treatment?

These are only a few of the questions that face individuals, families, physicians, and society today—questions involving the quality of life and the nature and circumstances of death. The field of medical ethics is expanding rapidly, in large part because of questions raised by recent technological advances: antibiotics that enable older patients to survive one illness only to succumb to another; respirators that keep people breathing when they are in a coma and show no brain activity or other physiological function; organ transplants that may achieve "miracles" at great risk and great cost. None of these questions has a simple answer. Each requires soul searching. Let's look at two subjects that have received much attention: suicide and euthanasia. Both involve the issue of the "right to die."

SUICIDE

Audience members at a Metropolitan Opera performance of Verdi's *Macbeth* were horrified when, during the intermission, an elderly man—Bantcho Bantchevsky—plunged to his death from a balcony. Bantchevsky was an 82-year-old vocal coach who had lived for his music and his friends. He had been lively and gregarious; but when his health began to deteriorate, he became depressed. His depression grew until he took his life, dying as theatrically as he had lived (Okun, 1988).

Many people find life so precious that they cannot understand why anyone would voluntarily end it. Yet in 1992 more than 30,000 Americans committed suicide, making it the ninth leading cause of death in the nation (USDHHS, 1995). And suicide rates in the United States are moderate compared with those in some other countries (see Figure 13-2).

Statistically, Bantcho Bantchevsky—an elderly white man—was likely to commit suicide. In most nations, suicide is most prevalent among elderly males (McIntosh, 1992; based on data from World Health Organization, 1991). White Americans end their own lives almost twice as often as African Americans, and men more often than women. In absolute numbers, more suicides occur among young white males; but by far the highest *rate* of suicide—the proportion of suicides in a given population—is among elderly white men, though this rate is falling (USDHHS, 1995; see Figure 13-3). Black men and women are more vulnerable in young adulthood, and white women in middle age. Most other minority groups also have lower overall rates than whites (USDHHS, 1995).

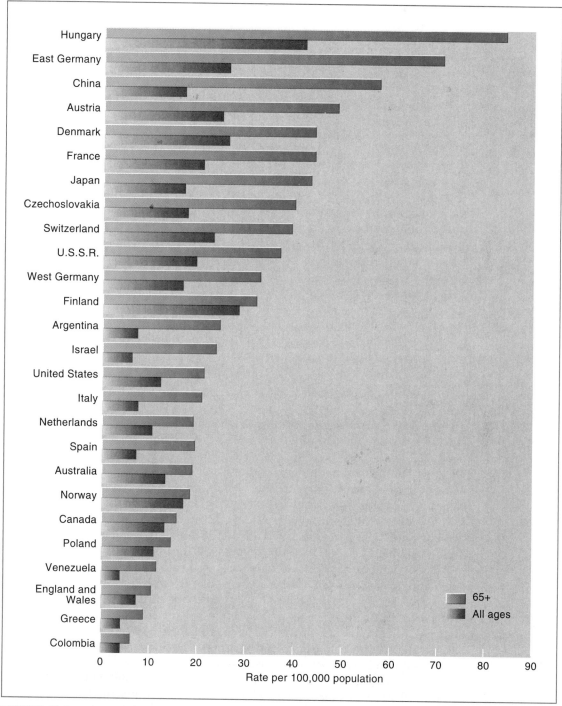

FIGURE 13-2

Suicide rates for all ages and for older adults in selected countries.

(SOURCE: McIntosh, 1992, fig. 5, p. 30; based on data from World Health Organization, 1991.)

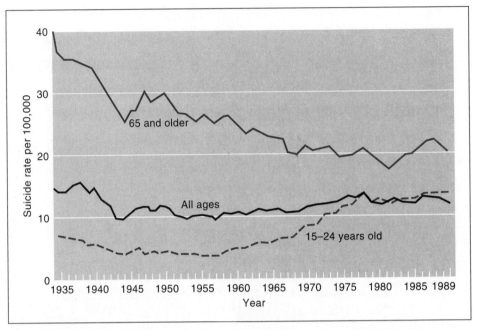

FIGURE 13-3
Suicide rates in the United States by age, showing changes from 1933 to 1989.
(SOURCE: National Center for Health Statistics, 1992.)

Older white men, after the sometimes high achievements of youth, may find it especially hard to face deprivation in old age—possibly because overidentification with work leaves them without a clear identity or social status in retirement. They may despair over a progression of losses that they are helpless to stop: of work, of friends, perhaps of a spouse, of children who may have moved away, of memory, of health, and finally of self-esteem and hope (Maris, 1981; M. Miller, 1979; Osgood, 1984; Seiden, 1981). Older African Americans seem less willing to consider suicide, in part because of religion and in part because they are used to coping with hard knocks (Kalish & Reynolds, 1976).

As with Bantchevsky, suicide often occurs in conjunction with depression or debilitating physical illness. About 15 percent of depressed people eventually kill themselves, accounting for some 30 to 70 percent of suicides in the United States (USDHHS, 1990). Other factors that increase the risk of suicide are being divorced, widowed, or unemployed; having relatives who attempted or committed suicide; having had psychiatric treatment; having undergone stressful life events; suffering from schizophrenia, substance abuse, or panic attacks; and keeping a handgun in the home. Personality factors associated with a high risk of suicide include dependency, helplessness, hopelessness, inability to accept help, difficulty in forming close relationships, poor problem-solving ability (especially under stress), extreme anxiety or irritability, difficulty in concentrating, and antisocial behavior (Boyer & Guthrie, 1985; Kellerman et al., 1992; Meehan, 1990;

Morbidity and Mortality Weekly Report, 1985; "Suicide," 1986; USDHHS, 1990, 1992; Weissman, Klerman, Markowitz, & Ouelette, 1989).

Statistics probably understate the number of suicides, since many go unreported and some are not recognized as such. Some suicides look like traffic accidents, accidental overdoses of drugs, or forgetfulness—unintentional failure to take life-preserving medicine. Studies show that 10 to 40 percent of people who commit suicide have attempted it at least once before (Meehan, 1990). The increased use of guns instead of less certain methods, such as poison, may indicate that more people who commit suicide are determined to succeed. Firearms are used in most suicides in the United States today (USDHHS, 1992).

Preventing Suicide: Warning Signs

Although some people intent on suicide carefully conceal their plans, there are often warning signs. A person who is truly determined to end his or her life will probably find a way to do it. But sometimes an attempted suicide is a call for help.

Warning signs of suicide include withdrawing from family or friends; talking about death, the hereafter, or suicide; giving away prized possessions; abusing drugs or alcohol; personality changes, such as unusual anger, boredom, or apathy; and typical signs of depression, such as unusual neglect of appearance, difficulty concentrating, staying away from work or other customary activities, complaints of physical problems when nothing is organically wrong, sleeping or eating much more or much less than usual, loss of self-esteem, and feelings of helplessness, hopelessness, extreme anxiety, or panic.

Many suicides are impulsive; if a convenient means is not at hand, a suicidal person may desist or defer action long enough to get help. Psychotherapy, medication, or increased social contacts can often help to lessen feelings of isolation, lift depression, and restore interest in life.

Survivors of people who take their own lives have been called "suicide's other victims." Many of them blame themselves for failing to recognize the signs. They "obsessively replay the events leading up to the death, imagining how they could have prevented it and berating themselves for their failure to do so" (L. L. Goldman & Rothschild, in press). Because of the stigma attached to suicide, they often struggle with their emotions alone rather than sharing them with others who might understand.

The Right to Die and Assisted Suicide

A 45-year-old Israeli filmmaker shot a video in which his 83-year-old father and 82-year-old mother stated that they planned to kill themselves while they were still healthy, to avoid deteriorating, suffering, or becoming a burden on their children. Four days later, the couple carried out their plan by taking an overdose of sleeping pills. At the funeral, the son read a letter in which his parents had said they hoped what they were about to do would help "break the taboo" on suicide (D. Perry, 1995, p. 10).

(C. Hillary/Reuters/Bettmann)

Physician-assisted suicide for the terminally ill has become a controversial issue. Jack Kevorkian, a doctor, defied Michigan's law banning the practice by aiding in the deaths of at least 21 people. The two women shown here, Marcella Lawrence (left) and Marguerite Tate (right), took their lives in Kevorkian's presence a few hours before the governor signed the bill into law.

In traditional Inuit (Eskimo) society, there is no such taboo. Given the belief that the personality survives death, an older man who feels that he can no longer be useful may ask his sons to help him strangle himself; and an older woman who feels that she cannot complete an arduous journey across the tundra may ask her children to leave her behind on the trail. Children usually attempt to change their parents' minds but soon grant this last wish (Guemple, 1983).

In some quarters, suicide is seen as a right to be defended and ending one's life as a rational decision, especially in circumstances such as terminal illness. In the United States, suicide is no longer a crime: "right to die" legislation has given mature people the right to end their lives when they see fit.

However, even among supporters of the right to die, many people hold that family, friends, and others should try to thwart a suicide. According to this view, suicide is often not so much a wish for death as a desire to avoid unbearable pain, either physical or emotional. Finding ways to reduce pain (for example, through hospice care) may prevent a suicide.

Recently, *assisted suicide,* in which a physician or someone else helps a person die, has become a controversial issue. Assisted suicide is illegal in many states. In Michigan, when Jack Kevorkian—a retired pathologist—devised and used a machine to help terminally ill people commit suicide by inhaling a lethal gas, the state legislature banned it. Kevorkian remained defiant; and by December 1994, when the Michigan Supreme Court upheld the law, he had attended 21 deaths

("Michigan Court," 1994). A Harris poll of 1,250 adults found that, of those who knew about Kevorkian, 58 percent supported him (Taylor, 1995).

Meanwhile, in November 1994, voters in Oregon adopted a law permitting terminally ill patients with less than 6 months to live to ask a doctor for a lethal prescription, with safeguards to make sure that the request is serious and all other alternatives have been considered. The Oregon law—the first in the world to specifically legalize assisted suicide—has been challenged in court. However, the Harris poll found 2-to-1 support nationwide for such a law (Taylor, 1995). This issue is one that will also have to be resolved elsewhere, as terminally ill people increasingly claim a right to die with help.

EUTHANASIA

A 79-year-old man visited his 62-year-old wife in a nursing home. Once a successful businesswoman, the wife, now suffering from advanced Alzheimer's disease, screamed constantly and was unable or unwilling to speak. The man pushed his wife's wheelchair into a stairwell, where he killed her with a pistol shot. The district attorney who prosecuted the husband called his action "classic first-degree murder." But the grand jury refused to indict, and he went free (Malcolm, 1984).

This husband claimed to be practicing euthanasia ("good death"), sometimes called *mercy killing.* If so, his act was an example of *active euthanasia,* action taken deliberately to shorten a life, in order to end suffering or allow a terminally ill person to die with dignity. *Passive euthanasia* is deliberately withholding or discontinuing treatment that might extend the life of a terminally ill patient, such as medication, life-support systems, or feeding tubes. Active euthanasia is generally illegal; passive euthanasia, in some circumstances and in some places, is not. *Voluntary active euthanasia,* which carries out the wishes of the patient, is similar in principle to assisted suicide, except that someone other than the person who wants to die performs the actual deed (Brock, 1992).

Changing Attitudes toward Euthanasia

A change in attitudes toward euthanasia can be attributed to revulsion against technologies that keep patients alive indefinitely after the brain has, for all practical purposes, stopped functioning. But there are thorny ethical questions for society and for patients and their families.

The President's Commission for the Study of Ethical Problems in Medicine and Biomedical and Behavioral Research proposed that mentally competent patients, and families acting on behalf of incompetent patients, be allowed to halt medical treatment that keeps the patients alive without any hope of cure or improvement. The commission recommended that ending a life intentionally be forbidden, but that doctors should be allowed to give drugs that are likely to shorten life if the reason for administering the drugs is to relieve pain (Schmeck, 1983). However, the Harris poll conducted in December 1994 found that 70 percent of adults would "allow doctors to comply with the wishes of a dying patient in severe distress who asks to have his or her life ended" (Taylor, 1995).

Advance Directives

The United States Supreme Court has held that a person whose wishes are clearly known has a constitutional right to have life-sustaining treatment discontinued (*Cruzan v. Director, Missouri Department of Health*, 1990). Since that decision, more people have specified in writing what measures they want—or do not want—taken if they become mentally incompetent or terminally ill, or if they are in a *persistent vegetative state*, a state in which, while technically alive, they have no awareness and only rudimentary brain functioning. The importance of putting these requests in legally enforceable form was highlighted by a survey of 1,400 doctors and nurses in five major hospitals around the United States. Nearly half of attending doctors and nurses and 70 percent of resident doctors reported prolonging life support for terminally ill patients—even though they knew the patients would not want such treatment—while failing to give them enough pain medication (M. Solomon, 1993).

A person's wishes can be spelled out in advance in a document called a *living will*. A person who signs a living will must be legally competent, and the document generally cannot be witnessed by anyone who stands to gain. The living will may contain specific provisions with regard to—for example—relief of pain, cardiac resuscitation, mechanical respiration, antibiotics, and artificial nutrition and hydration.

Some "living will" legislation applies only to terminally ill patients—not to patients who are incapacitated by illness or injury but may live many years in severe pain, or to patients in a coma, or to patients in some other extremely disabled state. Therefore, it may be advisable to draw up a *durable power of attorney*, which appoints another person to make decisions if someone becomes incapacitated. A number of states have enacted statutes expressly for decisions about health care, which provide for a simple form known as a *medical durable power of attorney*.

Active Euthanasia: The Next Step?

Some legal scholars and ethicists (Brock, 1992; R. A. Epstein, 1989) advocate legalizing all forms of voluntary euthanasia, active as well as passive. They argue that the key issue is not how death occurs but who makes the decision, and that a person sufficiently competent to control his or her own life should have the right to exercise that control through consent given either in advance or at the time. If a patient is unconscious, "decisions may have to be made by family acting in accordance with the patient's wishes" (R. A. Epstein, 1989, p. 9).

Opponents of active euthanasia warn that it could be subject to abuse—that voluntary euthanasia is a slippery slope, which could lead to involuntary euthanasia. Furthermore, they argue that involvement of doctors in killing patients (for example, by lethal injection) contradicts the essential role of the physician as healer. They claim that most of the pressure for euthanasia comes not from sick and dying people, but from healthy people who fear a long terminal illness, and that the needs of the terminally ill would be better served by improved palliative care (Latimer, 1992; Singer, 1988).

Although active euthanasia remains highly controversial, some observers predict that it will become increasingly common, perhaps following the pattern in the Netherlands (W. McCord, 1993). A law passed there in 1993 tolerates euthanasia under strict conditions. The request must be made freely and repeatedly over a period of time by the patient, unpressured by others; the patient's suffering must be unbearable and without hope of recovery; another physician must agree on the advisability of euthanasia and on the method; and a complete report must be written. A government study estimated that in 1990, even before passage of the new law, voluntary euthanasia accounted for 2,300 deaths, and doctor-assisted suicide for 400 deaths—a total of about 2 percent of all deaths in that year (Simons, 1993).

FINDING MEANING AND PURPOSE IN LIFE AND DEATH

▼

For most people, death comes at a time and in a way not of their choosing. As the end of their journey approaches, they look back over what they have made of themselves—how they have changed and grown. They ask themselves about the purpose of life and death and try to sum up what their lives have meant.

REVIEWING A LIFE

In Ingmar Bergman's film *Wild Strawberries,* an elderly doctor dreams and thinks about his past and his coming death. Realizing how cold and unaffectionate he has been, he becomes warmer and more open in his last days. In Charles Dickens's *A Christmas Carol,* Scrooge changes his greedy, heartless ways after seeing ghostly visions of his past, his present, and his future—his death. In Kurosawa's film *Ikiru* ("To Live"), a petty bureaucrat who discovers that he is dying of cancer looks back over the emptiness of his life and, in a final burst of energy, creates a meaningful legacy by pushing through a project for a children's park, which he has previously blocked. These three fictional characters make their remaining time more purposeful through *life review,* a process of reminiscence that enables a person to see the significance of his or her life as death draws nearer.

Life review, which commonly occurs in old age, can foster *ego integrity—* according to Erikson, the final critical task of the lifespan. Awareness of mortality may be an impetus for reexamination of one's values. By going over their lives, people may see their experiences and actions in a new light. They may be able to complete unfinished tasks—such as reconciliation with estranged family members or friends—and thus achieve a satisfying sense of closure.

Not all memories are equally conducive to life review or to mental health. One research team (Sherman, 1991, 1993; Sherman & Peak, 1991) identified three types of reminiscences. *Reminiscences for pleasure* (the most frequent kind) enhance mood and self-image. *Reminiscences for self-understanding* (reported by about 1 out of 4 older adults) help people resolve past problems and find meaning in life. *Reminiscences to solve present problems and cope with losses* are predominant among about 1 in 10 older people. People who use reminiscence for self-understanding show the greatest ego integrity and positive mental health, although those actively engaged in a life review may temporarily experience lower morale. Those who shut out all but pleasurable memories have high spirits but less ego integrity. Then there is a group who keep recalling negative events and are obsessed with regret, hopelessness, and fear of death. These people, from Erikson's perspective, have given way to despair and may need treatment (Sherman, 1993; Walasky, Whitbourne, & Nehrke, 1983–1984).

Another team of researchers (Wong & Watt, 1991) found that people who are "aging successfully" (according to the measures used) have more integrative or instrumental reminiscences and fewer obsessive or escapist reminiscences than people who are "aging unsuccessfully." *Integrative* reminiscences help people accept their lives, resolve old conflicts, and reconcile their idealized version of the past with reality. *Instrumental* reminiscences allow them to draw on coping strategies that have worked in the past to deal with current problems. *Escapist* reminiscences glorify the past over the present. *Obsessive* reminiscences are colored by guilt, bitterness, or despair.

Life-review therapy can help focus the natural process of life review and make it more conscious, purposeful, and efficient (Butler, 1961; M. I. Lewis & Butler, 1974). Box 13-3 describes methods often used for uncovering memories in life-review therapy, which may also be used by older adults to facilitate their own life review. (The questions listed in Table 12-6 offer additional possibilities.)

OVERCOMING FEAR OF DEATH

The central character in Leo Tolstoy's story "The Death of Ivan Ilyich" is racked by a fatal illness. But even greater than his physical suffering is his mental torment. He asks himself over and over what meaning there is to his agony, and he becomes more and more convinced that his life has been without purpose and his death will be equally pointless. At the last minute, though, he experiences a spiritual revelation, a concern for his wife and son, which gives him a final moment of integrity and enables him to conquer his terror.

What Tolstoy dramatized in literature is being confirmed by social scientists. A researcher who administered attitudinal scales to 39 women whose average age was 76 found that those who saw the most purpose in life had the least fear of death (Durlak, 1973). "There is no need to be afraid of death," Kübler-Ross wrote (1975, p. 164); facing the reality of death is a key to growth:

> It is the denial of death that is partially responsible for [people's] living empty, purposeless lives; for when you live as if you'll live forever, it becomes too easy to postpone the things you know that you must do. In contrast, when you fully understand that each day you awaken could be the last you have, you take the time *that day* to grow, to become more of who you really are, to reach out to other human beings. (p. 164)

Consciousness of impending death, then, can give adults a last chance to express their best qualities and to savor the sweetness of life.

BOX 13-3

THE ART OF AGING

Evoking Memories for a Life Review

The following methods for uncovering memories (adapted from M. I. Lewis & Butler, 1974) are often used in life review therapy and can also be used fruitfully outside a therapeutic situation. By engaging in such projects with younger family members or friends, older adults can creatively order their lives, build a bridge between generations, and give younger people insights that may help them in their own old age.

(Joel Gordon)

High school students interviewing an elderly man in a nursing home evoke memories for a life review, a process of reminiscence that helps people approaching death appreciate the significance of their lives.

- *Written or taped autobiographies.* What a person includes—or does not include—in an autobiography may be significant. One successful professional man put together an extensive record of his life, with practically no mention of his two middle-aged children. When the therapist explored this omission, the man revealed that he was estranged from both children—and was then able to use the therapy to examine his feelings about them.

- *Pilgrimages.* When possible, older people can make trips back to scenes of their birth, childhood, and young adulthood, taking photographs and notes to put their thoughts together. If they cannot do this in reality, they may be able to contact people still living in these places. Such pilgrimages can reawaken memories and provide new understanding. One woman, who was still angry with her parents for forbidding her to go into the attic and had for years fantasized about what they were hiding from her, discovered upon revisiting her childhood home that there were no stairs to the attic and that the prohibition had been simply for her safety.

- *Reunions.* Getting together with high school and college classmates, distant family members, or members of a religious or civic organization can give older adults a new view of themselves in relation to their peers and other important people in their lives.

- *Constructing a genealogy.* Developing a family tree can provide a sense of continuity. The search is interesting; it may include putting advertisements in newspapers, visiting cemeteries, and poring over town records, family documents, and records of churches, synagogues, or other religious institutions.

- *Scrapbooks, photo albums, old letters, and other memorabilia.* The items usually have a special, pleasurable meaning. By talking about them, older people can often recall forgotten events, acquaintances, and emotional experiences.

- *Focus on ethnic identity.* By describing special ethnic traditions they have enjoyed and valued, older persons can enhance their appreciation of their heritage and pass it on.

- *Summation of a life's work.* By summing up what they regard as their contributions to the world, older people can gain a sense of their meaningful participation in it. Some of these summations have grown into published books, poems, and music.

DEVELOPMENT: A LIFELONG PROCESS

In his late seventies, the artist Pierre-Auguste Renoir had crippling arthritis and chronic bronchitis and had lost his wife; he was confined to a wheelchair and was so pain-wracked that he could not sleep through the night. He was unable to hold a palette and could no longer grip a brush: he had to have his brush tied to his right hand. Yet he continued to produce brilliant, youthful paintings, full of color and vibrant life. Finally, stricken by pneumonia, he lay in bed, gazing at some anemones his maid had picked. He gathered enough strength to sketch the form of these beautiful flowers, and then—just before he died—lay back and whispered, "I think I am beginning to understand something about it" (L. Hanson, 1968).

Within a limited lifespan, no person can realize all capabilities, gratify all desires, engage all interests, or experience all the richness that life has to offer. The tension between virtually infinite possibilities for growth and a finite time in which to grow defines human life, particularly during late adulthood. By choosing which possibilities to pursue and by continuing to follow them as far as possible, even up to the very end, each person contributes to the unfinished story of adult development.

SUMMARY

CHANGING PERSPECTIVES ON DEATH AND DYING

- Dying has three interrelated aspects: biological, social, and psychological.
- Although denial of death has been characteristic of modern American society, there is now an upsurge of interest in understanding and dealing realistically and compassionately with death.

FACING DEATH

- Attitudes toward death are affected by culture and cohort and vary at different stages of adulthood.
- People often undergo cognitive and personality changes shortly before death.
- Elisabeth Kübler-Ross proposed five stages in coming to terms with death: denial, anger, bargaining, depression, and acceptance. These stages, and their sequence, are not universal.

FACING BEREAVEMENT

- Mourning customs vary greatly from one culture to another.
- Anticipatory grief may or may not help survivors handle actual bereavement.
- The most widely studied pattern of grief after a death moves from shock and disbelief to preoccupation with the memory of the dead person and finally to resolution. Research has found several variations: high to low distress, no intense distress, and prolonged distress.

■ Being widowed has been found to be the most stressful life event. Women are more likely to be widowed than men. Older adults seem better adjusted to widowhood than younger ones. Men are more likely to remarry than women.

■ Today, more people are losing parents later in life. Death of a parent can precipitate changes in the self and in relationships with others.

■ The loss of a child can be especially difficult because it is no longer normative.

CONTROVERSIAL ISSUES

■ Suicide is the ninth leading cause of death in the United States, is prevalent worldwide, and is often associated with depression or debilitating illness. The highest suicide rate in the United States is among elderly white men. The "right to die" and assisted suicide are controversial issues.

■ Passive euthanasia is generally permitted with the patient's consent or with advance directives. Active euthanasia is generally illegal, but voluntary active euthanasia is tolerated in the Netherlands under strict conditions.

FINDING MEANING AND PURPOSE IN LIFE AND DEATH

■ Life review helps people prepare for death and gives them a last chance to complete unfinished tasks.

■ The more purpose and meaning people find in their lives, the less they fear death.

■ Development can continue up to the moment of death.

KEY TERMS

▼

thanatology (page 492)
death education (492)
hospice care (492)
palliative care (492)
near-death experiences (498)
bereavement (503)
grief (503)
mourning (503)
anticipatory grief (504)

grief work (505)
grief therapy (505)
assisted suicide (518)
active euthanasia (519)
passive euthanasia (519)
persistent vegetative state (520)
living will (520)
durable power of attorney (520)
life review (521)

GLOSSARY

achieving stage Second of Schaie's five cognitive stages, in which young adults use knowledge to gain competence and independence.

acquired immune deficiency syndrome (AIDS) Failure of the immune system due to a viral infection, which leaves the body vulnerable to fatal disease.

acquisitive stage First of Schaie's five cognitive stages, characterized by a child's or adolescent's learning of information and skills largely for their own sake or as preparation for participation in society.

active euthanasia Deliberate action to shorten the life of a terminally ill person in order to end suffering or allow death with dignity; also called *mercy killing*. Compare *passive euthanasia*.

activity theory Theory of aging, proposed by Neugarten and others, which holds that in order to age successfully a person must remain as active as possible. Compare *disengagement theory*.

adaptation Adjustment to changing events, circumstances, and conditions of life.

adaptive mechanisms Characteristic ways in which an individual copes or interacts with the environment.

age structure Percentages of various age groups in a given population.

age-differentiated Life structure in which primary roles—learning, working, and leisure—are based on age; typical in industrialized societies. Compare *age-integrated*.

age-integrated Life structure in which all roles—learning, working, and leisure—are open to adults of all ages and can be interspersed throughout the lifespan. Compare *age-differentiated*.

ageism Prejudice or discrimination (most commonly against older people) based on age.

ageless self Concept of remaining the same person regardless of age.

aging in place Remaining in one's own home, with or without assistance, during late life.

Alzheimer's disease (AD) Degenerative brain disorder characterized by irreversible deterioration in memory, awareness, and control of bodily functions, eventually leading to death.

androgynous Personality type integrating characteristics typically thought of as masculine with characteristics typically thought of as feminine.

anticipatory grief Grief that begins before an expected death in preparation for bereavement.

antidepressant drugs Drugs used to treat depression by restoring the chemical balance of neurotransmitters in the brain.

archetypes In Jung's terminology, images of ideas important in a culture's mythic tradition, which survive in the "collective unconscious."

arteriosclerosis Age-related condition in which walls of the arteries become thickened and more rigid; also called *hardening of the arteries*.

arthritis Group of disorders involving painful inflammation of joints.

articulatory loop In information-processing models, component of working memory that allows information about sounds and language to be kept in consciousness.

artificial insemination Injection of sperm into a woman's cervix in order to enable her to conceive.

assisted suicide Suicide in which a physician or someone else helps a person take his or her own life.

assortative mating Tendency to fall in love with and marry a person similar to oneself.

atherosclerosis Buildup of fatty deposits on inner walls of arteries, obstructing the flow of blood; this can lead to heart attack. Also called *coronary artery disease*.

attentional resources In Craik's terminology, amount of mental energy a person has available to focus on a task.

autoimmunity Tendency of an aging body to mistake its own tissues for foreign invaders and to attack and destroy them.

balanced investment Pattern of retirement activity allocated among family, work, and leisure. Compare *family-focused lifestyle*.

behavior therapy Therapeutic method that uses positive and negative reinforcement to modify behavior.

bereavement Loss, due to death, of someone to whom one feels close and the process of adjustment to the loss.

biological age Measure of progress along the potential lifespan predicted by a person's physical condition.

biomarkers Specific biological measures of the rate at which a body is aging.

bisexual Sexually oriented toward both sexes.

blended family Family resulting from the marriage or cohabitation of an adult who already has children; also called *stepfamily, reconstituted family,* or *combined family*.

blood pressure Force of blood flow against arterial walls.

brief dynamic therapy Therapeutic method based on a genuine, nonmanipulative working alliance between therapist and client.

burnout Syndrome characterized by emotional exhaustion and a sense that one no longer can accomplish anything on the job.

cancer Group of diseases involving uncontrolled growth of abnormal cells, which invade and destroy healthy tissue.

carcinogens Cancer-causing agents in the environment.

cardiac reserve Heart's ability to pump faster under stress.

caregiver burnout Condition of physical, mental, and emotional exhaustion affecting adults who care for aged persons.

caregiving Informal or unpaid care of a person whose independence is physically, mentally, emotionally, or economically limited.

case study Research design covering a single case or life, based on observations, interviews, or biographical and documentary material.

cataracts Cloudy or opaque areas in the lens of the eye, which often cause blurring of vision in older adults.

central executive In information-processing models of memory, component of working memory that selects and processes sensory inputs and transforms them into meaningful mental representations; it also can retrieve information from long-term memory.

change Alteration or modification from one time to another.

child abuse Maltreatment of a child involving physical injury.

chronological age Number of years a person has lived.

classic aging pattern On Wechsler Adult Intelligence Scale (WAIS), greater and sharper age-associated decline in performance IQ than in verbal IQ.

classical conditioning Form of unconscious learning in which a previously neutral stimulus (one that does not ordinarily elicit a particular involuntary response) comes to elicit the response as a result of repeated association with a stimulus that normally produces the response.

climacteric Period of 2 to 5 years during which a woman's body undergoes physiological changes that bring on menopause.

cochlear implants Electronic devices, useful for people with hearing impairment, which transform sound waves into electrical signals to be transmitted to the brain.

cognitive-appraisal model Model, proposed by Lazarus and colleagues, that views coping as dynamic interaction between individual and environment, in which an individual chooses effortful coping strategies on the basis of cognitive appraisal of a situation that taxes or exceeds his or her resources.

cognitive-developmental theory Theory, proposed by Kohlberg and others, that children learn about gender and other aspects of their world by actively thinking about their experience and then organize their behavior around these perceptions.

cognitive therapy Therapeutic method aimed at teaching patients to recognize and correct negative thinking.

cohabitation Living together and maintaining a sexual relationship without being legally married.

cohort Group of people with a common experience; often, people of about the same age and cultural background.

commitment within relativism In Perry's terminology, final stage of college students' cognitive development, in which they commit themselves to self-chosen beliefs and values despite uncertainty and recognition of other valid possibilities.

compensation hypothesis Hypothesis that there is a negative correlation between intellectuality of work and of leisure activities because people seek leisure activities that make up for what they find missing in work. Compare *spillover hypothesis, resource provision-depletion hypothesis,* and *segmentation hypothesis.*

componential element In Sternberg's triarchic theory, the analytic aspect of intelligence, which determines how efficiently people process information and solve problems.

congestive heart failure Inability of the heart to pump an adequate supply of blood, as a result of cardiovascular disease.

congruence model Model, proposed by Kahana, which holds that life satisfaction or stress depends on the match between an individual's needs and an environment's ability to meet those needs.

consolidation stage In Super's terminology, fifth stage of career exploration and development, in which people in their mid-thirties strive for rapid advancement and consolidate gains.

construct validity Ability of a researcher to demonstrate that the manipulations and measures used in a study pertain to, or represent, the concept or phenomenon under study.

contextual element In Sternberg's triarchic theory, the practical aspect of intelligence, which determines how effectively people deal with their environment.

contextual perspective Metatheory that views development as the product of an ongoing process of interaction between an individual and the context within which the individual acts to achieve goals.

contingent career paths In Raynor's terminology, career paths in which workers are motivated by a perception that their future success hinges on their own actions. Compare *noncontingent career paths.*

continuity theory Theory of aging, proposed by Atchley, which holds that in order to age successfully people must maintain a balance of continuity and change in both the internal and the external structures of their lives.

control group In an experiment, a group of people who are similar to the people in the experimental group but who do not receive the treatment under study. Results obtained with the control group are compared with results obtained with the experimental group.

convergent thinking Thinking aimed at finding the single right answer to a problem, usually the conventional answer. Compare with *divergent thinking.*

convoy theory Theory, proposed by Kahn and Antonucci, that reduction of social contacts in outer circles after retirement may be offset by new contacts in those circles, as well as by maintenance of an inner core of close friends and family. Compare *selectivity theory.*

coping Adaptive thinking or behavior aimed at reducing or relieving stress that arises from harmful, threatening, or challenging conditions.

corneal disease Visual disorder characterized by clouding, scarring, or distortion of the cornea, the front surface of the eye.

correlational study Research design intended to discover whether a statistical correlation can be calculated showing the direction and strength of a relationship between variables.

cosmic perspective Viewpoint achieved in Kohlberg's proposed seventh stage of moral reasoning, characterized by a sense of unity with the cosmos, nature, or the divine.

cross-sectional study Quasi-experimental research design in which people of different ages are assessed on one occasion, providing comparative information about different age cohorts. Compare with *longitudinal study*.

crystallization stage In Super's terminology, first stage of career exploration and development, in which younger adolescents develop a general concept of occupation as a defining feature of the self.

crystallized intelligence Type of intelligence, proposed by Horn, that involves remembering and applying learned information; it is relatively dependent on education and cultural background. Compare *fluid intelligence*.

cultural bias Tendency of psychometric intelligence tests to include questions involving content or skills more familiar and meaningful to some cultural groups than to others.

data Information gathered from research.

death education Programs to educate people about death and to help them deal with issues concerning dying and grief in their personal and professional lives.

deceleration stage In Super's terminology, seventh stage of career exploration and development, in which people in their late fifties begin to anticipate retirement and distance themselves from their work.

declarative memory In information-processing models, memory for facts and events that can be recalled or recognized and stated verbally or can cause feelings of familiarity; compare with *nondeclarative memory*.

dementia Deterioration in cognitive and behavioral functioning due to physiological causes; sometimes inaccurately called *senility*.

dependency ratio Comparative size of productive and dependent portions of a population.

dependent variable In an experiment, the variable that may or may not change as a result of manipulation of the independent variable. Compare *independent variable*.

development Systematic process of adaptive change in behavior in one or more directions.

developmental reserve In Baltes's terminology, extent to which memory can be improved with training.

deviation IQ Measurement of intelligence based on distribution of raw scores and standard deviation from the mean.

digit span Number of digits a person can remember at one time; it usually consists of 5 to 9 digits but can be increased by chunking.

disengagement theory Theory of aging, proposed by Cumming and Henry, which holds that successful aging is characterized by mutual withdrawal between the older person and society. Compare *activity theory*.

divergent thinking Thinking that produces a variety of novel possibilities; believed to be a factor in creativity. Compare with *convergent thinking*.

dream In Levinson's terminology, a vision that spurs a young adult's personal and vocational development.

dual-process model Model of intellectual functioning in late adulthood, proposed by Baltes, which identifies and seeks to measure two dimensions of intelligence: mechanics and pragmatics.

durable power of attorney Legal instrument that appoints one person to make decisions in the event of another person's incapacitation.

dynamic visual acuity Ability to see moving objects clearly.

dysmenorrhea Menstrual cramps.

ecological approach Bronfenbrenner's system of understanding development, which identifies five levels of environmental influences, from most intimate to broadest.

ecological validity Characteristic of adult intelligence tests that indicate competence in dealing with real problems or challenges faced by adults.

E-I-E-I-O model Camp's model for classifying mnemonic techniques according to type of processing (explicit or implicit) and initial site of storage (external or internal).

elaboration Encoding strategy or mnemonic device, consisting of making associations, often between new information and information already in memory.

elder abuse Maltreatment or neglect of dependent older people, or violation of their personal rights.

electroconvulsive therapy (ECT) Electric shocks administered to treat severe depression; also called *shock therapy*.

emphysema Irreversible disease, often caused by smoking, which destroys lung tissue, causing progressive difficulty in breathing.

emotion-focused coping In Lazarus's cognitive-appraisal model, coping strategy directed toward managing the emotional response to a stressful situation so as to lessen its physical or psychological impact; also called *palliative coping*. Compare *problem-focused coping*.

empty nest Transitional phase of parenting following the last child's leaving home.

encapsulation In Hoyer's terminology, progressive dedication of information processing and fluid thinking to specific knowledge systems, making knowledge more readily accessible and compensating for declines in cognitive machinery.

encoding In information-processing models of memory, the process by which information is prepared for long-term storage and later retrieval.

environment Totality of nongenetic stimuli influencing development.

environmental press model Model, proposed by Lawton, which holds that stress and adaptation depend on the fit between environmental demands and an individual's competence to meet them.

episodic memory In information-processing models, memory for personal experiences, activities, and events linked with specific times and places; compare with *semantic memory.*

establishment stage In Super's terminology, fourth stage of career exploration and development, in which people in their late twenties seek advancement along a chosen career path, develop expertise, and see work as intrinsic to the self-concept.

estrogen-replacement therapy (ERT) Treatment with artificial estrogen, sometimes in combination with the hormone progesterone, to relieve or prevent symptoms caused by decline in estrogen levels after menopause. Also called *hormone-replacement therapy (HRT).*

executive stage Fourth of Schaie's five cognitive stages, in which middle-aged people responsible for societal systems deal with complex relationships on several levels.

experiential element In Sternberg's triarchic theory, the insightful aspect of intelligence, which determines how effectively people process both novel and familiar tasks.

experiment Rigorously controlled, replicable (repeatable) procedure in which a researcher (experimenter) manipulates variables to assess the effect of one on the other.

experimental group In an experiment, the group receiving the treatment under study; any changes in these people are compared with any changes in the control group.

explanatory style Person's habitual way of explaining misfortune.

explicit memory In information-processing models of memory, processing that is intentional and conscious; compare with *implicit memory.*

extended family Multigenerational family made up of parents, children, and more distant relatives, sometimes living together in an *extended-family household.*

external validity Generalizability of experimental results beyond the study situation.

factor analysis Statistical method that seeks to identify underlying factors common to a group of tests on which the same people score similarly.

factorial invariance Issue of whether a measure represents or pertains to the same construct in all age groups.

family-focused lifestyle Pattern of retirement activity that revolves around family, home, and companions. Compare *balanced investment.*

five-factor model Costa and McCrae's model of personality, consisting of five dimensions: neuroticism, extraversion, openness to experience, conscientiousness, and agreeableness.

fluid intelligence Type of intelligence, proposed by Horn, that is applied to novel problems and is relatively independent of educational and cultural influences. Compare *crystallized intelligence.*

free radicals Unstable, highly reactive molecules formed during metabolism, which can cause bodily damage.

frontal lobes Front portions of the brain's cerebral cortex, or outer layer, which form and direct strategies for encoding, storage, and retrieval of memories.

functional age Measure of a person's ability to function effectively in his or her physical and social environment.

fundamental pragmatics of life In Baltes's terminology, the area in which a wise person is expert, including knowledge of facts and procedures concerning the essence of the human condition.

gender identity Personal awareness of what it means to be male or female; includes gender roles and (sometimes) gender stereotypes.

gender roles Behaviors, interests, attitudes, abilities, and personality traits that a culture considers appropriate for men or women and expects them to display.

gender-schema theory Theory, proposed by Bem, that people develop gender schemas, patterns of behavior organized around gender, which help them sort out their observations of what it means to be male or female.

gender stereotypes Exaggerated generalizations about differences between men and women, which may form a part of a society's gender roles, though not all men and women conform to these generalizations.

gene therapy Experimental method of treating certain diseases by insertion of genetic material into the body to alter cellular composition or replace defective genes.

generativity In Erikson's terminology, middle-aged person's concern with establishing and guiding the next generation.

genes Basic functional units of heredity, composed of deoxyribonucleic acid (DNA), which determine inherited characteristics.

genetic-programming theories Theories that explain biological aging as resulting from a genetically determined developmental timetable; compare *variable-rate theories.*

geriatrics Branch of medicine concerned with processes of aging and age-related medical conditions.

gerontologists People engaged in gerontology, the study of the aged and processes of aging.

glaucoma Visual disorder caused by buildup of fluid pressure in the eye; it can cause blindness if not treated.

grief Emotional response experienced in the early phases of bereavement.

grief therapy Program of treatment to help the bereaved cope with loss.

grief work Common pattern of grief in which the bereaved person accepts the loss, releases the bond with the deceased, and rebuilds a life without that person.

Hayflick limit Limit, discovered by Hayflick, on the number of times an animal cell can divide (about 50 times for human cells).

heredity Inborn influences on development, carried on the genes.

heterosexual Sexually oriented toward the other sex.

hippocampus Structure in the medial temporal lobe of the brain, actively involved in initial encoding and storage and immediate retrieval of new information.

homeostasis Maintenance of vital functions within optimum range.

homosexual Sexually oriented toward the same sex.

hospice care Warm, personal, patient- and family-centered care for a person with a terminal illness, focused on relieving pain, controlling symptoms, and maintaining quality of life.

hypertension High blood pressure.

hypochondriasis Mental disorder characterized by preoccupation with fear of having a serious disease; this fear is based on misinterpretation of physical symptoms.

ideal self Person's concept of who he or she would like to be. Compare with *real self*.

identity accommodation In Whitbourne's terminology, adjusting the self-concept to fit new experience. Compare with *identity assimilation*.

identity assimilation In Whitbourne's terminology, effort to fit new experience into an existing self-concept. Compare with *identity accommodation*.

identity styles In Whitbourne's terminology, characteristic ways of confronting, interpreting, and responding to experience.

implementation stage In Super's terminology, third stage of career exploration and development, in which people in their early twenties try out entry-level jobs or start professional training and make a final choice of career.

implicit memory In information-processing models, processing that is unintentional and unconscious; compare with *explicit memory*.

impotence (erectile dysfunction) Inability of a man to achieve or maintain an erect penis sufficient for satisfactory sexual performance.

in vitro fertilization Fertilization of an ovum outside the mother's body.

independent variable In an experiment, the variable over which the experimenter has direct control; its manipulation is called the *treatment*. Compare *dependent variable*.

infertility Inability to conceive after 12 to 18 months of trying.

information-processing theory Study of mental processes that underlie intelligent behavior: these involve manipulation of symbols and perceptions to acquire, store, and retrieve information and solve problems.

integrated level Third and final level in Labouvie-Vief's model of adult cognitive development, characterized by openness, flexibility, and autonomous choice of principles; integration of subjectivity with objectivity; and judgment of truth claims on the basis of rational, disciplined reflection and collective thought and discussion.

intelligence quotient (IQ) Measurement of intelligence traditionally obtained by dividing a person's mental age by his or her chronological age and multiplying the result by 100.

intelligent behavior Behavior that is goal-oriented (conscious and deliberate) and adaptive (used to identify and solve problems effectively).

interiority In Neugarten's terminology, tendency toward introspection, or preoccupation with inner life, which usually appears in middle age.

internal validity Assurance that the conclusions of an experiment are valid for the participants; in other words, that the treatment, and only the treatment, caused the result.

interpersonal wisdom According to Achenbaum and Orwoll, one of three facets of wisdom, characterized by empathy, understanding, and maturity in social relationships.

intersystemic level Second level in Labouvie-Vief's model of adult cognitive development, characterized by awareness of multiple, contradictory systems of thought.

intrapersonal wisdom According to Achenbaum and Orwoll, one of three facets of wisdom, characterized by self-examination, self-knowledge, and integrity.

intrasystemic level First level in Labouvie-Vief's model of adult cognitive development, characterized by ability to reason only within a single system of thought.

intrinsic motivation Urge to solve problems for the gains achieved in solving them, rather than for external rewards; believed to be a factor in creativity.

intrusion errors "Remembering" information that was not originally presented, through associations retrieved from long-term memory.

kinship care Care of children living without parents in the home of grandparents or other relatives with or without a change of legal custody.

laboratory observation Research method in which the behavior of all participants is noted and recorded in the same situation, under controlled conditions. Compare *naturalistic observation*.

learned helplessness Adaptive pattern in which an organism learns to cope with an extremely stressful and uncontrollable situation by doing nothing.

learning Long-lasting change in behavior as a result of experience.

life expectancy Age to which a person in a particular cohort is statistically likely to live; this age is based on average longevity of a population.

life review Reminiscence about a person's life course in order to determine its significance.

life structure In Levinson's terminology, the underlying pattern of a person's life at a given time; this structure is built around whatever aspects of life the person finds most important.

lifelong learning Organized, sustained study by adults of all ages.

lifespan development Concept of development as a lifelong process of adaptation.

lifespan developmental psychology Branch of psychology whose primary task is the scientific study of lifespan development.

living will Document specifying the type of care wanted by the maker in the event of terminal illness.

long-term memory In information-processing models, storage of virtually unlimited capacity, which holds information for very long periods.

longevity Length of an individual's life.

longitudinal study Quasi-experimental research design in which data are collected about the same person or persons over a period of time, to assess developmental changes that occur with age. Compare with *cross-sectional study*.

lumpectomy Surgical treatment for breast cancer involving removal of the tumor and a small amount of surrounding tissue; compare *mastectomy*.

maintenance stage In Super's terminology, sixth stage of career exploration and development, in which people in their mid-forties focus on maintaining rather than acquiring prestige, authority, and responsibility.

major depressive episode Mental disorder lasting at least 2 weeks and not caused by substance abuse, medication, a medical condition, or recent bereavement, in which a person shows extreme sadness or loss of interest or pleasure in normal activities, as well as at least four of the following: change in weight or appetite; insomnia; agitation; fatigue; feelings of worthlessness or guilt; inability to think, concentrate, or make decisions; and thoughts of death or suicide.

male climacteric Period of physiological, emotional, and psychological change involving a man's reproductive and other body systems.

mammography Diagnostic x-ray examination of the breast to detect signs of breast cancer.

mastectomy Surgical treatment for breast cancer involving removal of all or part of the breast; compare *lumpectomy.*

maturation Unfolding of a biologically determined sequence of behavior patterns, including readiness to master new abilities.

mature-onset diabetes Type of diabetes, typically developed after age 30, in which blood sugar rises because of loss of ability to use insulin for metabolism.

mechanics of intelligence In Baltes's dual-process model, basic physiological functions or procedures used to process information (similar to fluid intelligence); the dimension of intellect in which there is often an age-related decline. Compare with *pragmatics of intelligence.*

mechanistic perspective Metatheory, based on the machine as a metaphor, that views development as a response to internal and external stimuli and studies phenomena by analyzing the operation of their component parts.

menopause Cessation of menstruation and of ability to bear children, typically around age 50.

mentor In Levinson's terminology, a slightly older person whose guidance and advice in both career and personal matters strongly influence a young adult's prospects for success.

metacognition Knowledge about what one knows and about one's own thinking processes.

metamemory Knowledge or beliefs about how one's own memory works.

metatheory Hypothesis about the operation of the universe, which embraces a group of theories having similar assumptions and values.

method of loci Mnemonic technique in which a series of places (loci) are associated with items to be remembered and then mentally revisited during recall.

microprocessor-enhanced hearing aids Hearing aids using microchip technology, which allows for precise, individualized tuning.

midlife crisis In some stage models, potentially stressful life period precipitated by review and reevaluation of one's past, typically occurring in the early to middle forties.

mnemonics Strategies for enhancing memory.

model Concrete image or structural representation of a theory, which helps visualize meaningful relationships among data.

morality of autonomous moral principles Kohlberg's third level of moral reasoning, in which morality is fully internal and principled. Also called *postconventional morality.*

morality of conventional role conformity Kohlberg's second level of moral reasoning, in which standards of authority figures are internalized. Also called *conventional morality.*

mourning Behavior of the bereaved and the community, including culturally accepted customs and rituals.

multidirectional In the lifespan developmental approach, descriptive of development that involves both growth and decline.

music therapy Therapeutic method used to treat depression by teaching the patient how to reduce stress by listening to music.

myocardial infarction Damage to part of the heart muscle due to stoppage of blood circulation through a coronary artery; also called *heart attack.*

naturalistic observation Method of research in which people's behavior is noted and recorded in natural settings without the observer's intervention or manipulation. Compare *laboratory observation.*

near-death experiences Profound, subjective experiences reported by people who have come close to death but have not died; these may include a feeling of well-being, enhanced clarity of thinking, out-of-body sensations, and visions of bright lights or mystical encounters.

necessary subjectivity In Sinnott's terminology, characteristic of social interactions in which each person's view of the situation inevitably affects the other's and the situation as a whole.

neglect Withholding of adequate care; usually refers to physical needs, such as food, clothing, and supervision.

noncontingent career paths In Raynor's terminology, career paths in which workers lack "achievement motivation" because they perceive that their actions will have little or no effect on their advancement. Compare *contingent career paths.*

nondeclarative memory In information-processing models, memory for procedures, habits, skills, or other types of information that generally do not require effort to recall; also called *procedural memory.* Compare with *declarative memory.*

nonnormative life events In the timing-of-events model, life experiences which are unusual and thus not normally anticipated, or are ordinary but come at unexpected times, and which may have a major impact on development. Compare with *normative life events.*

normative age-graded influences Biological and environmental influences on development that are highly similar for people in a given age group.

normative history-graded influences Biological and environmental influences on development that are common to a particular cohort.

normative life events In the timing-of-events model, commonly expected life experiences that occur at customary times. Compare with *nonnormative life events.*

normative personality change Age-related patterns of personality development that occur in most members of a population.

nuclear family Two-generational family made up of parents and growing children related by blood or adoption and living together.

obesity Overweight condition defined as skinfold measurement in the 85th percentile.

observer bias Tendency of an observer to misinterpret or distort data to fit his or her expectations.

organismic perspective Metatheory that views development as internally initiated and controlled and as occurring in a universal sequence of qualitatively different stages culminating in full maturation.

organization Encoding strategy or mnemonic device, consisting of arranging or categorizing material to be remembered.

osteoporosis Condition, most often affecting postmenopausal women, in which the bones become extremely thin, porous, and susceptible to fractures, and posture typically becomes stooped owing to compression and collapse of vertebrae.

ovum transfer Method of conception in which a woman who cannot produce normal ova receives an ovum donated by a fertile woman.

palliative care Care aimed at relieving pain and suffering and allowing the terminally ill to die in peace, comfort, and dignity.

Parkinson's disease Slowly progressive neurological disorder characterized by tremor, rigidity, slowed movement, and unstable posture.

partner abuse Violence directed against a current or former spouse or intimate partner.

passive euthanasia Deliberate withholding or discontinuation of life-prolonging treatment of a terminally ill person in order to end suffering or allow death with dignity. Compare *active euthanasia*.

passive smoking Inhaling smoke as a result of being in the presence of someone who is smoking.

periodontitis Gum disease.

persistent vegetative state State in which a patient, while technically alive, has lost all but the most rudimentary brain functioning.

personality Distinctive patterns of characteristic behavioral, mental, and emotional adaptations—that is, a person's unique and relatively consistent way of thinking, feeling, and behaving.

personality dimensions Groupings or categories of related personality traits, devised for research purposes.

personality inventory Instrument that yields psychometric ratings of personality traits or categories of traits.

plasticity In the lifespan developmental approach, modifiability of skills with training and practice, even in late life.

postformal thought Mature thinking, which relies on experience and intuition as well as logic, can transcend particular systems, and can deal with ambiguity, uncertainty, inconsistency, contradiction, imperfection, and compromise.

pragmatics of intelligence In Baltes's dual-process model, processes that involve application of the contents of the mind—an accumulation of culture-based factual and procedural knowledge; the dimension of intellect that tends to grow with age. Compare with *mechanics of intelligence*.

preconventional morality Kohlberg's first level of moral reasoning, in which right conduct is based on external control or self-interest.

premenstrual syndrome (PMS) Disorder producing physical discomfort and emotional tension before a menstrual period.

presbycusis Gradual loss of hearing, beginning with sounds at upper frequencies.

presbyopia Age-related decline in near vision, stemming from loss of elasticity of the lens of the eye.

primary aging Gradual, inevitable process of bodily deterioration throughout the lifespan.

priming Increase in ability to do a task or remember information as a result of a previous encounter with the task or information.

problem finding Ability to identify and formulate novel and important problems to be solved; believed to be a characteristic of creativity and postformal thought.

problem-focused coping In Lazarus's cognitive-appraisal model, coping strategy directed toward eliminating, managing, or improving a stressful situation. Compare *emotion-focused coping*.

production deficiency Failure to generate efficient encoding strategies in working memory.

productive aging Concept that older persons are potentially unlimited contributors to the goods, services, and products available for themselves and for society.

prospective memory Remembering to perform future actions.

pseudodementia Cognitive impairment due to major depression; sometimes called *transitory dementia*.

psychological age Measure of how effectively a person can adapt to environmental challenges.

psychometric approach Study of intelligence through quantitative measurements of intellectual functioning.

Q-sort Instrument that yields distribution of self-descriptive statements or characteristics.

qualitative development Changes, occurring at successive times of life, in kind, nature, structure, or organization of phenomena, such as new ways of telling a story. Compare *quantitative development*.

quality ratio Comparison between number of major works and total output of a highly creative person.

quantitative development Changes, occurring with age, in number or amount of something, such as how many items can be remembered. Compare *qualitative development*.

quasi experiment Study which resembles an experiment in that it attempts to measure change or to find differences among groups, but which lacks control based on random assignment.

radial keratotomy (RK) Surgical technique to correct myopia (nearsightedness) by means of microscopic incisions that reduce the cornea's curvature.

random assignment Technique used in assigning members of a study sample to experimental and control groups, in which each member of the sample has an equal chance to be assigned to each group and to receive or not receive the treatment.

random sample Type of study sample in which representativeness is ensured through random selection.

random selection Technique used to ensure representativeness of a sample by giving each member of a population an equal chance to be selected. Compare *random sample*.

real self Person's concept of who he or she actually is. Compare with *ideal self.*

rehearsal Conscious repetition of information to keep it in working memory or transfer it to long-term memory.

reintegrative stage Fifth of Schaie's five cognitive stages, in which older adults choose to focus limited energy on tasks that have meaning for them.

reliable With regard to a research method or tool, consistent in measuring performance.

reserve capacity Ability of body organs and systems to put forth 4 to 10 times as much effort as usual under stress; also called *organ reserve.*

resource provision-depletion hypothesis Hypothesis that work and leisure activities may be either positively or negatively related because work either promotes or constrains leisure activities by providing or depleting the resources (time, energy, and money) needed for those activities. Compare *spillover hypothesis, compensation hypothesis,* and *segmentation hypothesis.*

responsible stage Third of Schaie's five cognitive stages, in which middle-aged people are concerned with long-range goals and practical problems related to their responsibility for others.

retirement stage In Super's terminology, eighth stage of career exploration and development, in which people formally separate from their work, usually at age 65, and adjust their self-concept to lack of a career.

retrieval In information-processing models of memory, the process by which information is accessed or recalled from storage.

sample Group of research participants chosen to represent a population under study.

schemas Working conceptual models, or constructs of reality, around which behavior is organized.

schizophrenia Group of mental disorders involving loss of contact with reality and such symptoms as delusions, hallucinations, and thought disturbances.

scientific method System of established principles and processes of scientific inquiry, including careful observation and recording of data, testing of alternative hypotheses, and widespread dissemination of findings and conclusions so that other scientists can check, analyze, repeat, learn from, and build on the results.

secondary aging Bodily deterioration that results from disease, abuse, and disuse and is often preventable.

segmentation hypothesis Hypothesis that there is no correlation between work and leisure activities. Compare *spillover hypothesis, compensation hypothesis,* and *resource provision-depletion hypothesis.*

selective optimization with compensation In Baltes's dual-process model, strategy for maintaining or enhancing overall intellectual functioning by careful choice of tasks, increased practice, and use of stronger abilities to compensate for those that have weakened.

selectivity theory Theory, proposed by Carstensen, that reduction of social contacts directed toward information gathering and identity formation is adaptive to aging, while contacts that fulfill emotional needs become central. Compare *convoy theory.*

self-concept One's sense of self.

self-in-relation theory Theory, proposed by Jean Baker-Miller, that men develop gender identity by distancing from the mother, while women develop gender identity within the relationship with the mother.

semantic memory In information-processing models, memory for general factual knowledge about the world, social customs, and language; compare with *episodic memory.*

senescence Period of the lifespan during which adults experience decrements in bodily functioning associated with aging; begins at different ages for different people.

senile (or age-related) macular degeneration Visual disorder in which the central part of the retina loses ability to distinguish fine details; common cause of functional blindness in older adults.

sensory memory In information-processing models, initial storage facility where sensory information registers but decays rapidly without attention.

sequential designs Research designs that combine two or all three of the simple quasi-experimental designs (cross-sectional, longitudinal, and time-lag) to combat effects of confounding.

serial monogamy Pattern of involvement in a succession of sexually exclusive relationships.

serious leisure Leisure activity requiring skill, attention, and commitment.

sexual orientation Tendency to be consistently attracted to members of the other sex (heterosexual orientation), the same sex (homosexual orientation), or both sexes (bisexual orientation).

sleep apnea Disorder in which breathing stops for 10 seconds or more at a time, causing frequent awakening.

social age Measure of conformity to an expected progression of social roles at various phases of life.

social clock Set of cultural norms or expectations for the times of life when important events such as marriage, parenthood, work, and retirement should occur.

social-learning theory Theory, proposed chiefly by Bandura, which holds that behaviors, including gender roles, are learned by observing and imitating models and through reinforcement of socially approved behavior.

spaced retrieval Mnemonic technique involving priming or classical conditioning, in which people are trained to recall information for an increasingly long time.

specification stage In Super's terminology, second stage of career exporation and development, in which older adolescents or college-age adults gain information about occupations and working conditions and begin to focus on specific vocations.

spillover hypothesis Hypothesis that there is a positive correlation between intellectuality of work and of leisure activities because of a carryover of learning from work to leisure. Compare *compensation hypothesis, resource provision-depletion hypothesis,* and *segmentation hypothesis.*

stage Specific pattern of behavior typical of a certain period of development, which leads to a qualitatively different, usually more advanced pattern of behavior.

storage In information-processing models, the process by, or location in which, memories are retained for future use.

stress Organism's physiological and psychological reaction to difficult demands made on it.

stroke Cessation of blood flow to the brain, or hemorrhage in the brain, causing damage to brain cells and sometimes paralysis or death.

substance abuse Maladaptive behavior pattern, lasting more than 1 month, in which a person continues to use a substance after knowingly being harmed by it or uses it repeatedly in a hazardous situation.

substance dependence Physiological or psychological addiction to a substance.

substantive complexity Degree to which a person's work requires thought and independent judgment.

surrogate motherhood Method of conception in which a woman who is not married to a man agrees to bear his baby and then give the child to the father and his wife.

survival curves Curves, plotted on a graph, showing percentages of a population who survive at each age level.

tacit knowledge In Sternberg's terminology, information that is not formally taught or openly expressed but is necessary to get ahead; includes self-management and management of tasks and of others.

temperament Characteristic, biologically based emotional style with which a person approaches and reacts to people and situations. Also called *disposition.*

terminal drop Sudden decrease in intellectual performance shortly before death.

thanatology Study of death and dying.

theory Coherent set of related concepts that seeks to organize and explain data.

time-lag study Quasi-experimental research design in which data are collected about different age cohorts on two or more occasions when the groups of people being studied are the same age.

timing-of-events model Theoretical model, supported by Neugarten and others, that describes adult personality development as a response to whether the occurrence and timing of important life events is expected or unexpected.

tinnitus Hearing disorder characterized by persistent ringing or buzzing in the ears.

Torrance Tests of Creative Thinking Widely used psychometric tests of creativity.

transpersonal wisdom According to Achenbaum and Orwoll, one of three facets of wisdom, characterized by capacity for self-transcendence.

treatment Manipulation of an independent variable whose effects an experiment is designed to study.

triangular theory of love Sternberg's theory that the relative presence or absence of three elements of love—intimacy, passion, and commitment—affects the nature and course of a relationship.

undifferentiated Personality type consisting of low degrees of traits typically thought of as masculine and feminine.

valid With regard to research, yielding conclusions appropriate to the phenomena and population under study.

variable-rate theories Theories explaining biological aging as a result of processes that vary from person to person and are influenced by both the internal and the external environment; compare *genetic-programming theories.*

variables Phenomena that change or vary among members of a group, or can be varied for purposes of research.

visual acuity Ability of the eye to distinguish visual details.

visual scratch pad In information-processing models of memory, component of working memory that allows information about the shape and location of visual images to be kept in consciousness.

vital capacity Amount of air that can be drawn in with a deep breath and expelled; may be a biomarker of aging.

Wechsler Adult Intelligence Scale (WAIS) Intelligence test for adults, consisting of eleven subtests that yield verbal IQ, performance IQ, and total IQ scores.

working memory In information-processing models of memory, intermediate storage where information from sensory memory or from long-term memory is consciously manipulated or reorganized.

BIBLIOGRAPHY

NOTE: See also Addenda on page 582.

AARP. See American Association of Retired Persons.

Abbey, A., Andrews, F. M., & Halman, J. (1992). Infertility and subjective well being: The mediating roles of self-esteem, internal control, and interpersonal conflict. *Journal of Marriage and the Family, 54,* 408–417.

Abel, E. K. (1991). *Who cares for the elderly?* Philadelphia: Temple University Press.

Abrahams, B., Feldman, S. S., & Nash, S. C. (1978). Sex role self-concept and sex role attitudes: Enduring personality characteristics or adaptations to changing life situations? *Developmental Psychology, 14,* 393–400.

Abrahams, J. P., & Camp, C. J. (1993). Maintenance and generalization of object naming training anomia associated with degenerative dementia. *Clinical Gerontologist, 12,* 57–72.

Achenbaum, W. A., & Bengtson, V. L. (1994). Re-engaging the disengagement theory of aging: On the history and assessment of theory development in gerontology. *The Gerontologist, 34,* 756–763.

Achenbaum, W. A., & Orwoll, L. (1991). Becoming wise: A psychogerontological interpretation of the Book of Job. *International Journal of Aging and Human Development, 32,* 21–39.

Adamchak, D. J. (1993). Demographic aging in the industrialized world: A rising burden? *Generations, 17*(4), 6–9.

Adamchak, D. J., & Friedmann, E. A. (1983). Societal aging and generational dependency relationships: Problems of measurement and conceptualization. *Research on Aging, 5,* 319–338.

Adams, D. (1985). *So long and thanks for all the fish.* New York: Harmony.

Adams, R. G. (1986). Friendship and aging. *Generations, 10*(4), 40–43.

Adelman, M. (1991). Stigma, gay lifestyles, and adjustment to aging: A study of later-life gay men and lesbians. *Gay Midlife and Maturity, 4,* 7–32.

Adler, T. (1994, September 17). Just say no to prostate cancer screening. *Science News,* p. 180.

Aging and cholesterol. (1995, February). *University of California at Berkeley Wellness Letter,* pp. 4–5.

The aging eye. (1994, December). *Harvard Women's Health Watch,* pp. 4–5.

Akutsu, H., Legge, G. E., Ross, J. A., & Schuebel, K. J. (1991). Psychophysics of reading: Effects of age-related changes in vision. *Journal of Gerontology: Psychological Sciences 46*(6), P325–331.

Albert, M. S., & Kaplan, E. (1980). Organic implications of neuropsychological deficits in the elderly. In L. W. Poon, J. L. Fozard, L. S. Cremack, D. Arenberg, & L. W. Thompson (Eds.), *New directions in memory and aging: Proceedings of the George A. Talland Memorial Conference.* Hillsdale, NJ: Erlbaum.

Alcott, L. M. (1929). *Little women.* New York: Saalfield. (Original work published 1868)

Aldous, J. J. (1987). Family life of the elderly and near-elderly. *Journal of Marriage and the Family, 49*(2), 227–234.

Alexander, B. B., Rubinstein, R. L., Goodman, M., & Luborsky, M. (1992). A path not taken: A cultural analysis of regrets and childlessness in the lives of older women. *The Gerontologist, 32*(5), 618–626.

Alexander, C. N. (1982). Ego development, personality and behavioral change in inmates practicing the Transcendental Meditation technique or participating in other programs: A cross-sectional and longitudinal study (Doctoral dissertation, Harvard University). *Dissertation Abstracts International, 43*(2), 539B.

Alexander, C. N., et al. (in press-a, b). See following entries.

Alexander, C. N., Kurth, S. C., Travis, F., Warner, T., & Alexander, V. K. (1991). Cognitive stage development in children practicing the Transcendental Meditation program: Acquisition and consolidation of conservation. In R. A. Chalmer, G. Clements, H. Schenkluhn, & M. Weinless (Eds.), *Scientific research on Maharishi's Transcendental Meditation and TM-Sidhi programme: Collective papers* (Vol. 4, pp. 2352–2370). Vlodrop, Netherlands: MERU Press.

Alexander, C. N., Swanson, G., Rainforth, M., Carlisle, T., & Todd, C. (1991). The Transcendental Meditation program and business: A prospective study. In R. K. Wallace, D. W. Orme-Johnson, & M. C. Dillbeck (Eds.), *Scientific research on Maharishi's Transcendental Meditation and TM-Sidhi program: Collected papers* (Vol. 5, pp. 3141–3149). Fairfield, IA: MIU Press.

ALS Association. See Amyotrophic Lateral Sclerosis Association.

Altemeir, W. A., O'Connor, S. M., Sherrod, K. B., & Vietze, P. M. (1985). Prospective study of antecedents for nonorganic failure to thrive. *Journal of Pediatrics, 106,* 360–365.

Alternatives to hormone replacement. (1994, August). *Harvard Women's Health Watch,* pp. 2–3.

Altman, L. K. (1992, July 21). Women worldwide nearing higher rate for AIDS than men. *New York Times,* pp. C1, C3.

Alzheimer's and stress: Caregivers at risk. (1994, Fall). *Alzheimer's Association Newsletter,* pp. 1, 9.

Alzheimer's Association. (undated). *Is it Alzheimer's? Warning signs you should know.* Chicago: Author.

Amadiume, I. (1987). *Male daughters, female husbands.* Atlantic Highlands, NJ: Zed.

American Academy of Otolaryngology—Head and Neck Surgery. (1986). *Smell and taste disorders.* Alexandria, VA: Author.

American Academy of Pediatrics (AAP) Committee on Bioethics. (1992, July). Ethical issues in surrogate motherhood. *AAP News*, pp. 14–15.

American Association of Retired Persons (AARP). (1981). *A profile of older Americans*. Washington, DC: Author.

American Association of Retired Persons (AARP). (1986). *A profile of older Americans*. Washington, DC: Author.

American Association of Retired Persons (AARP). (1989a, March). *Working caregivers report*. Washington, DC: Author.

American Association of Retired Persons (AARP). (1989b). *Business and older workers: Current perceptions and new directions for the 1990s*. Washington, DC: Author.

American Association of Retired Persons (AARP). (1991). *A profile of older Americans*. Washington, DC: Author.

American Association of Retired Persons (AARP). (1992). *A profile of older Americans*. Washington, DC: Author.

American Association of Retired Persons (AARP). (1993a). *A profile of older Americans*. Washington, DC: Author.

American Association of Retired Persons (AARP). (1993b). *Understanding senior housing*. Washington, DC: Author.

American Association of Retired Persons (AARP). (1993c). *Abused elders or battered women?* Washington, DC: Author.

American Association of Retired Persons (AARP). (1994). *A profile of older Americans*. Washington, DC: Author.

American Cancer Society. (1994). *Cancer facts and figures—1994*. Atlanta: Author.

American Council on Science and Health. (1985). *Premenstrual syndrome*. Summit, NJ: Author.

American Diabetes Association. (1992). *Diabetes facts*. Alexandria, VA: Author.

American Heart Association. (1990). *The healthy American diet*. Dallas: Author.

American Heart Association. (1992). *Silent epidemic: The truth about women and heart disease*. Dallas: Author.

American Heart Association. (1993). *Heart and stroke fact statistics*. Dallas: Author.

American Heart Association. (1994). *Heart and stroke facts: 1994 statistical supplement*. Dallas: Author.

American Medical Association. (1992). *Diagnosis and treatment guidelines on elder abuse and neglect*. Chicago: Author.

American Psychiatric Association. (1994). *Diagnostic and statistical manual of mental disorders* (4th ed.). Washington, DC: Author.

Amory, M. (1987). The author. In G. O'Connor (Ed.), *Olivier: In celebration* (pp. 187–191). New York: Dodd, Mead.

Amyotrophic Lateral Sclerosis Association. (undated). Profiles in courage: Three stories of determination and hope. Woodland Hills, CA: Author.

Anastasi, A. (1988). *Psychological testing* (6th ed.). New York: Macmillan.

Anders, T. R., Fozard, J. L., & Lillyquist, T. D. (1972). Effects of age upon retrieval from short-term memory. *Developmental Psychology, 6*(2), 214–217.

Anderson, M. (1956). *My Lord, what a morning*. New York: Viking.

Anderson, M. (1992). *My Lord, what a morning*. Madison: University of Wisconsin Press.

Anderson, R. (1980). I never sang for my father. In R. G. Lyell (Ed.), *Middle age, old age* (pp. 55–110). New York: Harcourt Brace Jovanovich.

Anderson, S. A., Russell, C. S., & Schumm, W. R. (1983). Perceived marital quality and family life-cycle categories: A further analysis. *Journal of Marriage and the Family, 45*, 127–139.

Anderson, T. B. (1984). Widowhood as a life transition: Its impact on kinship ties. *Journal of Marriage and the Family, 46*, 105–114.

Angell, M. (1991). The case of Helga Wanglie. *New England Journal of Medicine, 325*, 511–512.

Angier, N. (1990, April 17). Diet offers tantalizing clues to long life. *New York Times*, pp. C1–C2.

Angier, N. (1993, March 4). Scientists find long-sought gene that causes Lou Gehrig's disease. *New York Times*, pp. A1, B8.

Anschutz, L., Camp, C. J., Markley, R. P., & Kramer, J. J. (1985). Maintenance and generalization of mnemonics for grocery shopping by older adults. *Experimental Aging Research, 11*, 157–160.

Anschutz, L., Camp, C. J., Markley, R. P., & Kramer, J. J. (1987). Remembering mnemonics: A 3-year follow-up on the effects of mnemonics training in elderly adults. *Experimental Aging Research, 13*, 141–143.

Ansley, J., & Erber, J. T. (1988). Computer interaction: Effects on attitudes and performance in older adults. *Educational Gerontology, 14*, 107–119.

Anson, O. (1989). Marital status and women's health revisited: The importance of a proximate adult. *Journal of Marriage and the Family, 51*, 185–194.

APA. See American Psychiatric Association.

Apostol, R. A., et al. (1993). Commitment to and role changes in dual career families. *Journal of Career Development, 20*(2), 121–129.

Aquilino, W. S., & Supple, K. R. (1991). Parent-child relations and parent's satisfaction with living arrangements when adult children live at home. *Journal of Marriage and the Family, 53*, 13–27.

Are we "in the middle of a cancer epidemic"? (1994, September). *University of California at Berkeley Wellness Letter*, pp. 4–5.

Arlin, P. K. (1975). Cognitive development in adulthood: A fifth stage? *Developmental Psychology, 11*, 602–606.

Arlin, P. K. (1984). Adolescent and adult thought: A structural interpretation. In M. L. Commons, F. A. Richards, & C. Armon (Eds.), *Beyond formal operations* (pp. 258–271). New York: Praeger.

Armitage, M. (1966). *Martha Graham*. New York: Dance Horizons.

Arthritis Foundation (1993). *Arthritis information: Basic facts: Answers to your questions*. Atlanta: Author.

Ashcraft, M. H. (1994). *Human memory and cognition* (2d ed.). New York: HarperCollins.

Assisted reproduction. (1995, April). *Harvard Women's Health Watch*, pp. 4–5.

Atchley, R. C. (1985). *Social forces and aging* (4th ed.). Belmont, CA: Wadsworth.

Atchley, R. C. (1989). A continuity theory of normal aging. *The Gerontologist, 29*, 183–190.

Atchley, R. C. (1991a). *Social forces and aging* (6th ed.). Belmont, CA: Wadsworth.

Atchley, R. C. (1991b, November). *Detachment and disengagement: Vedantic perspectives on wisdom.* Paper presented at the meeting of the Gerontological Society of America, San Francisco.

Atkinson, J. N., & Raynor, J. O. (1974). *Motivation and achievement.* New York: Halstead.

Atkinson, R. M., Ganzini, L., & Bernstein, M. J. (1992). Alcohol and substance-use disorders in the elderly. In J. E. Birren, R. Sloane, & G. D. Cohen (Eds.), *Handbook of mental health and aging* (2d ed., pp. 515–555). New York: Academic.

August, M. (1995, January 12). Compound may ease pains of growing old. *Chicago Sun-Times,* p. 48.

Ausubel, N. (Ed.). (1948). *A treasury of Jewish folklore.* New York: Crown.

Ausubel, N. (1964). *The book of Jewish knowledge.* New York: Crown.

Ayya, N. (1994, November-December). AIDS is of growing concern to professionals in aging. *Aging Today,* pp. 1, 4.

Babchuk, N. (1978-1979). Aging and primary relations. *International Journal of Aging and Human Development, 9*(2), 137–151.

Bachrach, C. A., London, K. A., & Maza, P. L. (1991). On the path to adoption: Adoption seeking in the United States, 1988. *Journal of Marriage and the Family, 53,* 705–718.

Bachu, A. (1993). *Fertility of American Women: June, 1992.* Washington, DC: U.S. Government Printing Office.

Backett, K. (1987). The negotiation of fatherhood. In C. Lewis & M. O'Brien (Eds.), *Reassessing fatherhood: New observations on fathers and the modern family.* London: Sage.

Baddeley, A. D. (1981). The concept of working memory: A view of its current state and probable future development. *Cognition, 10,* 17–23.

Baddeley, A. D. (1986). *Working memory.* London: Oxford University Press.

Baker, B. (1994, October). Outsmarting Alzheimer's: New research may speed prevention drug. *AARP Bulletin,* pp. 1, 14–15, 17.

Baker-Miller, J. (1976). *Toward a new psychology of women.* Boston: Beacon.

Balkwell, C. (1981). Transition to widowhood: A review of the literature. *Family Relations, 30,* 117–127.

Balkwell, C. (1985). An attitudinal correlate of the timing of a major life event: The case of morale in widowhood. *Family Relations, 34,* 577–581.

Baltes, P. B. (1983). Life span developmental psychology: Observations on history and theory revisited. In R. M. Lerner (Ed.), *Developmental psychology: Historical and developmental perspectives* (pp. 79–111). Hillsdale, NJ: Erlbaum.

Baltes, P. B. (1985). *The aging of intelligence: On the dynamics between growth and decline.* Unpublished manuscript.

Baltes, P. B. (1987). Theoretical propositions of life-span development psychology: On the dynamics between growth and decline. *Developmental Psychology, 23*(5), 611–626.

Baltes, P. B. (1993). The aging mind: Potential and limits. *The Gerontologist, 33,* 580–594.

Baltes, P. B., & Baltes, M. M. (1980). Plasticity and variability in psychological aging: Methodological and theoretical issues. In G. E. Gurski (Ed.), *Determining the effects of aging on the central nervous system* (pp. 41–66). Berlin: Schering.

Baltes, P. B., & Baltes, M. M. (1990). Psychological perspectives on successful aging: The model of selective optimization with compensation. In P. B. Baltes & M. M. Baltes (Eds.), *Successful aging: Perspectives from the behavioral sciences* (pp. 1–34). New York: Cambridge University Press.

Baltes, P. B., Dittman-Kohli, F., & Dixon, R. A. (1984). New perspectives in the development of intelligence in adulthood: Toward a dual-process conception and a model of selective optimization with compensation. In P. B. Baltes & O. G. Brim, Jr. (Eds.), *Life-span development and behavior* (Vol. 6, pp. 33–76). New York: Academic.

Baltes, P. B., & Kliegl, R. (1992). Further testing of limits of cognitive plasticity: Negative age differences in a mnemonic skill are robust. *Developmental Psychology, 28,* 121–125.

Baltes, P. B., Reese, H. W., & Lipsitt, L. (1980). Life-span developmental psychology. *Annual Review of Psychology, 31,* 65–110.

Baltes, P. B., Reese, H. W., & Nesselroade, J. R. (1977). *Life-span developmental psychology: Introduction to research methods.* Pacific Grove, CA: Brooks/Cole.

Baltes, P. B., & Schaie, K. W. (1974). Aging and IQ: The myth of the twilight years. *Psychology Today, 7*(10), 35–38.

Baltes, P. B., & Schaie, K. W. (1976). On the plasticity of intelligence in adulthood and old age: Where Horn and Donaldson fail. *American Psychologist, 31,* 720–725.

Baltes, Staudinger, Maercker, & Smith, 1993. See Baltes, Staudinger, Maercker, & Smith, 1995.

Baltes, P. B., Staudinger, U. M., Maercker, A., & Smith, J. (1995). People nominated as wise: A comparative study of wisdom-related knowledge. *Psychology and Aging, 10,* 155–166.

Baltes, P. B., & Willis, S. L. (1982). Enhancement (plasticity) of intellectual functioning in old age: Penn State's Adult Development and Enrichment Project (ADEPT). In F. I. M. Craik & S. Trehub (Eds.), *Aging and cognitive processes* (pp. 353–389). New York: Plenum.

Baltimore, D. (1995). Lessons from people with nonprogressive HIV infection. *New England Journal of Medicine, 332,* 259–260.

Banaji, M. R., & Crowder, R. G. (1989). The bankruptcy of everyday memory. *American Psychologist, 44*(9), 1185–1193.

Banner, C. (1992). Recent insights into the biology of Alzheimer's disease. *Generations, 16*(4), 31–35.

Barager, J. R. (Ed.). (1968). *Why Perón came to power: The background to Peronism in Argentina.* New York: Knopf.

Barchillon, J. (1961). Creativity and its inhibition in child prodigies. In *Personality dimensions of creativity.* New York: Lincoln Institute of Psychotherapy.

Barefoot, J. C., Dahlstrom, W. G., & Williams, R. B. (1983). Hostility, CHD incidence and total mortality: A 25-year follow-up study of 255 physicians. *Psychosomatic Medicine, 45*(1), 59–63.

Barfield, R. E., & Morgan, J. N. (1974). *Early retirement: The decision and the experience and a second look.* Ann Arbor, MI: Institute for Social Research.

Barfield, R. E., & Morgan, J. N. (1978). Trends in satisfaction with retirement. *The Gerontologist, 18,* 19–23.

Barinaga, M. (1991). How long is the human life-span? *Science, 254,* 936–938.

Barinaga, M. (1992). Mortality: Overturning received wisdom. *Science, 258,* 398–399.

Barnett, R. (1985, March 2). *We've come a long way—but where are we and what are the rewards?* Paper presented at the conference on Women in Transition, New York University School of Continuing Education, Center for Career and Life Planning, New York.

Barnett, R. C., Kibria, N., Baruch, G. K., & Pleck, J. H. (1991). Adult daughter-parent relationships and their association with daughters' subjective well-being and psychological distress. *Journal of Marriage and the Family, 53,* 29–42.

Barnett, R. C., Marshall, N. L, & Pleck, J. H. (1992). Men's multiple roles and their relationship to men's psychological distress. *Journal of Marriage and the Family, 54,* 358–367.

Barnett, R. C., et al. (1994). Gender and the relationship between marital-role quality and psychological distress. *Psychology of Women Quarterly, 18*(1), 105–127.

Barnhart, M. A. (1992, Fall). Coping with the Methuselah syndrome. *Free Inquiry,* pp. 19–22.

Barrett, C. J. (1978). Effectiveness of widows' groups in facilitating change. *Journal of Counseling and Clinical Psychology, 46*(1), 20–31.

Barrett, R. L., & Robinson, B. E. (1990). *Gay fathers.* Lexington, MA: Lexington.

Barrett-Connor, E., & Kritz-Silverstein, D. (1993, May 26). Estrogen replacement therapy and cognitive function in older women. *Journal of the American Medical Association, 269,* 2637–2641.

Barth, M. C., McNaught, W., & Rizzi, P. (1993). Corporations and the aging workforce. In P. H. Mirvis (Ed.), *Building the competitive workforce.* New York: Wiley.

Bartlett, F. (1958). *Thinking.* New York: Basic Books.

Bartlett, F. C. (1932). *Remembering.* Cambridge, England: Cambridge University Press.

Barton, P., & Lapointe, A. (1995). *Learning by degrees: Indicators of performance in higher education.* Princeton, NJ: ETS Policy Information Center.

Baruch, G., Barnett, R., & Rivers, C. (1983). *Lifeprints.* New York: McGraw-Hill.

Bates, J. E., & Wachs, T. D. (Eds.). (1994). *Temperament: Individual differences at the interface of biology and behavior.* Washington, DC: American Psychological Association.

Bateson, G. (1982). Totemic knowledge in New Guinea. In U. Neisser (Ed.), *Memory observed: Remembering in natural contexts* (pp. 269–273). San Francisco: Freeman.

Bayley, N., & Oden, M. (1955). The maintenance of intellectual ability in gifted adults. *Journal of Gerontology, 10,* 91–107.

Beard, G. M. (1874). *Legal responsibility in old age.* New York: Russell.

Beard, R. J. (1975). The menopause. *British Journal of Hospital Medicine, 12,* 631–637.

Bebbington, P. (1990). Population surveys of psychiatric disorder and the need for treatment. *Social Psychiatry and Psychiatric Medicine, 25,* 33–40.

Beck, S. H. (1982). Adjustment to and satisfaction with retirement. *Journal of Gerontology, 37,* 616–624.

Becker, G. S. (1992, December 7). Finding fault with no-fault divorce. *Business Week,* p. 23.

Belbin, R. M. (1967). Middle age: What happens to ability? In R. Owen (Ed.). *Middle age.* London: BBC.

Bell, A. P., Weinberg, M. S., & Hammersmith, S. K. (1981). *Sexual preference: Its development in men and women.* New York: Simon & Schuster.

Bell, J. (1992). In search of a discourse on aging: The elderly on television. *The Gerontologist, 32*(3), 305–311.

Belsky, J. (1980). A family analysis of parental influence on infant exploratory competence. In F. A. Pedersen (Ed.), *The father-infant relationship: Observational studies in a family setting.* New York: Praeger.

Belsky, J. (1984). *The psychology of aging: Theory, research, and practice.* Monterey, CA: Brooks/Cole.

Belsky, J., Lang, M., & Huston, T. L. (1986). Sex typing and division of labor as determinants of marital change across the transition to parenthood. *Journal of Personality and Social Psychology, 50,* 517–522.

Belsky, J., & Rovine, M. (1990). Patterns of marital change across the transition to parenthood: Pregnancy to three years postpartum. *Journal of Marriage and the Family, 52,* 5–19.

Bem, S. L. (1974). The measurement of psychological androgyny. *Journal of Consulting and Clinical Psychology, 42,* 155–162.

Bem, S. L. (1976). Probing the promise of androgyny. In A. G. Kaplan & J. P. Bean (Eds.), *Beyond sex-role stereotypes: Readings toward a psychology of androgyny.* Boston: Little, Brown.

Bem, S. L. (1981). Gender schema theory: A cognitive account of sex typing. *Psychological Review, 88,* 354–369.

Bem, S. L. (1983). Gender schema theory and its implications for child development: Raising gender-aschematic children in a gender-schematic society. *Signs, 8,* 598–616.

Bem, S. L. (1985). Androgyny and gender schema theory: A conceptual and empirical investigation. In T. B. Sondregger (Ed.), *Nebraska Symposium on Motivation, 1984: Psychology and gender.* Lincoln: University of Nebraska Press.

Bemon, P., & Sharma, A. S. (1994). *Growing up adopted: A portrait of adolescents and their families.* Minneapolis: Search Institute of Minnesota.

Bengtson, V., Cuellar, J. A., & Ragan, P. (1975, October 29). *Group contrasts in attitudes toward death: Variation by race, age, occupational status and sex.* Paper presented at the annual meeting of the Gerontological Society, Louisville, KY.

Benner, P. (1984). *From novice to expert: Excellence and practice in clinical nursing practice.* Reading, MA: Addison-Wesley.

Benson, M. (1986). *Nelson Mandela: The man and the movement.* New York: Norton.

Benzing, W. C., & Squire, L. R. (1989). Preserved learning and memory in amnesia: Intact adaptation-level effects and learning of stereoscopic depth. *Behavioral Neuroscience, 103,* 538–547.

Berardo, D. H., Sheehan, C. L., & Leslie, G. R. (1987). A residue of tradition: Jobs, careers, and spouses' time in housework. *Journal of Marriage and the Family, 49*, 381–390.

Berg, C. A., & Sternberg, R. J. (1992). Adults' conceptions of intelligence across the adult life span. *Psychology and Aging, 7*, 221–231.

Berger, R. M. (1982). *Gay and gray: The older homosexual male.* Urbana: University of Illinois Press.

Berger, R. M. (1984, January-February). Realities of gay and lesbian aging. *Social Work*, pp. 57–62.

Berger, R. M., & Kelly, J. J. (1986). Working with homosexuals of the older population. *Social Casework, 67*, 203–210.

Bergman, A. B., Larsen, R. M., & Mueller, B. A. (1986). Changing spectrum of serious child abuse. *Pediatrics, 77*(1), 113–116.

Bergman, S. J. (1991). *Men's psychological development: A relational perspective* (Work in Progress No. 48). Wellesley, MA: The Stone Center, Wellesley College.

Berkowitz, G. S., Skovron, M. L., Lapinski, R. H., & Berkowitz, R. L. (1990). Delayed childbearing and the outcome of pregnancy. *New England Journal of Medicine, 322*, 659–664.

Berman, C. (1981). *Making it as a stepparent: New roles/new rules.* New York: Bantam.

Bernard, J. L., & Bernard, M. L. (1984). The abusive male seeking treatment: Jekyll and Hyde. *Family Relations, 33*, 543–547.

Bernstein, J. (1995). *Where's the payoff?* Washington, DC: Economic Policy Institute.

Berrios, J. (1993, June–July). Partners in progress: Gannett Company profits from workplace diversity. *The National Voter*, pp. 12–13.

Berscheid, E., & Campbell, B. (1981). The changing longevity of heterosexual close relationships. In M. J. Lerner & S. C. Lerner (Eds.), *The justice motive in social behavior.* New York: Plenum.

Bettelheim, B. (1960). *The informed heart: Autonomy in a mass age.* Glencoe, IL: Free.

Better prostate cancer predictions. (1994, September). *Johns Hopkins Medical Center: Health after 50*, pp. 1–2.

Bianchi, S. M., & Spain, D. (1986). *American women in transition.* New York: Russell Sage Foundation.

Bielby, D., & Papalia, D. (1975). Moral development and perceptual role-taking egocentrism: Their development and interrelationship across the life span. *International Journal of Aging and Human Development, 6*(4), 293–308.

Bigger, J. T., Jr. (1985). Heart and blood vessel disease. In D. F. Tapley, R. J. Weiss, & T. Q. Morris, (Eds.), *The Columbia University College of Physicians and Surgeons complete home medical guide* (pp. 386–394). New York: Crown.

Binet, A. (1890). Perceptions d'enfants. *La Revue Philosophique, 30*, 582–611.

Binet, A., & Simon, T. (1905). Application des méthodes nouvelles au diagnostic du niveau intellectuel chez des enfants normaux et anormaux d'hospice et d'école primaire. *L'Année Psychologique, 11*, 245–336.

Binet, A., & Simon, T. (1908). Le développement de l'intelligence chez les enfants. *L'Année Psychologique, 14*, 1–94.

Binstock R. H. (1993). Healthcare costs around the world: Is aging a fiscal "blackhole"? *Generations, 17* (4), 37–42.

Bird, K. (1990, November 12). The very model of an ex-president. *The Nation*, pp. 545, 560–564.

Biringer, F., Anderson, J. R., & Strubel, D. (1988). Self-recognition in senile dementia. *Experimental Aging Research, 14*, 177–180.

Birren, J. E., & Cunningham, W. R. (1985). Research on the psychology of aging. In J. E. Birren & K. W. Schaie (Eds.), *Handbook of the psychology of aging* (2d ed., pp. 3–34). New York: Van Nostrand Reinhold.

Birren, J. E., & Morrison, D. F. (1961). Analysis of the WAIS subtests in relation to age and education. *Journal of Gerontology, 16*, 363–369.

Birren, J. E., & Renner, V. J. (1977). Research on the psychology of aging: Principles and experimentation. In J. E. Birren & K. W. Schaie (Eds.), *Handbook of the psychology of aging* (pp. 3–38). New York: Van Nostrand Reinhold.

Birren, J. E., Woods, A. M., & Williams, M. V. (1980). Behavioral slowing with age: Causes, organization, and consequences. In L. W. Poon (Ed.), *Aging in the 1980s.* Washington, DC: American Psychological Association.

Blackburn, J. A. (1984). The influence of personality, curriculum, and memory correlates on formal reasoning in young adults and elderly persons. *Journal of Gerontology, 39*, 207–209.

Blackburn, J. A., Papalia-Finlay, D., Foye, B. F., & Serlin, R. C. (1988). Modifiability of figural relations performance among elderly adults. *Journal of Gerontology: Psychological Sciences 43*(3), P87–89.

Blair, S. N., Kohl, H. W., Paffenbarger, R. S., Clark, D. G., Cooper, K. H., & Gibbons, L. W. (1989). Physical fitness and all-cause mortality: A prospective study of healthy men and women. *Journal of the American Medical Association, 262*, 2395–2401.

Blanchard-Fields, F. (1986). Reasoning on social dilemmas varying in emotional saliency: An adult developmental perspective. *Psychology and Aging, 1*, 325–333.

Blanchard-Fields, F., & Abeles, R. P. (in press). Social structural influences on behavior. In J. E. Birren & K. W. Schaie (Eds.), *Handbook of the psychology of aging* (4th ed.). San Diego: Academic.

Blanchard-Fields, F., Brannan, J. R., & Camp, C. J. (1987). Alternative conceptions of wisdom: An onion-peeling excercise. *Educational Gerontology, 13*, 497–503.

Blanchard-Fields, F., & Camp, C. J. (1990). Affect, individual differences, and real world problem solving across the adult life span. In T. Hess (Ed.), *Aging and cognition: Knowledge organization and utilization* (pp. 461–498). Amsterdam: North-Holland, Elsevier.

Blanchard-Fields, F., & Irion, J. (1987). Coping strategies from the perspective of two developmental markers: Age and social reasoning. *Journal of Genetic Psychology, 149*, 141–151.

Blanchard-Fields, F., Jahnke, H. C., & Camp, C. J. (1995). Age differences in problem solving style: The role of emotional salience. *Psychology and Aging, 10*, 173–180.

Blanchard-Fields, F., Suhrer-Roussel, L., & Hertzog, C. (1994). A confirmatory factor analysis of the Bem Sex

Role Inventory: Old questions, new answers. *Sex Roles, 30*, 423–457.

Blanksten, G. I. (1953). *Perón's Argentina*. Chicago: University of Chicago Press.

Blasko, J. C., Ragde, H., & Grimm, P. D. (1991). Transperineal ultrasound-guided implantation of the prostate: Morbidity and complications. *Scandinavian Journal of Urology and Nephrology Supplementum, 137*, 113–118.

Blazer, D. G. (1989). Depression in the elderly. *New England Journal of Medicine, 320*, 164–166.

Blazer, D. G., Kessler, R. C., McGonagle, K. A., & Swartz, M. S. (1994). The prevalence and distribution of major depression in a national community sample: The National Comorbidity Survey. *American Journal of Psychiatry, 151*, 979–986.

Blieszner, R. (1986). Trends in family gerontology research. *Family Relations, 35*, 555–562.

Blieszner, R., & Shifflett, P. A. (1990). The effects of Alzheimer's disease on close relationships between patients and caregivers. *Family Relations, 39*, 57–62.

Blieszner, R., Willis, S. L., & Baltes, P. B. (1981). Training research on induction ability: A short-term longitudinal study. *Journal of Applied Developmental Psychology, 2*, 247–265.

Block, J. (1981). Some enduring and consequential structures of personality. In A. I. Rabin et al. (Eds.), *Further explorations in personality*. New York: Wiley.

Block, J. (1993). Studying personality the long way. In D. C. Funder, R. D. Parke, C. Tomlinson-Keasey, & K. Widaman (Eds.), *Studying lives through time: Personality and development* (pp. 9–44). Washington, DC: American Psychological Association.

Bloom, D. E., & Pebley, A. R. (1982). Voluntary childlessness: A review of the evidence and its implications. *Population Research and Policy Review, 1*, 203–234.

Blue Cross and Blue Shield Association (BCBSA). (1988). *No-nonsense AIDS answers*. Chicago: Author.

Blum, L., & Rosner, F. (1983). Alcoholism in the elderly: An analysis of 50 patients. *Journal of the National Medical Association, 75*, 489–495.

Blumstein, P. W., & Schwartz, P. (1983). *American couples*. New York: Morrow.

Bogerts, B. (1993). Images in psychiatry: Alois Alzheimer. *American Journal of Psychiatry, 150*, 1868.

Bolger, N., DeLongis, A., Kessler, R. C., & Schilling, E. A. (1989). Effects of daily stress on negative mood. *Journal of Personality and Social Psychology, 57*, 808–818.

Bolles, R. N. (1979). *The three boxes of life*. Berkeley, CA: Ten Speed.

Bolton, R. (1981). Susto, hostility and hypoglycemia. *Ethnology, 20*(4), 227–258.

Bondi, M. W., Kaszniak, A. W., Bayles, K. A., & Vance, K. T. (1993). Contributions of frontal system dysfunctions to memory and perceptual abilities in Parkinson's disease. *Neuropsychology 7*(1), 89–102.

Bonfield, T. (1995, January 15). Prostate treatment has few certainties. *Chicago Sun-Times*, p. 61.

Borges, J. L. (1964). *Labyrinths: Selected stories and other writings*. New York: New Directions.

Borkowski, A., & Ozanne, E. (1993). New directions in aging policy in Australia. *Generations, 17*(4), 55–60.

Bossé, R., Aldwin, C. M., Levenson, M. R., & Ekerdt, D. J. (1987). Mental health among retirees and workers: Findings from the Normative Aging Study. *Psychology and Aging, 2*, 383–389.

Bossé, R., Aldwin, C. M., Levenson, M. R., Spiro, A., & Mroczek, D. K. (1993). Change in social support after retirement: Longitudinal findings from the normative aging study. *Journal of Gerontology: Psychological Sciences, 48*, P210–217.

Bossé, R., Aldwin, C. M., Levenson, M. R., & Workman-Daniels, K. (1991). How stressful is retirement? Findings from the Normative Aging Study. *Journal of Gerontology: Psychological Sciences, 46*, P9–14.

Botwinick, J. (1978). *Aging and behavior* (2d ed.). New York: Springer.

Botwinick, J. (1984). *Aging and behavior* (3d ed.). New York: Springer.

Botwinick, J., & Siegler, I. C. (1980). Intellectual ability among the elderly: Simultaneous cross-sectional and longitudinal comparisons. *Developmental Psychology, 16*, 49–53.

Boulton, M. G. (1983). *On being a mother: A study of women with pre-school children*. London: Tavistock.

Bouvier, L. F., & Simcox, D. (1994). *Foreign born professionals in the U.S.* Washington, DC: Center for Immigration Studies.

Bouza, A. V. (1990). *The police mystique: An insider's look at cops, crime, and the criminal justice system*. New York: Plenum.

Bowlby, J. (1973). *Separation: Anxiety and anger*. New York: Basic Books.

Boyer, J. L., & Guthrie, L. (1985). Assessment and treatment of the suicidal patient. In E. E. Beckham & W. R. Leber (Eds.), *Handbook of depression*. Homewood, IL: Dorsey.

Brabant, S. (1994). An overlooked AIDS affected population: The elderly parent as caregiver. *Journal of Gerontological Social Work, 22*, 131–145.

Bragg, M. (1984). *Laurence Olivier*. New York: St. Martin's.

Branch, L. G., Horowitz, A., & Carr, C. (1989). The implications for everyday life of incident of self-reported visual decline among people over age 65 living in the community. *The Gerontologist, 29*(3), 359–365.

Brandt, B. (1989). A place for her death. *Humanistic Judaism, 17*(3), 83–85.

Braungart, J. M., Plomin, R., DeFries, J. C., & Fulker, D. W. (1992). Genetic influence on tester-rated infant temperament as assessed by Bayley's Infant Behavior Record: Nonadoptive and adoptive siblings and twins. *Developmental Psychology, 28*, 40–47.

Braveman, N. S. (1987). Immunity and aging: Immunologic and behavioral perspectives. In M. W. Riley, J. D. Matarazzo, & A. Baum (Eds.), *Perspectives in behavioral medicine: The aging dimension* (pp. 93–124). Hillsdale, NJ: Erlbaum.

Brave new biology: Granny gives birth. (1993, February 13). *Science News*, p. 100.

Bray, D. W., & Howard, A. (1983). The AT&T longitudinal study of managers. In K. W. Schaie (Ed.), *Longitudinal studies on adult psychological development* (pp. 266–312). New York: Guilford.

The breast cancer genes. (1994, December). *Harvard Women's Health Watch*, p. 1.

Breast cancer: Up or down? (1995, June). *University of California at Berkeley Wellness Letter*, p. 2.

Breast imaging: Today and tomorrow. (1995, January). *Harvard Women's Health Watch*, p. 2.

Brecher, E., & the Editors of Consumer Reports Books. (1984). *Love, sex, and aging: A Consumers Union report.* Boston: Little, Brown.

Bremner, W. J., Vitiello, M. V., & Prinz, P. N. (1983). Loss of circadian rhythmicity in blood testosterone levels with aging in normal men. *Journal of Clinical Endocrinology and Metabolism, 56,* 1278–1281.

Brenner, M. H. (1991). Health, productivity, and the economic environment: Dynamic role of socio-economic status. In G. Green & F. Baker (Eds.), *Work, health, and productivity* (pp. 241–255). New York: Oxford University Press.

Brickfield, C. F. (1984). Attitudes and perceptions of older people toward technology. In P. K. Robinson & J. E. Birren (Eds.), *Aging and technological advances* (pp. 31–38). New York: Plenum.

Brigham, M. C., & Pressley, M. (1988). Cognitive monitoring and strategy choice in younger and older adults. *Psychology and Aging, 3,* 249–257.

Briley, M. (1980, July–August). Burnout stress and the human energy crisis. *Dynamic Years,* pp. 36–39.

Brim, O. G. (1977). Theories of male mid-life crisis. In N. Schlossberg & A. Entine (Eds.), *Counseling adults.* Monterey, CA: Brooks/Cole.

Brint, S. F. (1989). *Sight for a lifetime.* Metairie, LA: Plantain.

Brint, S. F., Nordan, L. T., & Herman, W. K. (1991). *Vision without glasses.* New York: J. B. Media.

Brocas, A., Cailloux, A., & Oget, V. (1990). *Women and social security: Progress towards equality of treatment.* Geneva: International Labour Office.

Brock, D. W. (1992, March–April). Voluntary active euthanasia. *Hastings Center Report,* pp. 10–22.

Brody, E. B., & Brody, N. (1976). *Intelligence: Nature, determinants, and consequences.* New York: Academic.

Brody, E. M. (1978). Community housing for the elderly. *The Gerontologist, 18*(2), 121–128.

Brody, H. (1955). Organization of the cerebral cortex: 3. A study of aging in the cerebral cortex. *Journal of Comparative Neurology, 102,* 511–556.

Brody, H. (1970). Structural changes in the aging nervous system. In H. T. Blumenthal (Ed.), *The regulatory role of the nervous system in aging: 7. Interdisciplinary topics in gerontology* (pp. 9–21). Basel, Switzerland: Karger.

Brody, J. E. (1990, October 11). Sedentary living, not cholesterol, is the nation's leading culprit in fatal heart attacks. *New York Times,* p. B12.

Brody, J. E. (1992a, June 16). Suicide myths cloud efforts to save children. *New York Times,* p. C1.

Brody, J. E. (1992b, December 9). Hip fracture: A potential killer that can be avoided. *New York Times,* p. C16.

Bronfenbrenner, U. (1979). *The ecology of human development.* Cambridge, MA: Harvard University Press.

Bronfenbrenner, U. (1994). Ecological models of human development. In T. Husen & T. N. Postlewaite (Eds.), *International Encyclopedia of Education* (2d ed., Vol. 3). Oxford, UK: Pergamon/Elsevier Science.

Bronte, L. (1993). *The longevity factor: The new reality of long careers and how it can lead to richer lives.* New York: HarperCollins.

Brown, D. (1994, September 15). Research race leads to breast cancer gene. *Chicago Sun-Times,* p. 27.

Brown, J. H. (1979). Suicide in Britain: More attempts, fewer deaths, lessons for public policy. *Archives of General Psychiatry, 36,* 1119–1124.

Brown, J. T., & Stoudemire, A. (1983). Normal and pathological grief. *Journal of the American Medical Association, 250,* 378–382.

Brown, M. B., & Tedrick, T. (1993). Outdoor leisure involvements of black older Americans: An exploration of ethnicity and marginality. In *Activities, adaptation, and aging* (pp. 55–65). New York: Haworth.

Brown, N. M. (1990). Age and children in the Kalahari. *Health and Human Development Research, 1,* 26–30.

Brown, N. M. (1993). Singular women. *Health and Human Development Research, 3,* 16–21.

Brown, P. (1993, April 17). Motherhood past midnight. *New Scientist,* pp. 4–8.

Browne, A., & Finkelhor, D. (1986). Impact of child sexual abuse: A review of research. *Psychological Bulletin, 99*(1), 66–77.

Brozan, N. (1990, November 29). Less visible but heavier burdens as AIDS attacks people over 50. *New York Times,* pp. A1, A16.

Brubaker, T. H. (1983). Introduction. In T. H. Brubaker (Ed.), *Family relationships in later life.* Beverly Hills, CA: Sage.

Brubaker, T. H. (1990). Families in later life: A burgeoning research area. *Journal of Marriage and the Family, 52,* 959–981.

Brubaker, T. H. (Ed.). (1993). *Family relationships: Current and future directions.* Newbury Park, CA: Sage.

Bruce, J., Lloyd, C. B., & Leonard, A. (1995). *Families in focus: New perspectives on mothers, fathers, and children.* New York: Population Council.

Brumberg, E. (1993, August–September). What price beauty? *Modern Maturity,* p. 74.

Buchwald, A. (1994). *Leaving home.* New York: Putnam.

Bühler, C. (1933). *Der menschliche lebenslauf als psychologisches problem.* Leipzig: Verlag von S. Hirzel.

Bühler, C. (1968a). The developmental structure of goal setting in group and individual studies. In C. Bühler & F. Massarik (Eds.), *The course of human life* (pp. 27–54). New York: Springer.

Bühler, C. (1968b). The general structure of the human life cycle. In C. Bühler & F. Massarik (Eds.), *The course of human life* (pp. 12–26). New York: Springer.

Bulcroft, K., & O'Conner, M. (1986). The importance of dating relationships on quality of life for older persons. *Family Relations, 35,* 397–401.

Bulcroft, R. A., & Bulcroft, K. A. (1991). The nature and function of dating in later life. *Research on Aging, 13,* 244–260.

Bumpass, L. L., & Sweet, J. A. (1988). *Preliminary evidence on cohabitation* (NSFH Working Paper No. 2). Madison: University of Wisconsin, Center for Demography and Ecology.

Bumpass, L., Sweet, J., & Martin, T. C. (1990). Changing patterns of remarriage. *Journal of Marriage and the Family, 52,* 747–756.

Bureau of Justice Statistics. See U.S. Bureau of Justice Statistics.

Burkhauser, R. V., Holden, K. C., & Feaster, D. (1988). Incidence, timing, and events associated with poverty: A dynamic view of poverty in retirement. *Journal of Gerontology: Social Sciences, 43,* S46–52.

Burkhauser, R. V., & Quinn, J. (1989). Work and retirement: The American experience. In Winfried Schmahl (Ed.), *Redefining the process of retirement: An international perspective.* Berlin: Springer-Verlag.

Burns, A. (1992). Mother-headed families: An international perspective and the case of Australia. *Social Policy Report of the Society for Research in Child Development, 6*(1).

Burns, B., & Taub, C. (1990). Mental health services in general medical care and nursing homes. In B. Fogel, A. Furino, & G. Gottlieb (Eds.), *Mental health policy for older Americans: Protecting minds at risk* (pp. 63–83). Washington, DC: American Psychiatric Press.

Burns, G. (1983). *How to live to be 100—or more: The ultimate diet, sex, and exercise book.* New York: Putnam.

Burton, L. M. (1992). Black grandparents rearing children of drug-addicted parents: Stressors, outcomes, and social service needs. *The Gerontologist, 32,* 744–751.

Bush, B. (1994). *Barbara Bush: A memoir.* New York: Scribner's.

Bush, T. L., Cowan, L. D., Barrett-Connor, E., Criqui, M. H., Karon, J. M., Wallace, R. B., Tyroler, H. A., & Rifkind, B. M. (1983). Estrogen use and all-cause mortality: Preliminary results from the Lipid Research Clinics program follow-up study. *Journal of the American Medical Association, 249*(7), 903–906.

Busse, E. W. (1987). Primary and secondary aging. In G. L. Maddox (Ed.), *The encyclopedia of aging* (p. 534). New York: Springer.

Butler, R. (1961). Re-awakening interests. *Nursing Homes: Journal of American Nursing Home Association, 10,* 8–19.

Butler, R. N. (1987a). Ageism. In G. L. Maddox (Ed.), *The encyclopedia of aging* (pp. 22–23). New York: Springer.

Butler, R. N. (1987b). Mental health and illness. In G. L. Maddox (Ed.), *The encyclopedia of aging* (pp. 439–440). New York: Springer.

Butler, R. N., & Lewis, M. (1982). *Aging and mental health* (3d ed.). St. Louis: Mosby.

Butler, R. N., Lewis, M. I., & Sunderland, T. (1991). *Aging and mental health: Positive psychosocial and biomedical approaches* (4th ed.). New York: Merrill.

Cadwell, S. (1994, August). The psychological impact of HIV on gay men. *The Menninger Letter,* pp. 4–5.

Cahan, S., & Cohen, M. (1989). Age versus schooling effects on intelligence development. *Child Development, 60,* 1239–1249.

Cain, W. S., Reid, F., & Stevens, J. C. (1990). Missing ingredients: Aging and the discrimination of flavor. *Journal of Nutrition for the Elderly, 9,* 3–15.

Camargo, C. A., Gaziano, M., Hennekens, C. H., Manson, J. E., & Stampfer, M. J. (1994, November). *Prospective study of moderate alcohol consumption and mortality in male physicians.* Paper presented at the 67th Annual Scientific Sessions of the American Heart Association, Dallas.

Camp, C. J. (1988). In pursuit of trivia: Remembering, forgetting, and aging. *Gerontological Review, 1,* 37–42.

Camp, C. J. (1989). World-knowledge systems. In L. W. Poon, D. C. Rubin, & B. A. Wilson (Eds.), *Everyday cognition in adulthood and late life* (pp. 457–482). Cambridge: Cambridge University Press.

Camp, C. J., Doherty, K., Moody-Thomas, S., & Denney, N. W. (1989). Practical problem solving in adults: A comparison of problem types and scoring methods. In J. D. Sinnott (Ed.), *Everyday problem solving: Theory and applications* (pp. 211–228). New York: Praeger.

Camp, C. J., Foss, J. W., Stevens, A. B., Reichard, C. C., McKitrick, L. A., & O'Hanlon, A. M. (1993). Memory training in normal and demented populations: The E-I-E-I-O model. *Experimental Aging Research, 19,* 277–290.

Camp, C. J., Markley, R. P., & Kramer, J. J. (1983). Spontaneous use of mnemonics by elderly individuals. *Educational Gerontology, 9,* 57–71.

Camp, C. J., Markley, R. P., & Spenser, M. (1987, May). *Directed forgetting and aging.* Paper presented at the first annual Cognition and Aging Conference, Atlanta.

Camp, C. J., & McKitrick, L. A. (1989). The dialectics of remembering and forgetting across the adult lifespan. In D. Kramer & M. Bopp (Eds.), *Dialectics and contextualism in clinical and developmental psychology: Change, transformation, and the social context* (pp. 169–187). New York: Springer.

Camp, C. J., & McKitrick, L. A. (1992). Memory interventions in Alzheimer's-type dementia populations: Methodological and theoretical issues. In R. L. West & J. D. Sinnott (Eds.), *Everyday memory and aging: Current research and methodology* (pp. 155–172). New York: Springer-Verlag.

Camp, C. J., & Pignatiello, M. F. (1988). Beliefs about fact retrieval and inferential reasoning across the adult lifespan. *Experimental Aging Research, 14,* 89–98.

Camp, C. J., & Stevens, A. B. (1990). Spaced-retrieval: A memory intervention for dementia of the Alzheimer's type (DAT). *Clinical Gerontologist, 10,* 58–61.

Campbell, F. L., Townes, B. D., & Beach, L. R. (1982). Motivational bases of childbearing decisions. In G. L. Fox (Ed.), *The childbearing decision: Fertility, attitudes, and behavior.* Beverly Hills, CA: Sage.

Campbell, J., & Moyers, W. (1988). *The power of myth with Bill Moyers.* New York: Doubleday.

Cantor, M. H. (1980). The informal support system: Its relevance in the lives in the elderly. In E. Borgatta & N. McClusky (Eds.), *Aging and society* (pp. 111–146). Beverly Hills, CA: Sage.

Cantor, M. H. (1983). Strain among caregivers: A study of experience in the United States. *The Gerontologist, 23*(6), 597–604.

Cargan, L. (1981). Singles: An examination of two stereotypes. *Family Relations, 30,* 377–385.

Carlson, E., & Crowley, S. L. (1992, September). The Friedan mystique. *AARP Bulletin,* pp. 20, 15.

Carroll, J. B. (1991a). No demonstration that *g* is not unitary, but there's more to the story: Comment on Kranzler and Jensen. *Intelligence, 15,* 423–436.

Carroll, J. B. (1991b). Still no demonstration that *g* is not unitary: Further comment on Kranzler and Jensen. *Intelligence, 15*, 449–453.

Carstensen, L. L. (1991). Selectivity theory: Social activity in life-span context. In *Annual review of gerontology and geriatrics* (Vol. 11, pp. 195–217). New York: Springer.

Carter, J. (1975). *Why not the best?* Nashville: Broadman.

Carter Center. (1995, Winter). *Carter Center News*, pp. 1, 3, 4–6, 9.

Carton, R. W. (1990). The road to euthanasia. *Journal of the American Medical Association, 263*(16), 2221.

Casey, P. H., Bradley, R., & Wortham, B. (1984). Social and nonsocial home environment of infants with nonorganic failure-to-thrive. *Pediatrics, 73*(3), 348–353.

Caspi, A. (1993). Why maladaptive behaviors persist: Sources of continuity and change across the life course. In D. C. Funder, R. D. Parke, C. Tomlinson-Keasey, & K. Widaman (Eds.), *Studying lives through time: Personality and development* (pp. 343–376). Washington, DC: American Psychological Association.

Cassel, C. (1992). Ethics and the future of aging research: Promises and problems. *Generations, 16*(4), 61–65.

Catania, J. A., Coates, T. J., Stall, R., Turner, H., et al. (1992). Prevalence of AIDS-related risk factors and condom use in the United States. *Science, 258*(5085), 1101–1106.

Cattell, R. B. (1965). *The scientific analysis of personality.* Baltimore: Penguin.

Cavanaugh, J. C., Kramer, D. A., Sinnott, J. D., Camp, C. J., & Markley, R. P. (1985). On missing links and such: Interfaces between cognitive research and everyday problem solving. *Human Development, 28*, 146–168.

Cavanaugh, J. C., & Morton, K. R. (1989). Contextualism, naturalistic inquiry, and the need for new science: A rethinking of everyday memory aging and childhood sexual abuse. In D. A. Kramer & M. Bopp (Eds.), *Transformation in clinical and developmental psychology* (pp. 89–114). New York: Springer-Verlag.

Ceci, S., & Liker, J. (1986). A day at the races: A study of IQ, expertise, and cognitive complexity. *Journal of Experimental Psychology: General, 114*, 255–266.

Celis, W. (1990). More states are laying school paddle to rest. *New York Times*, pp. A1, B12.

Center on Elderly People Living Alone. (1995a, January). *Medicaid and long-term care for older people* (Public Policy Institute Fact Sheet FS18R). Washington, DC: American Association of Retired Persons.

Center on Elderly People Living Alone. (1995b, January). *Nursing homes* (Public Policy Institute Fact Sheet FS10R). Washington, DC: American Association of Retired Persons.

Center on Elderly People Living Alone. (1995c, April). *Long-term care* (Public Policy Institute Fact Sheet FS27R). Washington, DC: American Association of Retired Persons.

Centers for Disease Control and Prevention. (1994). Annual summary of births, marriages, divorces, and deaths: United States, 1993. *Monthly Vital Statistics, 42*(13), 18–20.

Centers for Disease Control and Prevention. (1995). Differences in maternal mortality among black and white women: United States, 1990. *Morbidity and Mortality Weekly Report, 44*(1), 6–7, 13–14.

Central Bureau of Statistics. (1992). *Statistical pocket book 1992.* Kathmandu, Nepal: Ratna Offset Press.

Chafetz, M. D. (1992). *Smart for life.* New York: Penguin.

Chalfie, D. (1994). *Going it alone: A closer look at grandparents parenting grandchildren.* Washington, DC: AARP Women's Initiative.

Chambre, S. M. (1993). Volunteerism by elders: Past trends and future prospects. *The Gerontologist, 33*, 221–227.

Chan, W. (1963). *A source book in Chinese philosophy.* Princeton, NJ: Princeton University Press.

Chappell, N. L. (1991). Living arrangements and sources of caregiving. *Journal of Gerontology: Social Sciences, 46*(1), S1–8.

Chappell, N. L., & Penning, M. J. (1979). The trend away from institutionalization. *Research on Aging, 1*(1), 162–287.

Charness, N., Schumann, C. E., & Boritz, G. M. (1992). Training older adults in word processing: Effects of age, training technique, and computer anxiety. *International Journal of Technology and Aging, 5*, 79–106.

Chatters, L. M., & Taylor, R. J. (1989). Age differences in religious participation among black adults. *Journal of Gerontology: Social Sciences, 44*(5), S183–189.

Chawla, S. (1993). Demographic aging and development. *Generations, 17*(4), 20–23.

Checkoway, B. (1992). *Empowering the elderly: Gerontological health promotion in Latin America.* Unpublished manuscript.

Cherlin, A., & Furstenberg, F. F. (1986a). Grandparents and family crisis. *Generations, 10*(4), 26–28.

Cherlin, A., & Furstenberg, F. F., Jr. (1986b). *The new American grandparent.* New York: Basic Books.

Chernoff, A. S. (1989). A parent's grief. *Humanistic Judaism, 17*(3), 80–82.

Cherry, K. E., & Park, D. C. (1993). Individual differences and contextual variables influence spatial memory in younger and older adults. *Psychology and Aging, 8*, 517–526.

Child Welfare League of America. (1986). *Born to run: The status of child abuse in America.* Washington, DC: Author.

Chilman, C. W. (1980). *Adolescent sexuality in a changing American society: Social and psychological perspectives* (NIH Publication No. 80-1426). Bethesda, MD: National Institutes of Health.

Chinen, A. B. (1984). Modal logic: A new paradigm of development and late-life potential. *Human Development, 27*, 42–56.

Chinen, A. B. (1985). Fairy tales and transpersonal development in later life. *Journal of Transpersonal Psychology, 17*, 99–122.

Chiriboga, D. (1982). Adaptation to marital separation in later and earlier life. *Journal of Gerontology, 37*, 109–114.

Chiriboga, D. (1989). Mental health at the midpoint: Crisis, challenge, or relief? In S. Hunter & M. Sundel (Eds.), *Midlife myths.* Newbury Park, CA: Sage.

Chiriboga, D., & Thurnher, M. (1975). Concept of self. In M. F. Lowenthal, M. Thurnher, & D. A. Chiriboga (Eds.), *Four stages of life: A comparative study of women and men facing transitions.* San Francisco: Jossey-Bass.

Chissell, J. T. (1989, July 16). Paper presented at the 94th annual convention of the National Medical Association, Orlando, FL.

Cholesterol: Can you stop worrying? (1995, February). *The Johns Hopkins Medical Letter*, pp. 1–2.

Chumlea, W. C. (1982). Physical growth in adolescence. In B. B. Wolman (Ed.). *Handbook of developmental psychology*. Englewood Cliffs, NJ: Prentice-Hall.

Cicirelli, V. G. (1977). Relationship of siblings to the elderly person's feelings and concerns. *Journal of Gerontology, 12*(3), 317–322.

Cicirelli, V. G. (1980, December). *Adult children's views on providing services for elderly parents*. Report to the Andrus Foundation.

Cicirelli, V. G. (1981, April). *Interpersonal relationships of siblings in the middle part of the life span*. Paper presented at the biennial meeting of the Society for Research in Child Development, Boston.

Cicirelli, V. G. (1989a). Feelings of attachment to siblings and well-being in later life. *Psychology and Aging, 4*(2), 211–216.

Cicirelli, V. G. (1989b). Helping relationships in later life: A reexamination. In J. A. Mancini (Ed.), *Aging parents and adult children*. Lexington, MA: Heath.

Clark, L. F., & Collins, J. E. (1993). Remembering old flames: How the past affects assessment of the present. *Personality and Social Psychology Bulletin, 19*, 399–408.

Clarke, C. J., & Neidert, L. J. (1992). Living arrangements of the elderly: An examination of differences according to ancestry and generation. *The Gerontologist, 32*(6), 796–804.

Clausen, J. A. (1993). *American lives*. New York: Free.

Clayton, V. (1975). Erikson's theory of human development as it applies to the aged: Wisdom as contradictory cognition. *Human Development, 18*, 119–128.

Clayton, V. (1982). Wisdom and intelligence: The nature and function of knowledge in the later years. *International Journal of Aging and Development, 15*, 315–321.

Cleiren, M. P., Diekstra, R. F., Kerkhof, A. D., & van der Wal, J. (1994). Mode of death and kinship in bereavement: Focusing on "who" rather than "how." *Crisis, 14*, 22–36.

Clemens, A. W., & Axelson, L. J. (1985). The not-so-empty nest: Return of the fledgling adult. *Family Relations, 34*, 259–264.

Cm. 849. (1989). *Caring for people: Community care in the next decade and beyond*. London: HMSO.

Cobleigh, M. A., Berris, R. F., Bush, T., Davidson, N. E., Robert, N. J., Sparano, J. A., Tormey, D. C., & Wood, W. C. for the Breast Cancer Committees of the Eastern Cooperative Oncology Group. (1994, August 17). Estrogen replacement therapy in breast cancer survivors. *Journal of the American Medical Association, 272*, 540–545.

Cochran, W. G., Mosteller, F., & Tukey, J. W. (1953). Statistical problems of the Kinsey report. *Journal of the American Statistical Association, 48*, 674–716.

Cohen, G. (1989). *Memory in the real world*. Hillsdale: Erlbaum.

Cohen, G., & Faulkner, D. (1989). Age differences in source forgetting: Effects on reality monitoring and on eyewitness testimony. *Psychology and Aging, 4*, 10–17.

Cohen, G. D. (1987). Alzheimer's disease. In G. L. Maddox (Ed.), *The encyclopedia of aging* (pp. 27–30). New York: Springer.

Cohen, N. L, Waltzman, S. B., Fisher, S. G., Tyler, R., and Department of Veterans Affairs Cochlear Implant Study Group. (1993). A prospective randomized study of cochlear implants. *New England Journal of Medicine, 328*(4), 233–237.

Cohen, S., Lichtenstein, E., Prochaska, J. O., Rossi, J. S., Gutz, E. R., Carr, C. R., Orleans, C. T., Schoenbach, V. J., Biener, L., Abrams, D., DiClemente, C., Curry, S., Marlatt, G. A., Cummings, K. M., Emont, S. L., Grovino, G., & Ossip-Klein, D. (1989). Debunking myths about self-quitting: Evidence from 10 prospective studies of persons who attempt to quit smoking by themselves. *American Psychologist, 44*(11), 1355–1365.

Coke, M. M. (1992). Correlates of life satisfaction among elderly African-Americans. *Journal of Gerontology: Psychological Sciences, 47*(5), P316–320.

Colby, A., & Damon, W. (1992). Gaining insight into the lives of moral leaders. *Chronicle of Higher Education, 39*(20), 83–84.

Colby, A., Kohlberg, L., Gibbs, J., & Lieberman, M. (1983). A longitudinal study of moral development. *Monographs of the Society for Research in Child Development, 48*(1–2, Serial No. 200).

Colditz, G. A., Hankinson, S. E., Hunter, D. J., Willett, W. C., Manson, J. E., Stampfer, M. J., Hennekens, C., Rosner, B., & Speizer, F. E. (1995). The use of estrogens and progestins and the risk of breast cancer in postmenopausal women. *New England Journal of Medicine, 332*, 1589–1593.

Cole, M., & Cole, S. R. (1989). *The development of children*. New York: Freeman.

Cole, M., & Scribner, S. (1974). *Culture and thought: A psychological introduction*. New York: Wiley.

Cole, M., & Scribner, S. (1978). Literacy without schooling: Testing for intellectual effects. *Harvard Educational Review, 48*(4), 448–460.

Coles, R. (1970). *Erik H. Erikson: The growth of his work*. Boston: Atlantic/Little, Brown.

Colton, C. C. (1855). *Lacon: or, Many things in few words, addressed to those who think*. New York: Gowans.

Commonwealth Fund Commission on Elderly People Living Alone. (1986). *Problems facing elderly Americans living alone*. New York: Harris & Associates.

Commonwealth Fund Commission on Elderly People Living Alone. (1992). *Study of elderly people in five countries—U.S., Canada, Germany, Britain, and Japan: Key findings*. New York: Harris & Associates.

Connidis, I. A. (1992). Life transitions and the adult sibling tie: A qualitative study. *Journal of Marriage and the Family, 54*, 972–982.

Connidis, I. A., & Davies, L. (1992). Confidants and companions: Choices in later life. *Journal of Gerontology: Social Sciences, 47*(30), S115–122.

Conway, M. A. (1991). In defense of everyday memory. *American Psychologist, 46*(1), 19–26.

Cooper, K. L., & Gutmann, D. L. (1987). Gender identity and ego mastery style in middle-aged, pre- and post-empty nest women. *The Gerontologist, 27*(3), 347–352.

Cornelius, S. W., & Caspi, A. (1987). Everyday problem solving in adulthood and old age. *Psychology and Aging, 2*, 144–153.

Correa, P., Pickle, L. W., Fontham, E., Lin, Y., & Haenszel, W. (1983, September 10). Passive smoking and lung cancer. *The Lancet*, pp. 595–597.

Costa, P. T., Jr., & McCrae, R. R. (1980). Still stable after all these years: Personality as a key to some issues in adulthood and old age. In P. B. Baltes, & O. G. Brim, Jr. (Eds.), *Life-span development and behavior* (Vol. 3, pp. 65–102). New York: Academic.

Costa, P. T., Jr., & McCrae, R. R. (1988). Personality in adulthood: A six-year longitudinal study of self-reports and spouse ratings on the NEO Personality Inventory. *Journal of Personality and Social Psychology, 54*, 853–863.

Costa, P. T., Jr., & McCrae, R. R. (1994a). Set like plaster? Evidence for the stability of adult personality. In T. F. Heatherton, & J. L. Weinberger (Eds.), *Can personality change?* (pp. 21–41). Washington, DC: American Psychological Association.

Costa, P. T., Jr., & McCrae, R. R. (1994b). Stability and change in personality from adolescence through adulthood. In C. F. Halverson, G. A. Kohnstamm, & R. P. Martin (Eds.), *The developing structure of temperament and personality from infancy to adulthood*. Hillsdale, NJ: Erlbaum.

Costa & McCrae. 1994. See a or b.

Costa, P. T., Jr., McCrae, R. R., Zonderman, A. B., Barbano, H. E., Lebowitz, B., & Larson, D. M. (1986). Cross-sectional studies of personality in a national sample: 2. Stability in neuroticism, extraversion, and openness. *Psychology and Aging, 1*, 144–149.

Cotliar, S. (1994, July 27). Some cities innovating on promotions. *Chicago Sun-Times*, p. 6.

Council of Europe. (1993). *Recent demographic developments in Europe and North America: 1992*. Strasbourg: Council of Europe Press.

Council on Ethical and Judicial Affairs. (1990). Black-white disparities in health care. *Journal of the American Medical Association, 263*, 2344–2346.

Council on Scientific Affairs of the American Medical Association. (1991). Hispanic health in the United States. *Journal of the American Medical Association, 265*(2), 248–252.

Cousins, N. (1979). *Anatomy of an illness as perceived by the patient*. New York: Norton.

Cowell, A. (1994, September 14). U.N. population meeting adopts program of action. *New York Times*, p. 2.

Craik, F. I. M. (1977). Age differences in human memory. In J. E. Birren & K. W. Schaie (Eds.), *Handbook of the psychology of aging* (pp. 384–420). New York: Van Nostrand Reinhold.

Craik, F. I. M. (1994). Memory changes in normal aging. *Current Directions in Psychological Science, 5*, 155–158.

Craik, F. I. M., & Byrd, M. (1982). Aging and cognitive deficits: The role of attentional resources. In F. I. M. Craik & S. Trehub (Eds.), *Aging and cognitive processes* (pp. 191–221). New York: Plenum.

Craik, F. I. M., & Jennings, J. M. (1992). Human memory. In F. I. M. Craik & T. A. Salthouse (Eds.), *The handbook of aging and cognition* (pp. 51–110). Hillsdale, NJ: Erlbaum.

Craik, F. I. M., Morris, L. W., Morris, R. G., & Loewen, E. R. (1990). Aging, source amnesia, and frontal lobe functioning. *Psychology and Aging, 5*, 148–151.

Cramer, D. (1986). Gay parents and their children: A review of research and practical implications. *Journal of Counseling and Development, 64*, 504–507.

Crisp, A. H., Queenan, M., & D'Souza, M. F. (1984, March 17). Myocardial infarction and the emotional climate. *The Lancet*, pp. 616–618.

Crowley, S. L. (1993, October). Grandparents to the rescue. *AARP Bulletin*, pp. 1, 16–17.

Crowley, S. L. (1994a, May). Much ado about menopause: Plenty of information but precious few answers. *AARP Bulletin*, pp. 2, 7.

Crowley, S. L. (1994b, June). Estrogen: Friend or foe? *AARP Bulletin*, pp. 2, 5.

Crown, W. H. (1993). Projecting the costs of aging populations. *Generations, 17*(4), 32–36.

Crutchfield, R. S. (1962). Conformity and creative thinking. In H. E. Gruber, G. Terrell, & M. Wertheimer (Eds.), *Contemporary approaches to creative thinking* (pp. 120–140). New York: Atherton.

Cruzan v. Director, Missouri Department of Health, 110 S. Ct. 2841 (1990).

Csikszentmihalyi, M., & Rathunde, K. (1990). The psychology of wisdom: An evolutionary interpretation. In R. J. Sternberg (Ed.), *Wisdom: Its nature, origins, and development* (pp. 25–51). Cambridge: Cambridge University Press.

Cumming, E., & Henry, W. (1961). *Growing old*. New York: Basic Books.

Cutrona, C., Russell, D., & Rose, J. (1986). Social support and adaptation to stress by the elderly. *Psychology and Aging, 1*(1), 47–54.

Cvetanovski, J., & Jex, S. (1994). Locus of control of unemployed people and its relationship to psychological and physical well-being. *Work and Stress, 8*(1), 60–67.

Cytrynbaum, S., Bluum, L., Patrick, R., Stein, J., Wadner, D., & Wilk, C. (1980). Midlife development: A personality and social systems perspective. In L. Poon (Ed.), *Aging in the 1980s*. Washington, DC: American Psychological Association.

Dainoff, M. (1989). Death and other losses. *Humanistic Judaism, 17*(3), 63–67.

D'Amato, R. J., Loughnon, M. S., Flynn, E., & Folkman, J. (1994). Thalidomide as an inhibitor of angiogenesis. *Proceedings of the National Academy of Sciences of the United States of America, 91*, 4082–4085.

Dan, A. J., & Bernhard, L. A. (1989). Menopause and other health issues for midlife women. In S. Hunter & M. Sundel (Eds.), *Midlife myths*. Newbury Park, CA: Sage.

Daniels, D., & Plomin, R. (1985). Origins of individual differences in infant shyness. *Developmental Psychology, 21*, 118–121.

Darley, J., & Fazio, R. H. (1980). Expectancy confirmation processes arising in the social interaction sequence. *American Psychology, 35*, 867–881.

Datan, N., Rodeheaver, D., & Hughes, F. (1987). Adult development and aging. *Annual Review of Psychology, 38*, 153–180.

Davidson, G. P. (1985). *Family law and family therapy: A New Zealand history of convergent development*. Paper presented at the conference of the California Chapter of the Association of Family and Conciliation Courts, Anaheim.

Davies, B. (1993). Caring for the frail elderly: An international perspective. *Generations, 17*(4), 51–54.

Davis, B. W. (1985). *Visits to remember: A handbook for visitors of nursing home residents.* University Park: Pennsylvania State University Cooperative Extension Service.

Davis, K. E. (1985, February). Near and dear: Friendship and love compared. *Psychology Today,* pp. 22–30.

Davis, K. L., et al. (1992). A double-blind placebo-controlled multicenter study of tacrine for Alzheimer's disease. *New England Journal of Medicine, 327,* 1253–1259.

Davis-Friedmann, D. (1983). *Long lives: Chinese elderly and the Communist revolution.* Cambridge, MA: Harvard University Press.

Davis-Friedmann, D. (1985). Chinese retirement: Policy and practices. In Z. S. Blau (Ed.), *Current perspectives on aging and the life cycle* (Vol. 1). Greenwich, CT: JAI.

Dawson, J. M., & Langan, P. A. (1994, July). *Murder in families* (Bureau of Justice Statistics Special Report). Washington, DC: U.S. Government Printing Office.

Dawson-Hughes, B., Dallal, G. E., Krall, E. A., Sadowski, L., Sahyoun, N., & Tannenbaum, S. (1990). A controlled trial of the effect of calcium supplementation on bone density in postmenopausal women. *New England Journal of Medicine, 323,* 878–883.

Day, J. C. (1992). *Population projections of the United States, by age, sex, race, and Hispanic origin: 1992 to 2050* (Current Population Reports, P25–1092). Washington, DC: U.S. Government Printing Office.

DeAngelis, T. (1994, October). Loving styles may be determined in infancy. *American Psychological Association Monitor,* p. 21.

DeCarlo, D., & Gruenfeld, D. (1989). *Stress in the American workplace.* Horsham, PA: LRP.

Deimling, G., Harel, Z., & Noelker, L. (1983). Racial differences in social integration and life satisfaction among aged public housing residents. *International Journal of Aging and Human Development, 17,* 203–212.

de Lafuente, D. (1994, September 11). Fertility clinics: Trying to cut the cost of high-tech baby making. *Chicago Sun-Times,* p. 4C.

Delany, E., Delany, S., & Hearth, A. H. (1993). *The Delany sisters' first 100 years.* New York: Kodansha America.

de la Rochefordiere, A., Asselain, B., Campana, F., et al. (1993). Age as prognostic factor in premenopausal breast carcinoma. *The Lancet, 341* (8852), 1039–1043.

De Mille, A. (1991). *Martha: The life and work of Martha Graham.* New York: Random House. (Original work published 1956)

Denney, N. W. (1974). Classification ability in the elderly. *Journal of Gerontology, 29,* 309–314.

Denney, N. W., & Palmer, A. M. (1981). Adult age differences on traditional and practical problem-solving measures. *Journal of Gerontology, 36*(3), 323–328.

Denney, N. W., & Pearce, K. A. (1989). A developmental study of practical problem solving in adults. *Psychology and Aging, 4*(4), 438–442.

Dennis, W. (1954). Bibliographies of eminent scientists. *Scientific Monthly, 79,* 180–183.

Dennis, W. (1955). Variations in productivity among creative workers. *Scientific Monthly, 80,* 277–278.

Depression. (1995, March). *Harvard Women's Health Watch,* pp. 2–3.

de Vos, S. (1990). Extended family living among older people in six Latin American countries. *Journal of Gerontology: Social Sciences, 45,* S87–94.

Dien, D. S. F. (1982). A Chinese perspective on Kohlberg's theory of moral development. *Developmental Review, 2,* 331–341.

Differences in maternal mortality among black and white women—United States, 1990. (1995, January 13). *Morbidity and Mortality Weekly Report,* pp. 6–7, 13–14.

DiGiulio, J. F. (1992). Early widowhood: An atypical transition. *Journal of Mental Health Counseling, 14,* 97–109.

Dittmann-Kohli, F., & Baltes, P. B. (1990). Toward a neofunctionalist conception of adult intellectual development: Wisdom as a prototypical case of intellectual growth. In C. N. Alexander & E. J. Langer (Eds.), *Higher stages of human development: Perspectives on adult growth* (pp. 54–78). New York: Oxford University Press.

Dixon, R. A., & Baltes, P. B. (1986). Toward life-span research on the functions and pragmatics of intelligence. In R. J. Sternberg & R. K. Wagner (Eds.), *Practical intelligence: Nature and origins of competence in the everyday world* (pp. 203–235). New York: Cambridge University Press.

Dixon, R. A., Hultsch, D. F., & Hertzog, C. (1988). The metamemory in adulthood (MIA) questionnaire. *Psychopharmocology Bulletin, 24,* 671–688.

Dixon, R. A., Kurzman, D., & Friesen, I. C. (1993). Handwriting performance in younger and older adults: Age, familiarity, and practice effects. *Psychology and Aging, 8,* 360–370.

Dobbs, A. R., & Rule, B. G. (1987). Prospective memory and self-reports of memory abilities in older adults. *Canadian Journal of Psychology, 41,* 209–222.

Doering, C. H., Kraemer, H. C., Brodie, H. K. H., & Hamburg, D. A. (1975). A cycle of plasma testosterone in the human male. *Journal of Clinical Endocrinology and Metabolism, 40,* 492–500.

Doherty, W. J., & Jacobson, N. S. (1982). Marriage and the family. In B. Wolman (Ed.), *Handbook of developmental psychology.* Englewood Cliffs, NJ: Prentice-Hall.

Doka, K. J., & Mertz, M. E. (1988). The meaning and significance of great-grandparenthood. *The Gerontologist, 28*(2), 192–197.

Donn, A. (1985). The eyes. In D. F. Tapley, R. J. Weiss, T. Q. Morris, G. J. Subak-Sharpe, & D. M. Goetz (Eds.), *Columbia University College of Physicians and Surgeons complete home medical guide* (p. 659). New York: Crown.

Doppelt, J. E., & Wallace, W. L. (1955). Standardization of the Wechsler Adult Intelligence Scale for older persons. *Journal of Abnormal and Social Psychology, 51,* 312–330.

Dorris, M. (1989). *The broken cord.* New York: Harper and Row.

Dowling, C., & Hollister, A. (1993, June 16). The rebirth of an artist. *Life,* pp. 76–80.

Downs, H. (1993, February 28). My father's new life. *Parade,* p. 12.

Drachman, D. A. (1976). Memory and cholinergic function. In W. S. Fields (Ed.), *Neurotransmitter Function*. New York: Stratton International.

Drachman, D. A. (1977). Memory and cognitive function in man: Does the cholinergic system have a specific code? *Neurology, 27*, 783–790.

Drachman, D. A., & Leavitt, J. (1972). Memory impairment in the aged: Storage versus retrieval deficit. *Journal of Experimental Psychology, 93*, 302–308.

Dreyfus, H. L. (1993–1994, Winter). What computers still can't do. *The Key Reporter*, pp. 4–9.

Drinka, P., Jaschob, K., Schultz, S., & Rudman, D. (1992). Is male hip fracture a marker for low testosterone in elderly male nursing home residents? *Journal of the American Geriatrics Society, 41*(2), 192, 199.

Dube, E. F. (1982). Literacy, cultural familiarity, and "intelligence" as determinants of story recall. In H. C. Trandis & A. Heron (Eds.), *Handbook of cross-cultural psychology: Developmental psychology* (pp. 274–292). Boston: Allyn & Bacon.

Dubin, R. (1956). Industrial workers' worlds: A study in the central life interests of industrial workers. *Social Problems, 4*, 131–142.

Duffy, M. (1991, April 15). The deity of modern dance: Martha Graham, 1894–1991. *Time*, p. 69.

Dufour, M., Colliver, J., Stinson, F., & Grigson, B. (1988, November). *Changes in alcohol consumption with age: NHANES I epidemiologic followup*. Paper presented at the 116th annual meeting of the American Public Health Association, Boston.

Duncan, G. J., & Hoffman, S. D. (1985). Economic consequences of marital instability. In M. David & T. Smeeding (Eds.), *Horizontal equity, uncertainty, and economic well-being* (pp. 427–467). Chicago: University of Chicago Press.

Durlak, J. A. (1973). Relationship between attitudes toward life and death among elderly women. *Developmental Psychology, 8*(1), 146.

Dustman, R. E., Emmerson, R. Y., Steinhaus, L. A., Shearer, D. E., & Dustman, T. J. (1992). The effects of videogame playing on neuropsychological performance of elderly individuals. *Journal of Gerontology: Psychological Sciences, 47*(3), P168–171.

Dutta, R., Schulenberg, E., & Lair, T. J. (1986, April). *The effect of job characteristics on cognitive abilities and intellectual flexibility*. Paper presented at the annual meeting of the Eastern Psychological Association, New York.

Dychtwald, K. & Flower, J. (1990). *Age wave: How the most important trend of our time will change your future*. New York: Bantam.

Eastman, P. (1992, November). Won't you please speak up? High-tech solutions come to the rescue of the hard-of-hearing. *AARP Bulletin*, pp. 8–9.

Eastman, P., & Crowley, S. L. (1995, April). Prostate cancer dilemma: New hope, difficult choices. *AARP Bulletin*, pp. 8–9.

Eaves, L. J., Eysenck, H. J., & Martin, N. G. (1989). *Genes, culture, and behavior: An empirical approach*. San Diego: Academic.

Edelstein, S. (1990, December–1991, January). Do grandparents have rights? *Modern Maturity*, pp. 40–41.

Edlin, B. R., Irwin, K. L., Farugue, S., McCoy, C. B., Word, C., Serrano, Y., Inciardi, J. A., Bowser, B. P., Schilling, R. F., Holmberg, S. D., & Multicenter Crack Cocaine and HIV Infection Study Team. (1994, November 24). Intersecting epidemics—Crack cocaine use and HIV infection among inner-city young adults. *New England Journal of Medicine, 331*, 1422–1427.

Edson, L. (1968, August 18). To hell with being discovered when you're dead. *New York Times Magazine*, pp. 26–27, 29–31, 34–36, 41, 44–46.

Edwards, A. J. (1994). *When memory fails: Helping the Alzheimer's and dementia patient*. New York: Plenum.

Edwards, C. P. (1977). The comparative study of the development of moral judgment and reasoning. In R. Monroe, R. Monroe, & B. B. Whiting (Eds.), *Handbook of cross-cultural human development*. New York: Garland.

Effective solutions for impotence. (1994, October). *Johns Hopkins Medical Letter: Health after 50*, pp. 2–3.

Eichorn, D. H., Clausen, J. A., Haan, N., Honzik, M. P., & Mussen, P. H. (Eds.). (1981). *Present and past in middle life*. New York: Academic.

Einstein, A., & Infeld, L. (1938). *The evolution of physics*. New York: Simon & Schuster.

Einstein, G. (1992, April). *Aging and prospective memory: Examining the influence of self-initiated retrieval*. Paper presented at the Cognitive Aging Conference, Atlanta.

Einstein, G. O., & McDaniel, M. A. (1990). Normal aging and prospective memory. *Journal of Experimental Psychology: Learning, Memory, and Cognition, 16*, 717–726.

Eisenberg, L. (1980). Adolescent suicide: On taking arms against a sea of troubles. *Pediatrics, 66*, 315–320.

Eisenberg, L. (1995, Spring). Is the family obsolete? *The Key Reporter*, pp. 1–5.

Ekerdt, D. (1986). The busy ethic: Moral continuity between work and retirement. *The Gerontologist, 26*, 239–244.

Elder, G. H., Jr., & Pavalko, E. K. (1993). Work careers in men's later years: Transitions, trajectories, and historical change. *Journal of Gerontology: Social Sciences, 48*, S180–191.

Elderly driving poses challenges for families. (1994, February). *The Menninger Letter*, p. 6.

Eley, J. W., Hill, H. A., Chen, V. W., Austin, D. F., Wesley, M. N., Muss, H. B., Greenberg, R. S., Coates, R. J., Correa, O., Redmond, C. K., Hunter, C. P., Herman, A. A., Kurman, R., Blacklow, R., Shapiro, S., & Edwards, B. K. (1994, September 28). Racial differences in survival from breast cancer. *Journal of the American Medical Association, 272*, 199–208.

Elias, P. K., Elias, M. F., Robbins, M. A., & Gage, P. (1987). Acquisition of word-processing skills by younger, middle-age, and older adults. *Psychology and Aging, 2*, 340–348.

Elkind, D. (1984). *All grown up and no place to go*. Reading, MA: Addison-Wesley.

Emde, R. N., Plomin, R., Robinson, J., Corley, R., DeFries, J., Fulker, D. W., Reznick, J. S., Campos, J., Kagan, J., & Zahn-Waxler, C. (1992). Temperament, emotion, and cognition at 14 months: The MacArthur longitudinal twin study. *Child Development, 63*, 1437–1455.

Emery, V. O. B., & Oxman, T. E. (1994). *Dementia presentations, differential diagnosis, and nosology.* Baltimore: Johns Hopkins University Press.

Environmental tobacco smoke: Health effects and prevention policies. (1994, October). *Archives of Family Medicine, 3,* 865–871.

Epstein, E., & Gutmann, R. (1984). Mate selection in man: Evidence, theory, and outcome. *Social Biology, 31,* 243–278.

Epstein, R. A. (1989, Spring). Voluntary euthanasia. *The Law School Record* (University of Chicago), pp. 8–13.

Epstein, S. (1990). Cognitive-experiential self-theory. In L. A. Pervin (Ed.), *Handbook of personality theory and research* (pp. 165–192). New York: Guilford.

Epstein, W. (1977). Mechanisms of directed forgetting. In G. H. Bower (Ed.), *The psychology of learning and motivation: Advances in research and theory* (Vol. 6, pp. 147–191). New York: Academic.

Equal Employment Opportunity Commission (EEOC). (1994). Enforcement guidance on Harris v. Forklift systems. *Fair Employment Practices, No. 743* (Bureau of National Affairs, 405), 7165–7170.

Erdrich, L. (1984). *Love medicine.* New York: Holt Rinehart & Winston.

Erikson, E. H. (1950). *Childhood and society.* New York: Norton.

Erikson, E. H. (1985). *The life cycle completed.* New York: Norton.

Erikson, E. H., Erikson, J. M., & Kivnick, H. Q. (1986). *Vital involvement in old age: The experience of old age in our time.* New York: Norton.

Ershler, W. B. (1992). Cancer biology and aging. *Generations, 16*(4), 27–30.

Essex, M. J., & Nam, S. (1987). Marital status and loneliness among older women: The differential importance of close family and friends. *Journal of Marriage and the Family, 49,* 93–106.

Estés, C. P. (1992). *Women who run with the wolves: Myths and stories of the wild woman.* New York: Ballantine.

Estrogen and the heart. (1994, August). *Harvard Women's Health Watch,* p. 7.

Ettinger, B., Selby, J., Citron, J. T., Vangessel, A., Ettinger, V. M., & Hendrickson, M. R. (1994). Cyclic hormone replacement therapy using quarterly progestin. *Obstetrics and Gynecology, 83,* 693–700.

Evans, D. A., Funkenstein, H., Albert, M. A., Scherr, P. A., Cook, N. R., Chown, M. J., Hebert, L. E., Hennekens, C. H., & Taylor, J. O. (1989). Prevalence of Alzheimer's disease in a community population of older persons: Higher than previously reported. *Journal of the American Medical Association, 262*(18), 2551–2556.

Evans, J. (1994). *Caring for the caregiver: Body, mind and spirit.* New York: American Parkinson Disease Association.

Evans-Pritchard, E. E. (1970). Sexual inversion among the Azande. *American Anthropologist, 72,* 1428–1433.

Eveleth, P. B., & Tanner, J. M. (1976). *Worldwide variation in human growth.* London: Cambridge University Press.

Exton-Smith, A. N. (1985). Mineral metabolism. In C. E. Finch & E. L. Schneider (Eds.), *Handbook of the biology of aging* (2d ed., pp. 511–539). New York: Van Nostrand Reinhold.

Fackelmann, K. A. (1993a, October 23). Weighing risks, benefits of mammography. *Science News,* p. 262.

Fackelmann, K. A. (1993b, December 11). Nabbing a gene for colorectal cancer. *Science News,* p. 388.

Farlow, M., Gracon, S. I., Hershey, L. A., Lewis, K. W., Sadowsky, C. H., Dolan-Ureno, J., for the Tacrine Study Group. (1992). A controlled trial of tacrine in Alzheimer's disease. *Journal of the American Medical Association, 268,* 2523–2529.

Farooq, M. (1966). Importance of determining transmission sites in planning bilharziasis control: Field observations from Egypt-49 project area. *American Journal of Epidemiology, 83,* 603–612.

Farrell, C., Palmer, A. T., Atchison, S., & Andelman, B. (1994, September 12). The economics of aging: Why the growing number of elderly won't bankrupt America. *Business Week,* pp. 60–68.

Farrell, M. P., & Rosenberg, S. D. (1981). *Men at midlife.* Boston: Auburn.

Farrer, L. A., Myers, R. H., Cupples, L. A., St. George-Hyslop, P. H., Bird, T. D., Rossor, M. N., Mullan, M. J., Polinsky, R., Nee, L., Heston, L., Van Broeckhoven, C., Martin, J. J., Crapper-McLachlan, D., & Growdon, J. H. (1990). Transmission and age at onset patterns in familial Alzheimer's disease: Evidence for heterogeneity. *Neurology, 40,* 395–403.

Feazell, C. S., Mayers, R. S., & Deschner, J. (1984). Services for men who batter: Implications for programs and policies. *Family Relations, 33,* 217–223.

Feifel, H. (1977). *New meanings of death.* New York: McGraw-Hill.

Feldman, H. (1981). A comparison of intentional parents and intentionally childless couples. *Journal of Marriage and the Family, 43*(3), 593–600.

Feldman, R. D. (1982). *Whatever happened to the Quiz Kids? Perils and profits of growing up gifted.* Chicago: Chicago Review Press.

Feldman, R. D. (1985, August 6). Libraries open the books on local adult illiteracy. *Chicago Sun-Times School Guide,* pp. 10–11.

Feldman, R. S. (1993). *Understanding Psychology* (3d ed.). New York: McGraw-Hill.

Feldman, S. S., Biringen, Z. C., & Nash, S. C. (1981). Fluctuations of sex-related self-attributions as a function of stage of family life cycle. *Developmental Psychology, 17,* 24–35.

Fellin, P. A., & Powell, T. J. (1988). Mental health services and older adult minorities: An assessment. *The Gerontologist, 28*(4), 442–446.

Felson, D. T., Zhang, Y., Hannan, M., Kiel, D. P., Wilson, P. F. W., & Anderson, J. J. (1993, October 14). The effect of postmenopausal estrogen therapy on bone density in elderly women. *New England Journal of Medicine, 329,* 1141–1146.

Ferrante, L. S., & Woodruff-Pak, D. S. (1995). Longitudinal investigation of eyeblink classical conditioning in elderly human subjects. *Journal of Gerontology: Psychological Sciences, 50,* P42–50.

Ferstenberg, R. L. (1992). Mediation versus litigation in divorce and why a litigator becomes a mediator. *American Journal of Family Therapy, 20,* 266–273.

Fiatarone, M. A., Marks, E. C., Ryan, N. D., Meredith,

C. N., Lipsitz, L. A., & Evans, W. J. (1990). High-intensity strength training in nonagenarians: Effects on skeletal muscles. *Journal of the American Medical Association, 263,* 3029–3034.

Fiatarone, M. A., O'Neill, E. F., Ryan, N. D., Clemens, K. M., et al. (1994). Exercise training and nutritional supplementation for physical frailty in very elderly people. *New England Journal of Medicine, 330,* 1769–1775.

Field, D., & Millsap, R. E. (1991). Personality in advanced old age: Continuity or change? *Journal of Gerontology: Psychological Sciences, 46,* P299–308.

Field, D., & Minkler, M. (1988). Continuity and change in social support between young-old and old-old or very-old age. *Journal of Gerontology: Psychological Sciences, 43*(4), P100–106.

Field, D., Minkler, M., Falk, R. F., & Leino, E. V. (1993). The influence of health on family contacts and family functioning in advanced old age: A longitudinal study. *Journal of Gerontology: Psychological Sciences, 48*(1), P18–28.

Fielding, J. E., & Phenow, K. J. (1988). Health effects of involuntary smoking. *New England Journal of Medicine, 319*(22), 1452–1460.

Finn, R. (1993, February 8). Arthur Ashe, tennis champion, dies of AIDS. *New York Times,* pp. B1, B43.

Fiore, M. C., Novotny, T. E., Pierce, J. P., et al. (1990). Methods used to quit smoking in the United States: Do cessation programs help? *Journal of the American Medical Association, 263,* 2760–2765.

Fisher, B., Fisher, E. R., Redmond, C., et al. (1986). Tumor nuclear grade, estrogen receptor, and progesterone receptor: Their value alone or in combination as indicators of outcome following adjuvant therapy for breast cancer. *Breast Cancer Research and Treatment, 7,* 147–160.

Fisher, B., Redmond, C., Poisson, R., et al. (1989). Eight-year results of a randomized clinical trial comparing total mastectomy and lumpectomy with or without irradiation in the treatment of breast cancer. *New England Journal of Medicine, 320,* 822–828.

Fisher, L., & Lieberman, M. (1994, September). Alzheimer's disease: The impact of the family on spouses, offspring, and in-laws. *Family Process, 33*(3), 305–325.

Fitzpatrick, K. M., & Logan, J. R. (1985). The aging of the suburbs. *American Sociological Review, 50,* 106–117.

Flavel, J. H. (1985). *Cognitive development* (2d ed.). Englewood Cliffs, NJ: Prentice-Hall.

Flores, J. (1952). *The woman with the whip: Eva Peron.* Garden City, NY: Doubleday.

Folkman, S., & Lazarus, R. S. (1980). An analysis of coping in a middle-aged community sample. *Journal of Health and Social Behavior, 21,* 219–239.

Folkman, S., Lazarus, R. S., Pimley, S., & Novacek, J. (1987). Age differences in stress and coping processes. *Psychology and Aging, 2,* 171–184.

Folstein, M. F., Bassett, S. S., Anthony, J. C., Romanoski, A. J., & Nestadt, G. R. (1991). Dementia: Case ascertainment in a community survey. *Journal of Gerontology: Medical Sciences, 46*(4), M132–138.

Ford, C. S., & Beach, F. A. (1951). *Patterns of sexual behavior.* New York: Harper Torchbooks.

Foreman, J. (1994, May 16). Brain power's sliding scale. *Boston Globe,* pp. 25, 29.

Foster, D. (1991, May–June). Double vision: An interview with the authors. *Mother Jones,* pp. 26, 78, 80.

Foster, G. M., & Anderson, B. G. (1978). *Medical anthropology.* New York: McGraw-Hill.

Fowble, B. L., Solin, L. J., Schultz, D. J., et al. (1991). Ten year results of conservative surgery and irradiation for stage I and stage II breast cancer. *International Journal of Radiation Oncology, Biology, and Physics, 21,* 269–277.

Fowler, J. (1981). *Stages of faith: The psychology of human development and the quest for meaning.* New York: Harper & Row.

Foy, K. (1987, Fall). Family and divorce mediation: A comparative analysis of international programs. *Mediation Quarterly,* pp. 83–96.

Frank, A. (1958). *The diary of a young girl.* New York: Pocket.

Frank, S. J., Avery, C. B., & Laman, M. S. (1988). Young adults' perception of their relationships with their parents: Individual differences in connectedness, competence, and emotional autonomy. *Developmental Psychology, 24,* 729–737.

Frankl, V. (1965). *The doctor and the soul.* New York: Knopf.

Freeman, S. M., Whartenby, K. A., & Abraham, G. N. (1992). Gene therapy: Applications to diseases associated with aging. *Generations, 16*(4), 45–48.

Freud, S. (1947). *Leonardo da Vinci: A study in psychosexuality.* New York: Random House. (Original work published 1910)

Freud, S. (1949). The unconscious. In *Collected Papers* (Vol. 4). London: Hogarth. (Original work published 1915)

Freud, S. (1957). Leonardo da Vinci and a memory of his childhood. In J. Strachey, A. Freud, A. Strachey, and A. Tyson (Eds., Trans.), *The standard edition of the complete psychological works of Sigmund Freud* (Vol. 11, pp. 59–138). London: Hogarth and Institute of Psycho-Analysis. (Original work published 1910)

Frezza, M., DiPadova, C., Pozzato, G., Terpin, M., Baraona, E., & Lieber, C. S. (1990). High blood alcohol levels in women: The role of decreased gastric alcohol dehydrogenase activity and first-pass metabolism. *New England Journal of Medicine, 322,* 95–99.

Friedan, B. (1963). *The feminine mystique.* New York: Norton.

Friedan, B. (1976). *It changed my life: Writings on the women's movement.* New York: Random House.

Friedan, B. (1981). *The second stage.* New York: Summit.

Friedan, B. (1993). *The fountain of age.* New York: Simon & Schuster.

Friedan, B. (1994, March 20). How to live longer, better, wiser. *Parade,* pp. 4–6.

Friedman, H. S., & Booth-Kewley, S. (1987). The "disease-prone personality": A meta-analytic view of the construct. *American Psychologist, 42,* 539–555.

Friedman, M., & Rosenman, R. H. (1974). *Type A behavior and your heart.* New York: Knopf.

Friend, T. (1994, November 13). Alzheimer's is focus of new developments. *Chicago Sun-Times,* p. 59.

Fries, J. F., & Crapo, L. M. (1981). *Vitality and aging.* San Francisco: Freeman.

Frieze, I. H., Parsons, J. E., Johnson, P. B., Ruble, D. N., & Zellman, G. L. (1978). *Women and sex roles: A social psychological perspective.* New York: Norton.

Fulton, R., & Owen, G. (1987–1988). Death and society in twentieth-century America: Special issue—Research in thanatology. *Omega: Journal of Death and Dying, 18,* 379–395.

Funder, D. C. (1993). Judgments as data for personality and developmental psychology: Error versus accuracy. In D. C. Funder, R. D. Parke, C. Tomlinson-Keasey, & K. Widaman (Eds.), *Studying lives through time: Personality and development* (pp. 121–146). Washington, DC: American Psychological Association.

Furry, C. A., & Baltes, P. B. (1973). The effect of age differences in ability-extraneous performance variables on the assessment of intelligence in children, adults, and the elderly. *Journal of Gerontology, 28*(1), 73–80.

Furukawa, S. (1994). *The diverse living arrangements of children: Summer of 1991* (U.S. Bureau of the Census, Current Population Reports, Series P70, No. 38). Washington, DC: U.S. Government Printing Office.

Gagné, J. P. (1992). Ancillary aural rehabilitation services for adult cochlear implant recipients: A review and analysis of literature. *Journal of Speech, Language Pathology and Audiology, 16,* 121–128.

Gagné, J. P., Parnes, L. S., LaRocque, M., Hassan, R., & Vidas, S. (1991). Effectiveness of an intensive speech perception training program for adult cochlear implant recipients. *Annals of Otorhinolaryngology, 100,* 700–707.

Gallo, J. J., Anthony, J. C., & Muthen, B. O. (1994). Age differences in the symptoms of depression: A latent trace analysis. *Journal of Gerontology: Psychological Sciences, 49,* P251–264.

Gallup, G., & Proctor, W. (1982). *Adventures in immortality: A look beyond the threshold of death.* New York: McGraw-Hill.

Gallup, G. H. (1984). *The Gallup poll: Public opinion 1983.* Wilmington, DE: Scholarly Resources.

Galton, F. (1883). *Inquiries into human faculty and its development.* London: Macmillan.

Gardner, H. (1981, July). Breakaway minds. *Psychology Today,* pp. 64–71.

Gardner, H. (1983). *Frames of mind: The theory of multiple intelligences.* New York: Basic.

Gardner, H. (1986). Freud in three frames. *Daedalus,* 105–134.

Gardner, H. (1988). Creative lives and creative works: A synthetic scientific approach. In R. J. Sternberg (Ed.), *The nature of creativity: Contemporary psychological perspectives* (pp. 298–321). Cambridge: Cambridge University Press.

Gardner, H. (1989, December). Learning: Chinese-style. *Psychology Today,* pp. 54–56.

Gardner, J. (1994). Refocusing the family values debate. *Humanistic Judaism, 22*(1), 33–35.

Garfein, A. J., Schaie, K. W., & Willis, S. L. (1988). Microcomputer proficiency in later-middle-aged and older adults: Teaching old dogs new tricks. *Social Behavior, 3,* 131–148.

Garwick, A. W., et al. (1994, September). Family perceptions of living with Alzheimer's disease. *Family Process, 33*(3), 327–340.

Gatz, M., & Smyer, M. (1992). The mental health system and older adults in the 1990's. *American Psychologist, 47,* 741–751.

Gelfand, D. E. (1982). *Aging: The ethnic factor.* Boston: Little, Brown.

Geller, J. A. (1992). *Breaking destructive patterns: Multiple strategies for treating partner abuse.* New York: Free.

Gelles, R. J., & Maynard, P. E. (1987). A structural family systems approach to intervention in cases of family violence. *Family Relations, 36,* 270–275.

Genevay, B. (1986). Intimacy as we age. *Generations, 10*(4), 12–15.

George, L. K. (1980). *Role transitions in later life.* Monterey, CA: Brooks/Cole.

George, L. K. (1993). Depressive disorders and symptoms in later life. *Generations, 17*(1), 35–38.

George, L. K., Blazer, D. G., Winfield-Laird, I., Leaf, P. J., & Fischbach, R. L. (1988). Psychiatric disorders and mental health service use in later life: Evidence from the epidemiologic catchment area program. In J. Brody & G. Maddox (Eds.), *Epidemiology and aging.* New York: Springer.

Gerhard, G. S. & Cristofalo, V. J. (1992). The limits of biogerontology. *Generations, 16*(4), 55–59.

Getlin & Cristofalo (1992). See Gerhard & Cristofalo.

Getzels, J. W. (1964). Creative thinking, problem-solving, and instruction. In *Yearbook of the National Society for the Study of Education* (Part 1, pp. 240–267). Chicago: University of Chicago Press.

Getzels, J. W. (1984, March). *Problem finding and creativity in higher education.* Boston: Boston College, School of Education.

Getzels, J. W., & Csikszentmihalyi, M. (1968). The value-orientations of art students as determinants of artistic specialization and creative performance. *Studies in Art Education, 10*(1), 5–16.

Getzels, J. W., & Csikszentmihalyi, M. (1975). From problem solving to problem finding. In J. A. Taylor & J. W. Getzels (Eds.), *Perspectives in creativity* (pp. 90–116). Volente, TX: Aldine.

Getzels, J. W., & Csikszentmihalyi, M. (1976). *The creative vision: A longitudinal study of problem finding in art.* New York: Wiley.

Getzels, J. W., & Jackson, P. W. (1962). *Creativity and intelligence: Explorations with gifted students.* New York: Wiley.

Geyer, G. A. (1983). *Buying the night flight.* New York: Delacorte/Seymour Lawrence.

Giambra, L. M., & Arenberg, D. (1993). Adult age differences in forgetting sentences. *Psychology and Aging, 8,* 451–462.

Gibson, R. C. (1986). Older black Americans. *Generations, 10*(4), 35–39.

Gielen, U., & Kelly, D. (1983, February). *Buddhist Ladakh: Psychological portrait of a non-violent culture.* Paper presented at the annual meeting of the Society for Cross-Cultural Research, Washington, DC.

Gil, D. G. (1971). Violence against children. *Journal of Marriage and the Family, 33*(4), 637–648.

Gilbert, J. G., & Levee, R. F. (1971). Patterns of declining memory. *Journal of Gerontology, 26,* 70–75.

Gilbert, L. A. (1994). Current perspectives in dual-career families. *Current Directions in Psychological Science, 3,* 101–105.

Gilford, R. (1984). Contrasts in marital satisfaction throughout old age: An exchange theory analysis. *Journal of Gerontology, 39,* 325–333.

Gilford, R. (1986). Marriages later in life. *Generations, 10*(4), 16–20.

Gilford, R., & Bengtson, V. (1979). Measuring marital satisfaction in three generations: Positive and negative dimensions. *Journal of Marriage and the Family, 41,* 387–398.

Gilliand, P. (1989). Evolution of family policy in light of development in western European countries. *International Social Security Review, 42,* 395–426.

Gilligan, C. (1982). *In a different voice: Psychological theory and women's development.* Cambridge, MA: Harvard University Press.

Gilligan, C. (1987). Adolescent development reconsidered. In E. E. Irwin (Ed.), *Adolescent social behavior and health.* San Francisco: Jossey-Bass.

Gilligan, C., Murphy, J. M., & Tappan, M. B. (1990). Moral development beyond adolescence. In C. N. Alexander & E. J. Langer (Eds.), *Higher stages of human development* (pp. 208–228). New York: Oxford University Press.

Ginzberg, E. (1972). Toward a theory of occupational choice: A restatement. *Vocational Guidance Quarterly, 20,* 169–176.

Giovannucci, E., Rimm, E. B., Colditz, G. A., Stampfer, M. J., Ascherio, A., Chute, C. C., & Willett, W. C. (1993). A prospective study of dietary fat and risk of prostate cancer. *Journal of the National Cancer Institute, 85,* 1571–1579.

Gist, M., Rosen, B., & Schwoerer, C. (1988). The influence of training method and trainee age on the acquisition of computer skills. *Personnel Psychology, 41,* 255–265.

Gladue, B. A. (1994). The biopsychology of sexual orientation. *Current Directions in Psychological Science, 3,* 150–154.

Glantz, S. A., & Parmley, W. W. (1995). Passive smoking and heart disease: Mechanisms and risk. *Journal of the American Medical Association, 273,* 1047–1053.

Glasheen, L. K. (1993, September). A place to call your own. *AARP Bulletin,* pp. 1, 10–14.

Glass, R. B. (1986). Infertility. In S. S. C. Yen & R. B. Jaffe (Eds.), *Reproductive endocrinology: Physiology, pathophysiology, and clinical management* (2d ed., pp. 571–613). Philadelphia: Saunders.

Glenn, N. D. (1987, October). Marriage on the rocks. *Psychology Today,* pp. 20–21.

Glenn, N. D. (1991). The recent trend in marital success in the United States. *Journal of Marriage and the Family, 53,* 261–270.

Glenn, N. D., & McLanahan, S. (1981). The effects of offspring on the psychological well-being of older adults. *Journal of Marriage and the Family, 43*(2), 409–421.

Glick, J. (1975). Cognitive development in cross-cultural perspective. In F. Horowitz (Ed.), *Review of child development research* (Vol. 4, pp. 595–654). Chicago: University of Chicago Press.

Glick, P. C. (1988). Fifty years of family demography: A record of social change. *Journal of Marriage and the Family, 50,* 861–873.

Glick, P. C. (1989). Remarried families, stepfamilies, and stepchildren: A brief demographic profile. *Family Relations, 38,* 24–27.

Glick, P. C., & Lin, S.-L. (1986a). More young adults are living with their parents: Who are they? *Journal of Marriage and the Family, 48,* 107–112.

Glick, P. C., & Lin, S.-L. (1986b). Recent changes in divorce and remarriage. *Journal of Marriage and the Family, 48*(4), 737–747.

Glynn, R. J., Bouchard, G. R., LoCastro, J. S., & Laird, N. M. (1985). Aging and generational effects on drinking behaviors in men: Results from the Normative Aging Study. *American Journal of Public Health, 75,* 1413–1419.

Goldberg, E. L., Comstock, G. W., & Harlow, S. D. (1988). Emotional problems in widowhood. *Journal of Gerontology, 43*(6), S206–208.

Golden, D. (1994, July). Building a better brain. *Life,* pp. 63–70.

Goldman, H. (1994). *The Nootka of British Columbia: Natural resources and cultural change.* Unpublished manuscript.

Goldman, L. L., & Rothschild, J. (in press). Healing the wounded with art therapy. In B. Danto (Ed.), *Bereavement and suicide.* Philadelphia: Charles.

Goldman, L., & Tosteson, A. N. A. (1991). Uncertainty about postmenopausal estrogen. *New England Journal of Medicine, 325,* 800–802.

Goldstein, A. M. (1980). The "uncooperative" patient: Self-destructive behavior in hemodialysis patients. In N. L. Farberow (Ed.), *The many faces of suicide: Indirect self-destructive behavior.* New York: McGraw-Hill.

Goleman, D. (1990, April 24). Anger over racism is seen as a cause of blacks' high blood pressure. *New York Times,* p. C3.

Gonyea, J. G., Hudson, R. B., & Seltzer, G. B. (1990). Housing preferences of vulnerable elders in suburbia. *Journal of Housing for the Elderly, 7,* 79–95.

Goodrich, C. (1995, January 18). Mandela tells the story of his monumental life. *Chicago Sun-Times,* p. 45.

Goodwin, J. (1994). *Akira Kurosawa and intertextual cinema.* Baltimore: Johns Hopkins University Press.

Gorbach, S. L., Zimmerman, D. R., & Woods, M. (1984). *The doctors' anti-breast cancer diet.* New York: Simon & Schuster.

Gordon, A. (1975). The Jewish view of death: Guidelines for mourning. In E. Kübler-Ross (Ed.), *Death: The final stage of growth.* Englewood Cliffs, NJ: Prentice-Hall.

Gorman, M. (1993). Help and self-help for older adults in developing countries. *Generations, 17*(4), 73–76.

Gottman, J. M., & Krokoff, L. J. (1989). Marital interaction and satisfaction: A longitudinal view. *Journal of Consulting and Clinical Psychology, 57,* 47–52.

Graham, M. (1954). God's athlete. In E. R. Murrow (Ed.), *This I believe* (pp. 58–59). New York: Help.

Graham, M. (1991). *Blood memory.* New York: Doubleday.

Granger, D. (1987). The Granada factor. In G. O'Connor (Ed.), *Olivier: In celebration.* New York: Dodd, Mead.

Grant, B. S., Harford, T. C., Dawson, D. A., Chou, P., Dufour, M., & Pickering, R. (1994). Prevalence of *DSM-IV* alcohol abuse and dependency: United States, 1992. *Alcohol, Health, and Research World, 18,* 243–248.

Grant, L. (1994, March). Into the wind . . . Unemployment and welfare reform. *The NPG (Negative Population Growth) Forum,* pp. 1–8.

Greenberg, J., & Becker, M. (1988). Aging parents as family resources. *The Gerontologist, 28*(6), 786–790.

Greenhouse, L. (1990, June 26). Justices find a right to die, but the majority sees need for clear proof on intent. *New York Times,* pp. A1, A18, A19.

Greenwald, A. G. (1980). The totalitarian ego: Fabrication and revision of personal history. *American Psychologist, 35,* 603–618.

Greyson, B. (1992–1993). Near-death experiences and antisuicidal attitudes. *Omega, 26,* 81–89.

Greyson, B. (1993). Varieties of near-death experience. *Psychiatry, 56,* 390–399.

Gribbin, K., Schaie, K. W., & Parham, I. A. (1980). Complexity of lifestyle and maintenance of intellectual abilities. *Journal of Social Issues, 36,* 47–61.

Gruber, A., & Schaie, K. W. (1986, November 21). *Longitudinal-sequential studies of marital assortativity.* Paper presented at the annual meeting of the Gerontological Society of America, Chicago.

Gruber, H. (1981). *Darwin on man.* Chicago: University of Chicago Press.

Gruber-Baldini, A. L. (1991). *The impact of health and disease on cognitive ability in adulthood and old age in the Seattle Longitudinal Study.* Unpublished doctoral dissertation, Pennsylvania State University.

Gruson, L. (1992, April 22). Gains in deciphering genes set off effort to guard data against abuses. *New York Times,* p. C12.

Guemple, L. (1983). Growing old in Inuit society. In J. Sokolovsky (Ed.), *Growing old in different societies* (pp. 24–28). Belmont, CA: Wadsworth.

Gui, S.-X. (1989, December). *A new approach to the pension system in Shanghai suburbs.* Paper presented at the International Academic Conference on China's Population Aging, Beijing.

Guilford, J. P. (1956). Structure of intellect. *Psychological Bulletin, 53,* 267–293.

Guilford, J. P. (1959). Three faces of intellect. *American Psychologist, 14,* 469–479.

Guilford, J. P. (1960). Basic conceptual problems of the psychology of thinking. *Proceedings of the New York Academy of Sciences, 91,* 6–21.

Guilford, J. P. (1967). *The nature of human intelligence.* New York: McGraw-Hill.

Guilford, J. P. (1982). Cognitive psychology's ambiguities: Some suggested remedies. *Psychology Review, 89,* 48–59.

Guilford, J. P. (1986). *Creative talents: Their nature, uses and development.* Buffalo, NY: Bearly.

Gutmann, D. L. (1974). Alternatives to disengagement: Aging among the highland Druze. In R. LeVine (Ed.), *Culture and personality: Contemporary readings* (pp. 232–245). Chicago: Aldine.

Gutmann, D. (1975). Parenting: A key to the comparative study of the life cycle. In N. Datan & L. H. Ginsberg (Eds.), *Life-span developmental psychology: Normative life crises.* New York: Academic.

Gutmann, D. (1977). The cross-cultural perspective: Notes toward a comparative psychology of aging. In J. Birren & K. W. Schaie (Eds.), *Handbook of the psychology of aging* (pp. 302–326). New York: Van Nostrand Reinhold.

Gutmann, D. (1985). The parental imperative revisited. In J. Meacham (Ed.), *Family and individual development.* Basel, Switzerland: Karger.

Gutmann, D. (1992). Culture and mental health in later life. In J. E. Birren, R. Sloane, & G. D. Cohen (Eds.), *Handbook of mental health and aging* (2d ed., pp. 75–96). New York: Academic.

Haan, N. (1990). Personality at midlife. In S. Hunter & M. Sundel (Eds.), *Midlife myths.* Newbury Park: Sage.

Haan, N., & Day, D. (1974). A longitudinal study of change and sameness in personality development: Adolescence to later adulthood. *International Journal of Aging and Human Development, 5,* 11–39.

Haas, A. D. (1989, Winter). Adults in college. *Women's American ORT Reporter,* pp. 7, 14.

Hagestad, G. O. (1978). *Patterns of communication and influence between grandparents and grandchildren in a changing society.* Paper presented at the meeting of the World Conference of Sociology, Uppsala, Sweden.

Hagestad, G. O. (1982). *Issues in the study of intergenerational continuity.* Paper presented at the National Council on Family Relations Theory and Methods Workshop, Washington, DC.

Hagestad, G. O. (1984, November). *Family transitions in adulthood: Some recent changes and their consequences.* Paper presented at the annual meeting of the Gerontological Society of America, San Antonio, TX.

Haley, A. (1976). *Roots.* Garden City, NY: Doubleday.

Hall, C., & Lindzey, G. (1978). *Personality* (3d ed.). New York: Wiley.

Hall, G. S. (1922). *Senescence: The last half of life.* New York: Appleton.

Hammond, C. B., Jelovsek, F. R., Lee, K. L., Creasman, W. T., & Parker, R. T. (1979). Effects of long-term estrogen replacement therapy: 2. Neoplasia. *American Journal of Obstetrics and Gynecology, 133,* 537–547.

Hamon, R. R., & Blieszner, R. (1990). Filial responsibility expectations among adult child–older parent pairs. *Journal of Gerontology: Psychological Sciences, 45*(3), P110–112.

Hampton, R. L., Gelles, R. J., & Harrop, J. W. (1989). Is violence in black families increasing? A comparison of 1975 and 1985 national survey rates. *Journal of Marriage and the Family, 51,* 969–980.

Handy, C. (1991, October–November). Building small fires: Keep life sizzling—diversify! *Modern Maturity,* pp. 35–39.

Hankinson, S. E., Stampfer, M. J., Seddon, J. M., Colditz, G. A., Rosner, B., Speizer, F. E., & Willett, W. C. (1992). Nutrient intake and cataract extraction in women: A prospective study. *British Medical Journal, 305*(6849), 335–339.

Hanley, R. (1988a, February 4). Surrogate deals for mothers held illegal in Jersey. *New York Times,* pp. A1, B6.

Hanley, R. (1988b, February 4). Legislators are hesitant on regulating surrogacy. *New York Times,* p. B7.

Hanser, S. B., & Thompson, L. W. (1994). Effects of a music therapy strategy on depressed older adults. *Journal of Gerontology: Psychological Sciences, 49,* P265–269.

Hanson, L. (1968). *Renoir: The man, the painter, and his world.* New York: Dodd, Mead.

Hanson, R. O., & Carpenter, B. N. (1994). *Relationships in old age.* New York: Guilford.

Hare, P. H. (1993). Frail elders and the suburbs. In J. J. Callahan, Jr. (Ed.), *Aging in place* (pp. 61–72). Amityville, NY: Baywood.

Hare, P. H., & Haske, M. (1983–1984, December–January). Innovative living arrangements: A source of long-term care. *Aging,* pp. 3–8.

Hargrove, J. (1989). *Nelson Mandela: South Africa's silent voice of protest.* Chicago: Children's Press.

Harkins, E. (1978). Effects of empty nest transition on self-report of psychological and physical well-being. *Journal of Marriage and the Family, 40*(3), 549–556.

Harper, S., & Lund, D. (1990). Wives, husbands, and daughters caring for institutionalized and noninstitutionalized dementia patients: Toward a model of caregiving burden. *International Journal of Aging and Human Development, 30,* 241–262.

Harris, R., & Bologh, R. W. (1985). The dark side of love: Blue- and white-collar wife abuse. *Victimology.*

Harrison, M. (1982). *Self-help for premenstrual syndrome.* Cambridge, MA: Matrix.

Hart, S. N., & Brassard, M. R. (1987). A major threat to children's mental health: Psychological maltreatment. *American Psychologist, 42*(2), 160–165.

Hartley, A. A., Hartley, J. T., & Johnson, S. A. (1984). The older adult as computer user. In P. K. Robinson & J. E. Birren (Eds.), *Aging and technological advances* (pp. 347–348). New York: Plenum.

Hasher, L. (1992, April). Inhibitory mechanisms: Overview. Paper presented at the Fourth Cognitive Aging Conference, Atlanta.

Hasher, L., & Zacks, R. T. (1988). Working memory, comprehension, and aging: A review and a new view. In G. H. Bower (Ed.), *The psychology of learning and motivation: Advances in research and theory* (Vol. 22, pp. 193–225). New York: Academic.

Haug, M., Belkgrave, L., & Gratton, B. (1984). Mental health and the elderly: Factors in stability and change over time. *Journal of Health and Social Behavior, 25,* 100–115.

Havighurst, R. J., Neugarten, B. L., & Tobin, S. S. (1968). Disengagement and patterns of aging. In B. L. Neugarten (Ed.), *Middle age and aging* (pp. 161–172). Chicago: University of Chicago Press.

Hawking, S. W. (1988). *A brief history of time: From the Big Bang to black holes.* New York: Bantam.

Hayflick, L. (1974). The strategy of senescence. *The Gerontologist, 14*(1), 37–45.

Hayflick, L. (1981). Intracellular determinants of aging. *Mechanisms of Aging and Development, 28,* 177.

Hayward, M. D., & Wang, W. (1993). Retirement in Shanghai. *Research on Aging, 15,* 3–32.

Headache: Putting an end to pain. (1994, September). *Johns Hopkins Medical Letter: Health after 50, 6,* pp. 4–5.

Health Care Finance Administration. (1981). *Long-term care: Background and future directions.* Washington, DC: U.S. Department of Health and Human Services.

Healy, B. (1991). The Yentl syndrome. *New England Journal of Medicine, 325,* 274–276.

Healy, J. (1983). Bereavement issues and anticipatory grief. In *Symposium on death and dying: The role of the family and estate planner.* New York: Foundation of Thanatology.

Heckhausen, J., Dixon, R. A., & Baltes, P. B. (1989). Gains and losses in development throughout adulthood as perceived by different adult age groups. *Developmental Psychology, 25,* 109–121.

Heindel, W. C., Butters, N., & Salmon, D. P. (1988). Impaired learning of a motor skill in patients with Huntington's disease. *Behavioral Neuroscience, 102,* 141–147.

Heindel, W. C., Salmon, D. P., & Butters, N. (1989). Neuropsychological differentiation of memory impairments in dementia. In G. C. Gilmore, P. J. Whitehouse, & M. L. Wykle (Eds.), *Memory, aging, and dementia: Theory, assessment, and treatment* (pp. 112–139). New York: Springer.

Heindel, W. C., Salmon, D. P., & Butters, N. (1991). The biasing of weight judgments in Alzheimer's and Huntington's disease: A priming or programming phenomenon? *Journal of Clinical and Experimental Neuropsychology, 13,* 189–203.

Heindel, Salmon, & Butters (1991a). See 1991.

Heindel, Salmon, & Butters (1991b). See 1989.

Heller, R. B., & Dobbs, A. R. (1993). Age differences in word finding in discourse and nondiscourse situations. *Psychology and Aging, 8,* 443–450.

Heller, Z. I. (1975). The Jewish view of dying: Guidelines for dying. In E. Kübler-Ross (Ed.), *Death: The final stage of growth.* Englewood Cliffs, NJ: Prentice-Hall.

Helson, R. (1992). Women's difficult times and the rewriting of the life story. *Psychology of Women Quarterly, 16,* 331–347.

Helson, R. (1993). Comparing longitudinal studies of adult development: Toward a paradigm of tension between stability and change. In D. C. Funder, R. D. Parke, C. Tomlinson-Keasey, & K. Widaman (Eds.), *Studying lives through time: Personality and development* (pp. 93–120). Washington, DC: American Psychological Association.

Helson, R., & Moane, G. (1987). Personality change in women from college to midlife. *Journal of Personality and Social Psychology, 53,* 176–186.

Helson, R., & Picano, J. (1990). Is the traditional role bad for women? *Journal of Personality and Social Psychology, 59,* 311–320.

Helson, R., & Wink, P. (1992). Personality change in women from the early 40s to the early 50s. *Psychology and Aging, 7*(1), 46–55.

Henderson, V. W., & Finch, C. E. (1989). The neurobiology of Alzheimer's disease. *Journal of Neurosurgery, 70,* 335–353.

Henig, R. M. (1989, December 24). High-tech fortune-telling. *New York Times,* pp. 20–22.

Henker, F. O. (1981). Male climacteric. In J. G. Howells (Ed.), *Modern perspectives in the psychiatry of middle age.* New York: Brunner/Mazel.

Henrich, J. B. (1992). The postmenopausal estrogen/breast cancer controversy. *Journal of the American Medical Association, 268*(14), 1900–1902.

Herdt, G. (1981). *Guardians of the flutes.* New York: McGraw-Hill.

Herdt, G. (1987). *Sambia: Ritual and gender in New Guinea.* New York: Harcourt Brace.

Hermanson, B., Omenn, G. S., Kronmal, R. A., Gersh, B. J., & Participants in the Coronary Artery Surgery Study. (1988). Beneficial six-year outcome of smoking cessation in older men and women with coronary artery disease. *New England Journal of Medicine, 319*(21), 1365–1369.

Herrnstein, R. J., & Murray, C. (1994). *The bell curve: Intelligence and class structure in American life.* New York: Free.

Hertzog, C. (1989). Influences of cognitive slowing on age differences in intelligence. *Developmental Psychology, 25*(4), 636–651.

Hertzog, C., & Dixon, R. A. (1994). Metacognitive development in adulthood and old age. In J. Metcalfe & A. P. Shimamura (Eds.), *Metacognition: Knowing about knowing* (pp. 221–251). Cambridge, MA: MIT Press.

Hertzog, C., Dixon, R. A., & Hultsch, D. F. (1990). Relationships between metamemory, memory predictions, and memory task performance in adults. *Psychology and Aging, 5*(2), 215–227.

Hertzog, C., Saylor, L. L., Fleece, A. M., & Dixon, R. A. (1994). Metamemory and aging: Relations between predicted, actual and perceived memory task performance. *Aging and Cognition, 1,* 203–237.

Hertzog, C., Schaie, K. W., & Gribbin, K. (1978). Cardiovascular disease and changes in intellectual functioning from middle to old age. *Journal of Gerontology, 33,* 872–883.

Herzog, A. R., House, J. S., & Morgan, J. N. (1991). Relation of work and retirement to health and well-being in older age. *Psychology and Aging, 6,* 202–211.

Herzog, A. R., Kahn, R. L., Morgan, J. N., Jackson, J. S., & Antonucci, T. C. (1989). Age differences in productive activities. *Journal of Gerontology: Social Sciences, 44,* S129–138.

Hill, C. D., Thompson, L. W., & Gallagher, D. (1988). The role of anticipatory bereavement in older women's adjustment to widowhood. *The Gerontologist, 28*(6), 792–796.

Hill, R., Foote, N., Aldonus, J., Carlson, R., & MacDonald, R. (1970). *Family development in three generations.* Cambridge, MA: Schenkman.

Hjelle, L. A., & Ziegler, D. J. (1992). *Personality theories* (3d ed.). New York: McGraw-Hill.

Hochanadel, G. A. (1991). Neuropsychological changes in aging: A process-oriented error analysis. *Dissertation Abstracts International, 52*(4-B), 2347.

Hoff, B. (1982). *The Tao of Pooh.* New York: Dutton.

Holden, A. (1988). *Laurence Olivier.* New York: Atheneum.

Holland, J. (1985). *Professional manual for the self-directed search.* Odessa, FL: Psychological Assessment Resources.

Holland, M. J. (1990). No sweat: How heat and stress affect the elderly. *Health and Human Development Research, 1,* 31–33.

Holliday, S. G., & Chandler, M. J. (1986). *Wisdom: Explorations in adult competence.* Basel, Switzerland: Karger.

Holmes, T. H., & Rahe, R. H. (1976). The social readjustment rating scale. *Journal of Psychosomatic Research, 11,* 213.

Honigmann, J. J. (1967). *Personality in culture.* New York: Harper & Row.

Hooker, K., & Kaus, C. R. (1994). Health-related possible selves in young and middle adulthood. *Psychology and Aging, 9,* 126–133.

Hooker, K., Monahan, D., Shifren, K., & Hutchinson, C. (1992). Mental and physical health of spouse caregivers: The role of personality. *Psychology and Aging, 7*(3), 367–375.

Hooyman, N. R., Rathbone-McCuan, E., & Klingbeil, K. (1982). Serving the vulnerable elderly. *Urban and Social Change Review, 15*(2), 9–13.

Horn, J. C., & Meer, J. (1987, May). The vintage years. *Psychology Today,* pp. 76–90.

Horn, J. L. (1967). Intelligence—Why it grows, why it declines. *Transaction, 5*(1), 23–31.

Horn, J. L. (1968). Organization of abilities and the development of intelligence. *Psychological Review, 75,* 242–259.

Horn, J. L. (1970). Organization of data on life-span development of human abilities. In L. R. Goulet & P. B. Baltes (Eds.), *Life-span developmental psychology: Theory and research* (pp. 424–466) New York: Academic.

Horn, J. L. (1982a). The aging of human abilities. In B. B. Wolman (Ed.), *Handbook of developmental psychology* (pp. 847–870). Englewood Cliffs, NJ: Prentice-Hall.

Horn, J. L. (1982b). The theory of fluid and crystallized intelligence in relation to concepts of cognitive psychology and aging in adulthood. In F. I. M. Craik & S. Trehub (Eds.), *Aging and cognitive processes* (Vol. 8, pp. 237–278). New York: Plenum.

Horn, J. L., & Cattell, R. B. (1966). Age differences in primary mental ability factors. *Journal of Gerontology, 21,* 210–220.

Horn, J. L., & Donaldson, G. (1976). On the myth of intellectual decline in adulthood. *American Psychologist, 31,* 701–719.

Horn, J. L., & Donaldson, G. (1977). Faith is not enough: A response to the Baltes-Schaie claim that intelligence does not wane. *American Psychologist, 32,* 369–373.

Horn, J. L., & Donaldson, G. (1980). Cognitive development: 2. Adulthood development of human abilities. In O. G. Brim & J. Kagan (Eds.), *Constancy and change in human development.* Cambridge, MA: Harvard University Press.

Horner, R. D., Matchar, D. B., Divine, G. W., & Feussner, J. R. (1991). Racial variations in ischemic, stroke-related physical and function impairments. *Stroke, 22*(12), 1491–1501.

Horton, A. M., & Fogelman, C. J. (1991). Behavioral treatment of aged alcoholics and drug addicts. In P. A. Wisocki (Ed.), *Handbook of clinical behavioral therapy with the elderly client* (pp. 299–316). New York: Plenum.

House, S. J., Landis, K. R., & Umberson, D. (1988). Social relationships and health. *Science, 241,* 540–544.

Howard, D. V. (1991). Implicit memory: An expanding picture of cognitive aging. In K. W. Schaie & M. P. Lawton (Eds.), *Annual review of gerontology and geriatrics* (pp. 1–22). New York: Springer.

Hoyer, W. J., & Rybash, J. M. (1994). Characterizing adult cognitive development. *Journal of Adult Development, 1*(1), 7–12.

Hu, Y., & Goldman, N. (1990). Mortality differentials by marital status: An international comparison. *Demography, 27*(2), 233–250.

Hull, R. H. (1980). Talking to the hearing impaired older person. *ASHA, 22*, 194.

Hultsch, D. F. (1971). Organization and memory in adulthood. *Human Development, 14*, 16–29.

Hunt, B., & Hunt, M. (1974). *Prime time*. New York: Stein & Day.

Hunt, E., & Love, T. (1982). The second mnemonist. In U. Neisser (Ed.), *Memory observed: Remembering in natural contexts*. San Francisco: Freeman.

Hurd, M. D. (1989). The economic status of the elderly. *Science, 244*, 659–664.

Hurley, D. (1994, May 11). Pump better than CPR for heart attack: Study. *Chicago Sun-Times*, p. 5.

Huyck, M. H. (1990). Gender differences in aging. In J. E. Birren & K. W. Schaie (Eds.), *Handbook of the psychology of aging* (3d ed., pp. 124–132). San Diego: Academic.

Hyde, J. S. (1986). *Understanding human sexuality* (3d ed.). New York: McGraw-Hill.

Hyde, J. S., Krajnik, M., & Skuldt-Niederberger, K. (1991). Androgyny across the life span: A replication and longitudinal follow-up. *Developmental Psychology, 27*, 516–519.

Ickovics, J. R., et al. (1994). Limited effects of HIV counseling and testing for women: A prospective study of behavioral and psychological consequences. *Journal of the American Medical Association, 272*(6), 443–448.

Illinois Task Force on Gender Bias in the Courts. (1990). *Executive summary with status of recommendations.*

Insel, P. M., & Roth, W. R. (1988). *Core concepts in health*. Mountain View, CA: Mayfield.

Irons, R. R. (1994, December 1). Addiction affects all members of family. *The Menninger Letter*, p. 3.

Irving, H. H., & Benjamin, M. (1988). Divorce mediation in a court-based fee for service agency: An empirical study. *Conciliation Courts Review, 26*(1), 43–47.

Ivers, G. H. (1994, Fall). Working to end violence. *Literacy Advocate* (Laubach Literacy International), p. 5.

Ivy, G. O., MacLeod, C. M., Petit, T. L., & Markus, E. J. (1992). A physiological framework for perceptual and cognitive changes in aging. In F. I. M. Craik & T. A. Salthouse (Eds.), *The handbook of aging and cognition* (pp. 273–314). Hillsdale, NJ: Erlbaum.

Jacques, E. (1967). The mid-life crisis. In R. Owen (Ed.), *Middle age*. London: BBC.

Jaffe, I. M. D. (1985). Arthritis. In D. F. Tapley, R. J. Weiss, & T. Q. Morris, (Eds.), *The Columbia University College of Physicians and Surgeons complete home medical guide* (pp. 564–587). New York: Crown.

Jahoda, M. (1958). *Current concepts of positive mental health*. New York: Basic Books.

Jallinoja, J. (1989). Women between the family and employment. In K. Boh et al. (Eds.), *Changing patterns of European family life* (pp. 95–122). London: Routledge.

James, W. (1890). *The principles of psychology* (Vol. 2). New York: Holt.

Janowsky, J. S., Shimamura, A. P., & Squire, L. R. (1989). Memory and metamemory: Comparisons between patients with frontal lobe lesions and amnesic patients. *Psychobiology, 17*, 3–11.

Japanese Social Welfare Association. (1990). The conditions of caring for the elderly. Tokyo: Author.

Jaroff, L. (1992, June 8). Einstein's inspiring heir. *Time*, pp. 88–89.

Jaroff, L. (1995, January 25). New age therapy. *Time*, p. 52.

Jay, G. M., & Willis, S. L. (1992). Influence of direct computer experience on older adults' attitudes toward computers. *Journal of Gerontology: Psychological Sciences, 47*, P250–257.

Jefferson, J. W., & Greist, J. H. (1993). *Depression and older people: Recognizing hidden signs and taking steps toward recovery*. Madison, WI: Pratt Pharmaceuticals.

Jelicic, M., Bonke, B., Wolters, G., & Phaf, R. H. (1992). Implicit memory for words presented during anaesthesia. *European Journal of Cognitive Psychology, 4*, 71–80.

Jendrek, M. P. (1994). Grandparents who parent grandchildren: Circumstances and decisions. *The Gerontologist, 34*, 206–216.

Jensen, A. R. (1969). How much can we boost IQ and scholastic achievement? *Harvard Educational Review, 39*, 1–123.

Jensen, A. R. (1993). Test validity: g versus "tacit knowledge." *Current Directions in Psychological Science, 2*(1), 9–10.

Johnson, C. L., & Catalano, D. J. (1981). Childless elderly and their family supports. *The Gerontologist, 21*(6), 610–618.

Johnson, C. L., & Troll, L. (1992). Family functioning in late late life. *Journal of Gerontology: Social Sciences, 47*(2), S66–72.

Johnson, C. L., & Troll, L. E. (1994). Constraints and facilitators to friendships in late late life. *The Gerontologist, 34*, 79–87.

Johnson, F. L., Foxall, M. J., Kelleher, E., Kentopp, E., Mannlein, E. A., & Cook, E. (1986). Life satisfaction of the elderly American Indian. *International Journal of Nursing Studies, 23*, 265–273.

Johnson, F. L., Foxall, M. J., Kelleher, E., Kentopp, E., Mannlein, E. A., & Cook, E. (1988). Comparison of mental health life satisfaction of five elderly ethnic groups. *Western Journal of Nursing, 10*, 613–628.

Johnson, L. (1991). Bridging paradigms: The role of a change agent in an international technical transfer project. In J. D. Sinnott & J. C. Cavanaugh (Eds.), *Bridging Paradigms* (pp. 59–71). New York: Praeger.

Johnson, S. J., & Rybash, J. M. (1993). A cognitive neuroscience perspective on age-related slowing: Developmental changes in the functional architecture. In J. Cerella, J. M. Rybash, W. J. Hoyer, & M. L. Commons (Eds.), *Adult information processing: Limits on loss* (pp. 143–175). San Diego: Academic.

Johnson, T. E. (1990). Age-1 mutants of *Caenorhabditis elegans* prolong life by modifying the Gompertz rate of aging. *Science, 229*, 908–912.

Jones, E. (1961). *The life and work of Sigmund Freud*. New York: Basic Books.

Jones, H., & Conrad, H. (1933). The growth and decline of intelligence: A study of a homogeneous group between the ages of 10 and 60. *Genetic Psychology Monographs, 13,* 223–298.

Jones, J. H. (1981). *Bad blood: The Tuskegee syphilis experiment.* New York: Free.

Juggling family, job, and aged dependent. (1989, January 26). *New York Times,* p. B8.

Jung, C. G. (1933). *Modern man in search of a soul.* New York: Harcourt Brace & World.

Jung, C. G. (1953). The stages of life. In H. Read, M. Fordham, & G. Adler (Eds.), *Collected works* (Vol. 2). Princeton, NJ: Princeton University Press. (Original work published 1931)

Jung, C. G. (1961). *Memories, dreams, and reflections.* New York: Random House.

Jung, C. G. (1966). Two essays on analytic psychology. In *Collected works* (Vol. 7). Princeton, NJ: Princeton University Press.

Jung, C. G. (1969). *The structure and dynamics of the psyche.* Princeton, NJ: Princeton University Press.

Kabanoff, B. (1980). Work and nonwork: A review of models, methods, and findings. *Psychological Bulletin, 88,* 60–77.

Kadar, A. B., M. D. (1994, August). The sex-bias myth in medicine. *Atlantic Monthly,* pp. 66–70.

Kagan, J. (1989). *Unstable ideas: Temperament, cognition, and self.* Cambridge, MA: Harvard University Press.

Kahana, B., & Kahana, E. (1970). Grandparenthood from the perspective of the developing grandchild. *Developmental Psychology, 3,* 98–105.

Kahana, E. (1982). A congruence model of person-environment interaction. In M. P. Lawton & T. O. Byerts (Eds.), *Aging and the environment: Theoretical approaches* (pp. 97–121). New York: Springer.

Kahn, R. L., & Antonucci, T. C. (1980). Convoys over the life course: Attachment, roles, and social support. In P. B. Baltes & O. G. Brim, Jr. (Eds.), *Life-span development and behavior* (Vol. 3, pp. 253–286). New York: Academic.

Kahn, S., Zimmerman, G., Csikszentmihalyi, M., & Getzels, J. W. (1985). Relations between identity in young adulthood and intimacy at midlife. *Journal of Personality and Social Psychology, 49,* 1316–1322.

Kaiser, M. A. (1993). The productive roles of older people in developing countries: What are the implications of economic, social, and cultural participation? *Generations, 17*(4), 65–69.

Kalat, J. W. (1992). *Biological psychology.* Pacific Grove, CA: Brooks/Cole.

Kalish, R. A., & Reynolds, D. K. (1976). *Death and ethnicity: A psychocultural study.* Los Angeles: University of Southern California, Ethel Percy Andrus Gerontology Center.

Kalmuss, D., Davidson, A., & Cushman, L. (1992). Parental expectations, experiences, and adjustment to parenthood: A test of the violated expectations framework. *Journal of Marriage and the Family, 54,* 516–526.

Kalmuss, D. S., & Straus, M. A. (1982). Wife's marital dependency and wife abuse. *Journal of Marriage and the Family, 44,* 277–286.

Kamin, L. J. (1974). *The science and politics of IQ.* Potomac, MD: Erlbaum.

Kamin, L. J. (1981). Commentary. In S. Scarr (Ed.), *Race, social class, and individual differences in I.Q.* Hillsdale, NJ: Erlbaum.

Kandel, D. B., Davies, M., Karus, D., & Yamaguchi, K. (1986). The consequences in young adulthood of adolescent drug involvement. *Archives of General Psychiatry, 43,* 746–754.

Kane, R. I., Wales, J., Bernstein, L, Leibowitz, A., & Kaplan, S. (1984, April 21). A randomized controlled trial of hospice care. *The Lancet,* pp. 890–894.

Karas, R. H., Patterson, B. L., & Mendelsohn, M. E. (1994). Human vascular smooth muscle cells contain functional estrogen receptor. *Circulation, 89,* 1943–1950.

Karlinsky, H., Lennox, A., & Rossor, M. (1994). Alzheimer's disease and genetic testing. *Alzheimer's Disease and Associated Disorders, 8*(2), 63–65.

Karni, A., Tanne, D., Rubenstein, B. S., Askenasy, J. J., & Sagi, D. (1994). Dependence on REM sleep of overnight improvement of a perceptual skill. *Science, 265*(5172), 679–682.

Karp, D. A. (1989). The social construction of retirement among professionals 50–60 years old. *The Gerontologist, 29,* 750–759.

Kastenbaum, R. (1977). The kingdom where nobody dies. In S. Zarit (Ed.), *Readings in aging and death: Contemporary perspectives.* New York: Harper & Row.

Kastenbaum, R. (1993). Reconstructing death in postmodern society. *Omega, 27,* 75–89.

Kastenbaum, R., & Aisenberg, R. (1972). *The psychology of death.* New York: Springer.

Katchadourian, H. (1987). *Fifty: Midlife in perspective.* New York: Freeman.

Katz, S., Branch, L. G., Branson, M. H., Papsidero, J. A., Beck, J. C., & Greer, D. S. (1983). Active life expectancy. *New England Journal of Medicine, 309,* 1218–1224.

Katzman, R. (1993). Education and prevalence of dementia and Alzheimer's disease. *Neurology, 43,* 13–20.

Kaufman, S. R. (1986). *The ageless self: Sources of meaning in late life.* Madison: University of Wisconsin Press.

Kaufman, T. S. (1993). *The combined family: A guide to creating successful step-relationships.* New York: Plenum.

Kausler, D. H. (1990). Automaticity of encoding and episodic memory processes. In E. A. Lovelace (Ed.), *Aging and cognition: Mental processes, self-awareness and interventions* (pp. 29–67). Amsterdam: North-Holland, Elsevier.

Kawachi, I., Colditz, G. A., Stampfer, M. J., Willett, W. C., Manson, J. E., Rosner, B., Speizer, F. E., & Hennekens, C. H. (1993). Smoking cessation and decreased risk of stroke in women. *Journal of the American Medical Association, 269,* 232–236.

Kay, B., & Neelley, J. N. (1982). Sexuality and the aging: A review of current literature. *Sexuality and Disability, 5,* 38–46.

Kayser-Jones, J. A. (1982). Institutional structures: Catalysts of or barriers to quality care for the institutionalized aged in Scotland and the U.S. *Social Science Medicine, 16,* 935–944.

Keating, N., & Cole, P. (1980). What do I do with him 24 hours a day? Changes in the housewife role after retirement. *The Gerontologist, 20,* 84–89.

Keeping cancer at bay with diet. (1994, April). *Johns Hopkins Medical Letter: Health after 50*, pp. 3, 6.

Keith, P. M. (1983). A comparison of the resources of parents and childless men and women in very old age. *Family Relations, 32,* 403–409.

Kellermann, A. L., Rivara, F. P., Somes, G., Reay, D. T., Francisco, J., Banton, J. G., Prodzinski, J., Flinger, C., & Hackman, B. B. (1992). Suicide in the home in relation to gun ownership. *New England Journal of Medicine, 327,* 467–472.

Kelly, J. B. (1982). Divorce: The adult perspective. In B. Wolman (Ed.), *Handbook of developmental psychology* (pp. 734–750). Englewood Cliffs, NJ: Prentice-Hall.

Kelly, J. R. (1987). *Peoria winter: Styles and resources in later life.* Lexington, MA: Lexington.

Kelly, J. R. (1994). Recreation and leisure. In A. Monk (Ed.), *The Columbia retirement handbook* (pp. 489–508). New York: Columbia University Press.

Kelly, J. R., Steinkamp, M., & Kelly, J. (1986). Later life leisure: How they play in Peoria. *The Gerontologist, 26,* 531–537.

Kelly, O. (1978). Living with a life-threatening illness. In M. C. Garfield (Ed.), *Psychosocial care of the dying patient* (pp. 59–66). New York: McGraw-Hill.

Kelly, R. C. (1976). Witchcraft and sexual relations: An exploration in the social and semantic implications of the structure of belief. In P. Brown & G. Buchbinder (Eds.), *Man and woman in the New Guinea highlands* (pp. 36–53). Washington, DC: American Anthropological Association.

Kempe, C. H., et al. (1962). The battered child syndrome. *Journal of the American Medical Association, 181,* 17–24.

Kemper, T. L. (1994). Neuroanatomical and neuropathological changes during aging and dementia. In M. L. Albert & J. E. Knoefel (Eds.), *Clinical neurology of aging* (2d ed., pp. 3–67). New York: Oxford University Press.

Kennedy, R. (1994, December 5). Elizabeth Glaser dies at 47; crusader for pediatric AIDS. *New York Times,* p. A12.

Kenrick, D. T., & Funder, D. C. (1988). Profiting from controversy: Lessons from the person-situation debate. *American Psychologist, 43,* 23–34.

Kernan, M. (1993, June). The object at hand. *Smithsonian,* pp. 14–16.

Kerschner, H. K. (1992). *An incumbent versus a new candidate paradigm in aging.* Washington, DC: American Association for International Aging.

Kessler, R. C., McGonagle, K. A., Nelson, C. B., Hughes, M., Swartz, M., & Blazer, D. G. (1994). Sex and depression in the National Comorbidity Survey: 2. Cohort effects. *Journal of Affective Disorders, 30,* 15–26.

Kidder, T. (1993, October–November). Inside Linda Manor. *Modern Maturity,* pp. 52–55.

Kiecolt-Glaser, J. K., Malarkey, W. B., Chee, M., Newton, T. Cacioppo, J. T., Mao, H. Y., & Glaser, R. (1993). Negative behavior during marital conflict is associated with immunological down-regulation. *Psychosomatic Medicine, 55,* 395–409.

Kiernan, T. (1981). *Sir Larry: The life of Laurence Olivier.* New York: Times.

Kihlstrom, J. F. (1983). Instructed forgetting: Hypnotic and nonhypnotic. *Journal of Experimental Psychology: General, 112,* 73–79.

Kim, N. W., Piatyszek, M. A., Prowse, K. R., Harley, C. B., West, M. D., Ho, P. L. C., Coviello, G. M., Wright, W. E., Weinrich, S. L., & Shay, J. W. (1994). Specific association of human telomerase activity with immortal cells and cancer. *Science, 266,* 2011–2015.

Kimmel, D. C. (1980). *Adulthood and aging* (2d ed.). New York: Wiley.

Kimmel, D. C. (1988). Ageism, psychology, and public policy. *American Psychologist, 43*(3), 175–178.

Kimura, D. (1989, November). Monthly fluctuation in sex hormones affect women's cognitive skills. *Psychology Today,* pp. 63–66.

King, B. M. (1996). *Human sexuality today.* Englewood Cliffs, NJ: Prentice-Hall.

King, B. M., Camp, C. J., & Downey, A. M. (1991). *Human sexuality today.* Englewood Cliffs, NJ: Prentice-Hall.

King, D. (1993, March). Age-old questions [Letter to the Editor]. *New Woman,* p. 14.

Kinsbourne, M. (1980). Attentional dysfunctions in the elderly: Theoretical models and research perspectives. In L. W. Poon, J. L. Fozard, L. S. Cremack, D. Arenberg, & L. W. Thompson (Eds.), *New directions in memory and aging: Proceedings of the George A. Talland memorial conference.* Hillsdale, NJ: Erlbaum.

Kinsey, A. C., Pomeroy, W., & Martin, C. E. (1948). *Sexual behavior in the human male.* Philadelphia: Saunders.

Kinsey, A. C., Pomeroy, W., Martin, C. E., & Gebhard, P. H. (1953). *Sexual behavior in the human female.* Philadelphia: Saunders.

Kirsch, I. S., Jenkins, L., Jungeblut, A., & Kolstad, A. (1993). *Adult literacy in America: A first look at the results of the National Adult Literacy Survey.* Princeton, NJ: Educational Testing Service.

Kirschenbaum, M. J. (1994, August). Breaking the cycle of domestic violence. *The Menninger Letter,* pp. 1–2.

Kirschenbaum, R. J. (1990, November–December). An interview with Howard Gardner. *The Gifted Child Today,* pp. 26–32.

Kite, M. E., & Johnson, B. T. (1988). Attitudes toward older and younger adults: A meta-analysis. *Psychology and Aging, 3*(3), 232–244.

Kitson, G. C., & Morgan, L. A. (1990). The multiple consequences of divorce: A decade review. *Journal of Marriage and Family Therapy, 52,* 913–924.

Kitson, G. C., & Roach, M. J. (1989). Independence and social and psychological adjustment in widowhood and divorce. In D. A. Lund (Ed.), *Older bereaved spouses: Research with practical implications.* New York: Hemisphere.

Kivett, V. R. (1991). Centrality of the grandfather role among older rural black and white men. *Journal of Gerontology: Social Sciences, 46*(5), S250–258.

Kivnick, H. (1982). *The meaning of grandparenthood.* Minneapolis: UMI Research.

Kivnick, H. Q. (1993). Everyday mental health: A guide to assessing life strengths. *Generations, 17*(1), 13–20.

Klagsbrun, F. (1993, November). Marching in front. *Hadassah,* pp. 24–25.

Klass, D. (1986, November). *When is forgetting cognitive decline?* Paper presented at the annual meeting of the Gerontological Society of America, Chicago.

Klatzky, R. L. (1991). Let's be friends. *American Psychologist, 46*(1), 43–45.

Kleemeier, R. W. (1962). Intellectual changes in the senium. *Proceedings of the American Statistical Association, 1*, 181–190.

Klerman, G. L. (1989). Treatment of alcoholism. *New England Journal of Medicine, 320*(6), 394–395.

Kliegl, R., & Lindenberger, U. (1993). Modeling intrusions and correct recall in episodic memory: Adult age differences in encoding of list context. *Journal of Experimental Psychology: Learning, Memory, and Cognition, 19*, 617–637.

Kline, D. W., Kline, T. J. B., Fozard, J. L., Kosnik, W., Schieber, F., & Sekuler, R. (1992). Vision, aging, and driving: The problems of older drivers. *Journal of Gerontology, 47*(1), P27–34.

Kline, D. W., & Schieber, F. (1985). Vision and aging. In J. E. Birren & K. W. Schaie (Eds.), *Handbook of the psychology of aging* (2d ed., pp. 296–331). New York: Van Nostrand Reinhold.

Knapp, M. J., Knopman, D. S., Solomon, P. R., Pendlebury, W. W., Davis, C. S., & Gracon, S. I. (1994). A 30-week, randomized controlled trial of high-dose tacrine in patients with Alzheimer's disease. *Journal of the American Medical Association, 271*, 985–991.

Koenig, H. G., & Blazer, D. G. (1992). Mood disorders and suicide. In J. E. Birren, R. Sloane, & G. D. Cohen (Eds.), *Handbook of mental health and aging* (2d ed., pp. 379–407). New York: Academic.

Koenig, H. G., George, L. K., & Siegler, I. C. (1988). The use of religion and other emotion-regulating coping strategies among older adults. *The Gerontologist, 28*(3), 303–310.

Koenig, H. G., Kvale, J. N., & Ferrel, C. (1988). Religion and well-being in later life. *The Gerontologist, 28*(1), 18–28.

Kohlberg, L. (1966). A cognitive-developmental analysis of children's sex-role concepts and attitudes. In E. E. Maccoby (Ed.), *The development of sex differences* (pp. 82–173). Stanford, CA: Stanford University Press.

Kohlberg, L. (1969). Stage and sequence: The cognitive-developmental approach to socialization. In D. A. Goslin (Ed.), *Handbook of socialization theory and research*. Chicago: Rand McNally.

Kohlberg, L. (1973). Continuities in childhood and adult moral development revisited. In P. Baltes & K. W. Schaie (Eds.), *Life-span developmental psychology: Personality and socialization* (pp. 180–207). New York: Academic.

Kohlberg (1974). See a or b.

Kohlberg, L. (1974a). Education, moral development and faith. *Journal of Moral Education, 4*, 5–16.

Kohlberg, L. (1974b, March 24). More authority [Letter to the Editor]. *New York Times*, VII, p. 42.

Kohlberg, L. (1981). *Essays on moral development*. San Francisco: Harper & Row.

Kohlberg, L., & Kramer, R. B. (1969). Continuities and discontinuities in childhood and adult moral development. *Human Development, 12*, 93–120.

Kohlberg, L., & Ryncarz, R. A. (1990). Beyond justice reasoning: Moral development and consideration of a seventh stage. In C. N. Alexander & E. J. Langer (Eds.), *Higher stages of human development* (pp. 191–207). New York: Oxford University Press.

Kohn, M. L. (1980). Job complexity and adult personality. In N. J. Smelser & E. H. Erikson (Eds.), *Themes of work and love in adulthood*. Cambridge, MA: Harvard University Press.

Kolata, G. (1995, March 27). Tests to assess risks for cancer raising questions. *New York Times*, pp. A1, A9.

Kopp, C. B., & McCall, R. B. (1982). Predicting later mental performance for normal, at-risk, and handicapped infants. In P. B. Baltes & O. G. Brim (Eds.), *Life-span development and behavior* (Vol. 4). New York: Academic.

Kornhaber, A. (1986). *Between parents and grandparents*. New York: St. Martin's.

Kornhaber, A., & Forsyth, S. (1994). *Grandparent power: How to strengthen the vital connection among grandparents, parents and children*. New York: Crown.

Kornhaber, A., & Woodward, K. L. (1981). *Grandparents/grandchildren: The vital connection*. Garden City, NY: Anchor/Doubleday.

Kosnik, W., Winslow, L., Kline, D., Rasinski, K., & Sekuler, R. (1988). Visual changes in daily life throughout adulthood. *Journal of Gerontology, 43*(3), P63–70.

Kottak, C. P. (1994). *Cultural anthropology*. New York: McGraw-Hill.

Kramer, D. A. (1983). Post-formal operations? A need for further conceptualization. *Human Development, 26*, 91–105.

Kramer, D. A. (1990). *A scoring manual for assessing absolute, relativistic, and dialectical thinking*. Unpublished manuscript.

Kramer, D. A., Kahlbaugh, O. E., & Goldston, R. B. (1992). A measure of paradigm beliefs about the social world. *Journal of Gerontology: Psychological Sciences, 47*, P180–189.

Kranzler, J. H., & Jensen, A. R. (1991a). The nature of psychometric g: Unitary process or a number of independent processes? *Intelligence, 15*, 397–422.

Kranzler, J. H., & Jensen, A. R. (1991b). Unitary g: Unquestioned postulate or empirical fact? *Intelligence, 15*, 437–448.

Krauss, I. K., & Hoyer, W. J. (1984). Technology and the older person: Age, sex and experience as moderators of attitudes towards computers. In P. K. Robinson & J. E. Birren (Eds.), *Aging and technological advances* (pp. 349–350). New York: Plenum.

Krieger, D. (1982). Cushing's syndrome. *Monographs in endocrinology, 22*, 1–142.

Krishnamurti, J. (1989). *You are the world*. New York: HarperCollins.

Kristof, N. D. (1990, December 6). At 102, he's back in school, with many like him. *New York Times*, p. A4.

Kropp, J. P., & Haynes, O. M. (1987). Abusive and nonabusive mothers' ability to identify general and specific emotional signals of infants. *Child Development, 58*, 187–190.

Krueger, J., & Heckhausen, J. (1993). Personality development across the adult life span: Subjective conceptions vs. cross-sectional analyses. *Journal of Gerontology: Psychological Sciences, 48*, P100–108.

Kubie, L. S. (1958). *The neurotic distortion of the creative process*. Lawrence: University of Kansas Press.

Kübler-Ross, E. (1969). *On death and dying.* New York: Macmillan.

Kübler-Ross, E. (1970). *On death and dying.* (paperback ed.). New York: Macmillan.

Kübler-Ross, E. (Ed.). (1975). *Death: The final stage of growth.* Englewood Cliffs, NJ: Prentice-Hall.

Kucharsky, D. (1976). *The man from Plains.* New York: Harper & Row.

Kumar, C, & Puri, M. (1983). *Mahatma Gandhi: His life and influence.* New York: Franklin Watts.

Kunkel, S. R., & Applebaum, R. A. (1992). Estimating the prevalence of long-term disability for an aging society. *Journal of Gerontology: Social Sciences, 47*(5), S253–260.

Kupfersmid, J., & Wonderly, D. (1980). Moral maturity and behavior: Failure to find a link. *Journal of Youth and Adolescence, 9*(3), 249–261.

Kurosawa, A. (1981). *Something like an autobiography* (A. E. Bock, Trans.). New York: Knopf.

Labouvie-Vief, G. (1982). Dynamic development and mature autonomy: A theoretical prologue. *Human Development, 25,* 161–191.

Labouvie-Vief, G. (1985). Intelligence and cognition. In J. E. Birren & K. W. Schaie (Eds.), *Handbook of the psychology of aging* (pp. 500–530). New York: Van Nostrand Reinhold.

Labouvie-Vief, G. (1986). Modes of knowledge and the organization of development. In M. Commons, L. Kohlberg, F. Richards, & J. Sinnott (Eds.), *Beyond formal operations: 3, Models and methods in the study of adult and adolescent thought.* New York: Praeger.

Labouvie-Vief, G. (1990a). Modes of knowledge and the organization of development. In M. L. Commons, L. Kohlberg, R. Richards, & J. Sinnott (Eds.), *Beyond formal operations: 2, Models and methods in the study of adult and adolescent thought.* New York: Praeger.

Labouvie-Vief, G. (1990b). Wisdom as integrated thought: Historical and development perspectives. In R. J. Sternberg (Ed.), *Wisdom: Its nature, origins, and development* (pp. 52–83). Cambridge: Cambridge University Press.

Labouvie-Vief, G., Adams, C., Hakim-Larson, J., Hayden, M., & DeVoe, M. (1987). *Modes of text processing from preadolescence to mature adulthood.* Unpublished manuscript, Wayne State University, Detroit.

Labouvie-Vief, G., & Hakim-Larson, J. (1989). Developmental shifts in adult thought. In S. Hunter & M. Sundel (Eds.), *Midlife myths.* Newbury Park, CA: Sage.

Labouvie-Vief, G., Hakim-Larson, J., DeVoe, M., & Schoeberlein, S. (1989). Emotions and self-regulation: A lifespan view. *Human Development, 32,* 279–299.

Labouvie-Vief, G., Hakim-Larson, J., & Hobart, C. J. (1987). Age, ego level, and the life-span development of coping and defense processes. *Psychology and Aging, 2,* 286–293.

Labouvie-Vief, G., Schell, D. A., & Weaverdyck, S. E. (1982). *Recall deficit in the aged: A fable recalled.* Unpublished manuscript, Wayne State University, Detroit.

Lachman, J. L., & Lachman, R. (1980). Age and the actualization of knowledge. In L. W. Poon, J. L. Fozard, L. S. Cermak, D. Arenberg, & L. W. Thompson (Eds.), *New directions in memory and aging* (pp. 313–343). Hillsdale, NJ: Erlbaum.

Lachman, M. E. (1986). Locus of control in aging research: A case for multidimensional and domain-specific assessment. *Psychology and Aging, 1,* 34–40.

Lachman, R., Lachman, J. L., & Taylor, D. W. (1982). Reallocation of mental resources over the productive lifespan: Assumptions and task analyses. In F. I. M. Craik & S. Trehub (Eds.), *Aging and cognitive processes* (pp. 279–307). New York: Plenum.

Lacy, W. B., & Hendricks, J. (1980). Developmental model of adult life: Myth or reality? *Aging and Human Development, 11,* 89–110.

Lakatta, E. G. (1990). Changes in cardiovascular function with aging. *European Heart Journal, 11c,* 22–29.

Lake, S. R. (1989). *Rematch: Winning legal battles with your ex.* Chicago: Chicago Review Press.

Lakoff, R. T., & Coyne, J. C. (1993). *Father knows best: The use and abuse of power in Freud's case of Dora.* New York: Teacher's College Press.

Lamb, M. E. (1987). *The father's role: Cross-cultural perspectives.* Hillsdale, NJ: Erlbaum.

Lancy, D. F. (1977). Studies of memory in culture. *Annals of the New York Academy of Science, 285,* 297–307.

Landers, S. (1992a, March). "Second time around families" find aid. *National Association of Social Workers News,* p. 5.

Landers, S. (1992b, March). Family "kin care" trend increasing. *National Association of Social Workers News,* p. 5.

Landy, F. J. (1992, February 19). Research on the use of fitness tests for police and fire fighting jobs. Presentation at the Second Annual Scientific Psychology Forum of the American Psychological Association, Washington, DC.

Landy, F. J. (1994, July–August). Mandatory retirement age: Serving the public welfare? *Psychological Science Agenda: American Psychological Association,* pp. 10–11, 20.

Langer, E., & Rodin, J. (1976). The effects of choice and enhanced personal responsibility in an institutional setting. *Journal of Personality and Social Psychology, 34*(2), 191–198.

Langer, S. (1942). *Philosophy in a new key: A study in the symbolism of reason, rite, and art.* Cambridge, MA: Harvard University Press.

Lao-tzu. (1985). *Tao: The way of the ways.* New York: Schocken.

LaRossa, R. (1988). Fatherhood and social change. *Family Relations, 34,* 451–457.

LaRossa, R., & LaRossa, M. M. (1981). *Transition to parenthood: How infants change families.* Beverly Hills, CA: Sage.

Larsen, D. (1990, December–1991, January). Unplanned parenthood. *Modern Maturity,* pp. 32–36.

Larson, A. (1989). Social context of human immunodeficiency virus transmission in Africa: Historical and cultural bases of east and central African sexual relations. *Review of Infectious Diseases, 11,* 713–731.

Larson, R., Mannell, R., & Zuzanek, J. (1986). Daily wellbeing of older adults with friends and family. *Psychology and Aging, 1*(2), 117–126.

Larson, R., Zuzanek, J., & Mannell, R. (1985). Being alone versus being with people: Disengagement in the daily experience of older adults. *Journal of Gerontology, 40,* 375–381.

Latimer, E. J. (1992, February). Euthanasia: A physician's reflections. *Ontario Medical Review*, pp. 21–29.

Laudenslager, M. L., Ryan, S. M., Drugan, R. C., Hyson, R. L., & Maier, S. F. (1983). Coping and immunosuppression: Inescapable but not escapable shock suppresses lymphocyte proliferation. *Science, 221*, 568–570.

Lauer, J., & Lauer, R. (1985). Marriages made to last. *Psychology Today, 19*(6), 22–26.

Lave, J. (1989). *Cognition in practice*. New York: Cambridge University Press.

Lawton, M. P. (1981). Alternate housing. *Journal of Gerontological Social Work, 3*(3), 61–79.

Lawton, M. P. (1982). Competence, environmental press, and the adaptation of old people. In M. P. Lawton & T. O. Byerts (Eds.), *Aging and the environment: Theoretical approaches* (pp. 33–59). New York: Springer.

Lawton, M. P., & Nahemow, L. (1973). Ecology and the aging process. In C. Eisdorfer & M. P. Lawton (Eds.), *The psychology of adult development and aging*. Washington, DC: American Psychological Association.

Lazarus, R. S. (1981, July). Little hassles can be hazardous to health. *Psychology Today*, pp. 58–62.

Lazarus, R. S., & Folkman, S. (1984). *Stress, appraisal, and coping*. New York: Springer.

Leabo, K. B. (1962). *Martha Graham*. New York: Theatre Arts.

Lebowitz, B. D., & Niederehe, G. (1992). Concepts and issues in mental health and aging. In J. E. Birren, R. B. Sloane, & G. D. Cohen (Eds.), *Handbook of mental health and aging* (2d ed., pp. 3–26). San Diego: Academic.

Lee, D. J., & Markides, K. S. (1990). Activity and mortality among aged people over an eight-year period. *Journal of Gerontology: Social Sciences, 45*(1), S39–42.

Lee, G. R., Dwyer, J. W., & Coward, R. T. (1993). Gender differences in parent care: Demographic factors and some gender preferences. *Journal of Gerontology: Social Sciences, 48*, S9–16.

Lee, I.-M., & Paffenbarger, R. S. (1992). Changes in body weight and longevity. *Journal of the American Medical Association, 268*, 2045–2049.

Lee, P. R., Franks, P., Thomas, G. S., & Paffenbarger, R. S. (1981). *Exercise and health: The evidence and its implications*. Cambridge, MA: Oelgeschlager, Gunn, & Hain.

Lee, T. R., Mancini, J. A., & Maxwell, J. W. (1990). Sibling relationships in adulthood: Current patterns and motivations. *Journal of Marriage and the Family, 52*, 431–440.

Lefrancois, G. R. (1982). *Psychology for teaching: A bear rarely faces the front*. Belmont, CA: Wadsworth.

LeGuin, U. (1989). *Dancing at the edge of the world*. New York: Grove.

Leigh, G. K. (1982). Kinship interaction over the family life span. *Journal of Marriage and the Family, 44*(1), 197–208.

Lemmon, J. A. (1983). Divorce mediation: Optimal scope and practical issues. *Mediation Quarterly, 1*, 45–61.

Lemon, B., Bengtson, V., & Peterson, J. (1972). An exploration of the activity theory of aging: Activity types and life satisfaction among inmovers to a retirement community. *Journal of Gerontology, 27*(4), 511–523.

Lennox, A., Karlinsky, H., Meschino, J., Buchanan, J. A., Percy, M. E., & Berg, J. M. (1994). Molecular genetic predictive testing for Alzheimer's disease: Delibera-

tions and preliminary recommendations. *Alzheimer Disease and Associated Disorders, 8*, 126–147.

Lenz, E. (1993, August–September). Mirror, mirror . . . : One woman's reflections on her changing image. *Modern Maturity*, pp. 24, 26–28, 80.

Leonard, F. (1992, December–1993, January). Home alone. *Modern Maturity*, pp. 46–51, 77.

Lerner, M. J., Somers, D. G., Reid, D., Chiriboga, D., & Tierney, M. (1991). Adult children as caregivers: Egocentric biases in judgments of sibling contributions. *The Gerontologist, 31*(6), 746–755.

Lesgold, A. M. (1983). *Expert systems*. Paper presented at the Cognitive Science Meetings, Rochester, NY.

Levin, J. S., & Taylor, R. J. (1993). Gender and age differences in religiosity among black Americans. *The Gerontologist, 33*(1), 16–23.

Levin, J. S., Taylor, R. J., & Chatters, L. M. (1994). Race and gender differences in religiosity among older adults: Findings from four national surveys. *Journal of Gerontology: Social Sciences, 49*, S137–145.

Levine, R. (1980). Adulthood among the Gusii of Kenya. In N. J. Smelser & E. H. Erikson (Eds.), *Themes of work and love in adulthood* (pp. 77–104). Cambridge, MA: Harvard University Press.

Levinson, D. (1978). *The seasons of a man's life*. New York: Knopf.

Levinson, D. (1980). Toward a conception of the adult life course. In N. J. Smelser & E. H. Erikson (Eds.), *Themes of work and love in adulthood* (pp. 265–290). Cambridge, MA: Harvard University Press.

Levinson, D. (1986). A conception of adult development. *American Psychologist, 41*, 3–13.

Leviton, D. (1977). Death education. In H. Feifel (Ed.), *New meanings of death* (pp. 253–272). New York: McGraw-Hill.

Levy, B., & Langer, E. (1994). Aging free from negative stereotypes: Successful memory in China and among the American Deaf. *Journal of Personality and Social Psychology, 66*, 989–997.

Lewis, C., & Ventura, S. (1990, October). Birth and fertility rates by education: 1980 and 1985. In *Vital and Health Statistics, 21*(49), 1–40. Hyattsville, MD: National Center for Health Statistics.

Lewis, D. B. W. (1968). *The World of Goya*. New York: Potter.

Lewis, M. I., & Butler, R. N. (1974). Life-review therapy: Putting memories to work in individual and group psychotherapy. *Geriatrics, 29*, 165–173.

Lewis, R. (1992, March). Iowa: Back to the future. *AARP Bulletin*, pp. 1, 16.

Lichtenberg, P. A. (1994). *A guide to psychological practice in geriatric long-term care*. Binghampton, NY: Haworth.

Lickona, T. (Ed.). (1976). *Moral development and behavior*. New York: Holt.

Lieberman, M., & Coplan, A. (1970). Distance from death as a variable in the study of aging. *Developmental Psychology, 2*(1), 71–84.

Light, L. L. (1990). Interactions between memory and language in old age. In J. E. Birren & K. W. Schaie (Eds.), *Handbook of the psychology of aging* (3d ed., pp. 275–290). San Diego: Academic.

Lindeman, R. D., Tobin, J., & Shock, N. (1985). Longitudinal studies on rate of decline in renal function with age. *Journal of the American Geriatrics Society, 33,* 278–285.

Linder, K. (1990). *Functional literacy projects and project proposals: Selected examples.* Paris: United Nations Educational, Scientific, and Cultural Organization.

Lindsey, R. (1984, January 15). A new generation finds it hard to leave the nest. *New York Times,* p. A18.

Lipid Research Clinics Program. (1984a). The lipid research clinic coronary primary prevention trial results: 1. Reduction in incidence of coronary heart disease. *Journal of the American Medical Association, 251,* 351–364.

Lipid Research Clinics Program. (1984b). The lipid research clinic coronary primary prevention trial results: 2. The relationship of reduction in incidence of coronary heart disease to cholesterol lowering. *Journal of the American Medical Association, 251,* 365–374.

Listening to depression: The new medicines. (1995, January). *Johns Hopkins Medical Letter: Health after 50,* pp. 4–5.

Littman, M. (1991). *Poverty in the United States: 1990* (Current Population Reports, Series P-60, No. 175). Washington, DC: U.S. Government Printing Office.

Livson, F. (1976, November). *Sex differences in personality development in the middle adult years: A longitudinal study.* Paper presented at the annual meeting of the Gerontological Society, Louisville, KY.

Lock, M. (1991). Contested meanings of the menopause. *The Lancet, 337,* 1270–1272.

Lofland, L. H. (1986). When others die. *Generations, 10*(4), 59–61.

Loftus, E. F. (1991). The glitter of everyday memory . . . and the gold. *American Psychologist, 46*(1), 16–18.

Longino, C. F. (1987). *The oldest Americans: State profiles for data-based planning.* Coral Gables, FL: University of Miami Department of Sociology.

Longino, C. F. (1988). Who are the oldest Americans? *The Gerontologist, 28,* 515–523.

Longino, C. F., & Kart, C. S. (1982). Explicating activity theory: A formal replication. *Journal of Gerontology, 37*(6), 713–721.

Lopata, H. (1977, September–October). Widows and widowers. *The Humanist,* pp. 25–28.

Lopata, H. (1979). *Women as widows.* New York: Elsevier.

Lopata, H., Heinemann, G. D., & Baum, J. (1982). Loneliness: Antecedents and coping strategies in the lives of widows. In L. A. Peplau & D. Perlman (Eds.), *Loneliness: A sourcebook of current theory, research, and therapy* (pp. 310–326). New York: Wiley.

Lord, A. B. (1982). Oral poetry in Yugoslavia. In U. Neisser (Ed.), *Memory observed: Remembering in natural contexts* (pp. 243–257). San Francisco: Freeman.

Lovelace, E. A. (1990). Basic concepts in cognition and aging. In E. A. Lovelace (Ed.), *Aging and cognition: Mental processes, self-awareness, and interventions* (pp. 1–28). Amsterdam: North-Holland, Elsevier.

Lowenthal, M., & Haven, C. (1968). Interaction and adaptation: Intimacy as a critical variable. *American Sociological Review, 33,* 20–30.

Ludmer-Gliebe, S. (1994, Spring). Can Johnny read? The American illiteracy crisis. *The Reporter* (Women's American ORT), pp. 18–20.

Lund, D. A. (Ed.). (1989). *Older bereaved spouses: Research with practical applications.* Washington, DC: Hemisphere.

Lund, D. A. (1993a). Caregiving. In R. Kastenbaum (Ed.), *Encyclopedia of adult development* (pp. 57–63). Phoenix: Oryx.

Lund, D. A. (1993b). Widowhood: The coping response. In R. Kastenbaum (Ed.), *Encyclopedia of adult development* (pp. 537–541). Phoenix: Oryx.

Lund, D. A., Caserta, M. S., Van Pelt, J., & Gass, K. A. (1990). Stability of social support networks after later-life spousal bereavement. *Death Studies, 14,* 53–73.

Luria, A. R. (1968). *The mind of a mnemonist.* New York: Basic Books.

Luria, A. R. (1976). *Cognitive development: Its cultural and social foundations.* Cambridge, MA: Harvard University Press.

Lutjen, P., Trounson, A., Leeton, J., Findlay, J., Wood, C., & Renou, P. (1984). The establishment and maintenance of pregnancy using in vitro fertilization and embryo donation in a patient with primary ovarian failure. *Nature, 307,* 174–175.

Lystad, M. (1975). Violence at home: A review of literature. *American Journal of Orthopsychiatry, 45*(3), 328–345.

Lytton, H. (1990). Child and parent effects in boys' conduct disorder: A reinterpretation. *Developmental Psychology, 26,* 683–697.

MacAdam, M. (1993). Review of *Caring for an aging world: International models for long-term care, financing, and delivery. Generations, 17*(4), 77–78.

MacKinnon, D. W. (1962). The nature and nurture of creative talent. *American Psychologist, 7,* 488–495.

Maddox, G. (1968). Persistence of life style among the elderly. In B. Neugarten (Ed.), *Middle age and aging.* Chicago: University of Chicago Press.

Maddox, G. L. (Ed.). (1987). *The encyclopedia of aging.* New York: Springer.

Maddox, G. L. (1993). Review of *Family support for the elderly: The international experience. Generations, 17*(4), 79–80.

Main, M. (1987). *Working models of attachment in adolescence and adulthood.* Symposium presented at the Society of Research in Child Development, Baltimore.

Malatesta, V. J., Pollack, R. H., Crotty, T. D., & Peacock, L. J. (1982). Acute alcohol intoxication and female orgasmic response. *Journal of Sex Research, 18,* 1–17.

Malatesta, V. J., Pollack, R. H., Wilbanks, W. A., & Adams, H. E. (1979). Alcohol effects on the orgasmic-ejaculatory response in human males. *Journal of Sex Research, 18,* 1.

Malcolm, A. H. (1984, September 23). Many see mercy in ending lives. *New York Times,* pp. 1, 56.

Malcolm, A. H. (1990, June 9). Giving death a hand: Rending issue. *New York Times,* p. A6.

Mandela, N. (1994). *Long walk to freedom: The autobiography of Nelson Mandela.* Boston: Little, Brown.

Mannell, R. (1993). High investment activity and life satisfaction: Commitment, serious leisure, and flow in the daily lives of older adults. In J. Kelly (Ed.), *Activity and aging.* Newbury Park, CA: Sage.

Manning, C. A., Hall, J. L., & Gold, P. E. (1990). Glucose effects on memory and other neuropsychological tests in elderly humans. *Psychological Science, 1*(5), 307–311.

Mansfield, R. S., & Busse, T. V. (1981). *The psychology of creativity and discovery: Scientists and their work.* Chicago: Nelson-Hall.

Manton, K. G., Siegler, I. C., & Woodbury, M. A. (1986). Patterns of intellectual development in later life. *Journal of Gerontology, 41,* 486–499.

Manuelidis, E. E., deFigueiredo, J. M., Kim, J. H., Fritch, W. W., & Manuelidis, L. (1988). Transmission studies from blood of Alzheimer's patients and healthy relatives. *Proceedings of the National Academy of Science, USA, 85,* 4898–4901.

Margolin, L., & White, L. (1987). The continuing role of physical attractiveness in marriage. *Journal of Marriage and the Family, 49*(1), 21–27.

Maris, R. W. (1981). *Pathways to suicide.* Baltimore: Johns Hopkins University Press.

Markides, K. S., Coreil, J., & Rogers, L. P. (1989). Aging and health among Southwestern Hispanics. In K. S. Markides (Ed.), *Aging and health: Perspectives on gender, race, ethnicity, and class.* Newbury Park, CA: Sage.

Markman, H. J., Renick, M. J., Floyd, F. J., Stanley, S. M., & Clements, M. (1993). *Journal of Consulting and Clinical Psychology, 61,* 70–77.

Markus, H. (1977). Self-schemata and processing information about the self. *Journal of Personality and Social Psychology, 35,* 63–78.

Markus, H., & Cross, S. (1990). The interpersonal self. In L. Pervin (Ed.), *Handbook of personality: Theory and research* (pp. 576–608). New York: Guilford.

Markus, H., & Nurius, P. (1986). Possible selves. *American Psychologist, 41,* 954–969.

Marquis, K. S., & Detweiler, R. A. (1985). Does adopted mean different? An attributional analysis. *Journal of Personality and Social Psychology, 48,* 1054–1066.

Marshall, V. W. (1980). No exit: A symbolic interactionist perspective on aging. In J. Hendricks (Ed.), *Being and becoming old* (pp. 20–32). Farmingdale, NY: Baywood.

Marshall, V. W. (1994). Sociology, psychology, and the theoretical legacy of the Kansas City studies. *The Gerontologist, 34,* 768–774.

Martin, L. G. (1988). The aging of Asia. *Journal of Gerontology: Social Sciences, 43*(4), S99–113.

Martino-Salzman, D., Blasch, B. B., Morris, R. D., & McNeal, L. W. (1991). Travel behavior of nursing home residents perceived as wanderers and nonwanderers. *The Gerontologist, 31,* 666–672.

Marvell, T. B. (1989). Divorce rates and the fault requirement. *Law and Society Review, 23,* 543–567.

Maslach, C., & Jackson, S. E. (1985). Burnout in health professions: A social psychological analysis. In G. Sanders & J. Suls (Eds.), *Social psychology of health and illness.* Hillsdale, NJ: Erlbaum.

Masoro, E. J. (1985). Metabolism. In C. E. Finch & E. L. Schneider (Eds.), *Handbook of the biology of aging* (2d ed., pp. 540–563). New York: Van Nostrand Reinhold.

Masters, W. H., & Johnson, V. E. (1966). *Human sexual response.* Boston: Little, Brown.

Masters, W. H., & Johnson, V. E. (1970). *Human sexual inadequacy.* Boston: Little, Brown.

Masters, W. H., & Johnson, V. E. (1981). Sex and the aging process. *Journal of the American Geriatrics Society, 29,* 385–390.

Masters, W. H., Johnson, V. E., & Kolodny, R. C. (1988). *Human Sexuality* (3d ed.). Glenview, IL: Scott, Foresman.

Masur, D. M., Sliwinski, M., Lipton, R. B., Blau, A. D., & Crystal, H. A. (1994). Neuropsychological prediction of dementia and the absence of dementia in healthy elderly persons. *Neurology, 44,* 1427–1432.

Matheny, K. B., & Cupp, P. (1983). Control, desirability, and anticipation as moderating variables between life changes and illness. *Journal of Human Stress, 9*(2), 14–23.

Matlin, M. M. (1987). *The psychology of women.* New York: Holt.

Matsukura, S., Taminato, T., Kitano, N., Seino, Y., Hamada, H., Uchihashi, M., Nakajima, H., & Hirata, Y. (1984). Effects of environmental tobacco smoke on urinary cotinine excretion in nonsmokers. *New England Journal of Medicine, 311*(13), 828–832.

Matthews, A. M., & Brown, K. H. (1988). Retirement as a critical life event: The differential experience of women and men. *Research on Aging, 9,* 548–571.

Matthews, K. A. (1992). Myths and realities of menopause. *Psychosomatic Medicine, 54,* 1–9.

Matthews, K. A., & Rodin, J. (1989). Women's changing work roles: Impact on health, family, and public policy. *American Psychologist, 44,* 1389–1393.

Mazel, A. (1984). Reforme legislative et sociologie judiciaire: Le nouveau divorce [Legislative reform and judicial sociology: The new divorce]. *Informatica e diritto, 10,* 383–408.

McCann, I. L., & Holmes, D. S. (1984). Influence of aerobic exercise on depression. *Journal of Personality and Social Psychology, 46*(5), 1142–1147.

McClelland, D. C. (1993). Intelligence is not the best predictor of job performance. *Current Directions in Psychological Science, 2*(1), 5–6.

McCord, C., & Freeman, H. P. (1990). Excess mortality in Harlem. *New England Journal of Medicine, 322,* 173–177.

McCord, W. (1993, January/February). Death with dignity. *The Humanist,* pp. 26–29.

McCrae, R. R., & Costa, P. T., Jr. (1984). *Emerging lives, enduring dispositions.* Boston: Little, Brown.

McCrae, R. R., Costa, P. T., Jr., & Busch, C. M. (1986). Evaluating comprehensiveness in personality system: The California Q-set and the five factor model. *Journal of Personality, 54,* 430–446.

McCusker, J., Cherubin, C. F., & Zimberg, S. (1971). Prevalence of alcoholism in general municipal hospital population. *New York State Journal of Medicine, 71,* 751–754.

McDonagh, D. (1973). *Martha Graham: A biography.* Newton Abbot and London, England: David & Charles.

McFall, S., & Miller, B. H. (1992). Caregiver burden and nursing home admission of frail elderly patients. *Journal of Gerontology: Social Sciences, 47,* S73–79.

McFarland, R. A., Tune, G. B., & Welford, A. (1964). On the driving of automobiles by older people. *Journal of Gerontology, 19,* 190–197.

McGregor, M. (1994, May/June). Primary prevention and breast cancer: What's the science and who will lead the fight? *The Network News* (National Women's Health Network), pp. 1, 4–5, 7.

McGue, M., Bacon, S., & Lykken, D. T. (1993). Personality stability and change in early adulthood: A behavioral genetic analysis. *Developmental Psychology, 21,* 96–109.

McIntosh, J. L. (1992). Epidemiology of suicide in the elderly. *Suicide and Life-Threatening Behavior, 22,* 15–35.

McKay, N. Y. (1992). Introduction. In M. Anderson, *My Lord, what a morning* (pp. ix–xxxiii). Madison: University of Wisconsin Press.

McKinlay, J. B., McKinlay, S. M., & Brambilla, D. (1987). The relative contributions of endocrine changes and social circumstances to depression in mid-aged women. *Journal of Health and Social Behavior, 28,* 345–363.

McKinley, D. (1964). *Social class and family life.* New York: Free.

McKitrick, L. A., Camp, C. J., & Black, F. W. (1992). Prospective memory intervention in Alzheimer's disease. *Journal of Gerontology, 47*(5), 337–343.

McLeod, D. (1993, January). "How are things at home?" Watch for symptoms of elder abuse, AMA urges doctors. *AARP Bulletin,* pp. 2, 15.

McLeod, D. (1994, September). Forgotten victims of abuse: Older women have no place to turn. *AARP Bulletin,* pp. 1, 16–17.

McMullen, R. (1984). *Degas: His life, times, and work.* Boston: Houghton Mifflin.

McNally, J. W., & Mosher, W. D. (1991, May 14). AIDS-related knowledge and behavior among women 15–44 years of age: United States, 1988. *Advance Data,* 200.

Meacham, J. A. (1982). Wisdom and the context of knowledge: Knowing that one doesn't know. In D. Kuhn & J. A. Meacham (Eds.), *On the development of developmental psychology* (pp. 111–134). Basel, Switzerland: Karger.

Meacham, J. A. (1990). The loss of wisdom. In R. J. Sternberg (Ed.), *Wisdom: Its nature, origins, and development* (pp. 181–211). Cambridge: Cambridge University Press.

Meehan, P. J. (1990). Prevention: The endpoint of suicidology. *Mayo Clinic Proceedings, 65,* 115–118.

Meer, F. (1988). *Higher than hope: The authorized biography of Nelson Mandela.* New York: Harper & Row.

Meer, J. T. (1987, May). The oldest old: The years after 85. *Psychology Today,* p. 82.

Mendelson, J. H., & Mello, N. K. (Eds.). (1985). *Diagnosis and treatment of alcoholism* (2d ed.). New York: McGraw-Hill.

Menken, J., Trussell, J., & Larsen, U. (1986). Age and infertility. *Science, 233,* 1389–1394.

Menninger Foundation. (1994, March). Grandparenting after divorce still a key role for older persons. *The Menninger Letter,* p. 3.

Mergler, N. L., & Goldstein, M. D. (1983). Why are there old people: Senescence as biological and cultural preparedness for the transmission of information. *Human Development, 26,* 72–90.

Merva, M., & Fowles, R. (1992). *Effects of diminished economic opportunities on social stress: Heart attacks, strokes, and crime* [Briefing paper]. Washington, DC: Economic Policy Institute.

Meyers, H. (1989). The impact of teenaged children on parents. In J. M. Oldham & R. S. Liebert (Eds.), *The middle years.* New Haven, CT: Yale University Press.

Michael, R. T., Gagnon, J., Laumann, E. O., & Kolata, G. (1994). *Sex in America: A definitive survey.* Boston: Little, Brown.

Michigan court upholds ban on assisted suicide. (1994, December 14). *Chicago Sun-Times,* p. 28.

Miles, C., & Miles, W. (1932). The correlation of intelligence scores and chronological age from early to late maturity. *American Journal of Psychology, 44,* 44–78.

Miles, S. H. (1991). Informed demand for "non-beneficial" medical treatment. *New England Journal of Medicine, 325,* 512–515.

Milgram, S. (1963). *Obedience to authority: An experimental view.* New York: Harper & Row.

Miller, B. C., & Myers-Walls, J. A. (1983). Parenthood: Stresses and coping strategies. In H. I. McCubbin & C. R. Figley (Eds.), *Stress and the family: 1. Coping with normative transitions.* New York: Brunner/Mazel.

Miller, C. A. (1987). Infant mortality in the U.S. *Scientific American, 253,* 31–37.

Miller, G. A. (1956). The magical number seven, plus or minus two: Some limits on our capacity to process information. *Psychological Review, 63,* 81–97.

Miller, J. (1987). Aboard the victory O. In G. O'Connor (Ed.), *Olivier: In celebration* (pp. 125–129). New York: Dodd, Mead.

Miller, J. B. (1991). The development of women's sense of self. In J. V. Jordan, A. G. Kaplan, J. B. Miller, I. P. Stiver, & J. L. Surrey (Eds.), *Women's growth in connection: Writings from the Stone Center.* New York: Guilford.

Miller, K., & Kohn, M. (1983). The reciprocal effects of job condition and the intellectuality of leisure-time activities. In M. L. Kohn & C. Schooler (Eds.), *Work and personality: An inquiry into the impact of social stratifications* (pp. 217–241). Norwood, NJ: Ablex.

Miller, M. (1979). *Suicide after sixty: The final alternative.* New York: Springer.

Miller, N., & Rockwell, R. C. (Eds.). (1988). *AIDS in Africa: The social and policy impact.* Lewiston: Mellen.

Miller-Jones, D. (1989). Culture and testing. *American Psychologist, 44,* 360–366.

Mind and body. (1993, April 17). *New Scientist—Supplement,* p. 10.

Mindel, C. H. (1983). The elderly in minority families. In T. H. Brubaker (Ed.), *Family relationships in later life* (pp. 193–208). Beverly Hills, CA: Sage.

Ministry of Health and Welfare Population Research Center. (1988). *World population prospects.* Tokyo: Koseishu.

Minkler, H., & Roe, K. (1992). *Forgotten caregivers: Grandmothers raising the children of the crack cocaine epidemic.* Newbury Park, CA: Sage.

Mischel, W. (1986). *Introduction to personality* (4th ed.). New York: Holt Rinehart & Winston.

Mishel, L., & Bernstein, J. (1994). *The state of working America 1994–1995.* Armonk, NY: Sharp.

Mitchell, D. B., Brown, A. S., & Murphy, D. R. (1990). Dissociations between procedural and episodic memory: Effects of time and aging. *Psychology and Aging, 5,* 264–276.

Mitchell, V., & Helson, R. (1990). Women's prime of life: Is it the 50s? *Psychology of Women Quarterly, 16,* 331–347.

Mohs, R. C., Breitner, J. C. S., Silverman, J. M., & Davis, K. L. (1987). Alzheimer's disease: Morbid risk among first-degree relatives approximates 50% by 90 years of age. *Archives of General Psychiatry, 44,* 405–408.

Monat, A., & Lazarus, R. S. (Eds.). (1985). *Stress and coping: An anthology.* New York: Columbia University Press.

Monk, A. (1994). Retirement and aging: An introduction to the Columbia retirement handbook. In A. Monk (Ed.), *The Columbia retirement handbook* (pp. 3–11). New York: Columbia University Press.

Monnier, A., & de Guibert-Lamoine, C. (1993). La conjoncture démographique: L'Europe et les développés d'outre-mer. *Population, 48*(4), 1043–1067.

Monnier, C., & Wells, A. (1980). Does the formal operational stage exist? A review and critique of recent works on the subject of formal operations. *Cahiers de la Fondation Archives de Jean Piaget, 1,* 201–242.

Montepare, J. M., & Lachman, M. E. (1989). "You're only as old as you feel": Self-perceptions of age, fears of aging, and life satisfaction from adolescence to old age. *Psychology and Aging, 4*(1), 73–78.

Moon, A., & Williams, D. (1993). Perception of elder abuse and help-seeking patterns among African-American, Caucasian American, and Korean American families. *The Gerontologist, 33,* 386–395.

Morbidity and Mortality Weekly Report (MMWR). (1985, June 21). *Suicide—U.S.,* 1970–1980.

Morbidity and Mortality Weekly Report (MMWR). (1989a). *Apparent per capita ethanol consumption—United States, 1977–1986, 38*(46), 800–803.

Morbidity and Mortality Weekly Report (MMWR). (1989b). *Tobacco use by adults—United States, 1987, 38*(40), 685–687.

Morehouse III, W. (1994, March 9). Hepburn agrees: She's a legend. *Chicago Sun-Times,* p. 39.

Morgan, L. (1984). Changes in family interaction following widowhood. *Journal of Marriage and the Family, 46*(2), 323–331.

Morton, J. (1991). The bankruptcy of everyday thinking. *American Psychologist, 46*(1), 32–33.

Moscovitch, M., & Winocur, G. (1992). The neuropsychology of memory and aging. In F. I. M. Craik & T. A. Salthouse (Eds.), *The handbook of aging and cognition* (pp. 315–372). Hillsdale, NJ: Erlbaum.

Mosher, W. D., & Pratt, W. F. (1990). Fecundity and infertility in the United States. *Vital and Health Statistics, 192.*

Moskow-McKenzie, D., & Manheimer, R. J. (1994). *A planning guide to organize educational programs for older adults.* Asheville, NC: University Publications, UNCA.

Moss, F., & Halamandaris, V. (1977). *Too old, too sick, too bad.* Germantown, MD: Aspen Systems.

Moss, M. S., & Moss, S. Z. (1989). The death of a parent. In R. A. Kalish (Ed.), *Midlife loss: Coping strategies.* Newbury Park, CA: Sage.

Mui, A. C. (1992). Caregiver strain among black and white daughter caregivers: A role theory perspective. *The Gerontologist, 32*(2), 203–212.

Munck, A., Guyre, P., & Holbrook, N. (1984). Physiological functions of glucocorticoids in stress and their relation to pharmacological actions. *Endocrine Reviews, 5,* 25–44.

Murphy, M. D., Schmitt, F. A., Caruso, M. J., & Sanders, R. E. (1987). Metamemory in older adults: The role of monitoring in serial recall. *Psychology and Aging, 2,* 331–339.

Murstein, B. I. (1980). Mate selection in the 1970s. *Journal of Marriage and the Family, 42,* 777–792.

Muuss, R. E. H. (1988). *Theories of adolescence* (5th ed.). New York: Random House.

Myers, J. E., & Perrin, N. (1993). Grandparents affected by parental divorce: A population at risk? *Journal of Counseling and Development, 72,* 62–66.

Myerson, J., Shealy, D., & Stern, M. B. (Eds.). (1987). *The selected letters of Louisa May Alcott.* Boston: Little, Brown.

Myers-Walls, J. A. (1984). Balancing multiple role responsibilities during the transition to parenthood. *Family Relations, 33,* 267–271.

Nash, S. C., & Feldman, S. S. (1981). Sex role and sex-related attributions: Constancy and change across the family life cycle. In M. E. Lamb & A. L. Brown (Eds.), *Advances in developmental psychology* (Vol. 1, pp. 137–147). Hillsdale, NJ: Erlbaum.

Nathanson, C. A., & Lorenz, G. (1982). Women and health: The social dimensions of biomedical data. In J. Z. Giele (Ed.), *Women in the middle years.* New York: Wiley.

National Center for Education Statistics. (1989). *National higher education statistics: Fall, 1989* (Publication No. NCES-90-379). Washington, DC: U.S. Department of Education.

National Center for Education Statistics. (1991). *National higher education statistics: Fall, 1991* (Publication No. NCES 92-038). Washington, DC: U.S. Department of Education, Office of Educational Research and Improvement.

National Center for Health Statistics. (1990). *Health United States 1989 and prevention profile* (DHHS Publication No. 90-1232). Washington, DC: U.S. Government Printing Office.

National Center for Health Statistics. (1992). *Statistics on suicide rates in the United States, 1935–1989.* Washington, DC: U.S. Government Printing Office.

National Center for Health Statistics. (1994). *Health, United States, 1993.* Hyattsville, MD: Public Health Service.

National Council on the Aging. (1978). *Fact book on aging: A profile of America's older population.* Washington, DC: Author.

National Council on the Aging. (1981). *Aging in the eighties: America in transition.* Washington, DC: Author.

National Hospice Organization (undated). *Hospice: A special kind of caring.* Arlington, VA: Author.

National Institute on Aging (NIA). (1980). *Senility: Myth or madness.* Washington, DC: U.S. Government Printing Office.

National Institute on Aging (NIA). (1984). *Be sensible about salt.* Washington, DC: U.S. Government Printing Office.

National Institute on Aging (NIA). (1993). *Bound for good health: A collection of Age Pages.* Washington, DC: U.S. Government Printing Office.

National Institute on Alcohol Abuse and Alcoholism (NIAAA). (1981, October). *Fact sheet: Selected statistics on alcohol and alcoholism.* Rockville, MD: National Clearinghouse for Alcohol Information.

National Institute on Drug Abuse. (1993). *Monitoring the future survey.* Washington, DC: U.S. Government Printing Office.

National Institutes of Health (NIH). (1984). *Osteoporosis* [1984-421-132:4652, Consensus Development Conference Statement, 5(3)]. Bethesda, MD: U.S. Government Printing Office.

National Institutes of Health (NIH). (1985). *Health implications of obesity* [Consensus Development Conference Statement, 5(9)]. Washington, DC: U.S. Government Printing Office.

National Institutes of Health (NIH). (1992, December 7–9). *Impotence: NIH Consensus Statement, 10*(4), 1–31. Washington, DC: U.S. Government Printing Office.

National Institutes of Health/National Institute on Aging (NIH/NIA). (1993, May). *In search of the secrets of aging* (NIH Publication No. 93-2756). Washington, DC: Department of Health and Human Services, Public Health Service, National Institutes of Health.

Neff, W. S. (1985). *Work and human behavior.* New York: Aldine.

Negative stereotypes still plague older workers on the job. (1995, April). *AARP Bulletin,* p. 3.

Neisser, U. (1978). Memory: What are the important questions? In M. M. Gruneberg, P. E. Morris, & R. N. Sykes (Eds.), *Practical aspects of memory* (pp. 3–24). London: Academic.

Neisser, U. (1982). John Dean's memory: A case study. In U. Neisser (Ed.), *Memory observed: Remembering in natural contexts* (pp. 139–159). San Francisco: Freeman.

Neisser, U. (1991). A case of misplaced nostalgia. *American Psychologist, 46*(1), 34–36.

Neiswender, M., Birren, J., & Schaie, K. W. (1975, August). *Age and the experience of love in adulthood.* Paper presented at the annual meeting of the American Psychological Association, Chicago.

Nelan, B. W. (1994, May 9). Time to take charge. *Time,* pp. 27–28.

Nelson, E. N. P. (1954). Persistence of attitudes of college students fourteen years later. *Psychological Monographs, 68,* 1–13.

Nelson, J. (1994, December 18). Motive behind Carter's missions sparks debate. *Chicago Sun-Times,* p. 40.

Nesselroade, J. R. (1991). The warp and the woof of the developmental fabric. In R. Downs, L. Liben, & D. Palermo (Eds.), *Visions of aesthetics, the environment, and development: The legacy of Joachim F. Wohlwill* (pp. 213–240). Hillsdale, NJ: Erlbaum.

Neugarten, B. L. (1967). The awareness of middle age. In R. Owen (Ed.), *Middle age.* London: BBC.

Neugarten, B. L. (1968). Adult personality: Toward a psychology of the life cycle. In B. Neugarten (Ed.), *Middle age and aging.* Chicago: University of Chicago Press.

Neugarten, B. L. (1977). Personality and aging. In J. E. Birren & K. W. Schaie (Eds.), *Handbook of the psychology of aging* (pp. 626–649). New York: Van Nostrand Reinhold.

Neugarten, B. L., & Hagestad, G. (1976). Age and the life course. In H. Binstock & E. Shanas (Eds.), *Handbook of aging and the social sciences.* New York: Van Nostrand Reinhold.

Neugarten, B. L., Havighurst, R., & Tobin, S. (1968). Personality and patterns of aging. In B. Neugarten (Ed.), *Middle age and aging.* Chicago: University of Chicago Press.

Neugarten, B. L., Moore, J. W., & Lowe, J. C. (1965). Age norms, age constraints, and adult socialization. *American Journal of Sociology, 70,* 710–717.

Neugarten, B. L., & Neugarten, D. A. (1987, May). The changing meanings of age. *Psychology Today,* pp. 29–33.

Neugarten, B. L., Wood, V., Kraines, R., & Loomis, B. (1963). Women's attitudes toward the menopause. *Vita Humana, 6,* 140–151.

The new genetic screens for cancer. (1995, January). *Johns Hopkins Medical Letter: Health after 50,* pp. 1–2.

NIA. See National Institute on Aging.

Nickerson, R. S. (1981). Why interactive computer systems are sometimes not used by people who might benefit from them. *International Journal of Man-Machine Studies, 15,* 469–483.

Nickerson, R. S., & Adams, M. J. (1979). Long-term memory for a common object. *Cognitive Psychology, 11,* 287–307.

NIH. See National Institutes of Health.

Nisan, M., & Kohlberg, L. (1982). Universality and variation in moral judgment: A longitudinal and cross-sectional study in Turkey. *Child Development, 53,* 865–876.

Nishio, H. K. (1994). Japan's welfare vision: Dealing with a rapidly increasing elderly population. In L. K. Olson (Ed.), *The graying of the world: Who will care for the frail elderly?* (pp. 233–260). New York: Haworth.

Noberini, M., & Neugarten, B. (1975, November). *A follow-up study of adaptation in middle-aged women.* Paper presented at the annual meeting of the Gerontological Society, Portland, OR.

Nojima, M. (1994). Japan's approach to continuing education for senior citizens. *Educational Gerontology, 20,* 463–471.

Norton, A. J., & Miller, L. F. (1992). *Marriage, divorce, and remarriage.* Current Population Reports (Series P23-188). Washington, DC: U.S. Government Printing Office.

Norton, A. J., & Moorman, J. E. (1987). Current trends in marriage and divorce among American women. *Journal of Marriage and the Family, 49*(1), 3–14.

Notelovitz, M., & Ware, M. (1983). *Stand tall: The informed woman's guide to preventing osteoporosis.* Gainesville, FL: Triad.

NOW Legal Defense and Education Fund, & Chernow-O'Leary, R. (1987). *The state-by-state guide to women's legal rights.* New York: McGraw-Hill.

Nuss, S., Denti, E., & Viry, D. (1989). *Women in the world of work: Statistical analyses and projections to the year 2000.* Geneva: International Labor Office.

O'Bryant, S. L. (1988). Sibling support and older widows' well-being. *Journal of Marriage and the Family, 50,* 173–183.

O'Bryant, S. L. (1990–1991). Forewarning of a husband's death: Does it make a difference for older widows? *Omega, 22,* 227–239.

O'Bryant, S. L., & Morgan, L. A. (1989). Financial experience and well-being among mature widowed women. *The Gerontologist, 29*(2), 245–251.

Oclander, J. (1994, July 27). Test type called into question: Standardized exams unfair, say experts, rejected cops. *Chicago Sun-Times,* p. 6.

O'Connell, M. (1991). Late expectations: Childbearing patterns of American women for the 1990s. *Current Population Reports* (Series P23-176), 1–18. Washington, DC: U.S. Government Printing Office.

Offer, D. (1982). Adolescent turmoil. *New York University Education Quarterly, 13,* 29–32.

Offer, D. (1987). In defense of adolescents. *Journal of the American Medical Association, 25,* 3407–3408.

Offer, D., Ostrov, E., Howard, K. I., & Atkinson, R. (1988). *The teenage world: Adolescents' self-image in ten countries.* New York: Plenum.

Offer, D., & Schonert-Reichl, K. A. (1992). Debunking the myths of adolescence: Findings from recent research. *Journal of the Academy of Child and Adolescent Psychiatry, 31,* 1003–1014.

O'Grady-LeShane, R. (1993). Changes in the lives of women and their families: Have old age pensions kept pace? *Generations, 17*(4), 27–31.

Okun, M. A., Stick, W. A., Haring, M. J., & Witter, R. A. (1984). The social activity/subjective well-being relation: A quantitative synthesis. *Research on Aging, 6,* 45–65.

Okun, S. (1988, January 29). Opera coach died in his "house of worship." *New York Times,* pp. B1, B3.

Older Women's League. (1994). *Ending violence against midlife and older women.* Washington, DC: Author.

Older workers: The good, the bad, and the truth. (1993, April-May). *Modern Maturity,* p. 10.

O'Leary, K. D., Barling, J., Arias, I., Rosenbaum, A., Malone, J., & Tyree, A. (1989). Prevalence and stability of physical aggression between spouses: A longitudinal analysis. *Journal of Consulting and Clinical Psychology, 57*(2), 263–268.

Olmsted, P. P., & Weikart, D. P. (Eds). (1994). *Family speak: Early childhood care and education in eleven countries.* Ypsilanti, MI: High/Scope.

Olson, P. G. (1994). The changing role of the elderly in the People's Republic of China. In L. K. Olson (Ed.), *The graying of the world: Who will care for the frail elderly?* (pp. 261–288). New York: Haworth.

Ong, A. (1987). *Spirits of resistance and capitalist discipline: Factory women in Malaysia.* Albany: State University of New York Press.

Orentlicher, D. (1990). Genetic screening by employers. *Journal of the American Medical Association, 263,* 1005–1008.

Organization for Economic Cooperation and Development. (1988). *Reforming public pensions.* Paris: OECD.

Ortega, S., Crutchfield, R., & Rushing, W. (1983). Race differences in elderly personal well-being. *Research on Aging, 5,* 101–118.

Osgood, N. J. (1984). *Suicide in the elderly.* Rockville, MD: Aspen.

Otten, M. W., Teutsch, S. M., Williamson, D. F., & Marks, J. S. (1990). The effect of known risk factors on the excess mortality of black adults in the United States. *Journal of the American Medical Association, 263*(6), 845–850.

Ouslander, J. G. (1989). Medical care in nursing homes. *Journal of the American Medical Association, 262*(18), 2582–2591.

Outtz, J. H. (1993, June-July). A changing population's call to action. *The National Voter,* pp. 4–6.

Owens, J. E., Cook, E. W., & Stevenson, I. (1990). Features of "near-death experience" in relation to whether or not patients were near death. *The Lancet, 336,* 1175–1177.

Owens, J. F., Matthews, K. A., Wing, R., & Kuller, L. H. (1992). Can physical activity mitigate the effects of aging in middle-aged women? *Circulation, 85*(3), 1265–1270.

Owens, W. A. (1966). Age and mental abilities: A second adult follow-up. *Journal of Educational Psychology, 57*(6), 311–325.

Paganini-Hill, A., & Henderson, V. W. (1994). Estrogen deficiency and risk of Alzheimer's disease in women. *American Journal of Epidemiology, 140,* 256–261.

Palmore, E. B. (1982). Predictors of the longevity difference. *The Gerontologist, 22,* 513–518.

Palmore, E. B., Burchett, B. M., Fillenbaum, G. G., George, L. K., & Wallman, L. M. (1985). *Retirement: Causes and consequences.* New York: Springer.

Palmore, E. B., Fillenbaum, G. G., & George, L. K. (1984). Consequences of retirement. *Journal of Gerontology, 39,* 109–116.

Paloma, M. M. (1972). Role conflict and the married professional woman. In C. Safilious-Rothschild (Ed.), *Toward a sociology of women.* Lexington, MA: Xerox.

Papalia, D. (1972). The status of several conservation abilities across the life-span. *Human Development, 15,* 229–243.

Papalia, D., & Bielby, D. (1974). Cognitive functioning in middle and old age adults: A review of research on Piaget's theory. *Human Development, 17,* 424–443.

Pappas, G., Queen, S., Hadden, N., & Fisher, G. (1993). The increasing disparity in mortality between socioeconomic groups in the United States, 1960 and 1986. *New England Journal of Medicine, 329,* 103–109.

Park, D. C., Pugiisi, J. T., & Smith, A. D. (1986). Memory for pictures: Does an age-related decline exist? *Psychology and Aging, 1,* 11–17.

Park, D. C., Royal, D., Dudley, W., & Morrel, R. (1988). Forgetting of pictures over a long retention interval in young and older adults. *Psychology and Aging, 3,* 94–95.

Park, D. C., Smith, A. D., & Cavanaugh, J. C. (1990). Metamemories of memory researchers. *Memory and Cognition, 18,* 321–327.

Parkes, C. M., & Weiss, R. S. (1983). *Recovery from bereavement.* New York: Basic Books.

Parkin, A. J., & Walter, B. M. (1992). Recollective experience, normal aging, and frontal dysfunction. *Psychology and Aging, 7*(2), 290–298.

Parlee, M. B. (1983). Menstrual rhythms in sensory processes: A review of fluctuations in vision, olfaction, audition, taste, and touch. *Psychological Bulletin, 93*(3), 539–548.

Parnes, H. S., & Sommers, D. G. (1994). Shunning retirement: Work experience of men in their seventies and early eighties. *Journal of Gerontology: Social Sciences, 49,* S117–124.

Passaro, V. (1991, April 21). Tales from a literary marriage. *New York Times Magazine,* pp. 34–36.

Patterson, C. J. (1992). Children of gay and lesbian parents. *Child Development, 63,* 1025–1042.

Pattison, E. M. (Ed.). (1977). *The experience of dying.* Englewood Cliffs, NJ: Prentice-Hall.

Paveza, G. J., Cohen, D., Eisdorfer, C., Freels, S., Semla, T., Ashford, J. W., Gorelick, P., Hirschman, R., Luchins, D., & Levy, P. (1992). Severe family violence and Alzheimer's disease: Prevalence and risk factors. *The Gerontologist, 32*(4), 493–497.

Pavlov, I. P. (1927). *Conditioned reflexes.* London: Oxford University Press.

Pavur, E. J., Comeaux, J. M., & Zeringue, J. A. (1984). Younger and older adults' attention to relevant and irrelevant stimuli in free recall. *Experimental Aging Research, 11,* 207–213.

Paykel, E. S., et al. (1994). Incidence of dementia in a population older than 75 in the United Kingdom. *Archives of General Psychiatry, 51,* 325–332.

Payne, J. D., & Overend, E. (1990). Divorce mediation: Process and strategies—an overview. *Family and Conciliation Courts Review, 28,* 27–34.

Peacock, J. R., & Paloma, M. M. (1991, November). *Religiosity and life satisfaction across the life course.* Paper presented at the annual conference of the Society for the Scientific Study of Religion, Pittsburgh, PA.

Pearlin, L. I. (1980). Life strains and psychological distress among adults. In N. J. Smelser & E. H. Erikson (Eds.), *Themes of work and love in adulthood.* Cambridge, MA: Harvard University Press.

Pearlin, L. I., Lieberman, M. A., Menaghan, E. G., & Mullan, J. T. (1981). The stress process. *Journal of Health and Social Behavior, 22,* 337–356.

Peck, R. C. (1955). Psychological developments in the second half of life. In J. E. Anderson (Ed.), *Psychological aspects of aging.* Washington, DC: American Psychological Association.

Penick, S., & Solomon, P. R. (1991). Hippocampus, context, and conditioning. *Behavioral Neuroscience, 105,* 611–617.

Pepper, S. C. (1942). *World hypotheses.* Berkeley: University of California Press.

Pepper, S. C. (1961). *World hypotheses.* Berkeley: University of California Press.

Perkins, H. W., & Harris, L. B. (1990). Familial bereavement and health in adult life course perspective. *Journal of Marriage and the Family, 52,* 233–241.

Perón, E. (1951). *La razón de mi vida.* Buenos Aires: Ediciones Peuser.

Perricone, M. (1992). *From deadlines to diapers.* Chicago: Noble.

Perrucci, C. C., Perrucci, R., & Targ, D. B. (1988). *Plant closings.* New York: Aldine.

Perry, D. (1995, March 3–9). Merciful end? Couple's suicide raises profound questions. *Chicago Jewish News,* p. 10.

Perry, W. G. (1970). *Forms of intellectual and ethical development in the college years.* New York: Holt.

Petchers, M. K., & Milligan, S. E. (1988). Access to health care in a black urban elderly population. *The Gerontologist, 28*(2), 213–217.

Peterson, C., Seligman, M. E., & Vaillant, G. E. (1988). Pessimistic explanatory style is a risk factor for physical illness: A thirty-five-year longitudinal study. *Journal of Personality and Social Psychology, 55,* 23–27.

Pettit, E. J., & Bloom, B. L. (1984). Whose decision was it? The effects of initiator status on adjustment to marital disruption. *Journal of Marriage and the Family, 46*(3), 587–595.

Phillips, D. P. (1992). The birthday: Lifeline or deadline? *Psychosomatic Medicine, 54*(5), 532–542.

Phillips, D. P., & King, E. W. (1988, September 24). Death takes a holiday: Mortality surrounding major social occasions. *The Lancet,* pp. 728–732.

Phillips, D. P., Ruth, T. E., & Wagner, L. M. (1993, November 6). Psychology and survival. *The Lancet,* pp. 1142–1145.

Phillips, D. P., & Smith, D. G. (1990). Postponement of death until symbolically meaningful occasions. *Journal of the American Medical Association, 263,* 1947–1951.

Phillips, S. M., & Sherwin, B. B. (1992). Effects of estrogen on memory function in surgically menopausal women. *Psychoneuroendocrinology, 17,* 485–495.

Piaget, J., & Inhelder, B. (1969). *The psychology of the child* (H. Weaver, Trans.). New York: Basic Books. (Original work published 1932)

Pienta, K. J., & Esper, P. S. (1993a). Risk factors for prostate cancer. *Annals of Internal Medicine, 118,* 793–803.

Pienta, K. J., & Esper, P. S. (1993b). Is dietary fat a risk factor for prostate cancer? *Journal of the National Cancer Institute, 85,* 1538–1540.

Pillemer, K., & Finkelhor, D. (1988). The prevalence of elder abuse: A random sample survey. *The Gerontologist, 28*(1), 51–57.

Pillemer, K., & Moore, D. W. (1989). Abuse of patients in nursing homes: Findings from a survey of staff. *The Gerontologist, 29*(3), 314–320.

Pillemer, K., & Suitor, J. J. (1991). "Will I ever escape my child's problems?": Effects of adult children's problems on elderly parents. *Journal of Marriage and the Family, 53,* 585–594.

Pincus, T., Callahan, L. F., & Burkhauser, R. V. (1987). Most chronic diseases are reported more frequently by individuals with fewer than 12 years of formal education in the age 18–64 United States population. *Journal of Chronic Diseases, 40,* 865–874.

Pines, A. M. (1991, October-November). When the heat fades: Why do some marriages glow while others flicker out? *Modern Maturity,* pp. 30–34.

Pleck, J. H. (1975). Masculinity-femininity: Current and alternative paradigms. *Sex Roles, 1,* 161–178.

Plemons, J., Willis, S., & Baltes, P. (1978). Modifiability of fluid intelligence in aging: A short-term longitudinal training approach. *Journal of Gerontology, 33*(2), 224–231.

PMS: It's real. (1994, July). *Harvard Women's Health Watch,* pp. 2–3.

Pompi, K. F., & Lachman, R. (1967). Surrogate processes in the short-term retention of connected discourse. *Journal of Experimental Psychology, 75,* 143–150.

Poon, L. W. (1985). Differences in human memory with aging: Nature, causes, and clinical implications. In J. Birren & K. W. Schaie (Eds.), *Handbook of the psychology of aging* (2d ed., pp. 427–462). New York: Van Nostrand Reinhold.

Porcino, J. (1983). *Growing older, getting better: A handbook for women in the second half of life*. Reading, MA: Addison-Wesley.

Porcino, J. (1991). *Living longer, living better: Adventures in community housing for the second half of life*. New York: Continuum.

Porcino, J. (1993, April–May). Designs for living. *Modern Maturity*, pp. 24–33.

Porterfield, J. D., & St. Pierre, R. S. (1992). *Wellness: Healthful aging*. Guilford, CT: Dushkin.

Posner, M. C., & Wolmark, N. (1994). Indications for breast-preserving surgery and adjuvant therapy in early breast cancer. *International Surgery (GUP), 79*, 43–47.

Post, S. G. (1994). Ethical commentary: Genetic testing for Alzheimer's disease. *Alzheimer Disease and Associated Disorders, 8*, 66–67.

Powerful new evidence: Lowering cholesterol does save lives. (1995, February). *University of California at Berkeley Wellness Letter*, p. 1.

Pratt, C. C., Wilson, W., Benthin, A., & Schmall, V. (1992). Alcohol problems and depression in later life: Development of two knowledge quizzes. *The Gerontologist, 32*, 175–183.

Prestwood, K. M., Pilbeam, C. C., Burleson, J. A., Woodiel, F. N., Delmas, P. D., Deftos, L. J., & Raisz, L. G. (1994). The short-term effects of conjugated estrogen on bone turnover in older women. *Journal of Clinical Endocrinology and Metabolism, 79*, 366–371.

Prevention Research Center. (1992). *Prevention index '92: A report on the nation's health*. Emmaus, PA: Rodale.

Prevention Research Center. (1993). *Prevention index '93: A report on the nation's health*. Emmaus, PA: Rodale.

Prinz, P. (1987). Sleep disorders. In G. Maddox (Ed.), *The Encyclopedia of Aging* (pp. 615–617). New York: Springer.

Prohaska, T. R., Leventhal, E. A., Leventhal, H., & Keller, M. L. (1985). Health practices and illness cognition in young, middle-aged, and elderly adults. *Journal of Gerontology, 40*, 569–578.

Pryer, H. (1994, May). Actuarially, birthdays aren't so bad. *AARP Bulletin*, p. 18.

The PSA debate continues. (1995, February). *Johns Hopkins Medical Letter: Health after 50*, pp. 2–3.

Quinby, N. (1985, October) On testing and teaching intelligence: A conversation with Robert Sternberg. *Educational Leadership*, pp. 50–53.

Quinn, J. F. (1993). Is early retirement an economic threat? *Generations, 17*(4), 10–14.

Ragozin, A. S., Basham, R. B., Crnic, K. A., Greenberg, M. T., & Robinson, N. M. (1982). Effects of maternal age on parenting role. *Developmental Psychology, 18*(4), 627–634.

Raloff, J. (1993, October 9). Fat may spur spread of prostate cancer. *Science News*, p. 228.

Raloff, J. (1994a, October 22). Tamoxifen turmoil: New issues emerge as healthy women volunteer to take a potent drug. *Science News*, pp. 268–269.

Raloff, J. (1994b, November 5). Tamoxifen puts cancer on starvation diet. *Science News*, p. 292.

Raphael, B. (1983). *The anatomy of bereavement*. New York: Basic Books.

Raven, J. C. (1983). *Raven progressive matrices test*. San Antonio, TX: Psychological Corp.

Raynor, J. O., & Rubin, I. S. (1971). Effects of achievement motivation and future orientation on level of performance. *Journal of Personality and Social Psychology, 17*, 36–41.

Read, K. (1993, June 27). 100 years old—and counting. *Chicago Sun-Times*, p. 38.

Read, P. P. (1974). *Alive: The story of the Andes survivors*. New York: Lippincott.

Rebecca, M., Hefner, R., & Oleshansky, B. (1976). A model of sex-role transcendence. *Journal of Social Issues, 32*, 197–206.

Ree, M. J., & Earles, J. A. (1992). Intelligence is the best predictor of job performance. *Current Directions in Psychological Science, 1*(3), 86–89.

Ree, M. J., & Earles, J. A. (1993). *g* is to psychology what carbon is to chemistry: A reply to Sternberg and Wagner, McClelland, and Calfee. *Current Directions in Psychological Science, 2*(1), 11–12.

Regier, D. A., Boyd, J. H., Burke, J. D., Locke, B. Z., Rae, D. S., Myers, J. K., Kramer, M., Robins, L. N., George, L. K., Karno, M., & Locke, B. Z. (1988). One-month prevalence of mental disorders in the U.S.: Based on five epidemiologic catchment area sites. *Archives of General Psychiatry, 45*, 977–986.

Reichard, S., Livson, F., & Peterson, P. (1962). *Aging and personality: A study of 87 older men*. New York: Wiley.

Reid, J. R., Patterson, G. R., & Loeber, R. (1982). The abused child: Victim, instigator, or innocent bystander? In D. J. Berstein (Ed.), *Response structure and organization*. Lincoln: University of Nebraska Press.

Reid, R. L., & Yen, S. S. C. (1981). Premenstrual syndrome. *American Journal of Obstetrics and Gynecology, 139*(1), 85–104.

Rempel, J. (1985). Childless elderly: What are they missing? *Journal of Marriage and the Family, 47*(2), 343–348.

Research to Prevent Blindness. (1994). Progress report, 1994. New York: Author.

Research update: The more we learn, the more questions there are to be answered. (1995, Winter). *LINK* (Newsletter of Amyotrophic Lateral Sclerosis Association), pp. 1–2.

Rest, J. R. (1975). Longitudinal study of the Defining Issues Test of moral judgment: A strategy for analyzing developmental change. *Developmental Psychology, 11*(16), 738–748.

Revicki, D., & Mitchell, J. (1990). Strain, social support, and mental health in rural elderly individuals. *Journal of Gerontology: Social Sciences, 45*, S267–274.

Rexroat, C., & Shehan, C. (1987). The family life cycle of spouses' time in housework. *Journal of Marriage and the Family, 49*, 737–750.

Reyes, L. (1994, May–June). Yes, there is a known cause of breast cancer! *The Network News* (National Women's Health Network), pp. 3–5.

Reynolds, C. R. (1988, Winter). Race differences in intelligence: Why the controversy. *Mensa Research Journal*, pp. 4–7.

Rhodes, S. R. (1983). Age-related differences in work attitudes and behaviors: A review and conceptual analysis. *Psychological Bulletin, 93*(2), 328–367.

Ribot, H. (1882). *Diseases of memory: An essay in the positive psychology.* New York: Appleton-Century-Crofts.

Ribot, T. (1906). *Essays on the creative imagination.* London: Routledge & Kegan Paul.

Richie, D. (1965). *The films of Akira Kurosawa.* Berkeley: University of California Press.

Riegel, K. F. (1973). Dialectic operations: The final period of cognitive development. *Human Development, 16,* 346–370.

Riegel, K. F. (1977). History of psychological gerontology. In J. E. Birren and K. W. Schaie (Eds.), *Handbook of the psychology of aging* (pp. 70–102). New York: Van Nostrand Reinhold.

Riegel, K. F., & Riegel, R. M. (1972). Development, drop, and death. *Developmental Psychology, 6,* 309–316.

Riegel, P. S. (1981). Athletic records and human endurance. *American Scientist, 69,* 285–290.

Riley, K. P. (1992). Bridging the gap between researchers and clinicians: Methodological perspectives and choices. In R. L. West & J. D. Sinnott (Eds.), *Everyday memory and aging: Current research and methodology* (pp. 182–189). New York: Springer-Verlag.

Riley, M. W. (1994). Aging and society: Past, present, and future. *The Gerontologist, 34,* 436–444.

Rilke, R. M. (1984). The notebooks of Malte Laurids Brigge. In E. Schwarz (Ed.), *Rainer Maria Rilke: Prose and poetry* (pp. 12–13). New York: Continuum.

Rindfuss, R. R., Morgan, S. P., & Swicegood, G. (1988). *First births in America.* Berkeley: University of California Press.

Rindfuss, R. R., & St. John, C. (1983). Social determinants of age at first birth. *Journal of Marriage and the Family, 45,* 553–565.

Ring, K. (1980). *Life at death: A scientific investigation of the near-death experience.* New York: Coward McCann & Geoghegan.

Rix, S. E. (1994). Older workers: How do they measure up? (Pub. No. 9412). Washington, DC: AARP Public Policy Institute.

Roazen, P. (1976). *Erik H. Erikson: The power and limits of a vision.* New York: Macmillan.

Robbins, T. (1984). *Jitterbug perfume.* New York: Bantam.

Roberts, P., Papalia-Finlay, D., Davis, E. S., Blackburn, J., & Dellman, M. (1982). "No two fields ever grow grass the same way": Assessment of conservation abilities in the elderly. *International Journal of Aging and Human Development, 15*(3), 185–195.

Robins, L. N., Helzer, J. C., Weissman, M. M., Owaschel, H., Bruenberg, E., Burke, J. O., & Regier, D. A. (1984). Lifetime prevalence of specific psychiatric disorders in three sites. *Archives of General Psychiatry, 41,* 949–958.

Robinson, B., & Thurnher, M. (1981). Taking care of aged parents: A family cycle transition. *The Gerontologist, 19*(6), 586–593.

Robinson, L. C., & Blanton, P. W. (1993). Marital strengths in enduring marriages. *Family Relations, 42,* 38–45.

Rodehoffer, R. J., Gerstenblith, G., Becker, L. C., Fleg, J. L., Weisfeldt, M. L., & Lakatta, E. G. (1984). Exercise cardiac output is maintained with advancing age in healthy human subjects: Cardiac dilation and increased stroke volume compensate for a diminished heart rate. *Circulation, 69,* 203–213.

Rodin, J., Timko, C., & Harris, S. (1985). The construct of control: Biological and psychological correlates. *Annual Review of Gerontology and Geriatrics, 5,* 3–55.

Roediger, H. L. (1990). Implicit memory: Retention without remembering. *American Psychologist, 45,* 1043–1056.

Roediger, H. L. (1991). They read an article? A commentary on the everyday memory controversy. *American Psychologist, 46*(1), 37–38.

Roff, L. C., & Atherton, C. R. (1989). *Promoting successful aging.* Chicago: Nelson-Hall.

Rogoff, B., & Morelli, G. (1989). Perspectives on children's development from cultural psychology. *American Psychologist, 44*(2), 343–348.

Roosa, M. W. (1988). The effect of age in the transition to parenthood: Are delayed childbearers a unique group? *Family Relations, 37,* 322–327.

Rosen, D. R., et al. (1993). Mutations in Cu/Zn superoxide dismutase gene are associated with familial amyotrophic lateral sclerosis. *Nature, 362,* 59–62.

Rosenberg, L., Palmer, J. R., & Shapiro, S. (1990). Decline in the risk of myocardial infarction among women who stop smoking. *New England Journal of Medicine, 322,* 213–217.

Rosenblatt, P. (1983). *Bitter, bitter tears: Nineteeth-century diarists and twentieth-century grief theories.* Minneapolis: University of Minnesota Press.

Rosenburg, H. (in press). The elderly and the use of illicit drugs: Sociological and epidemiological considerations. *International Journal of Addictions.*

Roses, A. D. (1994, September). Apolipoprotein E affects Alzheimer's disease expression. Paper presented at workshop on Alzheimer's Disease: Advances in Understanding and Treatment, Philadelphia.

Ross, C. E., Mirowsky, J., & Goldsteen, K. (1990). The impact of the family on health: A decade in review. *Journal of Marriage and the Family, 52,* 1059–1078.

Ross, H. G., Dalton, M. J., & Milgram, J. I. (1980, November). *Older adults' perceptions of closeness in sibling relationships.* Paper presented at the annual meeting of the Gerontological Society of America, San Diego.

Ross, L. (1977). The intuitive psychologist and his shortcomings. In L. Berkowitz (Ed.), *Advances in experimental social psychology* (Vol. 10, pp. 174–214). San Diego: Academic.

Ross, L., & Nisbett, R. E. (1991). *The person and the situation: Perspectives of social psychology.* New York: McGraw-Hill.

Rossi, A. S. (1980). Aging and parenthood in the middle years. In P. B. Baltes & O. G. Brim (Eds.), *Life-span development and behavior* (Vol. 3). New York: Academic.

Rossi, A. S., & Rossi, P. H. (1990). *Of human bonding: Parent-child relations across the life course.* New York: Aldine de Gruyter.

Rowe, J. W., et al. (1976). The effect of age on creatinine clearance in men: A cross-sectional and longitudinal study. *Journal of Gerontology, 31,* 155–163.

Roybal, E. R. (1988). Mental health and aging. *American Psychologist, 43*(3), 184–189.

Ruberman, W., Weinblatt, E., Goldberg, J. D., & Chaudhary, B. S. (1984). Psychosocial influences on mortality after myocardial infarction. *New England Journal of Medicine, 311,* 552–559.

Rubin, K. H. (1973, August). *Decentration skills in institutionalized and noninstitutionalized elderly.* Paper presented at the annual meeting of the American Psychological Association.

Rubin, K. H., Attewell, P., Tierney, M., & Tumulo, P. (1973). Development of spatial egocentrism and conservation across the lifespan. *Developmental Psychology, 9*(3), 432.

Rubin, L. B. (1979). *Women of a certain age.* New York: Harper & Row.

Rubin, L. B. (1982). Sex and sexuality: Women at midlife. In M. Kirkpatricks (Ed.), *Women's sexual experiences: Exploration of the dark continent* (pp. 61–82). New York: Plenum.

Rubinstein, A. (1980). *My many years.* New York: Knopf.

Rubinstein, R. L., Alexander, B. B., Goodman, M., & Luborsky, M. (1991). Key relationships of never married, childless older women: A cultural analysis. *Journal of Gerontology: Social Sciences, 46,* S270–277.

Rudman, D., Feller, A. G., Cohn, L., Shetty, K. R., Rudman, I. W., & Draper, M. W. (1991). *Hormone Research, 36* (Supplement 1), 73–81.

Runco, M. A., & Albert, R. S. (Eds.). (1990). *Theories of creativity.* Newbury Park, CA: Sage.

Ryan, M. (1993, September 26). I couldn't bear the silence. *Parade,* p. 14.

Rybash, J. M., Hoyer, W. J., & Roodin, P. A. (1986). *Adult cognition and aging: Developmental changes in processing, knowing and thinking.* New York: Pergamon.

Ryden, S. (1941). *A study of the Siriono Indians.* Goteborg, Sweden: Elanders Boktryckeri Aktiebolag.

Ryff, C. D. (1989). In the eye of the beholder: Views of psychological well-being among middle-aged and older adults. *Psychology and Aging, 4*(2), 195–210.

Sabatelli, R. M., Meth, R. L., & Gavazzi, S. M. (1988). Factors mediating the adjustment to involuntary childlessness. *Family Relations, 37,* 338–343.

Sabom, M. B. (1982). *Recollections of death: A medical investigation.* New York: Harper & Row.

Sacco, R. L., Hauser, W. A., & Mohr, J. P. (1991). Hospitalized stroke in blacks and Hispanics in northern Manhattan. *Stroke, 22*(12), 1491–1496.

Sacks, O. (1985). *The man who mistook his wife for a hat.* New York: Summit.

Sagan, C. (1977). *The dragons of Eden: Speculations on the evolution of human intelligence.* New York: Random House.

Sagan, C. (1988). Introduction. In S. W. Hawking, *A brief history of time: From the Big Bang to black holes* (pp. ix–x). New York: Bantam.

Salthouse, T. A. (1980). Age and memory: Strategies for localizing the loss. In L. W. Poon, J. L. Fozard, L. S. Cermak, D. Arenberg, & L. W. Thompson (Eds.), *New directions in memory and aging: Proceedings of the George A. Talland memorial conference.* Hillsdale, NJ: Erlbaum.

Salthouse, T. A. (1985). Anticipatory processing in transcription typing. *Journal of Applied Psychology, 70,* 264–271.

Salthouse, T. A. (1991). *Theoretical perspectives on cognitive aging.* Hillsdale, NJ: Erlbaum.

Salthouse, T. A., Kausler, D. H., & Saults, J. S. (1988). Utilization of path-analytic procedures to investigate the role of processing resources in cognitive aging. *Psychology and Aging, 3,* 158–166.

Sammartino, F. J. (1987, January). The effect of health on retirement. *Social Security Bulletin,* pp. 31–47.

Sanchez, C. (1992). Mental health issues: The elderly Hispanic. *Journal of Geriatric Psychiatry, 25,* 69–84.

Sanders, S., Laurendeau, M., & Bergeron, J. (1966). Aging and the concept of space: The conservation of surfaces. *Journal of Gerontology, 21,* 281–285.

Sansone, C., & Berg, C. A. (1993). Adapting to the environment across the life span: Different process or different inputs? *International Journal of Behavioral Development, 16,* 215–241.

Sapolsky, R. M. (1992). Stress and neuroendocrine changes during aging. *Generations, 16*(4), 35–38.

Sattler, J. M. (1988). *Assessment of children* (3d ed.). San Diego: Author.

Sauer, M. V., Paulson, R. J., & Lobo, R. A. (1990). A preliminary report on oocyte donation extending reproductive potential to women over 40. *New England Journal of Medicine, 323,* 1157–1160.

Sauer, M. V., Paulson, R. J., & Lobo, R. A. (1993, March). *Pregnancy after age 50: Applying oocyte donation to women following natural menopause.* Paper presented at the 40th annual meeting of the Society for Gynecological Research, Toronto.

Saunders, J. (1981). A process of bereavement resolution: Uncoupled identity. *Western Journal of Nursing Research, 3,* 319–332.

Scandinavian Simvastatin Survival Study Group. (1994). Randomized trial of cholesterol lowering in 4444 patients with coronary heart disease: The Scandinavian simvastatin survival study (4S). *The Lancet, 344,* 1383–1389.

Schacter, D. L. (1992). Understanding implicit memory: A cognitive neuroscience approach. *American Psychologist, 47,* 559–569.

Schafer, R. (1980). *Narrative action in psychoanalysis.* Worchester, MA: Clark University Press.

Schaie, K. W. (1965). A general model for the study of developmental problems. *Psychological Bulletin, 64,* 91–107.

Schaie, K. W. (1977). Quasi-experimental designs in the psychology of aging. In J. E. Birren & K. W. Schaie (Eds.), *Handbook of the psychology of aging* (pp. 39–58). New York: Van Nostrand Reinhold.

Schaie, K. W. (1977–1978). Toward a stage theory of adult cognitive development. *Journal of Aging and Human Development, 8*(2), 129–138.

Schaie, K. W. (1978). External validity in the assessment of intellectual development in adulthood. *Journal of Gerontology, 33,* 696–701.

Schaie, K. W. (1979). The primary mental abilities in adulthood: An exploration in the development of psychometric intelligence. In P. B. Baltes & O. G. Brim (Eds.), *Life-span development and behavior* (Vol. 2, pp. 67–115). New York: Academic.

Schaie, K. W. (1983). The Seattle longitudinal study: A twenty-one-year investigation of psychometric intelligence. In K. W. Schaie (Ed.), *Longitudinal studies of adult personality development* (pp. 64–155). New York: Guilford.

Schaie, K. W. (1984). Midlife influences upon intellectual functioning in old age. *Journal of Behavioral Development, 7,* 463–478.

Schaie, K. W. (1988a). Ageism in psychological research. *American Psychologist, 43,* 179–183.

Schaie, K. W. (1988b). The delicate balance: Technology, intellectual competence, and normal aging. In G. Lesnoff-Caravaglia (Ed.), *Aging in a technical society* (Vol. 7, pp. 155–166). New York: Human Sciences Press.

Schaie, K. W. (1989). The hazards of cognitive aging. *The Gerontologist, 29*(4), 484–493.

Schaie, K. W. (1990a). Intellectual development in adulthood. In J. E. Birren & K. W. Schaie (Eds.), *Handbook of the psychology of aging* (pp. 291–309). San Diego: Academic.

Schaie, K. W. (1990b). Perceptual speed in adulthood: Cross-sectional and longitudinal studies: Correction. *Psychology and Aging, 5*(2), 171.

Schaie, K. W. (1993). Agist language in psychological research. *American Psychologist, 48*(1), 49–51.

Schaie, K. W. (1994). The course of adult intellectual development. *American Psychologist, 49*(4), 304–313.

Schaie, K. W., & Baltes, P. B. (1977). Some faith helps to see the forest: A final comment on the Horn-Donaldson myth of the Baltes-Schaie position on adult intelligence. *American Psychologist, 32,* 1118–1120.

Schaie, K. W., & Gribbin, K. (1975). Adult development and aging. *Annual Review of Psychology, 26,* 65–96.

Schaie & Herzog. See Schaie & Hertzog.

Schaie, K. W., & Hertzog, C. (1983). Fourteen-year cohort sequential analyses of adult intellectual development. *Developmental Psychology, 19*(4), 531–543.

Schaie, K. W., & Hertzog, C. (1986). Toward a comprehensive model of adult intellectual development: Contributions of the Seattle Longitudinal Study. In R. J. Sternberg (Ed.), *Advances in human intelligence* (Vol. 3, pp. 79–118). Hillsdale, NJ: Erlbaum.

Schaie, K. W., & Strother, C. (1968). A cross-sequential study of age changes in cognitive behavior. *Psychological Bulletin, 70,* 671–680.

Schaie, K. W., & Willis, S. L. (1986). Can decline in adult intellectual functioning be reversed? *Developmental Psychology, 22,* 223–232.

Schaie, K. W., & Willis, S. L. (1991). Adult personality and psychomotor performance: Cross-sectional and longitudinal analysis. *Journal of Gerontology: Psychological Sciences, 46,* P275–284.

Scharlach, A. E. (1987). Relieving feelings of strain among women with elderly mothers. *Psychology and Aging, 2*(1), 9–13.

Scharlach, A. E. (1991). Factors associated with filial grief following the death of an elderly parent. *American Journal of Orthopsychiatry, 61,* 307–313.

Scharlach, A. E., & Fredriksen, K. I. (1993). Reactions to the death of a parent during midlife. *Omega, 27,* 307–319.

Scharlach, A. E., & Fredriksen, K. I. (1994). Elder care versus adult care: Does care recipient age make a difference? *Research on Aging, 16,* 43–68.

Schellenberg, G. D., Bird, T., Wijsman, E., et al. (1992). Genetic linkage evidence for a familial Alzheimer's disease locus on chromosome 14. *Science, 258,* 668–671.

Scherer, M. (1985, January). How many ways is a child intelligent? *Instructor,* pp. 32–35.

Schick, F. L. (Ed.). (1986). *Statistical handbook on aging Americans.* Phoenix: Oryx.

Schick, F. L., & Schick, R. (1994). *Statistical handbook on aging Americans, 1994.* Phoenix: Oryx.

Schieffelin, E. (1976). *The sorrow of the lonely and the burning of the dancers.* New York: St. Martin's.

Schlossberg, N. K. (1987, May). Taking the mystery out of change. *Psychology Today,* pp. 74–75.

Schmeck, H. M. (1983, March 22). U.S. panel calls for patients' right to end life. *New York Times,* pp. A1, C7.

Schmeck, H. M. (1995, June 24). Jonas Salk, whose polio drug altered life in U.S., dies at 80. *New York Times,* pp. A1, A10.

Schmidt, W. E. (1988, April 6). Graying of America prompts new highway safety efforts. *New York Times,* pp. A1, A17.

Schmitt, B. D., & Kempe, C. H. (1983). Abusing neglected children. In R. E. Berhman & V. C. Vaughn (Eds.), *Nelson textbook of pediatrics* (12th ed.). Philadelphia: Saunders.

Schnall, P. L., Pieper, C., Schwartz, J. E., Karasek, R. A., Schlussel, Y., Devereaux, R. B., Ganau, A., Alderman, M., Warren, K., & Pickering, T. G. (1990). The relationship between "job strain," workplace diastolic blood pressure, and left ventricular mass index: Results of a case-control study. *Journal of the American Medical Association, 263,* 1929–1935.

Schneider, E. L. (1992). Biological theories of aging. *Generations, 16*(4), 7–10.

Schneider, E. L., & Guralnik, J. M. (1990). The aging of America: Impact on health care costs. *Journal of the American Medical Association, 263*(17), 2335–2340.

Schoen, R. (1992). First unions and the stability of first marriages. *Journal of Marriage and the Family, 54,* 281–284.

Schonberg, H. C. (1992). *Horowitz: His life and music.* New York: Simon & Schuster.

Schonfield, D. (1974). Translations in gerontology—from lab to life: Utilizing information. *American Psychologist, 29,* 228–236.

Schonfield, D., & Robertson, E. A. (1966). Memory storage and aging. *Canadian Journal of Psychology, 20,* 228–236.

Schonfield, D., & Robertson, E. A. (1968). The coding and sorting of digits and symbols by an elderly sample. *Journal of Gerontology, 23,* 318–323.

Schuckit, M. A. (1987). Biological vulnerability to alcoholism. *Journal of Consulting and Clinical Psychology, 55*(3), 301–309.

Schultz, D. P., & Schultz, S. E. (1986). *Psychology and industry today* (4th ed.). New York: Macmillan.

Schulz, J. H. (1993a). Why the "welfare state" will continue to spread around the world. *Generations, 17*(4), 43–46.

Schulz, J. H. (1993b). Introduction: And then Chicken Little said, "The sky is falling!" *Generations, 17*(4), 5.

Schulz, J. H. (1993c). Should developing countries copy Chile's pension system? *Generations, 17*(4), 70–72.

Schulz, R. (1978). *The psychology of death, dying, and bereavement.* Reading, MA: Addison-Wesley.

Schulz, R. (1985). Emotion and affect. In J. E. Birren & K. W. Schaie (Eds.), *Handbook of the psychology of aging* (2d ed., pp. 531–543). New York: Van Nostrand Reinhold.

Schumacher, M. (1991, June). Louise Erdrich and Michael Dorris: A marriage of minds. *Writer's Digest,* pp. 28–31, 59.

Schwartz, P. E. (1994). Gynecologic surveillance of women on tamoxifen. *Connecticut Medicine, 58,* 515–521.

Scogin, F., & Bienias, J. L. (1988). A three-year follow-up of older adult participants in a memory-skills training program. *Psychology and Aging, 3,* 334–337.

Scott, C. (1993). *Decade of the executive woman.* New York: Korn/Ferry International.

Scott, J. P., & Roberto, K. A (1981, October). *Sibling relationships in late life.* Paper presented at the annual meeting of the National Council on Family Relations, Milwaukee.

Scribner, S. (1979). Modes of thinking and ways of speaking: Culture and logic reconsidered. In R. O. Freedle (Ed.), *New directions in discourse processing* (Vol. 2). Norwood, NJ: Ablex.

Seccombe, K. (1991). Assessing the costs and benefits of children: Gender comparisons among childfree husbands and wives. *Journal of Marriage and the Family, 53,* 191–202.

Secter, B. (1995, January 1). Some stats count for nothing: Surveys often produce "data" from thin air. *Chicago Sun-Times,* p. 17.

Seibel, T. (1994, June 3). V.C. fights cancer with DNA. *Chicago Sun-Times,* p. 5.

Seibert, G. (1991, September 13). Breathing in & out: Martha Graham, R.I.P. *Commonweal,* pp. 516–517, 519.

Seiden, R. H. (1981). Mellowing with age: Factors influencing the non-white suicide rate. *Omega, 13,* 265–281.

Selkoe, D. A. (1991). The molecular pathology of Alzheimer's disease. *Neuron, 6*(4), 487–498.

Selkoe, D. J. (1992). Aging brain, aging mind. *Scientific American, 267,* 135–142.

Seltzer, J. A., & Garfinkel, I. (1990). Inequality in divorce settlements: An investigation of property settlements and child support awards. *Social Science Research, 19,* 82–111.

Selye, H. (Ed.) (1980). *Selye's guide to stress research* (Vol. 1). New York: Van Nostrand Reinhold.

Sen, A. (1993). The economics of life and death. *Scientific American, 268,* 40–47.

Sexual side effects of Prozac and other SSRIs. (1994, May). *The Menninger Letter,* p. 7.

Shapiro, L. (1991, April 15). Graph of the heart: Martha Graham gave dance a new vocabulary. *Newsweek,* p. 77.

Shapiro, P. (1994, November). My house is your house: Advance planning can ease the way when parents move in with adult kids. *AARP Bulletin,* p. 2.

Sharp, D., Cole, M., & Lave, C. (1978). *Education and cognitive development: The evidence from experimental research.* Chicago: University of Chicago Press.

Shaw, M. P. (1989). The eureka process: A structure for the creative experience in science and engineering. *Creativity Research Journal, 2,* 286–298.

Shaw, M. P. (1992a). Affective components of scientific creativity. In M. P. Shaw & M. A. Runco (Eds.), *Creativity and affect.* Norwood, NJ: Ablex.

Shaw, M. P. (1992b). Reason, emotionality, and creative thinking. *Humanistic Judaism, 20*(4), 42–44.

Sheehy, G. (1993, October). The flaming fifties. *Vanity Fair,* pp. 270–273.

Sherman, E. (1991). *Reminiscence and the self in old age.* New York: Springer.

Sherman, E. (1993). Mental health and successful adaptation in late life. *Generations, 17*(1), 43–46.

Sherman, E., & Peak, T. (1991). Patterns of reminiscence and the assessment of late life adjustment. *Gerontological Social Work, 16,* 59–74.

Sherman, L. W., & Berk, R. A. (1984, April). The Minneapolis domestic violence experiment. *Police Foundation Reports,* pp. 1–8.

Sherman, L. W., & Cohn, E. G. (1989). The impact of research on legal policy: The Minneapolis domestic violence experiment. *Law and Society Review,* pp. 118–144.

Sherwin, B. B., Gelfand, M. M., & Brender, W. (1985). Androgen enhances sexual motivation in females: A prospective, crossover study of sex steroid administration in the surgical menopause. *Psychosomatic Medicine, 47,* 339–351.

Shier, A. (1992). *Oh, Utopia, how we miss you.* Livonia, MI: Mini-Lectures Press.

Shimamura, A. P., Janowsky, J. S., & Squire, L. R. (1991). What is the role of frontal lobe damage in memory disorders? In H. D. Levine, H. M. Eisenberg, & A. L. Benton (Eds.), *Frontal lobe functioning and dysfunction* (pp. 173–195). New York: Oxford University Press.

Ship, J. A., & Weiffenbach, J. M. (1993). Age, gender, medical treatment, and medication effects on smell identification. *Journal of Gerontology: Medical Sciences, 48*(1), M26–32.

Shipp, E. R. (1988, February 4). Decision could hinder surrogacy across nation. *New York Times,* p. B6.

Should you take estrogen to prevent osteoporosis? (1994, August). *Johns Hopkins Medical Letter: Health after 50,* pp. 4–5.

Siano, B. (1993, July–August). False history, gas chambers, blue smoke, and cracked mirrors. *The Humanist,* pp. 31–33.

Siegler, I., McCarty, S. M., & Logue, P. E. (1982). Wechsler Memory Scale scores, selective attribution, and distance from death. *Journal of Gerontology, 37,* 176–181.

Simons, M. (1993, February 10). Dutch parliament approves law permitting euthanasia. *New York Times,* p. A10.

Simonton, D. K. (1983). Dramatic greatness and content: A quantitative analysis of 82 Athenian and Shakespearean plays. *Empirical Studies of the Arts, 1,* 109–123.

Simonton, D. K. (1985). Quality, quantity, and age: The careers of 10 distinguished psychologists. *International Journal of Aging and Human Development, 21,* 241–254.

Simonton, D. K. (1986). Popularity, content, and context in 37 Shakespearean plays. *Poetics, 15,* 493–510.

Simonton, D. K. (1989). The swan-song phenomenon: Last-works effects for 172 classical composers. *Psychology and Aging, 4,* 42–47.

Simonton, D. K. (1990). Creativity and wisdom in aging. In J. E. Birren & K. W. Schaie (Eds.), *Handbook of the psychology of aging* (pp. 320–329). New York: Academic.

Simpson, R., Kelly, S. F., Atkinson, H. P., Turner, M., Greiser, K., & Zhao, D. (1991). Abstract. In *Circulation, 84*(4), 11–334.

Singelakis, A. T. (1990). Real estate market trends and the displacement of the aged: Examination of the linkages in Manhattan. *The Gerontologist, 30,* 658–666.

Singer, P. A. (1988, June 1). Should doctors kill patients? *Canadian Medical Association Journal, 138,* 1000–1001.

Sinnott, J. D. (1984). Postformal reasoning: The relativistic stage. In M. L. Commons, F. A. Richards & C. Armon (Eds.), *Beyond formal operations: Late adolescence and adult cognitive development* (pp. 357–380). New York: Praeger.

Sinnott, J. D. (1989). Prospective memory and aging: Memory as adaptive action. In L. W. Poon, D. C. Rubin, & B. A. Wilson (Eds.), *Everyday cognition in adulthood and old age* (pp. 352–372). New York: Cambridge University Press.

Sitarz, D. (1990). *Divorce yourself.* Carbondale, IL: Nova.

Skaff, M. M., & Pearlin, L. I. (1992). Caregiving: Role engulfment and the loss of self. *The Gerontologist, 32*(5), 656–664.

Skinner, B. F. (1938). *The behavior of organisms: An experimental approach.* New York: Appleton-Century.

Skinner, J. H. (1993). Aging in place: The experience of African American and other minority elders. In J. J. Callahan, Jr. (Ed.), *Aging in place* (pp. 89–96). Amityville, NY: Baywood.

Sklar, L. S., & Anisman, H. (1981). Stress and cancer. *Psychological Bulletin, 89*(3), 369–406.

Skolnick, A. (1990). It's important, but don't bank on exercise alone to prevent osteoporosis. *Journal of the American Medical Association, 263*(13), 1751–1752.

Skoog, I., Nilsson, L., Palmertz, B., Andreasson, L., & Svanborg, A. (1993). A population-based study for dementia in 85-year-olds. *New England Journal of Medicine, 328,* 153–158.

Sleep: From apnea to zzzz's. (1995, March). *University of California at Berkeley Wellness Letter,* pp. 4–5.

Smith, D. W., & Brodzinsky, D. M. (1994). Stress and coping in adopted children: A developmental study. *Journal of Clinical Child Psychology, 23*(1), 91–99.

Smith, J., & Baltes, P. B. (1990). Wisdom-related knowledge: Age/cohort differences in response to life planning problems. *Developmental Psychology, 26*(3), 494–505.

Smith, L. (1965). *The journey.* New York: Norton.

Smith, T. W. (1991). Adult sexual behavior in 1989: Number of partners, frequency of intercourse and risk of AIDS. *Family Planning Perspectives, 23*(3), 102–107.

Smith, T. W. (1994). *The demography of sexual behavior.* Menlo Park, CA: Henry J. Kaiser Family Foundation.

Smith, T. W. (1995). *Holocaust denial: What the survey data reveal.* New York: American Jewish Committee, Institute of Human Relations.

Snarey, J. R. (1985). Cross-cultural universality of social-moral development: A critical review of Kohlbergian research. *Psychological Bulletin, 97,* 202–232.

Snyder, C. J., & Barrett, G. V. (1988). The Age Discrimination in Employment Act: A review of court decisions. *Experimental Aging Research, 14,* 3–47.

Snyder, M. (1987). *Public appearance/private realities: The psychology of self-monitoring.* New York: Freeman.

Snyderman, M., & Rothman, S. (1987). Survey of expert opinion on intelligence and aptitude testing. *American Psychologist, 42,* 137–144.

Soddy, K., & Kidson, M. (1967). *Men in middle life: Cross cultural studies in mental health.* Philadelphia: Lippincott.

Soldo, B. J., Wolf, D. A., & Agree, E. M. (1990). Family, households, and care arrangement of frail older women: A structural analysis. *Journal of Gerontology: Social Sciences, 45,* S238–249.

Solomon, M. (1993). Report of survey of doctors and nurses about treatment of terminally ill patients. *American Journal of Public Health, 83*(1), 23–25.

Solomon, P. R., Pomerleau, D., Bennett, L., James, J., & Morse, D. L. (1989). Acquisition of the classically conditioned eyeblink response in humans over the life span. *Psychology and Aging, 4*(1), 34–41.

Soltes, F. (1994, March 27). Does prostate cancer get too little attention? *Chicago Sun-Times,* p. 59.

Solzhenitsyn, A. (1973). *The Gulag archipelago.* New York: Harper & Row.

Sontag, S. (1972, September 23). The double standard of aging. *Saturday Review,* pp. 29–38.

Spearman, C. E. (1927). *The abilities of man.* New York: Macmillan.

Spearman, C. E. (1930). *Creative mind.* Cambridge: Cambridge University Press.

Spence, A. P. (1989). *Biology of human aging.* Englewood Cliffs, NJ: Prentice-Hall.

Spencer, C. W. (1987). *America's centenarians.* Washington DC: U.S. Government Printing Office.

Spicer, D. V., Ursin, G., Parisky, Y. R., Pearce, J. G., Shoupe, D., Pike, A., & Pike, M. C. (1994). Changes in mammographic densities induced by a hormonal contraceptive designed to reduce breast cancer risks. *Journal of the National Cancer Institute, 86,* 431–436.

Spielman, F. (1994, July 26). Mayor, consultants put to test: $5 million process comes under fire. *Chicago Sun-Times,* p. 5.

Spilich, G. W., June, L., & Renner, J. (1992). Cigarette smoking and cognitive performance. *British Journal of Addiction, 87,* 1313–1326.

Spirduso, W. W., & MacRae, P. G. (1990). Motor performance and aging. In J. E. Birren & K. W. Schaie (Eds.), *Psychology of aging* (3d ed., pp. 183–200). New York: Academic.

Spitze, G., & Miner, S. (1992). Gender differences in adult child contact among elderly black parents. *The Gerontologist, 32,* 213–218.

Spitzer, M. E. (1988). Taste acuity in institutionalized and noninstitutionalized elderly men. *Journal of Gerontology, 43*(3), 71–74.

Spoto, D. (1992). *Laurence Olivier: A biography.* New York: HarperCollins.

Sprott, R. L., & Roth, G. S. (1992). Biomarkers of aging: Can we predict individual life span? *Generations, 16,* 11–14.

Squire, L. R. (1992). Memory and the hippocampus: A synthesis of findings with rats, monkeys, and humans. *Psychological Review, 99,* 195–231.

Squire, L. R. (1994). Declarative and nondeclarative memory: Multiple brain systems supporting learning and memory. In D. L. Schacter & E. Tulving (Eds.), *Memory systems 1994* (pp. 203–232). Cambridge, MA: MIT Press.

St. George-Hyslop, P. H., Tanzi, R. E., Polinsky, et al. (1987). The genetic defect causing familial Alzheimer's disease maps on chromosome 21. *Science, 235,* 885–890.

Stadtman, E. R. (1992). Protein oxidation and aging. *Science, 257,* 1220–1224.

Staines, G. L. (1980). Spillover versus compensation: A review of the literature on the relationship between work and nonwork. *Human Relations, 33,* 111–129.

Stampfer, M. J., Colditz, G. A., Willett, W. C., Manson, J. E., Rosner, B., Speizer, F. E., & Hennekens, C. H. (1991). Postmenopausal estrogen therapy and cardiovascular disease. *New England Journal of Medicine, 325,* 756–762.

Stanford, E. P., & Du Bois, B. C. (1992). Gender and ethnicity patterns. In J. E. Birren, R. Bruce Sloane, & G. D. Cohen (Eds.), *Handbook of mental health and aging* (pp. 99–119). San Diego: Academic.

Starkweather, E. K. (1976). Creativity research instruments designed for use with preschool children. In A. M. Biondi & S. J. Parnes (Eds.), *Assessing creative growth: The tests—Book 1* (pp. 79–90). Buffalo, NY: Creative Education Foundation.

Starr, B. D., & Weiner, M. B. (1981). *The Starr-Weiner report on sex and sexuality in the mature years.* New York: Stein & Day.

Staudinger, U. M., Smith, J., & Baltes, P. B. (1992). Wisdom-related knowledge in a life review task: Age differences and the role of professional specialization. *Psychology and Aging, 7,* 271–281.

Steele, S. (1990). *The content of our character: A new vision of race in America.* New York: St. Martin's.

Stein, M. I. (1953). Creativity and culture. *Journal of Psychology, 36,* 311–322.

Steinbach, U. (1992). Social networks, institutionalization, and mortality among elderly people in the United States. *Journal of Gerontology: Social Sciences, 47*(4), S183–190.

Steinberg, L., & Silverberg, S. B. (1987). Influences on marital satisfaction during the middle stages of the family life cycle. *Journal of Marriage and the Family, 49,* 751–760.

Steinberg, S., Javitt, J. C., et al. (1993). The content and cost of cataract surgery. *Archives of Opthalmology, 111,* 1041–1049.

Stengel, R. (1994, May 9). The making of a leader. *Time,* pp. 36–38.

Stern, M. B. (1950). *Louisa May Alcott.* Norman: University of Oklahoma Press.

Stern, W. (1911). *Die differentielle Psychologie in ihren methodischen Grundlagen.* Leipzig, Germany: Barth.

Sternberg, R. J. (1985a). *Beyond IQ: A triarchic theory of human intelligence.* New York: Cambridge University Press.

Sternberg, R. J. (1985b, August). *A triangular theory of love.* Paper presented at the annual meeting of the American Psychological Association, Los Angeles.

Sternberg, R. J. (1986). *Intelligence applied: Understanding and increasing your intellectual skills.* San Diego: Harcourt Brace.

Sternberg, R. J. (1987, September 23). The uses and misuses of intelligence testing: Misunderstanding meaning, users overrely on scores. *Education Week,* pp. 28, 22.

Sternberg, R. J. (1990). Wisdom and its relations to intelligence and creativity. In R. J. Sternberg (Ed.), *Wisdom: Its nature, origins, and development* (pp. 142–159). Cambridge: Cambridge University Press.

Sternberg, R. J., & Barnes, M. L. (1985). Real and ideal other in romantic relationships: Is four a crowd? *Journal of Personality and Social Psychology, 49,* 1586–1608.

Sternberg, R. J., & Detterman, D. K. (1986). *What is intelligence?* Norwood, NJ: Ablex.

Sternberg, R. J., & Grajek, S. (1984). The nature of love. *Journal of Personality and Social Psychology, 47,* 312–329.

Sternberg, R. J., & Wagner, R. K. (1993). The g-ocentric view of intelligence and job performance is wrong. *Current Directions in Psychological Science, 2*(1), 1–4.

Sterns, H. L., Barrett, G. V., & Alexander, R. A. (1985). Accidents and the aging individual. In J. E. Birren & K. W. Schaie (Eds.), *Handbook of the psychology of aging* (2d ed., pp. 703–724). New York: Van Nostrand Reinhold.

Stevens, J. C. (1992). Aging and spatial acuity of touch. *Journal of Gerontology: Psychological Sciences, 47*(1), P35–40.

Stevens, J. C., Cain, W. S., Demarque, A., & Ruthruff, A. M. (1991). On the discrimination of missing ingredients: Aging and salt flavor. *Appetite, 16,* 129–140.

Stevens, R. (1983). *Erik Erikson: An introduction.* New York: St. Martin's.

Stewart, G. W. (1950). Can productive thinking be taught? *Journal of Higher Education, 21,* 411–414.

Stewart, M. A., & Olds, S. W. (1973). *Raising a hyperactive child.* New York: Harper & Row.

Sticht, T. G., & McDonald, B. A. (1990). *Teach the mother and reach the child: Literacy across generations—literacy lessons.* Geneva: International Bureau of Education.

Stodelle, E. (1984). *Deep song: The dance story of Martha Graham.* New York: Schirmer.

Stone, I. F. (1988). *The trial of Socrates.* Boston: Little, Brown.

Storandt, M. (1976). Speed and coding effects in relation to age and ability level. *Developmental Psychology, 12,* 177–178.

Strawbridge, W. J., & Wallhagen, M. I. (1991). Impact of family conflict on adult child caregivers. *The Gerontologist, 31*(6), 770–777.

Stroebe, M., Gergen, M. M., Gergen, K. J., & Stroebe, W. (1992). Broken hearts or broken bonds: Love and death in historical perspective. *American Psychologist, 47*(10), 1205–1212.

Strom, R., Collinsworth, P., Strom, S., & Griswold, D. (1992–1993). Strengths and needs of black grandparents. *International Journal of Aging and Human Development, 36,* 255–268.

Strong, M. (1988). *Mainstay.* Boston: Little, Brown.

Strube, M. J., & Barbour, L. S. (1984). Factors related to the decision to leave an abusive relationship. *Journal of Marriage and the Family, 46,* 837–844.

Suicide: Part 1. (1986, February). *Harvard Medical School Health Letter,* pp. 1–4.

Suitor, J. J., & Pillemer, K. (1987). The presence of adult children: A source of stress for elderly married couples? *Journal of Marriage and the Family, 49,* 717–725.

Suitor, J. J., & Pillemer, K. (1988). Explaining intergenerational conflict when adult children and elderly parents live together. *Journal of Marriage and the Family, 50,* 1037–1047.

Suitor, J. J., & Pillemer, K. (1993). Support and interpersonal stress in the social networks of married daughters caring for parents with dementia. *Journal of Gerontology: Social Sciences, 41*(1), S1–8.

Super, D. E. (1957). *The psychology of careers.* New York: Harper & Row.

Super, D. E. (1985). Coming of age in Middletown: Careers in the making. *American Psychologist, 40,* 405–414.

Surgery for nearsightedness. (1994, October). *University of California at Berkeley Wellness Letter,* p. 7.

Swann, W. B. (1983). Self-verification: Bringing social reality into harmony with the self. In J. Suls & A. B. Greenwald (Eds.), *Psychological perspectives of the self* (Vol. 2, pp. 33–66). Hillsdale, NJ: Erlbaum.

Swann, W. B. (1987). Identity negotiations: Where two roads meet. *Journal of Personality and Social Psychology, 53,* 1038–1051.

Sweeting, J. G. (1985). The middle years and aging. In D. F. Tapley, R. J. Weiss, & T. Q. Morris (Eds.), *The Columbia University college of physicians and surgeons complete home medical guide* (pp. 257–273). New York: Crown.

Tamir, L. M. (1989). Modern myths about men at midlife: An assessment. In S. Hunter & M. Sundel (Eds.), *Midlife myths.* Newbury Park, CA: Sage.

Tanfer, K., & Horn, M. C. (1985). Contraceptive use, pregnancy and fertility patterns among single American women in their 20's. *Family Planning Perspectives, 17*(1), 10–19.

Targ, D. B. (1979). Toward a reassessment of women's experience at middle-age. *Family Coordinator, 28*(3), 377–382.

Taub, R. N. (1985). Cancer. In Tapley, D. F., Weiss, R. J., & Morris, T. Q. (Eds.), *The Columbia University College of Physicians and Surgeons complete home medical guide* (pp. 395–424). New York: Crown.

Taylor, H. (1995, January 30). *Doctor-assisted suicide: Support for Dr. Kevorkian remains strong, and 2-to-1 majority approves Oregon-style assisted suicide bill.* New York: Harris and Associates.

Taylor, I. A. (1959). The nature of the creative process. In P. Smith (Ed.), *Creativity* (pp. 51–82). New York: Hastings House.

Taylor, J. M. (1979). *Eva Peron: The myths of a woman.* Chicago: University of Chicago Press.

Taylor, P. (1994, May 11). Mandela's moment comes: Inauguration draws crush of foreign leaders. *Chicago Sun-Times,* p. 3.

Taylor, R. J., & Chatters, L. M. (1991). Extended family networks of older Black adults. *Journal of Gerontology: Social Sciences, 46*(4), S210–217.

Taylor, S. C. (1993, October–November). The end of retirement. *Modern Maturity,* pp. 32–39.

Techner, D. (1994, February 6). *Death and dying.* Seminar presentation for candidates in Leadership Program, International Institute for Secular Humanistic Judaism, Farmington Hills, MI.

Tellegren, A., Lykken, D. T., Bouchard, T. J., Wilcox, K. J., Segal, N. L., & Rich, S. (1988). Personality similarities in twins reared apart and reared together. *Journal of Personality and Social Psychology, 54,* 1031–1039.

Testing for Alzheimer's disease. (1995, January). *Harvard Women's Health Watch,* p. 1.

Testing awareness of the Holocaust. (1993, May 5). *Christian Century,* p. 481.

Thomas, A., & Chess, S. (1984). Genesis and evolution of behavioral disorders: From infancy to early adult life. *American Journal of Orthopsychiatry, 141,* 1–9.

Thomas, J. L. (1986). Gender differences in satisfaction with grandparenting. *Psychology and Aging, 1*(3), 215–219.

Thompson, L., & Walker, A. J. (1989). Gender in families: Women and men in marriage, work, and parenthood. *Journal of Marriage and the Family, 51,* 845–871.

Thomson, E., & Colella, U. (1992). Cohabitation and marital stability: Quality or commitment? *Journal of Marriage and the Family, 54,* 259–267.

Thorndike, E. L. (1927). *The measurement of intelligence.* New York: Bureau of Publications, Teacher's College, Columbia University.

Thornton, A. (1989). Changing attitudes toward family issues in the United States. *Journal of Marriage and the Family, 51,* 873–893.

Thurstone, L. L. (1938). Primary mental abilities. *Psychometric Monographs* (No. 1).

Thurstone, L. L. (1952). Creative talent. In L. L. Thurstone (Ed.), *Applications of psychology* (pp. 18–37). New York: Harper & Row.

Tiger, L., & Shepher, J. (1975). *Women in the kibbutz.* New York: Harcourt Brace.

Timiras, P. S. (1972). *Developmental physiology and aging.* New York: Macmillan.

Tomkins, S. (1986). Script theory. In J. Aronoff, A. I. Rabin, & R. A. Zucker (Eds.), *The emergence of personality* (pp. 147–216). New York: Springer.

Tomlinson-Keasey, C. (1982). Structures, functions, and stages: A trio of unresolved issues in formal operations. In S. Modgil & C. Modgil (Eds.), *Jean Piaget: Consensus and controversy.* New York: Holt, Rinehart, & Winston.

Torrance, E. P. (1957). *Psychology of survival.* Unpublished manuscript, Air Force Personnel Research Center, Lackland Air Force Base, TX.

Torrance, E. P. (1965). *Rewarding creative behavior.* Englewood Cliffs, NJ: Prentice-Hall.

Torrance, E. P. (1966). *The Torrance Test of Creative Thinking: Technical-norms manual* (research ed.). Princeton, NJ: Personnel Press.

Torrance, E. P. (1972a). Career patterns and peak creative experiences of creative high school students 12 years later. *Gifted Child Quarterly, 16,* 75–88.

Torrance, E. P. (1972b). Predictive validity of the Torrance Test of Creative Thinking. *Journal of Creative Behavior, 6,* 236–252.

Torrance, E. P. (1974). *The Torrance Tests of Creative Thinking: Technical-norms manual.* Bensenville, IL: Scholastic Testing Service.

Torrance, E. P. (1981). Predicting the creativity of elementary school children (1958–1980)—and the teacher who made a "difference." *Gifted Child Quarterly, 25,* 55–62.

Torrance, E. P. (1987). *The blazing drive: The creative personality.* Buffalo, NY: Bearly Limited.

Torrance, E. P. (1988). The nature of creativity as manifests in its testing. In R. J. Sternberg (Ed.), *The nature of creativity: Contemporary psychological perspectives* (pp. 43–75). Cambridge: Cambridge University Press.

Torrance, E. P., & Ball, O. E. (1984). *Torrance Tests of Creative Thinking: Streamlined (revised) manual, Figural A and B.* Bensenville, IL: Scholastic Testing Service.

Tracy, M. B., & Pampel, F. C. (Eds.) (1991). *International handbook on old-age innocence.* Westport, CT: Greenwood.

Tribute: Martha Graham, the revolutionary mother of modern dance, takes her final leave of the spotlight. (1991, April 15). *People Weekly,* p. 96.

Trichopoulos, D., Molio, F., Tomatis, L., Agapitos, E., Delsedime, L., Zavitsanos, X., Kalandidi, K., Riboli, E., & Saracci, R. (1992). Active and passive smoking and pathological indications of lung cancer risk in an autopsy study. *Journal of the American Medical Association, 268*(13), 1697–1701.

Trickett, P. K., & Kuczynski, L. (1986). Children's misbehaviors and parental discipline strategies in abusive and nonabusive families. *Developmental Psychology, 22,* 115–123.

Trickett, P. K., & Susman, E. J. (1988). Parental perceptions of child-rearing practices in physically abusive and non-abusive families. *Developmental Psychology, 24*(2), 270–276.

Troll, L. E. (1975). *Early and middle adulthood.* Monterey, CA: Brooks/Cole.

Troll, L. E. (1980). Grandparenting. In L. W. Poon (Ed.), *Aging in the 1980s.* Washington, DC: American Psychological Association.

Troll, L. E. (1983). Grandparents: The family watchdogs. In T. H. Brubaker (Ed.), *Family relationships in later life.* Beverly Hills, CA: Sage.

Troll, L. E. (1985). *Early and middle adulthood* (2d ed.). Monterey, CA: Brooks/Cole.

Troll, L. E. (1986). Parents and children in later life. *Generations, 10*(4), 23–25.

Troll, L. E. (1989). Myths of midlife intergenerational relationships. In S. Hunter & M. Sundel (Eds.), *Midlife myths.* Newbury Park, CA: Sage.

Troll, L. E., Miller, S., & Atchley, R. (1979). *Families in later life.* Belmont, CA: Wadsworth.

Troll, L. E., & Smith, J. (1976). Attachment through the life span. *Human Development, 3,* 156–171.

Trotter, R. J. (1986, August). Profile: Robert J. Sternberg: Three heads are better than one. *Psychology Today,* pp. 56–62.

Tsai, M., & Wagner, N. (1979, March). Incest and molestation: Problems of childhood sexuality. *Resident and Staff Physician,* pp. 129–136.

Tschann, J., Johnston, J. R., & Wallerstein, J. S. (1989). Resources, stressors, and attachment as predictors of adult adjustment after divorce: A longitudinal study. *Journal of Marriage and Family Therapy, 51,* 1033–1046.

Tucker, M. B., Taylor, R. J., & Mitchell-Kernan, C. (1993). Marriage and romantic involvement among aged African Americans. *Journal of Gerontology: Social Sciences: 48,* S123–132.

Tulving, E. (1991). Memory research is not a zero-sum game. *American Psychologist, 46*(1), 41–42.

Turner, P. H., et al. (1985, March). *Parenting in gay and lesbian families.* Paper presented at the first meeting of the Future of Parenting Symposium, Chicago.

Twain, M. (1963). How to make history dates stick. In C. Neider (Ed.), *The complete essays of Mark Twain* (pp. 495–516). Garden City, NY: Doubleday.

Uhlenberg, P. (1988). Aging and the social significance of cohorts. In J. E. Birren & V. L. Bengtson (Eds.), *Emergent theories of aging* (pp. 405–425). New York: Springer.

Uhlenberg, P., Cooney, T., & Boyd, R. (1990). Divorce for women after midlife. *Journal of Gerontology, 45*(1), 53–11.

Uhlenberg, P., & Myers, M. A. P. (1981). Divorce and the elderly. *The Gerontologist, 21*(3), 276–282.

Umberson, D. (1992). Relationships between adult children and their parents: Psychological consequences for both generations. *Journal of Marriage and the Family, 54,* 664–674.

Umberson, D., & Chen, M. D. (1994). Effects of a parent's death on adult children: Relationship to salience and reaction to loss. *American Sociological Review, 59,* 152–168.

Umberson, D., Wortman, C. B., & Kessler, R. C. (1992). Widowhood and depression: Explaining long-term gender differences in vulnerability. *Journal of Health and Social Behavior, 33,* 10–24.

United Nations. (1991). *The world's women 1970–1990: Trends and statistics.* New York: Author.

United Nations. (1992a). *Developmental implications of population aging: Preliminary results of multi-country study.* Paper presented at meeting of the U.N. Expert Group on Population Growth and Demographic Structure.

United Nations. (1992b). *Patterns of fertility in low fertility settings.* New York: Author.

United Nations Committee for Development Planning. (1988). *Report on the twenty-fourth session.* New York: United Nations Economic and Social Council.

United Nations Educational, Scientific, and Cultural Organization (UNESCO). (1989). *International Literacy Year (ILY), 1990.* Paris: Author.

United Nations International Labor Organization (UNILO). (1993). *Job stress: The 20th-century disease.* New York: United Nations.

U.S. Bureau of the Census. (1983). *America in transition: An aging society* (Current Population Reports, Series P-23, No. 128). Washington, DC: U.S. Government Printing Office.

U.S. Bureau of the Census. (1989). *Marital status and living arrangements, March 1988.* Washington DC: U.S. Government Printing Office.

U.S. Bureau of the Census. (1990). *Who's minding the kids? Child care arrangements: 1986–1987* (Current Population

Reports, Series P-70, No. 20). Washington, DC: U.S. Government Printing Office.

U.S. Bureau of the Census. (1991a). *Household and family characteristics, March 1991* (Publication No. AP-20-458). Washington, DC: U.S. Government Printing Office.

U.S. Bureau of the Census. (1991b). *1990 census of population and housing.* Washington, DC: Data User Service Division.

U.S. Bureau of the Census. (1992a, July). Growth of America's oldest-old population. *Profiles of America's elderly, No. 2.* Washington, DC: U.S. Government Printing Office.

U.S. Bureau of the Census. (1992b). *Marital status and living arrangements: March 1991* (Current Population Reports, Series P-20, No. 461). Washington, DC: U.S. Government Printing Office.

U.S. Bureau of the Census. (1992c). *Sixty-five plus in America.* Washington, DC: U.S. Government Printing Office.

U.S. Bureau of the Census. (1993). *Sixty-five plus in America.* Washington, DC: U.S. Government Printing Office.

U.S. Bureau of the Census. (1995). *Sixty-five plus in the United States.* Washington, DC: U.S. Government Printing Office.

U.S. Bureau of Justice Statistics. (1983). *Report to the nation on crime and justice.* Washington, DC: U.S. Government Printing Office.

U.S. Bureau of Justice Statistics. (1994, November). *Selected findings: Violence between intimates.* Washington, DC: U.S. Government Printing Office.

U.S. Department of Education (1986). *Participation in adult education, May 1984* (Office of Educational Research and Improvement Bulletin CS 86-308B). Washington, DC: Center for Educational Statistics.

U.S. Department of Education (1993, September). *Adult literacy in America.* Washington, DC: U.S. Government Printing Office.

U.S. Department of Health and Human Services (USDHHS). (1982). *Prevention 82* (DHHS [PHS] Publication No. 82-50157). Washington, DC: U.S. Government Printing Office.

U.S. Department of Health and Human Services (USDHHS). (1984). *Child sexual abuse prevention: Tips to parents.* Washington, DC: Office of Human Development Services, Administration for Children, Youth, and Families, and National Center on Child Abuse and Neglect.

U.S. Department of Health and Human Services (USDHHS). (1985). *Health, United States, 1985* (DHHS Publication No. PHS 86-1232). Washington, DC: U.S. Government Printing Office.

U.S. Department of Health and Human Services (USDHHS). (1986). *Health, United States, 1986, and Prevention Profile* (DHHS Publication No. PHS 87-1232). Washington, DC: U.S. Government Printing Office.

U.S. Department of Health and Human Services (USDHHS). (1987). *Smoking and health: A national status report* (DHHS/PHS/Child Development Publication No. 87-8396). Washington, DC: U.S. Government Printing Office.

U.S. Department of Health and Human Services (USDHHS). (1988). *Social security programs throughout the world—1987* (Report No. 61). Washington, DC: U.S. Government Printing Office.

U.S. Department of Health and Human Services (USDHHS). (1990). *Health, United States, 1989* (DHHS Publication No. PHS 90-1232). Washington, DC: U.S. Government Printing Office.

U.S. Department of Health and Human Services (USDHHS). (1991). *Aging America: Trends and projections* (DHHS Publication No. [FCoA] 91-28001). Washington, DC: U.S. Government Printing Office.

U.S. Department of Health and Human Services (USDHHS). (1992). *Health, United States, 1991, and Prevention Profile* (DHHS Publication No. PHS 92-1232). Washington, DC: U.S. Government Printing Office.

U.S. Department of Health and Human Services (USDHHS). (1993a). *A cataract patient's guide* (Publication No. PHS A93-0544). Washington, DC: U.S. Government Printing Office.

U.S. Department of Health and Human Services (USDHHS). (1993b). *Monthly vital statistics report, 42*(3), supplement.

U.S. Department of Health and Human Services (USDHHS). (1995). *Health, United States, 1994* (DHHS Publication No. PHS 95-1232). Washington, DC: U.S. Government Printing Office.

U.S. Department of Labor. (1992). Statistics on employed civilians detailed by occupation, sex, race, and Hispanic origin. *Handbook of labor statistics.* Washington, DC: U.S. Government Printing Office.

U.S. Department of Labor—Women's Bureau. (1994). *Working women count.* Washington, DC: U.S. Government Printing Office.

U.S. Office of Technology Assessment. (1992). *The menopause, hormone therapy, and women's health.* Washington, DC: U.S. Government Printing Office.

U.S. Senate, Special Committee on Aging. (1991). *Aging America: Trends and projections.* Washington, DC: U.S. Government Printing Office.

University hospitals first to treat kidney-cancer patient with gene therapy. (1994, June 9). *University of Chicago Chronicle,* p. 9.

Ursin, H. (1980). Personality, activation and somatic health. In S. Levine & H. Ursin (Eds.), *Coping and health.* New York: Plenum.

Vachon, M., Lyall, W., Rogers, J., Freedmen-Letofky, K., & Freeman, S. (1980). A controlled study of self-help intervention for widows. *American Journal of Psychiatry, 137*(11), 1380–1384.

Vaillant, G. E. (1977). *Adaptation to life.* Boston: Little, Brown.

Vaillant, G. E. (1989). The evolution of defense mechanisms during the middle years. In J. M. Oldham & R. S. Liebert (Eds.), *The middle years.* New Haven, CT: Yale University Press.

Vaillant, G. E., & Vaillant, C. O. (1990). Natural history of male psychological health: 12. A 45-year study of predictors of successful aging. *American Journal of Psychiatry, 147,* 31–37.

van Baal, J. (1966). *Dema, description and analysis of Marindanim culture (South New Guinea).* The Hague: Nijhoff.

van Noord-Zaadstra, B. M., Looman, C. W. N., Alsbach, H., Habbema, J. D. F., teVelde, E. R., & Karbaat, J.

(1991). Delaying childbearing: Effect of age on fecundity and outcome of pregnancy. *British Medical Journal, 302,* 1361.

Vasudev, J. (1983). *A study of moral reasoning at different stage in India.* Unpublished manuscript, University of Pittsburgh, PA.

Verhaeghen, P., Marcoen, A., & Goossens, L. (1992). Improving memory performance in the aged through mnemonic training: A meta-analytic study. *Psychology and Aging, 7*(2), 242–251.

Veronesi, U., Luini, A., Del Vecchio, M., et al. (1993). Radiotherapy after breast-preserving surgery in women with localized cancer of the breast. *New England Journal of Medicine, 328,* 1587–1591.

Veronesi, U., Salvadori, B., Luini, A., et al. (1990). Conservative treatment of early breast cancer: Long-term results of 1232 cases treated with quadrantectomy, axillary dissection, and radiotherapy. *Annals of Surgery, 211,* 250–259.

Vinick, B. (1978). Remarriage in old age. *Family Coordinator, 27,* 359–363.

Visher, E. B., & Visher, J. (1983). Stepparenting: Blending families. In H. I. McCubbin & C. R. Figley (Eds.), *Stress and the family: 1. Coping with normative transitions.* New York: Brunner/Mazel.

Visher, E. B., & Visher, J. S. (1989). Parenting coalitions after remarriage: Dynamics and therapeutic guidelines. *Family Relations, 38,* 65–70.

Voydanoff, P. (1987). *Work and family life.* Newbury Park, CA: Sage.

Voydanoff, P. (1990). Economic distress and family relations: A review of the eighties. *Journal of Marriage and the Family, 52,* 1099–1115.

Wagner, D. A. (1978). Memories of Morocco: The influence of age, schooling and environment on memory. *Cognitive Psychology, 10,* 1–28.

Wagner, D. A. (1981). Culture and memory development. In H. C. Triandis & A. Heron (Eds.), *Handbook of cross-cultural psychology: Developmental psychology* (Vol. 4, pp. 187–232). Boston: Allyn & Bacon.

Wagner, R. K., & Sternberg, R. J. (1986). Tacit knowledge and intelligence in the everyday world. In R. J. Sternberg & R. K. Wagner (Eds.), *Practical intelligence: Nature and origins of competence in the everyday world.* Cambridge: Cambridge University Press.

Walasky, M., Whitbourne, S. K., & Nehrke, M. F. (1983–1984). Construction and validation of an ego-integrity status interview. *International Journal of Aging and Human Development, 81,* 61–72.

Walford, R. L. (1983). *Maximum life span.* New York: Norton.

Walford, R. L. (1986). *The 120-year-diet.* New York: Simon & Schuster.

Walker, A. J., & Allen, K. R. (1991). Relationships between caregiving daughters and their elderly mothers. *The Gerontologist, 31*(3), 389–396.

Walker, A. J., Martin, S. S. K., & Jones, L. L. (1992). The benefits and costs of caregiving and care receiving for daughters and mothers. *Journal of Gerontology, 47*(3), S130–139.

Walker, L. J. (1984). Sex differences in the development of moral reasoning: A critical review. *Child Development, 55,* 677–691.

Wallace, D. C. (1992). Mitochondrial genetics: A paradigm for aging and degenerative diseases? *Science, 256,* 628–632.

Wallach, M. A., & Kogan, N. (1967). Creativity and intelligence in children's thinking. *Transaction, 4*(1), 38–43.

Wallas, G. (1926). *The art of thought.* New York: Harcourt Brace.

Wallechinsky & Wallace (1993, September 26). Achievers after the age of 90. *Parade,* p. 17.

Wallis, C. (1995, March 6). How to live to be 120. *Time,* p. 85.

Walls, C., & Zarit, S. (1991). Informal support from black churches and well-being of elderly blacks. *The Gerontologist, 31,* 490–495.

Ward, R. A., & Kilburn, H. (1983). Community access and satisfaction: Racial differences in later life. *International Journal of Aging and Human Development, 16,* 209–219.

Ward, R., Logan, J., & Spitze, G. (1992). The influence of parent and child needs on coresidence in middle and later life. *Journal of Marriage and the Family, 54,* 209–221.

Watson, R. (1994, October 25). Ever the best of enemies. *Newsweek,* pp. 35–36.

Wayler, A. H., Kapur, K. K., Feldman, R. S., & Chauncey, H. H. (1982). Effects of age and dentition status on measures of food acceptability. *Journal of Gerontology, 37*(3), 294–299.

Webb, W. B. (1987). Disorders of aging sleep. *Interdisciplinary Topics in Gerontology, 22,* 1–12.

Wechsler, D. (1939). *The measurement of adult intelligence.* Baltimore: Williams & Wilkins.

Weg, R. B. (1989). Sensuality/sexuality of the middle years. In S. Hunter & M. Sundel (Eds.), *Midlife myths.* Newbury Park, CA: Sage.

Wegman, M. E. (1992). Annual summary of vital statistics—1991. *Pediatrics, 90*(6), 835–845.

Weindruch, R., & Walford, R. L. (1988). *The retardation of aging and disease by dietary restriction.* Springfield, IL: Thomas.

Weishaus, S., & Field, D. (1988). A half century of marriage: Continuity or change? *Journal of Marriage and the Family, 50,* 763–774.

Weiss, G., (1994, January). Women and psychotherapy. *The Lilac Tree Newsletter,* pp. 2–4. (Reprinted from *Health Resources for Women,* April 1990, newsletter of Illinois Masonic Medical Center's Women's Health Resources)

Weiss, L., & Lowenthal, M. (1975). Life-course perspectives on friendship. In M. Lowenthal, M. Thurner, & D. Chiriboga (Eds.), *Four stages of life.* San Francisco: Jossey-Bass.

Weiss, R. (1994, March 17). Second colon cancer gene identified. *Chicago Sun-Times,* p. 36.

Weissman, M. M., Klerman, G. L., Markowitz, J. S., & Ouelette, R. (1989). Suicidal ideation and suicide attempts in panic disorders and attacks. *New England Journal of Medicine, 321,* 1209–1214.

Weitzman, L. J. (1985). *The divorce revolution: The unexpected social and economic consequences for women and children in America.* New York:

Wellness facts. (1995, January). *University of California at Berkeley Wellness Letter,* p. 1.

We're not like men. (1994, October). *Harvard Women's Health Watch,* p. 6.

West, R. L. (1985). *Memory fitness over 40*. Gainsville, FL: Triad.

West, R. L. (1992). Everyday memory and aging: A diversity of tests, tasks, and paradigms. In R. L. West & J. D. Sinnott (Eds.), *Everyday memory and aging: Current research and methodology* (pp. 3–21). New York: Springer-Verlag.

Wharton, D. (1993, June–July). Through the glass ceiling: Minorities, women, and corporate America's human resource needs. *The National Voter*, pp. 10–11.

Which living arrangement is for you? (1993, April–May). *Modern Maturity*, pp. 32–33.

Whitbourne, S. K. (1985). *The aging body*. New York: Springer-Verlag.

Whitbourne, S. K. (1987). Personality development in adulthood and old age: Relationships among identity style, health, and well-being. In K. W. Schaie (Ed.), *Annual review of gerontology and geriatrics* (Vol. 7, pp. 189–216). New York: Springer.

Whitbourne, S. K. (1989). Psychological treatment of the aging individual. *Journal of Integrative and Eclectic Psychotherapy, 8,* 161–173.

Whitbourne, S. K., & Primus, L. A. (in press). Physical identity in later adulthood. In J. E. Birren (Ed.), *Encyclopedia of gerontology*. San Diego: Academic.

White, J. M. (1992). Marital status and well-being in Canada: An analysis of age group variations. *Journal of Family Issues, 13,* 390–409.

White, L. K. (1990). Determinants of divorce: A review of research in the eighties. *Journal of Marriage and the Family, 52,* 904–912.

White, L., & Edwards, J. N. (1990). Emptying the nest and parental well-being: An analysis of national panel data. *American Sociological Review, 55,* 235–242.

White, M., & Gribbin, J. (1992). *Stephen Hawking: A life in science*. New York: Dutton.

White, N., & Cunningham, W. R. (1988). Is terminal drop pervasive or specific? *Journal of Gerontology, 43*(6), 141–144.

White, R. W. (1959). Motivation reconsidered: The concept of competence. *Psychological Review, 66,* 297.

White House Conference on Aging. (1971). *Aging and blindness* (Special Concerns Session Report). Washington, DC: U.S. Government Printing Office.

Who's who in America. (1994). New Providence, NJ: Reed.

Wiggins, S., Whyte, P., Higgins, M., Adam, S., et al. (1992). The psychological consequences of predictive testing for Huntington's disease. *New England Journal of Medicine, 327,* 1401–1405.

Wilensky, H. L. (1960). Work, careers, and social integration. *International Social Science Journal, 12,* 543–560.

Willett, W. C., Hunter, D. J., Stampfer, M. J., Colditz, G., Manson, J. E., Spiegelman, D., Rosner, B., Hennekens, C. H., & Spiezer, F. E. (1992). Dietary fat and fiber in relation to risk of breast cancer. *Journal of the American Medical Association, 268,* 2037–2044.

Willett, W. C., Stampfer, M. J., Colditz, G. A., Rosner, B. A., & Speizer, F. E. (1990). Relation of meat, fat, and fiber intake to the risk of colon cancer in a prospective study among women. *New England Journal of Medicine, 323,* 1664–1672.

Williams, G. (1991, October–November). Flaming out on the job: How to recognize when it's all too much. *Modern Maturity*, pp. 26–29.

Williams, J. E., & Best, D. L. (1982). *Measuring sex stereotypes: A thirty-nation study*. Beverly Hills, CA: Sage.

Williams, R. B., Barefoot, J. C., & Shekelle, R. B. (1984). The health consequences of hostility. In M. A. Chesney, S. E. Goldston, & R. H. Rosenman (Eds.), *Anger: Hostility and behavior medicine*. New York: Hemisphere/McGraw-Hill.

Williams, S. A., Denney, N. W., & Schadler, M. (1983). Elderly adults' perception of their own cognitive development during the adult years. *International Journal of Aging and Human Development, 16,* 147–158.

Williams, T. F. (1992). Aging versus disease: Which changes seen with age are the result of "biological aging"? *Generations, 16*(4), 21–25.

Williamson, D. F., Kahn, H. S., Remington, P. L., & Anda, R. F. (1990). The 10-year incidence of overweight and major weight gain in U.S. adults. *Archives of Internal Medicine, 150,* 665–672.

Willis, S. L. (1985). Towards an educational psychology of the older learner: Intellectual and cognitive bases. In J. E. Birren & K. W. Schaie, (Eds.), *Handbook of the psychology of aging* (2d ed., pp. 818–847). New York: Van Nostrand Reinhold.

Willis, S. L. (1990). Current issues in cognitive training research. In E. A. Lovelace (Ed.), *Aging and cognition: Mental processes, self-awareness, and intervention* (pp. 263–280). Amsterdam: North-Holland, Elsevier.

Willis, S. L., & Baltes, P. B. (1980). Intelligence in adulthood and aging: Contemporary issues. In L. W. Poon et al. (Eds.), *Aging in the 1980s* (pp. 260–272). Washington, DC: American Psychological Association.

Willis, S. L., Blieszner, R., & Baltes, P. B. (1981). Intellectual training research in aging: Modification of performance on the fluid ability of figural relations. *Journal of Educational Psychology, 73,* 41–50.

Willis, S. L., Jay, G. M., Diehl, M., & Marsiske, M. (1992). Longitudinal change and prediction of everyday task competence in the elderly. *Research on Aging, 14,* 68–91.

Willis, S. L., & Nesselroade, C. S. (1990). Long-term effects of fluid ability training in old-old age. *Developmental Psychology, 26,* 905–910.

Willis, S. L., & Schaie, K. W. (1986). Training the elderly on the ability factors of spatial orientation and inductive reasoning. *Psychology and Aging, 2,* 239–247.

Wilson, R. C. (1956). The program for gifted children in Portland, Oregon, schools. In C. W. Taylor (Ed.), *The 1955 University of Utah research conference on the identification of creative scientific talent* (pp. 14–22). Salt Lake City: University of Utah Press.

Wilson, W. J. (1987). *The truly disadvantaged: The inner city, the underclass, and public policy*. Chicago: University of Chicago Press.

Wingfield, A., & Stine, E. A. L. (1989). Modeling memory processes: Research and theory on memory and aging. In G. C. Gilmore, P. J. Whitehouse, & M. L. Wykle (Eds.), *Memory, aging, and dementia: Theory, assessment, and treatment* (pp. 4–40). New York: Springer.

Wink, P. (1991). Self- and object-directedness in adult women. *Journal of Personality, 59,* 769–791.

Wink, P. (1992). Three types of narcissism in women from college to midlife. *Journal of Personality, 60,* 7–30.

Wink, P., & Helson, R. (1993). Personality change in women and their partners. *Journal of Personality and Social Psychology, 65,* 597–606.

Winsborough, H. H., Bumpass, L. L., & Aquilino, W. S. (1991). *The death of parents and the transition to old age.* Paper presented at the annual meeting of the Population Association of America, Washington, DC.

Witteman, P. A. (1993, February 15). A man of fire and grace: Arthur Ashe, 1943–1993. *Time,* p. 70.

Wolf, M. (1968). *The house of Lim.* Englewood Cliffs, NJ: Prentice-Hall.

Wolfe, D. A. (1985). Child-abusive parents: An empirical review and analysis. *Psychological Bulletin, 97*(3), 462–482.

Wolinsky, F. D., & Johnson, R. J. (1992a). Perceived health status and mortality among older men and women. *Journal of Gerontology: Social Sciences, 47*(6), S304–312.

Wolinsky, F. D., & Johnson, R. J. (1992b). Widowhood, health status, and the use of health services by older adults: A cross-sectional and prospective approach. *Journal of Gerontology: Social Sciences, 47*(1), S8–16.

Wolinsky, H. (1994, March 27). Hope for prostate problems: More than half of men over 60 will face them. *Chicago Sun-Times,* pp. 55, 59.

Wong, P. T. P., & Watt, L. M. (1991). What types of reminiscences are associated with successful aging? *Psychology and Aging, 6*(2), 272–279.

Woodruff, D. S. (1985). Arousal, sleep and aging. In J. E. Birren & K. W. Schaie (Eds.), *Handbook of the psychology of aging* (2d ed., pp. 261–295). New York: Van Nostrand Reinhold.

Woodruff-Pak, D. S. (1987). Sleep apnea. In G. L. Maddox (Ed.), *The encyclopedia of aging* (pp. 614–615). New York: Springer.

Woodruff-Pak, D. S. (1990). Mammalian models of learning, memory, and aging. In J. E. Birren & K. W. Schaie (Eds.), *Handbook of the psychology of aging* (3d ed., pp. 234–257). San Diego: Academic.

Woodruff-Pak, D. S., & Jaeger, M. (in preparation). Declarative and nondeclarative learning and memory across the adult age life span.

Woodward, C. V. (1989, February 20). The noble dream: The "objectivity question" and the American historical profession. *The New Republic,* p. 40.

Wooten, J. (1995, January 29). The conciliator. *New York Times Magazine,* pp. 28–33.

Working Women Education Fund. (1981). *Health hazards for office workers.* Cleveland: Author.

World Health Organization. (1991). *World health statistics annual, 1990.* Geneva: Author.

Worldwatch Institute. (1994). *Vital signs.* New York: Norton.

Worobey, J. L, & Angel, R. J. (1990). Functional capacity and living arrangements of unmarried persons. *Journal of Gerontology: Social Sciences, 45,* S95–101.

Wortman, C. B., & Silver, R. C. (1989). The myths of coping with loss. *Journal of Consulting and Clinical Psychology, 57*(3), 349–357.

Wright, G. C., & Stetson, D. M. (1978). The impact of no-fault divorce law reform on divorce in American states. *Journal of Marriage and the Family, 40,* 575–585.

The Writing Group for the PEPI Trial. (1995). Effects of estrogen or estrogen/progestin regimens on heart disease risk factors in post-menopausal women. *Journal of the American Medical Association, 273,* 199–208.

Wurtman, R. J., & Wurtman, J. J. (1989). Carbohydrates and depression. *Scientific American, 260*(1), 68–75.

Wykle, M. L., & Musil, C. M. (1993). Mental health of older persons: Social and cultural factors. *Generations, 17*(1), 7–12.

Wykle, M. L., Segal, N., & Nagley, S. (1992). Mental health and aging: Hospital care—a nursing perspective. In J. E. Birren, R. B. Sloan, & G. Cohen (Eds.), *Handbook of mental health and aging* (pp. 815–831). San Diego: Academic.

Yllo, K. (1984). The status of women, marital equality, and violence against women: A contextual analysis. *Journal of Family Issues, 5,* 307–320.

Yllo, K., & Straus, M. A. (1981). Interpersonal violence among married and cohabiting couples. *Family Relations, 30,* 339–347.

Zandri, E., & Charness, N. (1989). Training older and younger adults to use software. *Educational Gerontology, 15,* 615–639.

Zarate, A. O. (1994). *International mortality chartbook: Levels and trends, 1955–1991.* Hyattsville, MD: U.S. Public Health Service.

Zen Buddism. (1959). Mount Vernon, NY: Peter Pauper.

Zimmer, H. (1956). *Philosophies of India.* New York: Meridian.

Zoglin, R. (1994, February 28). Murder, they wheezed. *Time,* pp. 60–62.

Zube, M. (1982). Changing behavior and outlook of aging men and women: Implications for marriage in the middle and later years. *Family Relations, 31*(1), 147–156.

Zuckerman, M. (1994). Impulsive unsocialized sensation seeking: The biological foundation of a basic dimension of personality. In J. E. Bates & T. D. Wachs (Eds.), *Temperament: Individual differences at the interface of biology and behavior* (pp. 219–255). Washington, DC: American Psychological Association.

ADDENDA

Ashe, A., & Rampersad, A. (1993). *Days of grace: A memoir.* New York: Ballantine.

Elbert, S. E. (1984). *A hunger for home: Louisa May Alcott and "Little Women."* Philadelphia: Temple University Press.

Getlin, J. (1994, January 9). Eldrich gives novel voice to Native Americans. *Chicago Sun-Times,* p. 14.

MacDonald, R. K., (1983). *Louisa May Alcott.* Boston: Twayne.

Miller, P. H. (1983). *Theory of Developmental Psychology.* San Francisco: Freeman.

Modern Maturity (April-May, 1993). "Which living arrangement is right for you?" pp. 32–33.

World Book Yearbook 1977 (Vol 3, p. 53). Chicago: World Book.

ACKNOWLEDGMENTS

Figure 1-1: From *The Development of Children* by Cole and Cole. Copyright © 1989 by Michael Cole, Sheila R. Cole, and Judith Boies. Used with permission of W. H. Freeman and Company.

Figure 1-2: American Association of Retired Persons, 1994. From *A Profile of Older Americans: 1993.* Reprinted with permission.

Figure 1-4: Schick & Schick, from *Statistical Handbook of Aging Americans*, 1994. Reprinted by permission of Oryx Press.

Table 1-1: Baltes, adapted from "Theoretical propositions of life-span development psychology: On the dynamics between growth and decline," *Developmental Psychology*, Vol. 23, pp. 611–626. Copyright © 1987 by the American Psychological Association. Adapted with permission.

Table 1-2: From *Human Development*, Sixth Edition, by Diane Papalia and Sally Olds. Copyright © 1995. Reprinted by permission of McGraw-Hill, Inc.

Figure 2-1: From *Life-Span Developmental Psychology: Introduction to Research Methods* by P. B. Baltes, H. W. Reese, and J. R. Nesselroade. Copyright © 1977 Brooks/Cole Publishing Company, a division of International Thomson Publishing Inc. Reprinted by permission of the publisher.

Table 2-3: From *Human Development*, Sixth Edition, by Diana Papalia and Sally Olds. Copyright © 1995. Reprinted by permission of McGraw-Hill, Inc.

Figure 3-1: Adapted from *Fifty: Midlife in Perspective* by Katchadourian. Copyright © 1987 by Herant Katchadourian. Used with permission of W. H. Freeman and Company.

Figure 3-2: From *Fifty: Midlife in Perspective* by Katchadourian. Copyright © 1987 by Herant Katchadourian. Used with permission of W. H. Freeman and Company.

Figure 3-4: Donn, from "The eyes," from *Columbia University College of Physicians and Surgeons Complete Home Medical Guide* edited by D. F. Tapley, R. J. Weiss, T. Q. Morris, G. J. Subak-Sharpe, and D. M. Goetz. Copyright © 1989 by The Trustees of Columbia University in the City of New York and The College of Physicians and Surgeons of Columbia University. Reprinted by permission of Crown Publishing Group.

Figure 4-2: From *Fifty: Midlife in Perspective* by Katchadourian. Copyright © 1987 by Herant Katchadourian. Used with permission of W. H. Freeman and Company.

Figure 4-4: Sen, from "The economics of life and death," *Scientific American*, Vol. 268, p. 45. Copyright © 1993 by Scientific American, Inc. All rights reserved.

Table 4-1: Adapted from *Is It Alzheimer's? Warning Signs You Should Know.* Chicago: Alzheimer's Association, 1993.

Table 4-2: From *Wellness: Healthful Aging* by James D. Porterfield and Richard St. Pierre. Copyright © 1992, The Dushkin Publishing Group/Brown & Benchmark Publishers, a Times Mirror Higher Education Group, Inc., Company, Guilford, CT. All rights reserved. Reprinted by permission.

Table 4-3: Reprinted with permission from the *Journal of Psychosomatic Research*, Vol. 11, T. H. Holmes and R. H. Rahe, "Social Readjustment Rating Scale," 1967, Elsevier Science Ltd., Pergamon Imprint, Oxford, England.

Figure 5-1: Lovelace, adapted from "Basic concepts in cognition and aging," *Aging and Cognition: Mental Processes, Self Awareness, and Interventions*, Elsevier Science Publishing, 1990. Reprinted with permission.

Figure 5-2: Nickerson & Adams, 1979. From "Long-term memory for a common object," *Cognitive Psychology*, Vol. 11, pp. 287–307. Reprinted by permission of Academic Press.

Figure 5-3: Adapted from *The Dragons of Eden: Speculations on the Evolution of Human Intelligence* by Carl Sagan, after Hans-Lucas Teuber, Random House, 1977. Reprinted by permission of Dr. Carl Sagan.

Table 5-3: From *Experimental Aging Research*, Vol. 19, pp. 177–290, C. J. Camp, J. W. Foss, A. B. Stevens, C. C. Reichard, L. A. McKitrick, and A. M. O'Hanlon, "Memory training in normal and demented populations: The E-I-E-I-O model," Taylor & Francis, Inc., 1101 Vermont Ave., N.W., Ste. 200, Washington, D.C. 20005. Reproduced with permission. All rights reserved.

Figures 6-1 and 6-2: From *Understanding Psychology*, Third Edition, by R. S. Feldman. Copyright © 1993. Reprinted by permission of McGraw-Hill, Inc.

Figure 6-3: From *Aging and Behavior*, 3d Edition, by J. Botwinick. Copyright © 1984. Springer Publishing Company, Inc., New York 10012. Used by permission.

Figure 6-4: Raven, 1983. From *Raven Progressive Matrices Test* by J. C. Raven. Reprinted by permission of J. C. Raven Ltd.

Table 6-1: Schaie, from "The Hazards of Cognitive Aging," *The Gerontologist*, Vol. 29, pp. 484–493, 1989. Copyright © The Gerontological Society of America.

Table 6-2: Reprinted by permission of Transaction Publishers. "Creativity and intelligence in children's thinking," by M. A. Wallach and N. Kogan, *Transaction*, Vol. 4, 1967. Copyright © 1967; all rights reserved.

Figure 7-1: Schaie, from "Toward a stage theory of adult cognitive development," *International Journal of Aging and Human Development*, Vol. 8, 1977–1978, pp. 129–138. Copyright © 1977–1978. Reprinted by permission of Baywood Publishing Company, Inc.

Figure 7-2: Baltes, from "The aging mind: Potential and limits," *The Gerontologist*, Vol. 33, pp. 580–594, 1993. Copyright © The Gerontological Society of America.

Table 7-1: Sternberg, from "Wisdom and its relation to intelligence and creativity," *Wisdom: Its Nature, Origins, and Development*, 1990, pp. 142–159. Reprinted with the permission of Cambridge University Press.

Table 7-2: Kohlberg, from "Stage and sequence: The cognitive-developmental approach to socialization," in *Handbook of Socialization Theory and Research*, by David A. Goslin, Rand McNally, 1969. Reprinted by permission of David A. Goslin.
From *Higher Stages of Human Development* by C. N. Alexander and E. J. Langer, Oxford University Press, 1990, pp. 191–207.

Chapter 8, opening quotation: From "My Portrait," *The Frugal Chariot* by Rita Duskin, Wing Press, 1970.

Figure 8-1: Riley, from "Aging and society: Past, present, and future," *The Gerontologist*, Vol. 33, pp. 436–444, 1994. Copyright © 1944 The Gerontological Society of America.

Figure 8-2: From *Motivation and Achievement*, J. N. Atkinson and J. O. Raynor, "Raynor's model of career paths," Taylor & Francis, Inc., 1101 Vermont Ave., N.W., Ste. 200, Washington, D.C. 20005. Reproduced with permission. All rights reserved.

Figure 8-2: Raynor & Rubin, from "Effects of achievement motivation and future orientation on level of performance," *Journal of Personality and Social Psychology*, Vol. 17, 1971, pp. 36–41. Copyright © 1971 by the American Psychological Association. Reprinted with permission.

Figure 8-3: O'Grady-LeShane, from "Changes in the lives of women and their families: Have old-age pensions kept pace?" from "Progress and Prospects in Mental Health," *Generations*, Winter/Spring, Vol. 17, No. 1, 1993, pp. 27–31. Reprinted with permission from *Generations*, 833 Market St., Suite 511, San Francisco, California 94103. Copyright 1993, ASA.

Figure 8-4: From "Commonwealth Fund Commission on elderly people living alone," *Study of Elderly People in Five Countries— U.S., Canada, Germany, Britain, and Japan: Key Findings*, 1992. Reprinted by permission of Louis Harris & Associates.

Figure 8-4: Kaiser, from "The production roles of older people in developing countries: What are the implications of economic, social and cultural participation," *Generations*, Vol. 17, No. 4, 1993. Reprinted with permission from *Generations*, 833 Market St., Suite 511, San Francisco, California 94103. Copyright 1993, ASA.

Figure 8-5: American Association of Retired Persons, 1993. From "A Profile of Older Americans: 1993." Reprinted with permission.

Table 8-1: From Working Women Education Fund, 1981, p. 9. Reprinted by permission of National Association for Working Women.

Figure 9-1: From *The Social Organization of Sexuality*, by E. O. Laumann, J. Gagnon, R. T. Michael, and S. Michaels. Copyright © 1994. Reprinted by permission of The University of Chicago Press.

Figures 9-2 and 9-4: Reprinted with the permission of the Population Council from Judith Bruce, Cynthia B. Lloyd, and Ann Leonard, *Families in Focus: New Perspectives on Mothers, Fathers, and Children*, p. 20 and p. 73.

Table 9-1: From "A Triangular Theory of Love." Paper presented at the annual meeting of the American Psychological Association, Los Angeles, 1985. Reprinted by permission of R. J. Sternberg.

Table 9-3: White, from "Determinants of divorce: A review of research in the eighties," *Journal of Marriage and the Family*, Vol. 52, 1990, pp. 904–912. Schoen, from "First unions and the stability of first marriages," *Journal of Marriage and the Family*, Vol. 54, 1992, pp. 281–284. Copyright 1990 and 1992 by the National Council on Family Relations, 3989 Central Ave. NE, Suite 550, Minneapolis, MN 55421. Reprinted by permission.

Figure 10-1: From *The New American Grandparent* by A. Cherlin and F. F. Furstenberg, Jr., Basic Books, 1986, p. 74. Reprinted by permission of the authors.

Figure 10-2: Schick & Schick, from *Statistical Handbook of Aging Americans*, 1994. Reprinted by permission of Oryx Press.

Figure 10-3: American Association of Retired Persons, 1993. From *A Profile of Older Americans: 1993*. Reprinted with permission.

Figure 10-4: Nishio, from "Japan's welfare vision: Dealing with a rapidly increasing elderly population," in *The Graying of the World: Who Will Care for the Frail Elderly?* edited by L. K. Olson, 1994, pp. 233–260. Reprinted by permission of The Haworth Press, Binghamton, New York.

Table 10-1: Hamon & Blieszner, from "Filial responsibility expectations among adult child-older parent pairs," *Journal of Gerontology*, Vol. 45, P110–P112, 1990. Copyright © The Gerontological Society of America.

Table 10-2: American Association of Retired Persons, from "Which living arrangement is for you?" *Modern Maturity*, April–May, 1993, pp. 32–33.

Table 10-3: "The Caregivers," from "Juggling Family, Job, and Aged Dependent," *The New York Times*, January 26, 1989, p. B8. Copyright © 1989 by The New York Times Company. Reprinted by permission.

Figure 11-1: Helson & Moane, from "Personality change in women from college to midlife," *Journal of Personality and Social Psychology,* Vol. 53, 1987, pp. 176–186. Copyright 1987 by the American Psychological Association. Reprinted with permission.

Figure 11-2: Costa & McCrae, from "Personality in adulthood: A six-year longitudinal study of self-reports and spouse ratings on the NEO Personality Inventory," *Journal of Personality and Social Psychology,* Vol. 54, 1988, pp. 853–863. Copyright © 1988 by the American Psychological Association. Reprinted with permission.

Figure 11-5: Helson, from "Comparing longitudinal studies of adult development: Toward a paradigm of tension between stability and change," in *Studying Lives Through Time: Personality and Development,* edited by D. C. Funder, R. D. Parke, C. Tomlinson-Keasey, and K. Widaman, 1993, pp. 93–120. Copyright © 1993 by the American Psychological Association. Reprinted with permission.

Table 11-2: Helson & Wink, from "Personality change in women from the early 40s to the early 50s," *Psychology and Aging,* Vol. 7, 1992, pp. 46–55. Copyright © 1992 by the American Psychological Association. Reprinted with permission.

Figure 12-1: Lawton & Nahemow, from "Ecology and the aging process," in *The Psychology of Adult Development and Aging,* edited by C. Eisdorfer and M. P. Lawton, 1973, p. 661. Copyright © 1973 by the American Psychological Association. Reprinted with permission.

Table 12-1: Koenig, George, & Siegler, from "The use of religion and other emotion-regulating coping strategies among older adults," *The Gerontologist,* Vol. 28, pp. 303–310, 1988. Copyright © The Gerontological Society of America.

Table 12-2: Atkinson, Ganzini, & Bernstein, from "Alcohol and substance-use disorders in the elderly," in *Handbook of Mental Health and Aging,* Second Edition, edited by J. E. Birren, R. Sloane, and G. D. Cohen, 1992, pp. 515–555. Reprinted by permission of Academic Press.

Table 12-3: Pratt, Wilson, Benthin, & Schmall, adapted from "Alcohol problems and depression in later life: Development of two knowledge quizzes," *The Gerontologist,* Vol. 32, pp. 175–183, 1992. Copyright © The Gerontological Society of America.

Table 12-4: Adapted from *Diagnosis and Treatment Guidelines on Abuse and Neglect.* Copyright 1992, American Medical Association.

Table 12-5: Belsky, from *Aging in the Eighties: America in Transition,* Louis Harris and Associates, Inc., 1981, p. 17. Copyright by and reprinted with permission of The National Council on the Aging, Inc., 409 Third Street SW, Washington, DC 20024.

Table 12-6: Kivnick, adapted from "Everyday mental health: A guide to assessing life strengths," *Generations,* Vol. 17, 1993. Reprinted from *Generations,* 833 Market St., Suite 511, San Francisco, CA 94103. Copyright 1993, ASA.

Figure 13-1: Siegler, McCarty, & Logue, from "Wechsler Memory Scale scores, selective attribution, and distance from death," *Journal of Gerontology,* Vol. 37, pp. 176–181, 1982. Copyright © The Gerontological Society of America.

Figure 13-2: McIntosh, from "Epidemiology of suicide in the elderly," *Suicide and Life-Threatening Behavior,* Vol. 22, 1992. Reprinted by permission of Guilford Publications, Inc.

Table 13-1: Adapted with the permission of Simon & Schuster, Inc., and Tavistock Publications, from *On Death and Dying* by Elisabeth Kübler-Ross. Copyright © 1969 by Elisabeth Kübler-Ross.

Table 13-2: Reprinted with permission from *Omega,* Vol. 27, A. E. Scharlach and K. I. Fredricksen, "Reactions to the death of a parent during midlife," p. 311, 1993, Elsevier Science Ltd., Pergamon Imprint, Oxford, England.

INDEXES

NAME INDEX

AARP (*see* American Association of Retired Persons)
Abbey, A., 349
Abel, E. K., 372
Abeles, R. P., 434
Abraham, G. N., 87, 139
Abrahams, B., 434
Achenbaum, W. A., 264, 459
Adamchak, D. J., 31, 316, 317
Adams, C., 250
Adams, D., 52
Adams, R. G., 324
Adelman, M., 461
Agree, E. M., 387
Aisenberg, R., 490, 491
Akutsu, H., 96
Albert, R. S., 234
Alcott, Elizabeth, 487–488
Alcott, Louisa May, 487–488
Aldous, J. J., 365, 368
Aldwin, C. M., 313, 314, 315
Alexander, B. B., 356, 371
Alexander, C. N., 258
Alexander, R. A., 104
Alexander, V. K., 258
Alinsky, Saul, 495
Allen, Woody, 78
Allende, Isabel, 364
ALS (Amyotrophic Lateral Sclerosis) Association, 115
Altman, L. K., 134
Alzheimer, Alois, 137
Alzheimer's Association, 138
Amadiume, I., 332
Ameche, Don, 142
American Academy of Otolaryngology, 100
American Academy of Pediatrics (AAP), 349
American Association of Retired Persons (AARP), 18, 23, 25, 27, 119, 126, 128, 144, 286, 298, 306, 310, 313, 314, 365, 381, 382, 385, 388, 390, 469, 470, 471
American Cancer Society, 139, 140, 148
American Council on Science and Health, 105

American Diabetes Association, 131, 145, 146
American Health Foundation, 148
American Heart Association, 128, 129, 149
American Jewish Committee, 49, 51
American Medical Association, 471
American Psychiatric Association (APA), 105, 135, 325, 463, 465, 474, 475, 480
Amory, Mark, 159–169
Amyotrophic Lateral Sclerosis (ALS) Association, 115
Anastasi, A., 208, 230
Anda, R. F., 91
Andelman, B., 23, 308
Anders, T. R., 165
Anderson, Annie, 361–362
Anderson, J. R., 53
Anderson, John, 361–362
Anderson, Marian, 361–363, 374
Anderson, R., 513
Anderson, S. A., 353
Anderson, T. B., 508
Andreasson, L., 137
Andrews, F. M., 349
Angel, R. J., 387
Angier, N., 83, 115, 116
Anisman, H., 152
Anschutz, L., 188, 192
Ansley, J., 286
Anson, O., 147
Anthony, J. C., 137, 476
Antonucci, Toni, 315
APA (American Psychiatric Association), 105, 135, 325, 463, 465, 474, 475, 480
Apostol, R. A., 335
Aquilino, W. S., 381, 510
Arenberg, D., 165
Aristide, Jean-Bertrand, 282
Arjyal, B. P., 344
Arlin, P. K., 234, 248, 253, 256
Armitage, M., 77, 78
Arthritis Foundation, 126
Ashcraft, M. H., 169, 174
Ashe, Arthur, 445–447, 453
Askenasy, J. J., 177

Atchison, S., 23, 308
Atchley, Robert C., 258, 263, 264, 355, 365, 460, 461
Atherton, C. R., 130
Atkinson, J. N., 293
Atkinson, R., 415
Atkinson, R. M., 463, 464, 465
Attewell, P., 248
August, M., 91
Ausubel, N., 490
Avery, C. B., 366, 421
Axelson, L. J., 380, 381
Ayya, N., 134

Babchuk, N., 324
Bachrach, C. A., 350
Bachu, A., 346
Backett, K., 351
Bacon, S., 409
Baddeley, A. D., 167
Baker, B., 137
Baker-Miller, Jean, 430
Balkwell, C., 508
Ball, O. E., 229
Baltes, M. M., 221
Baltes, Paul B., 7, 8, 13, 44, 50, 100, 120, 186, 192, 210, 216, 219, 220, 221, 225, 226, 245, 258, 260, 261, 262, 263, 264
Baltimore, D., 133
Banaji, M. R., 163
Bandura, Albert, 431
Banner, C., 137, 138
Bantchevsky, Bantcho, 514, 516
Barager, J. R., 403, 404
Barbour, L. S., 467
Barchillon, J., 227
Barefoot, J. C., 129
Barfield, R. E., 313
Barinaga, M., 84
Barnes, M. L., 325
Barnett, R., 323
Barnett, R. C., 335, 352, 366, 423, 447
Barnhart, M. A., 389, 390, 391, 392, 470
Barrett, C. J., 508
Barrett, G. V., 104, 298
Barrett, R. L., 347

Barrett-Connor, E., 125
Barth, M. C., 298
Bartlett, F. C., 187, 227
Barton, P., 288
Baruch, G., 323, 423
Baruch, J. H., 366
Bassett, S. S., 137
Bates, J. E., 410
Bateson, G., 190
Bayley, N., 220
Beach, C. S., 327
Beach, L. R., 356
Beard, G. M., 236
Beard, R. J., 109
Bebbington, P., 476
Beck, S. H., 314
Becker, G. S., 339
Becker, M., 367, 368
Belbin, R. M., 96
Belkgrave, L., 472
Bell, J., 20
Belsky, J., 354, 473
Belushi, John, 463
Bem, Sandra, 430, 432
Bemon, P., 350
Bengtson, V., 324, 353, 459, 460, 495
Benjamin, M., 341
Benner, P., 245
Bennett, L., 174
Benson, M., 241, 242
Benthin, A., 466
Benzing, W. C., 174
Berardo, D. H., 334
Berg, C. A., 44
Berger, R. M., 331, 461
Bergeron, J., 248
Bergman, A. B., 469
Bergman, Ingmar, 521
Bergman, S. J., 431
Berk, R. A., 468, 470
Berkowitz, G. S., 347
Berkowitz, R. L., 347
Berlin, Irving, 236
Berman, C., 351
Bernard, J. L., 467, 468
Bernard, M. L., 467, 468
Bernhard, L. A., 108
Bernstein, Dorothy, 377
Bernstein, J., 297
Bernstein, L., 493
Bernstein, Leonard, 232
Bernstein, M. J., 463
Berra, Yogi, 172
Berrios, J., 297
Berscheid, E., 338
Best, D. L., 429
Bianchi, S. M., 333, 428
Bielby, D., 248, 267
Bienias, J. L., 192
Bigger, J. T., Jr., 128
Binet, Alfred, 203
Bingham, Wilma, 387

Binstock, R. H., 31
Bird, K., 281, 282
Biringen, Z. C., 434
Biringer, F., 53
Birren, J. E., 12, 101, 103, 135, 224
Bixby, Bill, 142
Black, F. W., 192
Blackburn, E. S., 248
Blackburn, J. A., 224, 226
Blair, S. N., 153
Blanchard-Fields, F., 249, 250, 261, 434, 455
Blanksten, G. I. 403
Blanton, P. W., 343, 354
Blasko, J. C., 142
Blazer, D. G., 324, 448, 476, 478
Blieszner, R., 139, 225, 369
Block, J., 406, 408
Bloom, B. L., 341
Bloom, D. E., 356
Blum, L., 465
Blumstein, P. W., 337
Bobbitt, Lorena, 467
Bogerts, B., 137
Bolger, N., 301
Bolles, R. N., 284
Bonfield, T., 142
Boone, Richard, 78
Booth-Kewley, S., 129
Borges, J. L., 193
Boritz, G. M., 287
Borkowski, A., 394
Bossé, R., 313, 314, 315
Botwinick, J., 63, 89, 202, 208, 209, 216, 217, 220, 224
Bouchard, G. R., 465
Boulton, M. G., 351
Bouvier, L. F., 297
Bouza, A. V., 467, 468
Bowlby, J., 417
Boyd, R., 337
Boyer, J. L., 516
Brabant, S., 368
Bragg, M., 159
Branch, L. G., 97
Brandt, B., 513
Brannan, J. R., 261
Braungart, J. M., 409
Braveman, N. S., 131
Bray, D. W., 293
Brecher, E., 111, 508
Breitner, J. C. S., 138
Bremner, W. J., 109
Brenner, Claude, 55
Brenner, M. H., 303
Brickfield, C. F., 286
Briggin, K., 222
Brigham, M. C., 188, 189
Briley, M., 302
Brim, O. G., 423
Brint, S. F., 94
Brocas, A., 340

Brock, D. W., 519, 520
Brody, E. B., 207
Brody, E. M., 386
Brody, H., 181
Brody, J. E., 124
Brody, N., 207
Brodzinsky, D. M., 350
Bronfenbrenner, Urie, 16, 205
Bronte, L., 27, 306
Brown, A. S., 175
Brown, J. T., 504, 505
Brown, K. H., 314
Brown, M. B., 313
Brown, N. M., 330, 363
Brown, P., 347, 348
Browne, A., 469
Brozan, N., 134
Brubaker, T. H., 343, 353, 372, 508
Bruce, J., 297, 337, 338, 346
Brumberg, E., 91
Buchwald, Art, 475
Bühler, Charlotte, 44
Bulcroft, K. A., 330
Bulcroft, R. A., 330
Bumpass, L., 332, 342
Bumpass, L. L., 510
Burchett, B. M., 208
Bureau of Justice Statistics, 467
Bureau of the Census, U. S. (see U. S. Bureau of the Census)
Burkhauser, R. V., 146, 311, 313
Burns, A., 337
Burns, B., 474
Burns, George, 305
Burstenberg, F. F., 372
Burton, L. M., 379
Busch, C. M., 413
Bush, Barbara, 475
Bush, T. L., 126
Busse, E. W., 89
Busse, T. V., 230
Butler, R., 522
Butler, R. N., 19, 447, 474, 499, 522, 523
Butters, N., 172, 174
Byrd, M., 164, 168

Cadwell, S., 494
Cailloux, A., 340
Cain, W. S., 100
Callahan, L. F., 146
Calment, Jeanne, 81
Camargo, C. A., 150
Camp, C. J., 109, 139, 143, 165, 170, 171, 175, 182, 188, 190, 191, 192, 193, 194, 246, 261, 328, 455
Campbell, B., 338
Campbell, F. L., 356
Campbell, J., 269
Campbell, Stuart, 64
Cantor, M. H., 324
Cargan, L., 329

Carlisle, T., 258
Carlson, E., 3, 4
Carr, C., 97
Carroll, J. B., 211
Carstensen, Laura, 316
Carter, James Earl, Jr., 281–283
Carter Center, 281
Casals, Pablo, 215
Caserta, M. S., 324
Caspi, A., 246, 409, 410, 417
Cassel, C., 28, 80, 86
Catalano, D. J., 356, 383
Catania, J. A., 329
Cattell, Raymond B., 208, 216, 219, 220, 225
Cavanaugh, J. C., 170, 190, 209
Ceci, S., 244
Census Bureau (*see* U. S. Bureau of the Census)
Center on Elderly People Living Alone, 388, 389, 390
Centers for Disease Control and Prevention (CDC), 132, 134, 143, 489, 513
Central Bureau of Statistics, 29
Chafetz, M. D., 165, 178
Chagall, Marc, 232
Chalfie, D., 379
Chambre, S. M., 311
Chandler, M. J., 257, 258
Chappell, N. L., 382, 383
Charness, S. A., 287
Chatters, L. M., 25, 456
Chaudhary, B. S., 150
Chauncey, H. H., 153
Chawla, S., 28, 32
Checkoway, B., 32
Chen, M. D., 510
Cherlin, A., 372, 373, 374, 375, 376, 377
Chernow-O'Leary, R., 467, 469
Cherry, K. E., 168
Cherubin, C. F., 465
Chess, S., 409
Child, Julia, 306
Child Welfare League of America, 469
Chinen, A. B., 258
Chiriboga, D., 341, 370, 423, 432
Chissell, J. T., 145
Chumlea, W. C., 90, 332
Cicirelli, V. G., 365, 370, 371, 392, 393
Clark, L. F., 325
Clark, Paul, 26
Clarke, C. J., 385
Clausen, John A., 64, 406
Clayton, Vivian, 260, 261
Cleiren, M. P., 371
Clemens, A. W., 380, 381
Clements, M., 343
Cm. 849, 395

CNN (*Time*-CNN poll), 347
Cobleigh, M. A., 125
Cochran, W. G., 48
Cohen, G., 170
Cohen, N. L., 95
Cohn, E. G., 468
Coke, M. M., 456
Colby, Anne, 269, 273, 274
Colditz, G. A., 126, 152
Cole, M., 16, 184, 185, 187
Cole, S. R., 16
Colella, U., 332
Coles, R., 37
Collins, J. E., 325
Collinsworth, P., 372
Colliver, J., 465
Comeaux, J. M., 194
Commonwealth Fund, 31, 306, 385
Congress, U. S., 289, 298
Connidis, I. A., 370, 371
Consumer Reports Books, Editors of, 111, 508
Conway, M. A., 163
Cook, E. W., 499
Cooney, T., 337
Cooper, K. L., 352, 432
Coplan, A., 497
Coppola, Francis Ford, 200
Coreil, J., 146
Cornelius, S. W., 246
Correa, P., 148
Costa, Paul T., Jr., 6, 406, 410, 411, 412, 413, 415, 422, 432, 422, 440
Council of Europe, 346
Council on Scientific Affairs of the American Medical Association, 146
Coward, R. T., 366
Cowell, A., 345
Coyne, J. C., 56
Craik, F. I. M., 164, 166, 167, 168, 169, 181, 184, 185, 188
Cramer, D., 347
Crapo, L. M., 123
Creasman, W. T., 126
Crick, Francis, 234
Crisp, A. H., 150
Cristofalo, V. J., 86, 87
Cross, S., 417
Crowder, R. G., 163
Crowley, S. L., 3, 4, 107, 125, 142, 379, 380
Crown, W. H., 31, 316, 317
Crutchfield, R., 473
Crutchfield, R. S., 227
Csikszentmihalyi, Mihaly, 234, 264, 425
Cuellar, J. A., 495
Cumming, E., 459
Cunningham, W. R., 12, 496
Cupp, P., 152

Cutrona, C., 324
Cvetanovski, J., 303
Cytrynbaum, S., 432

Dahlstrom, W. G., 129
Dainoff, M., 510
Dalton, M. J., 370
D'Amato, R. J., 97
Damon, William, 273, 274
Dan, A. J., 108
Daniels, D., 409
Darley, J., 417
Darwin, Charles, 231, 232, 233
Datan, N., 285
Davidson, G. P., 341
Davies, B., 395
Davies, L., 371
Davies, M., 464
Davis, 423
Davis, Bette, 78
Davis, D. W., 248
Davis, K. E., 323
Davis, K. L., 138, 139
Davis-Friedmann, D., 309
Dawson, J. M., 469
Dawson-Hughes, B., 124
Day, J. C., 24
Day, P., 406
DeAngelis, T., 325
DeCarlo, D., 301
DeFigueiredo, J. M., 138
DeFries, J. C., 409
Degas, Edgar, 97
Deimling, G., 473
de Klerk, F. W., 242
de Lafuente, D., 349
Delany, Elizabeth, 370, 371
Delany, Sarah, 370, 371
de la Rochefordiere, A., 141
Dellman, J., 248
DeLongis, A., 301
Demarque, A., 100
DeMille, A., 77
Dennis, W., 236
Denney, N. W., 202, 245, 246, 247
Denti, E., 295
DePriest, James, 362
Deschner, J., 468
Detterman, D. K., 201
DeVoe, M., 249, 250
de Vos, S., 364
Dickens, Charles, 521
Diehl, M., 226
Diekstra, R. F., 371
Dien, D. S. F., 269, 270
DiGiulio, J. F., 508, 509
Dittmann-Kohli, F., 210, 219, 258, 261
Dixon, Roger A., 172, 188, 189, 219, 226
Dobbs, A. R., 171, 185
Doherty, K., 246
Doherty, W. J., 147

Doka, K. J., 378
Donaldson, G., 216, 218, 219
Donn, A., 95
Dorris, Michael, 321, 322, 323, 325, 463
Downey, A. M., 109, 143, 328
Downs, Hugh, 474
Draper, Patricia, 14
Dreyfus, H. L., 245
Drinka, P., 103
Drugan, R. C., 152
D'Souza, M. F., 150
Dube, E. F., 185, 187
Dubin, R., 304
Du Bois, B. C., 465, 476
Dudley, W., 164
Duffy, M., 77
Dufour, M., 465
Duncan, G. J., 340
Durlak, J. A., 522
Duskin, Rita, 495
Dustman, R. E., 104
Dustman, T. J., 104
Dutta, R., 222
Dwyer, J. W., 366
Dychtwald, Ken, 22, 32

Earles, James A., 212, 213
Eastman, P., 100, 142
Eaves, L. J., 409, 410
Edelstein, S., 376
Edison, Thomas Alva, 236
Edlin, B. R., 134
Edson, L., 234
Education, U. S. Department of, 284, 286
Edwards, A. J., 137
Edwards, C. P., 269
Edwards, J. N., 352
EEOC (Equal Employment Opportunity Commission), 298, 302
Eichorn, D. H., 406
Einstein, Albert, 168, 215, 234
Einstein, G., 185
Eisenberg, L., 295, 297, 322, 332, 335, 338, 343, 345, 346
Ekerdt, D. J., 311, 314
Elbert, S. E., 487
Elder, G. H., 311
Eley, J. W., 145
Elias, M. F., 287
Elias, P. K., 287
Eliot, T. S., 215
Elkind, D., 494
Emde, R. N., 409
Emery, V. O. B., 479, 480
Emmerson, R. Y., 104
Energy, U. S. Department of, 117
Epstein, E., 325
Epstein, R. A., 520
Epstein, S., 417

Epstein, W., 193
Equal Employment Opportunity Commission (EEOC), 298, 302
Erber, J. T., 286
Erdrich, Louise, 321, 322, 323, 325
Erikson, Erik H., 3, 37, 42, 43, 54, 259, 290, 323, 378, 418, 419–422, 425, 432, 455, 460–461, 462, 495, 481, 521, 522
Erikson, J. M., 419
Ershler, W. B., 139
Esper, P. S., 142
Esptein, S., 417
Essex, M. J., 324, 330
Estés, C. P., 258
Evans, D. A., 137
Evans, J., 392, 393
Evans-Pritchard, E. E., 327
Eveleth, P. B., 90, 332
Ewis, D., 100
Exton-Smith, A. N., 124
Eysenck, D. H., 409

Fackelmann, K. A., 140, 141
Falk, R. F., 365
Farlow, M., 139
Farrell, C., 23, 308
Farrell, M. P., 310, 423
Farrer, L. A., 138
Faulkner, D., 170
Fazio, R. H., 417
Feaster, D., 313
Feazell, C. S., 468
Feldman, Ruth Duskin, 55, 193, 288, 377
Feldman, R. S., 153, 205, 206
Feldman, S. S., 434
Fellin, P. A., 474
Felson, D. T., 125
Ferrante, L. S., 174
Ferrel, C., 456
Ferstenberg, R. L., 341
Fiatarone, M. A., 103
Field, D., 324, 353, 365, 368, 371, 374, 413, 508
Fielding, J. E., 148
Fillenbaum, G. G., 208, 314
Finch, C. E., 138
Finkelhor, D., 468, 469, 470, 471
Finn, R., 445
Fiore, M. C., 149
Fischbach, R. L., 476
Fisher, B., 142
Fisher, C., 139
Fisher, G., 146
Fisher, L., 391
Fitzgerald, Ella, 232
Fitzpatrick, K. M., 386
Fleece, A. M., 189
Flores, J., 403, 405
Flower, J., 22, 32

Floyd, F. J., 343
Flynn, E., 97
Fogelman, C. J., 465
Folkman, J., 97
Folkman, R., 455
Folkman, S., 452, 453, 455
Folstein, M. F., 137
Fontham, E., 148
Ford, F. A., 327
Foreman, J., 223, 224
Forsyth, S., 374
Foster, D., 321
Fowble, B. L., 142
Fowler, James, 268
Fowles, R., 303
Foy, K., 341
Foye, B. F., 226
Fozard, J. L., 165
Frank, S. J., 366, 421
Franks, P., 153
Fredriksen, K. I., 390, 495, 510, 511, 512
Freedmen-Letofky, K., 508
Freeman, H. P., 145
Freeman, S., 508
Freeman, S. M., 87, 139, 140
Freud, Sigmund, 5, 38, 42, 43, 54, 56, 230, 231, 233, 234, 327, 419, 472
Friedan, Betty, 3–4, 8, 20, 77, 78
Friedman, H. S., 129
Friedmann, E. A., 316, 317
Friend, T., 137
Fries, J. F., 123
Friesen, I. C., 172
Frieze, I. H., 430
Fritch, J. H., 138
Fulker, D. W., 409
Fulton, R., 489
Funder, D. C., 408
Furstenberg, F. F., 372, 373, 374, 375, 376, 377
Furukawa, S., 343

Gage, P., 287
Gagné, J. P., 95
Gagnon, J., 327, 328
Gallagher, D., 504
Gallo, J. J., 476
Gallup, G., 498
Gallup, G. H., 22
Gallup Organization, 22
Gandhi, Mohandas K. (Mahatma), 38, 274–276
Ganzini, L., 463
Gárcia Márquez, Gabriel, 364
Gardner, Howard, 211, 214, 215, 230, 231, 232
Gardner, J., 344
Garfein, A. J., 287
Garfinkel, I., 339, 340
Garwick, A. W., 139, 391
Gass, K. A., 324

Gatz, M., 472
Gavazzi, S. M., 349
Gaziano, M., 150
Gehrig, Lou, 115
Gelfand, D. E., 25
Geller, J. A., 467, 468
Gelles, R. J., 468
Genevay, B., 324
George, L. K., 208, 314, 449, 456, 476
Gergen, K. J., 503
Gergen, M. M., 503
Gerhard, G. S., 86, 87
Getlin, J., 321
Getzels, Jacob W., 229, 234, 425
Geyer, Georgie Ann, 191
Giambra, L. M., 165
Gibbs, J., 269
Gibson, R. C., 25
Gielen, U., 270
Gilbert, L. A., 334, 335
Gilford, R., 353, 354, 355
Gilliand, P., 343, 346
Gilligan, Carol, 271–273, 425
Ginzberg, Eli, 292–293
Giovannucci, E., 142
Gist, G., 287
Gladue, B., 327
Glantz, S. A., 149
Glaser, Ariel, 513
Glaser, Elizabeth, 133, 513
Glaser, Paul Michael, 513
Glasheen, L. K., 387
Glass, R. B., 347
Glenn, N. D., 324, 333, 353
Glick, J., 17
Glick, P. C., 203, 329, 351, 380, 509
Glynn, R. J., 465
Gold, P. E., 177
Goldberg, J. D., 150
Golden, D., 226
Golding, William, 232
Goldman, L., 125
Goldman, L. L., 517
Goldman, N., 147
Goldsteen, K., 147, 334
Goldstein, M. D., 171, 184
Gonyea, J. G., 386, 387
Goodman, M., 356, 371
Goodrich, C., 241
Goodwin, J., 199, 200
Goossens, L., 192
Gordon, A., 490, 491
Gorman, M., 363, 379, 396
Gottman, J. M., 343
Goya, Francisco de, 284
Graham, Martha, 77, 78
Grajek, S., 325
Granger, D., 159
Grant, B. S., 465
Gratton, B., 472
Greenberg, J., 367, 368
Greenwald, A. G., 417

Greist, J. H., 476, 477
Greyson, B., 498, 499
Gribbin, K., 222
Grigson, B., 465
Grimm, P. D., 142
Griswold, D., 372
Gruber, A., 222, 353
Gruber, Howard, 231, 232, 233
Gruber-Baldini, A. L., 222
Gruenfeld, D., 301
Gruson, L., 118
Guemple, L., 518
Gui, S. X., 309
Guibert-Lamoine, C. de, 338
Guilford, Joy P., 211, 227, 229, 230
Guralnik, J. M., 26, 79
Guthrie, L., 516
Gutmann, David L., 247, 352, 432, 433, 434–435, 437, 459
Gutmann, R., 325
Guyre, P., 151

Haan, N., 406, 423
Haas, A. D., 284, 285
Hadden, N., 146
Haenszel, W., 148
Hagestad, G. O., 365, 376, 429
Hakim-Larson, J., 247, 248, 249, 250, 455
Halamandaris, V., 388
Haley, Alex, 503–504
Hall, C., 37
Hall, G. Stanley, 6, 7, 264
Hall, J. L., 177
Halman, J., 349
Hammer, Armand, 306
Hammond, C. B., 126
Hamon, R. R., 369
Handy, C., 295
Hankinson, S. E., 96, 97
Hanley, R., 349
Hanser, S. B., 478
Hanson, L., 524
Hare, P. H., 386, 387
Harel, Z., 473
Hargrove, J., 241
Haring, M. J., 460
Harkins, E., 353
Harpending, Henry, 14
Harper, S., 391
Harris, L. B., 509
Harris, S., 152
Harrison, M., 105
Hartley, A. A., 287
Hartley, J. T., 287
Hasher, L., 184
Haske, M., 387
Hassan, R., 95
Haug, M., 472
Hauser, W. L., 145
Haven, C., 324
Havighurst, R., 459–460

Hawking, Stephen, 115, 116, 117
Hayden, M., 250
Hayflick, Leonard, 81, 86
Hayghe, H., 295
Hayward, M. D., 309
Hazlitt, William, 401
Health and Human Services, U.S. Department of (see U. S. Department of Health and Human Services)
Health Care Finance Administration, 383
Healy, B., 129
Healy, J., 508
Hearth, A. H., 370
Heckhausen, J., 415, 416
Hefner, R., 431
Heindel, W. C., 172, 174, 181
Heller, R. B., 171
Heller, Z. I., 490, 491
Helson, Ravenna, 352, 408, 413, 418, 419, 422, 432, 435, 436, 437, 438, 439, 440
Henderson, V. W., 125, 138
Hendricks, J., 422
Henker, F. O., 109
Hennekens, C. H., 150
Henrich, J. B., 126
Henry, W., 459
Herdt, G., 327
Herman, W. K., 94
Herrnstein, R. J., 207, 208
Hertzog, C., 188, 189, 208, 220, 222, 434
Herzog, A. R., 314
Hill, C. D., 504
Hishio, H. K., 29
Hjelle, L. A., 406, 408
Hobart, C. J., 455
Hochanadel, G. A., 224
Hoffman, S. D., 340
Holbrook, N., 151
Holden, A., 159
Holden, K. C., 313
Holland, John, 290
Holland, M. J., 101
Holliday, S. G., 257, 258
Holmes, D. S., 153
Holmes, T. H., 150, 151, 449
Honigmann, J. J., 414
Honzik, M. P., 406
Hooker, K., 355, 472
Hooyman, N. R., 471
Hope, Bob, 91
Horn, John L., 89, 171, 180, 208, 216, 217, 218, 219, 220, 225
Horn, M. C., 327
Horowitz, A., 97
Horowitz, Vladimir, 172, 221, 222
Horton, A. M., 465
House, J. S., 314
House, S. J., 147, 323

Howard, A., 293
Howard, D. V., 192
Howard, K. I., 415
Hoyer, William J., 243, 244, 286, 287
Hu, Y., 147
Hudson, R. B., 386
Hudson, Rock, 132
Hughes, F., 285
Hull, R. H., 100
Hultsch, David F., 165, 188
Hunt, B., 143
Hunt, M., 143
Hurd, M. D., 27, 314
Hurley, D., 71
Huston, T. L., 354
Hutchinson, C., 355
Huyck, M. H., 429, 430, 432
Hyde, J. S., 327, 433
Hyson, R. L., 152

Ickovics, J. R., 329
Illinois Task Force, 340
Infeld, L., 234
Irion, J., 455
Irons, R. R., 463, 465
Irving, Amy, 339
Irving, H. H., 341
Ivy, G. O., 180
Izumi, Shirechiyo, 81

Jackson, P. W., 229
Jackson, S. E., 302
Jacobson, N. S., 147
Jacques, Elliott, 422
Jaeger, M., 174
Jaffe, I. M. D., 123
Jahnke, H. C., 455
Jahoda, M., 448
Jallinoja, J., 295
James, J., 174
James, William, 194
Janowsky, J. S., 181
Japanese Social Welfare Association, 396
Jaroff, L., 90, 116
Jaschob, K., 103
Javits, Jacob K., 115
Jay, G. M., 226, 287
Jefferson, J. W., 476, 477
Jefferson, Thomas, 502
Jelovsek, F. R., 126
Jendrek, M. P., 380
Jenkins, L., 288
Jennings, J. M., 164, 166, 167, 168, 169, 184, 185, 188
Jensen, A. R., 207, 211, 213
Jet, 361
Jex, S., 303
Johnson, Albert, 378
Johnson, B. T., 20
Johnson, C. L., 324, 356, 363, 383
Johnson, Earvin ("Magic"), 132

Johnson, F. L., 474
Johnson, J. R., 509
Johnson, L., 251, 252
Johnson, Mary Etta, 378
Johnson, P. B., 430
Johnson, R. J., 388
Johnson, S. A., 287
Johnson, S. J., 103
Johnson, Samuel, 342
Johnson, T. E., 83
Johnson, Virginia E., 47, 48, 106, 109, 111
Johnston, J. R., 341
Jones, Ernest, 230
Jones, J. H., 69
Jones, L. L., 392
Joplin, Janis, 463
June, L., 177
Jung, Carl, 258, 264, 422, 432, 437, 498
Jungeblut, A., 288

Kabanoff, B., 304
Kagan, J., 409
Kahana, B., 376
Kahana, E., 376, 450
Kahn, H. S., 91
Kahn, Robert, 315
Kahn, S., 425
Kaiser, M. A., 31, 32, 306, 307, 373
Kalat, J. W., 56
Kalish, R. A., 494, 516
Kalmuss, D. S., 467
Kamin, L. J., 207
Kandel, D. B., 464
Kane, R. I., 493
Kaplan, A., 295, 301
Kaplan, S., 493
Kapur, K. K., 153
Karlinsky, H., 138
Karni, Avi, 177
Karp, D. A., 305
Kart, C. S., 460
Karus, D., 464
Kastenbaum, Robert, 63, 490, 491, 492, 493, 494
Katchadourian, H., 20, 80, 82, 84, 91, 98, 99, 101, 102, 103, 106, 109, 121, 123, 129, 149
Katz, S., 24
Katzman, R., 56
Kaufman, S. R., 12, 312
Kaufman, T. S., 377
Kaus, C. R., 472
Kausler, D. H., 168, 170, 172, 173
Kawachi, I., 149
Kay, B., 112
Kayser-Jones, J. A., 389
Keith, P. M., 356
Keller, M. L., 455
Kellerman, A. L., 516
Kelly, D., 270
Kelly, J., 313

Kelly, J. B., 341
Kelly, J. J., 331, 461
Kelly, J. R., 311, 312, 313
Kelly, R. C., 327
Kempe, C. H., 469
Kemper, T. L., 135
Kennedy, Edward, 123
Kennedy, John F., 123, 232
Kennedy, R., 513
Kennedy, Rose, 123
Kenrick, D. T., 408
Kerkhof, A. D., 371
Kernan, M., 361
Kerschner, H. K., 32
Kessler, R. C., 301, 448, 476, 507
Kevorkian, Jack, 518–519
Kibria, N., 366
Kidder, T., 23
Kiernan, T., 159
Kihlstrom, J. F., 193
Kilburn, H., 474
Kim, J. H., 138
Kim, N. W., 140
Kimmel, D. C., 18, 109
King, B. M., 109, 110, 133, 134, 143, 328, 347
King, D., 455
King, E. W., 502
King, Martin Luther, 276
Kinner, J. H., 386
Kinsey, Alfred C., 47
Kirsch, I. S., 288
Kirschenbaum, M. J., 468
Kirschenbaum, R. J., 215
Kite, M. E., 20
Kitson, G. C., 341
Kivett, V. R., 376
Kivnick, Helen Q., 372, 376, 419, 447, 480, 481, 482
Klagsbrun, F., 3
Klass, D., 193
Klatzky, R. L., 163
Kleemeier, R. W., 496
Klerman, G. L., 517
Kliegl, R., 186, 187
Kline, D. W., 92, 93, 96
Kline, T. J. B., 92
Klingbeil, K., 471
Koenig, H. G., 456, 457, 478
Kogan, N., 229
Kohlberg, Lawrence, 71, 265–270, 271, 273, 274, 431
Kohn, M. L., 303, 304
Kolata, G., 118
Kolodny, R. C., 47
Kolstad, A., 288
Kopp, C. B., 205
Kornhaber, A., 372, 374
Kosnik, W., 92
Kottak, C. P., 207, 208, 332, 343
Kraines, R., 107
Krajnik, M., 433

Kramer, D. A., 170
Kramer, J. J., 188, 191
Kranzler, J. H., 211
Krauss, I. K., 286
Krieger, D., 151
Kristof, N. D., 285
Kritz-Silverstein, D., 125
Krokoff, L. J., 343
Krueger, J., 415, 416
Kubie, L. S., 227
Kübler-Ross, Elisabeth, 498–501, 506, 522
Kuczynski, L., 469
Kufman, S. R., 12
Kuller, L. H., 153
Kumar, C., 274
Kunin, Madelein M., 288
Kupfersmid, J., 273
Kurosawa, Akira, 199–200, 201, 229, 232, 236, 521
Kurth, S. C., 258
Kurzman, D., 172
Kvale, J. N., 456

Labor, U. S. Department of, 295, 297
Labouvie-Vief, Gisela, 203, 247, 248, 249, 250, 263, 264, 455
Lachman, J. L., 67, 171
Lachman, M. E., 11, 472
Lachman, R., 67, 171, 184
Lacy, W. B., 422
Lair, T. J., 222
Laird, N. M., 465
Lakatta, E. G., 151
Lake, S. R., 376
Lakoff, R. T., 56
Laman, M. S., 366, 421
Lamb, M. E., 334
Lancy, D. F., 172
Landers, S., 379, 380
Landis, K. R., 147, 323
Landy, Frank J., 298, 299–300
Lang, M., 354
Langan, P. A., 469
Langer, E., 183, 389
Lansbury, Angela, 19
Lapinski, R. H., 347
Lapointe, A., 288
LaRocque, M., 95
LaRossa, M. M., 351
Larossa, R., 351
Larsen, D., 378, 380
Larsen, R. M., 469
Larsen, U., 347
Larson, A., 134
Larson, D. A., 324
Larson, R., 264
Latimer, E. J., 520
Laudenslager, M. L., 152
Lauer, J., 342
Lauer, R., 342
Laumann, E. O., 327, 328

Laurendeau, M., 248
Lave, C., 185
Lawton, M. P., 386, 387, 450
Lazarus, Richard S., 449, 452, 453, 455
Leabo, K. B., 77
Leaf, P. J., 476
Lebowitz, B. D., 472
Lee, D. J., 460
Lee, G. R., 366, 390
Lee, K. L., 126
Lee, P. R., 153
Lee, T. R., 370
Lefrancois, G. R., 227
Legge, G. E., 96
Leibowitz, A., 493
Leino, E. V., 365
Lemmon, J. A., 341
Lemon, B., 324, 460
Lennox, A., 138, 139
Lenz, E., 20
Leonard, A., 297, 337, 338, 346
Leonard, F., 386
Leonardo da Vinci, 233
Lerner, M. J., 370
Lesgold, A. M., 243
Leslie, G. R., 334
Levenson, M. R., 313, 314, 315
Leventhal, E. A., 455
Leventhal, H., 455
Levin, J. S., 456
Levine, R., 426
Levinson, Daniel, 418, 419, 422–424, 423, 435, 446
Leviton, D., 492, 499
Levy, B., 183
Lewin, Kurt, 3
Lewis, D. B. W., 284
Lewis, M. I., 447, 499, 522, 523
Lewis, R., 385, 386
Lichtenberg, P. A., 465
Lickona, T., 267
Lieberman, M., 139, 269, 390, 497
Lieberman, M. A., 449
Light, L. L., 171
Liker, J., 244
Likun, Qian, 285
Lillyquist, T. D., 165
Lin, S. L., 329, 380, 509
Lin, Y., 148
Lindeman, R. D., 120
Lindenberger, U., 187
Linder, K., 289
Lindsey, R., 380
Lindzey, G., 37
Lipid Research Clinics Program, 152
Lipsitt, L., 13
Littman, M., 27
Livson, F., 406
Lloyd, C. B., 297, 337, 338, 346
Lloyd Webber, Andrew, 403
Lobo, R. A., 348

LoCastro, J. S., 465
Loeber, R., 469
Loewen, E. R., 181
Lofland, L. H., 489
Loftus, E. F., 163
Logan, J., 380
Logan, J. R., 386
Logue, P. E., 496
London, K. A., 350
Longino, C. F., 24, 26, 460
Lock, M., 108
Loomis, B., 107
Lopata, H., 508
Lord, A. B., 187
Lorenz, G., 144
Loughnon, M. S., 97
Lovelace, E. A., 162, 165, 166, 167, 169, 170, 173, 175
Lowe, J. C., 427
Lowenthal, M., 324
Luborsky, M., 356, 371
Lucas, George, 200
Ludmer-Gliebe, S., 288
Lund, D. A., 324, 389, 392, 393, 394, 470, 503, 504, 505, 508, 509
Luria, Alexander R., 186, 194, 202, 203
Luther, Martin, 38
Lutjen, P., 348
Lyall, W., 508
Lykken, D. T., 409
Lytton, H., 409

MacAdam, M., 30, 31
MacDonald, R. K., 487
MacKinnon, D. W., 229
MacLeod, C. M., 180
MacRae, P. G., 101, 102, 103
Madonna, 78
Maercker, A., 262
Maier, S. F., 152
Main, M., 247
Malcolm, A. H., 519
Malthus, Thomas, 233
Mancini, J. A., 370
Mandela, Nelson, 241–243, 267, 276, 446
Manheimer, R. J., 285
Mannell, M. S., 324
Mannell, R., 264
Manning, C. A., 177
Mansfield, R. S., 230
Manson, J. E., 150
Manton, K. G., 208
Manuelidis, E. E., 138
Manuelidis, L., 138
Marcoen, A., 192
Margolin, L., 20
Maris, R. W., 516
Markides, K. S., 146, 460
Markley, R. P., 170, 188, 191, 194
Markman, H. J., 343

Markowitz, J. S., 517
Marks, J. S., 145
Markus, E. J., 180
Markus, H., 417
Marshal, N. L., 447
Marshall, V. W., 460
Marsiske, M., 226
Martin, John, 78
Martin, L. G., 29
Martin, N. G., 409
Martin, S. S. K., 392
Martin, T. C., 342
Martino-Saltzman, D., 52
Marvell, T. B., 338
Marx, Karl, 309
Maslach, C., 302
Masoro, E. J., 88
Masters, William H., 47, 48, 106, 109, 111
Matheny, K. B., 152
Matlin, M. M., 430
Matsukura, S., 148
Matthews, A. M., 314
Matthews, K. A., 107, 153, 344
Maxwell, J. W., 370
Mayers, R. S., 468
Maynard, P. E., 468
Maza, P. L., 350
Mazel, A., 336
McCall, R. B., 205
McCann, I. L., 153
McCarty, S. M., 496
McClelland, D. C., 213
McCord, C., 145
McCord, W., 521
McCrae, Robert R., 6, 406, 410, 411, 412, 413, 415, 422, 432, 440
McCusker, J., 465
McDaniel, M. A., 185
McDonagh, D., 77
McDonald, B. A., 289
McEnroe, John, 446
McFall, S., 388
McFarland, R. A., 103
McGonagle, K. A., 448
McGue, M., 409
McIntosh, J. L., 476, 514, 515
McKay, N. Y., 361, 363
McKitrick, L. A., 139, 165, 175, 192, 193, 194
McLanahan, S., 324
McLeod, D., 469
McMullen, R., 97
McNally, J. W., 328
McNaugh, M., 298
McNeal, R. D., 52
Meacham, John A., 260
Meehan, P. J., 516, 517
Meer, F., 241
Meer, J. T., 27, 89
Menaghan, E. G., 449

Menken, J., 347
Menninger Foundation, 372
Mergler, N. L., 171, 184
Mertz, M. E., 378
Merva, M., 303
Meth, R. L., 349
Metropolitan Life Insurance Company, 143
Meyers, H., 352
Michael, R. T., 327, 328, 335, 337
Michaels, S., 327, 328
Milgram, J. I., 370
Milgram, Stanley, 70
Miller, B. H., 388
Miller, G. A., 167
Miller, J., 159
Miller, J. B., 431
Miller, K., 304
Miller, L. F., 333, 337, 338
Miller, M., 516
Miller, N., 134
Miller, P. H., 37
Miller, S., 365
Miller-Jones, D., 207, 208
Millsap, R. E., 413
Mills, Harold, 385
Mindel, C. H., 25
Miner, S., 366
Mingus, Charles, 115
Minkler, H., 379
Minkler, M., 324, 365, 368, 371, 374, 508
Mirowsky, J., 147
Mirowsky, J. W., 334
Mischel, W., 406
Mishel, L., 297
Mitchell, D. B., 175
Mitchell, J., 474
Mitchell, V., 352, 437, 440
Mitchell-Kernan, C., 330, 333, 385
Moane, G., 408, 432, 437, 439, 440
Modern Maturity, 384
Mohr, J. P., 145
Mohs, R. C., 138
Monahan, D., 355
Monat, A., 452
Monk, A., 307, 308
Monnier, A., 338
Montepare, J. M., 11
Moody, S., 246
Moody-Thomas, S., 246
Moon, A., 471
Moore, D. W., 389
Moore, J. W., 427
Morbidity and Mortality Weekly Report, 517
Morelli, G., 17
Morgan, J. N., 313, 314
Morgan, L. A., 341
Morgan, S. P., 347
Morrel, R., 164
Morris, B. B., 52

Morris, L. W., 181
Morris, R. G., 181
Morrison, D. F., 224
Morse, D. L., 174
Morton, J., 163
Morton, K. R., 209
Moscovitch, M., 179, 181, 182
Mosher, W. D., 328, 347
Moskow-McKenzie, D., 285
Moss, F., 388
Moss, M. S., 510
Moss, S. Z., 510
Mosteller, F., 48
Moyers, W., 269
Mroczek, D. K., 315
Mueller, B. A., 469
Mui, A. C., 392
Mullan, J. T., 449
Munck, A., 151
Murphy, D. R., 175
Murphy, J. M., 271
Murray, C., 207, 208
Murstein, B. I., 325
Mussen, P. H., 406
Musil, C. M., 448, 472, 474, 476
Muthen, B. O., 476
Muuss, R. E. H., 268
Myers, J. E., 377
Myers, M. A. P., 341
Myerson, J., 488

Nagley, S., 476
Nahemow, L., 450
Nam, S., 324, 330
Nash, S. C., 434
Nathanson, C. A., 144
National Center for Education Statistics, 284
National Center for Health Statistics, 131, 346, 347, 428, 516
National Council on the Aging, 473
National Hospice Organization, 492
National Institute on Aging (NIA), 81, 87, 83, 88, 98, 99, 106, 121, 124, 125, 126, 128, 129, 135, 148, 149, 153, 474
National Institute on Alcohol Abuse and Alcoholism, 150
National Institutes of Health (NIH), 49, 87, 109, 110, 117, 121, 124, 135, 152
National Opinion Research Center, 333
National Research Council, 284
Neelley, J. N., 112
Neff, W. S., 292
Nehrke, M. F., 522
Neidert, L. J., 385
Neisser, Ulrich, 163
Nelan, B. W., 241, 242
Nelson, Erland, 66

Nelson, J., 281
Nesselroade, J. R., 50, 225
Nestadt, G. R., 137
Neugarten, Bernice L., 6, 12, 107, 264,
    406, 422, 427, 428, 429, 432,
    459–460, 495
Neugarten, D. A., 12, 427, 428, 429,
    459–460
Newsweek, 347
Newton, Isaac, 115
New Yorker, The, 361
NIA (*see* National Institute on Aging)
NIH (*see* National Institutes of
    Health)
Nickerson, R. S., 286
Niederehe, G., 472
Nilsson, L., 137
Nisan, M., 269
Nisbett, R. E., 408
Nishio, H. K., 29, 372, 395, 396
Niven, David, 115
Nixon, Richard M., 282
Noberini, M., 406
Noelker, L., 473
Nojima, N., 285
Nordan, L. T., 94
Norton, A. J., 333, 337, 338
Notelovitz, M., 153
Novacek, J., 455
NOW Legal Defense and Education
    Fund, 467, 469
Nurius, P., 417
Nuss, S., 295

O'Bryant, S. L., 356, 504, 507
O'Connell, M., 356
O'Connor, M., 330
Oden, M., 220
Offer, D., 352, 415
Office of Technology Assessment,
    U. S., 107, 349
Oget, V., 340
O'Grady-LeShane, R., 295, 296, 307,
    308, 317, 322, 343
Okun, M. A., 460
Okun, S., 514
Older Women's League, 468
Olds, S. W., 406
O'Leary, K. D., 467
Oleshansky, B., 431
Olivier, Laurence, 159–161
Olmsted, P. P., 352
Olson, P. G., 396
Ong, A., 454
Organization for Economic
    Cooperation and Development,
    308
Ortega, Daniel, 282
Ortega, S., 473
Orwoll, L., 264
Osgood, N. J., 516
Ostrov, E., 415

Otten, M. W., 145
Ouelette, R., 517
Ouslander, J. G., 388
Outtz, J. H., 24, 343, 344
Overend, E., 341
Owen, G., 489
Owens, J. E., 499
Owens, J. F., 153
Owens, W. A., 220
Oxman, T. E., 479, 480
Ozanne, E., 395

Paffenbarger, R. S., 153
Paganini-Hill, A., 125
Palmer, A. M., 245
Palmer, A. T., 23, 308
Palmer, J. L., 149
Palmertz, B., 137
Palmore, E. B., 208, 314, 496
Pampel, F. C., 308
Papalia (Papalia-Finlay), Diane, 226,
    248, 267, 350
Pappas, G., 146
Parham, I. A., 222
Park, D. C., 164, 168, 190
Parker, R. T., 126
Parkes, C. M., 508
Parkin, A. J., 181
Parlee, M. B., 104
Parmley, W. W., 149
Parnes, H. S., 306, 307
Parnes, L. S., 95
Parsons, J. E., 430
Passaro, V., 321
Patterson, G. R., 469
Pattison, E. M., 494
Paulson, R. J., 348
Pavalko, E. K., 311
Paveza, G. J., 470
Pavlov, Ivan, 174
Pavur, E. J., 194
Paykel, E. S., 478
Payne, J. D., 341
Peak, T., 521
Pearce, K. A., 246
Pearlin, L. I., 355, 365, 449
Pebley, A. R., 356
Peck, Gregory, 78
Peck, Robert C., 458, 462, 495
Penick, S., 182
Penning, M. J., 382
People Weekly, 361
Pepper, S. C., 40, 42
Perkins, H. W., 509
Perón, Eva, 403–405, 409, 411, 412
Perón, Juan Domingo, 404
Perricone, M., 344
Perrin, N., 377
Perrucci, C. C., 303
Perrucci, R., 303
Perry, D., 517
Perry, William, 249

Peterson, C., 407
Peterson, J., 324, 460
Petit, T. L., 180
Pettit, E. J., 341
Phenow, K. J., 148
Phillips, David P., 122, 502
Phillips, S. M., 183
Phoenix, River, 463
Piaget, Jean, 42, 43, 243, 247, 248, 249,
    265, 267, 410
Picano, J., 439
Picasso, Pablo, 236
Pickle, L. W., 148
Pienta, K. J., 142
Pignatiello, M. F., 188
Pillemer, K., 367, 370, 381, 389, 468,
    470, 471
Pimley, S., 455
Pincus, T., 146
Pines, A. M., 338
Plato, 258
Pleck, G. K., 366
Pleck, J. H., 431, 447
Plemons, J., 225
Plomin, R., 409
Pomerleau, D., 174
Pompi, K. F., 184
Poon, L. W., 164, 165, 166, 167, 188
Porcino, J., 373, 382, 387, 394
Porterfield, J. D., 139, 147, 148
Posner, M. C., 142
Post, S. G., 118
Powell, T. J., 474
Pratt, C. C., 466
Pratt, W. F., 347
Presley, Elvis, 463
Pressley, M., 188, 189
Prestwood, K. M., 125
Prevention Research Center, 149, 153
Primus, L. A., 417, 461
Prinz, P., 130
Prinz, P. N., 109
Proctor, W., 498
Prohaska, T. R., 455
Pugiisi, J. T., 164
Puri, M., 274

Queen, S., 146
Queenan, M., 150
Quinby, N., 208
Quinn, J. F., 18, 21, 306, 308, 311

Ragan, P., 495
Ragde, H., 142
Rahe, R. H., 150, 151, 449
Rainforth, M., 258
Raloff, J., 141, 142
Rampersad, A., 445, 446, 453
Randall, Tony, 78
Raphael, B., 513
Rasinski, K., 92
Rathbone-McCuan, E., 471

Rathunde, K., 264
Raven, J. C., 218
Raynor, Joel, 293–295
Read, K., 20
Read, P. P., 251
Reagan, Ronald, 136, 138, 282
Rebecca, M., 431
Redgrave, Lynn, 510, 512
Redgrave, Michael, 510
Ree, Malcolm James, 212, 213
Reese, H. W., 13, 50
Regier, D. A., 448, 476
Reid, D., 370
Reid, F., 100
Reid, J. R., 469, 470
Reid, R. L., 105
Remington, P. L., 91
Rempel, J., 356
Renick, M. J., 343
Renner, J., 177
Renner, V. J., 12
Renoir, Pierre-August, 524
Research to Prevent Blindness, 96, 97
Rest, J. R., 273
Revicki, D., 474
Rexroat, C., 355
Reynolds, C. R., 207
Reynolds, D. K., 494, 516
Rhodes, S. R., 298
Ribot, T., 227
Richie, D., 199, 200
Rickover, Hyman G., 281
Riegel, K. F., 45, 220, 496
Riegel, R. M., 220, 496
Riley, K. P., 192
Riley, Matilda W., 283, 284, 317
Rilke, Rainer Maria, 237
Rindfuss, R. R., 347
Ring, K., 498
Rivers, C., 323, 423
Rivers, Eunice, 70
Rix, S. E., 298, 308, 310
Rizzi, P., 298
Roach, M. J., 341
Roazen, P., 37
Robbins, M. A., 287
Robbins, Tom, 82
Roberto, K. A., 370, 371
Roberts, P., 248
Robertson, E. A., 171, 216
Robins, L. N., 448
Robinson, B., 392
Robinson, B. E., 347
Robinson, L. C., 343, 354
Rockwell, R. C., 134
Rodeheaver, D., 285
Rodehoffer, R. J., 121
Rodin, J., 152, 344, 389
Roe, K., 379
Roediger, H. L., 163, 175
Roff, L. C., 130
Rogers, J., 508

Rogers, L. P., 146
Rogoff, B., 17
Rolff, L. C., 130
Romanoski, A. J., 137
Roodin, P. A., 243
Roosa, M. W., 429
Roosevelt, Eleanor, 361, 363
Roosevelt, Elliott, 363
Roosevelt, Franklin Delano, 363
Rose, J., 324
Rosen, B., 287
Rosen, D. R., 116
Rosenberg, L., 149
Rosenberg, S. D., 423
Rosenburg, L., 464
Rosenman, R. H., 129
Roses, Allen D., 138, 139
Rosner, B. A., 152
Rosner, F., 465
Ross, C. E., 147, 334
Ross, H. G., 370, 371
Ross, J. A., 96
Ross, L., 408
Rossi, A. S., 365, 423, 432
Rossi, P. H., 365
Rossor, M., 138
Roth, G. S., 90
Rothman, S., 201
Rothschild, J., 517
Rovine, M., 354
Rowe, J. W., 120
Royal, D., 164
Roybal, E. R., 474
Rubenstein, B. S., 177
Ruberman, W., 150
Rubin, I. S., 293
Rubin, K. H., 248
Rubin, L. B., 110, 352
Rubinstein, Arthur, 172, 221
Rubinstein, R. L., 356, 371
Ruble, D. N., 430
Rudman, D., 103
Rule, B. G., 185
Runco, M. A., 234
Rushing, W., 473
Russell, C. S., 353
Russell, S., 324
Ruth, T. E., 122, 502
Ruthruff, A. M., 100
Ryan, M., 510
Ryan, Nolan, 101
Ryan, S. M., 152
Rybash, J. M., 103, 243, 244, 245, 261
Ryff, C. D., 462
Ryncarz, R. A., 267, 268

Sabatelli, R. M., 349
Sabom, M. B., 498
Sacco, R. L., 145
Sagan, C., 115, 180
St. Denis, Ruth, 77
St. George-Hyslop, P. H., 138

St. John, C., 347
St. Pierre, R. S., 139, 147, 148
Salk, Jonas, 234, 306
Salmon, D. P., 172, 174
Salthouse, T. A., 101, 135, 168, 172,
    173, 185, 188, 189
Sammartino, F. J., 307
Sanchez, C., 474
Sanders, S., 248
Sansone, C., 44
Sapolsky, D., 151
Sapolsky, R. M., 135, 180
Sattler, J. M., 201, 215
Sauer, Mark V., 348
Saults, J. S., 173
Saunders, Cicely, 492
Saunders, J., 507
Saylor, L. L., 189
Scandinavian Simvastatin Survival
    Study Group, 152
Schacter, D. L., 169, 175
Schadler, M., 247
Schafer, R., 247
Schaie, K. Warner, 6, 67, 68, 208,
    216, 221, 220, 222, 223, 224,
    225, 226, 254, 255, 287, 353,
    413
Scharlach, A. E., 390, 393, 495, 510,
    511, 512
Schell, D. A., 247
Schellenberg, G. D., 138
Scherer, M., 215
Schick, F. L., 25, 27, 29, 119, 297, 303,
    306, 311, 379
Schick, R., 25, 27, 29, 119, 297, 303,
    306, 379
Schieber, F., 93, 96
Schieffelin, E., 327
Schilling, E. A., 301
Schlossberg, N. K., 423
Schmall, V., 466
Schmeck, H. M., 306, 519
Schmidt, W. E., 104
Schmitt, B. D., 469
Schnall, P. L., 300
Schneider, E. L., 26, 79, 81, 83, 84, 87,
    88
Schoeberlein, S., 249
Schoen, R., 332, 339
Schonberg, H. C., 172, 221
Schonert-Reichl, K. A., 352
Schonfield, D., 171, 216
Schuebel, K. J., 96
Schulesnberg, E., 222
Schultz, D. P., 293
Schultz, S., 103
Schultz, S. E., 293
Schulz, J. H., 31, 307
Schulz, R., 448, 472, 505
Schumacher, M., 321, 322
Schumann, C. E., 287
Schumm, W. R., 353

Schwartz, P., 337
Schwartz, P. E., 141
Schwoerer, C., 287
Scogin, F., 192
Scott, C., 297
Scott, J. P., 370, 371
Scribner, S., 184, 185, 187, 202
Seattle (Native American chief), 269
Seccombe, K., 351
Secter, B., 51
Segal, N., 476
Seibert, G., 77
Seiden, R. H., 516
Sekuler, R., 92
Seligman, M. E., 407
Selkoe, D. J., 121, 135
Seltzer, G. B., 386
Seltzer, J. A., 339, 340
Selye, H., 448
Senate, United States, 21
Seringue, J. A., 194
Serlin, R. C., 226
Shapiro, L., 77
Shapiro, P., 77, 387
Shapiro, S., 149
Sharma, A. S., 350
Sharp, D., 185
Shaw, M. P., 228, 234
Shawn, Ted, 77
Shealy, D., 488
Shearer, D. E., 104
Sheehan, C. L., 334
Sheehy, G., 20
Shehan, C., 355
Shekelle, R. B., 129
Shepher, J., 432
Sherman, E., 447, 448, 521, 522
Sherman, L. W., 468, 470
Sherwin, B. B., 183
Shier, A., 263
Shifflett, P. A., 139
Shifren, K., 355
Shimamura, A. P., 181
Ship, J. A., 101
Shipp, E. R., 349
Shock, N., 120
Shweder, 270
Siano, G., 51
Siegler, I., 496, 497
Siegler, I. C., 208, 456
Silver, R. C., 506
Silverberg, S. B., 354
Silverman, J. M., 138
Simcox, D., 297
Simon, Theodore, 203
Simons, M., 521
Simonton, Dean K., 229, 230, 235, 236, 256
Simpson, Nicole, 463, 467
Simpson, O. J., 463
Singelakis, A. T., 386
Singer, P. A., 520

Sinnott, J. D., 170, 185, 248, 250, 251, 253
Sitarz, D., 339, 340
Skaff, M. M., 355
Skinner, B. F., 406
Skinner, J. H., 386
Sklar, L. S., 152
Skoog, I., 137
Skovron, M. L., 347
Skuldt-Niederberger, K., 433
Smith, A. D., 164, 190
Smith, D. G., 502
Smith, D. W., 350
Smith, J., 261, 262, 513
Smith, T. W., 51, 325, 327, 329, 337
Smyer, M., 472
Snarey, J. R., 269, 270
Snyder, C. J., 298
Snyder, M., 417
Snyderman, M., 201
Socrates, 235, 258, 260
Soldo, B. J., 387
Solomon, M., 520
Solomon, P. R., 174, 182
Soltes, F., 142
Somers, D. G., 370
Sommers, D. G., 306, 307
Spain, D., 333, 428
Spearman, Charles E., 210, 227
Speizer, F. E., 152
Spence, A. P., 92, 102, 103, 106, 109, 123, 124, 128, 130, 131, 135, 140
Spenser, M., 194
Spicer, D. V., 126
Spielberg, Steven, 339
Spilich, G. W., 177
Spirduso, W. W., 101, 102, 103
Spiro, A., 315
Spitze, G., 366, 380
Spoto, D., 159, 160
Sprott, R. L., 90
Squire, L. R., 169, 174, 175, 178, 179, 181, 182
Stadtman, E. R., 88
Staines, G. L., 304
Stampfer, M. J., 125, 129, 150, 152
Stanford, E. P., 465, 476
Stanley, S. M., 343
Starkweather, E. K., 227
Starr, B. D., 111
Staudinger, U. M., 261, 262
Stein, M. I., 227
Steinbach, U., 324, 383, 387, 388
Steinberg, L., 354
Steinberg, S., 96
Steinhaus, L. A., 104
Steinkamp, M., 313
Stengel, R., 241
Stern, M. B., 487, 488
Stern, William, 204
Sternberg, Robert J., 201, 208, 211, 212, 213, 214, 227, 235, 245, 256,

Sternberg, Robert J. (Cont.):
257, 325, 326
Sterns, H. L., 104
Stetson, D. M., 338
Stevens, A. B., 192
Stevens, J. C., 100, 101
Stevens, R., 37
Stevenson, I., 499
Stewart, G. W., 227
Stewart, M. A., 406
Sticht, T. G., 289
Stick, W. A., 460
Stine, E. A. L., 162, 167, 168
Stinson, F., 465
Stiver, I., 301
Stodelle, E., 77
Stone, I. F., 235
Storandt, M., 216
Stoudemire, A., 504, 505
Straus, M. A., 467
Strawbridge, W. J., 391
Stroebe, M., 503
Stroebe, W., 503, 504
Strom, D., 372
Strom, R., 372, 376
Strong, M., 393
Strother, C., 220
Strube, M. J., 467
Strubel, D., 53
Suhrer-Rousell, L., 434
Suitor, J. J., 367, 370, 381
Sunderland, T., 447
Super, Donald E., 291–292
Supple, K. R., 381
Susman, E. J., 469
Svanborg, A., 137
Swann, W. B., 417
Swanson, G., 258
Swartz, M. S., 448
Sweet, J., 332, 342
Swicegood, G., 347

Taguiri, 423
Tamir, L. M., 293
Tandy, Jessica, 305
Tanfer, K., 327
Tanne, D., 177
Tanner, J. M., 90, 332
Tappan, M. B., 271
Targ, D. B., 303, 353
Taub, C., 474
Taub, R. N., 140
Taylor, D. W., 67
Taylor, H., 241, 519
Taylor, I. A., 228
Taylor, J. M., 403
Taylor, Maxwell, 115
Taylor, R. J., 25, 330, 333, 385, 456
Taylor, S. C., 311, 317
Techner, D., 490
Technology Assessment, U. S. Office of, 107, 349

Tedrick, T., 313
Tellegren, A., 409
Terman, Louis, 6
Teutsch, S. M., 145
Thomas, A., 409
Thomas, G. S., 153
Thomas, J. L., 376
Thomas, N. W., 246
Thompson, L., 334, 351
Thompson, L. W., 478, 504
Thomson, E., 332
Thornton, A., 322, 327, 356
Thurnher, M., 392, 432
Thurstone, Louis L., 210, 211, 220, 227
Tierney, M., 248, 370
Tiger, L., 432
Time Magazine, 347, 361
Timiras, P. S., 100
Timko, C., 152
Tobin, J., 120
Tobin, S., 459–460
Todd, C., 258
Tolstoy, Leo, 522
Tomkins, S., 417
Tomlinson-Keasey, C., 248
Torrance, E. Paul, 227, 228, 229, 230
Toscanini, Arturo, 361
Tosteson, A. N. A., 125
Townes, D. B., 356
Tracy, M. B., 308
Travis, F., 258
Trichopoulos, D., 148
Trickett, P. K., 469
Troll, L., 324, 363
Troll, L. E., 96, 98, 100, 101, 365, 366, 368, 372, 374, 390, 393, 513
Trotter, R. J., 211
Trussell, J., 347
Tschann, J., 341
Tucker, M. B., 330, 333, 385
Tukey, J. W., 48
Tulving, E., 163
Tumulo, P., 248
Tune, G. B., 103
Turner, P. H., 347
Twain, Mark, 193

Uhlenberg, P., 337, 341, 342, 373
Umberson, D., 147, 323, 365, 507, 508, 510
UNESCO, 289
United Nations, 295, 296, 297, 317, 329, 332, 340, 345, 346
United Nations Committee for Development Planning, 32
United Nations International Labor Organization (UNILO), 300
U. S. Bureau of the Census, 21, 23, 24, 25, 26, 27, 28, 79, 80, 84, 119, 120, 133, 134, 144, 295, 297, 306, 329,

U. S. Bureau of the Census *(Cont.)*:
330, 333, 337, 343, 344, 356, 372, 375, 381, 382, 385, 388, 428, 507
U. S. Bureau of Justice Statistics, 467
U. S. Department of Education, 284, 286
U. S. Department of Energy, 117
U. S. Department of Health and Human Services (USDDHS), 80, 96, 119, 128, 134, 139, 143, 144, 145, 146, 147, 149, 153, 308, 346, 381, 385, 489, 513, 514, 516, 517
U. S. Department of Labor, 295, 297
U. S. Office of Technology Assessment, 107, 349
U. S. Senate, 21
Ursin, H., 451

Vachon, M., 508
Vaillant, C. O., 421, 422, 451
Vaillant, George E., 407, 418, 419, 421, 422, 435, 451
van Baal, J., 327
van der Wal, J., 371
Van Pelt, J., 324
Vargas, Mario Llosa, 364
Vasudev, J., 270
Verhaeghen, P., 192
Veronesi, U., 142
Victoria, queen of England, 505
Vidas, S., 95
Vinci, Leonardo da, 233
Vinick, B., 509
Viry, D., 295
Visher, E. B., 351
Visher, J. S., 351
Vitiello, M. V., 109
Voydanoff, P., 303

Wachs, T. D., 410
Wagner, D. A., 186, 187
Wagner, L. M., 122, 502
Wagner, Richard K., 212, 213, 214
Walasky, M., 522
Wales, J., 493
Walford, Roy L., 83, 90, 130
Walker, A. J., 334, 351, 392
Walker, L. J., 273
Wallace, 20, 306
Wallace, D. C., 88
Wallach, Eli, 78
Wallach, M. A., 229
Wallas, G., 227
Wallechinsky, 20, 306
Wallerstein, J. S., 341
Wallhagen, M. I., 391
Wallman, L. M., 208
Walls, C., 456
Walter, B. M., 181
Wang, W., 309
Ward, R., 380
Ward, R. A., 474

Ware, M., 153
Warner, T., 258
Watson, James D., 55, 234
Watson, R., 241
Watt, L. M., 522
Wayler, A. H., 153
Weaverdyck, S. E., 247
Webb, W. B., 130, 177
Wechsler, David, 204
Weg, R. B., 109, 110
Wegman, M. E., 23, 79, 80, 489
Weiffenbach, J. M., 101
Weikart, D. P., 352
Weinblatt, E., 150
Weindruch, R., 83
Weiner, M. B., 111
Weishaus, S., 353
Weiss, G., 140
Weiss, R., 431
Weiss, R. S., 508
Weissman, M. M., 517
Weitzman, L. J., 340
Welford, A., 103
West, R. L., 171, 190, 191, 192
Whartenby, K. A., 87, 139
Wharton, D., 295
Whitbourne, Susan Krauss, 96, 417, 461, 472, 522
White, J. M., 147
White, L., 20, 352
White, L. K., 339
White, N., 496
Who's Who in America, 3
Wiggins, S., 118
Wilensky, H. L., 304
Willett, W. C., 152
Williams, D., 471
Williams, G., 300
Williams, J. E., 429
Williams, M. V., 101
Williams, R. B., 129
Williams, S. A., 247
Williams, T. F., 120
Williams, Ted, 92
Williams, William Carlos, 219
Williamson, D. F., 91, 145, 152
Willis, S. L., 225, 226, 285, 287, 288, 413
Wilson, R. C., 227
Wilson, W., 466
Wilson, W. J., 346
Winfield-Laird, I., 476
Wing, R., 153
Wingfield, A., 162, 167, 168
Wink, P., 437, 438, 439
Winocur, G., 179, 181, 182
Winsborough, H. H., 510
Winslow, L., 92
Witteman, P. A., 445
Witter, R. A., 460
Wolf, D. A., 387
Wolf, M., 269

Wolfe, D. A., 469, 470
Wolinsky, F. D., 388, 509
Wolinsky, H., 142
Wolmark, N., 142
Wonderly, D., 273
Wong, P. T. P., 522
Wood, V., 107
Woodbury, M. A., 208
Woodruff, D. S., 130, 177
Woodruff-Pak, D. S., 130, 174
Woods, A. M., 101
Woodward, C. Vann, 440
Woodward, Joanne, 78
Woodward, K. L., 374
Wooten, J., 281
Working Women Education Fund, 301

Workman-Daniels, K., 313
World Book Yearbook, 1977, 281
World Health Organization, 133, 514, 515
Worldwatch Institute, 79, 80
Worobey, J. L., 387
Wortman, C. B., 506, 507
Wright, G. C., 338
Writing Group for the PEPI Trial, 125
Wurtman, J. J., 105
Wurtman, R. J., 105
Wykle, M. L., 448, 472, 474, 476

Yamaguchi, K., 464
Yamamoto, Kajiro, 199, 200
Yen, S. S., 105
Yllo, K., 467

Zacks, R. T., 184
Zandri, E., 287
Zappa, Frank, 142
Zarate, A. O., 85
Zarit, S., 456
Zellman, G. L., 430
Zeringue, J. A., 194
Ziegler, D. J., 406, 408
Zimberg, S., 465
Zimmer, H., 425, 426
Zimmerman, G., 425
Zoglin, R., 19
Zube, M., 355
Zuckerman, M., 325
Zuzanek, J., 264, 324

SUBJECT INDEX

Abuse:
    child, 469–470
    elder, 470–471
    partner, 467–469
Acceptance, as stage of dying, 498, 500
Accommodation, as identity style, 462
Achieving stage of cognitive development, 254
Acquired immune deficiency syndrome (*see* AIDS)
Acquisitive stage of cognitive development, 254
Activated lifespace model, 44
Active euthanasia, 519–521
Activity, energy, and health, as dimension of personality, 413
Activity theory of successful aging, 459–460
Adaptation, 406
Adaptation level, in environmental-press model of coping, 450
Adaptive mechanisms, 451
ADEPT (Adult Development and Enrichment Project), 225–226
Adjustments, personality, in Peck's theory, 458, 495
Adoption, 349–350
    kinship, 380
Adult development and aging:
    aspects of, 9–10
    defined, 5–6
    influences on, 13–17
    long-term studies, 7–8
    periods of adulthood, 10, 11, 366–367
    study of, 6–7
Adult Development and Enrichment Project (ADEPT), 225–226
Adult Literacy Survey, 27

Adulthood, periods of, 10–11
Affect (*see* Emotion)
Affect tolerance, 234
African Americans:
    adoption and, 350
    demographics, 24–25, 27
    grandparenthood, 372, 376
    health problems, 144–145
    older adults living alone, 385
    religion, 456, 474
    in workplace, 297
    (*See also* Race)
African National Congress (ANC), 241–242
Age (aging):
    challenges and dilemmas, 28–32
    chronic ailments, 143–144
    classic aging pattern on WAIS, 216
    cultural views of, 14–15, 18–20
    demographics, 21–31
    "dread diseases," 136–143
    long-term memory and, 170–175
    meanings of, 10–13
Age curve, 235
Age-differentiated roles, 283
Age Discrimination in Employment Act (ADEA), 298, 299
Age-integrated roles, 284
Ageism, 19–20
Ageless self, 11–12, 312
Age mystique, 4
Agency for International Development (AID), 251–252
Age-related macular degeneration, 97
Age structure, 372
Age Wave (Dychtwald and Flower), 22, 32
Aging in place, 382, 385–386, 395

Aging successfully (*see* Successful aging)
Agreeableness, 411–412, 413
AIDS (acquired immune deficiency syndrome), 132–134, 143, 328–329, 445, 478, 489, 494, 513
Alcohol, 149–150, 465–466
Alimony, 339–340
ALS (amyotrophic lateral sclerosis), 115–116
Alzheimer's disease (AD), 53, 70, 135, 136–139, 478, 479
    caregiving, 139, 391, 393
    causes, 137–138, 478
    treatment, 138–139
American Cancer Society, 141, 142
American Psychological Association (APA), and ethics of research, 69
Americans with Disabilities Act (ADA), 118
America Windows (Chagall), 232
Amygdala, 182
Amyloid plaque, 137, 138–139
Amyotrophic lateral sclerosis (ALS), 115–116
ANC (African National Congress), 241–242
Androgynous, defined, 430
Anger, as stage of dying, 498, 500
Antibodies, 131
Anticipatory grief, 504
Antidepressant drugs, 477
Anxiety, test, 209
Apartheid, 241
APOE gene, 139
Archetypes, 258
Armor-defended style of aging, 460
Arteriosclerosis, 128
Arthritis, 101, 126–127
Articulatory loop, 167

Artificial insemination, 349
Artistic personality, 290
Asia, demographics, 29–31
  (*See also* China; Japan; Malaya)
Aspartame, 178
Assimilation, as identity style,
  461–462
Assisted living, 383, 387
Assisted suicide, 518–519
Assortative mating, 325
Astigmatism, 94
Astrology, medicine and, 122
Atherosclerosis, 128, 129
Attentional resources, 168
Attrition, 63
Autobiographies, 523
Autoimmune theory, 131
Autoimmunity, 131
Automobile driving, 104
Autonomic nervous system, 135
AZT (azidothymidine), 133

"Baby M" case, 349
Balanced investment, 313
Balance models of successful aging,
  460–462
Baltimore Longitudinal Study of
  Aging, 120, 413
"Bankruptcy of Everday Memory,
  The" (Banaji and Crowder), 163
"Bankruptcy of Everyday Thinking,
  The" (Morton), 163
Bargaining, as stage of dying, 498,
  500
Behavioral measure, 51
Behavioral models of coping, 448,
  451
Behavior therapy, 478
Beliefs:
  about memory, 188–189
  illnesses and, 122
Bem's Sex Role Inventory, 430, 433
Bereavement, 503–513
Berkeley Longitudinal Studies, 7,
  64–65
Bias:
  cultural, 50
  observer, 53, 56, 408
  sampling, 63, 413
Binet-Simon Scale, 203
Biographical approach to creativity,
  230–234
Biological age, defined, 12
Biological aging, 12
  theories of, 86–89
Biological death, 490
Biological research on memory, 161,
  176–182
Biomarkers, 89–90
Bisexual, defined, 325
Blended family, 351
Blood pressure, 128, 129

Blood sugar, 88
Bodily-kinesthetic intelligence, 214
Body systems, 123–135
  cardiovascular, 128–129
  immune, 131–134
  neurological, 134–135
  respiratory, 130–131
  skeletal, 12–127
Bones, calcium and, 123–125
Book of the Dead (Egyptian), 490
Boston Normative Aging Study, 315
Boston Veterans Administration
  Normative Aging Study, 314
Brain structure, and sexual
  orientation, 327
Breast cancer, 118, 126, 140–142, 145
Brief dynamic therapy, 478
Brief History of Time, A (Hawking),
  115, 116
Broken Cord, The (Dorris), 322
Buddhism, 258
Burnout:
  caregiver, 391–392
  occupational, 302

Calcitonin, 125
Calcium, 123–125
California Psychological Inventory,
  437
Caloric-restriction research, 83–84
Cancer, 80, 139–143, 152
  smoking and, 148–149
Carcinogens, 140
Cardiac reserve, 128
Cardiovascular disease, 128–129
Cardiovascular system, 128–129
Career, 289, 290–295
Career consolidation, 421
Caregiver burnout, 391–392
Caregiving, 389–394
  in Asian countries, 30–31
  burdens and strains, 391–393
  community support, 393–394
  international perspective on,
    395–397
  legal intervention, 394
Caring, in theories of morality, 273
Cars and driving, 104
"Case of Misplaced Nostalgia, A"
  (Neisser), 163
Case study, 54–56
Cataracts, 94, 96–97
Central executive (memory), 167
Central nervous system, 135
Cerebellum, 135, 182
Cerebrovascular disease, 129
Change, defined, 5–6
Chemotherapy, 140
Child abuse, defined, 469–470
Children:
  abuse and neglect of, 469–470
  adult, living at home, 380–381

Children (*Cont.*):
  caregiving, 390–393
  childlessness, as option, 356
  death of, 513
  and death of parent, 510–513
  filial responsibility, 369, 370, 372
  grandparents and great-
    grandparents as "parents by
    default," 378–380
  relationships with parents, mature,
    366–367, 369
  middle-aged, and elderly parents,
    365–369
  parents living with adult, 387
  sibling relationships, 370–371
  young adult, and middle-aged
    parents, 365
Child support, 339–340
China:
  caregiving in, 396–397
  demographics, 29–30
  diseases and traditional Chinese
    beliefs, 122
  and Kohlberg's theory of morality,
    270
  lifelong learning in, 285
  memory, cross-cultural study, 183
  work and retirement in, 309
Cholesterol, 152
Christmas Carol, A (Dickens), 521
Chronic ailments, 119, 143–144
  (*See also specific ailments*)
Chronological age, 12, 323–324
Chronosystem, 17
Cigarette smoking, 148–149, 177
Classic aging pattern on WAIS, 216
Classical conditioning, 173–174, 192
Climacteric, 106
  male, 109
Closed contingent career path, 294
Cochlear implants, 94–95
Cognex (tacrine), 139
Cognitive-appraisal model of coping,
  448, 452–453, 455
Cognitive (intellectual)
  development, defined, 9
Cognitive development and
  functioning, 90, 243
  gender, theories of, 431–432
  lifespan model, 254–255
  (*See also* Intellectual development
    and functioning)
Cognitive-developmental theories,
  defined, 431
Cognitive therapy, 478
Cohabitation, 332
Cohort, 13, 62, 63
  effect in substance use disorders,
    464
Cohort-sequential design, 67
College, 284–285
Commitment, 325

Commitment within relativism, 249
Companionate grandparents, 374
Compensation hypothesis, 304
Componential element of intelligence, 211
Computer training, 285–287
Conditioned responses, 173–174
Confounding, 62, 66
Congestive heart failure, 128
Congregate housing, 383
Congruence model of coping, 450
Conscientiousness, 411–412
Conscious memory, 178–181
Consolidation stage of career development, 292
Constants, 56
Construct, 60
Construct validity, 60, 230
Context, in lifespan development approach, 8, 121
Contextual element of intelligence, 213
Contextual perspective, 44–45
Contingent career paths, 293–294
Continuing care retirement community, 383
Continuity theory of successful aging, 460–461
Control group, 58–59
Conventional personality, 290
Convergent thinking, 229
Convoy theory, 315
Coordination, 103–104, 208
Coping, 448–455
  behavioral models, 451
  cognitive-appraisal model, 452–453, 455
  coping-style models, 451–452
  with economic changes, 454
  environmental models, 448–451
Corneal disease, 97
Coronary artery disease, 128, 129
Corpus callosum, 224
Correlational study, 54, 56, 62
Cosmic perspective, 268–269
Creative process, 227–228
Creativity, 227–237
  age and, 235–237
  intelligence and, 228–229, 256, 257
  studying and measuring, 228–235
  and wisdom, compared, 256, 257
Cross-linking theory, 88
Cross-sectional studies, 61–63, 65, 67
  defined, 61
  longevity and, 90
  (See also specific studies)
Crown of Columbus, The (Dorris and Erdrich), 321
Cruzan v. Director, Missouri Department of Health, 520

Crystallization stage of career development, 291
Crystallized intelligence, 216, 217–219
Culminating phase of life structure, 424
Cultural bias, 50
  in IQ tests, 207–208, 213
Culture:
  death and dying and, 502
  gender roles and, 434–435
  intelligence and, 224
  memory and, 183, 186–187
  personality and, 414–415, 425–427
  role of, 17
  views of aging and, 14–15, 18–20

Data, 38
Data collection, 49, 51–53
Death and dying, 489–501
  attitudes toward, 494–495
  bereavement, 503–513
  biological aspects, 490
  of child, 513
  culture and, 502
  euthanasia, 519–521
  grief, forms and patterns of, 504–506
  near-death experiences, 498–499
  of parents, 510–513
  psychological aspects, 491, 496–498
  social aspects, 490
  stage model, 498–501
  study of, 492–493
  suicide, 514–519
  surviving a spouse, 506–509
Death education, 492
"Death of Ivan Ilyich" (Tolstoy), 522
Deceleration stage of career development, 292
Declarative memory, 169–171, 178, 179
Defining Issues Test (DIT), 273
Degenerative joint disease, 126–127
Dementia, 135, 478–480
Demographics, 21–31
  life expectancy trends, 79–80, 85
  (See also specific groups, topics, and countries)
Dendrites, 121, 135
Denial:
  as coping strategy, 453
  as stage of dying, 498, 500
Dental care, 153
Deoxyribonucleic acid (DNA), 81
Dependency ratio, 316–317
Dependent variable, 58
Depression:
  clinical, 475–478
  as stage of dying, 498, 501

Destructive behavior patterns, 463–471
  child abuse and neglect, 469–470
  elder abuse, 470–471
  partner abuse, 467–469
  substance use disorders, 148–150, 463–466
Developing nations, graying of population, 31–32
Development, defined, 5–6
  (See also Adult development)
Developmental reserve, 187
Deviation IQ, 204, 205
DHEA (dehydroepiandrosterone), 90
Diabetes, mature-onset, 131–132
Diary, 49
Diet, 152
  memory and, 177–178
Dietary restrictions, 83–84
Digit span, 167
Dimensions of personality, 411
Direct (repetition) priming, 182
Discrimination:
  genetic information and, 118
  public safety and, 299–300
Diseases, and personality patterns, 129, 407
  (See also specific diseases)
Disengagement theory of successful aging, 459
Disposition, 409–410
DIT (Defining Issues Test), 273
Divergent thinking, 229, 230, 235
Divorce:
  blended families and, 344, 351
  economic consequences, 339–341
  emotional adjustment to, 341
  in France, 336
  grandparenting after, 376–377
  remarriage and, 337–338, 342
DNA (deoxyribonucleic acid), 81
Domestic violence, 467–471
Dominant trait, 81
Double-blind test, 58
Double standard, of sexuality, 325
"Dread diseases" of aging (see Alzheimer's disease; Cancer)
Dream, 423
Drinking, 149–150, 465–466
Driving Miss Daisy, 305
Druze sect, 434–435
Dual-career families, 334–335
Dual-process model of intelligence, 219, 221, 261
Duke University Longitudinal Study, 111, 208, 496
Dumping, 470
Durable power of attorney, 520
Dynamic visual acuity, 93
Dysmenorrhea, 105

ECHO (elder cottage housing opportunity), 383
Echoic memory, 165
Ecological approach to adult development, 16–17
Ecological validity, 255
Economic change, coping with, 454
Economic development, aging and, 31–32
ECT (electroconvulsive therapy), 477–478
Education, 6, 284–289
  college, 284–285
  computer training, 285–287
  demographics, 27
  and health problems, 146
  illiteracy, adult, 288–289
  and intelligence, 224
  lifelong learning, 285–288
E-I-E-I-O model of memory, 190
Elaboration (in memory), 167, 191–192
Elder abuse, 470–471
Elderly parents:
  care of, 370
  middle-aged children and, 365–369
Electroconvulsive therapy (ECT), 477–478
Embellishment, 183–184
Emotion:
  intellect and, 263
  in social reasoning, 250
Emotional conditioning, 182
Emotion-focused coping, 453, 455, 457, 495
Emphysema, 130
Empty nest, 293, 352–353
Emotional stability, as dimension of personality, 415
Encapsulation, 244–245
Encoding (memory), 162, 164, 173, 187, 189
Endurance, 102–103
Enterprising personality, 290
Environment, 13
  "aging avalanche," 22, 23
  ecological approach, 16–17
  (See also Culture)
Environmental constraints, in cognitive-appraisal model, 452
Environmental models of coping, 448–451
Environmental-press model of coping, 450–451
Episodic memory, 170
Equal Employment Opportunity Commission (EEOC), 118
Erectile dysfunction, 109–110
Error-catastrophe theory, 88
Error theories, 88–89, 131
Eskimo (Inuit) culture, 414–415, 518

Establishment stage of career development, 292
Estrogen, 106
Estrogen replacement therapy (ERT), 106, 125–126, 129
Ethical development (see Moral development)
Ethics of research, 68–71
Ethnic identity, 523
Ethnicity:
  demographics, 24–25
  and elder abuse, 470–471
  and health problems, 144–146
  and IQ tests, 207–208
  and older adults living alone, 385
  and leisure time during retirement, 313
  and work, 297
Etridronate, 125
Euthanasia, 519–521
Everyday memory research, 163
Evita (Lloyd Webber), 403
Evolutionary psychology, 20
Executive stage of cognitive development, 254
Exercise, 103, 153
Exosystem, 17
Experience, 243–247
  expertise and, 243–245
  integrative thinking and, 247
  morality and, 267
  problem solving and, 245–247
Experiential element of intelligence, 212
Experiment, 54, 57–61
Experimental group, 58–59
Expertise, 243–245
Expert thinking, 245
Explanatory style, 407
Explicit external aids, 190
Explicit internal aids, 191–192
Explicit memory, 169–170
Extended family, 363, 364, 374
External structures, in continuity theory, 460–461
External validity, 46, 50, 63
Extramarital sexual activity, 335, 337
Extraversion, 411–412, 413
Eye, structure and function, 93, 95, 96

Factor analysis, 210–211
Factorial invariance, 61
Falls, prevention of, 98
Family (family life), 313, 343–356
  caregiving, 389–394
  child abuse and neglect, 469–470
  as defined by Census Bureau, 344
  late-life, 372
  living arrangements, 380–389
  and mental health, 447

Family (family life) (Cont.):
  parenthood, 344–355
  partner abuse, 467–469
  sibling relationships, 370–371
  structure, changes in, 343–344, 363–372
  (See also Children; Grandparents; Great-grandparents; Marriage; Parents)
Family-focused lifestyle, 313
Family and Medical Leave Act, 393
Fels Research Institute Study, 7
Female reproductive system, 104–108
Feminine Mystique, The (Friedan), 4
Field experiment, 60
Films of Akira Kurosawa, 199–200, 236, 521
Five-factor model of personality, 411–413
Fluid intelligence, 216–219, 226, 243
Folk wisdom, 257–258
Food and Drug Administration, U. S., 49, 71
Forgetting, 160, 193–194
Foster-care home, 383
Fountain of Age, The (Friedan), 3, 4
Four Season, The (Chagall), 232
Framingham, Massachusetts, Longitudinal Study, 130
France, divorce in, 336
Free-radical theory, 88
Fried Green Tomatoes, 305
Friendship, 323–324
Frontal lobes, 178, 180–181
Fructose, 178
Functional age, 12–13
Fundamental pragmatics of life, 260

Gender:
  ageism and, 20
  bone loss and, 123–126
  cardiovascular disease and, 129
  demographics, 23–24
  grandparenthood and, 375–376
  health problems and, 143–144
  intelligence and, 223–224
  in Latin America, 364
  life expectancy and, 80
  marital expectations and, 334
  memory and, 183
  mental health and, 447
  occupational stress and, 301–302
  of older adults living alone, 385
  personality and, 429–440
  postformal morality and, 271–273
  spousal abuse, 467–469
  stage models, 425
  taste and smell, loss of, 101
  work and, 290, 295–297
Gender identity, 429–432
Gender roles, 429–434
  in adulthood, changes in, 432–434

Gender roles *(Cont.):*
  culture and, 434–435
Gender-role transcendence, 432
Gender-schema theory, 432
Gender stereotypes, 429–430
Genealogy, 523
General factor (*g*), 210, 211, 212–213, 224
Generativity, 420
Generativity vs. staganation (Erikson's seventh crisis), 420
Genes, 81
Gene therapy, 86, 140
Genetic-programming theories, 86–87, 89
Genetics (*see* Heredity)
Genetic testing, 117–118, 141
Geriatrics, 27
Gerontological Society of America, 86
Gerontologists, 12
g (general) factor, 210, 211, 212–213, 224
Ghana, 363
Glaucoma, 97
Glucose, 177–178
"*g*-ocentric View of Intelligence, The" (Sternberg and Wagner), 212
Graduate Record Examination (GRE), 211
Grandparents, 344, 372–377
  as "parents by default," 378–380
Grant Study of Adult Development (Harvard University), 6, 407, 421–422, 451
Graying of the population, 28–32
Great-grandparents, 377–380
  as "parents by default," 378–380
Grief, 503
  forms and patterns of, 504–506
Grief therapy, 505
Grief work, 505
Gusii society, stages of life in, 426–427

Harassment, sexual, 302
"Hardware" of memory (biological approach), 176–194
Harmful substances, 148–150, 463–471
Hayflick limit, 81
Health and well-being:
  cardiovascular system, 128–129
  demographics, 27–28
  immune system, 131–134
  indirect influences on, 143–147
  intelligence and, 224
  lifespan development approach, 119–121
  maintaining and improving, 147–154

Health and well-being *(Cont.):*
  neurological system, 134–135
  respiratory system, 130–131
  retirement and, 313–316
  skeletal system, 123–127
Health care, 31
  of oldest old, 26
Hearing aids, 22, 94–95, 100
Hearing loss, 50, 94–95, 98–100, 208
Heart, 128
Heart attacks, 128, 129
  stress and, 150
Heart disease, 80, 122, 128–129, 144
  drinking and, 150
"Heinz's dilemma," 265
Heredity (genetics), 13
  depression and, 477
  personality and, 409
  sexual orientation and, 327
Herero people (Botswana), 14–15
Heterosexual, defined, 325
Heterosexuality, 325, 327
  single life and, 329–330
Hinduism, stages of life in, 425–426
Hippocampus, 178–180, 181
Hispanics:
  demographics, 24–25, 27
  extended families, 364
  health problems, 146
  in workplace, 297
History, lifespan development approach and, 8, 13, 121
HIV (human immunodeficiency virus), 132–133, 478
Holocaust, Nazi, survey on, 49–50
Homeostasis, 123
Homosexual, defined, 325
Homosexuals (homosexuality), 110, 325, 327, 330–332, 344, 494
  parenting, 347
  successful aging, 461
Honduras, farm program in, 251–252
Hormonal changes, 86
Hormone-replacement therapy (HRT), 106, 125–126
Hospice care, 492–493
Human Genome Project, 117–118
Human immunodeficiency virus (HIV), 132–133
Human Sexual Inadequacy (Masters and Johnson), 48
Human Sexual Response (Masters and Johnson), 48
Humility, wisdom and, 260
Huntington's disease, 181–182
Hypertension, 128, 129
Hypochondriasis, 480

Iconic memory, 165
Ideal self, 407
Identity accommodation, 417

Identity assimilation, 417
Identity crisis, 37, 42, 43
Identity styles, 417, 461–462
Illiteracy, 288–289
Immature coping styles, 451
Immigration, 24
Immune system, 86, 131–134
Implementation stage of career development, 291
Implicit external aids, 192
Implicit internal aids, 192
Implicit memory, 169–170
Impotence (erectile dysfunction), 109–110
"In Defense of Everyday Memory" (Conway), 163
Independent variable, 58
India, and Kohlberg's theory of morality, 270
Infertility, 347, 349
Information-processing research on memory, 161–175
Information-processing theory, 41
Informed consent, 70–71
Inheritance, 370
Institutional care, 25, 30–31, 388–389, 395
Insulin, 131
Insulin-dependent diabetes, 131
Integrated level of cognitive development, 250
Integrated style of aging, 460
Integrative thinking, 247
Integrity vs. despair (Erikson's final crisis), 420, 495
Intellect, 263
  as dimension of personality, 415
Intellectual (cognitive) development, defined, 9
Intellectual development and functioning, 9–10, 249–250, 254–255
  (*See also* Experience; Intelligence; Moral development; Postformal thought; Wisdom)
Intellectual style, 256
Intelligence, 201–227
  creativity and, 228–229, 256, 257
  defined, 201
  gender differences, 223–224
  growth or decline during adolescence, 216–221
  one ability or many, 210–215
  plasticity, 225–226
  testing, 201–209, 212–213
  variation in individuals, 222–224
  and wisdom, compared, 256, 257, 260
Intelligence quotient (IQ), 204–205, 210, 228–229
  decline in older adults, 216
Intelligent behavior, 201

Intentional forgetting, 194
Interiority, 264, 422
Internal structures, in continuity
    theory, 460–461
Internal validity, 59, 61–63
International Plan of Action on
    Ageing, 32
Interpersonal intelligence, 214
Interpersonal relationships (*see*
    Relationships)
Interpersonal wisdom, 264
Intersystemic level of cognitive
    development, 249
Interventions, 41
Interviews, 49, 408
Intimacy, 324, 325
Intimacy vs. isolation (Erikson's
    sixth crisis), 419
Intimate relationships (*see* Marriage;
    Relationships)
Intrapersonal intelligence, 214
Intrapersonal wisdom, 264
Intrasystemic level of cognitive
    development, 249
Intrinsic motivation, 234
Intrusion errors, 183–184
Inuit (Eskimo) culture, 414–415, 518
Investigative personality, 290
In vitro fertilization, 349
Involved grandparents, 374
IQ (intelligence quotient), 204–205,
    210, 228–229
    decline in older adults, 216
Israeli kibbutzim, and Kohlberg's
    theory of morality, 270

Japan:
    aging population, 372
    caregiving in, 395–396
    demographics, 29, 30–31
    lifelong learning in, 285
    menopause in, 108
    perspectives on aging, 18
Jews, 491, 502
Jitterbug Perfume (Robbins), 82
Job, defined, 289
Job performance:
    age and, 298
    intelligence and, 224
    test scores and, 212–213
    (*See also* Work)
Judaism, Orthodox, 491
Justice, 265, 271
Juvenile-onset diabetes, 131

Kibbutzim, Israeli, and Kohlberg's
    theory of morality, 270
Kinship (*see* Family; Marriage;
    Parents; Sibling relationships)
Kinship adoption, 380
Kinship care, 379
Kpelle people (Liberia), 17, 185, 187,

Kpelle people (Liberia) (*Cont.*):
    203, 208
!Kung San Bushmen (Botswana),
    14–15
Kurosawa, Akiro, films of, 199–200,
    236, 521

Laboratory experiment, 60
Laboratory observation, 53
Laboratory research on creativity,
    234–235
Language, in semantic memory, 171
Late adulthood (*see* Older adults)
Late-life family, 372
Leadership, moral, 274–275
Learned helplessness, 451
Learning, defined, 6
    (*See also* Education)
Leisure:
    defined, 289
    retirement and, 312–313
    work and, 304
Lesbians, 331
    (*See also* Homosexuals)
"Let's Be Friends," (Klatzky), 163
Life change units (LCUs), 449
Life expectancy, 79
    trends in, 79–80
Lifelong learning, 285–288
Life review, 521–523
Life satisfaction, 448
    and mental health, 472–474
Lifespan development, defined, 7
Lifespan development approach,
    7–8, 78
    biological aging and, 153–154
    cognitive development and,
        254–255
    features, 7–8
    health and, 119–121
    intellectual performance and, 225
    memory and, 160, 182–183
    mental health and, 472–482
    metatheories, 44–45
Lifespan developmental psychology,
    defined, 7
Life strengths, 481–482
Life structure, 422–424
Lifestyles:
    intelligence and, 224
    marital and postmarital, 332–343
    memory and, 177–178
    nonmarital, 329–332
    and well-being, 147–154
Linguistic intelligence, 214
Literacy, 27, 288–289
Little Women (Alcott), 487–488
Living alone, 385
Living arrangements, 25, 380–389
    adult children at home, 380–381
    caregiving, 389–394
    choosing, 382–383

Living arrangements (*Cont.*):
    for older adults, 381–389
Living will, 520
Logical-mathematical intelligence,
    214
Logos, wisdom and, 263
Longevity, 79, 81–85
    biological aging theories, 86–89
    individual, predicting, 89–90
Longitudinal study, 63, 64–65
    longevity and, 90
    (*See also* specific studies)
Long-term care (*see* Caregiving;
    Institutional care)
Long-term memory, 165, 167,
    169–175, 177
Lord of the Flies (Golding), 232
Lou Gehrig's disease (ALS), 115–116
Love, 325, 326
Love Medicine (Erdrich), 321
Lumpectomy, 142
Lung cancer, 140
    smoking and, 148–149

Mabaans (Sudan), 50
Macrosystem, 17
Magnetic resonance imaging (MRI),
    178
Maintenance stage of career
    development, 292
Major depressive episode, 475
Malaya:
    death rituals, 490
    economic change, responses to,
        454
Male reproductive system, 109–110
Mammography, 141
Manual dexterity, 22
"Maple Leaf Gala" (Graham), 78
Marriage, 332–337
    childless, 356
    early years, 353–354
    happiness and, 333–334
    health problems and, 147
    later years, 354–355
    middle years, 354
    motherhood without, 346
    partner abuse, 467–469
    satisfaction with, 353–355
    sexual activity in, 335, 337
    success in, 342–343
    surveying a spouse, 506–509
    work and, 334–335
    (*See also* Divorce; Parents;
        Remarriage)
Mass (Bernstein), 232
Mastectomy, 142
Maturation, 6
Mature coping styles, 451
Mature-onset diabetes, 131–132
Mature thought (*see* Postformal
    thought)

Mechanics of intelligence, 219
Mechanistic perspective, 40–42, 45
Media stereotypes about aging, 19, 20
Medicaid, 369
Medical durable power of attorney, 520
Medicare, 26, 369
Medicine:
  astrology and, 122
  depression and, 476
Memory, 161–194
  biological research, 161, 176–182
  culture and, 183, 185–188
  directions for research, new, 182–183
  everyday memory research, 163
  forgetting and, 193–194
  healthy lifestyle and, 177–178
  information-processing research, 161–175
  intrusion errors, 183–184
  metamemory, 188–189
  mnemonics, 189–193
  production deficiency, 185–188
  prospective, 185
Men:
  mental health, 447
  reproductive system, 109–110
  (See also Gender)
Menopause, 106–108
  motherhood after, 348
Menstrual cycle, 104–105
Mental disorders, 474–480
  dementia, 478–480
  depression, 475–478
  hypochondriasis, 480
Mental health, 447–448
  coping models, 448–455
  destructive behavior patterns, 463–471
  in late life, 472–482
  life satisfaction and, 472–474
  successful aging, 455–462
Mental imaging, 191
Mentor, 423
Mesosystem, 17
Metacognition, 256
Metamemory, 188–189
Metamemory in Adulthood (MIA) questionnaire, 188
Metatheories, 39–45
  application, 45
  contextual perspective, 44–45
  defined, 40
  mechanistic perspective, 40–42, 45
  organismic perspective, 42, 45
Method of loci, 191
Microprocessor-enhanced hearing aids, 94
Microsystem, 16–17

Middle-aged adults, 10, 11
  ageism and, 20
  death, attitudes toward, 494–495
  elderly parents and, 365–369
  physical appearance, 91
  sibling relationships, 370
  young adult children and, 365
Midlife crisis, 420, 421, 422–423, 427
Midlife transition, 422–423
Mills College longitudinal study, 408, 435–440
Minorities:
  occupational stress, 301
  in workplace, 297
  (See also specific groups)
Mnemonics, 189–193
Mobility, physical, 22, 208
Model, 40
Modifiability (plasticity), 225–226
Moral development, 265–276
  experience and, 267
  gender and, 271–273
  moral reasoning, 265–270
Morality of autonomous moral principles, 265, 266
Morality of conventional role conformity, 265, 266
Moral leadership, 274–275
"Mortality revolution," 489
Motherhood:
  after menopause, 348
  daughters and, 366
  without marriage, 346
  (See also Parents)
Motor functions, 101–104
Motor memory, 172
Mourning, 503
Multidirectional, defined, 7
Multidirectionality, 7–8, 120–121, 220, 472
Multigenerational late-life family, 372
Multiple causation, 8
Multiple intelligences, 214–215
"Murder, They Wheezed" (article in Time), 19
Muscular conditioning, 182
Muscular strength and endurance, 102–103
Musical intelligence, 214
Music therapy, 478
Myocardial infarction, 128, 129
Myopia, 94
Myth, wisdom and, 257–258
Mythos, wisdom and, 263

National Aging Day (Thailand), 31
National Institutes of Health (NIH), 6
National Literacy Act, 289
National Organization for Women (NOW), 4
Natural experiment, 60

Naturalistic observation, 52–53
Natural law, and ethics, 268
Near-death experiences, 498–499
Nearsightedness, 94
Necessary subjectivity, 250
Neglect, 469–470
Neostriatum, 181
Nepal, life expectancy in, 29
Nervous (neurological) system, 134–135
Neurofibrillary tangles, 137, 138–139
Neurological system, 134–135
Neurons, 135
Neurotic coping styles, 451
Neuroticism, 411–412, 472
No-fault divorce, 336, 337–338, 341
Noncontingent career paths, 293–294
Nondeclarative memory, 169, 170, 172–175, 181
Non-insulin-dependent diabetes, 131–132
Nonmarital lifestyles, 329–332
Nonnormative life events, 14–15, 427–428
Nonviolence, philosophy of, 276
Normative, defined, 13
Normative age-graded influences, 13
Normative-crisis models, 418–419
Normative-history graded influences, 13
Normative life events, 427–428
Normative models of successful aging, 455, 458–460
Normative personality change, 418–427
Novice phase of life structure, 423
Nuclear family, 363
Nursing homes, 25, 388–389
Nutrition, 152, 177–178

Oakland Growth Study, 7
Obesity, 152
Object (sensory) cues, in remembering, 190
Objectivity, 38–39
Observation, 52–53
Observer bias, 53, 56, 408
Occupation, defined, 289
Occupational burnout, 302
Occupational patterns, 295–297
Occupational stress, 300–302
Older adults, 10, 11
  death, attitudes toward, 495
  living arrangements, 381–389
  mental health, 472–482
  personality development, 413
  physical appearance, 91
  roles, new, 32
  sibling relationships, 370–371
  test performance, 208–209
Oldest old, 26, 84, 103, 395–397

Old-old, 12
Olfactory bulb, 100
Omnibus Budget Reconciliation Act, 389
Open contingent career path, 294
Open-ended interview, 49
Openness to experience, 411–412
Organismic perspective, 42, 45, 499
Organization (in memory), 191–192
Organ reserve, 123
Orientation, sexual, 325
Orthodox Judaism, 491
Osteoarthritis, 126–127
Osteoporosis, 124–125
Ovarian cancer, 141
Ovum transfer, 348, 349

Pain, 101
Palliative care, 492–493
Palliative coping, 453
Parents (parenthood), 344–355
    adoption, 349–350
    adult children, at home, 380–381
    adult children, living with, 387
    child abuse and neglect, 469–470
    child support, 339–340
    death of, 510–513
    death of child, 513
    delayed, 347
    as developmental experience, 351–352
    elderly, middle-aged children and, 365–369
    empty nest and, 352–353
    filial responsibility for, 369, 370, 372
    grandparenthood, 372–377, 378–380
    great-grandparenthood, 377–380
    infertility and new ways to parenthood, 347, 349–350
    middle-aged, young adult children and, 365
    motherhood without marriage, 346
    relationships with children, mature, 366–367
    role changes and marital satisfaction, 353–355
    sexual orientation and, 347
    (See also Caregiving)
Parent-support ratio, 372
Parkinson's disease, 476, 479
Partner abuse, 467–469
Passion, 325
Passive-dependent style of aging, 460
Passive euthanasia, 519
Passive smoking, 148, 149
Penicillin, 69
Pension plans, 307–308, 309

Perceptual memory, 172–173
Perceptual skills, 173
Periodontitis, 153
Periods of adulthood, 10–11
Peripheral nervous system, 135
Persistent vegetative state, 520
Personal constraints, in cognitive-appraisal model, 452
Personal fable, 494
Personality, 405–441
    approaches to, synthesizing, 440–441
    culture and, 414–415, 425–427
    defined, 406
    disease and, 129, 407
    gender and, 429–440
    measuring, 406–408
    mental health and, 472
    origins, 408–410
    self-concept models, 410, 416–417
    stage models, 410, 418–427, 481–482, 495
    terminal drop and, 496–497
    timing-of-events model, 410, 427–429, 493–494
    trait models, 410, 411–416
Personality adjustments, in Peck's theory, 458
Personality development, defined, 9–10
Personality dimensions, 411
Personality inventory, 406–407
Personal resources, in cognitive-appraisal model, 452
PET (positron emission tomography), 178
Philosophy, wisdom and, 257–258
Physical appearance, 90–92
Physical development, defined, 9
Physical disorders (see specific disorders)
Physical health and development, 9–10
    motor functions, 101–104
    retirement and, 314
    (See also Health and well-being)
Physiological aging (see specific topics)
Pilgrimages, 523
Planful competence, 63
Plasticity, 8, 103, 121, 472
    intellectual performance and, 225–226
PMS (premenstrual syndrome), 104–105
Population statistics, 21–31
    life expectancy trends, 79–80, 85
    of United States, 21, 23–24
Positron emission tomography (PET), 178
Postformal thought, 248–254
    criteria, 253–254
    cultural change and, 251–253

Postformal thought (Cont.):
    development, 248–250
    postconventional morality and, 267
    social reasoning and, 250
Postmarital lifestyles, 332–343
Postponing death, 502–503
Poverty:
    demographics, 25–26, 27
    retirement and, 313–314
Pragmatics of intelligence, 219, 261
Preconventional morality, 265, 266
Premarital sex, 327
Premenstrual syndrome (PMS), 104–105
Presbycusis, 98–99
Presbyopia, 93, 96
Primary aging, 89
Primary memory, 165
Priming, 170, 174–175
    direct (repetition) priming, 182
Problem finding, 234
Problem-focused coping, 453, 455
Problem solving, 245–247
Procedural memory (see Nondeclarative memory)
Production deficiency, 185–188
Productive aging, 32
Profession, defined, 289
Progestin, 106
Programmed senescence, 86–87
Prospective memory, 185
Prostaglandin E1, 110
Prostate:
    benign enlargement, 143
    cancer, 142–143
Provident funds, 307
Pseudodementia, 480
Psychoanalysis, 38
Psychological age, defined, 12
Psychological aspects of death, 490–491
Psychometric approach to intelligence, 202–209
Psychometric testing, 209, 215, 254–255
    of creativity, 228–230
    cultural bias in, 207–208
Psychotherapies, 478
Psychotic coping styles, 451
Public Health Service, U.S., 69
Public safety, age discrimination and, 299–300

Q-sort, 407, 439
Qualitative development, 39
Quality vs. quantity of life, 85–86
Quality ratio, 236
Quantitative development, 39, 41
Quasi experiment, defined, 61
Quasi-experimental designs, 61–67
Questionnaires, 49

Quiz Kids (television program), 55

Race:
  demographics, 24–25, 27
  elder abuse and, 470–471
  grandparenthood and, 375–376
  health problems and, 144–146
  IQ tests and, 207–208
  and leisure time during retirement, 313
  life expectancy and, 80
  occupational stress and, 301
  older adults living alone and, 385
  religion and, 456
  single mothers, 346
  work and, 297
Race-norming, 213
Radial keratotomy (RK), 94
Radiation studies, 69, 70
Random assignment, 59
Random sample, 46–47
Random selection, 46
Rate-of-living theory, 88
Raven Progressive Matrices, 217
Reaction time, 103–104
Realistic personality, 290
Real self, 407
Rehearsal (in memory), 167, 191–192
Reintegrative stage of cognitive development, 254
Relationships, 323–329
  friendship, 323–324
  health problems and, 147
  life adjustments and, 421–422
  love, 325, 326
  middle-aged children and elderly parents, 365–369
  sexuality, 325, 327–329
  siblings, 370–371
  young adult children and middle-aged parents, 365
Reliable, defined, 46
Religion, mental health and, 456–457, 474
Remarriage:
  blended families and, 344, 351
  divorce and, 337–338, 342
  grandparenting after, 376–377
  widowhood and, 509
Reminiscences, 521–523
Remote grandparents, 374
Reproductive system:
  female, 104–108
  male, 109–110
Research designs, 54–61
  case studies, 54–56
  correlational studies, 56, 62
  experiments, 57–61
  quasi-experimental designs, 61–67
Research ethics, 68–71

Research methods, 46–53
  cultural bias in, 50
  data collection, 49, 51–53
  sampling, 46–47, 49
Reserve capacity, 123
Resource provision-depletion hypothesis, 304
Respect for the Aged Day (Japan), 31
Respiratory system, 130–131
Responsible stage of cognitive development, 254
Retirement, 283, 304–317
  in China, 309
  financing, 307–308
  leisure during, 312–313
  planning for, 310
  social support and, 315–316
  society and, 316–317
  well-being and, 313–316
  working after, 311
Retirement community, 382
Retirement hotel, 382
Retirement stage of career development, 292
Retrieval (memory), 162, 164, 165
Reunions, 523
Rheumatoid arthritis, 127
Right to die, 517–519
Rights of Passage (Golding), 232
Role-sharing, 335

Safer sex practices, 328
Safety aids, 22
Sample, 46
Sampling, 46–47, 49
Sampling bias, 63, 413
Satisfaction, as dimension of personality, 413
Satisfaction with life (morale), 448
Schemas, 417
Schizophrenia, 474
Scientific method, 46
Seattle Longitudinal Study of Adult Intelligence, 6, 208, 219–224, 226, 254
Secondary aging, 89
Secondary memory, 165
Secondhand smoke, 148–149
Secular trend, 90
Segmentation hypothesis, 304
Selective optimization with compensation, 221
Selectivity theory, 316
Self:
  ideal, 407
  real, 407
Self-concept, 411, 430
Self-concept models of personality, 410, 416–417
Self-in-relation theory, 430–431
Self-report, 49, 51, 408

Semantic memory, 170–171
Senescence, 86
Senescence: The Last Half of Life (Hall), 6
Senile macular degeneration, 97
Sensorimotor functioning, 92–104
  hearing, 98–100
  motor functions, 101–104
  taste and smell, 100–101
  touch, pain and temperature, 101
  vision, 92–98
Sensory (object) clues, in remembering, 190
Sensory memory, 165–166
Sequential designs, 66–67
Sequential testing, 220
Serial monogamy, 331
Serious leisure, 313
Sex Role Inventory (Bem), 430, 433
Sexual activity:
  longevity and, 82
  marital and extramarital, 335, 337
  premarital, 327
Sexual Behavior in the Human Female (Kinsey), 47
Sexual Behavior in the Human Male (Kinsey), 47
Sexual harassment, 302
Sexuality, 110–112, 325, 327–329
  early studies of, 47–48
Sexual orientation, 325, 327
  parenthood and, 347
  (*See also* Heterosexuality; Homosexuals)
Shakespeare for My Father (Redgrave), 510
Shared housing, 382
Shifting career patterns, 293
Shiva, 491
Shock therapy (electroconvulsive therapy), 477–478
Sibling relationships, 370–371
Singapore, care of elderly in, 30, 31
Single-blind test, 58
Single life, 329–330, 385
Single mothers, 346
Skeletal system, 123–127
Skin cancer, 140
Sleep, 177
Sleep apnea, 130
Smell, 100–101
Smoking, 148–149, 177
Social age, 13, 14–15, 323–324
Social aspects of death, 490
Social clock, 426
Social development, defined, 10
Social insurance, 307
Social knowledge, 171
Social-learning theory, 431
Social personality, 290
Social reasoning, 250

Social roles, 13, 32
Social security, 25
Socioeconomic status, 25, 27
  health problems and, 144–146
  retirement and, 313–314
"Software" of memory (information-processing approach), 162–175
Somatic-mutation theory, 88
South Africa, and Nelson Mandela, 241–242
Spaced retrieval, 192
Specialized knowledge, 243–244
Specification stage of career development, 291
Spillover hypothesis, 304
Spiritual development, wisdom and, 263–264
Spousal abuse, 467–469
Stable career patterns, 293
Stage, 42
Stage models of personality, 410, 418–427, 481–482, 495
  evaluation of, 424–427
Standard deviation from the mean, 204
Standardized norms, 203
Stanford Studies of Gifted Children, 6–7
Star Wars, 258
Stepfamilies, 351
Stereotypes:
  about aging, 19–20, 25
  gender, 429–430
Storage (memory), 162, 164, 165–170
Strategies:
  of coping (styles), 451–452
  for remembering, 189–193
Stratified random sample, 47
Stress, 150–152, 448
  defined, 150
  divorce and, 341
  friendship and, 324
  longevity and, 82
  occupational, 300–302
  parenthood and, 367
  physiological effects of, 150–152
  (*See also* Coping)
Stroke, 129, 476
Structural lag, 283
Structured interview, 49
Sublimation, 233–234
Substance dependence, 463
Substance use disorders, 148–150, 463–466
Substantive complexity, 303
Successful aging, 455–462
  balance models, 460–462
  laypeople's views, 462
  normative models, 455, 458–460
Suicide, 514–519
  assisted, 518–519
  in Japan, 30–31

Supertheory, 40
Supreme Court, U. S., 302
Surrogate motherhood, 349
Survival curves, 84, 85
Sweden, care of old-old in, 395
Syphilis, 69

Tacit knowledge, 214, 245
Tacrine (Cognex), 139
Tactile-visual cues, 192
Taiwan, 269–270
Tamoxifen, 141
Taste, 100–101
T cells, 131
Telomerase, 140
Temperament, 409–410
Temperature adjustments, 22, 101
Terminal drop, 220, 496–497
Tertiary memory, 165
Test anxiety, 209
Testing effects, 63
Testing of intelligence, 201–209, 212–213
Testosterone, 106
Thalidomide, 97
Thanatology, 492
  (*See also* Death and dying)
Theory, 38
  (*See also* Metatheories)
Thinking integratively, 247
Thymus gland, 131
Time-lag study, 65, 66–67
Time-sequential design, 67
Timing-of-events model of personality, 410, 427–429, 493–494
Tinnitus, 100
Tobacco, 148–149
Torrance Tests of Creative Thinking, 229–230
Touch, 101
Traditional family, 343
Trait models of personality, 410, 411–416
Transitory dementia, 480
Transpersonal wisdom, 264
Treatment, 58
Trial of Socrates, The (Stone), 235
Triangular theory of love, 325
Triarchic theory of intelligence, 211–214
Tuskegee study of syphilis, 69
Type A personality, 129
Type B personality, 129

Unconscious learning, 172–175, 181–182
Undifferentiated, defined, 430
Unemployment, 303, 309
Unintegrated style of aging, 460
Universal adolescent, 415

Universal pensions, 307
Universities, 284–285
U-shaped curve of marital satisfaction, 353

Valid, defined, 46
Variable-rate theories, 87–89
Variables, 56, 58
Vascular dementia, 479
Vedas, 258
Violence Against Women Act, 468
Vision, 22, 92–98, 208
Visual acuity, 93, 96
Visual impairments, 94, 96–97
Visual losses, 97–98
Visual scratch pad, 167
Vital capacity, 130
Vocation, 289, 290–295
Voluntary pension plans, 307
Volunteerism, 311

Wear-and-tear theory, 88
Wechsler Adult Intelligence Scale (WAIS), 205, 206
  decline in older adults, 216, 219
Well-being (*see* Health and well-being)
WHO (World Health Organization), 133, 134
Widowhood, 342, 506–509
"Widow's hump," 91
Wife battering, 467–469
Wild Strawberries (Bergman), 521
Wilful personality, 439
Wisdom, 243, 255–264, 420
  in folklore, myth, and philosophy, 257–258
  and intelligence and creativity, compared, 256, 257, 260
  psychological concepts and assessments, 259–264
  spiritual development and, 263–264
Women:
  bone loss, 123–126
  depression, 476
  mental health, 447
  occupational stress, 301–302
  personality development, in Mills studies, 434–440
  reproductive system, 104–108
  widowhood, 506–509
  (*See also* Gender)
Women's movement, 4–5
"Women's Strike for Equality" (1970), 4
Work, 289–304
  in China, 309
  gender and, 295–297
  intellectual growth and, 303–304
  intelligence and, 224
  leisure and, 304

Work *(Cont.)*:
  marriage and, 334–335
  mental health and, 447
  occupational patterns, 295–297
  occupational stress, 300–302
  performance and test scores,
    212–213
  after retirement, 311
  vocational choice and career
    development, 290–295
Workaholics, 293

Work force, 25
Working memory, 165, 167–168, 175,
  177
World Health Organization (WHO),
  133, 134
World knowledge, 170–171
Written reminders, 190

Yugoslavia, bards in, 187
Young adults, 10, 11
  children returning home, 380–381

Young adults *(Cont.)*:
  death, attitudes toward, 494
  demographics, 23
  middle-aged parents and,
    365
  physical appearance, 90–91
  relationships with parents,
    366–367
Young-old, 12, 372

Zinc, in diet, 178

NOTES

NOTES

NOTES

NOTES